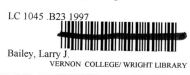

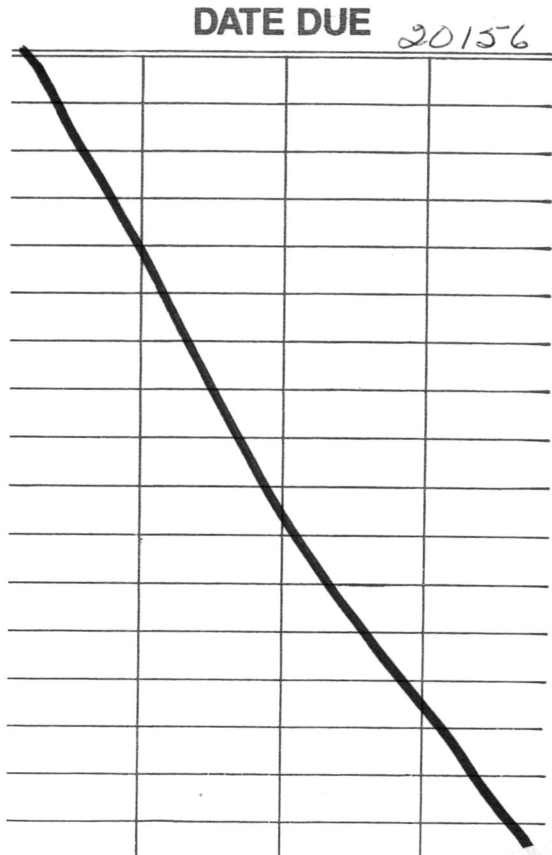
DATE DUE
20156
Demco, Inc. 38-293

Larry J. Bailey, Professor
Workforce Education and Development
Southern Illinois University
Carbondale, Illinois

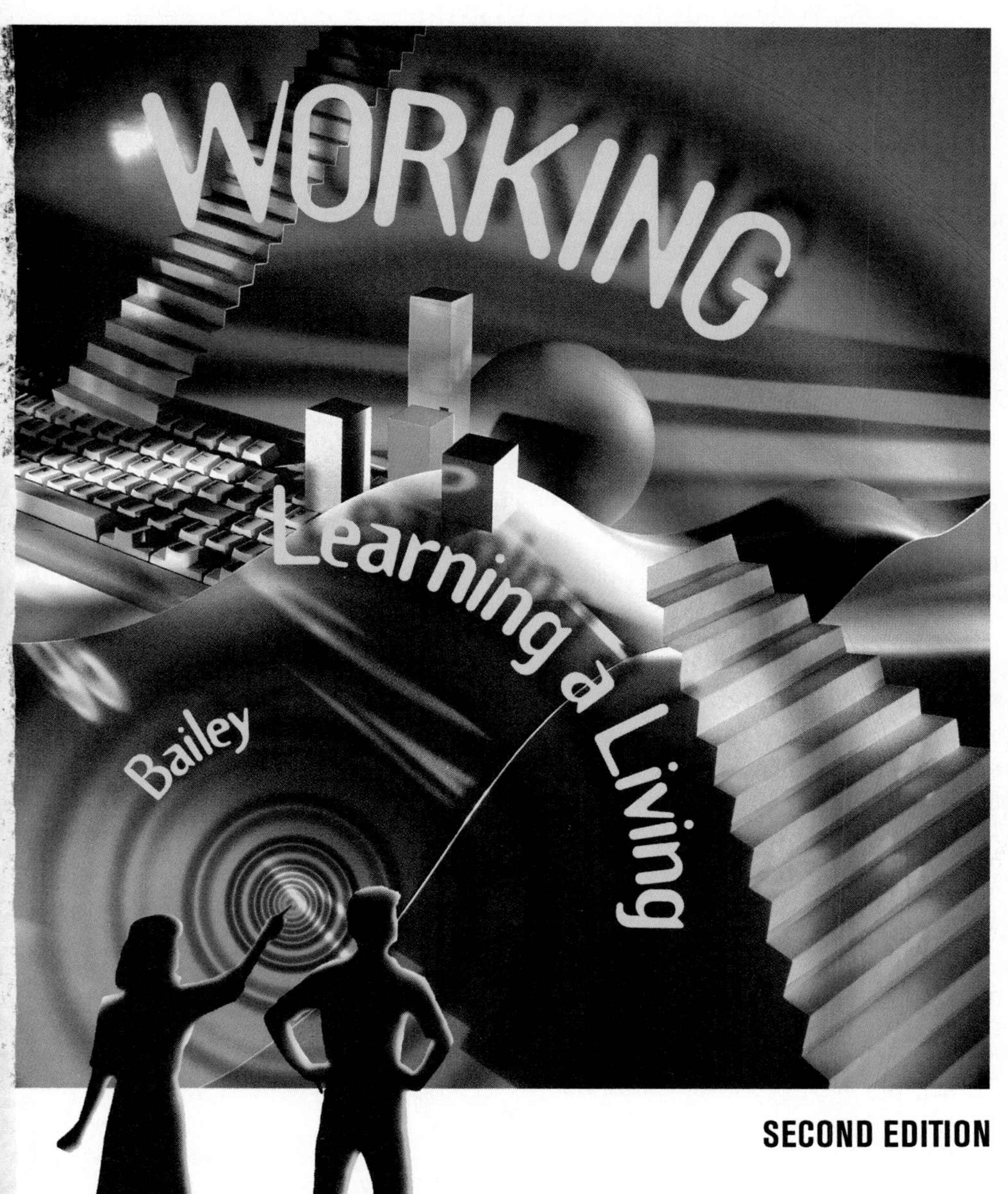

SECOND EDITION

SOUTH-WESTERN EDUCATIONAL PUBLISHING

I(T)P

International Thomson Publishing

South-Western Educational Publishing is a division of International Thomson Publishing Inc.
The ITP trademark is used under license.

ISBN:0-538-65096-6

Library of Congress Number 95–070256

VP/Editor-in-Chief: Peter McBride
Production Coordinator: Patricia M. Boies
Project Manager: Penny Shank
Editor: Edna D. Stroble
Marketing Manager: Carolyn Love
Photo Editor: Alix Roughen
Internal Illustrations: Angela Zawatsky, Photonics Graphics Inc.
Cover Design: Jim Brown, Design Crew Inc.

2 3 4 5 6 7 8 9 0 VH 99 98 97 96

Printed in the United States of America

WORKING
Learning a Living

PREFACE

Change is taking place in the United States and throughout the industrialized world. The world has become a global village in which countries compete for international standing and economic markets. Knowledge, information and skills have become the raw materials of international commerce. Learning is the essential investment required for success in this new era. We have entered the Information Age.

In response to these needs and challenges, American education is also undergoing change. Secondary schools across the country are reforming curricula and programs to meet increased academic requirements and higher standards. There is a clear recognition that yesterday's skills are inadequate for the world of tomorrow.

The attention being given education is not confined to basic academic skills. Some are proposing that *readiness for work* become education's fourth "R." There is a growing emphasis on integrating academic and vocational education. Numerous business and education partnerships are being created to help young people make successful transitions from school to work. Many educational authorities and respected organizations have called for increased emphasis on workforce preparation. For example:

> All American high school students must develop a new set of competencies and foundation skills if they are to enjoy a productive, full, and satisfying life. Whether they go next to work, apprenticeship, the armed services, or college, all young Americans should leave high school with the know-how they need to make their way in the world.[1]

> Academic and vocational integration, tech prep, and work experience programs such as cooperative education and new youth apprenticeships are usually regarded as critical to improving the school-to-work transition.[2]

> High-quality cooperative education programs can help youth prepare for the work force and make the transition from school to work. Quality programs establish school-employer linkages by offering students both training and employer contacts for entry to careers. Participating employers value co-op programs as a potential source of future employees.[3]

The culmination of more than a decade of federal reform efforts was the passage of two major education acts in spring 1994. One act is the *Goals 2000: Educate America Act* (P.L. 103-227) that includes a Goal 6 on Adult Literacy and Lifelong Learning. It states that every adult American will be literate and will possess the knowledge and skills necessary to compete in a global economy. To receive funding under the act, each state must prepare a state improvement plan. The plan must ". . . include a description of how secondary schools will be modified to provide career guidance, the integration of

---

1. *What work requires of schools.* Washington, DC: Secretary's Commission on Achieving Necessary Skills, June 1991, p. vi.

2. *Final report to Congress, Volume III program improvement: Education reform.* Washington, DC: National Assessment of Vocational Education, July 1994, p. 136.

3. *Transition from school to work.* Washington, DC: General Accounting Office, August 1991, p. 40.

academic and vocational education and work-based learning. . . ."

The second act is the *School-to-Work Opportunities Act* (P.L. 103-239) that provides states with federal assistance to develop and implement a statewide school-to-work transition system. A critical component of this legislation is the creation of partnerships between education and employers. It seeks to include employers as full partners in providing high-quality, worksite-based learning opportunities for students.

This book was written with a conscious awareness of changes that are taking place in the workplace and in the Nation's schools. The author and South-Western Educational Publishing enthusiastically support the Goals 2000 and school-to-work legislation. Further, we endorse the Learning a Living system proposed by the Secretary's Commission on Achieving Necessary Skills (SCANS), which calls for the creation of *high performance schools* and *high performance workplaces*. So committed are we to the Learning a Living concept, that a section is included in the appendix to explain the system and the role of SCANS. (See page 470.)

PURPOSE AND USE

This book was developed for use as a high school level text in several types of existing and emerging work experience education and school-to-work transition programs. Descriptions of specific applications follow.

Cooperative Vocational Education. In cooperative education, students learn occupational skills while working part-time at a training station in their community. Students also attend classes at their local high school, in which they participate in a "related" co-op class. This book is intended for use in such a class. Most related classes are one-year; a few are conducted for two years. This book can be conveniently covered in one year. Sufficient topics and activities are included, however, to allow the book to be profitably used for two-year programs.

Work-study. In work-study, part-time school is also combined with a part-time job. Unlike co-op education, however, this program seeks to develop general work habits and attitudes rather than specific occupational skills. Otherwise, the program is operated very similar to co-op. Work study students enroll in a related class, for which this text is ideally suited.

School-to-Work Transition. Many cities and states have developed a variety of apprenticeship, school-to-work, and youth employment programs. Some are privately supported and involve close collaboration between schools and employers. Others are funded under the federal Job Training Partnership Act and recently enacted school-to-work legislation. This book can be used as a primary text in such programs.

Related Courses. Because each of the six sections can stand alone, this book is appropriate for one-semester and short-term courses in career education, consumer education, introduction to occupations, and related courses.

Working: Learning a Living consists of 32 chapters organized into six sections. The contents and objectives meet requirements for vocational cooperative education and work-study programs in all states. The new edition benefits from feedback provided by many satisfied users of the first edition. Each chapter is organized, written, and produced in ways that foster successful teaching and learning.

- Each chapter begins with an outline of main headings and a listing of specific objectives to be achieved. These give students a good overview of the nature of the chapter.

- Carefully chosen headings are arranged to aid the teacher in presenting the material and the student in understanding it. In the teacher's annotated edition, each section is cross-referenced to SCANS foundation skills and competencies.
- Numerous examples, illustrations, and case studies are blended with the text narrative to make the material more relevant and to promote greater understanding.
- High quality, color photographs and figures are used throughout to generate interest and to illustrate and demonstrate application of concepts.
- Key words and phrases are italicized for emphasis. A complete *Glossary* is provided at the end of the book.
- Topical features dealing with work, workers, and the workplace are inserted in each chapter to enrich content and provide interesting, related material.
- At least two *What Would You Do?* features are included in each chapter to stimulate thinking and discussion. Many pose ethical questions that can be used to help students think about and clarify their values.
- A *Chapter Review* section summarizes important concepts and principles, lists words to define, and provides study questions to answer about the chapter. Supplemental *Activities to Do* and *Topics to Discuss* provide opportunities for advanced learning through a variety of individualized, team, and group activities.
- Communication, math and measurement, leadership, and human relation skills are applied and reinforced throughout the book.

RELATED MATERIALS

The student textbook and annotated teacher's edition are the primary components of a comprehensive set of work experience education materials. A number of ancillary student and teacher materials are also provided.

The primary student ancillary is a *Student Working Papers and Exploration Package*. In Part One, more than one hundred activities, problems, questions, forms, and puzzles are included to interest and challenge students. In Part Two, a "mini" *Occupational Outlook Handbook* is provided for students to explore occupational clusters and to investigate specific occupations of interest.

Teacher ancillary materials include a set of forty-eight transparencies designed to illustrate a concept or procedure or develop a solution directly on the transparencies. These can be used with both the student textbook and the student working papers and exploration package. Thirty-two chapter tests are provided in both printed and electronic formats (MicroEXAM software). Finally, a *Lesson Plan Guide and Supplemental Activities* is available to assist teachers in planning instruction and in augmenting the textbook with higher level SCANS skills. Teacher ancillary materials may be purchased separately or collectively within *The Working Box*.

ACKNOWLEDGMENTS

The author is grateful to the many Delmar sales representatives who promoted the first edition and to Penny Shank and the other South-Western editorial and production staff who prepared the second edition. Preparation of the book was aided by comments and suggestions provided by the following reviewers.

Dennis Brock
Murphysboro High School
Murphysboro, IL

Judy Coburn
Hernando High School
Hernando, MS

Glenn Eagle
Salisbury High School
Salisbury, NC

Jean Gordon
First Colonial High School
Virginia Beach, VA

Deborah Hinrichs
Kansas State Board of Education
Topeka, KS

Diane Lawrence
Central High School
West Allis, WI

Joy Little
Florida Department of Education
Tallahassee, FL

Mary McCloe
Newark Valley High School
Newark Valley, NY

Jerry Minatree
Marysville High School
Career Center
Marysville, CA

Carol Spracklen
Sam Houston High School
Arlington, TX

Kenne Turner
Montgomery College
Conroe, TX

Marcia Webber
Murphysboro High School
Murphysboro, IL

ABOUT THE AUTHOR

Larry J. Bailey was born and raised in rural Indiana where he learned to work as a farm laborer, carpenter, painter, factory worker, and janitor. He attended Ball State University on an academic scholarship where he graduated with honors. He taught high school industrial arts prior to completing the Doctor of Education degree in Vocational Education at the University of Illinois. He held faculty research appointments at the University of Illinois and the University of Iowa before joining Southern Illinois University in 1969. He is author of five books and more than 100 other book chapters, articles, papers, and reports. He has served as a member of the National Advisory Council on Career Education and the Advisory Council on Adult, Vocational, and Technical Education, State of Illinois.

CONTENTS

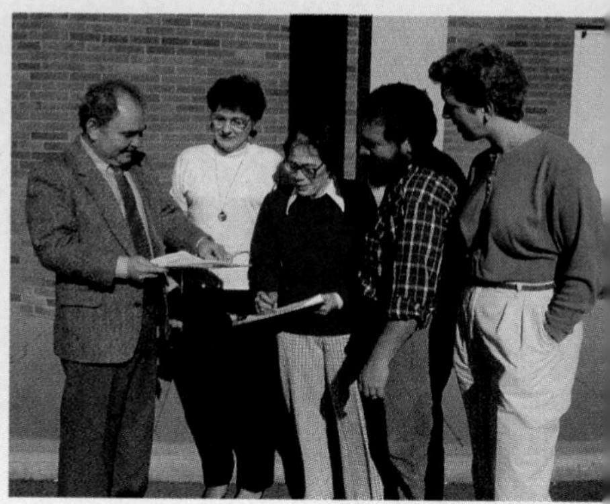

SECTION 1

PREPARING FOR WORK

Most adults in our society work. You need to learn about work and prepare for it. Having a paid job will enable you to establish your independence. In Chapter 1, you will learn about the role work plays in people's lives. You will discover how work experience education can benefit you as you begin your career.

The jobs you hold during your working life form your work history. In Chapter 2, you will examine different types of work histories. You will discover that there are many routes to a permanent, satisfying job. A career does not just happen. It is shaped and influenced by your own actions.

Chapter 3 encourages you to clarify your job goals. What you want out of a job will influence how and where you look for it. Six different sources of job leads are explained. A method is suggested for keeping track of information about job leads. Since most employees are eager to fill vacant jobs, the need to take quick action on job leads is emphasized.

How do you go about applying for a job? This is discussed in Chapter 4. You will learn how to develop a personal data sheet, how to prepare a job resume, and how to fill out a job application form. The three methods of contacting an employer about a job are explained. Guidelines in preparing for and taking a pre-employment test are also provided.

The job interview is generally the last and most important step in the job-search process. This is the focus of Chapter 5. You will discover what to do before, during, and after the interview. If a job offer is made, you will learn how to respond to it. Not all interviews will result in a job offer. There are recommended ways of dealing with that, also.

Co-op Career SPOTLIGHT ON

Liz Campbell, *Sports Marketer*

Liz Campbell is a star softball player. She is also interested in advertising and promotion, wants to own a business she can run from home, and plans to marry a professional athlete and have two or three children. Is sports marketing the career for her? It seems perfect—an idea that took shape in her co-op classes at Newberg High School, in Newberg, Oregon.

"I like working with people and know a lot about sports. I want to work with a professional sports team and promote the team and sports products through advertising and public relations," she said. Liz had always been a good athlete, but she got her first experiences in advertising and promotion in her co-op job. She worked for a florist/gift shop in several capacities, including salesperson, designing window and floor displays, delivering gift baskets, and opening and closing the store.

"My co-op job gave me an opportunity to actually be in a business and see how it runs . . . from manufacturer to consumer. I learned that business is a lot of work. I was given a great deal of responsibility and allowed to make mistakes. I learned what it takes to succeed." Liz said the co-op job gave her contact with mentors who gave her advice and support about what she was doing.

"They helped me plan my future—to look past high school, set goals, and make it happen," she said.

Liz is a marketing major in her junior year at Azusa Pacific University, a private four-year Christian college with strong sports emphasis and a work/study program. The university awarded her sports and academic scholarships, and the work/study program gave her valuable work experience in her field. She worked at Marshall's, a retail clothing store and at a sports marketing firm.

"This school works on the whole person—academic and spiritual. The coaches develop good athletes and the teachers are genuine and there to help you."

CHAPTER 1 Learning About Work

OUTLINE

- Why People Work
- Work, Occupation, and Job
- Work Experience Education
- Chapter Review

OBJECTIVES

After reading this chapter, you should be able to:

- Discuss reasons why people work.
- Define what is meant by the terms *work, occupation,* and *job.*
- Name three types of work experience education.
- Explain the role of a related class as part of a cooperative vocational education or work-study program.
- Identify the benefits of work experience education.

Most young people look forward to finishing school, leaving home, and starting out on their own. An important part of the transition from youth to young adult is getting a job. Working at a paid job will enable you to establish your independence and define your own life. As a working person, other people will see and respond to you in new ways. You will become more accepted as an adult and be granted greater rights and responsibilities of adulthood. This can be an exciting and enjoyable time of your life.

WHY PEOPLE WORK

People's views about work vary greatly. It would be untrue to say that all people value and enjoy their work. For most Americans, though, work is an important part of a well-rounded life. They generally like what they do. Many studies have shown that most people would work even

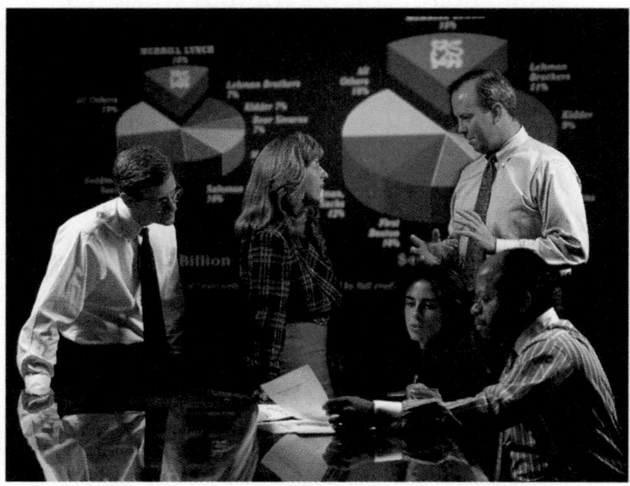

FIGURE 1–1 **Mature behavior is a basic requirement for any job.**
Courtesy of Merrill Lynch.

if they didn't have to. This view of work is not limited to adults. The interest of young people in learning about and preparing for work has never been greater.

People work for many different reasons. The reasons vary from person to person. The most common reasons for working follow.

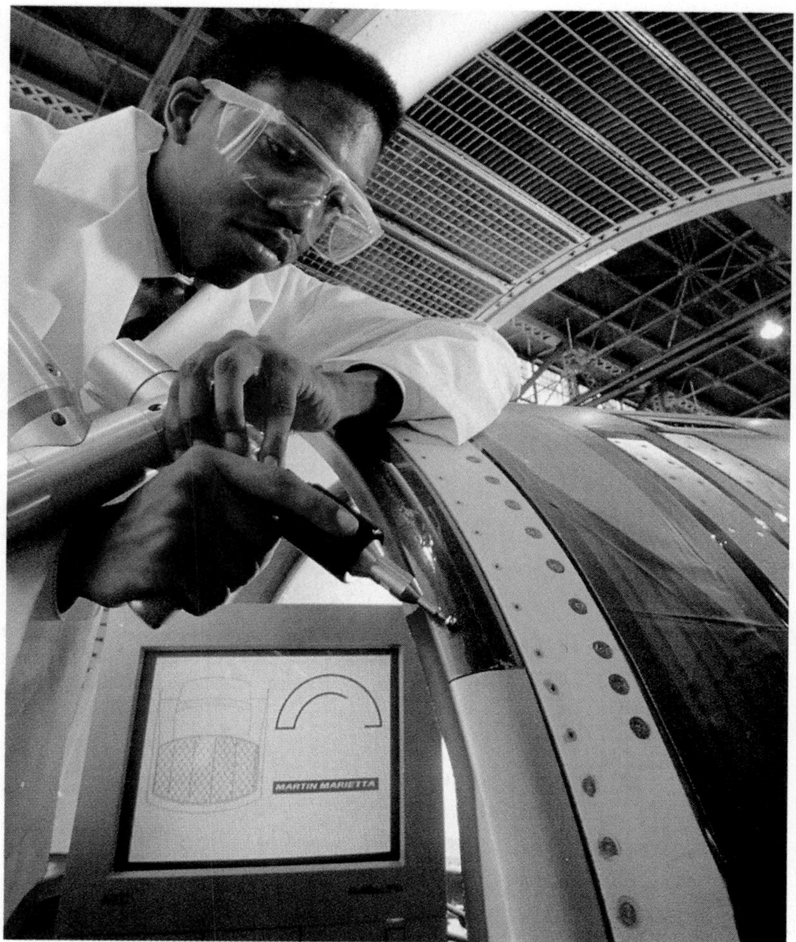

FIGURE 1–2 **A sense of accomplishment is one of the greatest rewards of working.**
Courtesy of Martin Marietta Corporation.

Earn Money

The major reason why people work is to earn money. Earnings are needed to buy food, shelter, clothing, and other necessities. Beyond meeting basic needs, money is used to purchase goods and services that provide comfort, enjoyment, and security.

Social Satisfaction

People are social creatures. Working gives people a chance to be with others and to make friends. In the work environment, people can give and receive understanding and acceptance.

Positive Feelings

People get satisfaction from their work. For instance, your work may give you a sense of accomplishment. Think of how you feel when you finish a school project or a difficult job task.

Working also gives people a feeling of self-worth. The feeling comes from knowing that other people will pay you for your skills.

Prestige

Some people work because of the prestige or status they enjoy. Prestige is an admiration that society has for an occupation. Prestige is separate from how well the job is performed. What occupations do you consider to have prestige?

Personal Development

Many people have a drive to improve themselves. Work can provide an opportunity to learn and grow. Work can often be a great teacher.

Contributions to Health

Work can be very important for mental and physical health. This results from the work itself as well as the physical activity and exercise involved. People who are active and happy in their work tend to feel better.

Self-expression

We all have interests, abilities, and talents. Work can be a way in which we express ourselves. It does not matter what kind of work it is as long as it suits the worker and is not illegal or immoral.

WORK, OCCUPATION, AND JOB

People often use the terms *work, occupation,* and *job* interchangeably. They do have a number of similarities. In this book, however, the terms will be used in different ways.

Work

Work can be defined as activity directed toward a purpose or goal that produces something of value to oneself and/or to society. For instance, work can provide you with money and a sense of accomplishment. Work by a teacher or nurse provides benefits to society. Another characteristic of work is that it may be paid or unpaid.

Occupation

All occupations carry out work. An *occupation* is the name given to a group of similar tasks that a person performs for pay. For example, typing, filing, maintaining records, placing phone calls, and scheduling meetings are tasks performed by the occupation of secretary. Carpenter, salesclerk, attorney, truck driver, and chef are examples of common occupations that involve groups of similar tasks.

FIGURE 1–3 **Some work may not have monetary payment; it may have even greater rewards.** *Courtesy of General Dynamics.*

Most occupations require specific knowledge and skills to perform them. Occupations are learned on the job or in various kinds of education and training programs. A person having an occupation can work at a number of different jobs.

Job

A *job* is a paid position at a specific place or setting. A job can be in an office, store, factory, farm, or mine. For example, a nurse (an occupation) can work at jobs in a doctor's office, clinic, hospital, home, school, factory, or nursing home. The relationship between work, occupation, and job is illustrated in Figure 1–4.

The typical relationship between occupation and job is that an occupation is acquired first. That is, an occupation is learned through education and training, after which a job is secured. Some jobs require no previous training. When this

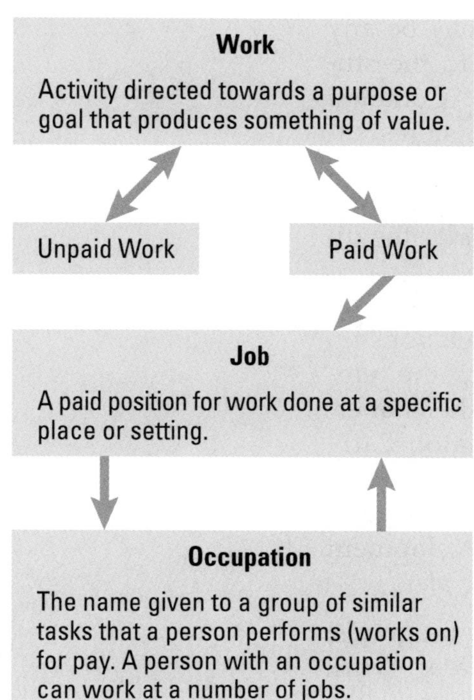

Work
Activity directed towards a purpose or goal that produces something of value.
Unpaid Work
Paid Work
Job
A paid position for work done at a specific place or setting.
Occupation
The name given to a group of similar tasks that a person performs (works on) for pay. A person with an occupation can work at a number of jobs.

FIGURE 1–4 The relationship between work, job, and occupation. Can you see the relationships among them?

type of job is obtained, occupational training may follow.

Most people change jobs a number of times throughout their lives. For instance, Lionel, a secretary, might leave a job at State Insurance to work at Merchants Bank. Later, he might leave Merchants Bank to work at Mercy Hospital.

Sometimes, people change both occupations and jobs. An example would be if Lionel leaves the secretarial position at Mercy Hospital to become an office manager for Suburban Realty Company.

WORK EXPERIENCE EDUCATION

During the last several decades, many kinds of education programs have been developed to help young people learn about and prepare for work. Programs of this type are called *work experience education.* Their purpose is to provide opportunities for students to explore or participate in work as an extension of the regular school environment.

Types of Work Experience Programs

Unlike many countries, the United States does not have a national system of education. As a result, state and local programs like work experience education are called by many different names. Whatever it is called, a work experience program is probably one of the following.

Cooperative (co-op) vocational education. Vocational education is a program in which students learn specific

? ? ? ? ? ? ? ? ? ? ? ? ? ?

WHAT WOULD YOU DO?

You have been working for about a year at a small nursery and garden center. You enjoy the informality, the variety of work, caring for plants, and being out-of-doors. You have learned about a job opening in the garden department of a large discount store. Your primary duties would be waiting on customers and operating the cash register. The job pays quite a bit more than you presently earn, but you do not think you would enjoy the new job as much as your present one. You cannot decide whether to give up a satisfying job for the opportunity to make more money.

What would you do?

occupational skills for employment. One kind of vocational education is taught in school-based classrooms, shops, and laboratories. Instruction may be provided in occupational areas such as agriculture, business, marketing, industrial-technical, home economics, and health occupations.

Another kind of vocational education is cooperative (co-op) vocational education. This is a cooperative program between a secondary school (or community college) and a local employer. Most cooperative education students attend classes at their school campus for part of the day. Students then spend the rest of the day working at a training site in a local business or industry. Students receive both pay and school credit for their co-op jobs.

In cooperative vocational education, the student learns and applies occupational skills on the job rather than only in a school shop or laboratory. Another part of cooperative vocational education is a related class. This is taught at the school to reinforce skills used at a job site. Students study topics such as job-seeking, consumer skills, independent living, and career planning. This textbook is probably being used as part of a related class.

Cooperative vocational education follows certain guidelines and procedures. A cooperative education teacher/coordinator employed by a school system usually manages the program. The coordinator reviews and approves student applications for the program. The coordinator also approves each student's place of employment, called the *training station.*

The training station may be any type of job that relates to the student's career objectives. Common training stations include stores, offices, hospitals, restaurants, and auto repair shops. At the training station, the student is under the direction of a supervisor.

The cooperative education program is a three-way relationship involving the student, the employer-supervisor, and the cooperative education coordinator. Early on, all three parties sign a *training agreement* (See Figure 1–5, page 9) and participate in the development of a step-by-step *training plan.*

Work-study. Work-study programs, sometimes called general work experience education, are like

? ? ? ? ? ? ? ? ? ? ? ? ? ? ?

WHAT WOULD YOU DO?

Your school has both school-based vocational education and cooperative vocational education. You cannot decide which one to enroll in. The advantages of the school-based program are that you know the teacher, you are familiar with the equipment, and you would be taking the course with your friends. In the co-op program, you would meet new people, earn some money, and work on more advanced equipment. You have been told by other students that in co-op you will work harder and that more will be expected of you.

What would you do?

SAMPLE TRAINING AGREEMENT

Student's Name ______________________ School ______________________ Date ____

Age __________ Social Security No. ______________ Job Title ______________________

Co. Name ______________________ Co. Address ______________________

Co. Phone ______________________ Employer Identification No. ______________

Co. Supervisor ______________________ Student Hours ______________

Wages ______________ Dates Covered by Agreement ______________________

Responsibilities of the Student-Learner:

1. The student-learner will keep regular attendance, both in school and on the job, and cannot work on any school day that he/she fails to atter school; he/she will notify the school and employer if unable to report.
2. The student's employment will be terminated if he/she does not remain in school.
3. The student will show honesty, punctuality, courtesy, a cooperative attitude, proper health and grooming habits, gooddress and a willingness to learn.
4. The student will consult the teacher-coordinator about any difficulties arising at the training station.
5. The student will conform to the rules and regulations of the training station.
6. The student will furnish the teacher-coordinator with all necessary information and complete all necessary reports.

Responsibilities of the Training Sponsor:

1. The training sponsor will endeavor to employ the student for at least the minimum number of hours each day and each week for the entire agreed training period.
2. The training sponsor will adhere to all Federal and State regulations regarding employment, child labor laws, minimumwages and other applicable regulations.
3. The training sponsor will see that the student is not allowed to remain in any one operation, job, or phase of the occupationbeyond the period time where such experience is of educational value.
4. The training sponsor will consult the teacher-coordinator about any difficulties at the training station.
5. The training sponsor will provide experiences that will contribute to the attainment of the students' career objective.
6. The training sponsor will assist in evaluating the student.
7. The training sponsor will provide time for consultation with the teacher-coordinator concerning the student.
8. The training sponsor will provide instructional material and occupational guidance for the student as needed and available.

Responsibilities of the Teacher-Coordinator:

1. The teacher-coordinator will coordinate related classroom instruction and on-the-job training to improve job performance and to better prepare the student for his/her occupational career objective.
2. The teacher-coordinator will see that the necessary related classroom instruction is provided.
3. The teacher-coordinator will make periodic visits as necessary to the training station to observe the student and consult with the employer a training sponsor.
4. The teacher-coordinator will assist in the evaluation of the student.

This agreement may be terminated by mutual consent of the training sponsor and the teacher-coordinator.
It is understood that the parties participating in this agreement will not discriminate in employment opportunities on the basis of race, religio color, sex, or national origin.

______________________ ______________________
Student (Date) Training Sponsor (Date)

______________________ ______________________
Parent (Date) Teacher Coordinator (Date)

Source: Gooch, B.G. *Handbook for Work-based Learning.* Carbondale, IL: Southern Illinois University, 1995.

FIGURE 1–5 Sample training agreement.

cooperative vocational education in several ways. Both allow students to attend school part-time while working part-time. For these jobs, students receive pay and school credit. Each program is supervised by a work experience coordinator.

Unlike cooperative vocational education, work-study is *not* a program of on-the-job training for a specific occupation. Rather, the program deals with the development of what are called *employability skills.* These are required in all jobs. They include things such as punctuality, dependability, and cooperation.

Many students find that the combination of school and work is more interesting than school alone. Also, the opportunity to earn money keeps some students in school who might otherwise drop out before graduation.

Exploratory work experience education. Many schools provide exploratory work experience education for the junior-high and early high-school-age students. The purpose of this type of program is to provide students with opportunities to observe work and to try out various work tasks. This is why the program is called "exploratory." Students explore various occupations in order to discover or to confirm occupational interests. Thus, the program

FIGURE 1–6 "Job shadowing" is often part of exploratory work experience. Why do you think this term is used?
Photo by Joe Schuyler.

is concerned with *career guidance* rather than the development of occupational or employability skills.

Exploratory programs may last only a few days or a few weeks. Students receive no pay for the work they do, but they usually receive school credit.

Benefits of Work Experience

Depending on the type of program in which you are enrolled, work experience can benefit you in the following ways. You can:

- ***Learn Occupational Skills.*** You can acquire marketable skills through on-the-job training in an actual work setting.
- ***Develop Employability Skills.*** Success on the job requires more than occupational skills. Work experience provides opportunities to develop the types of work habits and attitudes that employers expect.
- ***Establish a Work Record.*** It is often hard to get a job if you lack previous experience. Completing a work experience program will make it easier for you to get a job later.
- ***Earn While You Learn.*** Earning your own money will give you a sense of accomplishment. You will be able to save money, buy things that you might not otherwise be able to afford, or both. For some students, the money they earn can be the difference between staying in school and dropping out.
- ***Discover Career Interests and Goals.*** Work experience can help you find out what type of career you want. You may either confirm your present interests and goals or find new ones.

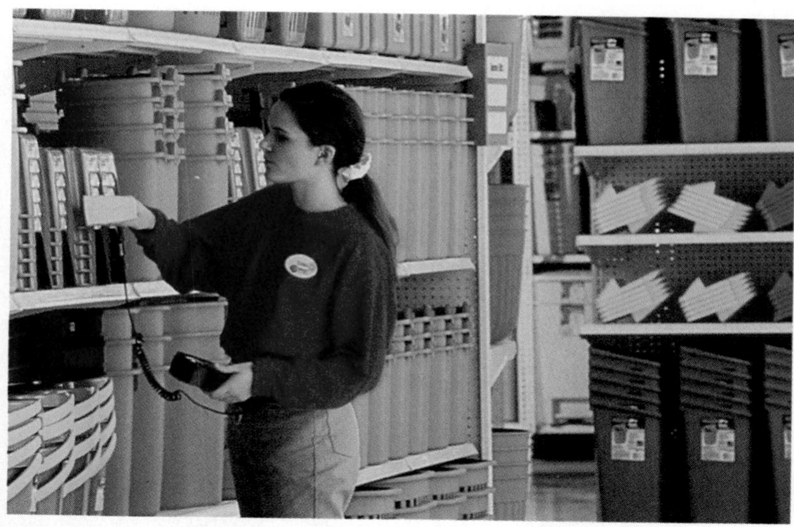

FIGURE 1–7 **Training sites often have tools and equipment that are not available in schools.**
Courtesy of Dayton Hudson Corporation/Steve Niedorf.

- ***Recognize the Relationship Between Education and Work.*** Work experience can provide something that may be missing in your present education. Education can take on new meaning as you come to recognize a greater connection between what you are learning in school and what you are doing on the job.
- ***Remain Employed After Graduation.*** Many students in work experience jobs are offered permanent jobs after graduation. This benefits both students and employers. If you are pleased with your job, you won't have to look for a new one. Hiring a work experience student saves the employer both interviewing and training time. Some students continue in co-op jobs while they attend post-high school education.

Let us see in more detail how work experience education has helped two young people.

Howard is enrolled in a business occupations program. This is a type

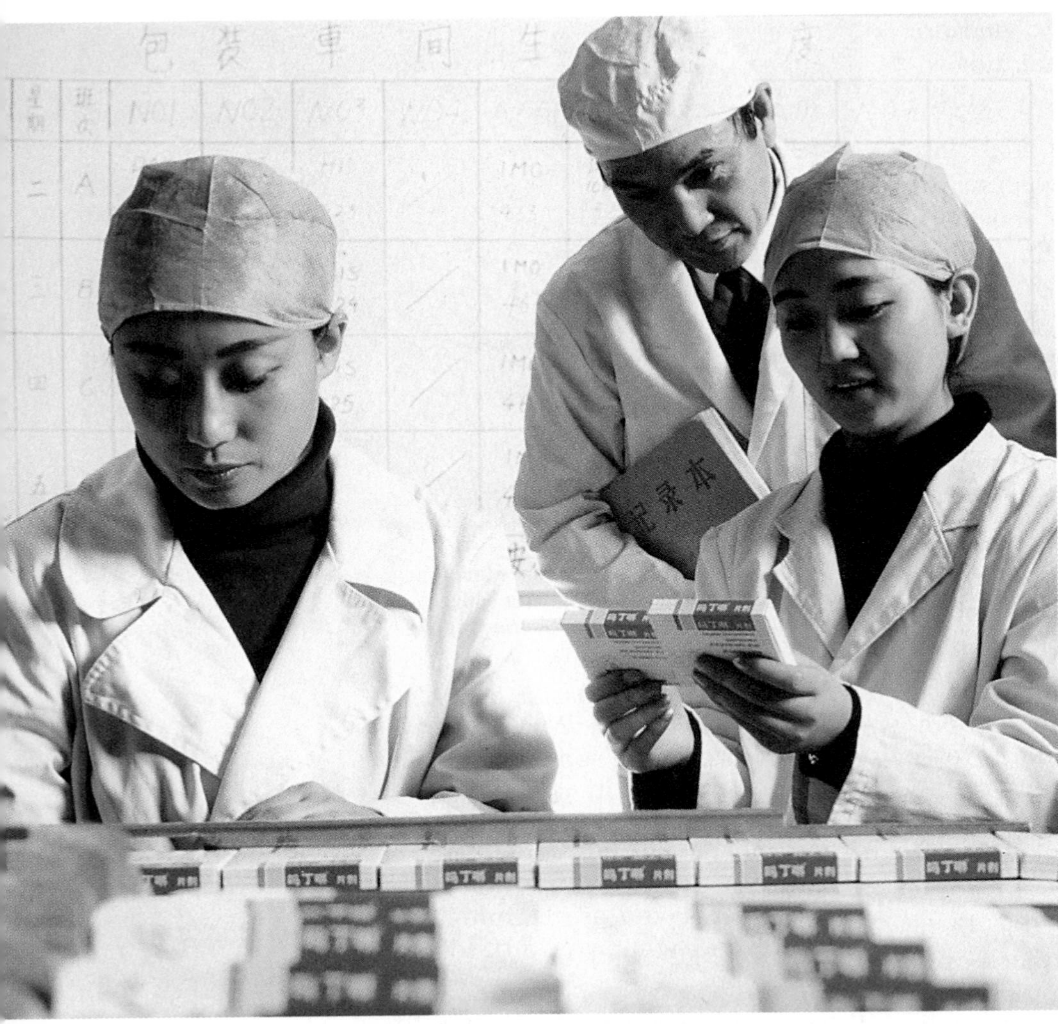

FIGURE 1–8 **A successful cooperative education often encourages students to continue their education or training beyond high school.**
© 1993 Ted Kawalerski and Johnson & Johnson.

of cooperative vocational education program for students interested in secretarial, accounting, information-processing, and similar occupations. Howard has a part-time job at a firm that distributes packaging equipment. He enters data and keyboards on a computer, files, and performs other office duties.

One day the sales manager asked Howard to sit in on a sales meeting and take notes. After the meeting, he prepared a short summary report. The manager was impressed and complimented Howard on his ability to organize and present the material well. Afterward, the manager began to give Howard more duties of this type.

Howard discovered a skill and an interest of which he was not aware. He also learned that there is a demand in the business world for skilled stenographers. After gradu-

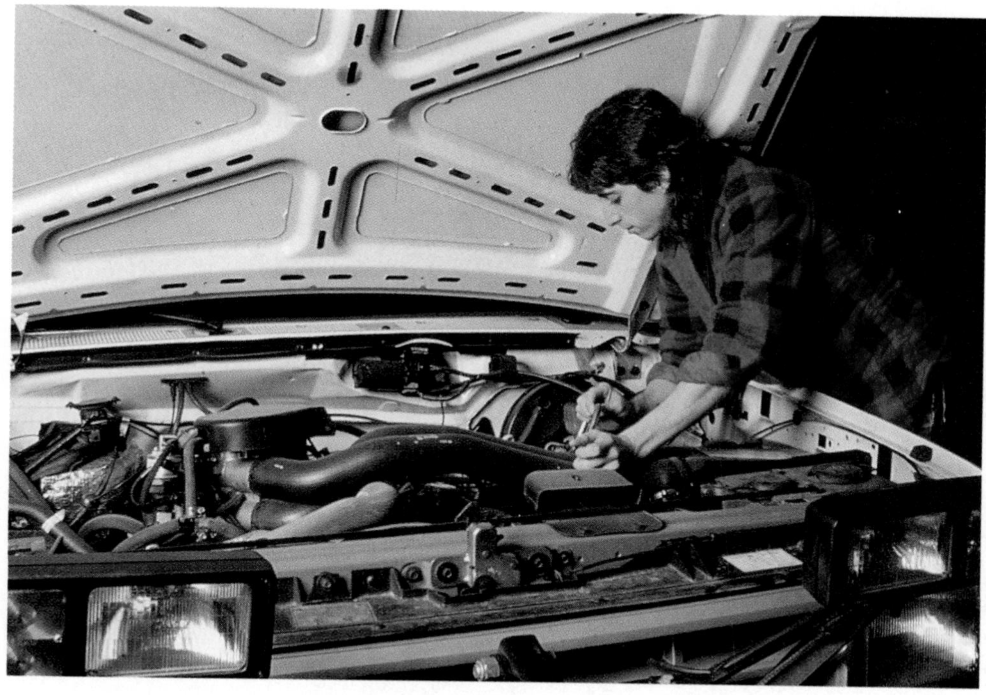

FIGURE 1–9 **Some students are motivated to stay in school by participating in a work-study program.**
Photo by David W. Tuttle.

ation, Howard will enroll in a new technical stenography program offered at a local community college. The program provides training in computer-aided transcription. This is a system in which a computer directly translates shorthand notes into English.

At the end of his junior year, Wilson had thoughts about not returning to school in the fall. He came from a large family supported only by his mother. There was little income available for extras. Wilson was discouraged with school. He did not have the nice clothes or money to participate in school activities like most other students.

A friend suggested that Wilson talk to the school's work experience coordinator. With the help of the coordinator, Wilson found a work-study job at the city highway garage. He helps clean and take care of the fleet of city-owned vehicles. While he does not want to do this type of work forever, Wilson is happy to have a paying job.

After signing up for work-study, Wilson decided to finish high school. The money he earns allows him to buy some new clothes and do a few things that he could not afford to do before. School has become enjoyable for him, and his grades are improving. Wilson is encouraging his younger brother and sister to enroll in a work experience program.

Which benefits of work experience education would be most important to *you?*

FOCUS ON

The Workplace

THE CHANGING WORKPLACE

When this country was founded, most people lived and worked on small, family-owned farms. The farm family raised livestock, poultry, and grain.

As trading increased, small villages grew along rivers and other transportation routes. The growth of towns provided new jobs for shop owners, bankers, blacksmiths, and others. Agriculture, however, remained the base of the economy.

In the second half of the 1800s, industry in the United States expanded rapidly. Growing towns and cities needed more and more goods. Typical workers in the early 1900s had factory jobs. They produced steel, machinery, and other manufactured goods.

Growing industry and a growing population needed many kinds of business, transportation, communication, personal, and government services. In response to these demands, service industries began to expand. Typical service occupations included secretary, clerk, salesperson, and manager. In 1995, over 70 percent of all workers were employed in services.

This service economy, however, is undergoing change. A new economy is evolving based on knowledge and information. Computers are the backbone of this information society. Influencing almost all industries and occupations, computers provide new ways of dealing with information.

With the computer has come many new occupations. These include laser nurse, computer animator, fiber-optics technician, and robotics repairer. "High-tech" industries will generate millions of new jobs into the next century. Many of you will probably work at some of these jobs.

Computer-driven industrial robots have launched many new industries and occupations.
Courtesy of Martin Marietta Corporation.

CHAPTER 1 REVIEW

CHAPTER IN BRIEF

- For most people, work is an important part of a well-rounded life. People work for many reasons, including money, social satisfaction, positive feelings, prestige, personal development, contributions to health, and self-expression. The specific reasons vary from person to person.
- The terms *work, occupation,* and *job* have different meanings. Work is activity directed toward a goal that produces something of value. It may be paid or unpaid. An occupation is the name given to a group of similar tasks that a person performs for pay. A job is a paid position at a specific place or setting.
- Work experience programs may be called different things depending on the state and community in which you live. Generally speaking, there are three common types of work experience education: cooperative vocational education, work-study, and exploratory work experience education.
- Work experience programs can benefit you in a number of ways. You can learn occupational skills, develop employability skills, establish a work record, earn while you learn, discover career interests and goals, recognize the relationship between education and work, and remain employed after graduation.

WORDS TO KNOW

career guidance
employability skills
job
occupation
occupational skills
training agreement
training plan
training station
work
work experience education

QUESTIONS TO ANSWER

1. Name the seven reasons why people work.
2. Name two ways you can get positive feelings from working.
3. Give examples that show the difference between an occupation and a job.
4. Identify and briefly explain the three kinds of work experience education programs.
5. How does cooperative vocational education differ from the other form of vocational education?
6. The term *exploratory* describes one type of work experience education. Explain why.
7. What is the benefit of establishing a work record? Give an example.
8. How can work experience make schooling more meaningful?

9. How can work experience education help you discover career interests and goals?
10. Name some ways in which Wilson benefitted from work-study.

ACTIVITIES TO DO

1. Interview a student who has taken a cooperative vocational education or work-study program. Ask the person what he or she thinks are the major benefits of the program. Ask also about whether the person found any disadvantages to the program. Discuss your findings in class.
2. Interview an employer who has provided a training site for a co-op or work-study student. List the ways in which the employer has benefitted from the program. Prepare an oral report and present it to the class.
3. Write a short statement (a paragraph or so) about what you hope to gain from being in a work experience program. Read your statement to the class. Compare and discuss the statements of different students.
4. Examine a copy of the training agreement used by your school. Discuss the purpose and requirements of the agreement. Make sure that you ask questions about any part that you don't understand.
5. Collect cartoons about work from your daily and weekend newspapers. You may be surprised at the number you find. Display them on a classroom bulletin board.

TOPICS TO DISCUSS

1. How would your future plans be changed if you suddenly won or inherited a great deal of money? Would you go to college? Would you plan on working? What type of work would you do?
2. In what ways can you influence and shape the direction of your career?
3. Are there any types of work experience programs in your school or community not mentioned in the chapter?
4. How might knowledge and skills learned in the following school subjects be applied on the job: English, mathematics, science, social studies, and foreign language?
5. In what ways might your interests and abilities be expressed in work? Cite examples of both paid and unpaid work.

CHAPTER 2 The Job Ahead

OUTLINE

- Sample Work Histories
- Moving Toward a Stable Job
- The Future Begins Now
- Chapter Review

OBJECTIVES

After reading this chapter, you should be able to:

- Explain what is meant by a work history.
- Discuss how different work histories can lead to a stable job.
- List characteristics of stable jobs.
- Identify what you can do to shape your own career.

The jobs you hold during your working life represent your unique *work history.* One person's work history may be a movement from job to job within the same occupation. Another person's work history may include one or more changes to entirely different occupations and jobs. A third person's work history may have no orderly pattern at all. Some people have long periods of unemployment with only an occasional short-term job. They are unable to establish a successful work history.

SAMPLE WORK HISTORIES

Knowing about different work histories can help you think about and plan for your own career. Let's examine the work histories of four different people.

Terry got a job in a small electronics sales and repair shop as part of a co-op program. After he graduated from high school, he took a full-time job in the electronics department of a large discount store. He often did small repair jobs for friends and neighbors during evenings and weekends.

Next, he got a job repairing televisions and installing antennas. He took this job in order to save enough money to open his own business. Terry now has a stable job as owner-manager of an electronics supply firm.

When Marie graduated from high school, she did not know what she wanted to do. After being out of work for several months, she found a full-time job. It was working as a salesclerk in a fashionable clothing store. From working in the store, Marie discovered that she enjoyed retail selling and had a talent for it.

After two years, she quit her job and enrolled in college to major in marketing. During college, she had a part-time job in a clothing store in the campus town. After she finished a marketing degree, she took a job as a sales manager for a national department store. She worked at that job for five years before staying at home two years with young children. Marie just started working again at a job that is similar to the one she left earlier.

Cindy was an outstanding athlete who never worked while attending high school or college. After college, her first job turned out to be a stable one. It was a high school teacher and coach. After six years, however, she had a desire to do something else.

A friend in the sporting goods business offered her a job. She was not sure whether she would like it, but quit her teaching job to give it a try. Somewhat to her surprise, Cindy enjoyed the challenge of the job. After a year in the job, she took another job with a large sporting goods manufacturer. She is now in charge of their school athletic sales. Cindy plans to make this a stable job.

Rick never liked school and could not wait to get out. After high school, he got a job stocking shelves in a grocery store. He worked a couple of months before getting into an argument with the store manager. Rick was fired.

His next job was working evenings and weekends as a service station attendant. After working at that job for about a year, Rick decided that he should learn a skill. Rick then moved to another town and got an apartment with a friend. He enrolled in a technical school to learn computer programming. He had heard this was a growing field.

FIGURE 2–1 People who work in sales and marketing fields often move from one stable job to another.
© 1993 Ted Kawalerski and Johnson & Johnson.

While going to school, Rick took a part-time job at another service station. He quit school after six months because he had to study too hard. Now Rick has another job driving a delivery truck while he decides whether to join the Armed Forces or start his own business!

The four work histories illustrate that jobs can serve different purposes at different times in one's life. Jobs are often used as a way to achieve something else. One purpose may be to learn occupational skills. Another purpose may be to earn money for college. Some jobs are used to gain experience in order to *qualify* for a better job. For most people, first jobs are only stepping stones to later ones.

MOVING TOWARD A STABLE JOB

Different work histories can lead to a stable job. You read how Terry, Marie, and Cindy followed different paths to a stable job. One route is not necessarily better than another. Some work histories like Rick's, however, only lead to detours and dead ends.

A *stable job* is one that you consider to be permanent and which may last several years. This does not mean, however, that you stay in the job forever. (Remember Cindy.) You may have a stable job at any time in your work life. Following are additional characteristics of stable jobs. Being aware of them can help you gain greater control over your work history.

Self-direction

Gaining a stable job does not usually happen by accident. Most successful careers come from hard work and *self-direction*. This means knowing what you want and taking steps to get there. Part of being self-directed is developing your skills through education or training.

Once you get a job, you want to keep it. This means performing well on the job tasks you are being paid to do. It also means learning and growing on the job. Much of this involves keeping up to date with what is going on in your field. Advancing in a job usually requires doing more than your share. To put yourself in a position for *promotion* or advancement you may also need to get more education or training.

Sometimes, advancing in a career also involves taking risks. For example, Robin was offered a promotion. To accept the new position would mean giving up a secure job, selling a house, and moving the family across the country. Decisions like these are not easy to make. A willingness to take a risk, though, often leads to greater personal and career success.

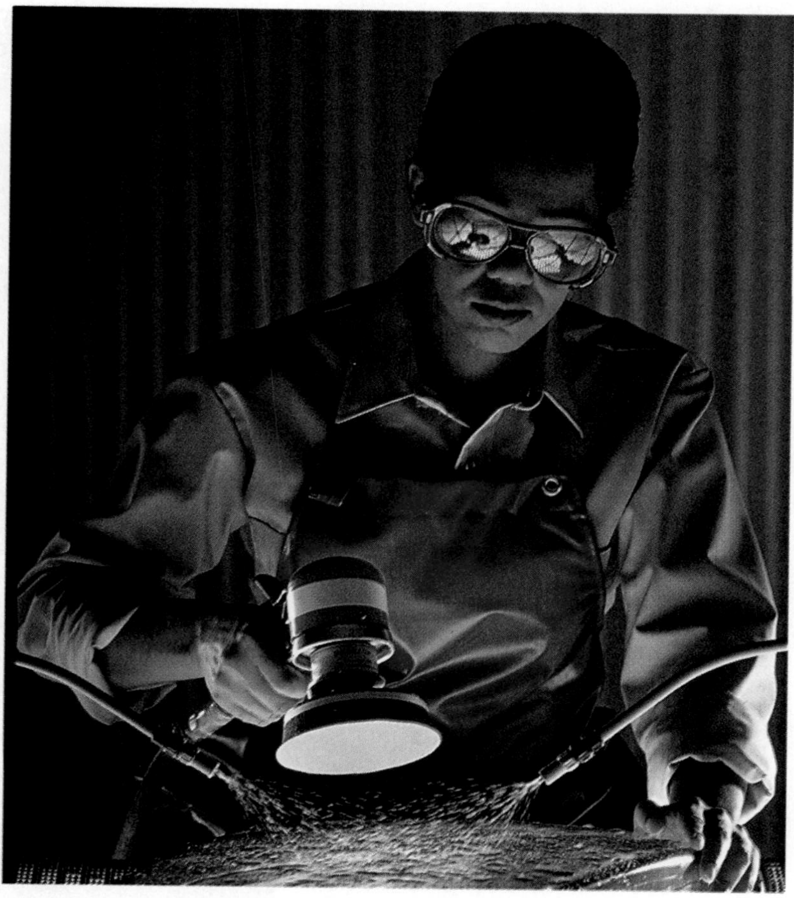

FIGURE 2–2 The first step to a stable job is to learn an occupational skill.
Courtesy of 3M.

? ? ? ? ? ? ? ? ? ? ? ? ? ?

WHAT WOULD YOU DO?

A fellow employee approaches you at work with some advice. "Listen," he says. "You are working too hard. Slow down a little bit. You are making the rest of us look bad. You do not want us all to be angry with you, do you?" The comments upset you. You are just trying to do the job the best way you know how. You are not trying to show anyone up. But now you wonder if you should slack off a bit.

What would you do?

Effort Pays Off

Not enough jobs are available for everyone who wants one. This is especially true for young people. If you want to work, you may have to accept any job that you can get. It may be low paying, boring, or undesirable in some other way. But a job is a job! Many adults started their careers this way.

It can be argued that there are no "bad jobs" as long as they are not illegal, immoral, or otherwise harmful. A job is a beginning. It is a way to earn money, get experience, learn skills, and prove yourself. Things can get better if you are cooperative, follow rules and directions, take an interest in what you are doing, and do your best. Employers tend to recognize and reward good work. Marcy's experience is a good example.

Marcy had finished her junior year in high school and started to look for a summer job. She went to the Job Service office. Little was available for students like her. Most of the job openings were permanent positions for people eighteen and over. Marcy was only seventeen and could not take a permanent job. One job was available. It was offered by someone who wanted a person to mow grass and do yard work one day a week. She took the job.

When Marcy showed up at the Porter's house, Mrs. Porter showed her what to do. For the rest of the day she mowed, raked, pruned, trimmed, and pulled weeds. The lawn and garden were beautiful and Marcy took pride in making them even more attractive. After

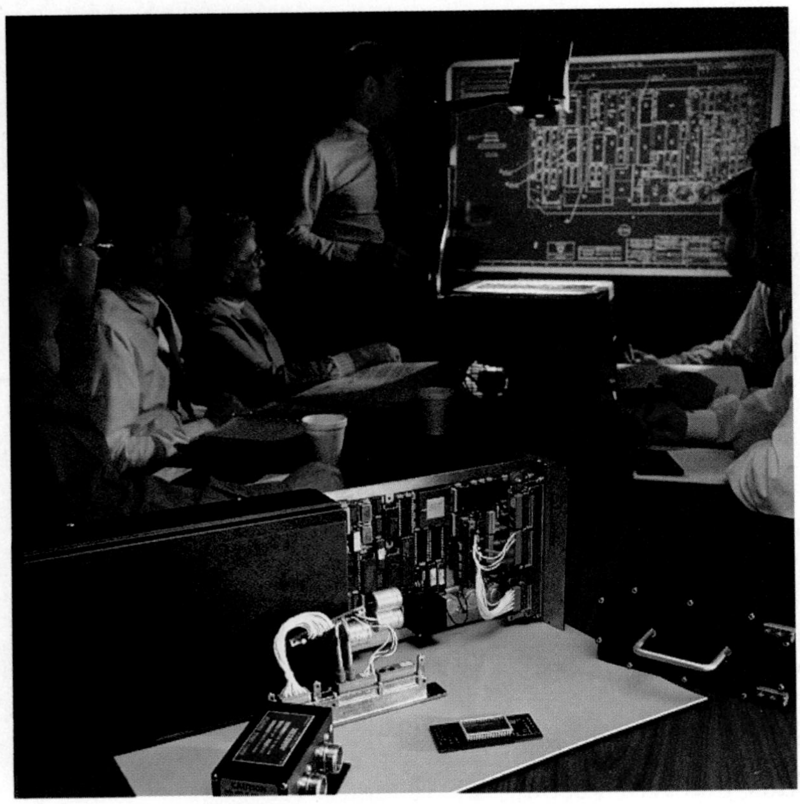

FIGURE 2–3 **Getting additional education or training often pays off in career advancement.**
© Ed Wheeler and AMETEK Inc.

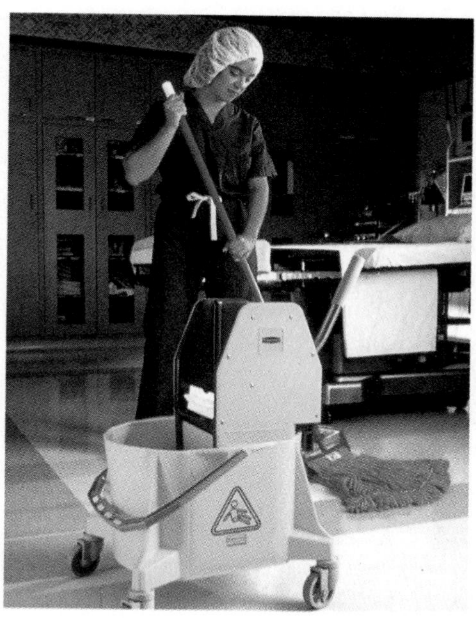

FIGURE 2–4 **Give your job your best effort, even if you would prefer a different kind of work.**

Photograph © 1993, Rubbermaid Incorporated. Used with permission.

she finished, she cleaned the mower, put away the tools, and swept the walk and driveway. Mrs. Porter thanked her and paid her.

She returned a week later and did a really good job. When Mrs. Porter paid her this time, she complimented her and gave her a bonus. She said that it was very difficult to find people willing and able to do good work. Mrs. Porter asked her if she would be interested in doing yard work for some of her neighbors.

Before long Marcy had all the jobs she was able to do. She learned that quality effort pays off. Because her work was appreciated, Marcy was able to use Mrs. Porter's name as a reference for a later job. Mrs. Porter was a well-respected member of the community. Her recommendations helped Marcy many times in later years.

Change is Certain

The world of work is continually changing. Some industries and occupations become *obsolete* (no longer used) as new ones are created. For example, the number of telephone operators has steadily decreased because of new electronic switching equipment. This *technology,* however, has created a need for new types of workers who can install and maintain such equipment. During your worklife, you will probably have to adjust to great change.

People who are more successful are generally those who anticipate and adapt to change. Marilyn and Bob are a good example. Marilyn and Bob own a typing and printing

? ? ? ? ? ? ? ? ? ? ? ? ? ? ?

WHAT WOULD YOU DO?

You have been operating your own small business for several years. You make a good income and are optimistic about the future. One day a salesperson calls on you to demonstrate a new piece of manufacturing equipment. He claims that this new machine will make the current method obsolete in a few years. He also says that most businesses like yours are already planning to install the equipment. You are not so sure. The new machine is very expensive. Since your business is currently doing very well, you question whether you actually need it.

What would you do?

FIGURE 2–5 **Technologies, such as fiber-optics, have created many new jobs.**
Courtesy of Corning Incorporated.

service. Most of their clients are small business owners and college students.

A few years ago, they began to get requests for desktop publishing. They had to decline the business. They explained that their office did only word processing. However, Marilyn and Bob saw the changes that were coming. They remembered years earlier having to switch from electric typewriters to computers.

To meet the needs of the clients, they purchased desktop publishing software and a laser printer. Bob, Marilyn, and the office staff took extra time to learn how to use the new software and equipment. They are glad they did. They now have more business and have been able to pay for the new equipment with the increased earnings.

Part of your preparation for a career should include planning for change. Become familiar with how the workplace is changing. Then try to develop the skills you will need in tomorrow's workplace. Look over the Contents for this book. You will find that much of the later material is concerned with preparing you for the challenge of change.

THE FUTURE BEGINS NOW

Some young people regard school as something to get through so they can be free to do what they want. What is the problem with this attitude? Well, school is a workplace, too. A prospective employer will look at your school record for clues as to what kind of an employee you might be. A poor school record is hard to defend. Blaming teachers or someone else for your problems will not impress anyone.

Perhaps you have done poorly in school thus far. What can you do now? You can always work harder during what is left of your high school career. A marked improvement in your attitude and performance will be helpful later. It will show teachers and employers that you have become a more mature person.

Now is the time to change habits and attitudes that may hold you back in the workplace. If, for example, you are frequently absent or late to school, make a greater effort to go to school and to be on time.

FIGURE 2–6 **It is never too late to change a negative attitude or behavior.**
Photo by Liane Enkelis.

Or, if you often commit careless errors in your schoolwork, take the time to reread or recheck your work before turning it in.

Consider taking more courses that will strengthen your academic background. Most jobs require basic mathematics and communication skills. You may want to take more math or English. If you haven't already, how about trying a computer course? Being familiar with computers is required in most jobs. Your work experience coordinator or school counselor may have other suggestions depending on your background and needs.

In Chapter 3, you will learn how to look for a job. You may discover that a job search can be frustrating. You may end up accepting a job that is less than what you had hoped for. If so, do not get discouraged. Remember what you have learned in this chapter about the different routes to a stable, satisfying job. *How you begin your career is less important than getting it started.* You can then use the beginning job as a stepping stone to something better.

FOCUS ON

The Workplace

Coping with Shift Work

You may apply for or be offered a job someday that requires you to work various shifts. The demand for round-the-clock shift workers has doubled since 1960. More than 25 million Americans now work the night shift (midnight to 8 A.M.). This trend is expected to continue as more businesses stay open 24 hours.

Some employees work the second and third shifts on a permanent basis. Others are rotated frequently from shift to shift. Time shuffling can have its price, however. The health and productivity of shift workers may suffer. An upside-down schedule disturbs the body's "inner clock." This can cause fatigue and digestive problems. Rotating shift workers also make more mistakes than workers with set shifts. For example, between midnight and dawn nurses dispense wrong medication more often and truckers have more single-vehicle accidents than do workers with set shifts.

A new breed of scientists called chronobiologists are beginning to solve some of these problems. Most problems are related to the direction and rate of shift rotation. Rotation can be clockwise (going to work later at each change) or counterclockwise (going to work earlier). Shifts may change every day or two, or every several weeks. It has been found that the body adjusts better to a clockwise rotation schedule; that is, rotating from the day shift to the swing shift to the night shift. At least three weeks should elapse between shift changes. Companies trying this pattern have found major improvement in production and less workers' complaints about schedules.

You may be asked to work nights sometime in your working career.

© Frank Herholdt/Tony Stone Images, Inc.

CHAPTER 2 REVIEW

CHAPTER IN BRIEF

- The jobs that you hold during your working life form a work history. People often have very different work histories. Knowing about work histories can help you think about and plan your own career.
- A job can serve different purposes at different times in your life. Beginning jobs are often used to achieve something else, for example, to learn a skill, save money for college, or qualify for a better job.
- A stable job is one that you consider to be permanent. It may last for several years. Many different routes can lead to a stable job. One route is not necessarily better than another.
- There are other common characteristics of stable jobs. One is that most stable jobs result from hard work and self-direction. Another is that quality effort on a job usually pays off. A third characteristic is that people with successful, stable jobs are generally ones who anticipate and adapt to change.
- You can take steps now to influence the direction of your career. Work harder during what is left of your high school years. Change habits and attitudes that may hold you back in the workplace. Consider taking additional courses to strengthen your academic background.

WORDS TO KNOW

obsolete
promotion
qualify
self-direction
stable job
technology
work history

QUESTIONS TO ANSWER

1. What are some reasons why people are unable to establish a successful work history?
2. Give an example to show how knowledge of work histories can help you think about and plan a career.
3. Name three reasons why a person might voluntarily leave a stable job.
4. Jobs can serve different purposes at different times in our lives. Give three examples.
5. Give an example to show how taking a risk can lead to greater success in a career.
6. How can technological change influence a career? Give one positive and one negative example.
7. Why are employers usually interested in how well you have done in school?

8. Name three things that you might begin to do now to influence your career.

ACTIVITIES TO DO

1. Ask a parent or other adult to list all the jobs he or she has held. Compare the work histories in class. What are the similarities and differences? Which types of work histories are the more common?
2. In doing Activity 1, did you note how work histories may be influenced by things such as illnesses, accidents, economic hard times, wars, and so on? List as many things as you can beyond one's control that may influence a career. Discuss your answers in class.
3. Think about your own work habits and attitudes. Write down two or three things that need improving. (We all have a few faults.) Go over the list with your work experience coordinator. Discuss what you can do to improve your performance.

TOPICS TO DISCUSS

1. Reread the case study about Rick's work history. Discuss why you think he has not progressed toward a stable job. What would you recommend that he do next?
2. If you are currently employed, do you think that your present job might develop into a stable job? Why or why not?
3. Do you think that hard work and quality effort pays off? Or is this just a myth that parents, teachers, and employers want you to believe?
4. Some young people not enrolled in a work experience program leave after school and go to a job. They often work from 3:30 or 4:00 in the afternoon to 10:30 or 11:00 at night. On weekends, they may put in eight to sixteen additional hours. Do you think that some teenagers are trying to work too much while attending high school? Share any relevant personal experiences that you may have.

CHAPTER 3 Looking for a Job

OUTLINE

- Thinking About Your Job Goals
- Getting Ready
- Finding Job Leads
- Keeping Track of Job Leads
- Chapter Review

OBJECTIVES

After reading this chapter, you should be able to:

- Describe the importance of clarifying job goals before looking for employment.
- Explain how to get a social security number and work permit.
- Identify different sources of job leads.
- Illustrate how to prepare a job-lead card.
- Summarize the benefits of using job-lead cards.

Students enrolled in work experience education programs get jobs in several ways. In cooperative vocational education, the coordinator plays a major role. The coordinator usually "sets up" training stations in the community and interviews and selects qualified students for admission to the program. The coordinator then takes into account students' interests, aptitudes, and job goals. These are matched with suitable jobs. It is up to the student, however, to interview with the employer and get the job.

In work-study programs, a student may get a job before or after entering the program. Some students will already have a job and ask to continue it for school credit. This may be done as

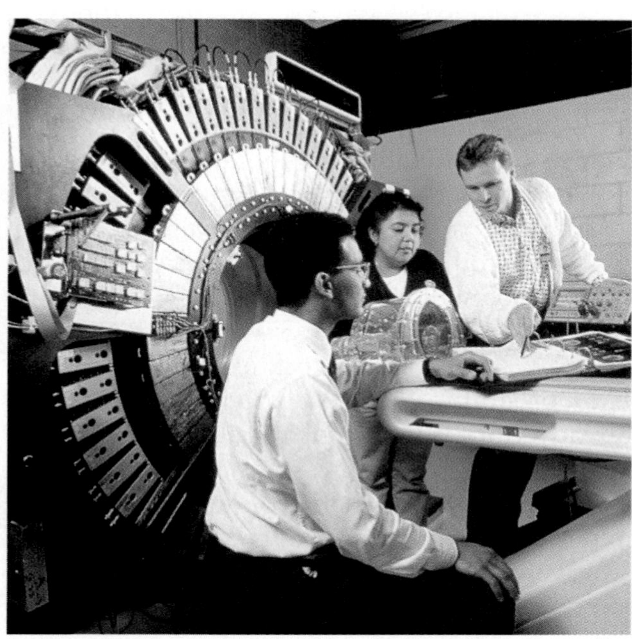

FIGURE 3–1 **The coordinator must approve your work-study job. Why is this a good idea?**
Photo by Tom Ferdebar, Courtesy of General Electric Company.

long as the coordinator approves the training station. Students who do not have jobs when they enroll in a work-study program will need to find one.

In this chapter and Chapters 4 and 5, you will learn how to find a job. If you do not have a job, you will be able to use the information right away. If you are working now, the material will help you in your next job search.

THINKING ABOUT YOUR JOB GOALS

Why do you want a job? Be prepared to answer this question. You will be hearing it often. Your work experience coordinator will certainly ask it. The coordinator wants to help you find a job that suits your interests and abilities. By getting to know you better, your coordinator can help you get a job you will enjoy. Counselors, placement officers, and others you approach for job leads will ask you about your job goals. And, of course, an interviewer will probably ask the question during a job interview.

Thinking about your job goals will help you, too. What you want out of a job will influence how and where you look for one. Since you are now enrolled in a work experience program, you have probably already done some thinking about your goals.

Reviewing the benefits of work experience education covered in Chapter 1 can help you clarify your job goals. If you recall, these are:

- Learning occupational skills
- Developing employability skills
- Establishing a work record
- Earning while you learn
- Discovering career interests and goals
- Recognizing the relationship between education and work
- Remaining employed after graduation

You may want to rank the benefits in order of their importance to you. Doing this can help you focus on your most important goals.

It was not difficult for Rachel to decide what she wanted out of a job. She had been interested in printing for a long time. In the ninth grade, she took a year of industrial education where she learned about the basic principles of offset printing.

Next, she took two years of vocational graphics and printing. In those courses, she learned about all aspects of offset printing. She liked

FIGURE 3–2 You will be asked why you want a particular job many times during your job search. Be prepared with a good answer.
Photo by David W. Tuttle.

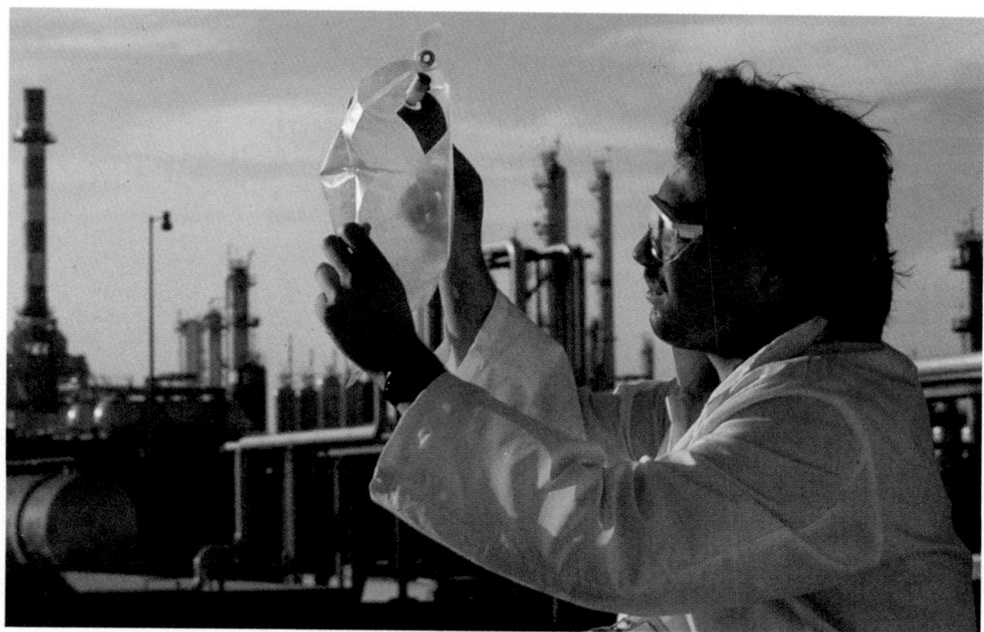

FIGURE 3–3 **Becoming an air quality technician is one possible occupational goal.**
Courtesy of Corning Incorporated.

the printing courses. What she was most interested in, however, was computer graphics. But the high school did not offer any courses in that area.

Rachel enrolled in a cooperative vocational education program so she could get a job in her area of interest. She now works for the publications department of a large company. Rachel is learning more about computer graphics. Rachel likes what she is doing. Her only regret is that she cannot work full time. She hopes that the company will hire her full time when she graduates. Can you name Rachel's goals?

GETTING READY

If you do not have a social security number, you should get one before you start a job search. (A Federal law took effect in 1988 requiring every person who is one year of age or older to have a social security number to be claimed as a dependent on tax form 1040.) You may also need to get a work permit.

Social Security Number

Social Security is a national program of social insurance. Your employer will withhold money from your paycheck for this. The money will go to the Social Security system. When you retire, you will receive income payments from Social Security. You will learn more about Social Security in Chapter 27.

In order for the government to keep a record of your earnings, you will need a social security number. The number will remain with you for life. No one else has the same number. An employer will ask for your number when you apply for a job or start work. Your social security number may have other uses, too. For example, in some states,

FIGURE 3–4 **Everyone in the work force must have a social security card. Be sure to apply for one if you do not have yours.**
Courtesy of Social Security Administration.

your driver's license identification number is the same as your social security number.

You can apply for a number at any Social Security office. You must fill out an application form and provide proof of your date of birth, identity, and U.S. citizenship. You will receive a social security card about two to four weeks after you apply.

Work Permit

At one time, employers were free to hire workers of any age for any type of job. It was not uncommon for young children to work long days in factories, mills, and mines.

Various federal and state laws now protect the health and safety of *minors.* Such laws regulate working conditions and working hours of students under the age of sixteen or eighteen. For instance, the Fair Labor Standards Act states that a person under the age of sixteen may not be employed during school hours. Some states have stricter laws than others regarding child labor.

A *work permit,* however, makes it legal for a "student learner" to work during school hours as part of a work experience education program. A work permit restricts the number of hours worked and the types of jobs a student can perform. School officials issue work permits for students under a certain age. In some states, the age is sixteen. In others, it is eighteen.

Besides a work permit, your state or school district may require other kinds of approval before you can work. Ask your school counselor or work experience coordinator about such rules.

FINDING JOB LEADS

It was the first day of the new school year. Sally was on the way to her work experience education class. "I wonder what job they will have for me," thought Sally.

The bell rang and students turned their attention to Mr. Amed, the teacher-coordinator. He took attendance and then began to explain about work experience education.

? ? ? ? ? ? ? ? ? ? ? ? ? ?

WHAT WOULD YOU DO?

You learn about a job opening for a part-time custodian at the shopping mall. The hours are good, and the pay is decent for a beginning job. You cannot decide whether to apply. You really do not want to empty waste-bas kets and mop floors. You wonder how you will feel if your friends see you working.

What would you do?

"A requirement of this program," he explained, "is that each of you must have a job. Some of you already have jobs. For the rest of you, your first 'job' will be to get a job. I do not have any jobs to assign."

Sally was somewhat surprised. She raised her hand to ask a question. "But I do not know where to get a job," she said.

"Do not worry," said Mr. Amed. "I will help you learn about sources of job leads and how to apply for a job."

If you do not have a job yet either, you will need to plan how to get one. At this point in your life, you will probably apply for an entry-level job. An *entry-level job* requires little or no experience. The following sources of job leads are those through which you are most likely to find a job.

Family and Friends

Start your job search by making a list of your relatives, neighbors, and friends. Include your working friends. They may know of job leads from their own job searches. Do not forget places where you and your family do business. You may want to have a family member review your final list.

Do not hesitate asking family or friends for help. However, do not expect them to find a job for you. Getting a job lead is the most you should hope for. It will be up to you to pursue the lead.

In-school Sources

Three good sources of job leads may be available within your school. One is your cooperative vocational education or work experience coordinator. He or she is probably already involved in helping you. Do not sit back and wait for the coordinator to find you a job.

Most schools also have a guidance office or guidance counselor. It is common for local employers to contact counselors when looking for workers. The counselor will usually keep a list of job openings or post them on a bulletin board. Tell the counselor that you are looking for a job and ask to see any information available about job openings.

A third source is job placement offices or career centers. Interested students generally register with the office. They may receive job counseling and other services. Job counselors help to match up students with job openings and make *referrals* for interviews. That is, they send students to employers who are hiring.

Students enrolled in postsecondary technical schools and community colleges usually have the same types of in-school assistance available as do secondary school students. In community preemployment training projects for out-of-school youth and unemployed adults, a job placement specialist is often available.

Newspaper Classified Ads

When employers have jobs to fill, they often advertise them in the newspaper. Most newspapers have a section that includes help-wanted ads. Four common kinds of ads are shown in Figure 3–5, on page 32.

The first kind is an *open ad.* It tells about the job requirements, identifies the employer, and tells how to apply. This is the best type of ad.

PART-TIME CLERK TYPIST. Approximately 20 hours per week, including some evenings and Saturdays. Experience with typing, filing, telephone reception, and work with public desirable. Must be dependable and able to work regular hours. $5.15 per hour. Applications accepted until Tuesday, Jan. 15, 1995 at 5 P.M. to Mary Campbell, Alton Public Library, 405 W. Main, Alton, MA 43331, 555-0135.

OPEN AD

Draftsperson
$18,000 & Up
Fee Paid

Male or female, at least 2 years experience. Call us or bring in your resume to compare your experience with our company requirements.

JOLEN
EMPLOYMENT AGENCY
17 Plaza Offices, P.O. Box 531
Tucker, TX 95313
555-0192

AGENCY SPOT AD

EARN
$100 TO $500

Write for details
P.O. Box 113
Sunnyvale, CA 75391

CATCH-TYPE AD

CLERICAL
Local manufacturer has immediate part-time clerical position open. Involves heavy computer entry, 4 hours a day, 5 days a week. Prefer afternoons.
Write: CLERICAL
P.O. Box 75A, Union Station,
Green Hills, NY 10112

BLIND AD

FIGURE 3–5 **Four common kinds of help-wanted ads.**

The second kind is the *blind ad.* The name, address, and phone number of the employer are not shown. Employers do this to keep from being bombarded with phone calls. It also allows them to screen applications carefully. Only qualified applicants are then invited for an interview.

A *catch-type ad* is the third kind. It tends to promise good salary and downplay the qualifications needed for the job. The "catch" is that the job is usually for door-to-door salespeople.

The last kind of ad is the *agency spot ad.* Note that the ad omits the name of the employer. It is used by private employment agencies to advertise jobs available only through the agency.

Job Service

Every state has a system of public employment offices usually called the *Job Service.* The services are provided free by the government. The primary purpose of the Job Service is to help workers who have lost jobs or been laid-off find jobs. Services are also provided to first-time job seekers, but preference is usually given to previously employed workers.

Some offices have a youth counselor who works mainly with young people. Job Service counselors often cooperate closely with local high school work experience programs and community job training projects.

To use the Job Service, you must fill out an application. A counselor will interview you to find out your interests and qualifications. You might be asked to take an interest inventory or aptitude test. If a job is available, the counselor will arrange an interview for you.

Private Employment Agencies

These are businesses that find people jobs for a *fee*. The fee is paid either by the employer or the employee. If you use a private employment agency, be sure that you understand the financial arrangements *before* signing a contract or accepting an interview.

Private agencies do not generally deal with clients under eighteen and those who are looking for part-time, entry-level jobs. So do not be discouraged if you are turned down by a private agency.

Direct Employer Contact

Many people find jobs by talking directly to employers. A help-wanted sign posted in a business is the oldest method of announcing a job opening. If you see such a sign, ask the employer for an application.

Employers often have unadvertised job openings. A list of the twenty-five leading occupations is shown in Figure 3–6. Study this list to get an idea of the types of employers that hire a number of young workers. You might then use the telephone Yellow Pages to make a list of companies to contact.

OCCUPATION

1. Cashiers
2. Cooks, except short order
3. Stock handlers and baggers
4. Waiters and waitresses
5. Janitors and cleaners
6. Secretaries
7. Laborers, except construction
8. Waiters' and waitresses' assistants
9. Sales workers, apparel
10. Receptionists
11. Child-care workers, except private household
12. Food counter, fountain, and related occupations
13. Nursing aides, orderlies, and attendants
14. Supervisors and proprietors, sales occupations
15. Child-care workers, private household
16. Truckdrivers, light
17. Bank tellers
18. Construction laborers
19. Garage and service station related occupations
20. Farm workers
21. Carpenters
22. Bookkeepers and accounting and auditing clerks
23. General office clerks
24. Groundskeepers and gardeners, except farm
25. Computer operators

FIGURE 3–6 **The twenty-five leading occupations for workers aged 16–24.**
Source: Occupational Outlook Quarterly.

Another means of direct employer contact is to visit a company employment office. Go dressed as you would for an interview. Be prepared to fill out an employment application form. Check bulletin boards outside the personnel office, too. Available jobs are often listed there. Some companies also have a separate telephone number that provides prerecorded messages about job openings.

? ? ? ? ? ? ? ? ? ? ? ? ? ?

WHAT WOULD YOU DO?

A schoolmate approaches you and says he heard you were looking for a job. He has a buddy who needs some people to deliver "packages" on weekends. The work is easy. You simply ride the bus around town and drop off packages at various places of business. The pay is $10 per hour in cash. You are told not to ask questions or to discuss the job with other people. You are concerned about taking the job because it sounds "fishy."

What would you do?

KEEPING TRACK OF JOB LEADS

"Hey, Steve," said Kevin. "I got my first job lead yesterday. I was eating lunch when I noticed the manager putting up a sign. It was for a part-time kitchen helper. So I wrote the information down."

"Great! What did the sign say?" asked Steve.

"Let me see," answered Kevin. "I have the information here someplace."

Kevin continued to search his backpack for the scrap of paper on which he took notes. Finally he said, "Darn, I must have lost it. Oh well, I will go back this weekend and get the information again."

Kevin is off to a shaky start in his search for a job. He was alert to notice the sign and to write down the information. Kevin was careless, though, in misplacing his notes. He also showed poor judgment in not going back or calling right away. When he returned on the weekend, he found the job was filled.

Job-lead Card

Whenever you learn about a job lead, make up a *job-lead card.* An example is shown in Figure 3–7. A five-by-eight-inch card works best because it gives you enough room to record information and make notes. The card has two parts.

On the "Job Lead" part (side one) record all important information

JOB LEAD

Source: *Daily Gazette*

Date: *1/20/--*

Type of Position: *Packing Clerk*

Person to Contact: *Steve*

Company Name:

Address: *Near Lindberg & Olive*

Phone Number: *555-0151*

PACKING CLERKS
PART-TIME JOB OPENINGS
Please: these are not full-time jobs. We have peak business seasons in Jan., Feb., Apr., Oct. Hours will vary from 0 to 40 a week. Also may have late afternoon (3 p.m.-7 p.m.) shift available. Job requires standing & using manual dexterity while preparing and packing women's clothing, shoes and gifts for UPS shipment. Perfect job situation for housewives, househusbands or students. Again—not a full-time job! Near Lindbergh & Olive. No smoking. $5.30 per hour. All applicants must pass a written test.
CALL STEVE, 555-0151

ACTION TAKEN

Call Made To: *Steve (555-0151)*

Date: *1/21/--*

Contact Made With:

Date:

Results: *Asked to come in and fill out job application and take a written test.*

Date, Time, and Place of Appointment: *1/23/--, 9:30 am, Mid-West Packaging Inc. Use main entrance.*

Follow-Up: *After test call back (ask for Steve) on 1/28/-- for possible interview.*

FIGURE 3–7 **Sample job-lead card.**

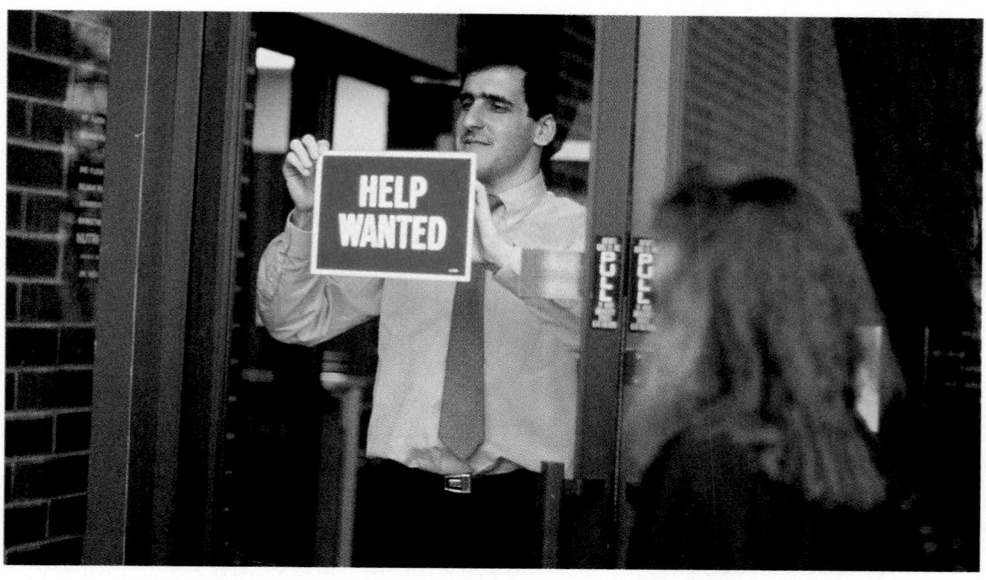

FIGURE 3–8 **When you find a job opening that interests you, apply quickly so you do not lose the opportunity.**
Photo by Paul E. Meyers.

about the job. If you have a newspaper help-wanted ad, tape it onto the card. If the lead comes from a different source, write on the card the company name, address, phone number, and the person to contact about the job.

On the "Action Taken" part (side two) record what you did to follow up the job lead. Write down the date when you contacted the employer and the name of the person with whom you talked. Also write down the results of the contact. If you get an appointment, record the date, time, and place. If you need directions to the interview, be sure to ask. Write the directions on the back of the card. Any follow-up you do after an interview should also be noted.

What are some benefits of using job-lead cards? They keep you from forgetting important information. They save you time, too. By being organized, you can get more results from the time you spend. Can you name other benefits?

Following Through

You read earlier how Kevin failed to act on a job lead. His big mistake was in not talking to the manager when he saw her posting a help-wanted sign. Had he done so, he might have gotten the job. Most employers want to fill job openings as quickly as they can.

You face stiff competition for jobs. Do not hold back. As soon as you learn about a job lead, follow through with quick action. The early applicant gets the job. If you do not get the job immediately, call or go back a few days later. Let the employer know that you are really interested in the job.

Motivation and persistence, so important in finding a job, are also qualities that make you a good employee. Employers recognize this. Demonstrating motivation and persistence in pursuing a job lead increases your chance of being rewarded with a job offer.

FOCUS ON The Workplace

TEMPORARY WORK

One of the fast-growing industries in America is the temporary services industry. These are companies like Kelly Services, Manpower, and others that provide listings of available workers to employers who need short-term help.

Temporary workers (temps) are hired to fill in when a permanent employee quits, gets sick, or goes on vacation. Some are hired to help out when a special project requires extra people for a short time. The most common temporary jobs involve secretaries, receptionists, and bookkeepers.

Who are these temporary workers? There are five categories:

1. *Rusty Skills.* Some people have not worked for a while and are uncertain of their abilities. "Temping" gives them a chance to brush up on old skills before looking for a permanent job.
2. *Uncertain Goals.* Some people are not sure what type of work they want to do. Temping allows them to sample different jobs before deciding.
3. *Between Jobs.* New high school or college graduates often cannot find the right position. Temping is a way to finance a job hunt so they don't have to accept the first offer.
4. *Supporting Another Occupation.* Some people who work as writers, artists, or performers do not have permanent jobs. They do temp work to pay the bills while they pursue their preferred line of work.
5. *Extra Money.* Students working their way through college are a major source of temps. So are retirees looking for additional income.

A temporary job may be as short as a day or as long as a year. The average length is one to two weeks. At some point in your life, a temporary job may meet your needs.

Conventions and trade shows are opportunities for many temporary jobs.

CHAPTER 3 REVIEW

CHAPTER IN BRIEF

- What you want out of a job will influence how and where you look for it. Therefore, think about your job goals before beginning the job search. Do this by reviewing the seven benefits of work experience education.
- Apply for a social security number as soon as possible. An employer will ask for your number when you apply for a job or start work. In some states, you may also need to get a work permit.
- To be enrolled in cooperative vocational education or work-study, you must have a job. If you do not already have one, your first "job" will be to get a job. The most common sources of entry-level jobs are: (a) family and friends, (b) in-school sources, (c) newspaper classified ads, (d) Job Service, (e) private employment agencies, and (f) direct employer contact.
- Whenever you learn about a job lead, make up a job-lead card. It will help you remember important information, save you time, and help you get more positive results. After recording all important information about a job lead, follow through with quick action. Most employers want to fill job openings as soon as possible.

WORDS TO KNOW

entry-level job
fee
job-lead card
Job Service
minors
referrals
work permit

QUESTIONS TO ANSWER

1. Sarah has a part-time job. She is starting a work experience program. How can she keep her job and get school credit?
2. Why is it important to clarify your job goals before beginning the job search?
3. Why must you get a social security number before you start work?
4. Andrea hesitates about asking friends and family for job leads. She says she would "feel funny" about doing so. Do you agree with her? Why or why not?
5. Your school may have three sources of job leads. Name them.
6. Name the four kinds of newspaper help-wanted ads.
7. What are the main differences between a public and a private employment agency?
8. Employers use various methods to announce job openings. Name the oldest method.
9. Name the two parts of a job-lead card?
10. Why should you follow through with quick action on a job lead?

ACTIVITIES TO DO

1. Find out your state's requirements on student employment during school hours. If a work permit or other type of approval is required, take the necessary steps to complete the approval process.
2. Get the help-wanted section of a Sunday newspaper that serves your geographic area. Cut out examples of the four types of ads described earlier in the chapter. Tape the examples onto a sheet of paper and label each type of ad. Then give the paper to your instructor. When you get your paper back, discuss your ads with the class.
3. Perhaps your instructor can arrange to make copies of a job-lead card. Or someone in the class might volunteer to make a sample. Duplicate enough so that each person has at least ten. Divide the printing cost among class members.
4. Using the telephone Yellow Pages, list the names and phone numbers of four possible job leads in each of the following categories: (a) employment agencies, (b) temporary agencies, (c) charitable organizations, (d) labor organizations, and (e) trade and professional associations.

TOPICS TO DISCUSS

1. What role does the teacher-coordinator play in helping students find jobs in work experience education programs?
2. Why have state and federal laws been passed restricting the hours of employment and regulating the working conditions of minors?
3. Six major sources of job leads are discussed in this chapter. Can you think of other sources in your city or community that have not been mentioned?
4. The ease or difficulty of finding a job may be influenced by where you live, for example, whether you live in a city or rural area. What other environmental, economic, or occupational factors influence job availability?

CHAPTER 4 Applying for a Job

OUTLINE

- Personal Data Sheet
- Job Application Form
- Writing a Resume
- Contacting Employers
- Pre-employment Tests
- Chapter Review

OBJECTIVES

After reading this chapter, you should be able to:

- Prepare a personal data sheet.
- Complete a job application form.
- Prepare a job resume.
- Explain the three methods of contacting employers about a job.
- Describe the two most common types of pre-employment tests.

Finding job leads may seem to take a long time. It does indeed take a great deal of time to contact family and friends, search the newspaper help-wanted ads, and identify other leads. Once you find a good job lead, however, things can speed up very quickly.

Richard learned from his Uncle Geraldo about a bowling buddy who was expanding his hardware store. Uncle Geraldo thought his friend might be hiring some new employees and suggested Richard should call him.

The next day Richard called Mr. Stevenson at the hardware store. He explained that he was looking for a job and that his uncle had told him to call. Mr. Stevenson said that he had already received several inquiries about the job.

"However," he went on to say, "I would be happy to have you fill out a job application form. Why not stop by and see me after school tomorrow?"

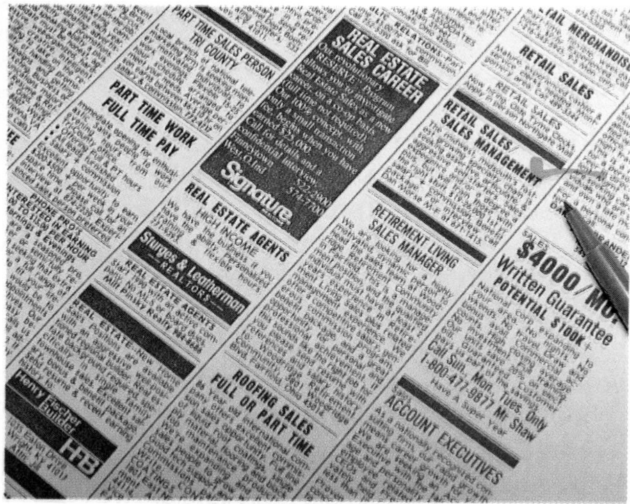

FIGURE 4–1 **The newspaper is a good source for job leads, either in the help-wanted ads or through local business news.**

"Thank you very much," said Richard. "I will be there at four o'clock tomorrow afternoon."

Donna is also on the trail of a hot job lead. She read an ad in the newspaper for a Hair Stylist/Shampoo Assistant. "Experience helpful but not necessary," the ad said. "Full training available. Send a resume to The Hair Performers, 638 North Walnut St., Muncie, IN, 47396."

"This sounds like what I am looking for," Donna told her family. "I'd better get a letter of application typed and put my resume in the mail at once."

Richard and Donna were ready to take quick action on job leads. Richard already had a *personal data sheet* prepared to assist him in filling out a *job application form.* Likewise, Donna had a stack of job *resumes* (pronounced REZ-oo-may) ready and waiting. She also knew how to write a *letter of application.* Richard and Donna have learned some valuable skills needed to apply for a job. In this chapter, you will learn how to do these things, too.

PERSONAL DATA SHEET

Let us say that you are in Richard's shoes and have to fill out a job application form tomorrow. Will you be prepared? Can you, for example, remember the name, address, and telephone number of each employer for whom you have worked? Or do you know your high school class rank and grade point average? How about references? Will you be prepared to list the names of people who could provide an evaluation of you?

Most employers require job seekers to fill out an application form. Some applications ask for very brief information. Others, however, may be very detailed. To be ready, you need to prepare a personal data sheet. You will not give it directly to an employer. You will take it with you and *use it to fill out the job application form.* You will also *use it to prepare a job resume.*

A personal data sheet contains four primary types of information. A sample data sheet is shown in Figure 4–2, on pages 41 and 42. You can add to or take out parts to meet your own needs. Some parts of the form, such as early educational background, may require you to obtain help from a family member. Similarly, the part on employment history may require you to search past records for specific information.

- *A. Identification.* Included in this part are personal identification and family information. In-school and extracurricular activities, interests, awards received, and the like are also recorded. The intent here is to provide information that explains who and what type of a person you are.
- *B. Educational Background.* In the next section record information about your educational background. You want to include data on all schools attended. Repeat the basic information for as many schools as required. Employers will be interested in what type of a student you are.
- *C. Employment History.* Information about all previous paid employment is included here. Start with present or most recent

PERSONAL DATA SHEET

IDENTIFICATION

Name ______________________ Soc. Sec. # ______________

Address ____

________________________________ Zip Code __________

Telephone (   ) ________________________________

Hobbies/Interests ______________________________

Honors/Awards/Offices __________________________

Sports/Activities ______________________________

Other ____

____

EDUCATIONAL BACKGROUND

School Name and Address	Dates Attended From:	To:
Elementary:		
Junior High:		
High School:		

Course of Study ________________ Rank ________ GPA ________

Favorite Subject(s) ____________________________

FIGURE 4–2A **Follow this general outline when you prepare a personal data sheet. Use it to fill out a job application form and create a resume.**

EMPLOYMENT HISTORY
(Start with present or most recent employer.)

1. Company ______________________ Telephone (___)__________

Address ______________________________________

Employed from Mo. ____ Yr. ____ / to Mo. ____ Yr. ____ Supervisor ____________

Position/Title ______________________________________

Last Wage __________ Reason for Leaving ______________________

2. Company ______________________ Telephone (___)__________

Address ______________________________________

Employed from Mo. ____ Yr. ____ / to Mo. ____ Yr. ____ Supervisor ____________

Position/Title ______________________________________

Last Wage __________ Reason for Leaving ______________________

3. Company ______________________ Telephone (___)__________

Address ______________________________________

Employed from Mo. ____ Yr. ____ / to Mo. ____ Yr. ____ Supervisor ____________

Position/Title ______________________________________

Last Wage __________ Reason for Leaving ______________________

REFERENCES

1. Name ______________________ Title ______________________

Address ______________________________ Zip Code ______

Relationship ______________________ Telephone (___)__________

2. Name ______________________ Title ______________________

Address ______________________________ Zip Code ______

Relationship ______________________ Telephone (___)__________

3. Name ______________________ Title ______________________

Address ______________________________ Zip Code ______

Relationship ______________________ Telephone (___)__________

FIGURE 4–2B **Personal Data Sheet continued.**

employment. Add employers as necessary.

- *D. References.* List here the names of persons who can provide information about your personal, school, and employment background. Examples include teachers, coaches, club advisors, previous employers, and clergy.

JOB APPLICATION FORM

When employers have jobs to fill, they usually ask interested people to fill out a job application form. The information provided on the form helps employers to sort out the best qualified persons for the job. After screening the application forms, a small number of people are invited for an interview.

If you have done a personal data sheet, you will have taken a big step toward filling out a job application form. You will be able to copy facts and information from the personal data sheet directly onto the job application form. Take your personal data sheet with you each time you contact an employer or employment office.

The type of job application form used will differ from company to company. A typical form is shown in Figure 4–3, on page 44. Follow these tips in filling out a job application form.

- Before you begin to fill out the form, read it over carefully. Study the instructions so you will know what information to provide. Note which parts are "for employer use only."

  You may receive an application form through the mail or have a chance to fill it out on your own and return it later. If your typing is fair to poor, print your answers in black ink. You may want to get an erasable ballpoint pen. This will allow you to correct mistakes easily. Be as neat as possible.
- You will probably be asked to print the information. It is a good idea to print even if it does not say to. Be sure to sign your name in those places where it asks for your signature. Use your correct name, not a nickname.
- Answer all questions on the form. If a question does not apply to you, put "NA" for "not applicable." Do not leave a blank space; the employer might think you forgot to answer the question.
- Answer all questions honestly. Giving false information can catch up with you later. If you do not have the information or do not know the answer, write in "unknown."
- List the specific position or job for which you are applying. Do not write "anything" in the space. You may be willing to accept any job; however, what you want to convey is that you are interested in and qualified for a certain job.
- Misspelled words give a poor impression of your ability. Take a small pocket or electronic dictionary with you (and use it).
- You may be asked to name the "wages or salary expected." It is best to discuss salary in a personal interview with the employer. So write "open" in the space provided.
- In the employment history part, you may be asked to give the reason for leaving a previous job. Do not put down anything that criticizes a past employer or

APPLICATION FOR EMPLOYMENT

(PRE-EMPLOYMENT QUESTIONNAIRE) (AN EQUAL OPPORTUNITY EMPLOYER)

PERSONAL INFORMATION

DATE April 15, 19--

NAME Fisher Ronald R.

SOCIAL SECURITY NUMBER 351-44-5751

PRESENT ADDRESS 6428 Valley Rd. Cambden Ohio 67423

PERMANENT ADDRESS same

PHONE NO. 627-555-0127 ARE YOU 18 YEARS OR OLDER? Yes ☒ No ☐

ARE YOU EITHER A U.S. CITIZEN OR AN ALIEN AUTHORIZED TO WORK IN THE UNITED STATES? Yes ☒ No ☐

EMPLOYMENT DESIRED

POSITION engine and powertrain mechanic DATE YOU CAN START May 1 SALARY DESIRED Open

ARE YOU EMPLOYED NOW? Yes IF SO MAY WE INQUIRE OF YOUR PRESENT EMPLOYER? Yes

EVER APPLIED TO THIS COMPANY BEFORE? No WHERE? ______ WHEN? ______

REFERRED BY Ken Jenkins

EDUCATION	NAME AND LOCATION OF SCHOOL	NO. OF YEARS ATTENDED	DID YOU GRADUATE?	SUBJECTS STUDIED
GRAMMAR SCHOOL	Cambden Elementary School District 95	8	Yes	general curriculum
HIGH SCHOOL	Cambden High School	4	Yes	vocational curriculum automotive
COLLEGE	Hillside Community College	2	Yes	automotive technology
TRADE, BUSINESS OR CORRESPONDENCE SCHOOL				

FORMER EMPLOYERS (LIST BELOW LAST THREE EMPLOYERS, STARTING WITH LAST ONE FIRST)

DATE (M/Y)	NAME AND ADDRESS OF EMPLOYER		POSITION	REASON FOR LEAVING
FROM June 19-- TO present	Goodman's Tire & Auto Center Cambden, OH	6.85 hr.	service technician	currently employed
FROM June 19-- TO May 19--	Hunter's Auto Repair — Eastbrook, OH	4.30 hr.	general auto repair	part-time only
FROM Aug. 19-- TO May 19--	Texacon Service Station — Cambden, OH	3.75 hr	auto maintenance	co-op student learner
FROM TO				

WHICH OF THESE JOBS DID YOU LIKE THE BEST? Hunter's Auto Repair

WHAT DID YOU LIKE MOST ABOUT THIS JOB? engine diagnosis

REFERENCES: GIVE THE NAMES OF THREE PERSONS NOT RELATED TO YOU, WHOM YOU HAVE KNOWN AT LEAST ONE YEAR.

NAME	ADDRESS	BUSINESS	YEARS ACQUAINTED
1 Earl Thompson	Goodman's Tire & Auto 219 E. Sycamore Cambden, OH	service manager	1.5
2 Archie Hunter	Hunter's Auto Repair 2025 W. Walnut Eastbrook, OH	owner/manager	2.0
3 Frank Hopkins	Hillside Community College – Eastbrook, OH	auto instructor	2.0

FIGURE 4–3 **This is a job application form that has been filled out correctly.**

? ? ? ? ? ? ? ? ? ? ? ? ? ?

WHAT WOULD YOU DO?

You see an ad in the newspaper for a computer operator. The job is exactly what you are looking for. However, the ad states that "prior work experience is required." You have not had any prior employment as a computer operator, but you have been operating your own computer for five years. You are confident that you can do the job. Should you ignore the stated requirement and apply for the job?

What would you do?

shows that you were not an acceptable employee. Examples of appropriate reasons for leaving a job are "returned to school," "left for a better job," and "job terminated."

- After you have filled out the form, check it over carefully before mailing it or handing it in.

What happens after you submit the job application form? Do you wait to hear from the employer? Are you supposed to go for an interview or make contact later with the employer? Some employers collect job applications for a position that begins on a certain date. Other employers, who may have no jobs available at the moment, collect applications for future use. Make sure you find out what to do next. Write the information down on the job-lead card that you are using to keep track of job leads.

WRITING A RESUME

When applying in person for a job, you may be asked for a resume. You should send a resume when applying for a job by letter.

If you have done a personal data sheet, you already have the basic information you will include in your resume. You will need to choose which parts of that information to use. Then you will have to arrange the information into a neat, organized format.

Your resume should be detailed enough to give an employer the information needed to judge your qualifications. It should also be brief. A busy employer wants the important facts in as few words as possible. In describing your work experience, for example, the sentence, "I was responsible for analyzing the cost sheets from the production department" is too lengthy. It can be condensed into a shorter phrase that provides the same information: "Analyzed production cost sheets."

An example of a completed resume is shown in Figure 4–4, on page 46. The resume provides five kinds of information. Personal information is given at the top of the page. Your name, address, and phone number are all that is needed.

In the next section, give a short statement of your career goals. Be specific about the type of job you are seeking. Do not limit yourself to one particular employer, though. (You want to be able to give the resume to many different employers.) Examples of possible goals might be:

- ". . . to obtain training and acquire experience in retail sales."

Ronald R. Fisher
6428 Valley Road
Cambden, Ohio 67423
(627) 555-0127

CAREER GOALS

My immediate objective is to obtain a job at a new car dealership as an engine and power train mechanic. My long-range goal is to become a shop supervisor or service manager. I am willing to complete additional training as required.

EDUCATIONAL BACKGROUND

19-- graduate of Hillside Community College in Eastbrock, Ohio. Received Associate of Applied Science Degree in Automotive Technology. Member of first-place team in regional engine troubleshooting competition.

July 19-- Licensed as a state auto and truck inspector (Ohio).

19-- graduate of Cambden High School. Completed two years of vocational auto and one year of cooperative vocational education. President of local Vocational Industrial Clubs of America (VICA).

WORK EXPERIENCE

June 19-- to present: Goodman's Tire and Auto Center, Cambden, Ohio. Duties include tune-ups, general engine repair, front wheel alignment, and wheel and brake work.

June 19-- to May 19--: Hunter's Auto Repair, Eastbrook, Ohio. Part-time and weekend work while attending college. Performed engine diagnosis, general engine repair, tune-ups, and transmission repair.

August 19-- to May 19--: Texacon Service Station, Cambden, Ohio. Part-time cooperative vocational education student-learner. Performed routine auto maintenance service and minor engine repair.

REFERENCES

Mr. Earl Thompson (Service Mgr.)
Goodman's Tire & Auto Center
219 E. Sycamore
Cambden, OH 67423
(627) 555-0164

Mr. Frank Hopkins (Automotive Inst.)
Vocational Education Department
Hillside Community College
Eastbrook, OH 67513
(314) 555-0173

Mr. Archie Hunter (Owner-Mgr.)
Hunter's Auto Repair
2025 W. Walnut
Eastbrook, OH 67513
(314) 555-0192

FIGURE 4–4 **Sample resume.**

- ". . . to gain practical work experience while saving money for college."
- ". . . to further develop my skills as a licensed practical nurse."

The third kind of information is about your education. List all high schools, colleges, technical schools, and so on. Begin with the most recent one. List any diplomas, degrees, licenses, and certificates you earned. Also mention any honors or awards you received. Name any job-related activities in which you participated. For example, Ronald Fisher's performance in an engine troubleshooting contest proves he has diagnostic and mechanical skills.

The fourth section is a summary of paid work experience. Begin with your present or most recent job. Identify previous employers, the time period worked, and the type of job duties you performed. Include co-op or work-study jobs here rather than in the section on educational background.

If you have limited paid work experience, it is proper to list paid or unpaid experiences, such as babysitting, yardwork, newspaper delivery, and so on. You can also mention volunteer work experience, such as being a junior volunteer, camp counselor, or campaign worker. If you think about it, you can probably identify many kinds of work experience that can compensate for having limited paid job experience.

The last section of the resume is a listing of *references.* These are individuals who have direct knowledge of your job performance. Two or three references are satisfactory. Present and previous employers and supervisors are best. A prospective employer will probably contact the references listed to inquire about your work habits, attitudes, and skills. If you are a recent graduate, you can list teachers who are familiar with your school work. A personal reference, such as a family friend, who can comment about your character may be listed as one of the references.

The resume should have a neat, error-free, professional appearance. Try to limit the length to one page. Type the resume on the same typewriter that was used for the letter of application. After it is typed, have multiple copies of the resume reproduced on a good quality paper.

CONTACTING EMPLOYERS

As you have learned, filling out a job application form is one way to apply for a job. Other methods include applying in person, by phone, and by letter.

Applying in Person

A help-wanted ad or sign will often contain the phrase "apply in person." The ad or sign may give the name of a person to contact or it may say to "ask for the manager." In some cases, though, the ad only tells you the name of the company.

When you apply for a job in person, first impressions are very important. Some employers, in fact, judge an applicant's appearance, self-confidence, and social skills this way. You want to be well-groomed and appropriately dressed. Introduce yourself and explain who you are. (For example, you may want to say you are a high school work experience education student.) In some instances, you may have been referred by an employment agency or were encouraged to apply by a placement counselor, teacher, or other person. In such a case, also share this information. Being referred or recommended by someone known to the employer can give you an immediate edge over other applicants. State your interest in the job advertised. If the first meeting goes well, the employer will probably ask you to fill out a job application form or leave a resume. Be prepared. Take along your personal data sheet and a copy of your resume.

Applying in person for a job is similar to going for a job interview. Most of the material in Chapter 5 on interviewing for a job will apply to this situation.

FIGURE 4–5 A help-wanted sign outside a business establishment should be answered in person.
Photo by Paul E. Meyers.

Applying by Telephone

Skillful use of the telephone is very important to a successful job search. By using the telephone you can make many contacts in the time it takes to make one personal visit. Of course, applying in person will still be necessary and desirable for some job leads.

??????????????

WHAT WOULD YOU DO?

One of your job-lead cards is for an opening at a business owned by your best friend's mother. You are not sure how to apply for the job. Should you call her at home or at work? Should you have your friend ask his mother for you? Should you give her a resume even though she already knows you? Should you address her as Betty, which you normally do, or as Mrs. Thompson?

What would you do?

The purpose of telephoning is to convert a job lead into an appointment for a job interview. In some cases, you may be following a suggestion from a family member or friend. An opening might not exist. For other leads, you know a certain opening is available. Perhaps you are answering a help-wanted ad.

Whatever your reasons for making the call, the following guidelines should help you:

- Get organized before you call. Have your job-lead card, pen, and paper ready. Know the purpose of your call. Plan what you are going to say. Write down information quickly so you do not have to ask the person to repeat what was said.
- Call from a quiet place. You do not want any background noise during the call.
- Speak clearly and directly into the telephone mouthpiece. Do

not have anything in your mouth when you talk.

- Give your name when calling and state your business as briefly as you can. Use the employer's name several times during the conversation. (Make sure it is correct.)
- Be courteous, friendly, and interested. Speak with a pleasant, even tone of voice. Put a "smile" in your voice, but talk naturally.
- Ask for a definite appointment, but do not sound pushy. If you get an appointment, write down the time, place, and the interviewer's name.

Letter of Application

Another way to act on a job lead is to write a letter of application. You might do this when acting on a suggestion from another person or responding to a newspaper help-wanted ad. A letter of application is often known as a *cover letter* when it is mailed along with a resume.

An example of a combination cover letter and letter of application is shown in Figure 4–6. Such a letter should have four parts.

1. In the first paragraph, you should explain your reason for writing. Name the job for which

6428 Valley Road
Cambden, OH 67423
April 16, 19--

Mr. Donald Young
Service Manager
Smith Auto Sales Inc.
274 Oakland Street
Cambden, OH 67423

Dear Mr. Young:

One of your employees, Ken Jenkins, told me that you plan to hire a new mechanic in a few weeks. I would like to apply for the position.

My training and experience fit your job. For the last two years, I worked at Goodman's Tire and Auto Center, primarily doing tune-ups, general engine repair, front wheel alignments, and wheel and brake work. While my present job is satisfying, I would like to work for a new car dealership where I can use my diagnostic and mechanical abilities. I hold a state inspection license and own my own tools.

The copy of my resume enclosed provides further details about my background. I could be available for employment following a two-week notice to my present employer.

I would be happy to meet you for an interview at your convenience. I can be reached after 4:00 p.m. at 555-0127.

Sincerely,

Ronald Fisher

Ronald Fisher

FIGURE 4–6 Sample letter of application.

you are applying. Also, tell how you learned about the job.

2. Use the second paragraph to briefly point out your qualifications. Give the facts, but do not brag. (Employers will look carefully at this paragraph.)
3. The third paragraph calls attention to the resume. It may also be wise to give a date when you are available for employment.
4. In the last paragraph, ask for an appointment. Tell how you can be contacted. Close the letter with a courteous comment or a thank-you.

Notice that the sample letter is short and to the point. The purpose of the letter is to attract and hold the reader's interest. It should not attempt to give facts that are better stated in a resume and job interview. If you are qualified for the job, the letter and resume should make the employer want to invite you for an interview.

The form and appearance of the letter is also very important. Write several drafts of the letter until you feel it is correct. Then have a teacher or parent check it over for correct spelling and grammar. Key the letter neatly, following a standard business-letter format. Use a good typewriter or word processor that will produce clean copy.

Proofread the letter carefully to check for errors. Ask a friend or family member to do the same. Make a copy of the letter for your files. You will be able to use it in the future as a guide in writing additional letters.

PRE-EMPLOYMENT TESTS

Dorothy lives in the city that is her state's capital. A large state university is nearby. The state government and university are two of the city's major employers.

Because they hire many employees, Dorothy applied for work at both offices. She was surprised to learn that she would have to take a test before she would be asked to interview for a job. Dorothy found something that is very common.

To apply for almost all state and federal government jobs, applicants must take one or more *pre-employment tests.* A test that people take before being considered for a government job is called a *civil service test.* The intent of civil service testing is to promote fairness in employment. Job applicants with the highest civil service test scores are given preference in hiring.

Nongovernment (private) employers may also give pre-employment tests. Large employers often give them as part of the job application process. For entry-level jobs with the government or private employers, the most common types of tests are general ability tests and performance tests.

General Ability Tests

A general ability test measures basic learning skills such as reading, spelling, vocabulary, and arithmetic. These written tests are similar to the types of tests that you have taken throughout your school years.

Performance Tests

In a performance test you demonstrate skills needed for a specific occupation. Some performance tests are paper-and-pencil tests. An example would be a clerical skills test that requires you to proofread a business letter for possible errors.

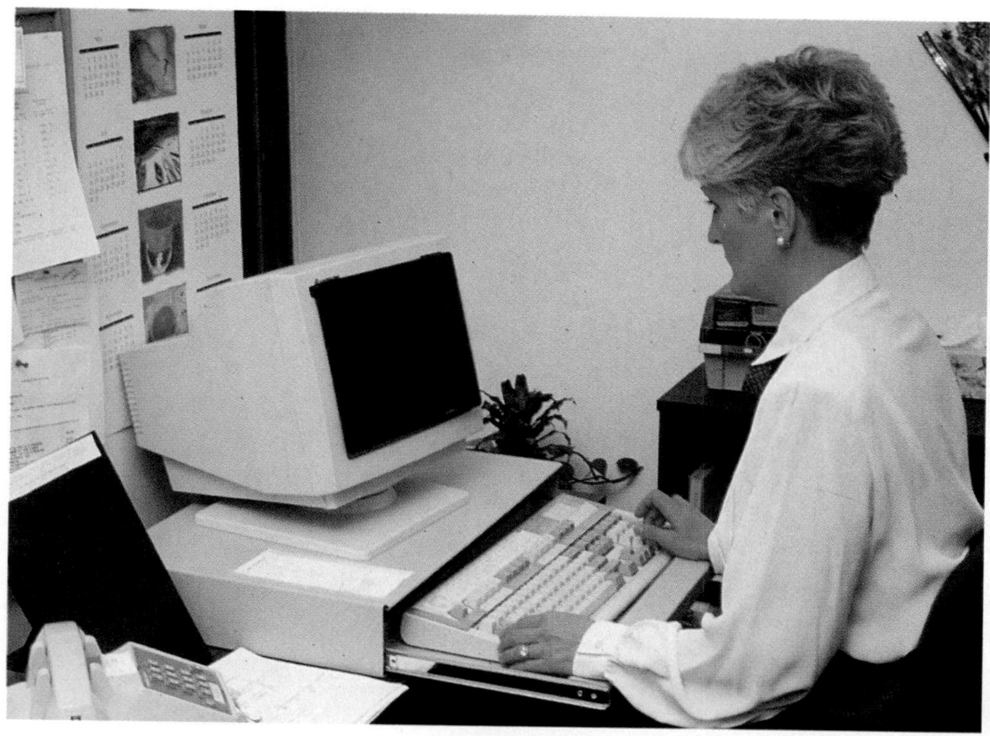

FIGURE 4–7 **A performance test can be written or hands-on.**
Photo by Paul E. Meyers.

Many performance tests are hands-on tests. They require you to use actual tools or machines. Suppose you are applying for a job as a data processing operator. Before being considered, you might be tested on a computer. By testing your skills now, employers avoid possible surprises later.

Taking a Test

Do not let the thought of taking a pre-employment test scare you away from a possible job. You will do better on the test if you do not spend time worrying about it.

Almost everyone experiences some test anxiety. You may be surprised to learn that mild test anxiety (stress) can be good. Studies have shown that mild stress actually improves the performance of athletes, entertainers, public speakers, and yes, test-takers. Stress can sharpen your attention, keep you alert, and give you greater energy.

Most tests don't require any advance preparation. However, if you haven't used your skills for a while, you may want to do some practicing before you take a performance test. The best preparation, though, is probably to prepare yourself mentally and physically to take the test. Be positive. Think of the test as a chance to show what you know and can do. During the days before the test, try to exercise, relax, eat well, and get plenty of sleep.

Many tests have time limits. You will be told how much time you have. Listen carefully to the instructions you receive. If you do not

FIGURE 4–8 **The best preparation for a pre-employment test may be to relax and go to the test mentally and physically alert.**

understand what you are expected to do, be sure to ask questions *before* the test begins. After you start the test, work steadily and carefully. Do not spend too much time on any one question. If math is required, double check each answer. If you finish ahead of time, use the remaining time to go back and complete unanswered questions or recheck answers.

Once the test is over, do not worry about it. Employers do not expect perfection. They just want some idea of whether or not you can do the work. Do not leave until you know what the next step will be. Ask when and how you will be told the test results. Some employers will hold an interview immediately after a pre-employment test. The test may even be scored at that time. Other employers will invite applicants back after they have examined the job application and the test results. Regardless of the procedure, if your test scores are good, you probably will get a job interview. (Chapter 5 covers what to do in the interview.)

FOCUS ON

The Workplace

LIE DETECTOR AND HONESTY TESTS

If you apply for a job in which money, merchandise, or drugs are handled, you may have to take an "honesty test." One type is a polygraph (lie detector) test. A polygraph is an electronic machine that is connected to the body of a subject. The person is asked a series of questions, while the machine records electronic impulses on a graph. If the person tells a lie, the device supposedly detects slight changes in the body's chemistry.

Many experts in the field question the accuracy of polygraph tests. As a result, Congress passed a law in 1988 to restrict the use of such tests.

The law prohibits polygraph tests for screening job applicants. An exception is for those seeking jobs in government, as security guards, or who will be handling narcotics. The law also curtails the use of polygraphs for workers already on the job. Managers cannot ask employees to take the test unless there is a "reasonable suspicion" that they have committed a crime. Even then, the test is voluntary. An employee cannot be fired for refusing to take it.

To avoid the problems and cost of polygraph tests, some companies use written honesty tests. These consist of multiple choice or yes-no items. For example:

- Have you every stolen anything from an employer? yes no
- Have you ever cheated in school? yes no
- Have you ever lied to a teacher or boss? yes no

The written test is interpreted by comparing an applicant's answers to those of persons already judged to be honest. Whether they help screen out the most honest job applicant is open to debate. But unless laws are passed restricting their use, millions of job applicants will probably be required to take them.

Written tests are given to job applicants and employees more often now than they were in the past because the legal use of polygraph tests has been limited.
Courtesy of Scantron Corporation, a subsidiary of John H. Harland Company.

CHAPTER 4 REVIEW

CHAPTER IN BRIEF

- To aid in filling out a job application form, prepare a personal data sheet. A personal data sheet contains the types of information most often requested by employers. You will also use the personal data sheet in preparing a job resume.
- Job application forms are used by employers to help sort out qualified people from a pool of applicants. Follow the recommended guidelines in this chapter to increase your chances of being selected for an interview.
- A job resume is often used when applying for a job in person or by letter. It should be limited to one page and contain the five types of information discussed in this chapter. The resume should have a neat, error-free, professional appearance.
- You can contact an employer about a job in person, by phone, or by letter. Applying in person usually also serves as a job interview. The purpose of phone and letter contacts is to gain an interview. In all three approaches, do everything possible to present yourself and your qualifications in the best possible light.
- Many employers administer pre-employment tests to job applicants. These may be either general ability tests or performance tests. After beginning the test, work steadily and carefully.

WORDS TO KNOW

civil service test
cover letter
job application form
personal data sheet
pre-employment test
references
resume

QUESTIONS TO ANSWER

1. What are the two main uses for a personal data sheet?
2. What kinds of people might you give as job references?
3. Why do employers use job application forms? Give an example.
4. If a question on a job application form does not apply to you, how should you answer it?
5. Name the five kinds of information provided in a job resume.
6. You can contact employers about jobs in three ways. Name them.
7. What is the main advantage of using the telephone in a job search?
8. What is the main thing you should do in the last paragraph of a letter of application?
9. What are the two most common types of pre-employment tests? What is the purpose of each?

10. If you finish a pre-employment test before the time limit is up, what should you do?

ACTIVITIES TO DO

1. Develop a personal data sheet following the outline shown in Figure 4–2. Ask your instructor to look it over before it is typed.
2. Using your personal data sheet, practice filling out the sample job application forms provided by the teacher.
3. Prepare a job resume according to the format shown in Figure 4–4. After the resume is finished, write a sample letter of application. Turn in both of them to your instructor.
4. Practice role playing in class how you would use a telephone to contact an employer for a job interview. One student can be the applicant and one the employer. Follow the guidelines on telephone use given earlier in this chapter.

TOPICS TO DISCUSS

1. People sometimes make mistakes during their lifetime. This might include getting into trouble at school, getting arrested for a minor infraction, or getting fired from a job. If a question is asked about things like this on a job application, how should you respond? What if it means that your answer will keep you from getting the job?
2. If you had an option to apply for a job in person or by letter, which would you choose? Discuss the advantages of each and why you chose the option you did.
3. What do you think about the practice of requiring a lie detector test as part of the job application process? Discuss both your and the employer's point of view.

CHAPTER 5 Interviewing for a Job

OUTLINE

- Before the Interview
- During the Interview
- After the Interview
- Accepting or Rejecting a Job
- Chapter Review

OBJECTIVES

After reading this chapter, you should be able to:

- Name and describe the five things to do in preparation for a job interview.
- List and discuss types of questions asked by interviewers.
- Summarize how one should act during a job interview.
- Name and describe the two things to do after an interview.
- Discuss how to respond to a job offer.

Ron Fisher had just gotten home from work when the telephone rang. He answered it: "Hello, Ron Fisher speaking."

"Hello, Ron, this is Donald Young at Smith Auto Sales. I have your letter of application and resume in front of me. It seems as if you would like to get out of your present job."

"No, sir, 'getting out' is not the main reason I am looking for a job. I like my job at Goodman's, but most of our work involves doing routine repairs on older cars. I have some training and skills that I am not able to use there. I would like to work on newer cars and be able to specialize in diagnostic work."

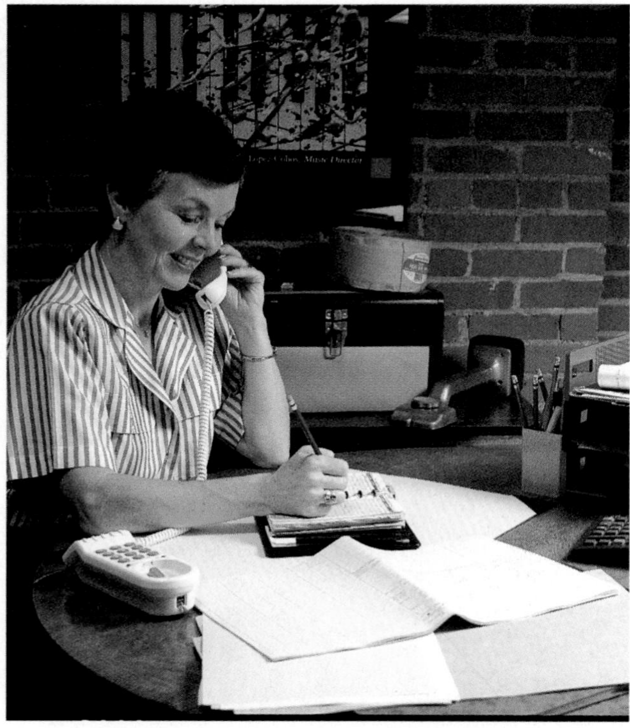

FIGURE 5–1 **A job applicant may receive an invitation for a job interview after sending a letter of application and a resume.** *Photo by Alan Brown/Photonics.*

"That is good to hear. I called Frank Hopkins at Hillside Community College and he said this is one of your strong areas."

"Yes, it is. Diagnostic work is often very simple if you know how to use testing equipment."

"Ron, I would like to talk further with you and show you around our shop. Could you come in Saturday morning at 9:00?"

"Yes, I would be happy to. I will see you on Saturday at 9:00, Mr. Young. Thank you for calling."

BEFORE THE INTERVIEW

The *job interview* is a face-to-face meeting between you and an employer. It is generally the last and most important step in the job-seeking process. An interview for an entry-level job usually lasts about 15 to 30 minutes. You will not be invited for an interview unless the employer thinks you may be qualified for the job. The employer wants to find out in person if you have the skills for the job. Another purpose is to help the employer decide if you will be able to work well with supervisors and co-workers. Your task is to show the employer that you *are* the person for the job.

An interview gives you a chance to "sell" what you can do for the employer. During the interview, an employer will judge your qualifications, appearance, and behavior. Equally important, the interview gives you a chance to *appraise* the job and the company. It enables you to decide if the position meets your job goals and interests, and whether this is the type of company for which you want to work. Before each interview, though, you should take the attitude that the job you are applying for is the one you want. To present yourself in the best possible light, you will need to do several things to prepare for the interview.

Practice your Interview Skills

You may be a little nervous when you think about going for a job interview. That is normal. To reduce your anxiety and help build your confidence, you may want to role play some practice interviews. Something as important as a job interview deserves advance preparation. You would not go for your driver's license exam without practicing your driving skills, would you?

You may be able to set up a classroom interview situation. Arrange a desk and a couple of chairs the way you might find them in an office. The instructor or a fellow student can play the role of an employer. Take turns being interviewed for a *hypothetical* job. Try to make "the interview" as realistic as possible.

Before you practice the interview, though, work together as a group to develop a list of questions for the interviewer to ask. These are some examples of the types of questions the employer may ask:

- I have already read your application form, but tell me something about yourself.
- Do you like school?
- What is your favorite subject? Why?
- What do you do in your spare time?
- Tell me why you applied for a job with us.

- How much do you know about the type of work we do here?
- Why do you think you would like this kind of work?
- Have you ever worked on this type of equipment before?
- Were you ever late to work in your last job?
- If I hired you, how long would you expect to stay with us?
- How much do you expect to make?
- What would you want to be doing in five years?
- When will you be available to start work?
- Do you have any questions?

As you can see from these examples, some questions can really put you on the spot if you are not prepared for them. By practicing the interview, you will become more aware of what is involved in thinking about a question and answering it out loud. It can be a valuable learning experience to discover, for example, how much you stumble and hesitate. Do not try to memorize answers, but do practice until you can respond easily. Make special efforts to rid your speech of "uhs," "you knows," and similar responses.

In addition to participating yourself, you can learn a great deal by watching others during practice interviews. Kevin, for example, noticed how some individuals pause for long periods before answering a question and repeatedly change positions in their chair. He has made a mental note to try to avoid these behaviors.

Learn About the Company

Find out as much as possible about the job and the company *before* your interview. Start by asking people you know who might have information on the company. From personal contacts you may learn inside information. For example, you might find out about the working conditions or the turnover rate of personnel. Further information may be available from the company itself. Ask about whether the company has any brochures, catalogs, annual reports, or other types of descriptive materials. If the potential place of employment is a restaurant, retail store, or similar public place, it may be possible to get first-hand information. Visit the establishment to get a feel for the atmosphere. You can observe the type of work done and perhaps have the opportunity to ask employees a few questions.

Next comes library research. A librarian can help you find several reference directories that tell about corporations by name. Some facts to look for include products or services produced, growth rate, and standing in the industry.

If information about the company is not available, find out something about the company's type of industry. Let's say that you are going to interview for a job in a property management firm. Find out what services these firms provide.

When you finish your research, write up a list of questions that you would like to ask about the job or the company. For example, you might ask: "Why did the job become vacant? Will any more training be required? What are the

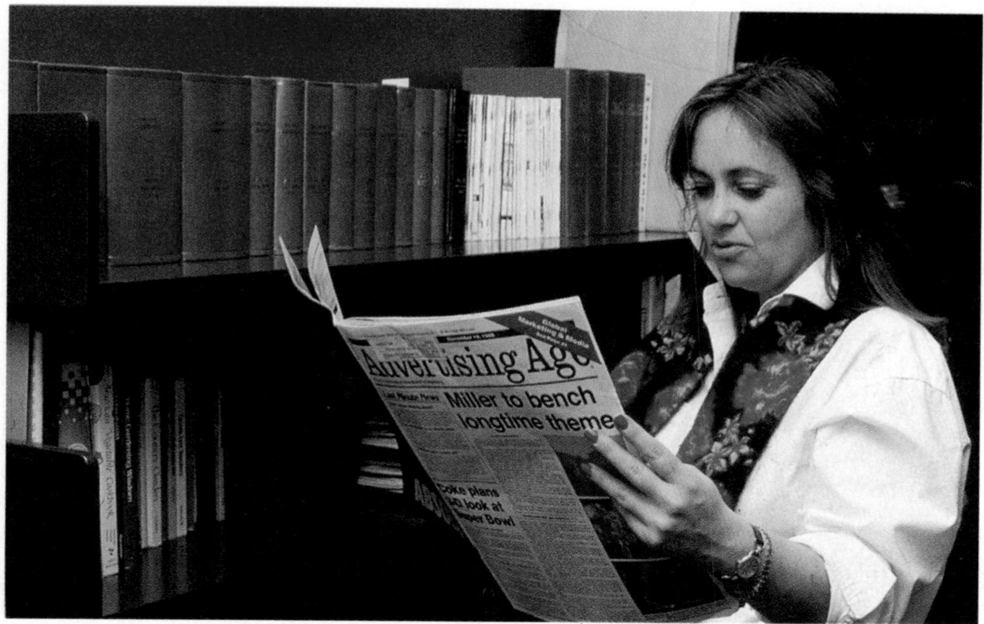

FIGURE 5–2 **It pleases interviewers when applicants show they have made an effort to learn about the company.**
Photo by Paul E. Meyers.

working hours? Who will my supervisor be if I get the job?" It is generally best to avoid asking about salary or benefits. If the information is not provided by the interviewer, you can ask after you have been offered the job.

Assemble Needed Materials

Have the materials you plan to take to the interview ready to go. These include the job-lead card, personal data sheet, resume, copies of any correspondence, pen and paper, a list of questions you will ask, and work permit, if needed. Also, take samples of your work if possible. Carry all of the materials in a large envelope or briefcase so you will not lose anything.

Attend to Appearance

Your grooming and dress will influence the interviewer's final decision. Choose clothes that are appropriate for the job setting. Ron, for example, has an interview for a job as an auto mechanic. It is not necessary that he wear a coat and tie. On the other hand, jeans, a T-shirt, and sneakers are too casual. Loud colors are never acceptable, nor are fad clothes. If you have doubts about what to wear, ask your work experience coordinator or counselor for advice. Or you might visit the company a day ahead of time and look around to see how people are dressed. Remember, though, you are dressing for an interview, not the job you will be doing.

Whatever clothes you decide to wear, they should be clean, pressed, and in good condition. Clothes do not have to be expensive to look neat. Do not forget to clean or shine your shoes. Heavy use of jewelry and other accessories should be avoided.

Careful grooming is also very important. If you need a haircut, plan ahead to get it done. On the day of the interview, a shower or bath is a must. Also, wash your hair, clean your nails, and brush your teeth. Men should shave or trim beards and mustaches. No heavy smelling colognes or aftershaves, please. Women may use make-up and lipstick sparingly.

Check Last-minute Details

Going to an interview at the wrong place or at the wrong time may seem dumb. People do it all the time, though. Do not miss an interview by making a silly mistake like that. It will help if you write the date, time, and place of the interview on a job-lead card. Check and then double-check the information. You may want to make a trial run so you will know where the company is located.

? ? ? ? ? ? ? ? ? ? ? ? ?

WHAT WOULD YOU DO?

You have an allergy to various food products. Occasionally, you unknowingly eat something that causes an allergic reaction. An unpleasant-looking skin rash appears on your face and hands. The day before a job interview you have such a reaction. You are very upset and discouraged. You don't want to go to the interview like this.

What would you do?

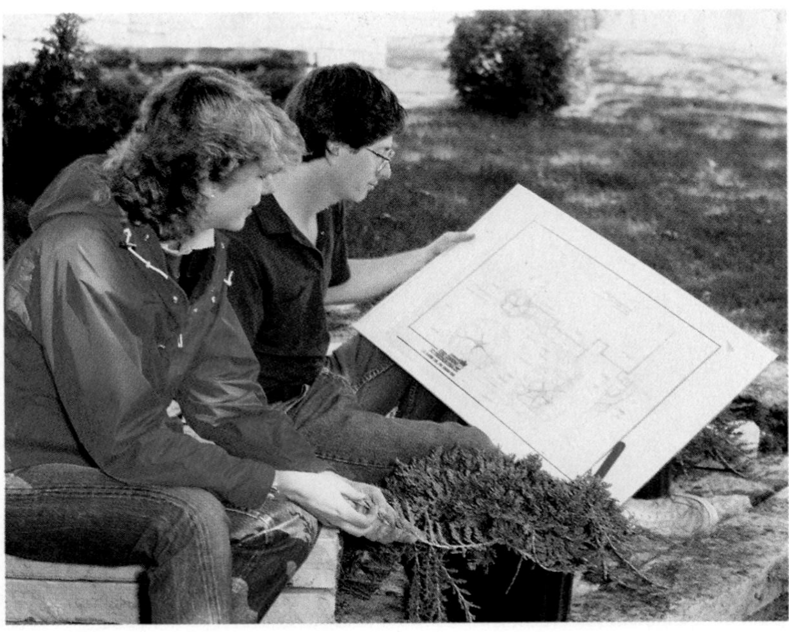

FIGURE 5–3 Take samples of your work with you when you go for an interview if your work is the kind you can show.
Reproduced from Better Homes and Gardens Magazine.

If more than a week goes by between the time you made the appointment and the actual interview, call to *confirm* it. Here is what Ellen did.

"Good morning, Solar Products Company."

"Hello, this is Ellen Simon. I'm calling to confirm my appointment for 10:00 tomorrow with Ms. Han."

"Wait just a moment, I'll check her calendar. Yes, Ms. Simon, she has you down."

"Good. Thank you. I'll be there tomorrow at 10:00."

Plan to arrive at the interviewer's office five to ten minutes ahead of schedule. Introduce yourself and tell why you are there. Do not take anyone with you to the interview. You do not want to give the impression that you cannot do things on your own.

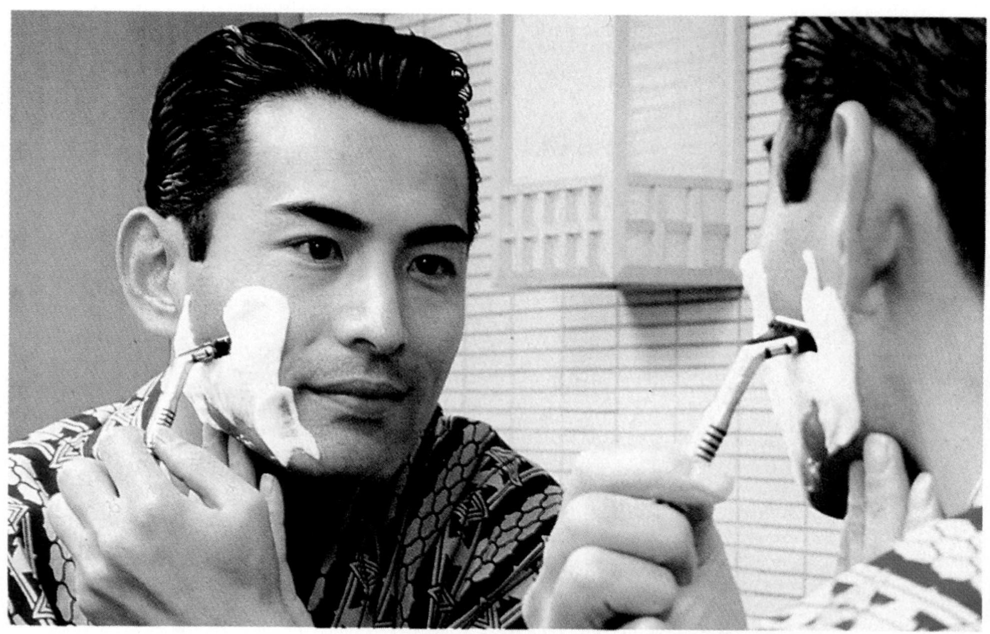

FIGURE 5–4 **Good grooming can help make a good first impression.**
Courtesy of The Gillette Company.

You may have to wait a short time in an outer office or reception area. During that time, you should relax, read, or look over your list of questions. Be pleasant toward others in the reception area. Do not smoke, chew gum, or do anything distracting. The interviewer may later ask for the receptionist's opinion of you.

DURING THE INTERVIEW

You may wonder what type of person the interviewer will be. Unfortunately, you have no way of knowing. If you have five job interviews, you will probably find five completely different personalities. It is not necessary for you to like the interviewer or for the interviewer to like you. The interviewer is looking for the best person to fill a job. You are not there to be social. You are looking for a job.

Prepare yourself to deal with whatever you may find. Remain calm and do your best. If you have prepared well for the interview, you have done your homework up to this point.

Effective Communication

Let the interviewer set the tone and pace of the interview. Adjust yourself to the style of the interviewer. For example, if the interviewer is serious and businesslike, your style should be similar. If the interviewer is cheerful and outgoing, you may need to brighten up a little. Try to establish a *compatible* relationship with the interviewer.

Communication skills, which are important at every step of the job search, are more so in the job interview. Be sure to listen carefully and

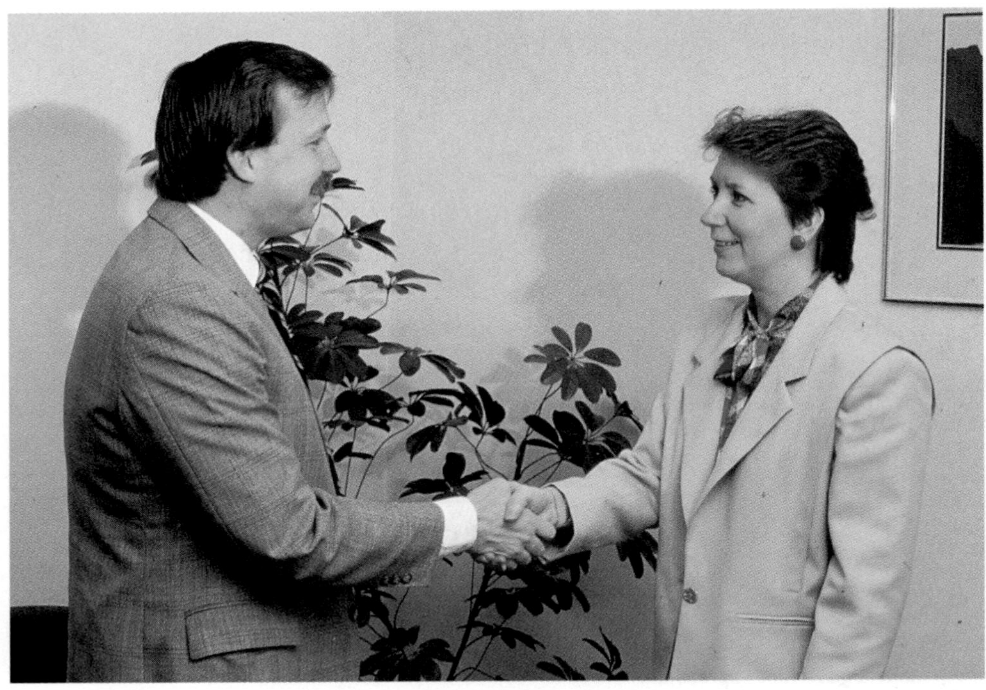

FIGURE 5–5 **Greet your interviewer with a firm handshake, not a limp or bone-crushing one.**
Photo by Paul E. Meyers.

speak clearly. Answer each question briefly, but do not give one-word or one-line answers. If you think that the interviewer has not understood your answer or that you have not made yourself clear, try again. Stay on the topic until you are sure that the interviewer has understood your message.

Answer a question only after the interviewer is completely finished. Otherwise, you risk making a bad impression. You may also never find out the exact question or hear important information that may be added to the question.

Listening to the interviewer is as important as speaking thoughtfully and clearly. The ability to listen shows your attentiveness and reflects on your interest in the job. At times, you may want to ask the interviewer the meaning of a word or phrase. Do so. You must understand a question before you can answer it.

Nonverbal Communication

Proper *body language* (nonverbal communication) may help or hinder communication. During the interview, sit comfortably; but do not slouch. Keep your hands on your lap. Do not look at your hands or feet during the interview. Maintain good eye contact throughout the interview, but do not stare. During the interview, keep a pleasant expression on your face.

Also be aware of the interviewer's body language. Watch for nonverbal clues. If the interviewer's body language conveys something negative, think about what you are doing or saying. Then modify what needs to be changed.

FIGURE 5–6 **Be pleasant and friendly, but businesslike, during your interview.**
Reprinted with permission from Communispond Inc. Management Consultants in Business Communication.

Asking Questions

An interview involves two-way communications. Of course, the interviewer will ask you questions. Did you know that the interviewer will also expect *you* to ask questions? It is wise to refer to a list of questions you have made beforehand. Hold the list near your lap so you can glance at it as you talk.

Do not be in a hurry to ask questions. Wait until the interviewer invites them. A pause in the conversation once the interview is well underway may be the time for you to bring up your questions. Be careful, though, not to interrupt the interviewer. By all means, if you have not already been invited to do so, request an opportunity to ask your questions before the interview ends.

Your questions should indicate a sincere interest in the company and the job. Good questions are concrete and show that you have prepared for the interview. For example, you might ask, "What opportunities are there to advance within the company?"

Use good judgment in deciding how much time to take up with questions. Try to sense whether or not the interviewer is on a tight schedule. If time seems pressing, ask only your most important questions.

Concluding the Interview

Suppose the interview is almost over. The employer has not said when a decision will be made about the job. What do you do? Ask about it. If the interviewer asks you to call back or supply more information, note it on the job-lead card.

Try to get a feeling for when the interview has run its course. The interviewer may stand or simply say right out, "Well, I think that I have enough information about you at this time." To help bring an interview to its conclusion you can ask, "Are there any more questions I can answer?"

Many job applicants fail to ask for the job. This is a big mistake. Tell the interviewer if you want the job. Say something like, "I know I can do the work, Mr. Young; and I would like to have the job."

Seldom does an interviewer make a job offer or reject an applicant at the conclusion of an interview. Usually the interviewer wants to think about and compare all applicants before making a final decision. In some cases, the interviewer's role is to evaluate and make recommendations only (refer to the bottom of the form in Figure 5–7). The actual employment

SOUTHWEST REALITY COMPANY
Applicant Evaluation

Name ______________________ Interview date ______________________

Position applied for ______________________

Criteria/comments	Poor	Good	Excellent
1. Appearance:			
2. Poise:			
3. Responses:			
4. Grammar and speech:			
5. Background:			
6. Knowledge of job requirements:			
7. Interest in company:			
8. Potential:			

SUMMARY AND RECOMMENDATION

Strengths:

Weaknesses:

*Based on interview, review of application, and follow-up, should an offer of employment be made? Yes ____ No ____

Date ______________________ Interviewer ______________________

FIGURE 5–7 **Some interviewers use forms like this to help them rate a job candidate.**

decision may be made by another person.

If you do learn that the company cannot use you, ask about other employers who may need a person with your skills. Thank the interviewer, shake hands, and leave. On the way out, thank the secretary or receptionist.

AFTER THE INTERVIEW

You can benefit from every interview, no matter what the outcome. Take time to think about the experience as soon as possible after the interview. Review any mistakes you think you made and consider how you could have avoided them. Could you have been better prepared? Did you mention everything about yourself that the employer needed to know? Think about what you did well. Would these things help you in other interviews?

Promptly send a *follow-up letter* to the interviewer. Such a letter may accomplish many things:

1. It helps to build a courteous relationship.
2. Having your letter keeps your name in front of the interviewer.
3. Taking time to write a letter tells the interviewer of your continued interest.
4. The letter allows you to reinforce key points you discussed during the interview.
5. If you forgot to mention something important during the interview, you can put it in your follow-up letter.

A sample follow-up letter is shown in Figure 5–8.

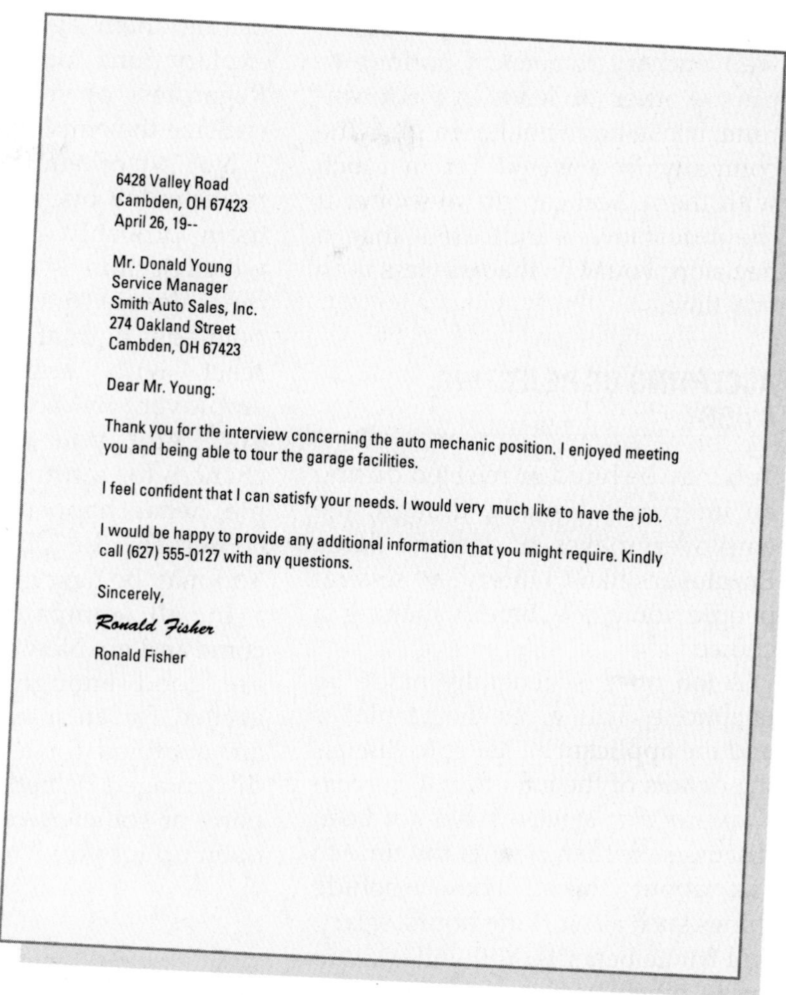

6428 Valley Road
Cambden, OH 67423
April 26, 19--

Mr. Donald Young
Service Manager
Smith Auto Sales, Inc.
274 Oakland Street
Cambden, OH 67423

Dear Mr. Young:

Thank you for the interview concerning the auto mechanic position. I enjoyed meeting you and being able to tour the garage facilities.

I feel confident that I can satisfy your needs. I would very much like to have the job. I would be happy to provide any additional information that you might require. Kindly call (627) 555-0127 with any questions.

Sincerely,

Ronald Fisher

Ronald Fisher

FIGURE 5–8 **Sample follow-up letter.**

Suppose the interviewer told you that you would not be hired. Or, perhaps you are no longer interested in the job. Send a letter to thank the interviewer for considering you.

When writing a follow-up letter, refer to the guidelines given about preparing a letter of application. The rules are similar for both types of letters. If someone helped arrange your interview, send a note of appreciation to him or her. This should be a simple, handwritten thank-you note.

After completing these steps, wait and try to relax. Continue to pursue other job leads in the meantime. If you have not heard from the company in a week, get in touch with them. You can do so sooner if the interviewer indicated that a decision would be made in less than this time.

ACCEPTING OR REJECTING A JOB

You may be hired or rejected during an interview. Usually, though, the employer makes a decision later. Employers like to interview several people for a job before making a choice.

A job offer is generally made by telephone. This gives the employer and the applicant a chance to discuss the details of the job offer. If the *conditions of employment* have not been discussed earlier, now is the time to ask about them. These include things such as working hours, salary, and fringe benefits. You will want to know when you start work and if there is anything special that you need to bring or be prepared to do the first day. For example, you might need to pick up a uniform.

It is possible to be considered for a job at different places at the same time. Let's say that you have been interviewed for jobs at both Burger Barn and Chicken Shack. If Burger Barn offers you a job and you accept it, you should phone Chicken Shack and tell them you have taken another job.

What if a company offers you a job you do not want? Be polite. (You never know when you may be contacting them again.) Give a brief explanation of your reasons. Regardless of your reasons *do not* criticize the employer.

Not all of your interviews will result in job offers. In fact, most of them probably will not. Dealing with rejection is something we all must learn to do. Being disappointed is normal. Do not, however, react with anger toward an employer. By accepting rejection gracefully, you keep alive your chances for a future job. For example, what happens if the person chosen for the job turns it down? You may be next in line for it.

In all companies, employees come and go. New jobs open. If you are good enough to have been invited for an interview, then you are qualified for a job. Do not get discouraged. Whether at that company or somewhere else, a job will open up for you.

? ? ? ? ? ? ? ? ? ? ? ? ? ? ?

WHAT WOULD YOU DO?

You have been offered two jobs. The first job would be acceptable. It is a traditional job for a person of your sex. The second job is a nontraditional job. You would be the only person of your sex out of eight employees who work there. You cannot decide which job to take.

What would you do?

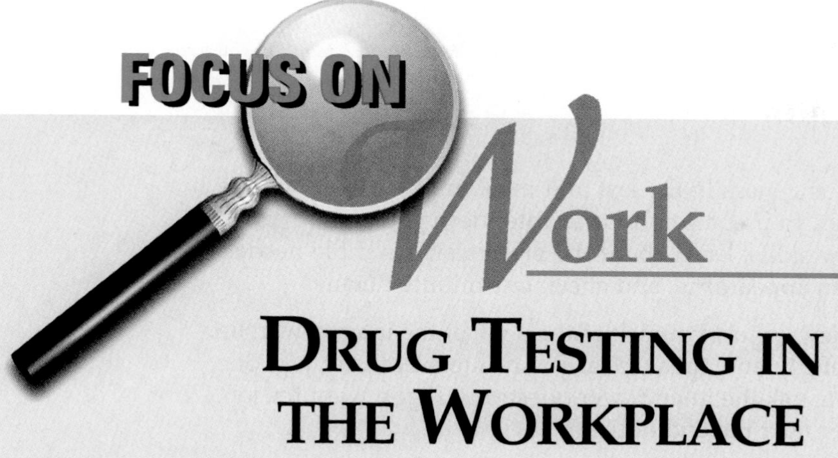

Drug Testing in the Workplace

During the job interview, Frank was surprised to learn that his potential employer has a drug testing program. After the first month of employment, all workers at Allied Receiving are subject to random drug testing. The purpose of such tests is to identify employees who use illegal (illicit) drugs, such as marijuana and cocaine. Not only is the use of such drugs illegal and dangerous, but the drugs have also been linked to accidents, absenteeism, and low productivity. (For example, it was found that drugs were a factor in a recent train crash that killed 16 passengers and injured 176 others. The engineer had been smoking marijuana.)

To identify drug users, employers often require each employee to submit a urine sample for analysis. The analysis can detect traces of cocaine up to two days after the drug was taken. Marijuana has been known to show up in the urine as long as a month after use.

Currently, more than half of the nation's 500 largest corporations have drug testing programs. Testing may be required for job applicants, employed workers, or both. Some employers test workers for "cause"; for instance, if they notice a worker is not performing well. Others test randomly, without announcement and without even suspecting wrongdoing.

Even though drug testing is widely used, the practice remains controversial. Some people claim that the tests are often inaccurate. Others claim that tests violate the Fourth Amendment's prohibition on unreasonable searches. A number of lawsuits have been filed to stop drug testing. It will probably be many years before the courts decide on these issues.

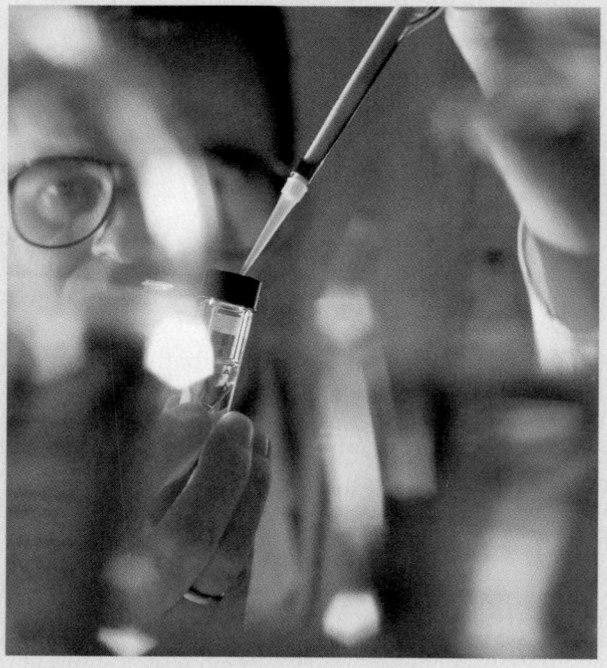

Unpleasant as it might be, employers have the right to test applicants and employees for illegal drug use.
© Andrew Brookes/Tony Stone Images, Inc.

CHAPTER 5 REVIEW

CHAPTER IN BRIEF

- The job interview is generally the last and most important step in the job-seeking process. In preparation for an interview, you should: practice your interview skills, learn about the employer, assemble needed materials, attend to appearance, and check last-minute details.
- During the interview, adjust yourself to the style of the interviewer. Be sure to listen carefully and speak clearly. An interview isn't just one way. Be prepared to ask the interviewer questions. If you want the job, tell the interviewer near the end of the interview.
- After the interview, take time to think about the experience. Review any mistakes you made and consider how to correct them next time. Promptly send a follow-up letter to the interviewer.
- A job offer may be made following the interview or later by phone or letter. Before accepting the offer, make sure you understand the conditions of employment. If you are rejected for a job, accept it gracefully. Don't do anything to close the door on a possible later offer or opportunity.

WORDS TO KNOW

appraise
body language
compatible
conditions of employment
confirm
follow-up letter
hypothetical
job interview

QUESTIONS TO ANSWER

1. A job interview provides you with a chance to do two things. Name them.
2. From the interviewer's standpoint, what is the purpose of the job interview?
3. Name the five things that you should do to prepare for a job interview. Why is each important?
4. Is it necessary that you like the interviewer? Why or why not?
5. Give an example to show how you might adjust your interview style to that of the interviewer.
6. Why shouldn't you give one-word or one-line answers in an interview?
7. What is a major mistake that applicants make at the end of a job interview?
8. What five things may a follow-up letter accomplish?
9. You are being considered for two jobs at the same time. You receive one job offer and accept it. What should you do next?
10. Why is it important to accept a job rejection gracefully?

ACTIVITIES TO DO

1. Choose a well-known company. Go to a public library and ask a librarian to direct you to information about business corporations. (*Standard and Poor's Register of Corporations* is one resource.) Look up the company you selected. Write down a half page or so of information that you think would be important for a job applicant to know about the company. Turn in the paper to your instructor.
2. In class, practice role playing a job interview.
3. If equipment is available, videotape the role-playing interview. View and discuss the tapes later. Seeing yourself on tape can often be quite informative.
4. Prepare a follow-up letter to a hypothetical job interview. Turn it in to your instructor for evaluation.

TOPICS TO DISCUSS

1. Some class members have probably already had job interviews. Those who have had interviews should describe their experiences with the class. Ask your classmates about things you would like to know regarding a job interview.
2. Despite your best planning efforts, an unexpected emergency or problem arises that prevents you from attending a job interview. How should you handle a situation like this?
3. A person with advanced education or highly marketable skills can often negotiate favorable conditions of employment following a job offer. Discuss realistically how much bargaining power a person has in applying for an entry-level job.

SECTION 2

WORKING ON THE JOB

Once you find a job, you will need to turn your thoughts and energies to working on the job. Your first few days and weeks will be busy, exciting, and sometimes confusing. In Chapter 6, you will learn what to expect as you begin a new job.

After a short adjustment period, you will need to perform the same as other employees. In Chapter 7, you will learn what your employer expects regarding job performance and work habits and attitudes. An employer will evaluate your on-the-job performance. You will learn how such performance evaluations are conducted.

What rights and protections do you have on the job? As a worker, you are entitled to fair and honest treatment regarding wages, hours, and equal pay. You have a right to work in a safe and healthful environment. You are entitled to be treated fairly regardless of your sex, race, or other factors. These are all explained in Chapter 8.

Chapter 9 deals with human relations at work. Your job success will depend on how well you get along with bosses, co-workers, and customers. In addition to working with individuals, you need to be able to work with groups. Guidelines are provided to help you be a more effective member of a work group.

Everyone looks forward to receiving a paycheck. In Chapter 10, you will learn about different forms of compensation and how your paycheck is figured. You will also discover what to do in order to advance on the job.

Chapter 11 deals with the importance of a good appearance. You will learn how to groom and dress in a way that fits your job.

Co-op Career SPOTLIGHT ON

Michael Fast Horse, *Agriculture Specialist*

Mike Fast Horse is a member of the Lakota Sioux tribe of South Dakota. He combines a heritage of deep respect and love for the environment with modern education and technology. He plans to use this combination of commitment and skills to help guide farmers toward the most productive ways to produce food while preserving the balance of nature.

"I understand my heritage and tradition. I want to move ahead without forgetting my heritage," he says. Mike took the agriculture education co-op program at Lyman High School in Presho, South Dakota, where he graduated in 1990. He is finishing a four-year agriculture education program at South Dakota State University and plans to get a job with DuPont selling agricultural products when he graduates. His job will be the next step toward his long-term goals, ones he got a taste for in his high school co-op program.

"Now I need to make money to reach my ultimate goal—to have a cattle ranch and work as an environmental consultant." While Mike was in the high school co-op program, he worked as a consultant, helping farmers develop plans to meet federal conservation guidelines for reducing erosion. He participated in a federal program surveying wetlands and building dams. He also worked on a 3,500-acre cattle ranch and wheat farm. He took care of the cattle and worked the wheat farm from preparing the soil for planting to harvesting the wheat with a combine. In the fall he was a guide for pheasant hunters on part of the ranch. During his junior and senior years in high school, he worked on a hog farm in the farrowing barn where the piglets are born.

"I cared for the piglets, giving them vaccinations, adding minerals to their feed, and clipping their teeth. I kept the barn clean, ground their feed from sorghum, and kept records of everything we did," he said. Mike says co-op and the local and district offices of FFA president and treasurer he held gave him many of the skills he needed for his work and for his studies at the university.

"Co-op helped me improve my personal skills for working with people, doing interviews, and speaking in front of large groups at FFA events." He says it taught him how to keep the detailed records needed to do scientific projects like taking care of the pigs.

"It also gave me a good feel for how to hold a job and take responsibility for my decisions, good and bad and I made contact with people in business."

CHAPTER 6 Beginning a New Job

OUTLINE

- Pre-employment Anxiety
- Reporting for Work
- Orientation to the Workplace
- Organizational Structure
- Working Under Supervision
- Payroll Withholding
- Chapter Review

OBJECTIVES

After reading this chapter, you should be able to:

- Recognize that anxiety toward beginning a new job is normal.
- Explain what to expect from an employer when beginning a new job.
- Describe how an organization chart shows the flow of authority and responsibility within an organization.
- List areas for which employers have policies and rules.
- Identify ways to work effectively with a supervisor.
- Illustrate how to fill out a Form W-4.

The job search is over. Your new job is about to start. You will be leaving or at least spending less time in the familiar world of the classroom. The changes you will experience may be scary at first. Remember what it was like going from junior high to high school? A similar experience awaits you now. You are going from the known into the unknown. This can be exciting and frightening at the same time. You are going from high school into the world of work. By taking the time now to learn what to expect, you can prepare yourself for a smooth transition into your new role as a worker.

FIGURE 6–1 **Becoming a worker will mark the start of a new phase of your life.**
Courtesy of California Edison, G. O'Loughlin.

PRE-EMPLOYMENT ANXIETY

Anxiety is the state of feeling worried or uneasy about what may happen in the future. You may have feelings of anxiety about beginning a new job. Try to relax. Remember that the employer chose your job application from among many others. You were interviewed because the employer thought you were qualified. You were hired because the employer believed you were the best person for the job.

Starting a new job is not like wilderness training. Your employer will not expect you to endure extreme temperatures, sleep on the hard ground, and eat cold beans. Your employer probably isn't going to test you to see if you can make it. Believe it or not, your employer wants you to succeed.

Your employer more than likely understands that you are going through a stressful time. He or she understands that it will take time for you to learn the company's rules, procedures, and any other policies.

? ? ? ? ? ? ? ? ? ? ? ? ? ?

WHAT WOULD YOU DO?

You have just been hired as a clerk at a grocery store. Your new supervisor tells you to report for work tomorrow at 4:00 sharp. You agree to do this and leave the store. Later, you remember that you have to take a make-up exam at school tomorrow afternoon.

What would you do?

REPORTING FOR WORK

What you do on the first day of work depends on the type and size of the company you have joined. Let's look at Francine Gordon's first day.

Francine applied for a job at Northeast Electric Power Company. Two weeks later, she received a telephone call from the assistant personnel manager, who offered Francine a job as an equipment operator. Since this was the job Francine wanted, she accepted right away. Francine was told to report to work at 9:30 on Monday morning for a new employee orientation. She was also told that a parking decal for her car and a map showing the location of the meeting room would be sent to her in the mail.

Francine arrived at the plant about 9:15 on Monday. A uniformed guard at the entrance motioned for her to stop. Before Francine could say anything, the guard asked her if she was a new employee. The guard pointed out the building entrance and the lot in which she was to park.

Francine parked her car and took out her map. She was glad to have the map. The building seemed to be as long as three football fields. She entered the building and walked down the hall. She finally found the correct meeting room. There, Mr. Walsh, the assistant personnel manager, gave Francine a name tag and directed her to a seat.

At 9:35, a woman went to the front of the room. Mr. Walsh introduced here as Mrs. Ramos, the personnel manager. Mrs. Ramos welcomed the twelve new employees and introduced several staff

FIGURE 6–2 **Most employers and co-workers will help you adjust to your job.**
Photo by Alan Brown/Photonics.

members. Then she gave a fifteen-minute slide presentation about the company. Before seeing the program, Francine had not thought much about the number of people and businesses that depended on Northeast Electric Power Company. She was already feeling proud about working for such an important company.

Mr. Walsh then took over the meeting. After answering some questions, he passed out a folder to each person. The folder contained a "Policies and Procedures Manual" and many forms. The group filled out forms and discussed the information in the folder for the rest of the day.

Some large companies, such as Northeast Electric Power Company, have a very formal employee orientation program. Because of the large number of employees that Northeast Electric Power Company hires, such a program is efficient. The company can orient several new workers at once. This kind of detailed program assures that all employees have received the same information. Many problems can be prevented when all employees are following the same set of rules.

Now, let's contrast Francine's first day with that of another beginning worker. Denny Liu was hired as a salesclerk at Rogers', a small men's store in North Plaza Mall. Denny learned about the job opening at Rogers' while he was working as a cooperative education student at another mall store. He applied for the job in person. After a short interview with Bob Brown,

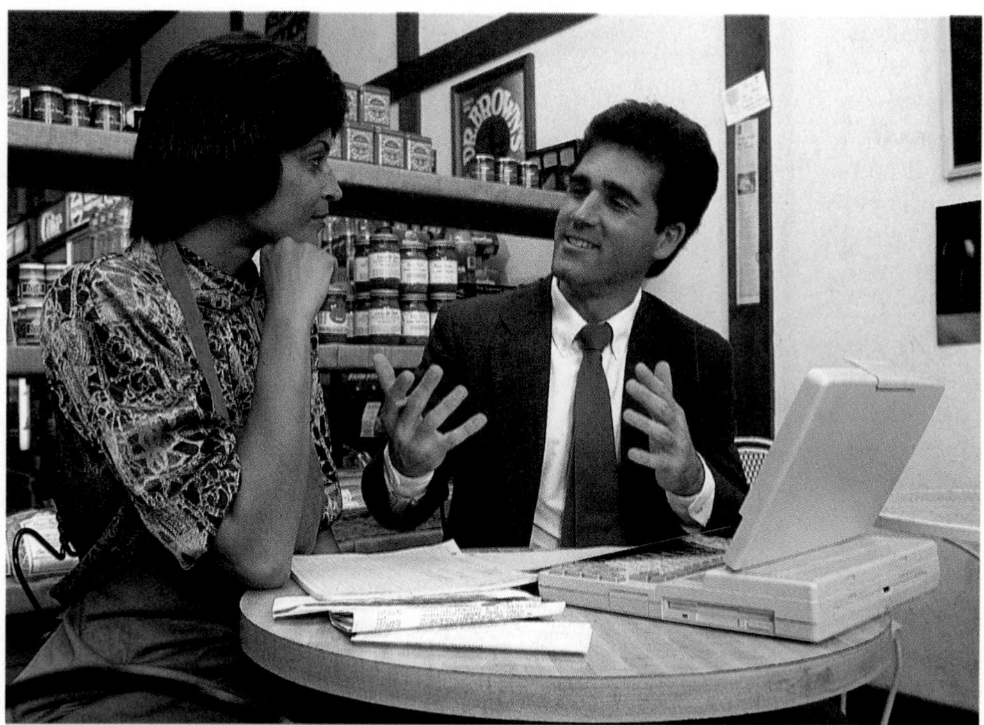

FIGURE 6–3 **At some companies, job orientation is very informal.**

the manager, he was hired on the spot. Denny agreed to report for work after giving the other store two weeks notice.

Three weeks later Denny arrived for his first day at work. Bob was unlocking the entrance. After greeting each other, Bob and Denny walked to the rear of the store. Along the way, Bob flipped on the lights. Denny smiled to himself. He was amused at how different the back of the shop looked compared to the shop's front display area. Bob pointed toward the coffee pot and asked Denny to start it while he checked the mail.

While the coffee was brewing, Denny and Bob exchanged small talk as Bob sorted the mail. A few minutes later Courtney and Evan, two other employees, came into the shop. Bob introduced Denny to them. They all chatted for a few minutes. Courtney and Evan then went to get the shop ready for its 10:00 opening.

Bob gave Denny a few forms to sign and a payroll card. He told Denny how to keep track of the number of hours he worked. They then walked around the shop while Bob explained procedures and pointed out features of certain merchandise.

Bob told Denny that he wanted him to begin working at the ties and accessories counter. If the other salesclerks got busy, he was to leave the counter area to help out.

"Denny, you know what goes on in a men's store," Bob said. "If you have questions or need help, ask us. We'll just play it by ear."

By 10:10, Denny had waited on his first customer and made his first sale. He was so busy that it was almost 1:30 before he had time for lunch. Business during the afternoon was also good. He even waited on several customers that he knew from his previous sales job. Overall, Denny had a good first day. He had to ask a few questions, and Bob made a few suggestions. Denny knew he was going to like working at Rogers'.

What a difference between Francine's and Denny's first days! Denny spent most of his first day waiting on customers. Francine, on the other hand, spent much of her first day learning about Northeast Electric Power Company. In fact, Francine didn't actually start work until two weeks later. She spent the first two weeks in class learning how to be an equipment operator.

Clearly, one person's first day at work may be quite different from another person's first day at work. However, Francine and Denny did many similar things and were provided with similar kinds of information. This was just done in different ways. Can you think of some ways that Francine's and Denny's first days were similar?

ORIENTATION TO THE WORKPLACE

During your first days on a new job, you will find out how the company is organized and what the written rules are. You will also begin to learn about the unwritten rules. Information about unwritten rules

FIGURE 6–4 **Some employees spend their first days on the job learning about the company and how to perform their jobs.**
Courtesy of Niagara Mohawk Power Corporation.

? ? ? ? ? ? ? ? ? ? ? ? ? ? ?

WHAT WOULD YOU DO?

Upon beginning a new job, you may know very little about a company or its management. This can happen despite your best efforts to research the company and ask thoughtful questions in a job interview. Suppose that during the orientation meeting you discover things about the company that disturb you. Perhaps the company manufactures products that are in conflict with your moral or religious beliefs. Perhaps the company officials have an attitude that is completely different from your own. You begin to wonder if this is the right job for you.

What would you do?

is included in Chapters 7 and 8. The company will want to know more about you, too. You will have to fill out many forms. The most common one is Form W-4.

Francine and Denny learned many of the same things during their first day on the job. They learned:

- How the workplace was laid out.
- Where they would be working (their workstations).
- How to keep track of hours worked.
- Where to look for posted notices such as work schedules.
- What to do if they needed help or had questions.

These are important things that all workers need to learn during their first day on the job. In the rest of this chapter, you will study other concerns of new workers.

ORGANIZATIONAL STRUCTURE

Every company, business, or school has lines of authority and responsibility. *Authority* has to do with the power to assign work to be done. For instance, a teacher has authority in the classroom. *Responsibility* deals with the duty to carry out a work assignment. In school, for example, you, as a student, are responsible to complete your assignments. The flow of authority and responsibility can be shown in an organization chart.

In a typical large company, the stockholders have the ultimate authority. That is, they "own" the company. However, thousands of stockholders cannot manage a company. So, the stockholders elect a board of directors to represent them. A board of directors is normally composed of people outside the company. They meet regularly to review management, establish policy, and make recommendations. The board hires a president to manage the company on a day-to-day basis. The president then *delegates* responsibility to lower-ranking executives who are responsible for various company operations. In practical terms, the company president has the greatest authority and the greatest responsibility in an organization.

A sample organization chart for a small kitchen equipment manufacturing company is shown in Figure 6–5, on page 78. Each person or group of workers in the organization does different tasks. Note how each level in the organization is responsible to another level. Also note that some workers have more authority than other workers.

When you begin work, you will be given a job title. Where will your job fit into the overall organization? If you start out in an entry-level job, you will probably have a lot of responsibility and little or no authority. You will probably report to a supervisor who will assign work for you to do.

Answering to a supervisor or boss is called reporting to authority. You may do this in two ways. One is *formal reporting*, which is based on rank or the chain of command. For example, Figure 6–5 shows that the production workers formally report to the plant manager.

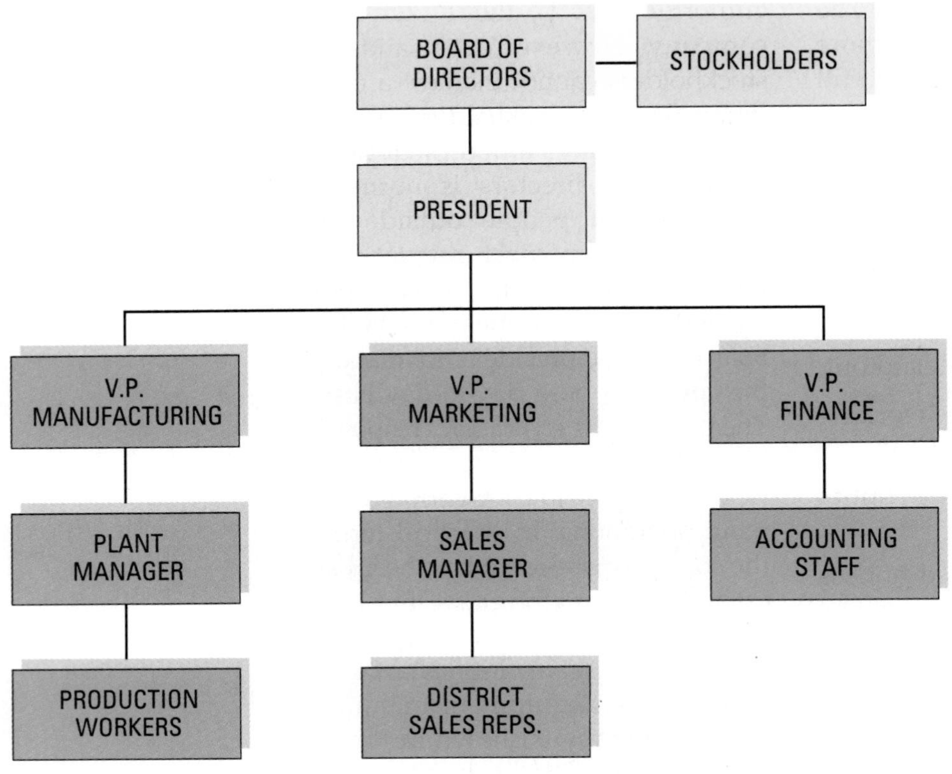

FIGURE 6–5 **Sample organization chart.**

Another way of reporting to authority is *informal reporting*. This usually involves reporting to a specific person for a short time or for a certain work assignment. Suppose, for example, that you work on the accounting staff for the company shown in Figure 6–5. Your regular supervisor, the vice-president for finance, assigns you to help out the sales manager on a new project. The supervisor tells you to follow what the sales manager tells you to do. In this case, you will be informally reporting to the sales manager for a while.

It is important to follow your company's lines of authority, both formal and informal. Take time to become familiar with these by listening, watching, and asking questions.

Policies and Rules

Most companies have written policies and rules. These help the organization to run smoothly. Imagine, for example, what would happen to production if large numbers of workers took their vacations at the same time. Or, how disruptive it would be if people came to work and left whenever they wanted.

Policies and rules also ensure that all employees receive fair and equal treatment. Some policies and rules are required by federal and state laws. Others are desirable simply to promote good *morale* and positive working relationships among employees.

The formal rules often appear in a company *policy manual.* If your company has one, you will be given a copy when you start work. If the workplace is unionized, the policy manual may contain both the employer's and the union's rules.

An employer may also present policies and rules in several other ways. For instance, rules may be explained at a formal meeting or program for new employees, as was done for Francine's orientation. In some cases, important rules appear on a sign or bulletin board somewhere in the work area (see figure 6–6). Your supervisor or co-workers may also be useful sources of such information.

Here are some of the most common items for which employers have written policies and rules.

STATE INSURANCE

POLICY NO. 106 DATE: 08/01/––
SUBJECT: NO-SMOKING POLICY

State Insurance has established a No-Smoking Policy aimed at protecting the overall health and environment in our workplace.

1. Smoking is not permitted by any person anywhere within State's portion of the building. Person is defined as all State's employees, temporaries, visitors, and customers.
2. All potential new hires must be advised of this policy and must abide by it as a condition of employment.
3. Employees in violation of this policy will be subject to the following:

First offense:	Written reprimand
Second offense:	30-day probation
Third offense:	Two-weeks' suspension without pay
Fourth offense:	Immediate dismissal

FIGURE 6–6 **Employees learn about company policies and rules in many different ways.**

- ***Salaries, Wages, and Benefits.*** Many employers outline in writing how pay rates, benefits, and raises are decided.
- ***Attendance, Absences, and Punctuality.*** You must report to work on time every workday unless you have a good reason. If you are going to be late or absent, follow your employer's policy for reporting it. In cases of illness, you may need a medical excuse.
- ***Leave.*** Most employers provide time off, with and without pay, for various reasons. Find out your employer's policies for sick leave, vacation time, jury-duty leave, and other time off.
- ***Work Schedule and Records.*** You must follow company rules for hours worked, meals, breaks, and overtime work. This often means clocking in and out on time *in person.*

Don had a friend, Kim, clock in for him on mornings he wanted to sleep late. When the boss found out, both Don and Kim almost lost their jobs. If they do this again, the employer's policy is to fire them both.

- ***Expenses and Reimbursement.*** If you travel on company business or buy materials for company use, those expenses are really company costs. The company should *reimburse* you for them. This means that the company should pay you back the money you spent. Company policy will explain what can be reimbursed and how to go about getting reimbursement.
- ***Due Process.*** Suppose you have a complaint about something or your boss has a complaint about you. The company may have formal procedures for solving this

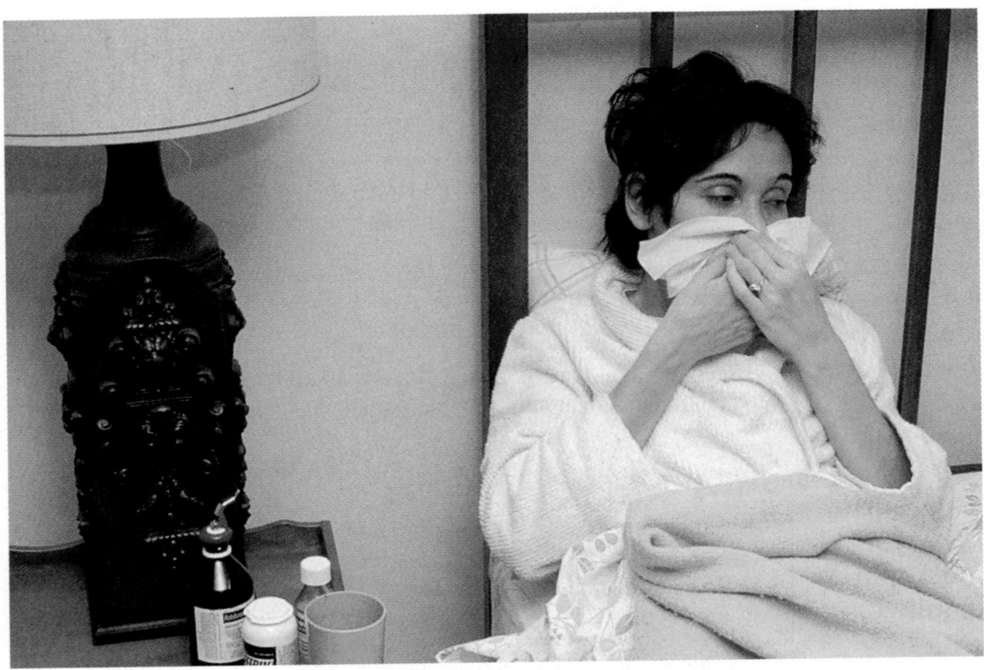

FIGURE 6–7 **Being too sick to go to work is acceptable. Failing to tell your employer about it is not.**
Photo by Paul E. Meyers.

problem. *Due process* refers to the right to state your case before a decision is made.

- ***Probation and Review.*** As a new employee, you may work for a period of time on *probation.* During this time, supervisors will carefully evaluate your work and attitude. At the end of your probation period, the employer will decide whether or not to consider you for permanent employment. Once you are a permanent employee, a supervisor will review your performance from time to time. Most employers have written policies about when and how you are to be reviewed.

Read and carefully study your company's policy manual. If you can't find rules covering these items or other items of interest, ask your supervisor about them. You are responsible for obeying all policies and rules. Not knowing the policies and rules is not a good excuse.

Unwritten Rules

Not all of a company's rules are written down. You will gradually learn rules that are not in the policy manual. Some of these rules relate to appearance, work habits, attitudes, and job performance. These rules will be discussed in Chapters 7 and 8.

Victor was doing some home repairs over the weekend. He left for work Monday morning with several of his tools still laying in the garage. Later in the morning when he reached into his toolbox for a screwdriver, he remembered where it was. He had to ask another crew member to borrow one. The look on his co-worker's face suggested that there is an unwritten rule about borrowing tools.

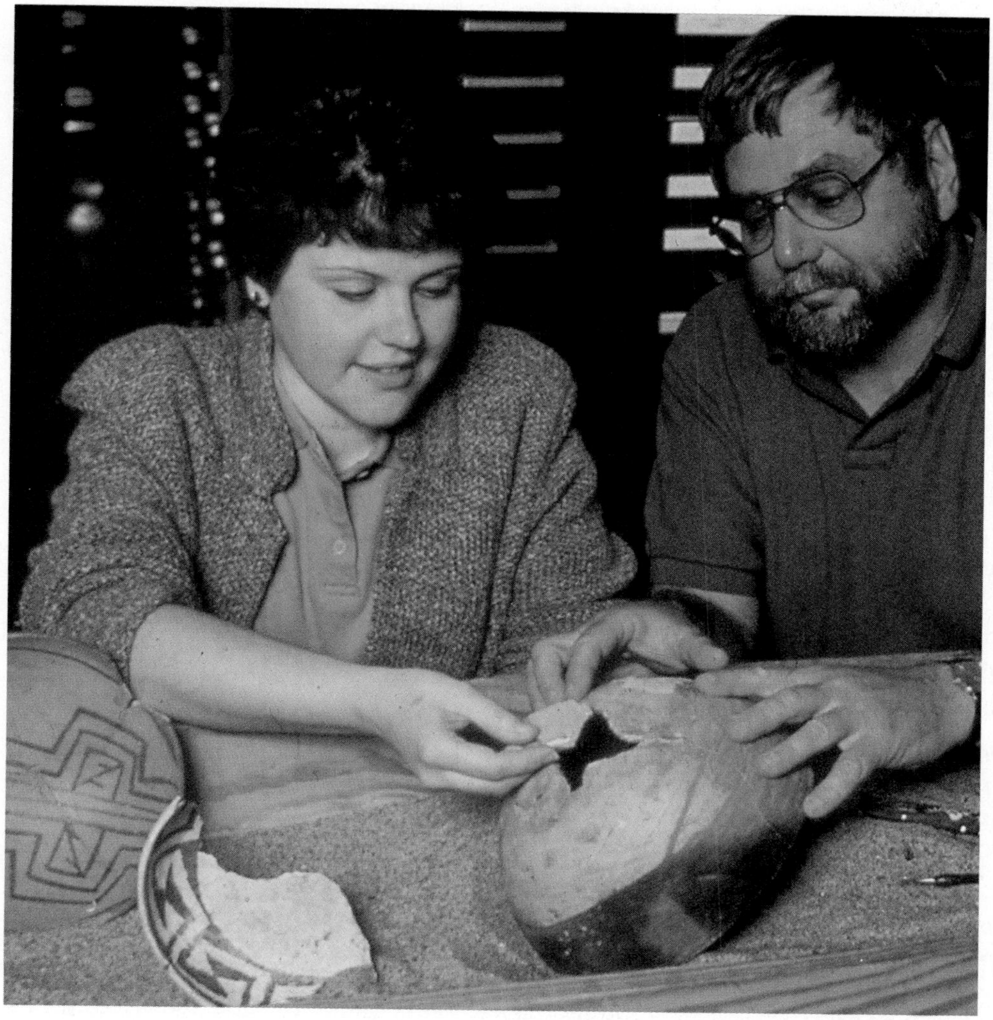

FIGURE 6–8 **Even in an informal workplace, do not call supervisors and managers by their first names unless they ask you to.**
Courtesy of SIUC Photocommunications.

One unwritten rule that needs to be discussed here relates to how people deal with each other in day-to-day activities. In some cases, managers, supervisors, and employees are very casual. Everyone is on a first-name basis. In other cases, the workers are more formal. All workers may be addressed by last names. Ann Morales, for instance, is called Mrs. Morales, and Paul Cramer is known as Mr. Cramer.

Some organizations have a formal way of getting work done. Ways of doing things that differ from the accepted way may be frowned upon. In less formal organizations, the most important thing may be getting the work done. How the work gets done may be left to each worker. By paying attention, you will learn how your company expects you to relate to others and to get the work done.

WORKING UNDER SUPERVISION

In the workplace, every employee is responsible to someone else. This is not unlike school. In your job as a student, you are responsible to your teachers. They, in turn, report to the principal, and so on. On the job, unless you are self-employed, you will work under the direction of a *supervisor.* Your supervisor will be responsible for training you and seeing that you learn company rules. He or she will also observe how well you perform on the job. Your success as an employee relates strongly to how well you work under supervision. Some suggestions for getting started on the right foot with your supervisor follow.

- ***Use the Supervisor for Communication.*** If you want to send messages to someone higher up in the organization, do so through your supervisor.
- ***Ask the Supervisor for Direction.*** Remember, the supervisor is responsible for your work, training and safety. Before starting job tasks for the first time, go over them with the supervisor. For example, you might say, "After I get these cartons unpacked and the contents shelved, then I should come back and see you, right?" Understanding beforehand what you are to do saves everyone time. If you are ever unsure of how to do something, ask for help. Most supervisors respect people who know when to ask for help.
- ***Don't Ask For or Expect Special Treatment.*** Most supervisors are responsible for many workers. All should be treated the same, so don't ask for special favors.
- ***Accept and Use the Supervisor's Suggestions.*** Your supervisor is more experienced at the work than you. Carla thought she had a better way of doing a job task. Because she was a new worker, though, she kept quiet. Later she learned that there were good reasons, such as safety, for following standard procedures.

Your supervisor is there to direct and assist you. Be aware, however, that your supervisor has other work to do. Your goal should be to learn your job quickly and perform it well with only a minimum of supervision. Your supervisor will appreciate not having to tell you everything to do.

PAYROLL WITHHOLDING

Every worker must pay federal income tax. The tax system operates on a pay-as-you go basis. This means that the employer takes income tax out of each paycheck. The amount of tax the employer withholds depends on three things:

- The amount of money you earn.
- Whether you are married or not (your marital status).
- The number of *allowances* you claim. This refers to the number of tax exemptions you are entitled to claim. For instance, a single person is entitled to one allowance.

Your employer will keep track of how much money you earn. On Form W-4, you will provide information about your marital status and the number of allowances you are entitled to claim.

John Nye is single and only claims one allowance. His completed Form W-4 is shown in Figure 6–9. Christina Comito is a single parent with two children. She claims three allowances—one for herself and one for each child. Based on each employee's earnings and allowances, an employer looks on a table to find how much tax to withhold.

Some people may be *exempt* from tax withholdings. This means that they don't have to pay taxes. People who earn less than a certain amount of money in a year are usually exempt. What was the amount last year that a single person with one allowance could earn before having to pay federal income tax?

Form **W-4** Department of the Treasury Internal Revenue Service

Employee's Withholding Allowance Certificate

▶ **For Privacy Act and Paperwork Reduction Act Notice, see reverse.**

OMB No. 1545-0010 **19 --**

1 Type or print your first name and middle initial: John R. | Last name: Nye | 2 Your social security number: 315 20 4024

Home address (number and street or rural route): 1612 Fredrick St.

3 ☒ Single ☐ Married ☐ Married, but withhold at higher Single rate.
Note: *If married, but legally separated, or spouse is a nonresident alien, check the Single box.*

City or town, state, and ZIP code: Carbondale, IL 72901

4 If your last name differs from that on your social security card, check here and call 1-800-772-1213 for a new card . . . . . ▶ ☐

5 Total number of allowances you are claiming (from line G above or from the worksheets on page 2 if they apply) . **5** 1

6 Additional amount, if any, you want withheld from each paycheck . . . . **6** $ 0

7 I claim exemption from withholding for 19-- and I certify that I meet **BOTH** of the following conditions for exemption:
- Last year I had a right to a refund of **ALL** Federal income tax withheld because I had **NO** tax liability; **AND**
- This year I expect a refund of **ALL** Federal income tax withheld because I expect to have **NO** tax liability.

If you meet both conditions, enter "EXEMPT" here . . . . ▶ **7**

Under penalties of perjury, I certify that I am entitled to the number of withholding allowances claimed on this certificate or entitled to claim exempt status.

Employee's signature ▶ *John R. Nye* **Date** ▶ *March 6* , 19 --

8 Employer's name and address (Employer: Complete 8 and 10 only if sending to the IRS) | 9 Office code (optional) | 10 Employer identification number

Cat. No. 10220Q

FIGURE 6–9 **Your employer will ask you to fill out one of these forms. A worksheet is provided to help you figure withholding allowances.**

High-performance Work Organizations

Work in America is largely patterned after the mass production system made famous by Henry Ford in the early 1900s. In mass production, jobs are broken down into a number of simple tasks. Each worker specializes in one task, which is done over and over.

Managers do the thinking and planning for the organization. Supervisors direct the work of front-line employees. Workers under this system need only be reliable, steady, and willing to follow directions.

The mass production system has helped make our nation a great economic power. It has also resulted in a high standard of living for workers. This system still determines the way most factories, offices, banks, hospitals, and schools are organized.

As we approach a new century, our nation faces increasing global economic competition. To remain competitive, we must increase productivity and improve quality.

The book *America's Choice: High Skills or Low Wages* describes a new style of work being adopted by some companies. It is called a high performance work organization. The basic idea is to give greater authority to front-line workers. Layers of managers disappear as teams of workers take over such tasks as quality control and production scheduling. Workers are asked to use judgment and make decisions at the point where goods and services are produced.

This type of work organization requires retraining of workers and managers. The high cost of retraining, however, is offset by gains in quality and productivity. High-performance work organizations are becoming the model for a successful future.

In a high-performance work organization, input from front-line workers is encouraged.
Photo courtesy of Chrysler Corporation.

CHAPTER 6 REVIEW

CHAPTER IN BRIEF

- It is normal to experience some anxiety when beginning a new job. Many companies provide an orientation to help new employees get started properly. Your employer wants you to be successful on the job.
- One person's first day at work may be quite different from another person's first day. However, most new employees do similar things and are provided with similar kinds of information.
- An organization chart shows the flow of authority and responsibility within an organization. It is important to follow your company's formal and informal lines of authority and responsibility.
- Companies have written policies and rules to help them run smoothly. You are responsible for obeying all policies and rules. Companies also have unwritten rules that you will need to learn.
- On the job, you will probably work under the direction of a supervisor. Use the supervisor for communication and direction. Accept and use the supervisor's suggestions, but don't ask for or expect special treatment.
- Employers are required to withhold money from your paycheck for federal income tax. The amount withheld is based on information that you provide on Form W-4.

WORDS TO KNOW

allowances
anxiety
authority
delegates
due process
exempt
morale
policy manual
probation
reimburse
responsibility
supervisor

QUESTIONS TO ANSWER

1. What are two reasons why companies like Northeast Electric Power Company conduct employee orientation programs?
2. Which is usually greater for beginning workers, level of authority or level of responsibility?
3. What is the difference between formal reporting and informal reporting?
4. What two purposes do written policies and rules serve in a company?
5. What are the four ways in which a company may communicate policies and rules to employees?
6. What should you do if a subject of interest is not covered in the company's policy manual?
7. Give an example of an area that is often covered by unwritten rules.
8. How is the job of student similar to that of a paid employee?

9. What are four ways to start a good relationship with a supervisor? Briefly explain each.
10. What three things determine the amount of income tax withheld from your paycheck?

ACTIVITIES TO DO

1. Some of your classmates may already have jobs. Ask these people to explain what their orientation to a new job was like. Ask them questions about their experiences on the job.
2. As a group activity, develop an organization chart for the employees in your school. At the top of the chart, start with the school district's board of education. How many levels are there? Suppose a teacher has a complaint about a board policy. To whom would he or she file a complaint? Discuss the process the teacher should follow.
3. Obtain an example of a company policy manual. You may already have one from your job, or perhaps you can borrow one from a family member or a friend. Look through the manuals in class and discuss examples of each of the seven types of policies and rules explained. Do the manuals contain types of policies and rules that are not explained in the chapter? If so, discuss the merits of these policies and rules.
4. Does your school provide students with a written code of conduct or something similar that outlines school policies and rules? If so, discuss how it is similar to a company policy manual. If your school does not have a code of conduct or something similar, discuss possible policies or rules that could go into such a manual.

TOPICS TO DISCUSS

1. What are some of the reasons why employers want new employees to make a quick and successful transition from school to the workplace?
2. Think of an instance in your life in which your anxiety about a situation turned out to be worse than the situation itself. What might this suggest regarding anxiety toward beginning a new job?
3. Some supervisors try not to get too friendly or informal with employees whom they supervise. Do you think this is a good idea or a bad idea? Explain why.
4. Under what circumstances might someone choose to specify an additional amount of withholding on line 6 of form W-4?

CHAPTER 7 Expectations of Employers

OUTLINE

- Job Performance
- Work Habits and Attitudes
- Rating Work Behavior
- Chapter Review

OBJECTIVES

After reading this chapter, you should be able to:

- Name and describe the five things that employers expect regarding job performance.
- Name and describe the six things that employers expect regarding work habits and attitudes.
- Describe the purposes of performance evaluation.
- Explain the two-step process of performance evaluation used by most large companies.

Everyone needs time to adjust to a new job. After that, you will need to meet the same expectations as other employees. Accepting a job means you make a contract with an employer. You agree to perform certain duties in return for a certain salary or wage. Your responsibility is to do the tasks you were hired to do, in the way and at the time the employer wants them done.

JOB PERFORMANCE

Work organizations either produce goods or provide services. Whether you are involved in producing goods or providing services, your employer will expect certain things from you.

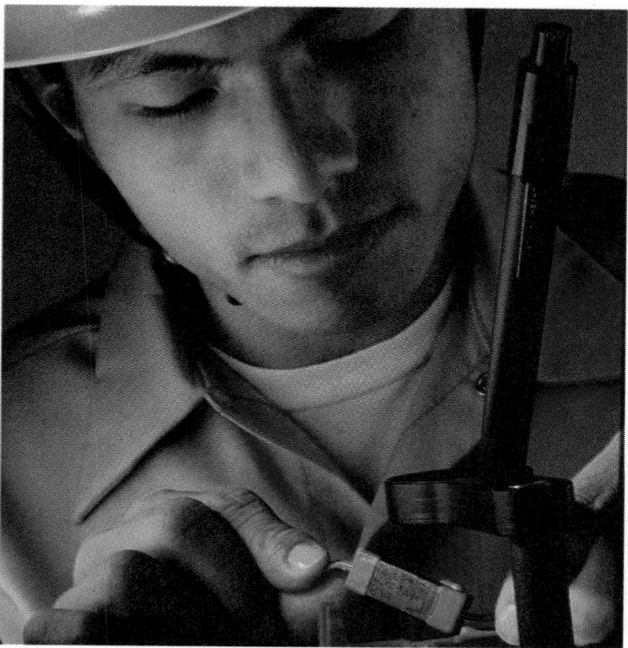

FIGURE 7–1 **An employer has a right to expect a certain level and quality of performance from the employee.**
Courtesy of 3M Corporation.

Productivity

Employers expect employees to complete a certain amount of work. The output of a worker is known as *productivity.* Suppose Worker A does more work than Worker B. This means that Worker A is more productive.

Productivity is usually thought of in terms of goods-producing occupations such as welder, bricklayer, or factory worker. Productivity is also important in service occupations. Service-producing occupations include barber, flight attendant, salesclerk, and nurse. Whether you hammer nails or wait on tables, the employer will expect you to give a day's worth of work for a day's pay.

Being productive means working at a steady pace during your time on the job. "Goofing off" is never okay. Susan learned this the hard way.

Susan was the sales manager of a small company. She liked her work, but wasted a lot of time. During the workday, she often visited with coworkers and talked on the phone with friends. The boss warned her to manage her time more efficiently. Susan paid no attention. Last week, she was let go.

Quality of Work

An employer expects you to do your work carefully, accurately, and thoroughly. Quality of work means how well a job is performed. Poor work quality may cancel out high productivity. For example, a secretary who types fast but makes a lot of errors is not doing the job well. Likewise, a production worker who solders many electrical components but whose soldered joints do not hold is not doing the job well.

FIGURE 7–2 **In some jobs, productivity is easy to observe.**
Courtesy of Simpson Industries Inc.

The quality of work is very important to a company's success. Customers who receive high-quality goods or services come back for repeat business. This is why employers want their workers to do good work.

Employees who perform high-quality work take *pride* in their work. Pride has to do with feeling proud and satisfied with what you have accomplished. Take the case of Kim, who works as a physical fitness instructor. She is proud to see her students progress and improve their health.

Good Judgment

Have people ever said to you, "Use your head"? What they meant was to think about what you are doing or figure it out yourself. You cannot run to a boss every time you have a problem or must make a

? ? ? ? ? ? ? ? ? ? ? ? ? ?

WHAT WOULD YOU DO?

You have been instructed to call a supplier and order replacement parts for several broken pieces of equipment. You are careful to provide all important information on quantities, part numbers, prices, and the like. After you finish, the supplier asks, "How do you want this shipped?"

"Gee, the boss did not tell me that," you think. There is no one else in the office to ask.

What would you do?

decision. Your employer will want you to think about a problem and come to the right decision.

Using good *judgment* is a sign of maturity. It is something that employers look for when promoting people to better jobs. If you are known as someone who makes quick decisions and has poor judgment, your time with the company may be short.

Safety Consciousness

Many jobs involve working with tools, machines, and equipment. Some of these may be dangerous. For your benefit as well as that of co-workers, the employer will expect you to work safely. Part of being a safe worker is knowing how to do a job. You will have learned this through education or on-the-job training. For instance, if you are working as a carpenter, you should already know how to safely use a circular saw.

Your employer will expect you to perform your job in the way that you have been trained. In addition, the company will probably have safety rules that you will be expected to follow. For example, workers who go to certain areas of the plant may need to wear a hard hat or safety glasses. Or, there may be certain containers that workers must use when disposing of cleaning rags or solvents.

If an accident or emergency does happen, you will be expected to follow certain steps. Let's say that a machine part gets stuck in a punch press. Your boss has told you that when this happens you should turn off the machine right away and go for help. Do what you are told. Do not try to fix the problem yourself.

Learn your company's safety rules and procedures. Do this by reading and studying printed company material that you may have. If you have any questions, be sure to ask your boss. Once you know the safety rules, practice them. Knowledge of them alone is not enough. Additional information on safety will be presented in Chapter 17.

Care of Equipment

An employer often has money tied up in expensive tools and equipment. You will be expected to take care of them and use them properly. Damaged tools and equipment cost money in two ways. First, the item must be repaired or replaced. Then, while the repairs are going on, work time is lost. Should you have questions about tools or equipment, ask them. Not doing so could cause serious problems.

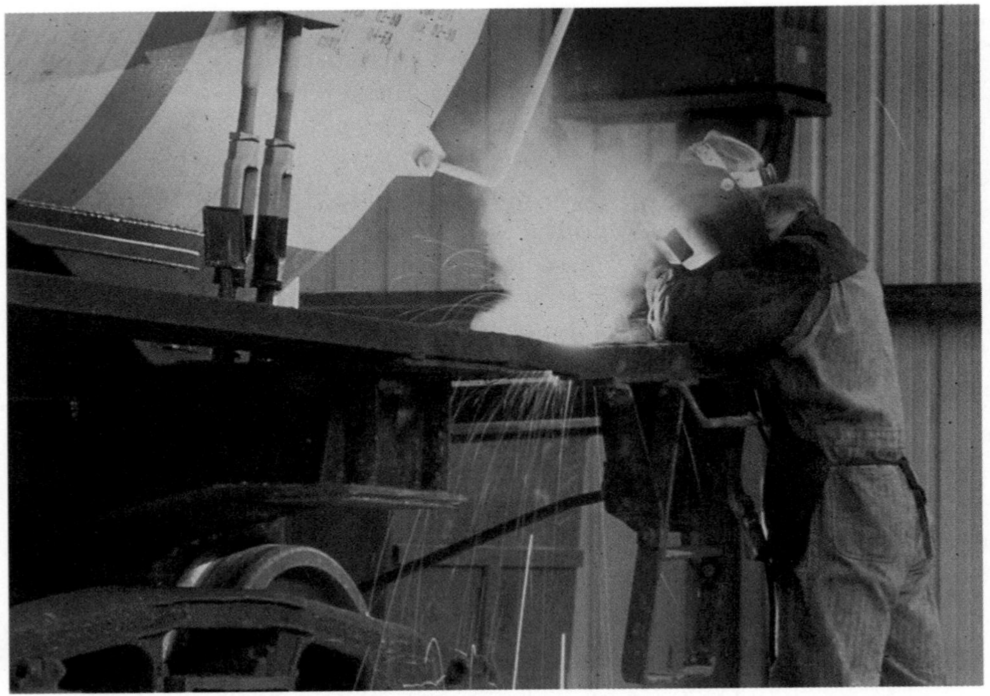

FIGURE 7–3 **If equipment is broken, production has to be stopped while the repair is made.**
Courtesy of Miller Electric Mfg. Co. of Appleton, WI.

Let's say, for instance, that you are working summers as a farm laborer. The boss asks you if you know how to drive the tractor. You say that you do. The new tractor has some features that are unfamiliar to you. You decide to drive it anyhow. After a few minutes, the tractor stops dead. The mechanic says that your mistake caused several thousands of dollars of damage to the tractor. Even though the boss fires you because of your carelessness, it could have been worse. In some cases, improper use of tools and equipment injures and kills workers.

Use tools and equipment as if they are your own. Think of them as if you have to pay for repairing or replacing them.

WORK HABITS AND ATTITUDES

Another type of employer expectation has to do with work habits and attitudes. These are the ways employees behave on the job. Poor work habits and a negative attitude are the main reasons most people lose their jobs. You may, for example, be a great hair stylist. You will not keep your job, though, if you cannot get along with your boss, coworkers, or clients.

Attendance and Punctuality

To avoid work delays or interruptions, employers expect workers to be on the job regularly (attendance). Let's see what happened on a construction site when a worker "took off" regularly.

A crew was building townhouses in the Dallas suburbs. All of the workers showed up unless they had a good reason. Yvonne frequently missed work. When she was absent, the others covered for her. Sometimes, though, the others were too busy with their own work to do hers, too. Yvonne's work did not get done on those days. The boss told Yvonne that if other crew members missed work as she did, the job could shut down. Yvonne got the point and changed her ways.

Punctuality is also necessary. Workplaces that are open at certain times need employees there to deal with business. An employer's profits and public image may suffer if employees are not there to take care of business. Suppose a restaurant opens for business at 6:00 a.m. If some workers do not arrive until 6:30, customers will get poor service. They will eat elsewhere and tell others to do the same. Be ready to work at starting time, stay until quitting time, and take only the time set aside for lunch periods and breaks. Remember that most workers are not paid for time they miss when they are absent or tardy.

If you must be absent or late, try to tell your supervisor as far ahead of time as possible. If you get sick one evening, for instance, notify the boss that you will miss work the next day.

1. Absent from work too frequently or for questionable reasons.
2. Has to be supervised too much of the time.
3. Takes no initiative when something needs to be done.
4. Isn't very observant; fails to recognize errors or problems.
5. Doesn't listen well.
6. Arrives late or leaves early too often.
7. Doesn't consider the consequences of decisions or actions.
8. Too much socializing with other workers or visitors.
9. Can't accept suggestions or criticism.
10. Doesn't seem to care about doing a job well.

FIGURE 7–4 **One study of employers identified these as the ten most serious problems of young, entry-level workers (in rank order).**

Cooperation

"He or she just refuses to cooperate" is a common employer complaint about a worker. *Cooperation* involves getting along with others. One aspect of cooperation is following orders. Another way of saying this is doing what you are told. Since you are likely to be a beginning worker, you will probably receive many orders.

Your job may include many boring tasks, such as sweeping floors, cleaning equipment, or making coffee. After all, someone has to do them. If you won't, the employer will hire someone who will. So, accept your assignments cheerfully (or at least, willingly) and do your best. If you do so, the employer will notice.

Cooperation also means being able to take criticism. When you accept wages, you agree to do the job the way the employer wants it done. The employer has a right to criticize or correct you. The employer wants you to improve your work performance. (You do, too, hopefully.) Accept and profit from constructive criticism. Thank

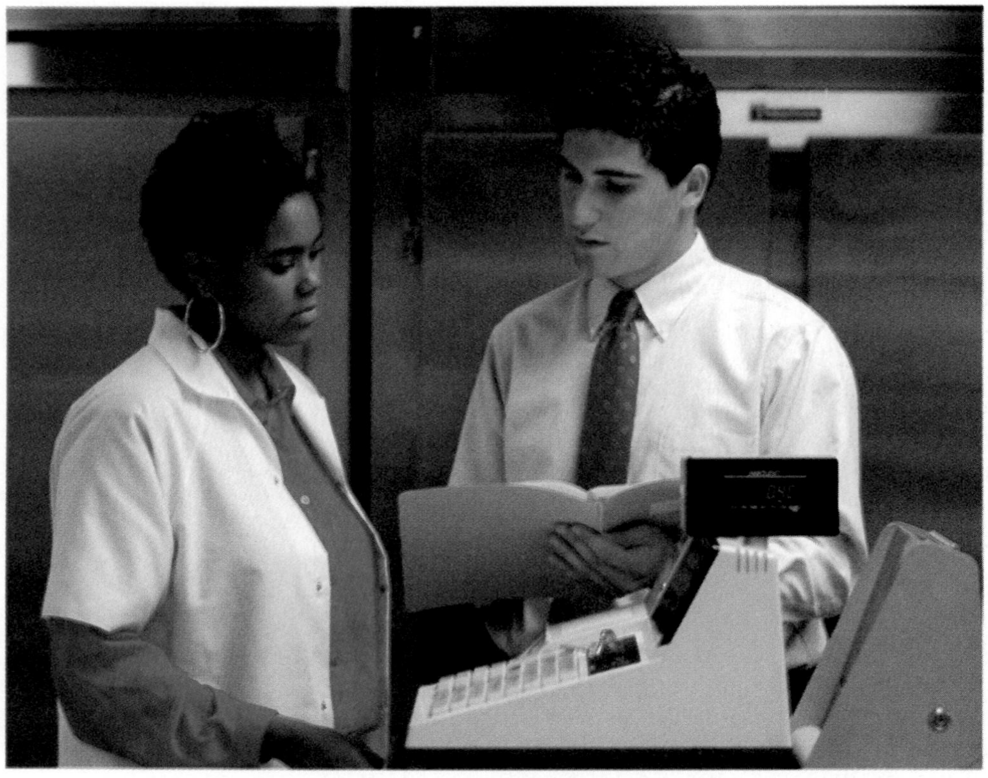

FIGURE 7–5 **Following orders is the most common way that an employee demonstrates cooperation.**

the employer, tell him or her you will improve, and then do so.

Courtesy and cooperation go hand-in-hand. You can build good working relationships by being respectful, friendly, and considerate toward others. A smile or a friendly greeting tells others that you are trying to help create a positive work setting.

Interest and Enthusiasm

Employers like employees who show *interest* and *enthusiasm* toward their work. Such people are often the most productive and cooperative workers. Few people, of course, find everything about their job to be interesting and enjoyable. Do, however, show your enthusiasm for those parts that you like.

Your company and your coworkers also deserve your interest and enthusiasm. Keep up to date on the company's plans. If your employer has an employee newsletter or company magazine, read it. Try to take part in company social events and activities. You may be just the shortstop the company softball team needs. If help is needed with company charities or service projects, volunteer your time. You, the company, and society will all benefit.

Honesty

Stealing is a serious problem in many businesses and industries. Employers usually deal firmly with theft. Most employees caught stealing are fired. They may face criminal charges as well.

Most stealing involves the theft of money or expensive tools and equipment. But taking office supplies and using the photocopy machine for personal use are also forms of stealing.

Art is an insurance agent. He also serves as secretary of the area's youth soccer association. Over the weekend, he needed to prepare a mailing for the group. So after business on Friday, he loaded up his briefcase with supplies from the company's storeroom. He picked up a computer diskette, a couple of pens, a legal pad, a ream of printer paper, a roll of tape, and a box of envelopes. "They won't miss it," Art thought to himself, "The company made $230 million last year."

Art tried to justify his behavior, but what he did is stealing. Had he been caught, the company would not have been impressed by his excuses. He may have been fired. Surely, his chances for future advancement in the company would have been lessened.

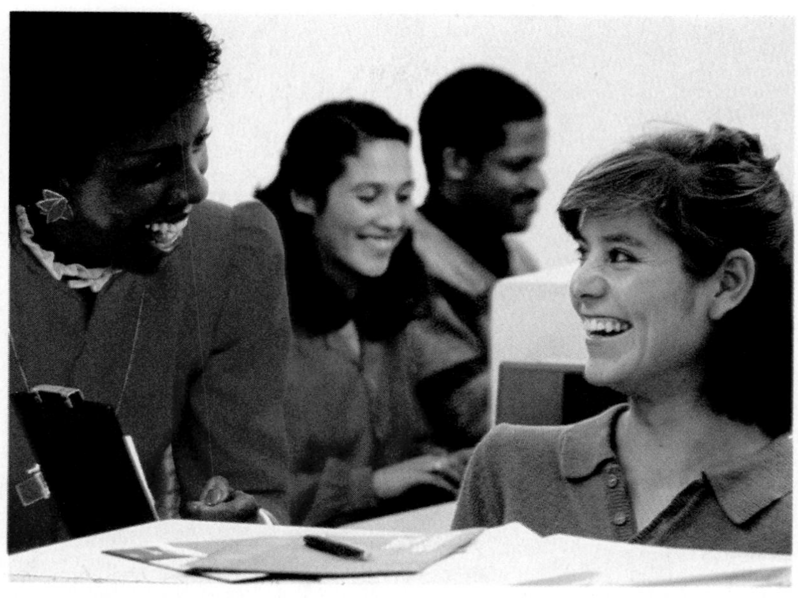

FIGURE 7–6 **Workers who show interest and enthusiasm benefit themselves and their company.**

You have a promising future. Don't risk it by being like Art. Practice honesty by not taking anything owned by the company regardless of its worth.

? ? ? ? ? ? ? ? ? ? ? ? ? ?

WHAT WOULD YOU DO?

You and two other employees work as clerks at a Quick-Mart convenience food store. One afternoon you notice that a co-worker lays $.75 from a purchase beside the cash register. You think it is odd that he does not ring it up. When you look back again, the money is gone. Over the next several days, you watch him more closely. You discover that he is stealing money. You wish you had not seen him. You do not know whether to say something to him, tell your boss, or keep quiet.

What would you do?

Loyalty

Your employer would like you to feel a sense of devotion to the company. This means, for example, that you should not criticize the company when talking with coworkers, friends, or strangers. *Loyalty* means being proud of what you do and where you work. It is believing in your company and defending it, if necessary.

No company, of course, is perfect. If you disagree with a company policy or action, discuss it with your supervisor. If things cannot be

FIGURE 7–7 **These workers wear their company name proudly.**
Courtesy of Martin Marietta Corporation.

worked out, it may be time to find another job.

RATING WORK BEHAVIOR

As a student, teachers have been evaluating you for many years. On the job, your employer will also evaluate your work. The evaluation of employees is usually known as *performance evaluation.* The employer rates your job performance, your work habits, and your attitudes.

Purposes of Evaluation

Employee evaluation allows employers to determine how well workers are doing their jobs. Performance evaluations have several purposes.

One purpose is to decide if you deserve a pay raise and how much to give you. Employers know it is important to provide pay raises as a reward for good work.

Evaluation also helps employees become better workers. This benefits both the employee and the

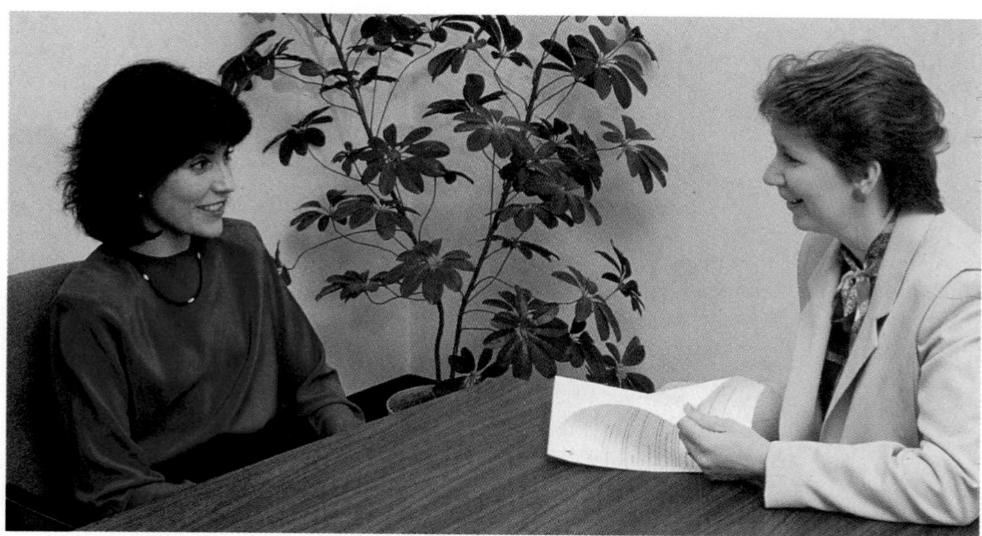

FIGURE 7–8 **Evaluation in the school classroom or on the job has many of the same purposes.**
Photo by Paul E. Meyers.

employer. For you, the employee, the feedback you get helps you learn and improve. You find out what your strengths and weaknesses are, and where you may need improvement. For the employer, the evaluation may suggest places where you need more on-the-job training.

Finally, evaluation provides a basis for future job assignments. Let's say that an opening exists for a department supervisor. Management might review employee evaluations to see which (if any) employee could be promoted. Or, suppose your evaluation results suggest that you would do better in a different job. The employer might then transfer you to another department.

How You Are Evaluated

The way in which you will be evaluated differs from company to company. Donna, who works for a very small company, does not often realize that her boss is evaluating her. From time to time, she and her boss discuss Donna's work over a cup of coffee. All feedback is verbal, no forms are used, and no records are kept.

Most large firms, however, have a standard procedure for employee evaluation. The evaluations usually take place once a year, although every six months is not uncommon.

Most evaluations are done in two steps. Your boss or supervisor fills out an evaluation form. A sample form is shown in Figure 7–9, on page 96. Then you meet with the supervisor or boss. The two of you will go over the form and discuss your strengths and weaknesses. The tone of this meeting should be positive and constructive (unless you are doing a really poor job).

The discussion between you and your supervisor will not be one-sided. You should have a chance to discuss what you like and dislike about your current position. This is a good time for you to discuss your future goals. Do not use the time to

Student-Trainee Evaluation Sheet
COOPERATIVE EDUCATION PROGRAMS

Reporting Month ____________________

Please Return By ____________________

Swinburn Public Schools

Student's Name ____________________ Supervisor's Name ____________________

Training Station ____________________

INSTRUCTIONS: Please rate the student by circling the number on each scale below at the point which most accurately describes the student learner's progress to date. (Please feel free to make comments on the back of this paper.)

Categories	OUTSTANDING	ABOVE AVERAGE	AVERAGE	BELOW AVERAGE	UNSATISFACTORY
Personal Appearance	5	4	3	2	1
Attendance and Tardiness	5	4	3	2	1
Rate of Progress	5	4	3	2	1
Follows Directions	5	4	3	2	1
Job Judgment Decision Making	5	4	3	2	1
Attitude Toward Job	5	4	3	2	1
Ability to Get Along with People	5	4	3	2	1
Initiative (Does Things Without Being Told)	5	4	3	2	1
Safety	5	4	3	2	1
Dependability (Overall)	5	4	3	2	1

OUTSTANDING ☐ ABOVE AVERAGE ☐ AVERAGE ☐ BELOW AVERAGE ☐ UNSATISFACTORY ☐

Supervisor's Signature ____________________ Date __________ Letter Grade __________

Student's Signature ____________________

FIGURE 7–9 Sample performance evaluation form.

FIGURE 7–10 **Approach your work as if you are being evaluated every day. In fact, you are!**
Courtesy of Rotary Lift.

complain about the job or co-workers, though.

After the Evaluation

An evaluation is not just a once-a-year thing. Your boss is continually watching your job performance, work habits, and attitudes. The ratings you receive from time to time result from a process that goes on all the time. This is why it pays to do your best work each and every day.

If you get a negative evaluation, you will need to face up to your shortcomings. Make sure you understand what you can do to correct the problem. Your future in the company will depend on showing that you can improve your work behavior before the next evaluation. If you ignore what your boss tells you, your next evaluation could be your last.

FOCUS ON

The Worker

Labor Unions

A labor union is a group of workers who have joined together to protect their rights. The two main types of unions are craft and industrial. A craft union is made up of skilled workers in a craft or trade, such as plumbers, musicians, or barbers. Workers in the same industry often belong to an industrial union. Perhaps you have heard of the United Auto Workers or the United Mine Workers. These are industrial unions.

Throughout its history, organized labor has fought for three main goals. These have been improvements in:

1. Wages, hours, and benefits,
2. Job security, and
3. Safe and healthful working conditions.

Unions also provide apprenticeship programs that teach work skills to young union members. Some unions have hiring halls where workers can go to find out about job openings.

Most unions are in the Midwest and Northeast parts of the United States. These areas have large construction, manufacturing, transportation, and mining industries.

An employer that has an agreement with a union is called a union shop. In a union shop, the employer can hire whomever he or she chooses. However, the employee must join the union within a certain period of time. About twenty states have so-called "right-to-work" laws that do not allow union shops. These states have open shops in which an employee does not have to join a union.

When you start a job, a co-worker or supervisor may ask you to join a union. Members of the local union must vote on your membership. Usually, though, anyone who applies is accepted. You will probably pay an initiation fee to join, and you must pay regular dues.

This truck driver is a union member. Does he belong to a craft union or an industrial union?
Courtesy of Fluor Daniel Inc.

CHAPTER 7 REVIEW

CHAPTER IN BRIEF

- After a short period of adjustment, you will need to meet the same expectations as other employees. Your responsibility is to do the job tasks in the way and at the time the employer wants them done.
- Your employer will expect the following in terms of your job performance:
  a. *Productivity*—completing a certain amount of work in the time provided.
  b. *Quality of work*—doing your work carefully, accurately, and thoroughly.
  c. *Good judgment*—thinking about a problem and then doing the right thing.
  d. *Safety consciousness*—learning and following safety rules and procedures.
  e. *Care of equipment*—using and handling tools and equipment correctly.
- Another type of employer expectation has to do with work habits and attitudes. Your employer will expect the following:
  a. *Attendance and punctuality*—showing up for work every day, on time.
  b. *Cooperation*—getting along with supervisors, co-workers, and customers.
  c. *Interest and enthusiasm*—showing you like and care about your company and co-workers.
  d. *Honesty*—not taking anything owned by the company regardless of what it is worth.
  e. *Loyalty*—believing in and being proud of your company.
- An employer will evaluate your on-the-job performance. Both your job performance and your work habits and attitudes will be evaluated. Employee evaluation allows employers to determine how well workers are doing their jobs.
- Most evaluations are done in two steps. First, your supervisor will fill out an evaluation form. Next, your supervisor will meet with you to go over the ratings. If you get a negative evaluation, you will need to improve your performance before the next rating.

WORDS TO KNOW

cooperation
enthusiasm
honesty
interest
judgment
loyalty
performance evaluation
pride
productivity
punctuality

QUESTIONS TO ANSWER

1. Suppose your work always falls below the employer's expectations. What will probably happen?
2. How does the quality of employees' work relate to a company's success?
3. Name three things that an employee can do to perform a job more safely.
4. A damaged tool or piece of equipment may cost an employer in two ways. Explain how.
5. Give three examples of why a person might get fired.
6. What should you do if you must be absent or late to work?
7. List four ways that an employee can be cooperative on the job.
8. Is taking a few stamps and some tape from the company considered stealing? Why or why not?
9. What are the three purposes of employee evaluation from the employer's standpoint?
10. Most companies follow a two-step evaluation procedure. Describe both steps.

ACTIVITIES TO DO

1. Work with your instructor to develop a rating sheet based on the ten items from Figure 7–4. Type the items in random order without the rankings. Make copies of the form. Each person in class should ask one or more employers or supervisors to complete the form. The instructions should ask employers to rank the items from one to ten in terms of what they see as the most serious problems of young workers. Tally the survey results in class and compare them with the rankings shown in Figure 7–4.
2. Assume you are an employer. What would you do or say to an employee in each of the following situations?
   a. An employee puts the wrong kind of lubricant in a chain saw, causing it to burn up.
   b. An employee calls in sick; then, on your way to lunch, you see the person playing tennis.
   c. An employee has been making personal, long-distance calls on company phones.
   d. An employee has been bad-mouthing the company to co-workers.

   Discuss your answers in class.

TOPICS TO DISCUSS

1. During the last decade or so, many U.S. companies have moved their manufacturing plants overseas. The reason, they claim, is that U.S. workers are less productive and less concerned about quality than foreign workers. Do you think this is true?
2. Some companies make employees pay for any tools or equipment they damage or lose. Do you think this practice is fair?

3. Some American manufacturers, particularly in the auto industry, have begun to use Japanese-style management techniques. For instance, workers are given uniforms with the company name on them. Production and management workers all wear the same uniform. This is supposed to help build enthusiasm and loyalty toward the company. Do you think things like this make a difference?
4. As an employee, which would you rather receive: (a) a guaranteed 4% annual raise, or (b) the possibility of a raise between 0% and 8% based on the results of an annual evaluation of your performance? Why?

CHAPTER 8 Worker Rights and Protections

OUTLINE

- Honesty and Respect
- Fair Employment Practices
- Protection from Discrimination
- Worker Safety and Health
- Agencies Providing Services to Workers
- Chapter Review

OBJECTIVES

After reading this chapter, you should be able to:

- Name and describe six things employers owe their workers.
- Discuss the importance of employers treating workers with honesty and respect.
- Name and describe the three types of fair employment practices.
- Explain workers' rights regarding protection from discrimination.
- Explain the roles of employers and workers regarding safety and health in the workplace.
- Identify agencies that deal with workers' complaints.

In Chapter 7, you learned that an employee has certain responsibilities to an employer. An employment contract, however, isn't a one-way deal. Employers also owe certain things to their employees. One of these, of course, is payment for their work. Other things include:

- *Training and Supervision.* An employer should provide the necessary on-the-job training. Once the worker starts the job, the employer should give proper supervision and feedback. Workers need to know what to do, and how well they are performing.
- *Orientation to the Workplace.* A worker deserves to have information about company policies and rules. When these change, the employer should tell its workers.
- *Honesty and Respect.* An employer owes all its workers honesty and respect.

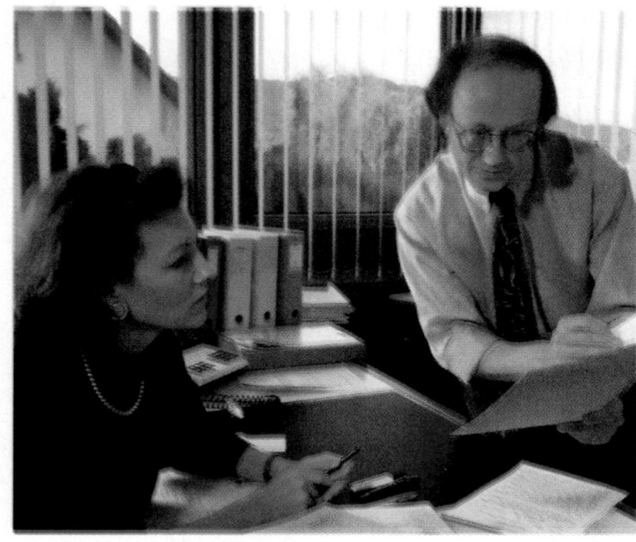

FIGURE 8–1 **Most employers treat workers fairly.**
Courtesy of Corning Incorporated.

- ***Fair Employment Practice.*** Laws cover child labor, work hours, and payment of wages. An employer who wants to avoid legal hassles must obey such laws.
- ***Protection from Discrimination.*** Laws prohibit discrimination against workers.
- ***Safety and Health.*** Years ago, employers did not have to provide safe working conditions. Many workers paid with their lives. Employers now must follow certain health and safety standards.

The first two responsibilities in the preceding list were discussed in Chapter 6. The four remaining ones will be covered here.

HONESTY AND RESPECT

An employer who pays your salary has a right to tell you what to do as long as it is not unlawful. Most employers and supervisors, however, realize that honesty and respect toward their employees are essential. Workers are not robots. They are human beings with pride and self-worth. The following important historical case shows what can happen when a company forgets about the feelings of its workers.

Lordstown is a city in Ohio where a General Motors assembly plant is located. The plant was built to be the world's fastest, most fully automated auto assembly line. In 1971, the assembly line was producing 104 cars per hour. (The industry average was 55 per hour.) Some GM officials thought the line could produce even more cars. They cut back workers on the line and increased the number of jobs each person had to do.

The result was that many workers could not keep up with the pace. Some workers were literally riding down the line with the cars as they tried to bolt on parts. Workers complained, but GM officials ignored them. Out of frustration, workers began intentionally leaving pieces off the cars. In some cases, workers inflicted costly damage to the cars. Many cars came off the line with broken windshields, torn upholstery, or other damage. Eventually, the workers went on strike.

Between March 3 and March 24, 1972, approximately 8,000 workers participated in the strike. After three weeks and $150 million in lost production, workers and management agreed to a settlement. The episode at Lordstown marked a turning point in employer-worker relations.

This example illustrates that employers cannot always force workers to do what they want them to do. The best relationship is one where employers treat workers as they wish to be treated. Honesty and respect is the foundation for a good relationship between employers and workers.

FIGURE 8–2 Employees are more productive when treated with honesty and respect than when they are not.
Courtesy of Hewlett Packard.

FAIR EMPLOYMENT PRACTICES

Many state and federal laws deal with *employment practices.* A very important federal law is the Fair Labor Standards Act (FLSA). It applies to employers or companies that do business in more than one state and have annual sales above a certain amount. The FLSA covers three types of practices. These are child labor, wages and hours, and equal pay.

Child Labor

The FLSA includes laws covering workers under the age of eighteen. For instance, people fifteen years and younger cannot work in factories or during school hours. Nor can those under eighteen work in dangerous occupations such as mining.

Each of the fifty states also has its own child-labor laws. If both federal and state laws apply to a situation, the employer must obey the stricter standard. For instance, David is seventeen and wants to work at a sawmill in his town. His state's laws would let him work there. Federal law, though, says that such jobs are too dangerous for workers under eighteen. David will have to wait until his next birthday to apply for a mill job.

You read in Chapter 3 that the law is flexible to allow students to take part in work experience education programs. In most states, schools issue work permits to those between fourteen and seventeen years of age. This allows students to work during school hours. The program helps protect the health and welfare of minors. It regulates the types of work they may do and the hours they can work. Can you think of how a work permit benefits employers as well?

FIGURE 8–3 **Not all businesses are covered by minimum wage laws.**

Wages and Hours

The FLSA sets standards for minimum wages and maximum hours for most workers in the U.S. Many states also have laws about workers' pay. The *minimum wage* is the lowest wage the law permits employers to pay workers. (Remember, not all employers are covered by this law.) In 1938, the national minimum wage was $.25 an hour. By April 1991 the figure had risen to $4.25 an hour. The same law permits employers to pay a *training wage* to workers under age 20. This wage is set at 85 percent of the minimum wage ($3.62). Employers can pay this wage for the first 90 days of

? ? ? ? ? ? ? ? ? ? ? ? ? ?

WHAT WOULD YOU DO?

Your employer asks you to work a few extra hours on Saturday to help him catch up on an important order. Even though you have already put in 40 hours this week, you agree to do so. The next week, you eagerly open your pay envelope. You discover that you have been paid straight time for 45 hours. You call this to the boss's attention. He tells you that he does not pay overtime and that you should be glad that you have a job. You are not satisfied with his explanation.

What would you do?

employment. Congress periodically raises the minimum wage. Is it still $4.25 an hour?

The FLSA also sets the length of the *standard workweek.* Time worked beyond 40 hours is called *overtime.* For overtime hours, employers must pay workers at a rate of 1½ times their regular rate. The discussion of overtime pay in Chapter 10 holds special interest for us all. That material deals with figuring overtime on a paycheck.

Equal Pay

John and Ruth were assistant managers for a small hotel chain. They started working for the chain at the same time. They had equal qualifications. Ruth learned that John was making a lot more money than she was. Ruth tried to figure out the problem. She knew that workers sometimes receive different salaries because of shift work, skill level, seniority, and things like that. Ruth ruled out all those reasons. The only difference she could name was that she was a woman. She knew that the Equal Pay Act of 1963 outlawed different wage scales for equal work. This means that workers doing the same job must receive the same wage. An employer may still pay workers different wages based on things such as seniority, skill level, and shift worked. What would you do if you were Ruth?

FIGURE 8–4 **These workers receive equal pay for equal work.**
Courtesy of Ford Motor Company.

PROTECTION FROM DISCRIMINATION

As you can see, laws protect workers from being discriminated against. *Discrimination* means treating someone differently than another. For example, if an employer will not hire you only because of your race, that is discrimination. Another example is being "passed over" for promotion because of your sex. So, too, is getting fired because you are older. What about equal treatment in such areas as hiring, promotion, and job security? Laws covering these areas exist. They deal with the broad areas of *equal employment opportunity and affirmative action.*

SALES

NEWSPAPER SALES REP

A national newspaper is seeking a sales representative for St. Louis/Kansas City. Responsibilities include the development of retail, vending, corporate and college sales. Excellent salary and benefits. Car provided. Send resume and salary history to:

ARC INC.
78 WEST 5TH STREET
SUITE 100
HICKORY HEIGHTS, OH 45492
ATTENTION: JOHN GOODMAN

Equal Opportunity Employer

FIGURE 8–5 Some companies advertise that they are an "Equal Opportunity Employer."

Equal Employment Opportunity

The passage of the Civil Rights Act of 1964 gave the government a strong legal tool to prevent job discrimination. It thus paved the way for equal employment opportunity. Under equal opportunity, employers, unions, and employment agencies cannot discriminate against people because of race, color, religion, sex, or national origin. The Equal Employment Opportunity Commission (EEOC) administers the Civil Rights Act and related laws.

In 1964, Warren Johnson lost his job as a landscaper. His employer had gone out of business. Warren was fifty-six at the time. With his experience, he figured that he would easily find a job. The first two places he applied told him he was "too old." Warren was upset. He could not legally fight the employers. Today, he could take action against them.

The Age Discrimination Act of 1967 was passed to prohibit discrimination against people between forty and seventy years of age. The Rehabilitation Act of 1973 extended protection to those with physical or mental handicaps.

The most recent legislation prohibiting discrimination in employment practices is the Americans with Disabilities Act that took effect in 1992. It gives civil rights projections to individuals with disabilities similar to those provided on the basis of race, sex, national origin, age, and religion. The EEOC also administers these laws.

Another recent employment-related law is the Family and Medical Leave Act, which took effect in August 1993. It requires employers with 50 or more workers to grant up to 12 weeks' unpaid leave a year. This allows workers to take time off to help care for a new baby or an ill family member without fear of losing their jobs.

Affirmative Action

Equal employment opportunity laws forbid job discrimination. What about those people who have been victims of past discrimination, though? For instance, many women and other minorities have been unjustly passed over for job promotions. This is an example of a condition that *affirmative action* tries to

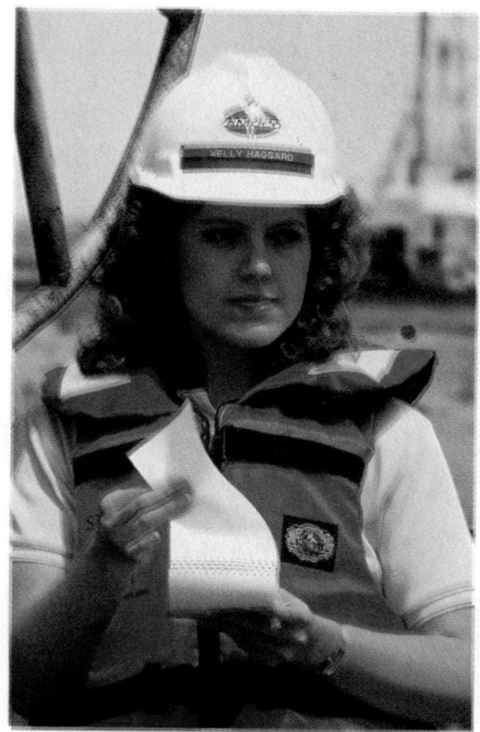

FIGURE 8–6 **The number of women and minority employees has increased in many occupations because of affirmative action programs.** *Courtesy of Amoco Corporation.*

correct. Affirmative action is not a federal law. Instead, it refers to a series of policies and programs designed to correct *past discrimination.* Most affirmative action programs include special efforts to hire and promote women, minorities, handicapped people, and Vietnam veterans.

WORKER SAFETY AND HEALTH

Have you seen workers wearing hard hats and safety glasses? Perhaps you have worn such gear yourself. Such equipment helps protect workers from injury. Years ago, many employers were often unconcerned if their employees failed to use safety equipment or otherwise acted unsafely. Some employers even made employees work under unsafe or unhealthful conditions. If workers complained, they lost their jobs. In 1971, such situations changed for the better. That year marked the beginning of the Occupational Safety and Health Administration (OSHA). This organization sets and enforces standards for safe and healthful working conditions.

Examples of OSHA rules include the following:

- Each high-radiation area shall contain a sign having the radiation caution symbol and the words: CAUTION, HIGH-RADIATION AREA.
- Safety shoes shall conform to certain standards.
- Tools and other metal objects shall be kept away from the top of uncovered batteries.
- Exposed hot water and steam pipes shall be covered with insulating material whenever necessary to protect employees from contact with them.
- All workplaces shall be kept as clean as the nature of the work allows.

All employers having at least one employee must obey OSHA standards. To help employers, OSHA offers free on-site visitations. Most employers welcome suggestions that will create a better work environment. Exceptions exist, though. To discourage these, OSHA makes random inspections as well. If inspectors find hazards, the employer can be fined and the business shut down.

A restaurant server in Kansas complained to her employer that it was too hot in the restaurant's kitchen area. The employer ignored her complaint. She took her complaint to OSHA. When the employer found out, he tried to get even with the server. He threatened her, began giving her the least desirable work, and rearranged her work schedule. The server tried to reason with the employer, but finally quit because of the harassment.

The server filed a complaint with OSHA. After investigating the case, OSHA ordered the employer to pay the server back wages and to remove all papers about the case from her files. (Most employers keep records on each employee.) OSHA also required the employer to post a notice that advised other employees of the settlement.

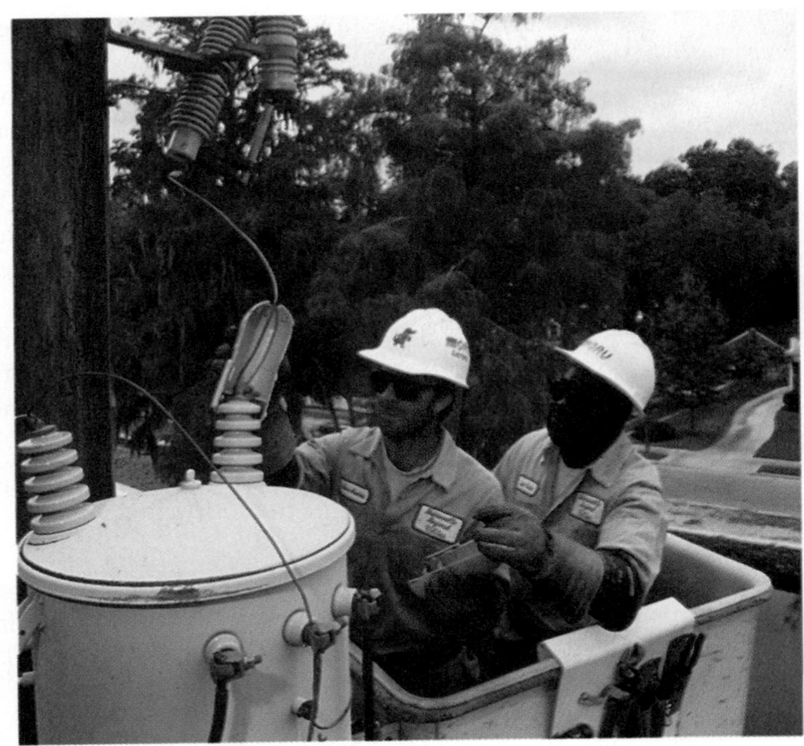

FIGURE 8–7 Think safety every minute you are on the job.
Courtesy of Union Pacific Corporation.

Protecting New Workers

New employees have a much higher risk of injury than experienced workers. The Bureau of Labor Statistics (BLS) reports that about half of all work-related injuries occur during the first year of employment. Why are new workers more likely to be hurt? Studies show that new workers often do not know enough to protect themselves. One BLS study found that:

- Of 724 workers hurt while using scaffolds, 27 percent said they had received no information on safety requirements for installing the kind of scaffold on which they were hurt.

? ? ? ? ? ? ? ? ? ? ? ? ? ? ?

WHAT WOULD YOU DO?

The production machine on which you work was repaired over the weekend. As you begin work on Monday morning, you notice that the safety guard has not been replaced. You immediately go to the supervisor. He tells you to go ahead and get started and he will replace the guard when he gets time. But you do not want to work on the machine unless the safety guard is in place.

What would you do?

FIGURE 8–8 **Ask about anything on the job that you do not understand. What you don't know can hurt you or your chances for advancement.**
Courtesy of Lab-Volt Systems Division of Buck Engineering Inc.

- Of 868 workers who suffered head injuries, 71 percent said they had no instruction about hard hats.
- Of 554 workers hurt while servicing equipment, 61 percent said they were not informed about lockout procedures.

In nearly every type of injury studied by the BLS, the same story is repeated. Workers often do not receive the safety information they need. Or, if they do, they do not apply it.

What Workers Can Do

During your on-the-job training, your employer is responsible for your safety education. You, too, play an important role. Before starting to work, be sure that you understand all necessary safety measures. If an explanation is unclear, ask again. Practice and use what you have learned. Do not take shortcuts that could endanger your health or safety.

Following are some general safety rules. Can you think of others?

- Never use a tool or piece of equipment that lacks a safety guard or has a nonworking one.
- If earplugs or other personal protective devices such as gloves or aprons are required, use them all the time.
- Do not "horse around" or play practical jokes at the workplace.
- Be especially careful when you get tired. This is when accidents are more likely to happen.
- If you work where dangerous substances are used, find out what something is before you handle it.
- Accept responsibility for your own safety on the job.

FIGURE 8–9 **Try to resolve an employment problem informally before contacting an outside agency.**
Courtesy of Deere and Company.

Besides taking care of their own safety and health, workers should be on the lookout for possible dangers. Employers should correct any problems that employees call to their attention. If an employer does not correct a problem, it is up to the employee to call on OSHA for help if needed. OSHA protects your right to complain to your employer, your union, and to OSHA itself. It is illegal for your employer to punish you for exercising this or any other OSHA right.

AGENCIES PROVIDING SERVICES TO WORKERS C13, F9

What should you do if you have a work problem dealing with fair employment practices, discrimination, or health and safety? If you are a work experience student, contact your school coordinator. He or she can help solve the problem. Apprentices and union workers can speak to the union representative. Civil service employees also have representatives they can turn to for help. Wherever you work, follow any procedures that may appear in your company's policy manual.

If you do not have certain procedures to follow or anyone else to help you, try to work out the problem with your boss or employer. Ask for a meeting to informally discuss your complaint. Present your point of view and then listen patiently to the other person's side of the story.

If an informal meeting does not work, file a formal complaint. Write a letter to the proper company official. State your complaint clearly and briefly. Ask for an answer by a reasonable date. Be polite and businesslike in your letter. Do not make demands. Ask that the problem be solved. Keep a copy of the letter for your file.

If all your efforts to solve the problem meet dead ends, you can then turn to outside help. Many federal laws and government agencies protect the rights of workers. A summary of the major types of complaints and agencies that handle them is provided in Figure 8–10. Ask for help at your public library if you have any trouble finding the addresses or phone numbers you need.

Most employers support and respect laws and rules that protect workers. Employers may sometimes overlook a law or rule. Other times, though, an employer violates a law on purpose. In either case, it is up to you to identify and then to report any violations you find. Learn your rights so you can be in control of your health, safety, and welfare.

Type of Complaint	Federal Agency
Child labor Wages and hours	Employment Standards Administration U.S. Department of Labor 200 Constitution Ave., N.W. Washington, D.C. 20210
Equal pay Discrimination based on race, color, religion, sex, national origin, age or disability	Equal Employment Opportunity Commission (EEOC) 2401 E. St. N.W. Washington, D.C. 20507
Safety and health	Occupational Safety and Health Administration (OSHA) U.S. Department of Labor 200 Constitution Ave., N.W. Washington, D.C. 20210

Note: *Federal agencies also maintain state and local offices. Look in the telephone Yellow Pages under "Governmental Offices—Federal."*

FIGURE 8–10 **These are the primary federal agencies that handle complaints regarding fair employment practices, discrimination, and health and safety.**

Collective Bargaining

Labor (workers) and management (owners/managers) share a common interest. Both want to see the company grow and succeed. Occasionally, the two groups may disagree regarding wages, benefits, working conditions, or other matters. If the workers are union members, the two sides engage in collective bargaining to settle their differences.

In typical collective bargaining, union representatives present demands. Management may accept or reject the demands. It may also make a counteroffer. The two sides often negotiate back and forth for days or even weeks.

Eventually, the two sides usually agree. The agreement, called a labor contract, is put into writing. The union membership must then vote on the agreement. As a legal document, the labor contract can be enforced in a court of law. The contract usually covers a specified time period, such as three years.

After a labor contract is signed, the agreement is put into practice. A contract presents certain rules that labor and management are to follow. Sometimes, though, a complaint or grievance arises over what the rules mean or how they are carried out. For instance, a grievance might result from the firing of a worker or the violation of a safety practice.

The procedure for settling grievances is an important part of the labor contract. An employee with a grievance, along with the union representative, usually discusses the matter with the boss. Most problems are resolved at this level. If the problem is not resolved, the employee may file a complaint with a higher level of management.

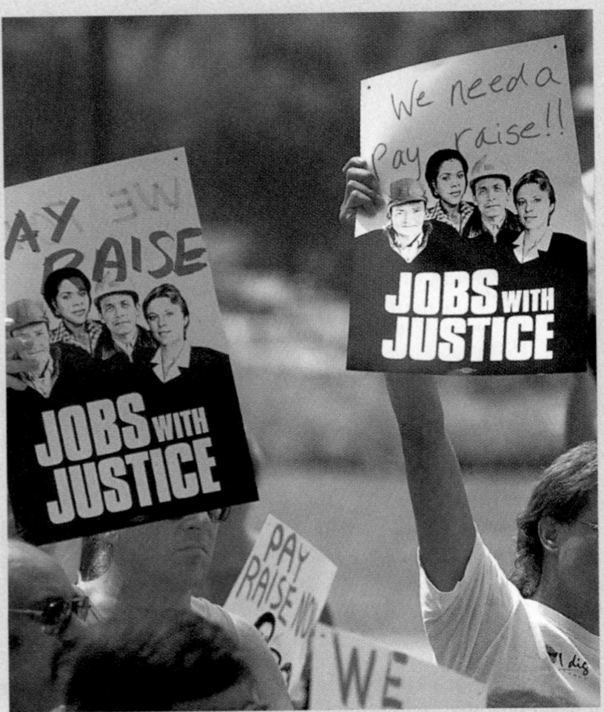

A strike, or threat of one, is a major bargaining tool for organized labor. These workers are threatening to strike if they do not receive their wage demands.
Courtesy Daemmrich/Uniphoto.

CHAPTER 8 REVIEW

CHAPTER IN BRIEF

- An employment contract is not a one-way deal. Employers owe certain things to their employees.
- An employer who pays your salary has a right to give you orders as long as they are not unlawful. Most employers and supervisors, however, realize that honesty and respect toward their employees are essential.
- Many state and federal laws deal with employment practices. The most important one is the Fair Labor Standards Act (FLSA). The FLSA covers three types of practices: child labor, wages and hours, and equal pay.
- Laws also exist to promote equal treatment in areas such as hiring, promotion, and job security. It is illegal for employers, unions, and employment agencies to discriminate against people because of race, color, religion, sex, national origin, age, or physical or mental disabilities.
- Affirmative action policies and programs have been established to help victims of past discrimination. These include special efforts to hire and promote women, minorities, handicapped people, and Vietnam veterans.
- The Occupational Safety and Health Administration (OSHA) was created in 1971 to set and enforce standards for safe and healthful working conditions. Workers can file a complaint with OSHA if an employer refuses to correct unsafe or unhealthful working conditions.
- New employees have a much higher risk of injury than experienced workers. A reason seems to be that workers often do not receive the safety information they need. Or, if they do, they do not apply it. You play an important role in learning and practicing safety rules.
- If you have a problem at work regarding fair employment practices, discrimination, or health and safety, try to solve it informally. If this does not work, file a formal complaint with the proper company official. If this does not solve the problem, you can turn to outside agencies for help.

WORDS TO KNOW

affirmative action
discrimination
equal employment opportunity
Equal Employment Opportunity Commission (EEOC)
employment practices
minimum wage
Occupational Safety and Health Administration (OSHA)
overtime
standard workweek
training wage

QUESTIONS TO ANSWER

1. How does the Lordstown case show an employer's lack of respect toward workers?
2. When federal and state fair labor standards conflict, which law applies? Give an example.
3. Name three things the FLSA covers.
4. What is the purpose of the Equal Pay Act of 1963?
5. The Civil Rights Act of 1964 prevents discrimination on what five things? What things were added in 1967 and 1973?
6. Affirmative actions seeks to correct past discrimination. Give an example.
7. To which employers do OSHA rules and standards apply?
8. Why are new employees more likely to be hurt on the job than more experienced workers?
9. To protect your health and safety, what four things should you do before you start to work?
10. Suppose a work problem arises between you and your employer. List the steps that you should follow in trying to correct it.

ACTIVITIES TO DO

1. Find out what your state laws are on child labor, wages and hours, and equal pay. Report your findings to the class.
2. The Americans with Disabilities Act (ADA) goes beyond The Rehabilitation Act of 1973 in extending equal protection to individuals with mental and physical disabilities. Find out who is covered under ADA? Also, find out what is meant by the "reasonable accommodation" requirement of the act? Report and discuss your findings in class.
3. Find out the location of your nearest OSHA office. Pick up or request copies of booklets that explain workers' rights under OSHA. Discuss these in class. After studying them, you may want to make a bulletin board display.
4. Write an imaginary letter to an employer complaining of a work-related problem. Follow the guidelines presented in this chapter. Turn it into your instructor for evaluation.

TOPICS TO DISCUSS

1. Federal law and some state laws permit employers to pay a training wage for the first 90 days of employment. What is the justification for this? Do you think this is fair?
2. Affirmative action programs give special advantages to groups that were discriminated against in the past. Discuss in class the pros and cons of such programs.
3. Have you ever had a work accident or been hurt on the job? If so, how might it have been prevented? Discuss your answers in class.

CHAPTER 9 Human Relations at Work

OUTLINE

- Bosses, Co-workers, and Customers
- Group Participation
- Chapter Review

OBJECTIVES

After reading this chapter, you should be able to:

- Explain the importance of good human relations to success on the job.
- Discuss ways to get along with co-workers.
- Identify three reasons why customers patronize a particular business.
- Discuss ways to participate effectively in a task group.

You deal with people every day of your life. You may talk, joke, plan, study, argue, and so on. Some of these dealings are more important than others. For instance, you go into a store to buy a quart of milk. Chances are that your conversation with the clerk will not influence life much. On the other hand, a talk with your boss, co-workers, or teacher just might. Your dealings with others influence your happiness and success. They also may affect others. Ask Kevin.

Guy was supposed to pick up his friend Kevin on the way to school. Guy got up late, and in his hurry to get to school, forgot Kevin. So an unhappy Kevin had to walk two miles to school. He got to school late, missed a test, and had to go to detention after school. Guy's mistake caused problems for Kevin.

Some *human relations* are pleasant. Others are very difficult. Unless we become hermits, we cannot get away from other people. So we need to develop human relations skills. This is especially true for workers. It is a fact that many fired workers lose their jobs because they cannot get along with others.

FIGURE 9–1 **Relationships with others are part of what makes us human.**
Photo by Jeffry W. Meyers/Uniphoto.

BOSSES, CO-WORKERS, AND CUSTOMERS

Suppose you and another student whom you do not get along very well with find yourselves in the same English class. Chances are that you will not need to work closely with the other student. On the job, though, you may have to work closely all week with someone you really do not like. In such cases, you will both need to put personal feelings aside.

At work we have to deal with all kinds of people. These include bosses, co-workers, and customers. We may like some of these people more than others. Even so, we must try to get along with everyone. Understanding our bosses, co-workers, and customers can make this task easier.

FIGURE 9–2 Students who relate well to teachers tend to get along well with their bosses.
Photo by Jeffry W. Meyers/Uniphoto.

Getting Along with Bosses

Most employees have a boss. The boss may be the company's owner, a crew chief, a foreman, or a department head. Whomever your boss is, you will need to form a working relationship with him or her (reviewed in Chapters 6 and 7).

Good employees try to understand the boss's position. Being a boss is never easy. For instance, how would you feel if you had to fire someone? Bosses sometimes must do this. They must always provide workers with instructions and helpful criticism. Good bosses act in the interest of the company. They do not act out of friendship. Sometimes, workers and bosses become friends. Even so, this should not influence their work behavior. The company should still come first. If you and your boss are not friends, that is fine. You can still have a good relationship. (Some bosses make it a policy not to be friends with people they supervise.)

Getting Along with Co-workers

Strong friendships depend on *interpersonal attraction.* Think about it. Why do people become your friends? Well, they are probably somewhat like you. We enjoy being with people who are like us in at least some ways. We choose such people for friends, and they choose us. At work, though, interpersonal attraction is not as important. What *is* important is doing your share of the work and following rules.

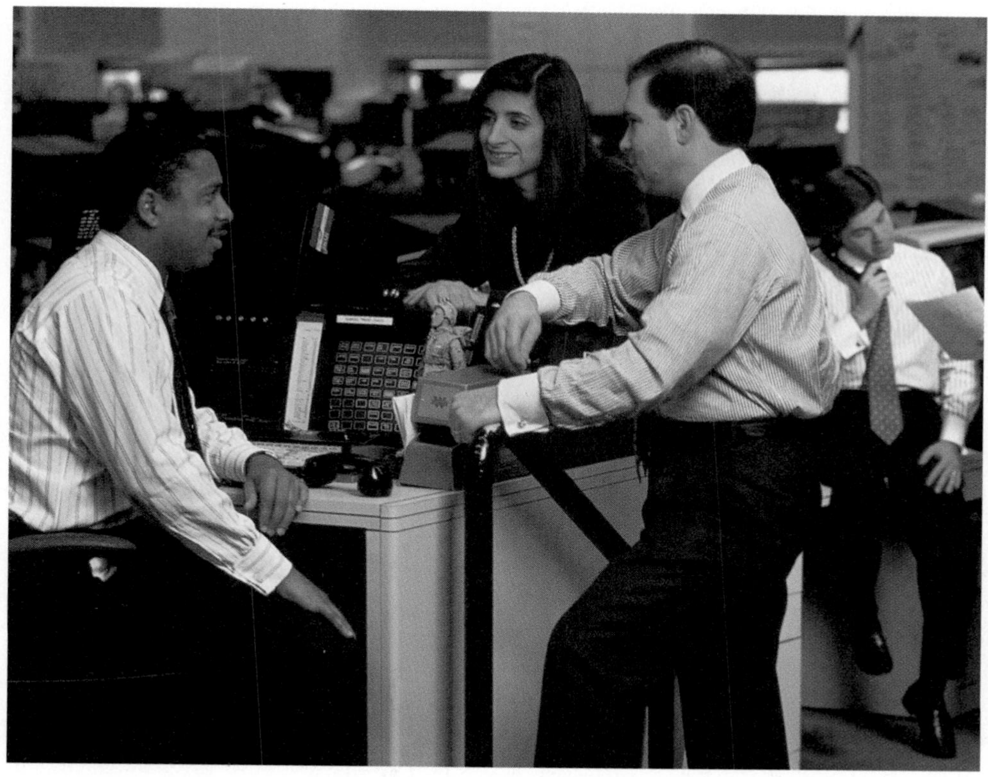

FIGURE 9–3 **You can learn a great deal from co-workers. They are usually glad to share information and advice.**
Courtesy Merrill Lynch.

As a new worker, you can be sure that your co-workers will be watching you. They will expect you to do your share of the work. Your co-workers probably will not mind helping you out from time to time. They will expect you to do the same when they need help. But your co-workers will not put up with doing their work and yours, too. At least, they will not for very long.

Following the rules is important. Rules make sure that employees in similar jobs receive equal treatment. If you ignore the rules, you are indicating that you are different or better than the other workers. Your co-workers will not like your ignoring the same rules that they are expected to follow.

Sometimes, being different has its place at work. Two examples involve seniority and territorial rights. *Seniority* refers to the length of time someone has worked for a company. Workers with the most seniority have the most privileges. Respecting seniority rules will help you get along with co-workers.

In January, Tina requested to take a week's vacation during the first week in June. Mrs. Soria, the boss, came to talk to her. It turned out that Sven, who had the same job title as Tina, wanted the same week off. Mrs. Soria told Tina that she could not do without both of them that week. Since Sven had been there two years longer than Tina, he would get to take that week. Tina

FIGURE 9–4 **Bosses are usually not impressed with workers who are LIFOs (Last In/First Out.)**

thanked Mrs. Soria for telling her. She then started to think about choosing some other week.

In a work setting, certain unwritten rules about *territorial rights* may develop. Some workers come to feel that they control a certain office, area, or sales territory. When you are on their turf, they expect you to behave as they wish. An example might be that you are not to bring food into a certain person's office. Or, maybe you are not supposed to use someone's tools without asking permission first. Be alert for such things. Try to respect others' territorial rights.

Doing your share of the work and following the rules leads to good feelings among co-workers. Other ways to maintain good relationships with co-workers include the following:

- ***Appearance.*** Maintain good personal hygiene and grooming. Do not underdress or overdress.
- ***Courtesy.*** Be pleasant, friendly, and courteous. Do not force relationships with co-workers. In time, some may become your friends.
- ***Attitude.*** Be positive. Do not complain about your job. Clint sometimes gets tired of being a "go-fer" for everyone in the shop. He doesn't let it discourage him, though. Clint is glad to have a job, and looks forward to a promotion soon.

- *Interest.* Show interest in the job. Pay attention to what co-workers are doing and show them that you feel their interests are important.
- *Loyalty.* Do not criticize the company or gossip about bosses or co-workers. Those you talk to will wonder what you are saying about them!
- *Tolerance.* Try to tolerate the opinions, habits, and behaviors of co-workers. Being different is all right. Martha, for instance, is a vegetarian. She eats bean, cucumber, and alfalfa sandwiches for lunch. Through her, some co-workers have learned more about good eating habits.
- *Maturity.* Be agreeable and avoid arguments. If conflicts arise with co-workers, talk them out.
- *Dependability.* Always do what you say you will do. Quinn agreed to work overtime on Saturday afternoons. Last Saturday would have been a great sailing day. Quinn went to work because he had given his word. He would have preferred to have gone to the bay.
- *Openness.* Be open to suggestions and change. Ask co-workers for advice and offer to help them.
- *Ethics.* Do not try to get ahead at the expense of others. Heather is the department's most creative layout artist. She lets her work speak for itself. Heather never criticizes the other artists' work to make herself look better.

Getting Along with Customers

The purpose of a business is to make a profit. Some businesses sell goods, such as clothing, hardware, or autos. Other businesses sell services. Examples of services include insurance, haircuts, and dry cleaning. A business sells its goods or services to customers. Not all customers are called by that name. An accountant may speak of *clients,* and a nurse of *patients.* What about users of library services? In a sense, they are customers of a service, even though they do not pay for it directly. Librarians call their customers *patrons.*

Relationships between employees and customers are important to the success of a business. Let's look at some reasons why a customer deals with a certain business. We will also give some hints as to how employees can encourage customers to return.

? ? ? ? ? ? ? ? ? ? ? ? ? ? ?

WHAT WOULD YOU DO?

You have been cutting and styling Mrs. Laird's hair for about 6 months. You are beginning to dread her coming into the shop. You like Mrs. Laird, but her young son is a terror. You wish she would not bring him along. He is loud and obnoxious and disturbs the other patrons. He always wants something from his mother and cries when he does not get his way. You do not want to make Mrs. Laird angry, but something has to be done about the boy.

What would you do?

One reason why customers *patronize* a business is that they like the product or service provided. Leigh, for instance, goes to Andrews-Evans because she likes their almond ice cream. Rafael has his hair cut at Rich's because he likes Rich's work. Customers who patronize a business have certain wants or needs. A competent worker who treats customers well encourages business.

Darcy is a landscaper for Sunrise Nursery. Last month, Mr. Clements, a client, said he wanted some more flowers and shrubs around his house. He did not have anything special in mind. So Darcy said she would think about it and call him. She did so and then made an appointment with Mr. Clements. Darcy brought with her design sketches, catalogs, and a price estimate of the work to be done. She had everything Mr. Clements would need before making a decision. Her efforts paid off. She got that job and other new customers in the neighborhood.

Businesses that provide services after a sale also encourage customers. The services may include things such as product repair, refunds, or quick processing of a claim. Let's look at a couple of contrasting examples.

In the first example, a customer is returning a defective product to a store. Here is the conversation between the customer and a salesclerk:

"I bought this clock-radio a couple of weeks ago. For some reason, the alarm doesn't work."

"Did you drop it or something?"

"No, it just quit on its own."

FIGURE 9–5 A company cannot stay in business without customers.
Courtesy Dayton Hudson.

"Are you sure it's broken? Maybe you're not setting it properly."

"I can assure you that I know how to set it."

"Did you buy it here?"

"Of course, I bought it here. You can see that the box has your sales sticker on it."

"Do you have the receipt?"

It is easy to see the direction this conversation took. Here is a second example, a conversation between another customer and a second salesclerk:

"I bought this food processor here some time ago and now it has quit working."

"I'm sorry you have had a problem. Do you remember about when you bought it?"

"Yes, it was right after Christmas. Here is the receipt."

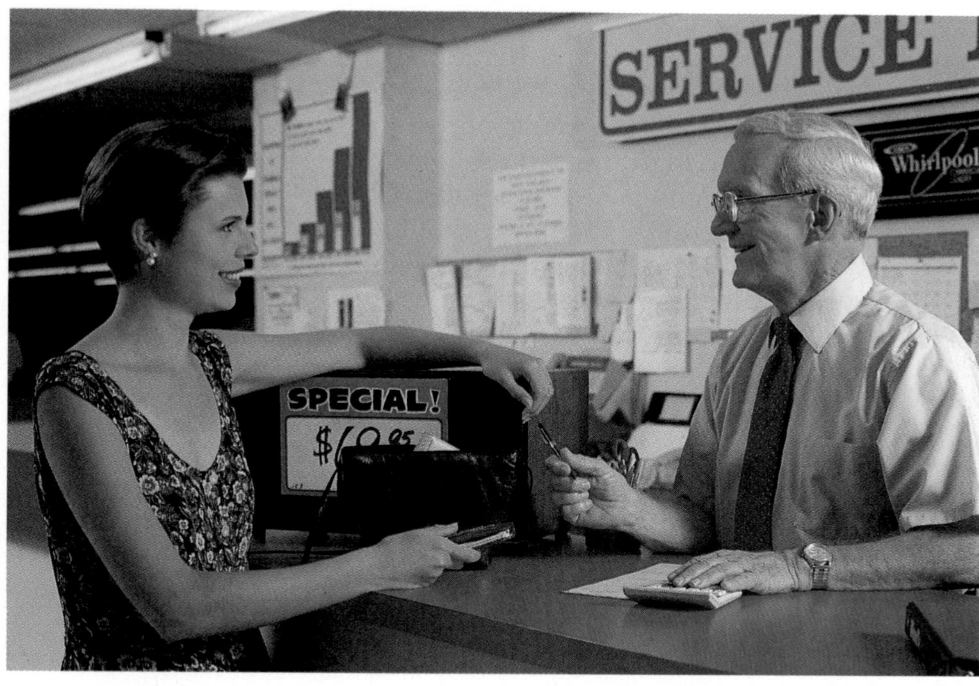

FIGURE 9–6 **Treat customers the way you want to be treated.**
Photo by Alan Brown/Photonics

"Good. The warranty is still valid. Why don't you go pick out another one, while I write up an exchange ticket."

"This is the same model and price, but it's a different color."

"Is that color okay?"

"Yes, I actually like it better."

"Well, that worked out nicely, didn't it? Will you please sign this form, while I put it in a bag for you? You shouldn't have any trouble with this one. Come back and see us."

A third reason customers return to a business is because of what is called *goodwill.* These are the little things about a business. Examples include reputation, honesty, and attitude toward customers. Employees promote goodwill in many ways.

- Jana calls as many customers as possible by name. She also

? ? ? ? ? ? ? ? ? ? ? ? ? ? ?

WHAT WOULD YOU DO?

You enjoy being in the club and are always eager to help out. In fact, you probably do more than anyone else. It is getting to the point that whenever something needs to be done, club members automatically look to you. You have been asked a number of times recently to substitute for someone who has other plans. Some of the club members seem to be taking advantage of your willingness to always pitch in.

What would you do?

knows which ones like to be called by their first names and which by their last.

- Ingmar knows that many people come into the store just to look around. He makes them feel welcome and then stays back until they ask for or seem to need help.
- Many adults come into Mia's store to buy toys or gifts for their children or young friends. They seem to appreciate it when she offers suggestions about the items that children like best.
- Some customers at the ice cream shop where Cleveland works have trouble deciding what flavor they want. He offers uncertain customers free samples.
- Jillian remembers what it was like when she was in college and didn't have much money. Her restaurant is the most popular one in the campus town. Why? Heaping plates of good food, of course.

GROUP PARTICIPATION

Most people, at least some of the time, work in groups. These are called *task groups* (or work groups). Groups are often formed to brainstorm a new product, discuss quality control problems, or plan a new sales strategy. There is a trend in business and industry to use more and different types of task groups. But do groups really perform better than individuals?

Groups are generally superior to most individuals at many (but not all) tasks. A school newspaper, for example, benefits by having different people write columns on current events, club activities, sports, and the like. It would be hard for one person to write about all these things. For tasks requiring a lot of effort, groups are faster than individuals. An example would be building a house. Following are guidelines for working effectively in a group.

- ***Show Your Readiness to Help the Group.*** A group depends on the willingness of each member to accomplish its work. Do your share of the work on a regular basis, and volunteer your effort from time-to-time for special group projects.
- ***Accept the Role the Group Gives You.*** Groups have leaders and followers. Followers are often in greater demand. Pitch in and do whatever the group needs, whether it is recording minutes, stuffing envelopes, or cleaning up after a meeting.
- ***Carry Out Your Role as Best You Can.*** Sports teams often have role players who go into the game to do certain things. Can you think of examples? Role players make a valuable contribution to a team or a group. Do your job well; the group and you will both benefit.
- ***Share Your Views with Others.*** Do not hold back on a good idea or suggestion. Your solution may be perfect. Offer your feelings and opinions, even if they differ from what others think. Groups sometimes make poor decisions or choices. If you believe this is the case, say so.

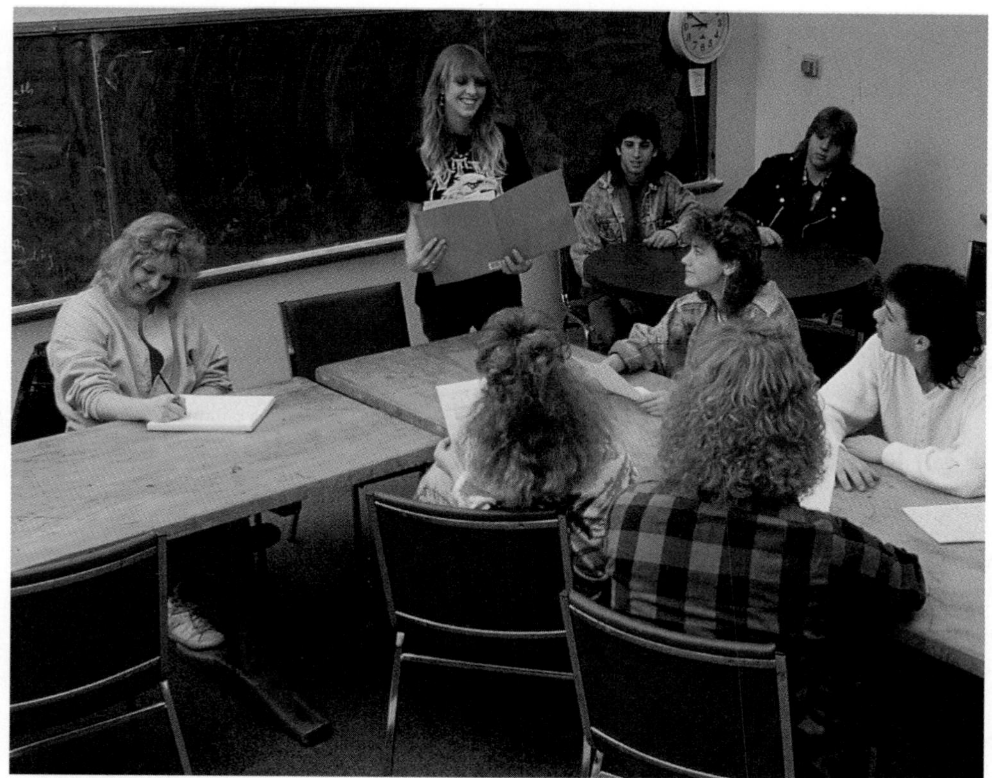

FIGURE 9–7 **A vocational student organization often functions as a task group. Are you part of any task groups?**
Photo by David W. Tuttle.

- *Do not Dominate Meetings.* Someone who talks too much irritates other group members. Do not over-power others, even though you may have the right answers or the best ideas.
- *Accept Group Decisions.* Offer your views when a group is discussing something. But once the group makes a decision, do not argue about it.
- *Encourage Other Members.* Doing your best on a job will encourage others to do likewise. A kind word from time to time always helps. Remember to pass out compliments and congratulations for a job well done.
- *Think of Solutions, Not Past Problems.* Suppose you have a fight with a family member. Dwelling on the problem will not help. Thinking of how to solve it will. The same is true in task groups. Focus on finding solutions to problems.
- *Be Proud of Group Success.* Completing a hard task, or winning a game is very satisfying. Should success come, enjoy it with your fellow members.

Getting along well with others is an important work and life skill. As a skill, it must be learned and practiced.

FOCUS ON

The Worker

Relating to Workaholics

At some point in your career, you may work for or with a workaholic (or become one yourself). Understanding and getting along with workaholics is a special case in human relations.

Workaholics are people who are addicted to their work. In her book *Workaholics,* Marilyn Machlowitz provides two examples of workaholics. An elderly attorney sat at his desk working while his office building was on fire. He ignored the fire and sirens until he was forcibly removed by firefighters. A pregnant publicist felt labor pains. She rushed to her doctor's office. When she found out that delivery was still hours away, she went back to work.

Workaholics not only work hard, but often play hard, too.

Workaholics exist in every occupation. It is not necessary to be employed to be one. Many homemakers are workaholics. As a group, workaholics are surprisingly happy. They are doing what they love. They cannot seem to get enough of it. If they are in the right job, they can be extremely productive.

There is another side to the workaholic at work. According to Machlowitz, workaholics may be among the world's worst workers. They suffer few ills themselves. But they often wind up doing damage to their companies. They often create a pressure-cooker atmosphere. They demand a great deal. They expect everyone to be as dedicated to work as they are.

Workaholics often have difficulty delegating work to others. They tend to be critical of co-workers. Even their high energy level causes problems. Workaholics may try to do everything themselves.

As you see, it can be difficult to work with a workaholic. The truth is, says Machlowitz, that workaholics are better suited to be entrepreneurs. They just do not do well in a business organization managing people.

CHAPTER 9 REVIEW

CHAPTER IN BRIEF

- Human relations are very important to job success. Many fired workers lose their jobs because they cannot get along with others.
- Bosses act in the interest of the company. They do not act out of friendship. Workers and bosses sometimes become friends. It is more important, though, to learn to work effectively with the boss than to become friends.
- Doing your share of the work and following the rules lead to good feelings among co-workers. Other ways of maintaining good relationships with co-workers include:
  a. *Appearance.* Maintain good personal hygiene, grooming, and dress.
  b. *Courtesy.* Be pleasant, friendly, and courteous.
  c. *Attitude.* Be positive and do not complain about your job.
  d. *Interest.* Show interest in the job and what your co-workers are doing.
  e. *Loyalty.* Do not criticize the company or gossip about bosses or co-workers.
  f. *Tolerance.* Try to tolerate the opinions, habits, and behaviors of co-workers.
  g. *Maturity.* Be agreeable and avoid arguments.
  h. *Dependability.* Always do what you say you will do.
  i. *Openness.* Be open to suggestions and change.
  j. *Ethics.* Do not try to get ahead at the expense of others.
- Relationships between employees and customers are important to the success of a business. Customers deal with a certain business for several reasons. One is that customers like the product or service provided. A second reason is the types of follow-up services provided. A third is the goodwill provided.
- Most people work in groups from time to time. Do the following to be an effective group member.
  a. Show your readiness to help the group.
  b. Accept the role a group gives you.
  c. Carry out your role as best you can.
  d. Share your views with others.
  e. Do not dominate meetings.
  f. Accept group decisions.
  g. Encourage other members.
  h. Think of solutions, not past problems.
  i. Be proud of group success.
- Effective human relations is a skill. As a skill, it must be learned and practiced.

WORDS TO KNOW

clients
goodwill
human relations
interpersonal attraction
patients
patronize
patrons
seniority
task group
territorial rights

QUESTIONS TO ANSWER

1. Why do most workers lose their jobs?
2. How important is it for you to be friends with the boss?
3. Name two ways to start out on the right foot with co-workers.
4. How should you relate to a co-worker whose opinions, habits, or behavior are different from yours?
5. What should you do if a co-worker offers advice or suggestions?
6. What are the three reasons why customers deal with a certain business?
7. Why is it important to know how to work in groups?
8. Groups are generally superior to most individuals at many tasks. Give an example.
9. What should you do if a task leader assigns you a job to do?
10. When is the best time to provide an opinion regarding a group decision?

ACTIVITIES TO DO

1. Identify a human relations problem that you have had with another student or a co-worker. What was the nature of the problem? Based on what you have learned in this chapter, how could you have helped avoid the problem? Share your answers in class.
2. This chapter gave several reasons why customers deal with certain businesses. Think about your favorite businesses. Can you add any reasons to those the text gives? As a class, list the reasons on the board.
3. Invite an employer who uses task groups to speak. Ask the person to talk about how to get along in task groups. Prepare a list of questions beforehand.

TOPICS TO DISCUSS

1. Human relations skills are also important for bosses. What does it take (beyond being a good co-worker) to be an effective boss?
2. Even though people work in groups, they still like to maintain their individuality. What are some of the ways that people express their individuality on the job?
3. Certain occupations like police officers, nurses, and attorneys deal with people who are often emotionally upset. What types of special human relations skills do these people need? What other occupations require these skills?

CHAPTER 10 Earnings and Job Advancement

OUTLINE

- Your Job Earnings
- Your Paycheck
- Pay Raises
- Job Advancement
- Chapter Review

OBJECTIVES

After reading this chapter, you should be able to:

- Identify and describe different forms of compensation.
- Describe how a paycheck is figured.
- State three guidelines regarding working for a pay raise.
- Identify the most common reasons for changing jobs.
- Explain what to do when voluntarily leaving a job.

When you get paid, you will receive a paycheck and an attached statement of earnings. Some people cash or deposit their paycheck and throw away the pay statement. This is not a good idea. You may have lost money because of an error. Or too much money may have been withheld for certain deductions. In this chapter, you will learn about how your earnings are figured and about different types of payroll deductions. You will also learn about pay raises, promotions, and what is involved in changing jobs.

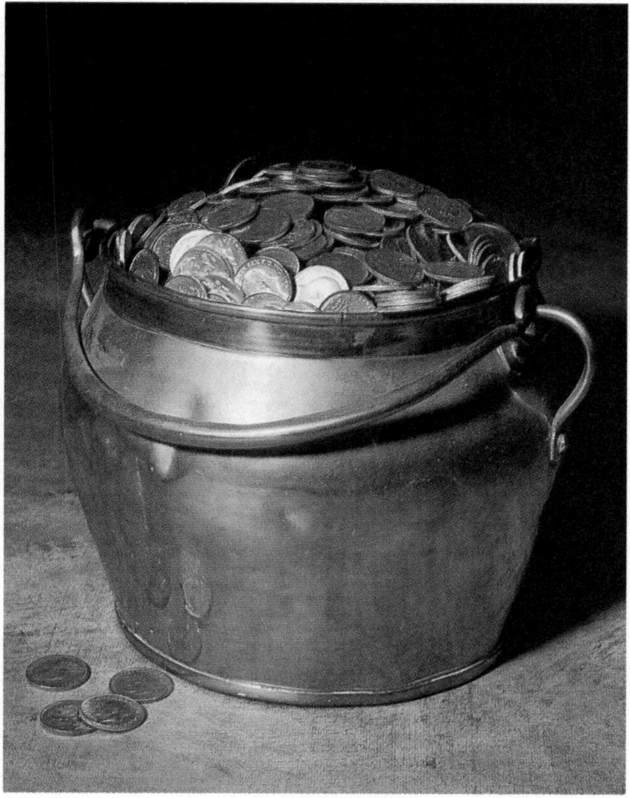

FIGURE 10–1 Payday is a favorite day for most people.
© Uniphoto, Inc.

YOUR JOB EARNINGS

The amount of your paycheck depends on how you are paid and on the deductions taken out. How do you know if your paycheck is accurate? Read on.

Forms of Compensation

The total amount of income and benefits you receive makes up your *compensation.* Employees are compensated in many ways.

- *Wages.* Most workers receive a set hourly wage. To arrive at the amount of pay, the hourly wage is multiplied by the number of hours worked. For example, if Sean receives $5.30 an hour and he works a 40-hour week, his weekly wages are $212.00 ($5.30 × 40). Most hourly workers are paid weekly.

  For working over 40 hours a week, most hourly workers get *overtime pay.* The overtime wage is usually 1½ times the normal hourly wage. Let's say that Sean worked 45 hours one week. He would receive $5.30 an hour for the first 40 hours and $7.95 ($5.30 × 1½) for the five extra hours. His weekly wages would be $251.75 ($212.00 + 39.75).

- *Salary.* Some workers receive a salary instead of an hourly wage. The salary is paid per month or per year. Teachers' salaries are usually a certain amount for 9 or 10 months. Some salaried workers are paid weekly. Others receive checks every other week. Some people must really plan ahead! They get paid only once a month. Salaried workers may put in more than 40 hours a week. Even so, they usually do not receive any extra pay. Do you think this is fair?

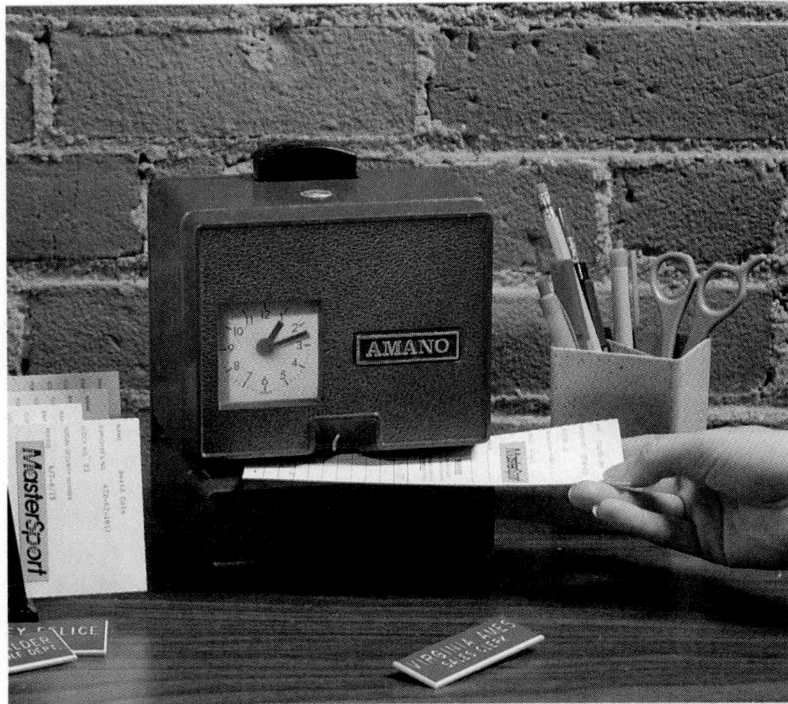

FIGURE 10–2 **Most hourly workers punch a time clock. Money is "docked" or deducted when a worker is late or leaves early.**
Photo by Alan Brown/Photonics.

- *Piece-rate.* In this method, the worker is paid for the amount of work performed. A sewing machine operator, for example, might be paid $.50 for each piece of goods completed. If 112 such pieces were done in one day, the worker would get $56.00 (112 × $.50) for that day.

- *Commissions.* Most sales workers receive all or part of their compensation through commissions. A commission is an amount the worker receives for making a sale. Real estate agents and insurance brokers are some workers that receive commissions. Can you name others?

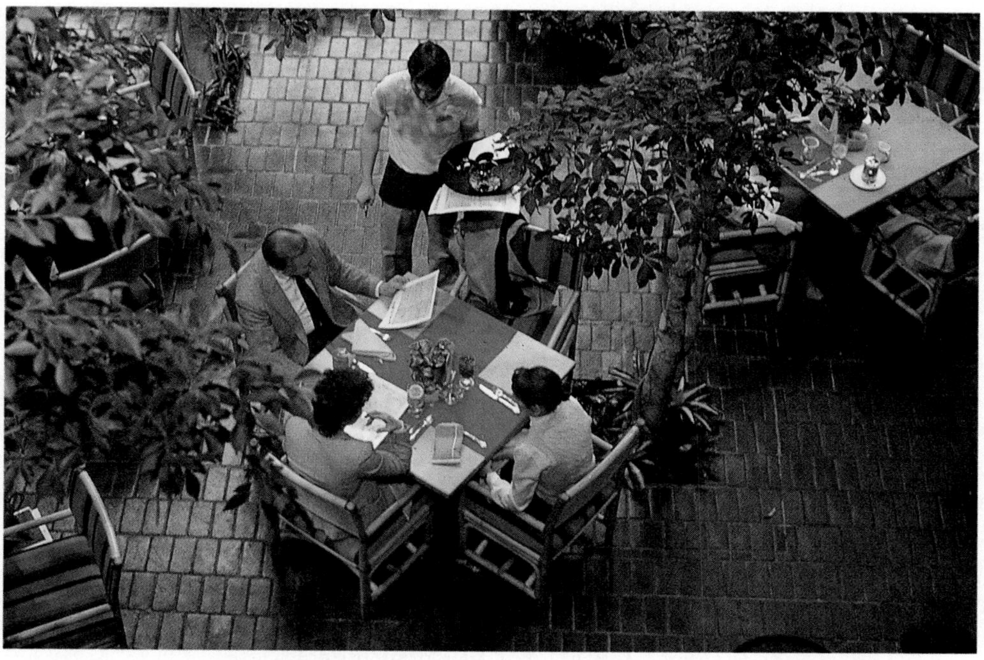

FIGURE 10–3 **A large part of the pay for service workers is tips.**

Most commissions are a certain percentage of the total sale. Rita Yang, for example, is a real estate agent. She gets a 2 percent commission on each house she sells. (If she owned the agency, she would get 6 percent or more.) Last week, Rita sold a house for $116,000. This meant a $2,320 commission ($116,000 × 0.02). She does not do that every day, though.

- ***Tips.*** Some workers receive a minimum hourly wage and earn the rest of their compensation from tips. Examples include restaurant servers, porters, and cab drivers. Can you think of any others? A *tip* (or gratuity) is an amount of money given in return for a favor or service. (Tips is an acronym for the phrase "to insure prompt service.")
- ***Bonuses.*** A bonus is extra money a company gives workers as a gift or a reward for good work. Most bonuses come from employers that are willing to share some of the company profits. A few years ago, for instance, Ford Motor Company distributed $640 million in profit sharing to salaried and hourly workers. The payout was the largest ever by a major U.S. corporation for a single year. Each hourly worker received a bonus check averaging $4,000.
- ***Fringe Benefits.*** Fringe benefits are indirect forms of compensation. That is, they are given instead of cash. Do you or your family members get company-paid insurance? How about paid holidays, vacations, and sick days? These are the most common fringe benefits. If you do not get fringe benefits, don't be discouraged. Most entry-level and part-time jobs offer few fringe benefits. Chances are you will get some later.

YOUR PAYCHECK

When you get your first check, look it over carefully. Make sure that your name is spelled right and your address and social security number are correct. Even employers make mistakes!

Your first paycheck may surprise you. Most new workers don't take home the pay they expect. Why is this so? You are right if you said that the employer has taken money out for certain reasons. Let's go back and see how the employer figures your earnings.

The amount of salary or wages that you earn during a certain time period is your *gross pay.* For example, if you work 20 hours a week at $4.85 an hour, your gross pay is $97.00 (20 × $4.85). From this amount, certain *deductions* are made for taxes, retirement, and so on. After these deductions are subtracted from your gross pay, you are left with *net pay* or take-home pay.

PERIOD FROM 02/18 TO 02/24 19 --

NAME

20	REG. HR. @	4	85	97	00
	OT. HR. @				
TOTAL EARNINGS ►				97	00
F.I.C.A.		7	28		
WITHHOLDING U.S. INCOME TAX		11	92		
STATE INCOME TAX		5	14		
TOTAL DEDUCTIONS ►				24	34
NET PAY				72	66

FIGURE 10–4 Always check your paycheck and statement. Ask your supervisor about any item on them you do not understand.

A pay statement or *statement of earnings* attached to your paycheck shows your gross pay, deductions, and net pay. A sample pay statement for a person paid weekly is shown in Figure 10–5.

Payroll deductions are of many types. The employer must take out (withhold) some of them. Other deductions, though, depend on what you request the employer to withhold. The most common types of payroll deductions are:

- ***Income Taxes.*** Your employer must withhold federal income tax from your earnings and send it to the federal government. When you start your job, you will need to fill out a Form W-4. (This was covered in Chapter 6.) Based on your answers on the form, the employer figures the amount of federal tax to withhold each payday. Depending on where you live, the employer may withhold state and local taxes, too.
- ***FICA.*** The acronym FICA stands for Federal Insurance Contributions Act tax. It is better known as the Social Security tax. Most jobs in the United States are part of the federal Social Security program. Both you and your employer pay into this fund. Social Security is discussed further in Chapter 27. Notice in Figure 10–5 that the employer withheld $33.50 for Social Security from Esther Robert's paycheck.
- ***Insurance.*** Many employers offer group life and health insurance programs to full-time employees.

FIRST TRUST CORPORATION

2 COMPUTER DRIVE TROY, NY 12347

Pay Statement

Co. Code	Department	File No.	Clock No./ID.	Name	Pay Period	Pay Date
5XQ	301712	35637	05502	Roberts, Esther	Ending 01/24/--	01/22/--

Hours/Units	Rate	Earnings	Type	Deduction	Type	Deduction	Type
40	452 00	452 00	REG B	2 63	DENTAL	16 95	HEALTH

	Gross	Fed. With Tax	Social Security	State With. Tax	City With. Tax	Sui/Dis	Net Pay
This Pay	452 00	67 71	33 50	15 06		60	315.55
YTD	1317 31	198 29	98 93	42 60		1 80	

FIGURE 10–5 **Sample statement of earnings.**

Employers often pay all or part of the insurance cost. If you must pay, the employer may withhold the premium from your paycheck. Esther Roberts' employer contributes 70 percent toward health insurance and provides free life insurance. Esther Roberts pays $16.95 per week for health insurance, $2.63 for optional dental insurance and $.60 for supplemental income and disability coverage.

- ***Union Dues.*** Most union members can pay their dues through payroll deductions.
- ***Charity.*** Many workers donate to charity through payroll deductions. A common example is The United Way.
- ***Savings.*** Do you find it hard to save? If so, see if your employer can withhold money for savings. For instance, the employer may be willing to deduct money for a savings account or U.S. Savings Bonds.

When you start a job, the employer should explain your deductions to you. If no one does, ask. After all, the deductions are your money.

PAY RAISES

Pay raises benefit both employees and their employers. As an employee, the idea of a pay raise may provide you with an *incentive* to do a good job. After getting the raise, you may feel better about your job. This, in turn, may make you continue to improve your work.

Improved work makes employees more valuable to the company. Most companies want to keep their good employees, so they give them raises. Good workers who do not get raises may go elsewhere.

Alice worked in the claims department of an insurance company for over 3 years. Eight other

? ? ? ? ? ? ? ? ? ? ? ? ? ?

WHAT WOULD YOU DO?

Each payday you carefully go over your check. Several times, you have found mistakes in which you were underpaid. The boss always apologizes and makes the correction. This payday, however, you discover that you have been overpaid by $20. You share this information with a co-worker. He tells you to forget it, since you have probably been cheated out of more than $20 by the company. You have been thinking about this all weekend.

What would you do?

FIGURE 10–6 **This man will be eligible for a pay raise because he is a very careful worker. Pay raises are performance rewards and incentives. Can you explain how?**
Courtesy of AMETEK Inc.

people worked in the same department. Alice was clearly the best worker. One of her co-workers said that Alice always did the work of two people.

All workers in the department get regular pay raises. Last year, Alice was upset when she got the same raise as the other workers. Her boss could have gotten her a higher raise.

Alice made an appointment to discuss a raise with Ms. Lorch, her boss. Alice asked why she kept getting the same average raise as everyone else even though she did more work. Ms. Lorch agreed that Alice was the most valuable employee in the department. But she explained that if she gave Alice a higher raise, it would create bad feelings within the department. That was enough for Alice. She started looking for another job. It did not take her long to find one either.

Later, a friend at the old job told Alice that things have not been going well in the claims department. Alice's replacement cannot do the amount of work that Alice could. The new person also makes a lot of errors, something that Alice seldom did. One day the friend heard Ms. Lorch say that she wished she had Alice back.

Getting a Pay Raise

In many jobs, employees receive *automatic raises* every 6 months, 12

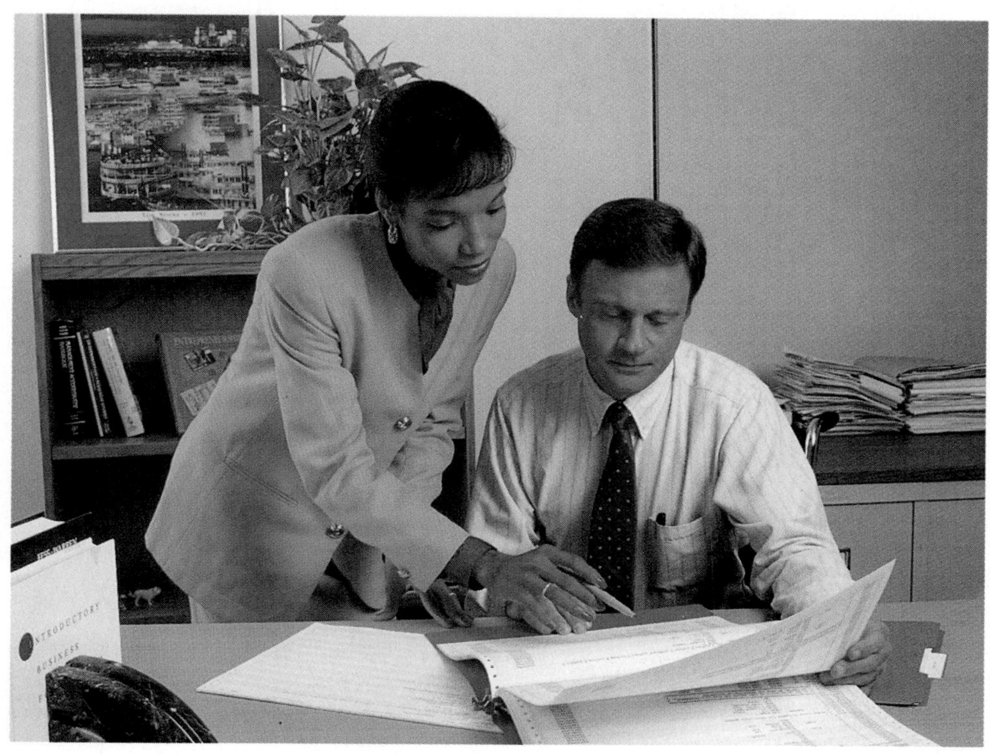

FIGURE 10–7 **Most employers use some type of performance evaluation as a basis for merit raises.**
Photo by Alan Brown/Photonics

months, and so on. All employees may get the same dollar amount or the same percentage amount. In some cases, the amount of the raise depends on the type of job. Production employees may get higher raises than office workers, for instance.

Some employers give *merit raises* instead of, or in addition to, automatic raises. A merit raise is based on the amount and quality of an employee's work. Most employers use a performance evaluation to determine these.

Not all employers have a set policy on pay raises. In such cases, it may be up to the employer to decide when an employee deserves a raise. Or the employee may be expected to ask for a raise. This type of situation is common in small businesses.

Suppose that you decide to ask for a raise. First of all, if you are a new employee, do not expect one until after you have learned the job and shown that you can do it well. You must earn a raise. Some workers want a pay raise because they are not making as much money as they would like. An employer will not be impressed by a worker who asks for a raise because he or she wants to buy a VCR, for instance.

When asking for a pay raise, tell the boss why you deserve one. Steve, for example, pointed out to his boss that sales had increased 18 percent since he started working in the department.

Ask for a raise when the company is doing well and the boss has had a good week. Do not ask for a raise during a time when you should be working. Ask for an appointment to discuss a raise during break, lunch, or after work.

When you meet with the boss, ask what workers must do to get a pay raise. If you have done all those things, tell the boss. Be clear. Talk about exactly what you have done. If the boss says there is no rule for granting raises, present your case. When asking for a raise, show confidence and respect. If you are turned down, do not argue with the decision. Just say that you will keep working hard and hope that you get a raise later. If you feel strongly that you deserve a raise, you may want to follow Alice's example.

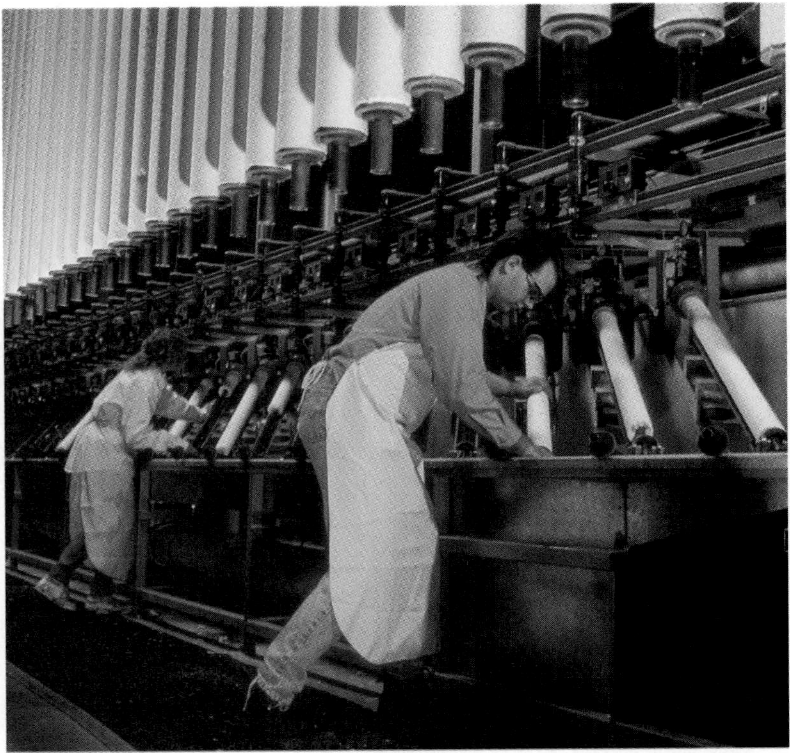

FIGURE 10–8 Production workers usually have fewer opportunities for promotion than workers in service industries.
Courtesy of AMETEK Inc.

JOB ADVANCEMENT

Most people start working in a low-paying, entry-level job. An entry-level job is a good way to earn money and gain valuable experience. Usually, though, an entry-level job is not one that you want to keep forever. You may want to advance within the company or move to a better job in another company.

Job Promotions

A *promotion* is an advancement from one position to another within a company. The new position usually brings a new title, more money, and more responsibility. Some promotions also bring the chance to supervise others. Opportunities for promotion differ among occupations and industries. For example, most workers in skilled trades have less chance for promotion than do sales representatives. Large businesses offer more chances for promotion than do small ones.

Promotion opportunities occur for two reasons: a new position is created within the company; or a vacancy occurs because someone was promoted or left the company. How can you put yourself in line for a promotion? You can begin during the job interview. Ask, "What are my chances for advancement if I perform well?" Suppose you work where you can advance. Do the best work you can every day. Employers notice workers who do their jobs well and get along with others.

FIGURE 10–9 Not everyone has the emotional control to be a good manager or boss.
Photo by Paul E. Meyers.

Even if you are a good employee, remember that promotions take time. Employers want to watch you over a period of time. Even when an employer thinks you are ready, an opening may not yet exist. Or a worker who has the same job as you may have more seniority. If so, the person with seniority will probably get promoted first.

While many people want promotions, not all of us want to be the boss or have a better job. A higher level job is not for everyone, as shown in the following example about Seymour.

When the job of office manager opened up, Seymour's co-workers encouraged him to apply. He was the most experienced accounting clerk in the company, got along with everyone, and knew the business well. He applied for the job and got it.

Seymour soon found out that being an office manager was different than he had thought. He had to assign work, manage the office budget, make on-the-spot decisions, and do many other things. To get everything done, he began to come to work earlier and stay later. Once he started giving orders, Seymour sensed tension between himself and the other employees. His most painful moment was when his boss ordered him to fire one of the clerk typists.

Seymour is not alone. All businesses have people like him. They are great workers, but are not suited to be supervisors. No matter what your job, try to work toward something that you will like. For many workers, that is the job they have now.

Changing Jobs

Years ago, most people stayed on a job for most of their working lives. Things have changed since then. While some people stay on the same job, most of us do not. The most common reasons for changing jobs are:

- *Lack of Opportunity with Present Employer.* You may be in a dead-end job that offers little chance for pay raises and promotions.
- *Better Opportunity Elsewhere.* Perhaps you like the job you have, but another company offers you something you would like even better. Often such a change involves a pay raise.
- *Dislike for Present Occupation or Job.* Not everything looks as good up close as it did from afar. Perhaps you thought you would really enjoy your present occupation. After doing it for a while, though, you see that you were wrong. It's just not what you want to do the rest of your life. You may want to train for another occupation.

Or, you may like your occupation (what you do) but dislike your job (where you work). In this case, changing jobs is probably the answer.

- *Change in Personal or Family Situation.* You may need to quit a job because of such things as illness or a move to a new area.
- *Loss of Job.* Perhaps your company slows down and lays you off. Maybe the employer even goes out of business. These things are not your fault. Being fired probably is though. Either way, you are out of a job.

No matter what the reason, plan the change carefully if you can. Do not make a quick decision. Some workers get angry and quit. Later, most of these people regret what they did. Earlier in the chapter, you read about Alice being turned down for a raise. It would have been a mistake for her to quit on the spot. Instead, she made sure she had a new job first. Another mistake would have been to threaten her boss with the statement, "If you don't give me a raise, I'm going to quit." What do you think would have happened then?

Once you have decided to leave, find out if the company has rules about quitting a job. If so, follow them. If not, give your employer *at least a two-week notice.* Tell your boss *before* you mention it to your co-

? ? ? ? ? ? ? ? ? ? ? ? ? ? ?

WHAT WOULD YOU DO?

You have been working at a farm implement dealership since your senior year in high school. You like the job and the people who work there. The business, however, is barely making enough profit to stay alive. You have only had one small raise in three years. You have been laid off a couple of months each winter. The prospects for additional raises or promotions do not look good. You understand the dealer's financial problems, but you have your future to think about.

What would you do?

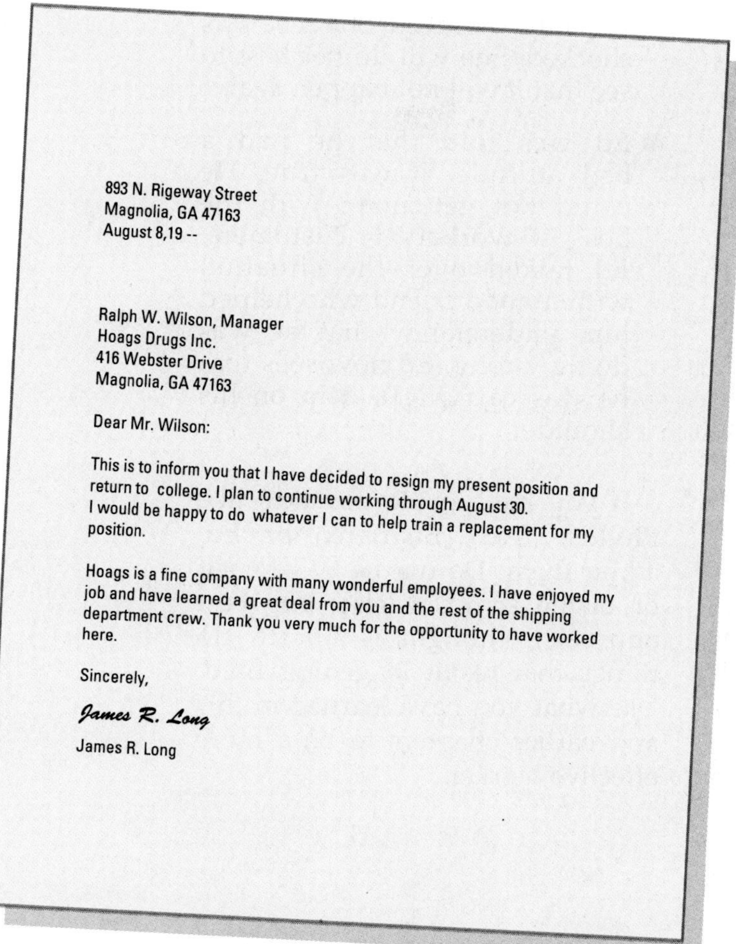

893 N. Rigeway Street
Magnolia, GA 47163
August 8,19 --

Ralph W. Wilson, Manager
Hoags Drugs Inc.
416 Webster Drive
Magnolia, GA 47163

Dear Mr. Wilson:

This is to inform you that I have decided to resign my present position and return to college. I plan to continue working through August 30. I would be happy to do whatever I can to help train a replacement for my position.

Hoags is a fine company with many wonderful employees. I have enjoyed my job and have learned a great deal from you and the rest of the shipping department crew. Thank you very much for the opportunity to have worked here.

Sincerely,

James R. Long

James R. Long

FIGURE 10–10 **Sample letter of resignation.**

workers. Follow up your verbal notice with a written *letter of resignation*, Figure 10–10.

Such a letter should contain the following points: (a) the fact that you are leaving, (b) a date when you plan to leave, (c) the reason you are leaving, (d) an offer to help train your replacement, and (e) a thank-you for the chance to work there.

Once you have told your employer you are leaving, do not let up. Do your job as best you can through the last day. Do not criticize your boss on the last day or brag to your co-workers about your new job. Your employer will watch and evaluate you through your last day. Try to leave on good terms with your employer.

Being Fired

Being fired is much different than leaving a job on your own. Some employers may ask you to leave, but give you the chance to resign.

Remember that resigning will make it easier for you to find another job. If you are fired outright, try to turn disaster into a learning experience. Never make the same mistake twice.

The following people were fired. Each, however, learned from the experience.

- Phyllis was fired but was not sure why. It would have been easy for her to never go back. Instead, she made an appointment with her former boss to find out why she was fired. After learning about some of her poor work habits, she decided to improve on her next job.
- Theo was let go because he did not have the skills for the job. He decided to start classes at the community college.
- Sharlene lost her job because of too many absences. She did not think the boss would fire her. When the boss did, Sharlene was shocked. She will do her best to see that it will not happen again.
- Ed was told that he had a bad attitude. It was true. He could not get along with the boss, co-workers, or customers. Ed talked over the situation with a good friend who helped him understand what he was doing wrong. Ed now sees that he was carrying a chip on his shoulder.

If you have made mistakes like Phyllis, Theo, Sharlene, or Ed, admit them. Do not lie to yourself or blame someone else. The best approach, though, is not to do things that result in getting fired. Use what you have learned in this and earlier chapters to be a more effective worker.

FOCUS ON

The Workplace

EMPLOYER-SPONSORED CHILD-CARE ASSISTANCE

About two out of three American mothers work outside the home. As a result, millions of children spend part of their day being cared for by other people. This has led to child-care assistance becoming the hot new fringe benefit.

One recent report estimates that about 15 percent of major companies and 65 percent of state governments provide on-site child care. Over half of the companies sponsor referral services to help employees find out about child-care options in their community. Businesses that cannot provide child care sometimes offer dependent-care-assistance plans. These allow parents to set aside up to $5,000 a year in tax-free dollars to help pay for child care.

Employer-sponsored child-care assistance has increased in response to growing numbers of mothers with small children who are joining the work force.
Courtesy of Unisource.

The major reason that companies offer child-care assistance is to attract and hold good employees. For instance, one department head turned down a job across town that offered a large salary increase. She put it this way: "I spend the lunch hour with my six-month-old son. They couldn't put a price tag on having my child within a few minutes of me."

Child-care assistance is an expensive undertaking. Very few companies pay 100 percent of the costs. Usually, employees pay tuition that amounts to about one-third to one-half of the cost of private, community child-care. Experts predict that more employers will offer child-care assistance in the future. The future is also likely to bring more workplace options, such as flextime, job sharing, and home offices. Such options can help working parents regain a more balanced family life.

CHAPTER 10 REVIEW

CHAPTER IN BRIEF

- The amount of your paycheck depends on how you are paid and on the deductions taken out. Employees are compensated in many ways. These include: wages, salary, piece-rate, commissions, tips, bonuses, and fringe benefits.
- The total amount of salary or wages that you earn is your gross pay. From this, certain deductions are made. After deductions are subtracted from the gross pay, you are left with net pay.
- The most common types of payroll deductions are: income taxes, FICA, insurance, union dues, charity, and savings.
- Pay raises benefit both employees and employers. Some workers receive automatic raises every so often. Merit raises may be given instead of or in addition to automatic raises. Not all employers have a set policy on pay raises.
- A promotion is an advancement from one position to another. Opportunities for promotion differ among occupations and employers. Earning a promotion usually takes time and is based on outstanding performance.
- People frequently change jobs. There are many different reasons for changing a job. No matter what the reason, try to plan a job change carefully. Try to leave on good terms with your employer. Follow company guidelines for resigning and leaving a job.
- Some people are fired or given a chance to resign. If this happens to you, try to learn from the experience.

WORDS TO KNOW

automatic raise
compensation
deductions
gross pay
incentive
letter of resignation
merit raise
net pay
overtime pay
promotion
statement of earnings

QUESTIONS TO ANSWER

1. The amount of money you receive from your paycheck depends on two things. Name them.
2. List and briefly explain each form of compensation.
3. What type of workers are most likely to be paid on commission?
4. Which payroll deductions are generally automatic? Which ones are optional?

5. What is the FICA tax?
6. Why is it important to check your pay statement often?
7. Name two reasons why promotion opportunities occur.
8. Is a promotion for everyone? Why or why not?
9. List five common reasons for changing jobs.
10. Why is it best to leave a job on good terms with your employer?

ACTIVITIES TO DO

1. Suppose that you earn $4.80 an hour. One week, you work 48 hours. You are paid the normal rate for the first 40 hours, and time-and-a-half for overtime. What is your gross pay for the week?
2. Nat earns $200 a week salary plus a 5% commission on his total sales. This month his sales amounted to $18,500. His deductions are as follows:
   - Federal income tax, $188.50
   - State sales tax, $37.46
   - FICA, $121.61
   - Credit union, $48.00
   - Charity, $25.00

   Based on these figures, what is Nat's gross pay for the month? How much are his total deductions? What is his net pay?
3. Let's say that you are going to leave your job for a better one. Write a sample letter of resignation. Hand it in to your teacher for evaluation.
4. Role play a conversation you might have with your supervisor to ask for a raise. Plan out what you are going to say beforehand.

TOPICS TO DISCUSS

1. If you were a salesperson, would you rather be paid a salary or a straight commission? Discuss the advantages and disadvantages of each.
2. In recent years, workers in a number of industries have been forced to take pay cuts and give up benefits in order to save their jobs. Would you be willing to take a pay cut to keep a job?
3. Do you think that you would like to be a supervisor? Why or why not?
4. The decision to change jobs and move elsewhere is often complicated for married couples who both work. Discuss how you might feel in giving up a good job in order to move with your spouse.

CHAPTER 11 Appearance on the Job

OUTLINE

- Grooming and Appearance
- Dressing for the Job
- Chapter Review

OBJECTIVES

After reading this chapter, you should be able to:

- Explain why good hygiene, grooming, and proper dress are important on the job.
- List five rules for good grooming and appearance.
- Describe the benefits of good posture.
- Summarize guidelines on dressing for the job.

Janet had been on her job for only 10 days when Mr. Bedrava, the boss, called her in. "Janet," Mr. Bedrava began, "Your appearance and grooming impressed me a lot when I interviewed you for this job. In fact, that is one of the reasons I hired you. But since you have started work, your looks have changed. Some of your co-workers have complained about body odor, too. I am disappointed. I do not want our customers to think that your appearance is an indication of how we do business. Please think about cleaning up your act. I hope we will not have to talk about this again."

This straight talk embarrassed Janet. "Gee, I am sorry," said Janet. "I did not think it mattered that much how warehouse workers looked. I see what you are saying, though. Many people *do* see me in this job. Thanks for giving me another chance."

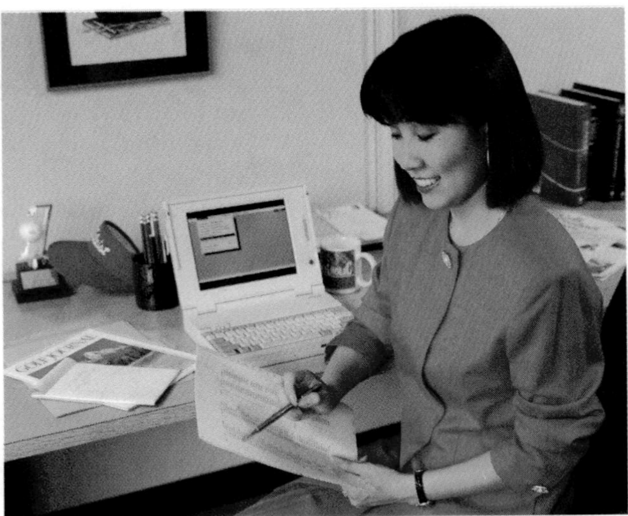

FIGURE 11–1 **Good grooming and proper dress will help you get a job and keep it.**
Photo by Alan Brown/Photonics.

Like Mr. Bedrava, most employers and bosses take note of their employees' appearance. In fact, many performance evaluations have a section on appearance. No matter what your job, your employer will expect you to groom and dress properly.

FIGURE 11–2 **Make sure your hairstyle suits you and your job.**
Photo by Alan Brown/Photonics.

GROOMING AND APPEARANCE

An appropriate appearance on the job begins with *personal hygiene.* In most jobs, being clean is not enough. It is also necessary to be neat and attractive as well. This is what *grooming* is all about. Rules for personal hygiene apply to everyone. What is considered to be attractive or good grooming varies from person to person and job to job. For instance, a hairstyle that looks good on one person may not suit another. What is considered to be proper makeup in one job setting may be inappropriate in another. Some of the following grooming tips may apply to you and your job situation, while others may not.

Hairstyling

For most jobs, hair should be neat, trimmed, and not too faddish. Beyond this, how you wear your hair is up to you. Whatever style you choose, hair should be neatly combed or brushed.

A hairstylist can help you choose a style that goes best with your features and your type of hair. When deciding on a hairstyle, be sure to think about the amount of care it will need. Twila chose a style that required her to roll it every day. She soon tired of the routine. After a while, Twila chose a style that was easier to care for.

? ? ? ? ? ? ? ? ? ? ? ? ? ? ?

WHAT WOULD YOU DO?

You have always wanted long, polished nails. One Saturday you go to the Sculptured Nails Salon for artificial nails. You think they are gorgeous. Back at work on Monday, things are not so good. The longer nails interfere with your keyboarding. Your work has slowed down and you are making more mistakes. The supervisor has noticed also. She has suggested that you have the nails trimmed. "I cannot," you think. "I paid a lot of money for these nails."

What would you do?

Shaving

A grooming choice for men is whether to be clean shaven or to grow a mustache or beard. Going to work with a growth of stubble is not a good choice. Should you decide to grow facial hair, start during a vacation. If you do grow a mustache or beard, shave your neck and the uncovered parts of the face. Weekly trims are in order, too.

Deodorants and Antiperspirants

Even after bathing, underarm perspiration odor can develop quickly. To control this, many people use a deodorant (for odor) or an antiperspirant (for wetness). Choose whatever fits your needs.

Wendy, a Houston realtor, has always perspired heavily. Moving to Texas made her problem even worse. Deodorant was no longer enough. Perspiration stains on her clothing embarrassed Wendy—especially when she was with clients. Antiperspirants reduced the amount of perspiration—and Wendy's embarrassment.

Skin Care and Cosmetics

Your skin may need care beyond daily bathing. The most common problem is dry skin. In colder climates, heated homes and low humidity cause the skin to become dry and itchy. In such cases, moisturize your skin often with lotion.

Hands may need special attention. Abused hands get rough, sore, and look bad. To help heal and soothe rough, sore hands, use hand lotion often. This applies to both men and women.

Many women choose to use cosmetics or beauty aids to improve their appearance. If you do, don't overdo them. Too much makeup can dry out the skin and cause irritation. Cosmetic counters in large department stores often have people who can advise you on proper cosmetic use.

Posture

Matthew is always clean and well groomed. His poor posture, however, ruins his appearance. *Posture* is the way you stand, walk and sit.

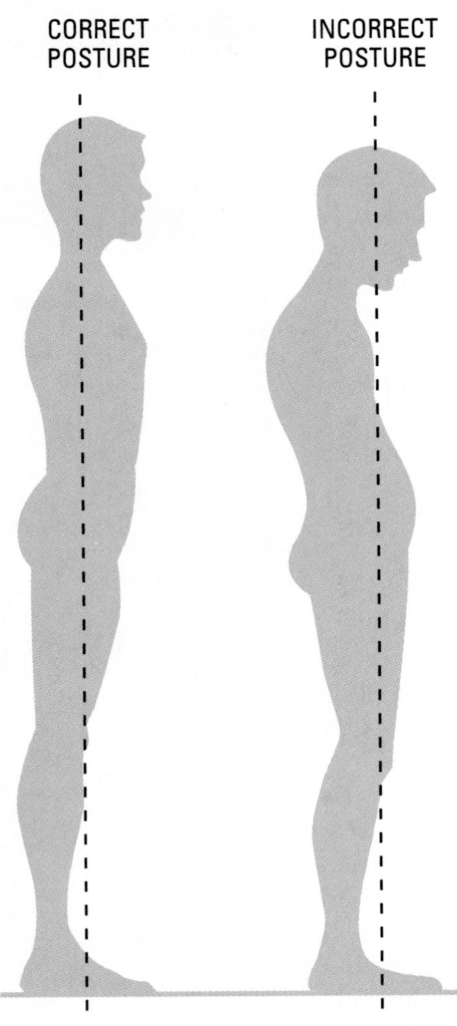

FIGURE 11–3 **Make an effort to demonstrate good posture.**

Like Matt, people with poor posture have a stooping head and shoulders and a belly that sticks out. They appear to be lazy and lacking in self-confidence. This may be untrue, but poor posture sends out the wrong message.

A person with good posture appears to be poised and self-confident. Good posture, like good grooming, is necessary if you want to make a good impression on the job. Good posture also makes you feel better and helps fight fatigue. The difference between correct and incorrect posture is shown in Figure 11–3.

DRESSING FOR THE JOB

Clothes are important to your overall appearance on the job. Some jobs require a uniform. If yours does, make sure the uniform you wear is *always* clean and pressed.

If your job does not require a uniform, deciding how to dress will be more difficult. On most jobs, however, the employer expects workers to dress in a certain way. A bank teller, for instance, is supposed to look professional. For a man, this usually means a suit (or nice slacks and jacket), together with a dress shirt and tie. For a woman, professional dress includes a suit or dress, or a nice skirt, blouse, or sweater. If in doubt, notice what the other employees wear. If you have any questions, ask your boss. Here are several rules:

- ***Wear What Fits Your Job.*** Think about your type of job. Will you get dirty and greasy? Will you need protection from sun, wind, rain, or cold? Will you be handling food? Buy the type of clothing that is best suited for the work you will do.
- ***Wear What Looks Good on You.*** Within the expectations or requirements for the job, wear clothes that look good on you. Do not try to dress like someone else. Choose clothes that best match your physical features and personality.
- ***Plan Your Wardrobe Carefully.*** You will not be able to buy your entire *wardrobe* all at once. So build around a number of basic items. For instance, a pair of gray slacks will go with many different shirts, blouses, or sweaters. You can wear a navy blazer formally or informally.

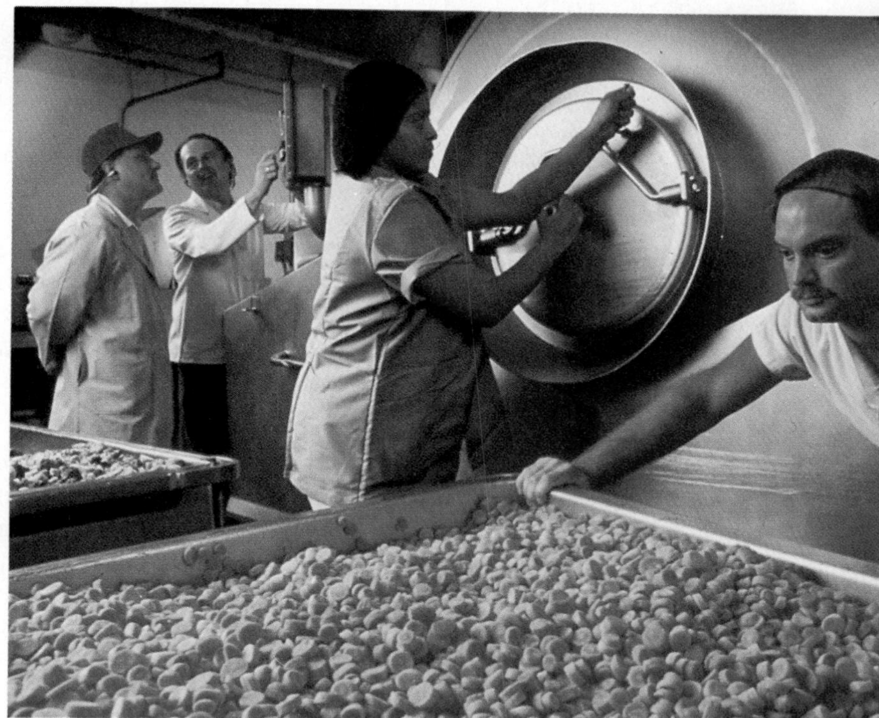

FIGURE 11–4 It is easy to decide what to wear when your job requires a uniform.
Courtesy of Campbell Soup Company.

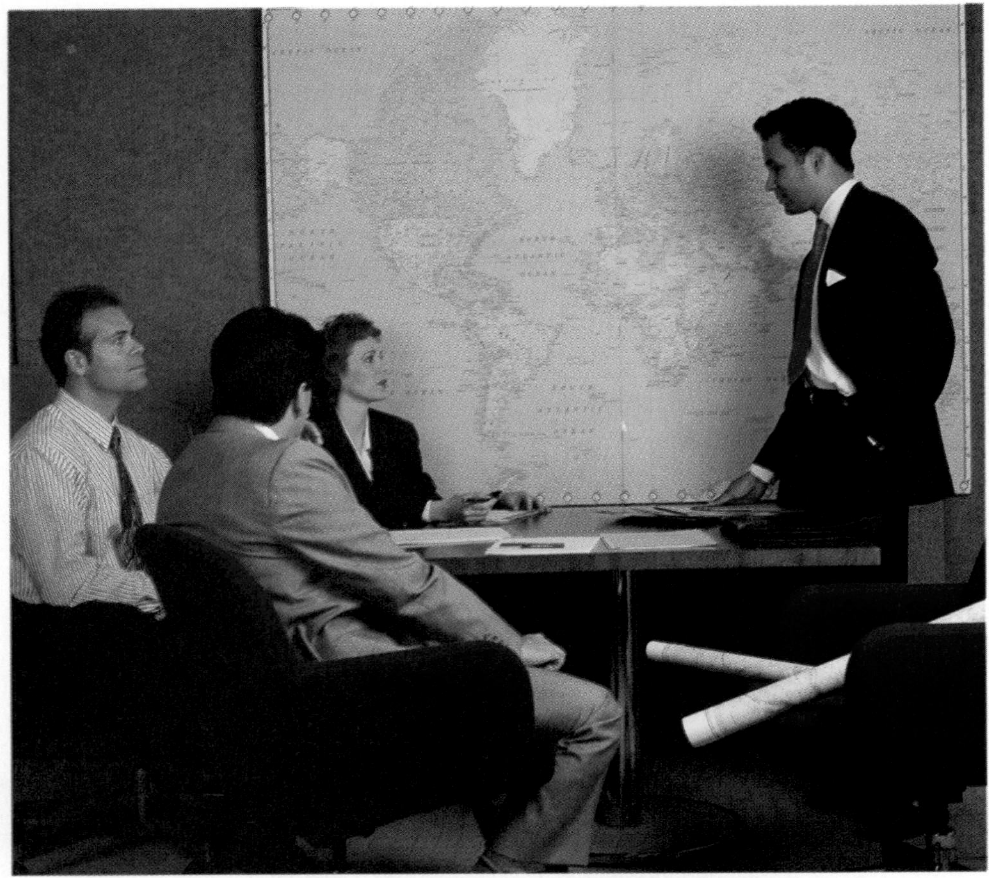

FIGURE 11–5 **Dark blazers are part of a basic business wardrobe for both men and women.**
Photo by Mimi Ostendorf/Photonics.

Fad clothes may be fun off the job. But, unless such clothes are required on your job, do not wear them to work.

- ***Learn How to Coordinate Clothes.*** Teach yourself how to mix and match your clothes. For instance, do not wear a plaid shirt or blouse with different plaid slacks. Libraries have magazines and books that can help you learn about fashion.

- ***Choose Quality, Well-made Clothing.*** The most expensive clothes are not always the best quality. Nor are clothes with a popular name or label always the best. Compare clothes and prices in many different stores before you decide to buy. After all, you will live with your choice for a long time.

- ***Take Proper Care of Your Clothes.*** Think about clothing care before you buy. Easy-care fabrics are more practical than ones that require frequent ironing or dry cleaning. Do not go to work in clothes that look as if you slept in them. To prevent heavy wrinkling, hang up or fold clothes properly. If wrinkles do appear, iron them. Dirty clothes are out, too. Clothes have attached tags

FIGURE 11–6 **When you take good care of your clothes, you save money having them cleaned.**
Photo by Paul E. Meyers.

that tell how to care for them. Follow the instructions carefully.

Michele's clothes are well chosen and fit her nicely. She is careless, however, in taking care of them. Her winter coats have been missing buttons for two years. Today, she wore a dress that has a ripped arm seam. In spite of her nice clothes, Michele often looks sloppy. Her co-workers joke about her appearance.

It is a fact that the way you look influences how other people see you. Your appearance will greatly influence your job success. Everyone can look good. Remember that a winning appearance depends more on knowledge and effort than it does on physical beauty.

? ? ? ? ? ? ? ? ? ? ? ? ? ?

WHAT WOULD YOU DO?

You just started a co-op job at a large savings and loan association. You are aware of how important it is to look good on the job. Everyone at work dresses so nicely. But you only have a couple of decent outfits. You do not have the money to go out and buy new clothes. You feel very self-conscious at work. You know you look more like a student than a real employee. You are thinking about looking for a new job where you could wear a uniform or more casual clothes.

What would you do?

FOCUS ON

Health and Safety

Sun Protection

Jobs requiring outdoor work pose a special skin care problem. Long-term exposure to the sun will cause your skin to become wrinkled and leathery. Premature aging of the skin is not the main problem, though. Dermatologists believe that continued exposure to the sun leads to skin cancer. The process can be likened to filling up a bottle with liquid. Each day's sun gets added to a lifetime's worth of exposure. After enough exposure, skin cancer may result.

The National Cancer Institute estimates that more than 300,000 cases of skin cancer occur each year in the United States. Between one and two percent of the cases result in death. Death rates for skin cancer have increased ten times in the last sixty years. The rate of increase is expected to continue.

What should you do if you have to work in the sun for long periods of time? The best protection is to keep the skin covered. Wear a hat, long-sleeved shirt, and long pants. What also works are special lotions and creams called *sunscreens.* These are rated according to a numerical "sun protection factor" (SPF). A lotion with an SPF of 2, for example, allows you to stay in the sun two times longer than you could without any protection. Many dermatologists, however, recommend nothing less than a SPF of 15, especially on the face. Sunscreens are not just for weekends on the beach. They should be used each day that you are outside exposed to the sun.

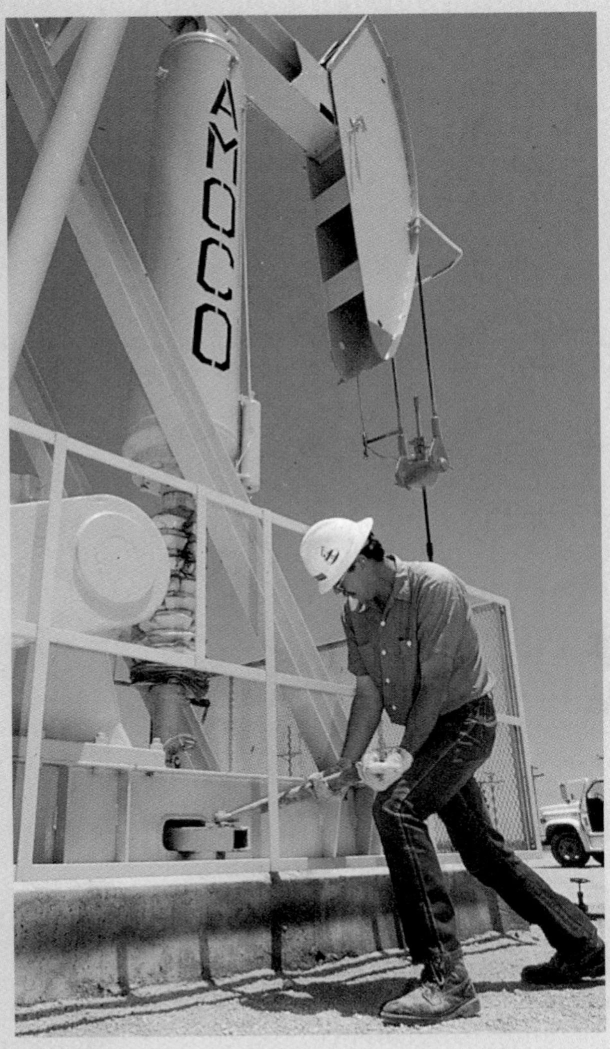

Individuals who work outdoors should wear protective clothing and use sunscreens.
Courtesy of Amoco Corporation.

CHAPTER 11 REVIEW

CHAPTER IN BRIEF

- No matter what your job, remember your employer will expect you to groom and dress properly. What is considered to be a good appearance, however, varies from job to job.
- In addition to personal hygiene, grooming is important on the job. Hair should be neat, trimmed, and not too faddish. Beyond this, how you wear your hair is up to you. A grooming decision for men is whether to be clean shaven or to grow a mustache or beard. To control underarm odor, use a deodorant or antiperspirant. Your skin may need care beyond daily bathing. Women should use cosmetics and other beauty aids properly.
- Posture is the way you stand, walk, and sit. Good posture, like good grooming, is necessary if you want to make a good impression on the job.
- Clothes are important to your overall appearance on the job. Wear what fits your job. Wear what looks good on you. Plan your wardrobe carefully. Learn how to coordinate clothes. Choose quality, well-made clothes and take proper care of them.

WORDS TO KNOW

grooming
personal hygiene
posture
sunscreen
wardrobe

QUESTIONS TO ANSWER

1. Why was Mr. Bedrava so concerned about Janet's poor hygiene and grooming?
2. For most jobs, what is the basic rule about hairstyles?
3. Suppose Kyle, a medical laboratory technician, wants to grow a beard. When should he start?
4. What is the purpose of a deodorant? An antiperspirant?
5. What are the possible dangers of too much sun exposure? How can you prevent overexposure?
6. How does good posture help you to make a good impression on the job?
7. If you aren't sure about how to dress on the job, what two things might you do?
8. List the six basic rules for clothing choice, wear, and care.

ACTIVITIES TO DO

1. Invite a hairstylist to class to discuss hair care and hairstyling as they relate to appearance on the job.
2. Invite a clothing store representative to class to discuss how to make the most of a basic wardrobe.
3. Prepare a bulletin board that shows proper dress and appearance for different occupations. Each person in the class should contribute something from a magazine or other source. Try to show occupations for which students in the class are preparing.
4. The sunscreens contained in suntan products are rated by numbers. The numbers correspond to the degree of protection provided. Prepare a chart or poster explaining the numbering system.

TOPICS TO DISCUSS

1. What are your feelings toward someone who has poor personal hygiene or inappropriate appearance? Pretend that you have a friend or co-worker with such a problem. Discuss your feelings and how you might go about telling the person.
2. Good appearance varies from job to job. Discuss different examples. Give examples that illustrate both different grooming practices and different types of dress.
3. Hairstyles, use of beauty aids, and clothing styles often differ from one region of the country to another. Perhaps you have lived or traveled in regions different from where you live now. Discuss some of these differences.

SECTION 3

CAREER PLANNING

Throughout your lifetime, you will be faced with making educational and occupational decisions. The more important the decision, the more time and effort you should spend on it. In Chapter 12, you will learn how to use a five-step process of decision-making. By using a systematic approach, you can gain greater control over your life. Your chances of being satisfied with your decisions will also be increased.

Occupational decision-making should be based on self-information. By learning more about what you like to do (interests), what you are able to do (aptitudes), and what you believe is important (work values), you will make better choices about what you want to be. These three types of self-information (interests, aptitudes, work values) are explained in Chapter 13.

Occupational information is also an important part of decision-making. The ways in which information about occupations and industries is collected, classified, and disseminated are explained in Chapter 14. The most useful and up-to-date occupational resource is the *Occupational Outlook Handbook (OOH)*. You will learn in this chapter how to use the *OOH* to conduct an occupational search.

Co-op Career SPOTLIGHT ON

Renata Cannon, *Navy Nurse*

"I took an anatomy and physiology course in co-op, and I knew nursing was what I wanted. I like caring for people. In my sophomore year in high school a Navy recruiter told me about the 44 different Navy nursing specialty schools. I knew there were things I would be able to do as a hospital corpsman that I could never do on the outside," said Renata Cannon, who left for boot camp a week after graduating from Deere Valley High School in Glendale, Arizona, in 1988.

"I thought the Navy would be exciting," said Renata, who received the Navy Achievement Medal for performance of duty in 1993, "and it was." She said in the Navy she was able to administer IV (intravenous) feeding, suture, do some surgery, put on splints, and drive an ambulance before she would be allowed to perform these tasks in civilian hospitals.

Renata took as many courses as she could squeeze into her schedule and when she finished, she was trained to do any nursing job that needed doing. Her many accomplishments include graduating from hospital corpsman school with distinction, becoming an emergency medical technician (EMT) instructor, clinical education coordinator, advanced cardiac life support coordinator, and pediatrics advanced life support coordinator. She was in charge of keeping over 1,000 Navy medical personnel up-to-date in their certifications to practice, and she established the IV certification education program. She took charge of running a military sick call in which nearly 200 people were processed daily. She was also a test site coordinator for a computer system that connected doctors to medical services.

Even with all her training and accomplishments, Renata had to leave the service to prepare for a Bachelor of Science in nursing degree in order to be promoted to a commissioned officer. She took a leave from the service in 1993 and enrolled in the nursing program at Glendale Community College. She plans to enroll in a four-year nursing program after graduating from Glendale. When she graduates and becomes an RN, she plans to "get right back in the Navy as a commissioned officer and teach in emergency medicine" until she retires in 15 years. Then, she says, she will collect her Navy pension and teach emergency medicine as a civilian.

Renata says her co-op experience gave her a solid foundation for her Navy career. "I made the transition into hospital corpsman with no difficulty. Co-op completely set me up for the very difficult courses. I knew so much, I didn't have to study at night." She says the certified nursing assistant (CNA) certificate she received in high school is still current and the position pays more than the more advanced certification EMT she received in the Navy.

CHAPTER 12 Career Decision-making

OUTLINE

- The Decision-making Process
- Individuals and Decision-making
- Other Influences on Decision-making
- Chapter Review

OBJECTIVES

After reading this chapter, you should be able to:

- Discuss instances in which an organized decision-making process is needed.
- List and summarize each step in the decision-making process.
- Identify and describe different decision-making styles.
- Discuss the need to accept responsibility for career planning.
- Explain how previous decisions, environment and experience, and real-world restrictions influence decision-making.

During the past year, Terrance has worked part-time in a local clothing store as part of a cooperative vocational education program. Since the store is rather small, he has learned many different skills.

Terrance sells, prices merchandise, operates the cash register, and prepares advertising. From time to time, he helps with payroll records and tax reports. His window display for an Easter sales promotion brought many compliments from customers and co-workers. His most interesting experience to date was going with the store manager on a buying trip.

FIGURE 12–1 **Most everyday decisions are made easily. Important career decisions, however, require more thought and effort.**
Courtesy of Texaco Inc.

The store manager has already offered him a full-time job after graduation. Terrance had planned to go away to college. He cannot decide whether to turn down the offer of a full-time job or go to college. What should he do? How should he go about making his decision?

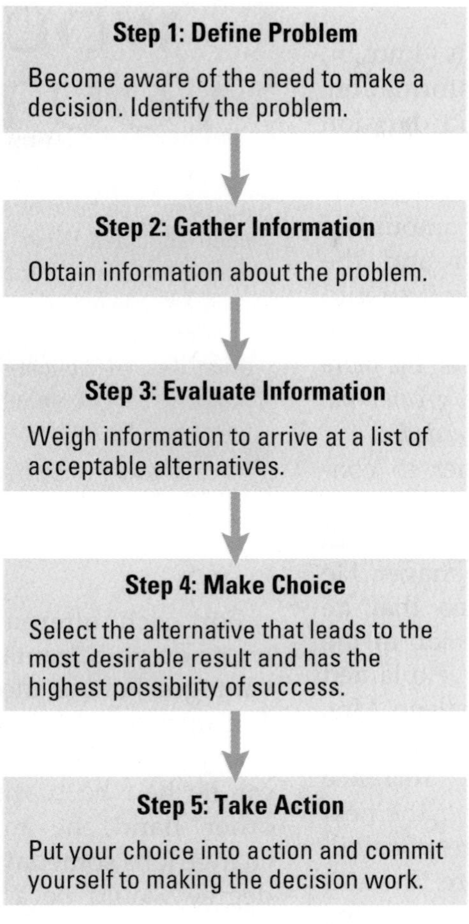

Step 1: Define Problem
Become aware of the need to make a decision. Identify the problem.
Step 2: Gather Information
Obtain information about the problem.
Step 3: Evaluate Information
Weigh information to arrive at a list of acceptable alternatives.
Step 4: Make Choice
Select the alternative that leads to the most desirable result and has the highest possibility of success.
Step 5: Take Action
Put your choice into action and commit yourself to making the decision work.

FIGURE 12–2 **Learning this five-step process can help you to plan your career better.**

THE DECISION-MAKING PROCESS

Decision-making involves choosing between two or more choices or *alternatives.* Some people make no effort to identify the choices available to them. Be aware that choosing not to decide is also a choice. Most everyday decisions such as "What shall I wear today?" are made without much thought. But decisions like the one facing Terrance are not as easy to make. He needs to follow a systematic decision-making process that will help him organize important information and make the decision that is best for him.

A simple five-step decision-making process is shown in Figure 12–2 and explained in the following paragraphs. The same steps are followed whether you are making a decision about a career, choosing a college, or buying a used car.

Defining the Problem

The term *problem* here refers to a question in need of a solution. The decision-making process begins when you become aware of a problem and see the need to make a decision. Perhaps the problem is broad and long-range, such as, "What are my goals in life?" Maybe it is an intermediate-range problem, such as "For what occupation do I want to prepare?" A problem like, "How can I earn some money to pay for Saturday's date?" is an immediate one.

Terrance has partially answered his long-range goal in that he would like to work in some area related to business after graduation. He still must answer the more immediate problem of whether to continue working at the clothing store. After making a choice, he may have to decide on future educational plans.

Gathering Information

Once the problem is known, gather the necessary information. You cannot make a good decision without it. Unfortunately, how do you know how much information is enough? You don't. The amount of information you gather and the time you spend gathering it should be related to how important the decision is. In other words, *the more important the decision, the greater the amount of information is needed.*

To help decide whether to continue working at the clothing store, Terrance made an appointment with Mrs. Enrico, the store manager. He explained to Mrs. Enrico that he liked retail sales and his job at the clothing store. He also explained that he wanted to go to college. Mrs. Enrico was very understanding and encouraging. She told Terrance what he could expect over the next several years in terms of responsibilities and salary at the store. She also gave Terrance the choice of working at the store part-time.

Evaluating the Information

In this step, you organize the information you have gathered into categories. You then identify the pros and cons of each possible choice. A rating scale or checklist may be of help as you do this.

After talking to Mrs. Enrico, Terrance wrote down the three choices he had:

1. Work full-time at the store and not go to college.
2. Quit the job at the store and go away to college.
3. Go to the nearby community college part-time and work at the store part-time.

? ? ? ? ? ? ? ? ? ? ? ? ? ? ?

WHAT WOULD YOU DO?

You plan to go to a business school next year. You have already applied and been accepted. Now, you are using a decision-making process to choose a program of study. You have collected information and given the problem a great deal of thought. The difficulty is that you like two programs (specializations) equally well.

What would you do?

For each alternative, Terrance wrote down advantages and disadvantages. For instance, if he chose 1, Terrance would have a full-time salary. He could probably buy the car he had been wanting. On the other hand, he might want to change jobs someday. In that case, a degree would be a strong advantage. He also went over the alternatives with his parents to see if they could add any information.

Making a Choice

At this point, you choose one of your alternatives. Making a choice is often difficult because rather than choosing between desirable and undesirable alternatives, you must choose from among several desirable alternatives.

It was finally time for Terrance to choose. He decided on choice 3—working part-time and going to college part-time. By working, he could pay for his education without having to borrow money. Going to a community college would also be cheaper than a four-year school, since he could live at home. And who knows? Maybe he will want to transfer to a four-year college in two years.

Taking Action

At this point, you begin to carry out the alternative you chose in step four. Suppose that you have weighed alternatives and decided to seek a job in a distant city. The best thing to do before you leave home is to find a job in the new place. Or, at least try to identify several promising job leads.

Taking action also involves committing yourself to making the decision work. In moving to a new city, for example, it might be a while before you find a job there. It would be easy to give up. Stick with your job search, but make sure your expectations are realistic.

Having made his choice, Terrance informed his parents and Mrs. Enrico. They all agreed with Terrance's decision and thought that he was wise to have made it. Terrance felt good about having put the decision behind him. Now it was time for him to start deciding what courses to take in school.

Occupational Decision-making

Let's see how the decision-making process might be used in making an occupational choice. As each step is explained, refer occasionally to Figure 12–3. The first step is defining the problem. In this case, the question is: "Which occupation should I choose?"

In step two, you collect information. In choosing an occupation, information about your own (self) characteristics and occupations are required. The three major types of self-information are interests, aptitudes, and work values. (You will learn more about self-information in Chapter 13.) You will use self-information to develop a preliminary list of occupational alternatives. You will then explore each

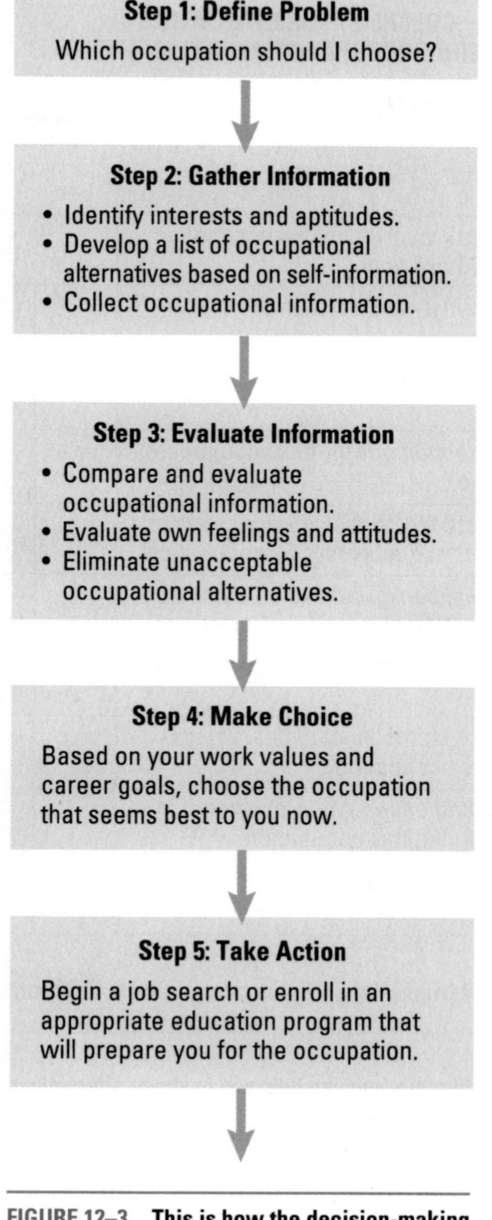

Step 1: Define Problem
Which occupation should I choose?
Step 2: Gather Information
• Identify interests and aptitudes.
• Develop a list of occupational alternatives based on self-information.
• Collect occupational information.
Step 3: Evaluate Information
• Compare and evaluate occupational information.
• Evaluate own feelings and attitudes.
• Eliminate unacceptable occupational alternatives.
Step 4: Make Choice
Based on your work values and career goals, choose the occupation that seems best to you now.
Step 5: Take Action
Begin a job search or enroll in an appropriate education program that will prepare you for the occupation.

FIGURE 12–3 This is how the decision-making process is applied to making an occupational choice.

CHECKLIST FOR EVALUATING POSSIBLE OCCUPATIONAL ALTERNATIVES

Name of occupation ____________________

	Yes	No	Not Sure
1. The nature of the work involved in this occupation is the type of work I'd *like to do.*			
2. I believe I have the *ability to do well* in this occupation.			
3. This occupation involves doing work that is *important to me.*			
4. The typical *working conditions* for this occupation are acceptable to me.			
5. I'm willing to complete the necessary *education* or *training requirements* to qualify for this occupation.			
6. I have the *educational background* to be admitted to any required education or training program.			
7. The future *employment outlook* for this occupation is good.			
8. I would be satisfied with the *amount of earnings* that is typical for this occupation.			
9. There are other *related occupations* in which I could work after learning this occupation.			
10. I believe I have *enough information* about this occupation to make a decision.			

On a scale of 1 (low) to 10 (high), I'd give this occupation a final ranking of_____

FIGURE 12–4 **Using a checklist like this one can help you evaluate alternatives.**

occupation on the list. (In Chapter 14, you will learn how to do an occupational search.)

In the third step, you consider the information and *eliminate* those occupations that are unacceptable for one reason or another. A form like the one shown in Figure 12–4 is helpful at this point.

By the fourth step, you have only a few alternatives left. Each of the choices seems to be equally desirable. You may be happy with any one of the choices. What you try to do, though, is choose the one alternative that seems best at this time. There is no guarantee that your choice will work out. You must choose based upon your best judgment.

Once you have made a decision, you are ready to put your choice into action. Starting a cooperative education program is an example of taking action. Perhaps you are not sure what type of educational program will meet your needs. If this is the case, you should start the decision-making process again. This time the problem is "What type of educational program should I choose?"

16 During any of the five steps, you may wish to seek help from a counselor, teacher, parent, or other adult. Talking about goals and alternatives often helps people make decisions. The final decision, though, will be yours.

INDIVIDUALS AND DECISION-MAKING

The decision-making process is a tool. How well you use this tool depends largely on your style of decision-making, and your willingness to accept responsibility and take action.

? ? ? ? ? ? ? ? ? ? ? ? ? ?

WHAT WOULD YOU DO?

You are attending a two-year technical institute, majoring in automotive technology. After two semesters, you have decided to change your major to machine tool technology. The counselor says you can make the change, but you will have to take overload hours and attend an additional semester beyond two years. You are anxious to finish school and begin work. You cannot decide whether the additional time and effort will be worthwhile.

What would you do?

Decision-making Styles

In watching a baseball game, you will notice that players have different batting styles. For example, one batter will move quickly into the batter's box, crowd the plate, and swing at the first ball that comes near the strike zone. Another batter will delay stepping into the box, stand deep in the batter's box, step out of the box if the pitcher is too slow, and will not swing until the pitch is exactly right.

People also have different *decision-making styles.* These styles are gained over a long period of time. Seven styles of decision-making are most common.

The Agonizer. These people collect information and spend a lot of time evaluating it. In fact, they spend so much time doing this that they end up not knowing what to do! They get overwhelmed with all the data.

The Mystic. Have you heard someone say a decision was made because it "feels right." Such a decision is based on *intuition* or hunch. Some people make most of their choices this way.

The Fatalist. These people do not believe that they have much control over their choices. So, they do not spend much time gathering information.

Leon's parents insist that he live at home and attend the local university. They will pay his tuition and expenses if he does this. Leon will be an education major even though the school's education department is weak. State University, 200 miles away, has a strong department. Leon, an excellent student, would like to go there. But he is convinced that he has no choice.

The Evader. John is a junior in high school. He has taken a general program of study because he has made no career decision. He hopes that by delaying long enough, the problem will go away. In its worst form, this style of decision-making is known as "the ostrich style." Ostriches stick their heads in the sand. John is behaving like an ostrich. He hasn't made any career decision at all.

The Plunger. These people eagerly make decisions. In fact, they are usually too eager to do so. The plunger frequently chooses the first alternative that comes to mind.

The Submissive. "What do you want me to do?" Sound familiar? Such people always want someone else to make a decision for them. If no one will make the decision for them, submissives will make it themselves based on what they think someone else would want them to do.

The Planner. These people are likely to use a good decision-making strategy. They are thorough and weigh all the information. Such people seek to maintain a balance between facts and emotions. Is this your decision-making style?

Benefits of Good Planning

Being a planner can have several benefits. For instance, it can increase your chances of being satisfied with your decision. By *collecting information about a number of alternatives* and carefully weighing the facts, you increase the chances of choosing what is best for you.

Using an organized decision-making process will provide you with more choices. A skilled decision-maker usually develops many alternatives from which to choose. Having several alternatives gives you more freedom than if you had only one or two.

Taking Charge of Your Life

The benefits of successful decision-making are achieved only if the process is used. And that depends on your willingness to accept responsibility for making decisions and for taking action to carry them out.

Part of becoming a mature person is accepting responsibility for what happens to you. This does not mean

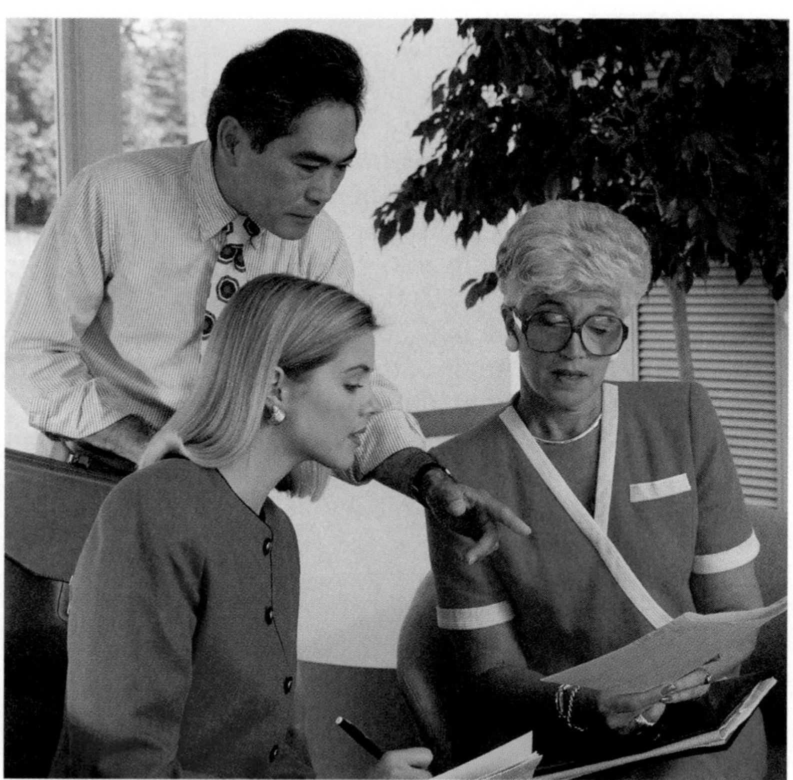

FIGURE 12–5 **What type of decision-making style is being used here?**
Courtesy of Chrysler Corporation.

that luck, natural ability, family advantages, or discrimination do not play a part. It is clear that they do. For instance, John Kennedy's being elected President of the United States was certainly helped by the wealth and name he inherited from his family. The success of Ted Williams at baseball was influenced by his nearly perfect eyesight.

On the other hand, it is possible to identify many examples of famous or successful people who did not have these advantages or who had only average ability. Success and happiness often depend on the choices you make.

Too many people blame someone or something for what happens to them. For example, in conversations about grades, students often say things like: "Mr. Anderson *gave me* a D in English." In truth, teachers do not give grades at all. Teachers simply assign grades to student's work. If you receive an A, you have earned it. The same is true if you receive a D.

OTHER INFLUENCES ON DECISION-MAKING

We have discussed how information, decision-making style, and willingness to accept responsibility all influence decision-making. Now, let's discuss three more factors related to decision-making. These are previous decisions, environment and experience, and real-world restrictions.

Previous Decisions

One decision may influence later ones. To illustrate, let's consider the case of Dee Dee, a tenth-grade student who is deciding what courses to take next year. She picks a health occupations course. By making this decision, Dee Dee will begin to move *toward* a health career and *away* from such fields as business, food service, and communications. Her decision isn't final, though. Dee Dee may change direction later—even as an adult. Important choices that influence later career decisions include selecting school courses and college majors, gaining work experience, marrying, and joining the military.

Environment and Experience

Your *environment* is your surroundings. It includes your family, your neighborhood, your friends, your school, your church, and the like. Your *experiences* are what you do and what happens to you in your environment. Environmental

FIGURE 12–6 **It is often easy to blame someone else for your shortcomings.**

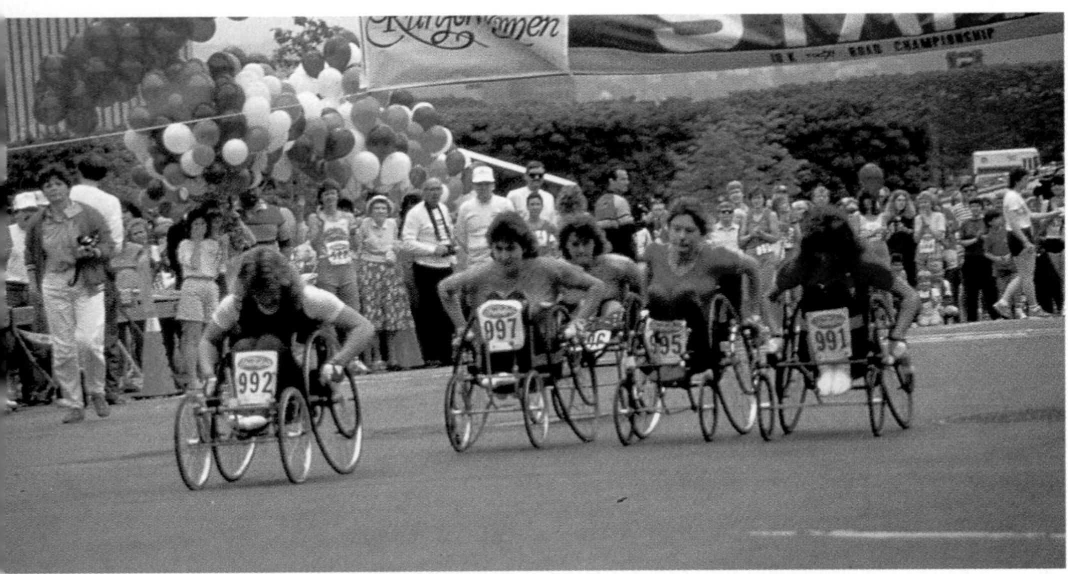

FIGURE 12–7 **Ways can often be found around many of life's roadblocks.**
Photo by Kenneth Deitcher.

and experience factors may strongly influence your choices. Let's see what influenced Luis.

Luis decided to become a veterinary assistant. His decision was heavily influenced by three environmental and experience factors. He grew up on a farm where he developed a love for animals. He worked part-time at his uncle's animal hospital and enjoyed that experience. And he lives near a community college that offers the only veterinary assistant's program in the state.

Real-world Restrictions

There are a number of *reality factors* over which we have little control that often influence decisions. These are persons, events, or situations that exist. Sam would like to be a musician, but the reality is that he would have trouble supporting himself. So he chooses another occupation and plays for parties on the weekend. Someday he may be able to work as a musician full-time.

Often what appears to be real-world restrictions are not. For instance, Sarah didn't think she would have enough money to attend a certain school. She was happy when the school gave her the scholarship she applied for. That, and a student loan, will get her through the program.

Other reality factors include age, experience, qualifications, abilities, physical characteristics, and so on. For example, someone with poor eyesight cannot become a commercial airline pilot. In making career decisions, everyone faces real-world restrictions. When you face such a situation, either try harder or choose another alternative.

FOCUS ON

The Worker

Envy in the Workplace

This chapter has stressed that success and happiness depend on your own efforts. This does not mean, however, that other people cannot help or hinder you. In her book, *The Snow White Syndrome,* Betsy Cohen points out that envy is often a by-product of success. Envy is dissatisfaction or dislike at the success or good fortune of another. In the fairy tale, Snow White's beauty led the Wicked Queen to try to kill her.

Unfortunately, envy exists in the workplace. The more successful you are, the more envy you are likely to cause. In the workplace, an envious person can hurt you. This is because your success often depends on others' cooperation. If someone is envious, he or she can make you look bad. Here are some ways that envy is expressed:

- "Forgetting" instructions or deadlines.
- Gossiping or lying behind your back.
- Being continually late, stubborn, or resistant.
- Clever put-downs.
- Excessive compliments and flattery.
- Outright destruction of your work.

Envious people act to control you. They want to bring you back to their level. To avoid being a victim of envy, learn to recognize it. Try to develop a tolerance for it. Do not make it worse by flaunting your strengths. Be considerate toward co-workers. Build on the other person's achievements. Remember that envy reflects what other people may see, not the real you.

If you are ambitious and aspire to be successful, be prepared to face envy. It exists in many workplaces. If you achieve success, someone is probably going to be envious.

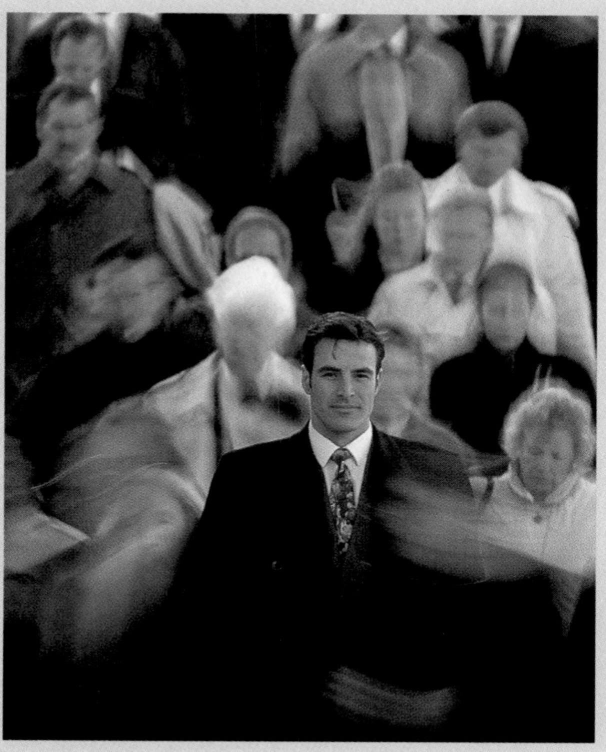

Successful people must be prepared to face the envy of others.
©/Tony Stone Images, Inc.

CHAPTER 12 REVIEW

CHAPTER IN BRIEF

- Decision-making involves choosing between two or more alternatives. The more important the decision, the more time and effort should be devoted to it. Decision-making involves the following five steps:
  1. Defining the problem
  2. Gathering information
  3. Evaluating the information
  4. Making a choice
  5. Taking action

  In making an occupational decision, step two involves collecting information about self-characteristics and occupations. During any of the five steps, you may wish to seek help from a counselor, teacher, parent, or other adult.
- How well you use the decision-making process depends on your style of decision-making and your willingness to accept responsibility and take action. Seven styles of decision-making are common: the agonizer, the mystic, the fatalist, the evader, the plunger, the submissive, and the planner. The planner is the preferred style.
- Being a planner can have several benefits. It can increase your chances of being satisfied with your decision. It can provide you with more choices. It will help you gain greater control over your life.
- A very important part of growing up is accepting responsibility for what happens to you. Your success and happiness will depend largely on the choices you make. Too many people blame someone or something for what happens to them.
- Three other factors also influence decision-making. These are previous decisions, environment and experience, and real-world restrictions.

WORDS TO KNOW

alternatives
decision-making
decision-making styles
environment
experiences
intuition
problem
reality factors

QUESTIONS TO ANSWER

1. When is a systematic decision-making process best used?
2. Name and briefly explain each step in the decision-making process.
3. In choosing an occupation, two types of information are collected in step two. Name them.
4. Identify the decision-making style that is described below:
   a. These people delay making a career decision.

b. These people get overwhelmed with all the data.
c. These people choose the first alternative that comes to mind.
d. These people make decisions based on what they think someone else would want them to do.

5. Which is the best type of decision-making style to use?
6. Using a decision-making process can have several benefits. Name three.
7. Explain what is meant by the phrase "accepting responsibility for what happens to you."
8. Give an example to illustrate how previous decisions may influence later ones.
9. What is the difference between your environment and your experiences?
10. Name three reality factors that can limit career decisions.

ACTIVITIES TO DO

1. You have probably used a problem-solving method in one of your science or math classes. Compare the problem-solving method with the decision-making process. How are they similar and different? Discuss your answers in class.
2. Find out which type of decision-making style is most common in your class. Be honest and write on a piece of scrap paper which of the seven styles you use. (No names on papers.) Summarize results on the board and discuss the outcome in class.
3. Groups as well as individuals can use the decision-making process. As a class, apply the decision-making method to a real or hypothetical situation. For example, what type of computer would be best for use in the class?

TOPICS TO DISCUSS

1. Identify and discuss a variety of situations in which a systematic decision-making process should be used.
2. How is an occupational decision different from a job decision?
3. Decisions are influenced by previous decisions made and not made. Identify and discuss some of the important decisions you have made and not made. How did they turn out? Might the outcome have been different had you used a systematic decision-making process?
4. Do you believe that you have the power to influence the direction of your life and career?
5. We tend to think of reality factors as negative things, such as not having enough money or lacking qualifications. Can you think of positive reality factors that also limit or restrict choices?

CHAPTER 13 Information About Your Self

OUTLINE

- Types of Self-information
- Relationships Among Self-information Factors
- Self and Other Life Roles
- Chapter Review

OBJECTIVES

After reading this chapter, you should be able to:

- Discuss how self-information can help you make more satisfying occupational decisions.
- Name and describe the three types of self-information.
- Describe how interests, aptitudes, and work values are measured.
- Explain how interests, aptitudes, and work values may be similar or different.
- Illustrate how interests, aptitudes, and work values may be expressed outside of one's job.

If you are in your teens, you can look forward to forty or more years of working. That is a long time—especially if you work at an occupation that you dislike. Wouldn't you rather have an occupation that you enjoy doing, that you are good at, and that involves work which is important to you?

Before you select an occupation, you should first answer the question, "Who am I?" This means that you should learn more about your *self.* The self includes your physical characteristics, your behavior, how you think, and many other things. Self is the sum of everything you are. Knowledge about your self is called *self-information.* This information can help you make more satisfying career decisions.

FIGURE 13–1 **Your complete self is much more than just what you see in the mirror.**

In this chapter, you will learn about three types of self-information. By learning more about what you like to do (interests), what you are able to do (aptitudes), and what work is important to you (work values), you will make better choices about what you want to be.

TYPES OF SELF-INFORMATION

When making an occupational decision, you should have information about your interests, aptitudes, and work values.

Interests

We all make choices based on likes and dislikes. We choose from different types of food, music, clothes, hobbies, and so on because we enjoy one thing more than another. For instance, if you enjoy Chinese food, you may choose to go to Chinese restaurants when eating out. If you dislike Greek food, you probably won't go to many Greek restaurants. Things that we like to do are called *interests.* William, for instance, enjoys hunting, fishing, camping, and hiking. His interests relate to outdoor activities.

Your interests can lead to occupations that might suit you. William's interest in the outdoors suggests that he would do well in occupations such as forester, game warden, or recreation worker.

Debbie likes working with her personal computer. She enjoys creating computer graphics. Debbie is also experimenting with a program that will play music on the computer. For what kinds of occupations do you think Debbie might be suited?

FIGURE 13–2 What type of interests do you think this person has?
Courtesy of Knight-Ridder Inc.

By thinking about your likes and dislikes, you are taking the first step toward learning about your self. Do you prefer indoor or outdoor activities? Would you rather work alone or with people? Do you like to work with tools and machines or data and figures? Do you enjoy music or art?

School courses and activities can offer clues to occupations that might be of interest. What school subjects do you like best? Think about school activities, such as clubs, plays, musicals, and fundraising events. Don't forget about hobbies. What do activities and hobbies reveal about your interests?

Vera, for example, belongs to the Journalism Club and works on the staffs of the yearbook and school newspaper. English has always been her favorite school subject. All of Vera's interests point in the direction of a career in the communications field.

Rather than only thinking about your interests, you might want to complete an occupational interest inventory. An interest inventory contains a list of work activities. For each activity, you indicate if you like it, dislike it, or don't know. Figure 13–3 shows several statements taken from the *Interest Checklist.* Most interest inventories use a similar approach.

An interest inventory is not a test. There are no right or wrong answers. However, responses to the items need to be carefully interpreted. Assistance from a teacher or counselor is usually required.

Chances are that your answers will form a pattern. Let's see how the *Interest Checklist* can help you identify occupational interests. Go back to Figure 13–3. You will see that the statements of work activities are listed in groups of three. To the left of each group is a four-digit number. This number corresponds to one of 66 work groups found in a government publication called the *Guide for Occupational Exploration (GOE).* Copies are in many school libraries.

Let's say that you marked "like" for the three work activities in group "02.04." Work group 02.04 is called "Laboratory Technology." This means that you have shown an interest in work activities relating to laboratory technology.

		L	?	D
02.01	Develop chemical processes to solve technical problems	___	___	___
	Analyze data on weather conditions	___	___	___
	Develop methods to control air or water pollution	___	___	___
02.02	Study causes of animal diseases	___	___	___
	Develop methods for growing better crops	___	___	___
	Develop new techniques to process foods	___	___	___
02.03	Examine teeth and treat dental problems	___	___	___
	Diagnose and treat sick animals	___	___	___
	Give medical treatment to people	___	___	___
02.04	Prepare medicines according to prescription	___	___	___
	Study blood samples using a microscope	___	___	___
	Test ore samples for gold or silver content	___	___	___
03.01	Manage a beef or dairy ranch	___	___	___
	Operate a commercial fish farm	___	___	___
	Manage the use and development of forest lands	___	___	___

FIGURE 13–3 **Here are sample items from the Interest Checklist.**
U.S. Employment Service.

Having identified your interests, you can relate them to occupations by using one of several common occupational resources. The *Interest Checklist,* for instance, is keyed to the *GOE.* The *GOE* explains each work group and lists occupations in that group. Occupations in the laboratory technology group include, for example, medical technologist, food tester, seed analyst, and film laboratory technician.

The results of an interest inventory do not mean that the occupations which are revealed are the

? ? ? ? ? ? ? ? ? ? ? ? ? ? ?

WHAT WOULD YOU DO?

You have always been interested in electronic gadgets. You enjoy taking things apart to find out how they work. The two electronics courses you took were your favorite courses. This year, you are working as a co-op student at Apollo TV and Electronics. Most of your time is spent as a "go-fer" helping to install antennas and satellite dishes. Occasionally, you get to do a minor repair job like clean the heads on a VCR or solder a loose connection on a radio receiver. The job is nothing like you thought it would be. You are beginning to wonder if you made the wrong occupational decision.

What would you do?

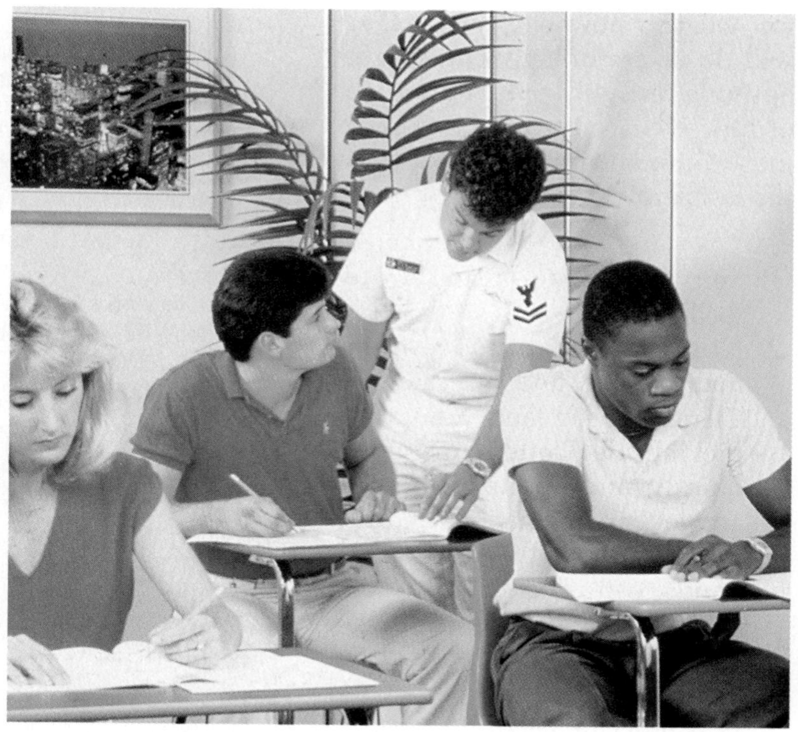

FIGURE 13–4 **The military uses the Armed Services Vocational Aptitude Battery (ASVAB) to help place military recruits in appropriate training programs.**
Courtesy of U.S. Navy Recruiting.

only ones for you. They simply represent alternatives that you should investigate. Learn more about the suggested occupations and others as well. And learn more about your self. Don't base your occupational choice solely on the results of an interest inventory.

Aptitudes

Are there occupations in which you are interested, but you wonder if you would do well in them? Karen, for instance, thinks that she might like to be an architect. But she isn't sure if she has the ability to become one. She needs to look at her *aptitudes*. An aptitude is a developed ability. Your aptitudes represent things you are good at doing.

Karen can get some idea about her aptitudes by looking at her grades. She has taken algebra and geometry and done well in both. Architects need math ability. Also, her art teacher has said that Karen has a talent for designing and illustrating. Karen thought about the two mechanical drawing courses she took. She got an A in both. Overall, it seems that Karen might do well in her occupation of interest.

How else can you find out if you are suited for a certain occupation? Well, you can take an aptitude test. These tests are ones that measure how well you *should* be able to do in a certain field. An aptitude test does not tell you how well you *actually* will do or are doing. Scores on an aptitude test will give you an idea of how well you *might* do. The six most common aptitudes covered by the tests are:

1. Verbal aptitude—using words well.
2. Numerical aptitude—doing math quickly and accurately.
3. Clerical speed and accuracy—picking out letters or words quickly, and arranging number and letter combinations in order.
4. Manual dexterity—moving the hands easily and skillfully.
5. Mechanical reasoning—understanding mechanical principles, how things work, and how tools are used.
6. Spatial visualization—forming mental pictures of the shape, size, and position of objects.

The types of questions included in an aptitude test vary widely depending on the aptitude being measured. Several different examples are shown in Figure 13–5. Each question has only one correct answer.

A separate score is given for each aptitude that is being tested. The scores are often reported as percentile ranks. For example, Joe received a percentile rank of 85 on mechanical reasoning. This means that out of every 100 people who took the test, Joe scored better than 84 of them.

Your teacher or counselor will help you interpret your aptitude test results. After you speak with him or her, the rest will be up to you.

1. Which two words have the same meaning?
   (a) open (b) happy (c) glad (d) green
2. Which two words have the opposite meaning?
   (a) old (b) dry (c) cold (d) young
3. Add (+)
   766 (A) 677 (C) 777
   11 (B) 755 (D) 656
4. Julie works 8 hours a day, 40 hours a week. She earns $4.20 an hour. How much does she earn each week?
   (A) 120.00 (C) 151.80
   (B) 133.80 (D) 168.00
5. At the left is a drawing of a flat piece of metal. Which object at the right can be made from this piece of metal?

A B C D

Which pairs of names are the same (S) and which are different (D)?

6. W. W. Jason . . . W. W. Jason
7. Johnson & Johnson . . . Johnson & Johnsen
8. Harold Jones Co. . . . Harold Jones and Co.

For questions 9 through 12 find the lettered figure exactly like the numbered figure.

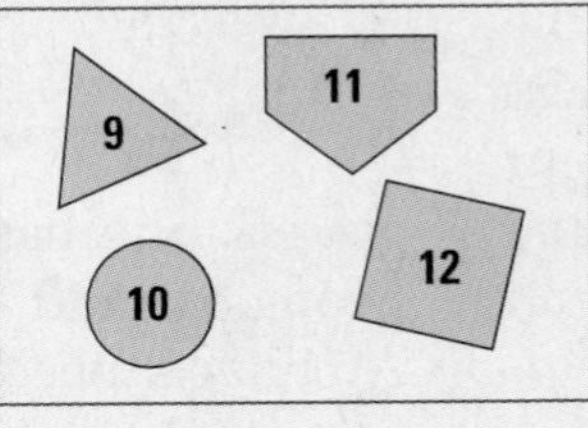

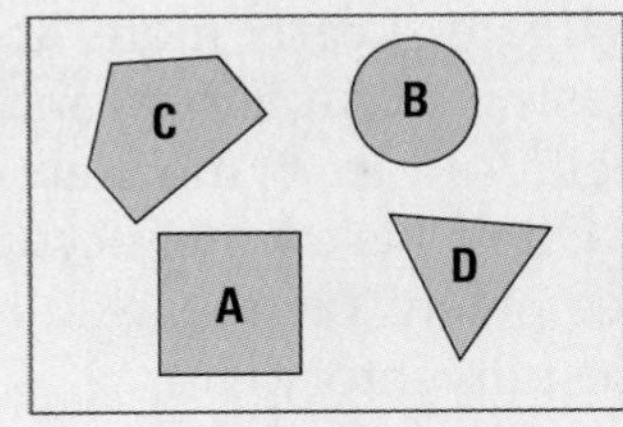

FIGURE 13–5 Here are sample aptitude test questions.
Doing Your Best on Aptitude Tests, GPO.

Work Values

Values are attitudes and beliefs about things we think are important in life. For instance, Americans believe strongly in the right of free speech. This is a basic democratic value that we think is important.

Values that relate to work and career are called *work values.* These are feelings about the importance or worth of an activity or occupation. For instance, if you would like to have an occupation in which you could help other people, you are expressing a value for a certain kind of work.

Work values can also be thought of as needs that we try to meet in our work. For example, Fred gave up a good job with a large insurance company to start his own business. He did so because he wanted to make his own decisions. For Fred, the need for independence was not being met in his former job.

What are some work values? Following are several examples.

- Altruism—helping other people.
- Creativity—inventing things, designing products, or developing new ideas.
- Achievement—having feelings of accomplishment from doing a job well.
- Independence—being able to work in your own way.
- Prestige—wanting to be looked up to.
- Money—earning enough to buy the things you want.
- Security—having a steady job even in hard times.
- Surroundings—being in a pleasant work environment.
- Variety—having the opportunity to do many types of tasks.

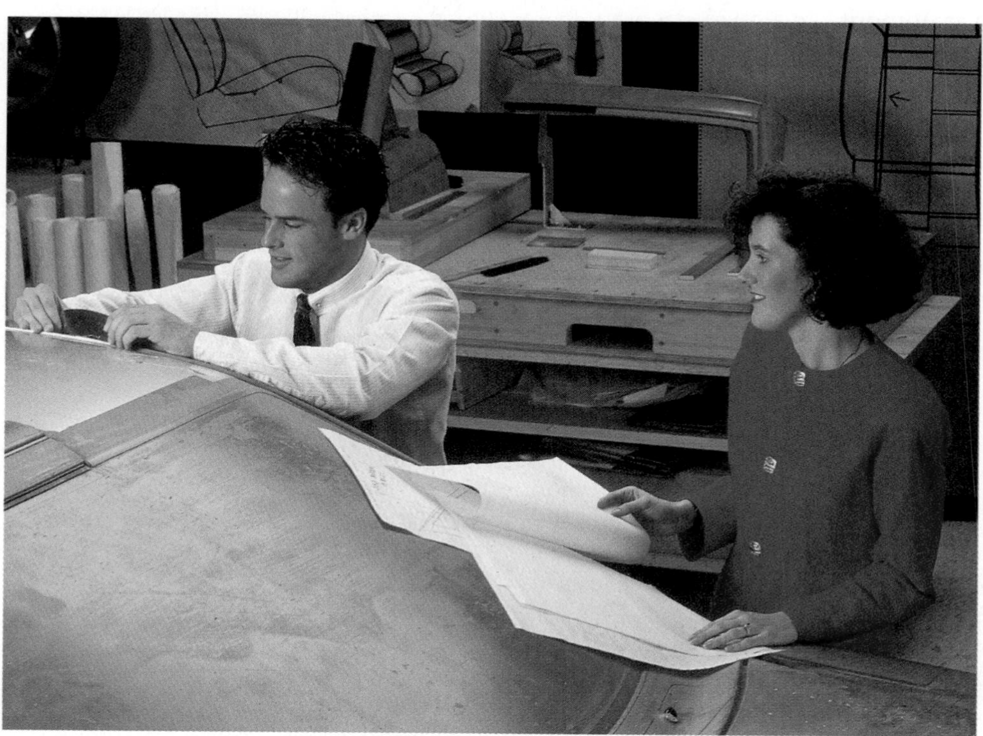

FIGURE 13–6
Creativity is an important work value for these designers.
Courtesy of Ford Motor Company.

You can identify your work values by taking a work values measure. Such measures generally include statements describing things that people look for in their work. The following five sample statements drawn from *The Values Scale,*[1] show the types of items included in a work values measure.

It is now or will in the future be important for me to:

5. **help people with problems.**
8. **discover, develop, or design new things.**
23. **know that my efforts will show.**
42. **have a regular income.**
65. **do something at which I am really good.**

The Values Scale consists of 106 such items. You read each statement and indicate how important it is according to a four-point rating scale: (1) little or no importance, (2) some importance, (3) important, or (4) very important. Interpretation of this measure is very simple, For instance, questions 23 and 65 in the example relate to the *Achievement* work value. Let's say that you assigned a rating of 4 to questions 23 and 65. This means that work that gives you a feeling of achievement is very important. Most occupations, of course, involve several kinds of work values.

Unlike interest inventories and aptitude tests, the results of a work values measure are not as easily related to specific occupations. This is because work values come from feelings that are more personal. As a result, work values scores are not as useful in helping to identify which occupations to explore. A work values measure is better used in step four of the decision-making process than in step two (refer back to figure 12–3). You will recall that step four is one in which you make a choice from among a small number of desirable occupational alternatives. Knowledge of work values can help you make final career choices that will lead to your future goals.

Earl took a work values measure. It suggested that altruism, security, and surroundings are important to him. These results tend to confirm his interest in becoming a technology education teacher. Norma found out that creativity and variety are the most important values for her. She is leaning toward becoming a floral designer or interior designer.

? ? ? ? ? ? ? ? ? ? ? ? ?

WHAT WOULD YOU DO?

You have completed a work values measure. In going over the results with the counselor, you learn that your highest rated values are money, independence, and prestige. It is true. You would like to be wealthy, independent, and have people look up to you.

"Big deal," you think. "Now all I have to do is go out and find someone that will give me an important job and pay me a lot of money. That is a joke. Work values measures are a waste of time. I will probably end up working in the mines like the rest of my family."

What would you do?

[1]Super, Donald E. and Nevill, Dorothy D. *The Values Scale.* Palo Alto, CA: Consulting Psychologists Press, 1985.

RELATIONSHIPS AMONG SELF-INFORMATION FACTORS

Interests, aptitudes, and work values relate to each other. Sometimes they agree and sometimes they conflict. For some people, interests, aptitudes, and work values may all point to the same choice. Robert, for example, wants to be a fashion designer. He has been interested in fashion design ever since he was a child. He has the aptitude, having already won several ribbons and awards in design competitions. Fashion design is usually done in pleasant surroundings, which is important for Robert.

For other people, though, interests, aptitudes, and work values may seem to point in different directions. This is not unusual. Nor is it something to worry about. Jean, for example, has a high aptitude for mechanical reasoning and manual dexterity. But mechanical principles and using tools and machines don't interest her much. What she really wants to do is some type of work that is mentally challenging and involves working with people.

Suppose *your* self-information conflicts. Choose based on the interest, aptitude, or work value that means the most to you. Then, try out your choice and see how it works. If you are not satisfied, look for something else. Your first occupational choice does not have to be a permanent one. You can learn from your decisions. Each decision you make will provide you with information that will help you make better decisions in the future.

FIGURE 13–7 Self knowledge can help you make good career decisions. Be aware, however, that some occupations are highly competitive and exclude all but a few highly talented people.
Courtesy of Lockheed Corporation; photo by Eric Schulzinger.

SELF AND OTHER LIFE ROLES

An occupation can be a very important part of your life. However, it is only one part of a total *lifestyle. Life roles* in addition to worker may include those of citizen, spouse, parent, and student. Many people lead happy and productive lives even though their jobs do not satisfy all of their interests, aptitudes, and work values. People pursue hobbies, sports, and leisure activities. Many people also participate in organizations, clubs, church, and the like. Let's take a look at some examples.

Gregorio works as a heavy equipment operator. His work is okay, but his first love is old cars. He has a 1964 Mustang that he has been restoring for about 6 years. He found the car rusting away in a junkyard. For Gregorio, working on his Mustang is a satisfying hobby and a major source of enjoyment.

Jerry is a personnel officer of a large company and really enjoys his work. He also is a very talented artist. Jerry manages to set aside about ten hours each week to work on his painting. By continuing to paint, he can satisfy his strong need for creative expression.

Bill is a manufacturing sales representative and a former minor league baseball player. He is successful in his work, but misses being involved in baseball. To satisfy his interests, Bill coaches a little league baseball team. He is a good coach and teacher of baseball. His young players respect him for taking the time to help them. They are not aware, however, that he gets more enjoyment out of it than they do.

Andy is an operating room nurse. He helps during surgery. His job involves a great deal of stress and anxiety. Andy sometimes wishes that the job was less demanding. To help him deal with the stress, he sings in the church choir. Singing allows him to satisfy interests and abilities that he doesn't use on his job.

All of these people have found ways to express themselves outside of their jobs. You may be fortunate enough to work at an occupation that uses all your interests, aptitudes, and work values. If not, many outside activities can provide you with outlets for expressing your self.

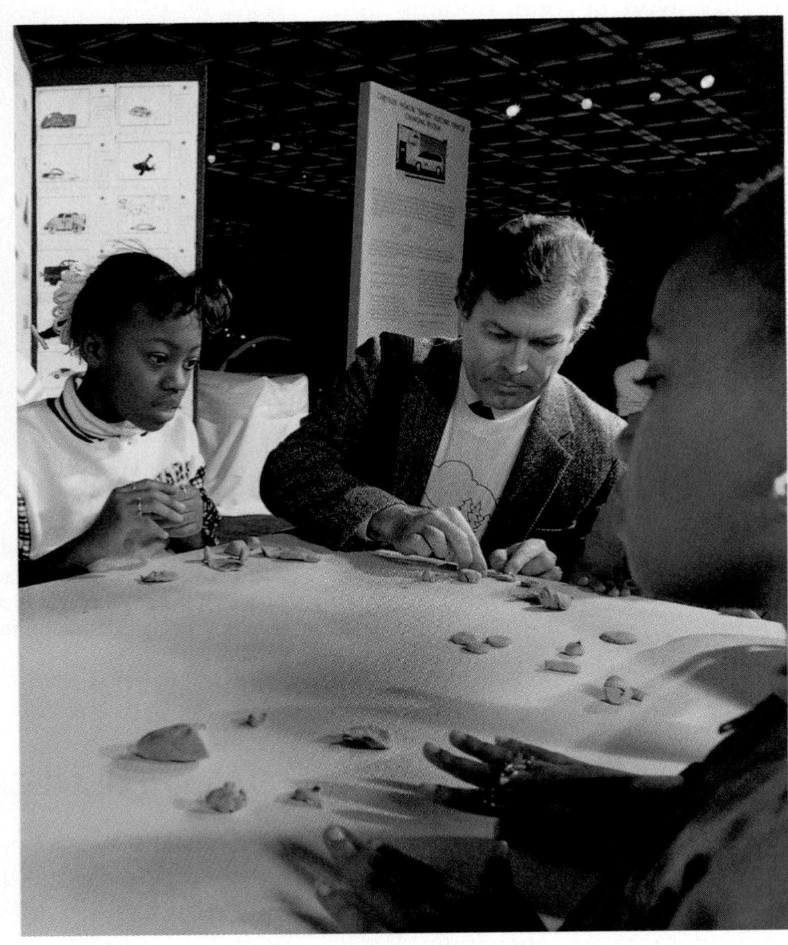

FIGURE 13–8 This engineer expresses some of his work values through community volunteer work.
Courtesy of Chrysler Corporation.

FOCUS ON The Worker

MID-CAREER CHANGE

Information about your self can help you make more satisfying occupational decisions. For young people, interests and aptitudes tend to be the more meaningful types of self-information. For adults, however, work values are usually the most important factor. An estimated 6 to 10 percent of U.S. workers over age 24 voluntarily change occupations every year. The main reason is to pursue work values not presently being met.

Earl, for example, was an engineer for a large manufacturing company. After 15 years, he had climbed the corporate ladder to become a manager. But he found he was working harder and enjoying it less. So, at age 37 he left the company to become a community college instructor. He hoped to gain more freedom in his work and spend more time with his family.

Arlene and her husband, Joe, owned and managed an automotive parts business for 10 years. She had always been fascinated by the stock market. At age 40, she decided to leave the family business to train as a stockbroker. She now says it was the best move she ever made.

Mid-career changes are usually brought on by the desire for greater earnings, achievement, or happiness. Or simply the realization that one is not suited for a certain occupation. Usually it is a combination of age, unhappiness, and a feeling of being trapped in an occupation.

Changing occupations, however, is not something to be taken lightly. It involves considerable risk. It can lead to a sharp drop in income and lots of insecurity and anxiety. Mid-career decisions are usually successful if they are well-planned and based on good self-information.

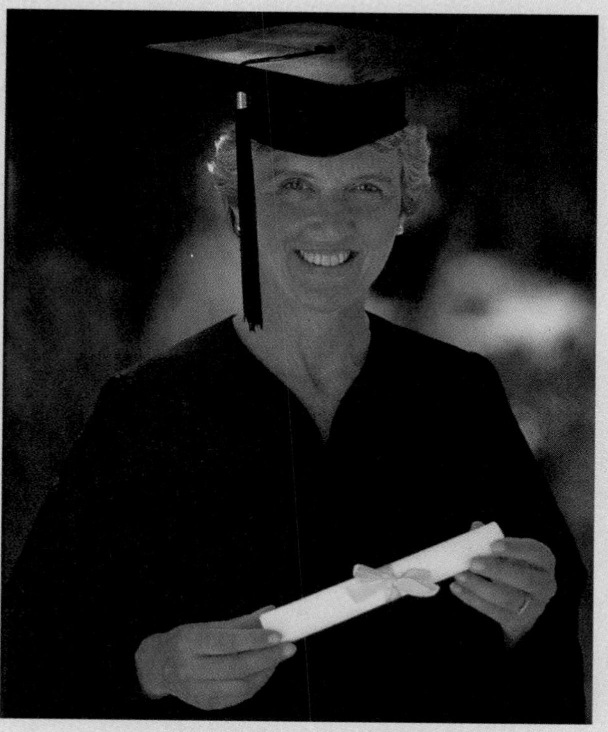

More and more people change educational and occupational goals throughout their lifetime.
© Michael Keller, 1990/Uniphoto Picture Agency.

CHAPTER 13 REVIEW

CHAPTER IN BRIEF

- Before you choose an occupation, first answer the question, "Who am I?" Such information about your self can help you make a more satisfying occupational decision. When making an occupational decision, you should have information about your interests, aptitudes, and work values.
- Things that you like to do are called interests. You can identify your interests by thinking about your likes and dislikes or by taking an interest inventory. Interests can be related to occupations that you may wish to investigate or explore.
- An aptitude is a developed ability. Your aptitudes represent things you are good at doing. Like interests, aptitudes can be related to occupations. By knowing your aptitudes, you can get some idea of occupations that you might be good at.
- Work values are your feelings about the importance or worth of an activity or occupation. Knowledge of work values are not as useful as interests and aptitudes in identifying occupations to explore. But you can use your work values to help you make a final choice from among a number of desirable occupational or educational alternatives.
- Interests, aptitudes, and work values sometimes all agree. When this happens, decision-making is not difficult. In other cases, interests, aptitudes, and work values conflict. This is not unusual, nor is it something to worry about. If the information conflicts, base your choice on the interest, aptitude, or work value that means the most to you. Then, try out your choice and see how it works.
- You may be fortunate enough to work at a job that uses all your interests, aptitudes, and work values. If not, outside activities (hobbies, sports, clubs, church) can provide you with a variety of outlets for expressing your self.

WORDS TO KNOW

aptitudes
interests
life roles
lifestyle
self
self-information
work values

QUESTIONS TO ANSWER

1. What is the first question to ask yourself before choosing an occupation?
2. There are three types of self-information used in career decision-making. Name them.

3. What does participation in school activities reveal about your self?
4. Why is it incorrect to call an interest inventory a "test"?
5. Without taking an aptitude test, how can you find out about your aptitudes?
6. If you are good at diagnosing and repairing auto engines, what two aptitudes do you have?
7. Name three occupations that would be suitable for a person who values independence.
8. At what point in the career decision-making process is knowledge of work values important? Explain.
9. What should you do if your interests, aptitudes, and work values point in different directions?
10. Why do people often pursue hobbies and other activities very different from what they do in their jobs?

ACTIVITIES TO DO

1. Make an appointment with the school guidance counselor to review your student records. Find out if you have taken any type of interest, aptitude, or work values inventory or test. If you have, ask the counselor to interpret the results for you.
2. To what extent are your interests, aptitudes, and work values being met in your work experience job? Rate the job in the terms of your overall satisfaction on a scale of 1 (low) to 10 (high). What are you doing or can you do to express interests, aptitudes, and work values not being met on your job? Discuss your answers in class.
3. Perhaps your teacher or counselor can arrange to have you take an interest inventory, aptitude test, and work values measure. If so, such information can be helpful to you in later occupational exploration and career decision-making.

TOPICS TO DISCUSS

1. This chapter has explained self-information in relation to occupational decision-making. Discuss how self-information may also be used to assist in making educational decisions.
2. As you mature, new interests develop and old ones are left behind. Think of examples of how your interests have changed from the time when you were younger. What does this suggest in terms of your occupational interests?
3. Self-information can help you identify occupations that you might wish to do. Discuss why it is important to investigate and explore these occupations prior to making a final decision.

CHAPTER 14 Career Information

OUTLINE

- The World of Work
- Tomorrow's Jobs
- Exploring Occupations
- Chapter Review

OBJECTIVES

After reading this chapter, you should be able to:

- Explain how occupations and industries are grouped.
- Describe trends in the growth of goods and service industries.
- Discuss reasons for the rapid growth of service industries.
- Identify occupations having the fastest rate of growth and those having the greatest numerical increase between 1990–2005.
- Use the *Occupational Outlook Handbook* to conduct an occupational search.

The school guidance counselor gave Mel an interest inventory. The results suggest that Mel might like certain occupations. These are electrician, aircraft mechanic, refrigeration mechanic, and tool and die maker.

These indeed are occupations that appeal to Mel, but he does not know very much about them. He wonders for example, what workers in those occupations actually do. How much education or training do they need? Do the occupations have a good outlook for the future? How much money do people in such occupations earn? To answer his questions, Mel needs to collect information about these occupations. Learning how to use resources on occupational information is an important part of career decision-making.

THE WORLD OF WORK

By the year 2005, it is estimated that 147 million people will be employed in the United States labor force. People work in hundreds of different types of offices, stores, factories, mines, farms, and other workplaces. Workers are employed in over 35,000 different occupations! This network of occupations and workplaces (industries) is often called the *world of work.*

Because of the large number of occupations and industries, special grouping systems are used to make it easier to collect and publish information about the world of work. A group is a collection of two or more things that are alike in some way. For example, rock, country, and classical are types of music. Groups are sometimes labeled as "categories," "classifications," "families," or "clusters."

About a dozen different systems classify information about the world of work. The two

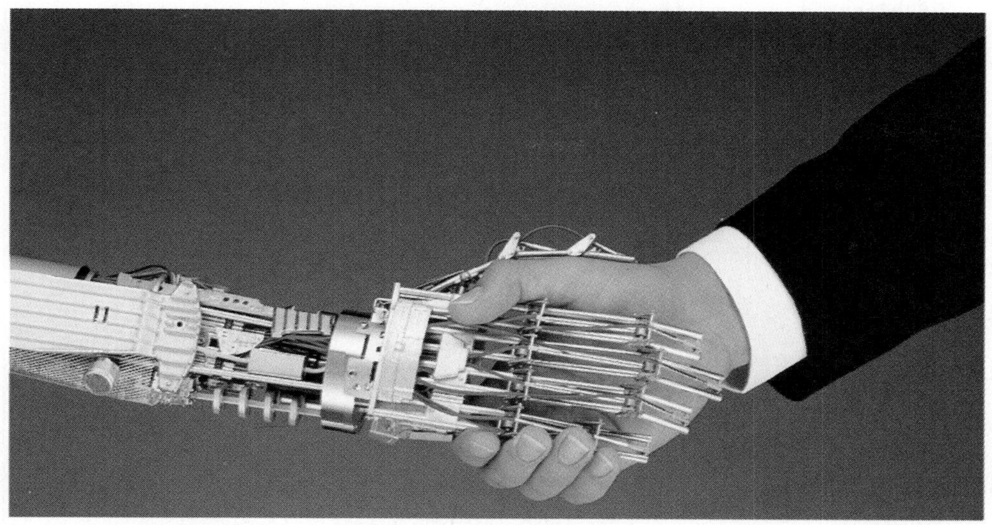

FIGURE 14–1 **Workers in the 21st Century will have more help from robots and computers than we have today.**
© Uniphoto, Inc.

most important classifications are occupational and industrial.

Classifying Occupations

The U.S. Department of Commerce has developed a grouping system called the *Standard Occupational Classification* (SOC) system. The SOC classifies occupations based on the type of work performed. For instance, the mechanics, installers, and repairers division includes workers who maintain and repair various kinds of machines and equipment. These include motor vehicles, appliances, communication equipment, electrical and electronic equipment, and related equipment and machines.

The *SOC* consists of the divisions shown in Figure 14–2. These divisions are used as the basis for the *Occupational Outlook Handbook* (OOH). The *OOH* is an excellent resource for occupational information. You will learn more about the OOH later in this chapter.

Classifying Industries

Another important grouping system is the *Standard Industrial Classification* (SIC). The SIC basically describes where people work. It is a grouping of different workplaces according to the type of product produced or service provided. The manufacturing division, for instance, includes industries that use machines or chemical processes to change materials or substances into new products. In the SIC system, all places of employment are called *industries.* In other words, hospitals, schools, food stores, restaurants, banks, and hundreds of other types of workplaces are industries. The SIC system is divided into the two broad categories and ten major divisions shown in Figure 14–3. It is important to understand the SOC and SIC classifications. This is because the government collects and reports information this way. The following section provides illustrations of how the SOC and SIC are used.

OCCUPATIONAL GROUPS	SAMPLE OCCUPATIONS
1. Managerial and Management-related Occupations	accountants, bank officers, health inspectors, purchasing agents, school administrators, insurance underwriters
2. Engineers, Surveyors, and Architects	architects, drafters, surveyors, engineers, cartographers
3. Natural, Computer, and Mathematical Scientists	computer systems analysts, chemists, geologists, meteorologists, statisticians
4. Lawyers, Social Scientists, Social Workers, and Religious Workers	psychologists, social workers, ministers, lawyers, economists
5. Teachers, Librarians, and Counselors	elementary teachers, secondary teachers, professors, librarians, counselors
6. Health Diagnosing and Treating Practitioners	chiropractors, dentists, optometrists, physicians, veterinarians
7. Registered Nurses, Pharmacists, Dietitians, Therapists, and Physician Assistants	dietitians, pharmacists, registered nurses, speech pathologists, physical therapists
8. Health Technologists and Technicians	dental hygienists, surgical technicians, health record technicians, licensed practical nurses, radiologic technologists
9. Writers, Artists, and Entertainers	radio and TV announcers, photographers, dancers, musicians, commercial artists
10. Technologists and Technicians, Except Health	air traffic controllers, legal assistants, broadcast technicians, electronics technicians, computer programmers
11. Marketing and Sales Occupations	cashiers, insurance agents, real estate brokers, travel agents, securities sales workers
12. Administrative Support Occupations, Including Clerical	bank tellers, bookkeepers, secretaries, telephone operators, postal clerks
13. Service Occupations	firefighters, correction officers, chefs, barbers, flight attendants
14. Agricultural, Forestry, Fishing, and Related Occupations	farmers, ranchers, animal caretakers, timbercutters, gardeners
15. Mechanics, Installers, and Repairers	automotive mechanics, appliance repairers, millwrights, office machine repairers, TV service technicians
16. Construction Trades and Extractive Occupations	carpenters, bricklayers, electricians, coal miners, rotary drill operators
17. Production Occupations	meatcutters, typesetters, dental laboratory technicians, machine tool operators, welders
18. Transportation and Material Moving Occupations	pilots, truckdrivers, construction machinery operators, oil pumpers, locomotive engineers
19. Handlers, Equipment Cleaners, Helpers, and Laborers	construction laborers, dock hands, garbage collectors, parking attendants, vehicle cleaners
20. Job Opportunities in the Armed Forces	officers, sonar operators, missile engineers, troop leaders, ship captains, navigators, demolition experts, and thousands of occupations with the same title as in the civilian sector

NOTE: The SOC actually consists of 22 divisions, but only these 20 are used in the *Occupational Outlook Handbook.*

FIGURE 14–2 **This is the primary way the federal government classifies occupations.**

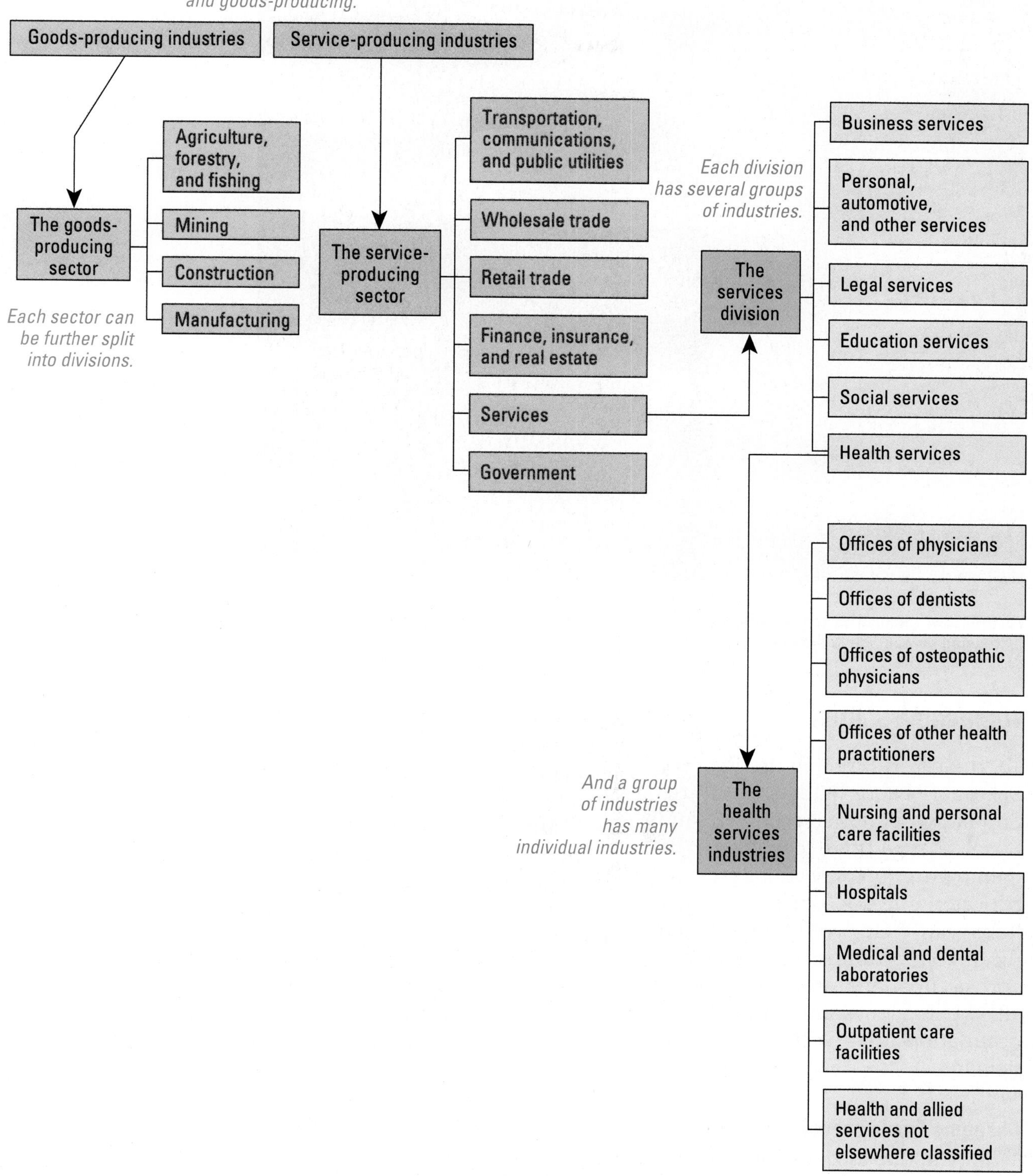

FIGURE 14–3 **Industries are classified by sector, division, group, and industry in the SIC system.**

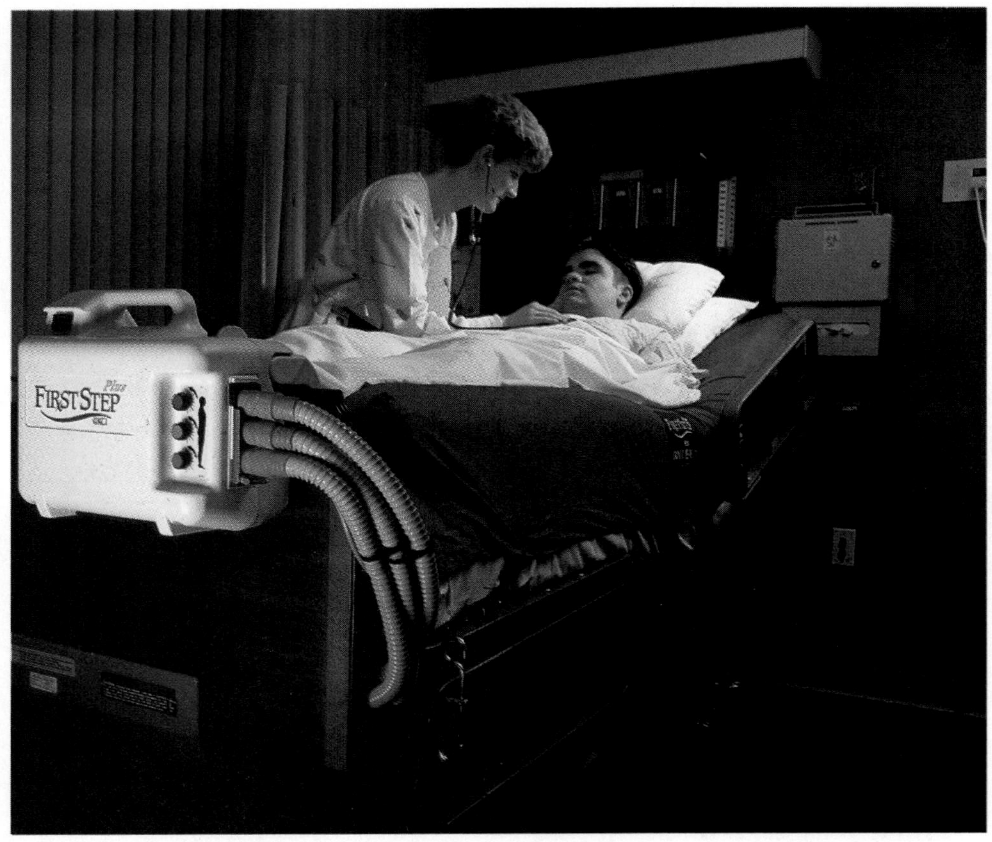

FIGURE 14–4 **Industries that provide services, like doctors and nurses, will continue to employ an increasing percentage of the work force.**
Courtesy AMETEK Inc.

TOMORROW'S JOBS

To project future job trends, the Bureau of Labor Statistics analyzes population patterns, economic and social change, and technology. By their nature, job projections are only educated guesses. But such projections can help you know about future opportunities in industries and occupations of interest. After all, you may not want to train for an occupation that will be in little demand.

Changing Employment in Industries

Since about 1960, employment in *service-producing industries* has been increasing at a faster rate than employment in *goods-producing industries*. About seven of every ten jobs are in service industries, such as health care, trade, education, repair and maintenance, transportation, banking, and insurance.

Rising incomes, higher living standards, and an aging population have helped contribute to the rapid growth of service industries. The result has been greater demand for health care, entertainment, and business and financial services. People with higher incomes may spend heavily on eating out, personal fitness, recreation and the like. The large group of "baby

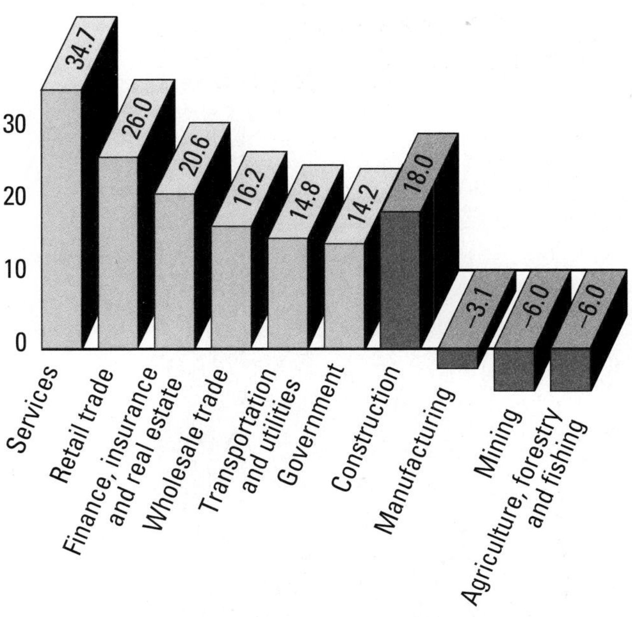

FIGURE 14–5 Some industries will grow more rapidly than others.
Source: Bureau of Labor Statistics.

boomers" (76 million) born between 1946 and 1964 are also using more health services. In addition, the growth of cities and suburbs has brought a need for more local government services.

Through the year 2005, employment is expected to increase faster in service-producing industries than in goods-producing ones. In fact, service-producing industries are expected to account for almost all new jobs between now and 2005. Employment in these industries is expected to increase to 118.8 million jobs, an increase of 24.5 million over 1990.

Within industries, growth will vary widely, Figure 14–5. It will be the greatest in services and retail trade. In the goods-producing sector, construction is the only division that will grow as a whole.

Sandra is interested in a job in the agriculture, forestry, and fishing industry. She was discouraged to read that jobs in this industry will probably decline in the future. Upon further reading, however, she found that some specific industries in the group (such as forest conservation) may actually grow.

Changing Employment in Occupations

Like industries, future employment among occupational groups will vary greatly. The fastest growth will be in technician and technologist occupations (SOC divisions 8 and 10). Growth will also vary within a specific occupational group. Therefore, it may be better to examine the outlook for specific occupations than for various occupational divisions.

? ? ? ? ? ? ? ? ? ? ? ? ?

WHAT WOULD YOU DO?

You have read so much recently about work, career decision-making, and occupations. You have found it to be interesting. You guess that you will probably work after leaving high school. However, what you really hope to be someday is a wife, mother, and homemaker. You are afraid to even mention it, because you think other students might laugh at you.

What would you do?

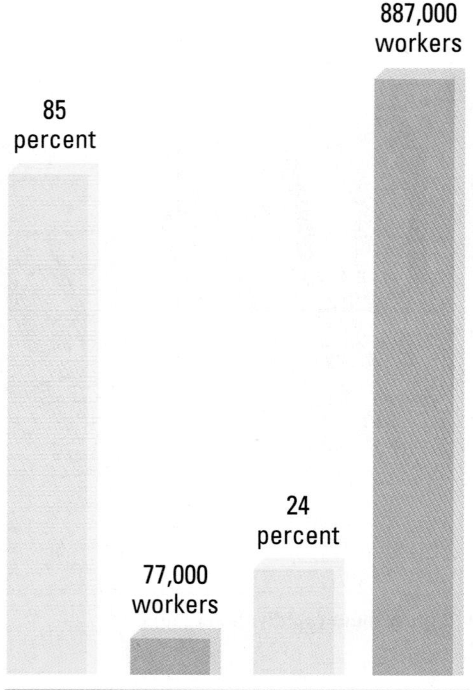

FIGURE 14–6 **Even though an occupation is expected to grow rapidly, it may provide fewer openings than a slower growing, but larger employment sector.**
Source: Bureau of Labor Statistics.

Information about projected trends is useful in several ways. It might, for instance, suggest to a person planning a career that he or she select an occupation for which future employment is expected to grow. On the other hand, it might suggest to a worker in a declining occupation that he or she consider retraining for a different one.

To obtain a complete picture of occupational trends, you will need to know two things. One is the *rate of growth* (percent) of an occupation. The other is the *numerical increase* of workers. The relationship between rate of growth and size of change for two occupations is shown in Figure 14–6.

From the chart, you can see that between 1990 and 2005 the rate of growth for paralegals will increase by 85 percent. Yet, the number of *new* jobs for paralegals between 1990 and 2005 will only be about 77,000. On the other hand, the growth rate for retail sales workers will increase only about 24 percent. But the actual number of *new* jobs in that area between 1990 and 2005 will be about 887,000. Study the chart in Figure 14–6 until you understand the difference.

Figure 14–7 shows the occupations that are projected to have the fastest growth rate between 1990 and 2005. You can see that health-related occupations will account for 12 of the 30 fastest-growing ones. Overall, Figure 14–7 shows that the

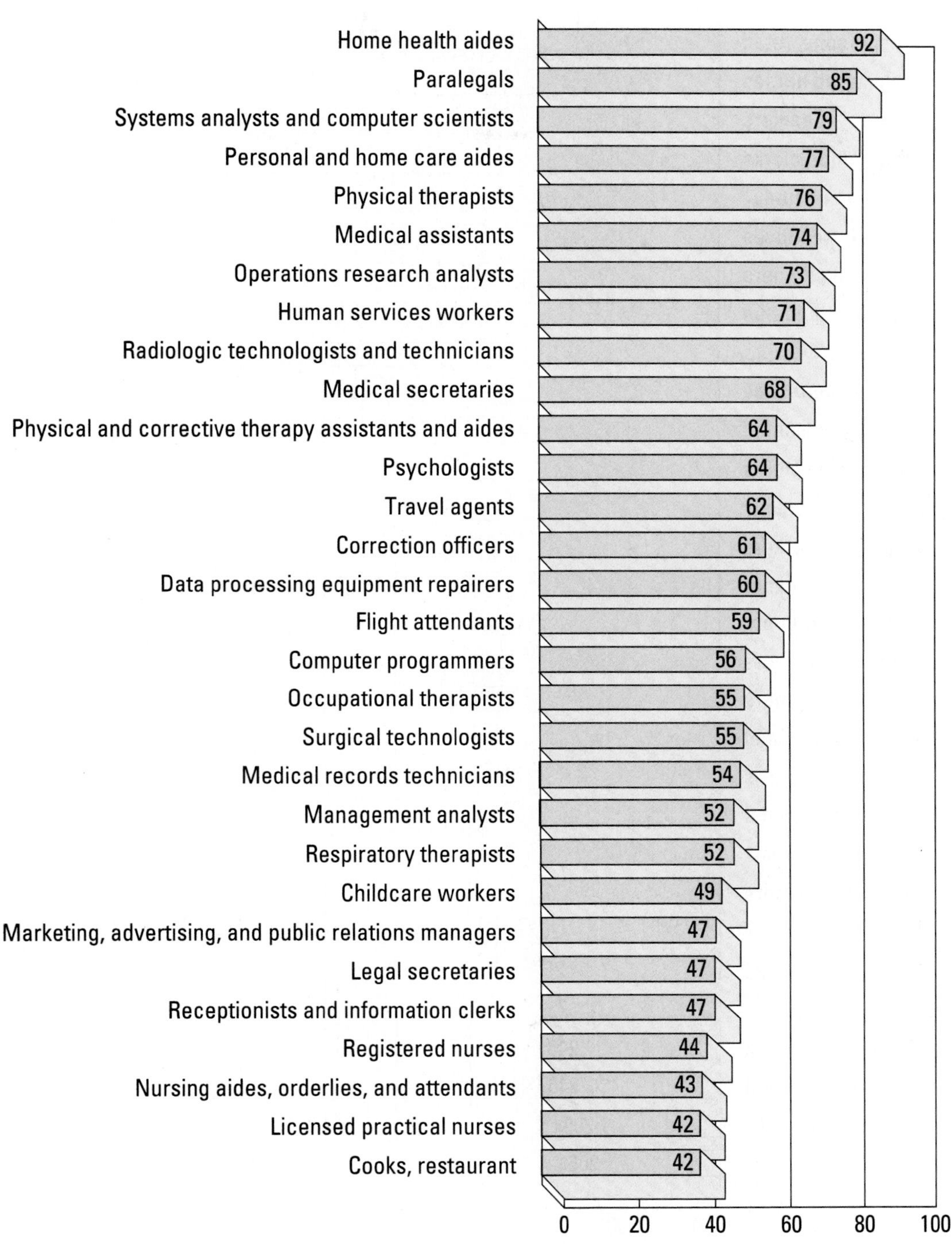

FIGURE 14–7 **The thirty fastest-growing occupations, projected 1990–2005 by percent.**
Source: Occupational Outlook Quarterly.

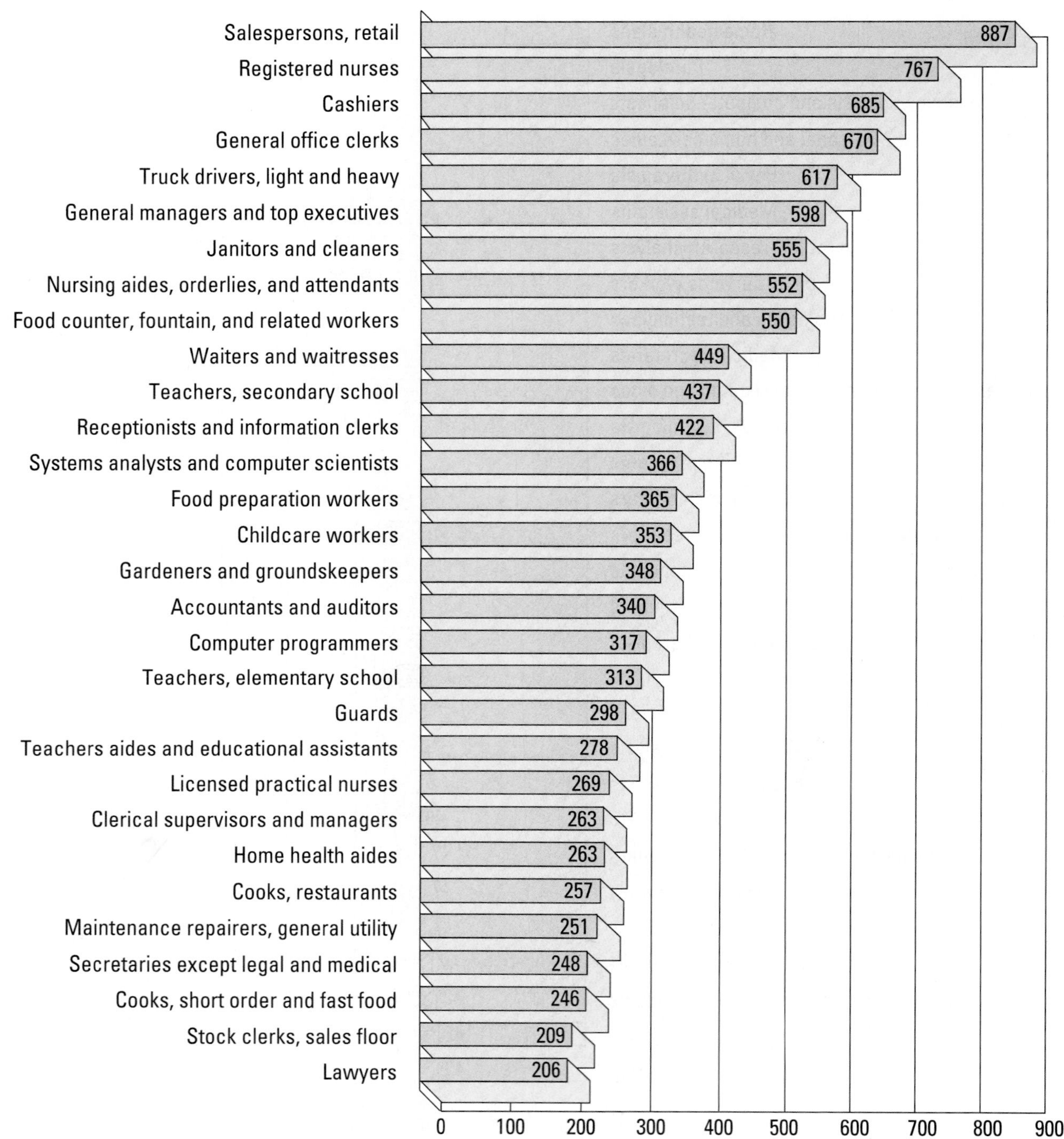

FIGURE 14–8 **These occupations will have the largest numerical increases, projected 1990–2005. Numbers shown are in thousands.**
Source: Occupational Outlook Quarterly.

fastest-growing occupations will be those requiring a college degree or some type of technical training. Why do you think that most of the occupations are in the health field?

In Figure 14–8, the 30 occupations shown are projected to have the greatest actual growth in number of jobs during the period 1990 to 2005. Note that 3 of the 4 top occupations are in the Business and Marketing cluster.

Another important fact shown in Figure 14–8 is that most new jobs will require on-the-job training or skills learned through vocational and technical education. Only about 7 of the 30 occupations shown are ones that normally require a college degree.

EXPLORING OCCUPATIONS

With the information you now have about your self and employment trends, you are ready to start an occupational search. Many resources exist to help you. One of the easiest to use is the *Occupational Outlook Handbook (OOH).*

Why is it useful to know how to use the *OOH?* Well, the *OOH* is available in more guidance offices and public libraries nationwide than any other occupational resource. And since the *OOH* is revised every two years, the information included is up-to-date.

Using the Occupational Outlook Handbook

The occupations included in the *OOH* are mostly ones in growing fields. Most of the occupations require some degree of education or training beyond high school. The *OOH* describes about 250 occupations in detail. These occupations comprise 87 percent of the labor force. A listing of about 80 additional occupations is provided in the appendix. These comprise an additional 4 percent of the labor force. Each occupational description in the *OOH* is organized as follows:

1. Nature of the work
2. Working conditions
3. Employment
4. Training, other qualifications, and advancement
5. Job outlook
6. Earnings
7. Related occupations
8. Sources of additional information

Having the same information makes it easier to compare occupations.

Doing a Search

Let's say you are following the five-step decision-making process explained in Chapter 12. In step two, you used self-information to identify a list of occupations that might suit you. Now it is time to learn more about each of your choices. Such a study is called an *occupational search.* In doing a search, it is helpful to use a form like the one shown in Figure 14–9. That way you can organize information from each of the occupational descriptions. Your instructor will provide you with copies of the form.

Now get a copy of the most recent edition of the *OOH.* At the top of your form, write the name of the occupation. Then turn to the "Index to Occupations" near the end of the *OOH.* This will give you the page numbers that discuss your

OCCUPATIONAL SEARCH FORM

TITLE OF OCCUPATION: ____________________

NATURE OF THE WORK

A. List five major tasks that workers in this occupation perform.

1. ____________________
2. ____________________
3. ____________________
4. ____________________
5. ____________________

WORKING CONDITIONS

B. What are the normal working hours? ____________________

C. Describe the typical working conditions. ____________________

D. Are there any unpleasant or dangerous aspects to this occupation? ____________________

EMPLOYMENT

E. In 19___, how many jobs were in this occupation? ____________________

F. In what type of industries or locations do people in this occupation work? ____________________

TRAINING, OTHER QUALIFICATIONS, AND ADVANCEMENT

G. What is the preferred or required level of education or training? ____________________

H. Is licensure or certification required? ____________________

I. Are any special abilities or qualifications recommended or required? ____________________

J. What opportunities are there for advancement? ____________________

JOB OUTLOOK

K. Check (✓) the statement in each column below that best describes the future outlook for this occupation.

Change in Employment

____ faster than average growth
____ average growth
____ slower than average growth
____ little change
____ decline

Opportunities and Competition

____ very good to excellent opportunities
____ good opportunities
____ may face competition
____ keen competition

FIGURE 14–9 **This form allows you to summarize information from the eight parts of a typical *OOH* occupational description.**

EARNINGS

L. The average yearly starting salary in 19 __ was $ ______________________.

M. In 19 __, the average yearly earnings ranged from $ __________ to $ __________.
(low) (high)

RELATED OCCUPATIONS

N. List the titles of any other related occupations.

1. ______________________ 5. ______________________
2. ______________________ 6. ______________________
3. ______________________ 7. ______________________
4. ______________________ 8. ______________________

SOURCES OF ADDITIONAL INFORMATION

O. List the names and addresses of places where further information may be obtained. ______________________

____

____

____

____

____

____

____

____

What is the source of this information? *Occupational Outlook Handbook:* 19 __/__ Edition, pages ________.

FIGURE 14–9 **Continued.**

designated occupation. As you read the *occupational description,* fill out your search form. Feel free to make notes on the form or add other information that you think is important. Repeat this process for as many occupations as you want to research.

After you have finished collecting information, compare and evaluate your information. For help in doing this, refer back to Figure 12–4, "Checklist for Evaluating Possible Occupational Alternatives."

Other Sources of Career Information

The *OOH* is not the only available resource. Many publishing companies produce resources to be used in occupational exploration and decision-making. Your teacher or career counselor may introduce you to such materials. Or you may find them on your own. (Librarians will be glad to help you.)

The greatest change in the use of occupational information is the development of computerized information systems. Many high schools, community and junior colleges, career centers, and Job Service offices have access to such systems. Most of you have or will be using a computer at some point in your decision-making.

It does not matter whether you use a book or a computer to find occupational information. The important thing is that you find it. A thorough occupational search will expose you to many possible choices. From these, you can make your decision. Good decisions, like the one you are trying to make, result from using complete, up-to-date information.

? ? ? ? ? ? ? ? ? ? ? ? ?

WHAT WOULD YOU DO?

You have identified three occupations that you want to learn more about. You get an *Occupational Outlook Handbook (OOH)* and look up information on the first occupation. You copy down important facts and data for later study. You follow the same procedure for the second occupation. For the third occupation, however, no information is available in the *OOH*.

What would you do?

Military Occupations

The largest employer in the country is the military services (Army, Navy, Air Force, Marine Corps, Coast Guard). In mid-1990, about 2 million persons were on active duty in the Armed Forces. About 11 percent of those were women.

The major occupational groups in the military are similar to those in the civilian sector. Over 75 percent of military occupational specialties have civilian counterparts. Nearly one out of every four enlisted persons are involved with electrical, electronic, mechanical, and related equipment. This reflects the highly technical and mechanical nature of the military. Officers (about 15 percent of all military personnel) are concentrated in administration, medical specialties, and directing combat activities.

Military life is more disciplined and structured than civilian life. There are dress and grooming requirements. Certain formalities, such as saluting officers and obeying military laws and regulations, must be followed.

Hours and working conditions vary. Most military personnel usually work 8 hours a day, 5 or 5½ days a week. Some assignments, however, require night and weekend work, or being on call at all hours. All may require travel and periodic relocation.

The Armed Forces has planned a personnel reduction of about 25 percent by the late 1990s. This is due primarily to the reduction in the threat from the Soviet Union. In spite of this reduction, job opportunities should be good in all branches of the Armed Forces through 2005. A section on Military Occupations may be found in the Occupational Outlook Handbook. A separate resource called Military Careers is also available.

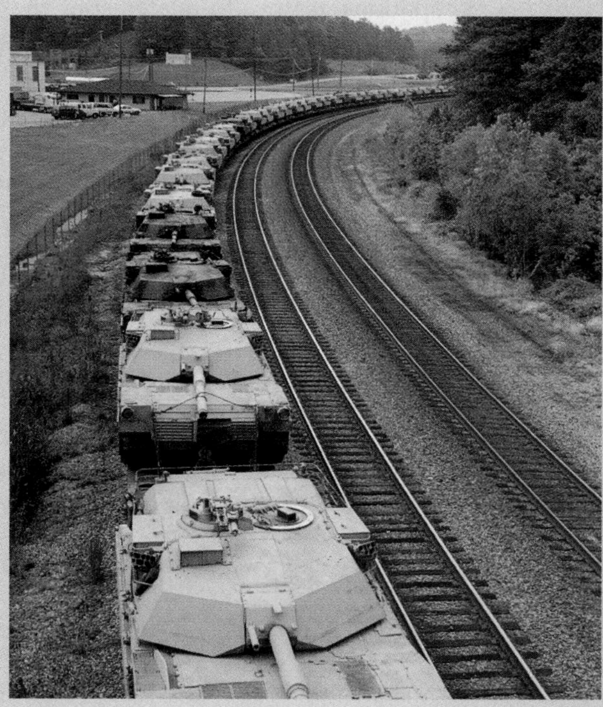

Repair and maintenance is the largest occupational segment in the U.S. military. These U.S. Army tanks are moving toward the 1,800-acre repair depot in Anniston, Alabama.
Courtesy U.S. Army.

CHAPTER 14 REVIEW

CHAPTER IN BRIEF

- The network of occupations and industries is called the world of work. Because the number of different occupations and industries, grouping systems are used to organize information about the world of work. The two most important grouping systems are the *Standard Occupational Classification* (SOC) and the *Standard Industrial Classification* (SIC).
- The SOC classifies occupations according to the type of work performed. The SOC divisions are used as the basis for the *Occupational Outlook Handbook.* The SIC describes where people work. In the SIC system, all places of employment are called industries.
- About eight out of every ten jobs are in service industries. Through the year 2005, employment is expected to increase faster in service-producing industries than in goods-producing ones. Services are supposed to account for about all new jobs between now and 2005.
- To understand occupational trends, it is necessary to look at both rate of growth and numerical increase of workers. The fastest growing occupations are health-related. But the occupations with the largest increase in number of jobs are primarily low-skilled and semi-skilled sales and clerical occupations.
- The *Occupational Outlook Handbook* (OOH) is a very important resource that you need to learn how to use. The *OOH* contains detailed occupational descriptions for about 250 occupations. These comprise 87 percent of the labor force. Follow the recommended procedure in conducting an occupational search.

WORDS TO KNOW

goods-producing industries
industries
occupational description
Occupational Outlook Handbook (OOH)
occupational search
service-producing industries
Standard Industrial Classification (SIC)
Standard Occupational Classification (SOC)
world of work

QUESTIONS TO ANSWER

1. Why are classification systems used to organize information about the world of work?
2. In the SOC system, how are occupations grouped? In the SIC system, how are industries grouped?
3. What type of industries are projected to grow the fastest? Explain why.

4. How can projections about future occupational trends help you in career decision-making?
5. To understand future occupational trends, it is necessary to know two types of information. Name them.
6. What characteristics do the fastest growing occupations shown in Figure 14–7 have in common?
7. How many of the occupations with the largest growth shown in Figure 14–8 require a college degree?
8. Why is it useful to know how to use the *OOH?*
9. Does the *OOH* contain information on all occupations? Explain.
10. Every occupational description in the *OOH* contains eight kinds of information. Name them.

ACTIVITIES TO DO

1. Use an *Occupational Outlook Handbook* and copies of Figure 14–9 to conduct an occupational search. (Your instructor can arrange to have copies of the form duplicated.) Follow the steps described in this chapter.
2. After completing an occupational search, you may want to collect first-hand information about a given occupation. With the help of your teacher or counselor, identify a person who works in your occupation of interest. Interview the person to find out his or her feelings about the occupation. If possible, also arrange to visit his or her place of employment.

   Before the interview, work with classmates to develop an interview form. Going over the information that you have already collected on the occupational search form may help you identify the types of questions you want to ask.

   After the interview, report to the class on what you have learned. Discuss whether the interview confirmed or changed your interest in the occupation.
3. Invite your school guidance counselor to class. Ask the counselor to describe and demonstrate any additional career information resources located in your school's guidance office, library, or career center.

TOPICS TO DISCUSS

1. If you are really interested in a particular occupation, how concerned should you be about its future job outlook?
2. How do civilian occupations differ from those in the military?
3. To make a good occupational decision, you should consider several types of information (nature of the work, working conditions, job outlook earnings, and so on). In the final analysis, however, there are very few perfect occupations. Most occupational decisions involve a compromise among various factors. Provide examples and discuss how occupational decision-making involves compromise.

SECTION 4

SUCCESS SKILLS

To be successful on the job, you need occupational skills, employability skills, and basic academic skills. The first two types of skills were explained in previous chapters. Communication skills, one type of academic skills, are dealt with in Chapter 15. Communication involves listening, speaking, reading, and writing. A second type of academic skills, math and measurement skills, is reviewed in Chapter 16.

Chapter 17 describes types and causes of accidents. For teenagers and young adults, accidents are the leading cause of death. You will examine things to do and avoid in order to prevent accidents at home, school, on the job, and elsewhere. Safety is everyone's business.

Leadership is the process of influencing people to accomplish the goals of an organization. In Chapter 18, you will learn about six characteristics of leaders. Vocational student organizations are presented as ways to help students develop leadership skills. The last part of the chapter deals with parliamentary procedures. These are rules used by businesses and other groups to conduct effective meetings.

Do you know how to use a computer? If not, you may be lacking one of the most important job skills of the future. In Chapter 19, you will learn about the importance of keyboarding skills. What a computer is and how it works will be explained. Application of computers in the workplace will also be illustrated. The chapter concludes with predictions about the future of computers in the workplace.

In the future, you may work as an employee for someone or go into business for yourself. Owning your own business is explored in Chapter 20. You will learn about the advantages and disadvantages of entrepreneurship and what it takes to operate a successful business.

Co-op Career SPOTLIGHT ON

David Hedstrom, *Mr. Neon, Super Salesman*

His neon creations range from the basic "OPEN" sign to the neon brains for manikins with glass heads in a Ripley's Believe It Or Not exhibit in Wisconsin Dells, Wisconsin. Several of his signs have made brief appearances in the movies, Pretty Woman and Terminator II. Yet David Hedstrom, owner of Green Bay Sign Company in Green Bay, Wisconsin, says he is a super salesman above all.

"Primarily, I am a super salesman. I bend great tubes but no matter how good they are, nobody would know about them if I wasn't a good salesman." He says the secret to good salesmanship is honesty and the ability to make your customers feel that you are their friend. David says the experiences of his childhood and what he learned in co-op helped him become the successful salesman he is.

David's father was a traveling engineer for the Milwaukee Railroad, so the family moved many times during David's childhood. "I was always the new kid in school, and I learned how to make friends fast," David said.

The co-op program he took at Southwest High School in Green Bay, Wisconsin, where he graduated in 1975, helped him turn his friend-making skills into money-making opportunities. "Co-op gave me a lot of confidence and skills to apply myself in the world of sales." He says co-op gave him interpersonal skills as well as practical business skills. "Co-op put me in a position to meet new people everyday and learn interpersonal skills, like how to handle objections and negotiations. It also taught me basic business skills like how to use a sign press in DECA, how to make signs, how to make change, and how to interview for a job."

Now there is no stopping David. He has the confidence to try anything. He plays the guitar, has a black belt in karate, a pilot's license, and a scuba diving certificate. He plans to add to his sign enterprise and sell commercial real estate before he runs for mayor of Green Bay.

CHAPTER 15 Communication Skills

OUTLINE

- Listening
- Speaking
- Reading
- Writing
- Chapter Review

OBJECTIVES

After reading this chapter, you should be able to:

- State guidelines for good listening.
- Discuss rules for effective speaking.
- Identify ways to improve reading skills.
- Explain why writing is the most important form of business communication.
- Illustrate different forms of business communication.

To be successful on the job, you need three types of skills: (a) occupational skills, (b) employability skills, and (c) basic academic skills. Occupational skills are the technical or manual abilities unique to a certain occupation. People learn these skills through vocational education or other types of education and training programs. Certain skills, such as honesty, good grooming, and a positive attitude, are required in all jobs. These are called employability skills. You read about employability skills in Chapters 7, 9, and 11.

Workers need basic academic skills, too. Joyce learned this during her first week as a stockhandler at Meadows Garden Center. She thought that all she would have to do is care for the plants—she was mistaken. Mrs. Wilkinson, Joyce's boss, often had to correct her grammar, spelling, and math. She told her that workers need many kinds of skills. Knowing how to do the work itself isn't enough. Many employers feel as Mrs. Wilkinson does.

This chapter deals with communication skills, one type of academic skills. *Communication* involves sending information, ideas, or feelings from one person to another. This is done through language. Language may be spoken or written. Before communication can take place, a receiver must understand the language. Communication, therefore, involves writing, reading, listening, and speaking.

According to *Effective Business Communication*, typical workers spend about 70 percent of their workday hours communicating. About 45 percent of communication time is spent listening; 30 percent, speaking; 16 percent, reading; and 9 percent, writing. In the following material, we will examine these four skills.

FIGURE 15–1A **Effective communication skills are needed for most jobs. Airline attendants must communicate with the pilot and passengers to give customers safe, comfortable flights.**
Courtesy of Delta Air Lines Inc.

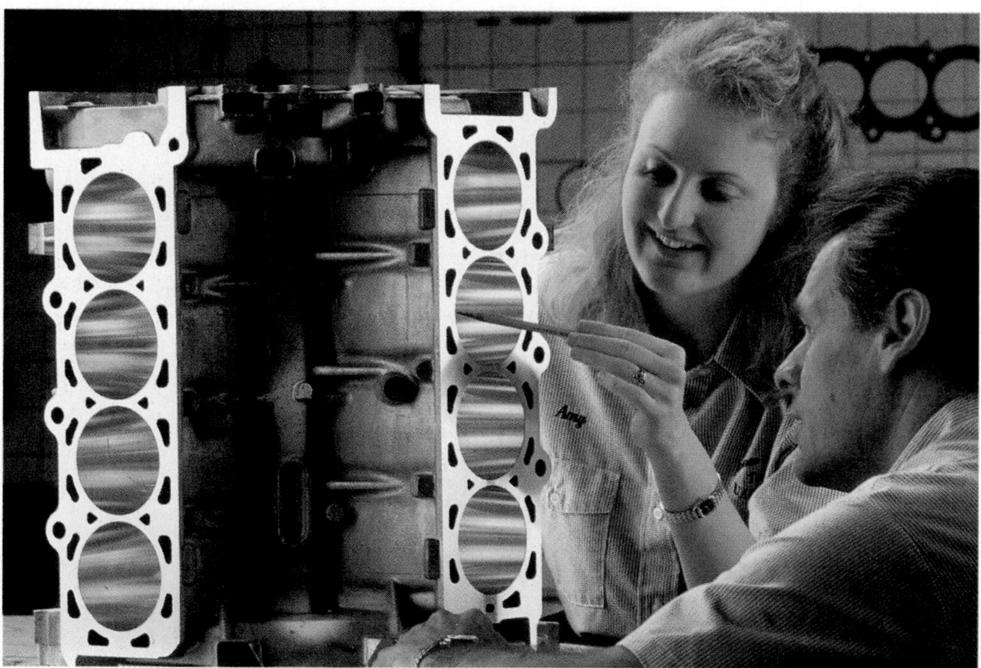

FIGURE 15–1B **Engineers who design automobile engines communicate to other technicians how each part works.**
Courtesy of Ford Motor Company.

LISTENING

Communication links the working world. Listening may be its weakest link. It has been said that poor listening costs employers billions of dollars every year.

Poor listening takes many forms. For instance, the boss told Murray to send the district sales agents both of the new price lists. A couple of days after Murray sent the report, the phones started ringing. The agents wondered where their price lists were. Murray knew he had goofed. He sent out a second mailing right away. By not following directions, he cost the company time and money. Common causes of poor listening include distractions, prejudging and overstimulation, and partial listening.

Distractions

Have you ever thought of something else while someone was talking? It's often hard *not* to do this. Most of us talk at a rate of about 125 words per minute. The average mind can handle about 600 to 800 words per minute. This means that there is a gap between the rate at which people are able to speak and the rate at which listeners are capable of thinking. Therefore, the mind tends to wander.

A distraction is something that you notice while you are listening to someone talk. For instance, suppose you are talking to the boss and someone turns on a noisy machine. Perhaps the workplace lighting flickers on and off. Your mind might pay attention to the distraction. Other common distractions are telephone calls, changes in temperature, and the appearance of a new smell. What kinds of problems could these cause later?

FIGURE 15–2 **This person missed an important meeting. He thought the boss said the meeting started at 2:30 P.M., when the boss said 10:30 A.M.**
Photo by Paul E. Meyers.

Prejudging and Overstimulation

Sometimes listeners try to outguess the speaker. This is called prejudging. Here is an example. Mrs. Krause asked to meet with the salesclerks a few minutes before the store opened. Carla began to feel nervous. She thought that Mrs. Krause was going to criticize her for something she had done. She started to think what her answer would be. Mrs. Krause just wanted to review check-approval policies. Carla had prejudged what Mrs. Krause was going to say. As it

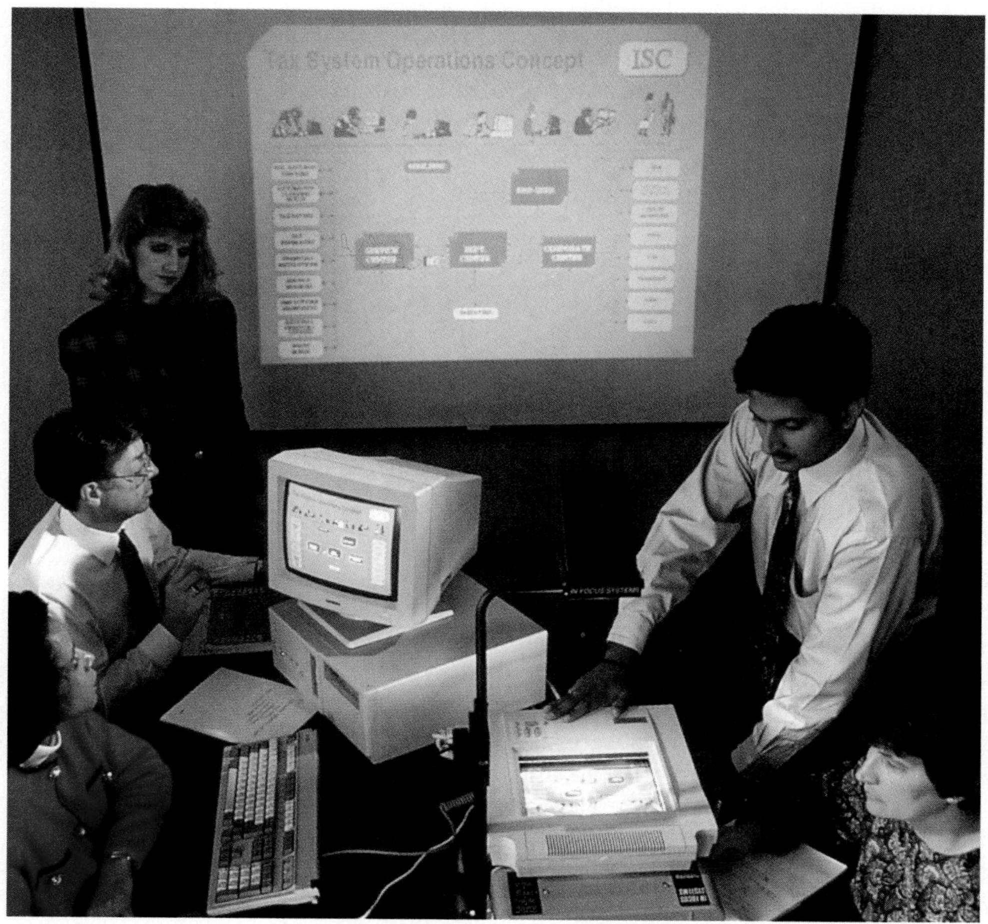

FIGURE 15–3 Observing a multi-media presentation may require listening as well as reading skills.
Courtesy TRW Inc.

turned out, Mrs. Krause complimented Carla. She was the only one who was doing that task correctly!

Another cause of poor listening is called overstimulation. A listener becomes too eager to respond to the speaker, as shown in the following example. Mr. Costa was demonstrating to Lee and the other apprentices how to adjust an air compressor and spray gun. He said that enamel requires a higher air pressure than lacquer. He misspoke—lacquer requires higher air pressure.

Lee caught the error and couldn't wait to correct him. But Lee was so eager to point out the mistake that she didn't pay attention to the rest of the demonstration.

Partial Listening

This can take several forms, including fragmented listening and pretend listening. Fragmented listening is when the listener listens only for certain things. For example, Harold works as a graphic artist for a large department store. Twice a year, the store manager talks to all employees about company goals. The only time Harold pays attention is when the manager says something about the art department.

Pretend listening is when the listener either doesn't care what is going on or is waiting for a turn to talk. Margo is a maintenance worker for the same company as Harold. She thinks it is a waste of time for maintenance workers to attend the store manager's presentation. Though she pretends to listen, she thinks about everything but company plans and goals. By not concentrating on the message being delivered, Harold and Margo miss very important information.

Following are a number of guidelines for good listening. Rate yourself in terms of how good a listener you are. You should:

1. Have a questioning attitude. Good listeners want to understand what is being said.
2. Concentrate on what is being said. Listening requires effort and active participation.
3. Eliminate distractions by turning off noisy machines, closing doors, moving closer to the speaker, and so on.
4. Use your eyes as well as your ears and mind. Observe facial expressions and body language of the speaker. These are often as important as what is said.
5. Listen "between the lines" for what the speaker *doesn't* say. The Coldwell Company's president told workers that someone had bought the company. Though he didn't say so, it sounded as if the plant might be relocated.
6. Get all the facts before evaluating it or reacting to it.
7. Write down important things before you forget them.
8. Ask questions if you do not understand something.

SPEAKING

Effective speaking requires correct pronunciation, clear enunciation, use of standard English, and good grammar. Each of these will be summarized. A section on telephone skills is also included.

Correct Pronunciation

Most words have several syllables. For instance, the word *advertisement* has four syllables: ad-ver-tise-ment. Correct *pronunciation* means saying the proper sound for each syllable and accenting the right syllable. Thus, the word *advertisement* is actually pronounced as "ad-vur'-tiz-ment." The accent is on the second syllable. Also, notice that the third syllable is pronounced as "tiz" rather than "tise."

Clear Enunciation

Clear *enunciation* means speaking distinctly. Many people, for instance, don't enunciate contractions such as "we're." That is, they say "we're" like "weer." How do you say "we're"? Poor enunciation and bad pronunciation often go together. As a result words like "are" and "our" often sound alike. The same is true for "fire" and "far." Say these two pairs of words out loud to find out how clearly you enunciate.

Use of Standard English

American English takes many forms. One is the informal slang

FIGURE 15–4 **Some of the words and phrases you use with your peer group may not be appropriate to use with people with whom you work.**
Courtesy of Siena College, Loudonville, NY.

that many teenagers use. Can you give examples of some of these words? It's fun to speak like this with friends. Informal slang is nonstandard English. So is poor grammar. *Standard English,* on the other hand, is the customary form of language used by the majority of Americans. Most employers will expect you to use standard English on the job.

Rules of Good Grammar

Since grade school, you have studied *grammar* in language arts and English classes. A language's grammar is a set of rules about correct speaking and writing. All languages have dozens of rules.

Grammar rules are pretty easy to understand. Even so, many people continue to say things like "they ain't here" instead of "they aren't here." Can you think of reasons why people break so many grammar rules when they speak?

Why should you use good grammar? Well, your getting and keeping a job may depend on it! How you speak makes an impression on an employer. Suppose you are interviewing people for a job. Two applicants have strong job skills. One says things such as "I done it" and "I couldn't find it nowhere." The other person speaks correctly. Whom would you hire? Poor grammar may create doubt in an employer's mind about your ability. It can also turn away customers and clients.

Telephone Skills

In Chapter 4, you learned how to use the telephone as part of a job search. Proper use of the telephone is also required on the job. An employee represents the company in a business transaction. An employee's time also costs the business money. Therefore, an effective speaker conducts telephone conversations with courtesy and efficiency.

When answering a business call, you should observe these guidelines:

- Answer in a pleasant, helpful tone of voice. Identify the company at once. For example, "Hello, Edwards and Company" or "Edwards and Company, may I help you?"
- Listen attentively as the caller gives the reason for calling. Be prepared to record a phone message. If you take a message, record complete information, i.e., date and time, caller's name and number, nature of the call, and the follow-up action required.
- Route the call to the person best able to meet the caller's need. An appropriate response would be, "Thank you, I'll transfer you to Mr. Weber, our sales manager."
- If the caller wants to talk to a specific person, you might ask, "May I tell her who is calling?"
- Often, the desired person will not be able to accept the call. In this case, your response might be, "I'm sorry, Mrs. Knight is away from her desk. May I ask her to return your call?"
- Always fulfill your promise to the caller. Pass on the message, track down the correct information, return the call yourself, or whatever else is required.
- Pleasantly conclude all calls; for example, "Thank you for calling."

Similar courtesies should be used when placing a business call. Follow these rules:

- Before placing a call, have your purpose clearly in mind. Write down the points you want to make. Have any necessary reference material at hand.
- If you are placing an order, complete a written order form beforehand.
- Identify yourself at once and state your reason for calling. For example, "Hello, this is Arnold Swartz at Midwest Publishers. I'm calling to inquire if our order is ready to be picked up."
- If necessary, name the person or department with whom you want to do business. After identifying yourself, state something like, "I would like to speak with Mr. Sullivan in the service department."
- Your call should be direct and businesslike. But don't forget to talk in a warm and friendly tone.

READING

Like listening, reading is a way to receive information. Both require concentration and understanding. More so than listening, however, reading also requires recognizing words before you can understand their meaning. To show this, look at the three lines in Figure 15–5. The first line is Spanish; the second is shorthand; and the third is English. You may understand only the third line. Some of you may understand only lines 1 and 3, and so on. Language is like a code. Unless you can recognize and attach meaning to it, you can't understand it.

Let's see if you can recognize and understand these four English words: *glabella, larrikin, neap,* and *scrieve.* Are any of them familiar to you? Probably not. The words might as well be written in Italian (unless, of course, you know that language). This points out the importance of *vocabulary.* Your vocabulary is the total of all the words you know. You cannot understand what you read unless you know the meaning of the words used.

Improve Your Vocabulary

Your vocabulary already consists of thousands of different words. Keep adding new words to your vocabulary. Don't just pass over words that you don't know. As you find new words, look up their meanings in a dictionary. (Small, electronic dictionaries are very convenient.) After you learn a word, use it in your speaking and writing. Vocabulary-building is a lifelong task.

Practice Reading

Because reading is a skill, people can improve it through practice.

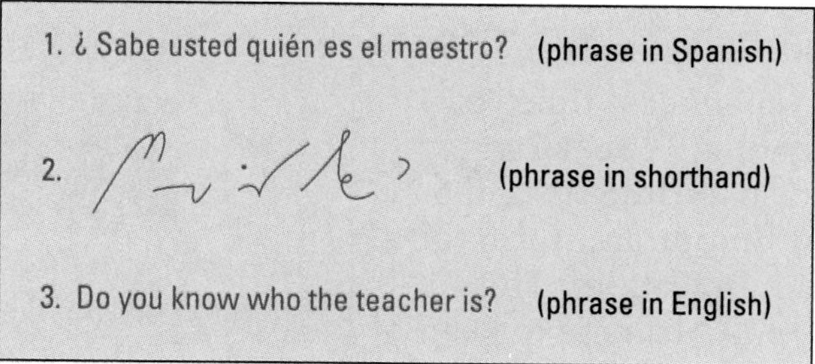

1. ¿Sabe usted quién es el maestro? (phrase in Spanish)
2. (phrase in shorthand)
3. Do you know who the teacher is? (phrase in English)

FIGURE 15–5 These three lines mean the same thing in different languages.

Reading newspapers and magazines are good ways to practice. So, too, is reading material in your field of work. Not only will you improve your reading, you will also be learning at the same time.

It is pretty boring to read things that are not interesting to you. Of course, we all must do some of this. On your own time, though, follow your interests, hobbies, and so on. If you don't want to spend money, check out materials from the public library.

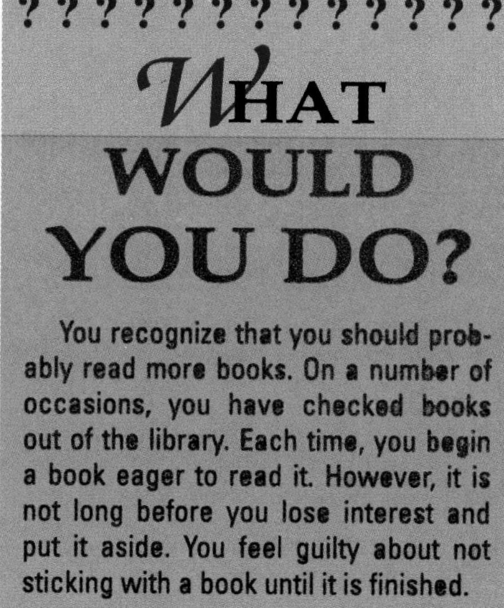

You recognize that you should probably read more books. On a number of occasions, you have checked books out of the library. Each time, you begin a book eager to read it. However, it is not long before you lose interest and put it aside. You feel guilty about not sticking with a book until it is finished.

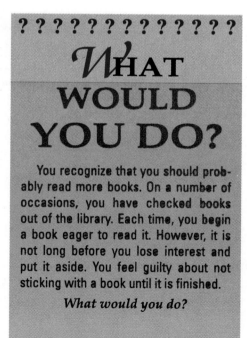

What would you do?

WRITING

Most workers spend less time writing than listening, speaking, or reading. Even so, writing is probably the most important form of business communication. This is because it is good business to keep permanent records of all business operations, transactions, and agreements. Denny learned this the hard way.

Denny was asked to answer the phone while the boss stepped out for a moment. He took two calls and left messages on her desk. A few moments after she returned, Denny saw the boss approaching.

"Who are these messages from?" she said. "I can't read them."

What could Denny say?

Written communication takes place within a company and between organizations. Internal communication takes the form of notes, business forms, and memorandums. External communication mainly takes the form of business letters.

Notes and Business Forms

A note is the most informal type of written business communication. Many notes are short, handwritten messages. Electronic fax messages are common examples, Figure 15–6. A wide variety of preprinted notes are used in business to record phone messages, route information, send directions, and so on.

Business forms are another type of written communication. Businesses often use preprinted forms to record business operations. Some examples of common business forms include:

ABC FAX

American Boating Corporation
1 Riverside Plaza, Apex, OH 42308

Public Affairs Department FAX 614/555-0167

No. of pages (including this page) 1

To: Sam Davis

Company: SIU 618-555-0190

From: Ted Bortz 614/555-0165

If copy is unreadable, call ________ 614/555-____

MESSAGE

Finally able to put my hands on all 3 slides you asked to use.

You should have them very soon.

FIGURE 15–6 Messages on FAX forms are often handwritten.

- Petty cash form
- Sales call report
- Purchase order
- Quotation form
- Job work order
- Stock requisition
- Packing list
- Receiving form

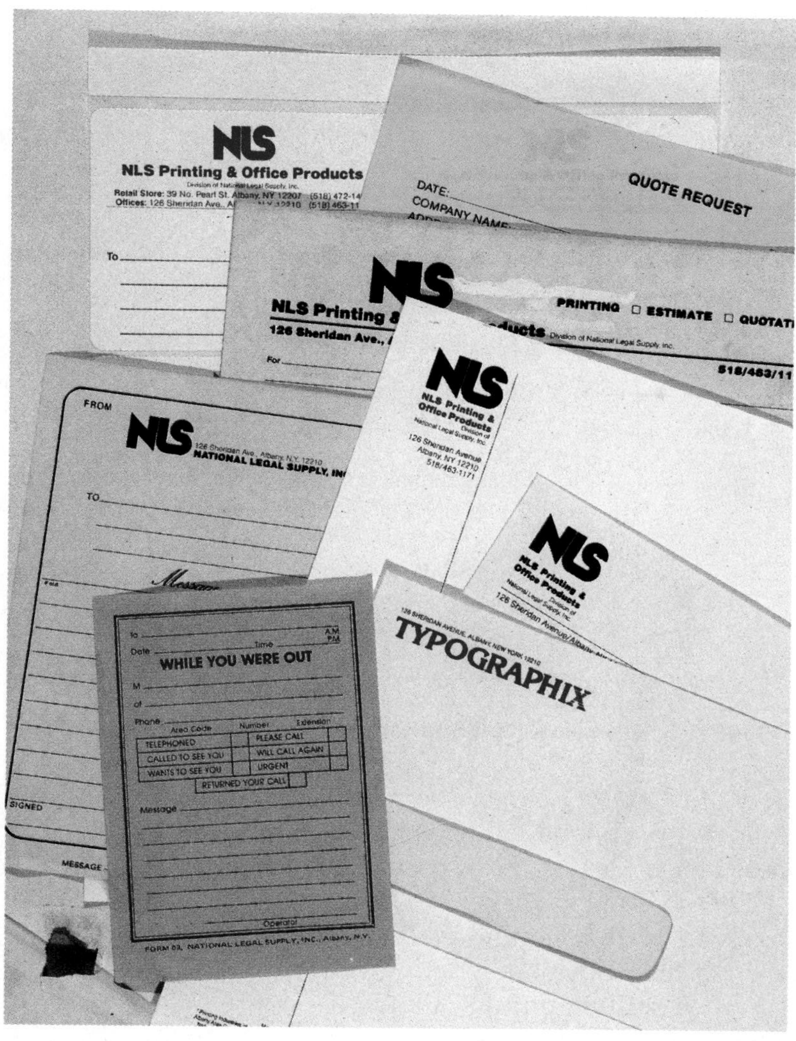

FIGURE 15–7 **Businesses use a variety of preprinted forms.**
Courtesy of NLS Printing and Office Products, Albany, NY.

- Production form
- Invoice

Notes and business forms are usually simple to complete. However, they need to be readable and accurate. For a message to be readable, write (or type) it neatly. Spell words correctly. If you aren't sure about the spelling of a word, check a dictionary. Finally, always check over written messages for possible errors before transmitting them.

Memorandums

Within companies, memorandums are the main form of written communication. Memorandums are also called "memos." Memos carry messages upward, downward, and across departmental lines. For instance, a stockclerk may write a memo to a boss. The boss may respond with a memo to the department. Or the boss may send a memo to someone in another department.

Most memos deal with daily business matters. They are usually brief. Their tone tends to be rather informal. Memos are used to communicate four types of information:

1. Instructions or explanations
2. Announcements and reports
3. Requests for information, action, or reaction
4. Answers to requests

A typical memo with its major parts labeled is shown in Figure 15–8. What type(s) of information does this memo communicate?

Little introductory information is necessary in a memo. But the first paragraph is often used to explain the purpose of the memo. A memo is usually limited to one main topic. Headings, underlining, or capitalization of words can be used to call attention to key points.

Business Letters

Why are business letters so common when it is so easy to place phone calls? Phone calls aren't permanent records. Business letters

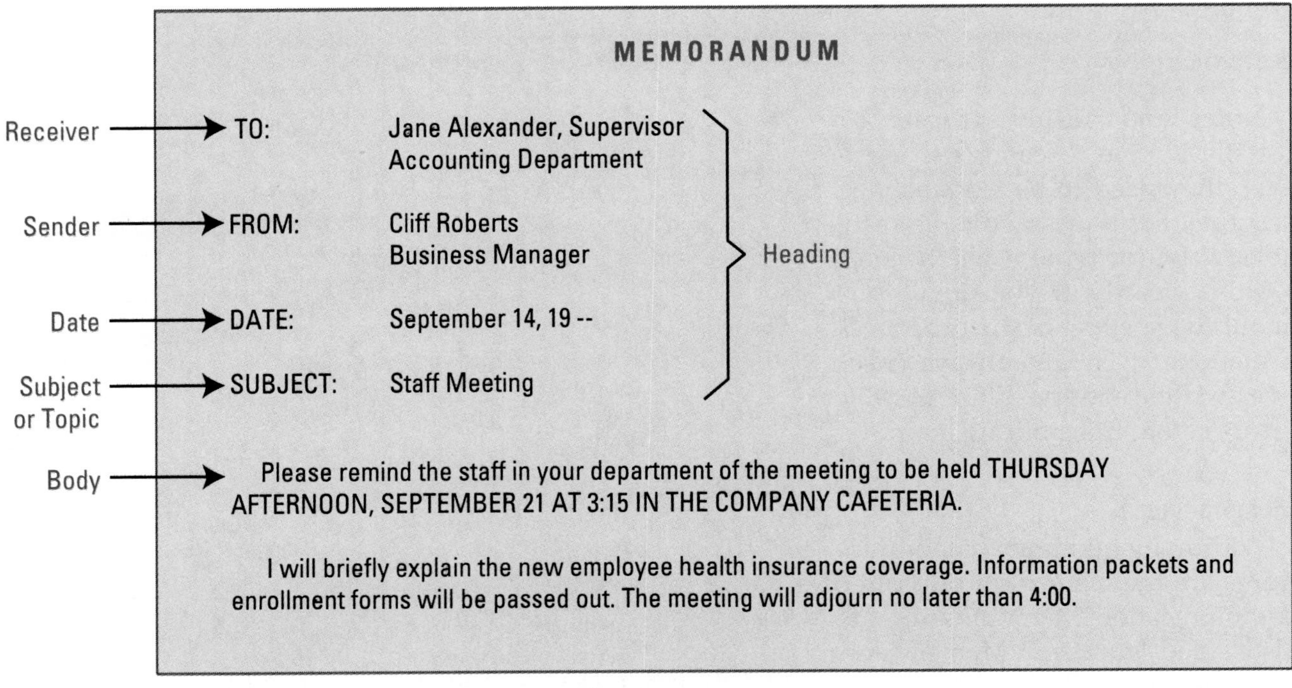

MEMORANDUM
Receiver
TO: Jane Alexander, Supervisor
Accounting Department
Sender
FROM: Cliff Roberts
Business Manager
Date
DATE: September 14, 19 --
Subject or Topic
SUBJECT: Staff Meeting
Heading
Body
Please remind the staff in your department of the meeting to be held THURSDAY AFTERNOON, SEPTEMBER 21 AT 3:15 IN THE COMPANY CAFETERIA.
I will briefly explain the new employee health insurance coverage. Information packets and enrollment forms will be passed out. The meeting will adjourn no later than 4:00.

FIGURE 15–8 The main parts of a typical interoffice memo.

are. In many cases, someone follows up a phone call with a business letter.

The average worker is more likely to write notes and memos on the job than business letters. Even so, it is still important to know how to write a good business letter. You saw in earlier chapters, for example, several cases where people wrote business letters during a job search. A good business letter should:

- Communicate a clear message.
- Convey a professional, businesslike tone.
- Be well organized.
- Use correct grammar, spelling, and punctuation.
- Have an attractive appearance.

WHAT WOULD YOU DO?

You come home from school grumbling about the grade you received on a written assignment. The teacher always marks off for misspelled words regardless of how good the paper is otherwise. You tell your sister Amy that you do not think it is fair.

"If I were you, I would not worry about it," says Amy. "You do not have to be concerned about spelling when you get out of school. At work, we use word processing software that automatically identifies and then corrects any spelling errors."

What would you do?

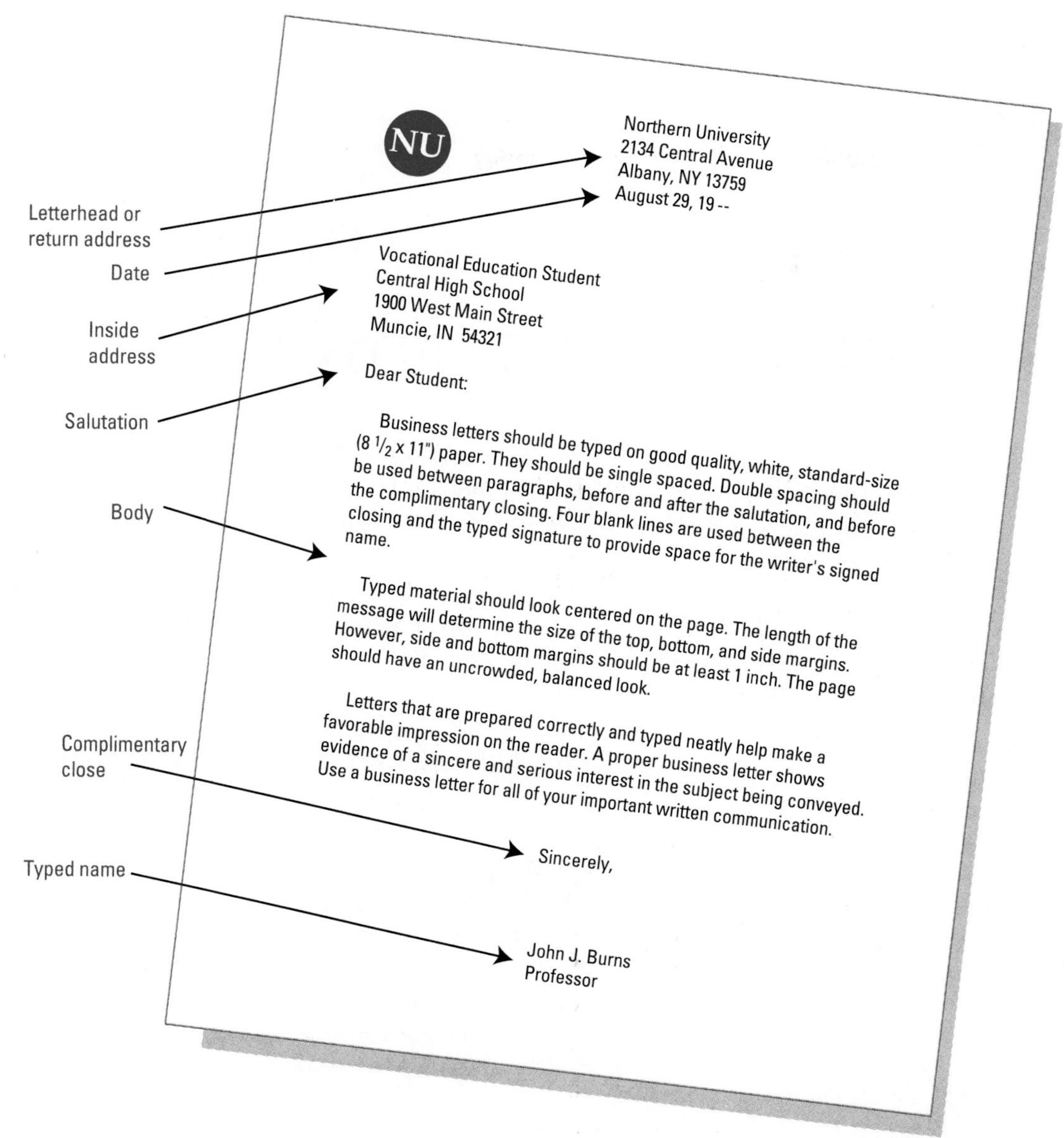

FIGURE 15–9 The main parts of a business letter.

A sample letter with its major parts labeled is shown in Figure 15–9. The letter uses what is called a "modified block style." Most parts of the letter begin at the left margin except for the return address, date, complimentary close, and signature line, which begin at the center of the page. In a "block style" letter, all lines (except a printed letterhead) begin at the left margin.

When writing a business letter, make a draft copy first. Then, rewrite the letter as necessary. Before sending it, read the letter carefully for errors. As a final step, make a copy for your records. If you are using a word processor, save the letter on disk.

The Workplace

ELIMINATING GOBBLEDYGOOK

The term *gobbledygook* was coined years ago by a Texas congressman. He had been reading government reports mixed with bloated, empty words. Gobbledygook, then, refers to "wordy, vague, unclear language." This language disorder (also called "double-speak") is found in education, government, science, and all other fields. Here are some examples:

- *Articulate*—talking to one another.
- *Vertical insertion*—invasion by paratroopers.
- *Social-expression product*—greeting card.
- *Protein spill*—to vomit.
- *Guest-relations facility*—restroom.
- *Atmospheric deposition of anthropogenically derived acidic substances*—acid rain.

Gobbledygook seems to be used for several reasons. Sometimes, people want to make common things seem more important. So an elevator operator becomes a *vertical-transportation-corps member.* A toothpick becomes a *wood interdental stimulator.*

Jargon is sometimes used to discourage or hide the truth. In one medical report, a *therapeutic misadventure* was used to refer to an operation that killed the patient. An airline's report referred to a plane crash as the *involuntary conversion of a 727.*

Gobbledygook should never be used. It lowers the value of language. It makes words and ideas more difficult to understand. Clear, simple speaking and writing are always the best approach. Word pollution, like other forms of pollution, needs to be cleaned up.

WORLD'S LARGEST PRE-OWNED SHOWROOM
THOMPSONVILLE
Main St. and Lincoln Ave.
555-0160
Call Toll Free:
1-800-555-0182

Why did this auto dealer use the word "pre-owned" instead of "used" when describing the cars the dealership sold? Can you provide other examples of vague, unclear, or misleading language?

CHAPTER 15 REVIEW

CHAPTER IN BRIEF

- In addition to occupational and employability skills, basic academic skills are required for job success.
- Communication links the working world. Listening may be its weakest link. Common causes of poor listening include distractions, prejudging and overstimulation, and partial listening.
- Effective speaking requires correct pronunciation, clear enunciation, use of standard English, and good grammar. An important application of effective speech is use of the telephone.
- Reading requires recognizing words before you can understand their meaning. Therefore, effective readers need a large vocabulary. Because reading is a skill, it can be improved through practice.
- Writing is probably the most important form of business communication. It is good business to keep records of what goes on. Internal communication within a company takes the form of notes, business forms, and memorandums. External communication between organizations mainly takes the form of business letters.

WORDS TO KNOW

communication
enunciation
grammar
pronunciation
standard English
vocabulary

QUESTIONS TO ANSWER

1. What three types of skills are needed to be successful on the job?
2. Which type of communication skill is used most by the average worker? Which type is used least?
3. Name and provide an example of each of the four common causes of poor listening.
4. When listening, what does it mean to have a "questioning attitude"?
5. What are the four things required to be an effective speaker?
6. In what ways are listening and reading the same?
7. List two ways to improve reading skills.
8. Why is writing the most important form of business communication?
9. Memos are used to communicate four types of information. Name them.
10. What four steps should be followed in writing a business letter?

ACTIVITIES TO DO

1. Throughout your school years, you have probably taken several achievement tests. Make an appointment with the school counselor to review your performance regarding language and communication skills. If you have done average or better on such tests, you probably have the basic communication skills for most entry-level jobs. If your skills are below average, ask the counselor for suggestions on how to improve your skills.
2. Keep a list for one day of slang words and phrases that you hear classmates and other people using. The next day, share the list with the class. Discuss what words and phrases of standard English could be substituted for them.
3. Assume that you are in charge of organizing the annual company picnic. Write a pretend memo to company employees. The memo should provide all important details about the picnic. Hand the memo in to your teacher for evaluation.
4. List several of your hobbies or recreational interests. Go to the library and find out what books are available on these subjects. Choose a book and read it. Make a short oral report to the class about the book you read.
5. For some individuals, giving a presentation to co-workers or a speech to a community group is part of their job. Effective public speaking depends on: (a) knowing the subject, and (b) preparing the presentation. Give a 5-minute speech to the class concerning some aspect of your job that you know well. Follow these guidelines:
   a. Select a subject that you can explain well in 5 minutes.
   b. Outline the main points to be covered. Write them down on note cards.
   c. Practice the speech beforehand so that it will not be too short or too long.
   d. Give the speech with confidence and enthusiasm.

   Afterward, discuss the strengths and weaknesses of each speech.

TOPICS TO DISCUSS

1. Computers, robots, and other forms of technology are changing many types of occupations and businesses. How is business communication changing as a result of new technology?
2. There are geographic differences in the way people use language. You may have lived or traveled in areas different from where you now live. Discuss some of the interesting and colorful words and phrases that people use in different parts of the country.
3. An *acronym* is a word formed from the first letter of consecutive words. An example is ASAP (as soon as possible). Identify and discuss some of the acronyms that are used in personal and business communication.

CHAPTER 16 Math and Measurement Skills

OUTLINE

- Basic Math
- Basic Measurement
- Systems of Measure
- Chapter Review

OBJECTIVES

After reading this chapter, you should be able to:

- Identify occupations requiring math and measurement skills.
- Apply math skills to computation of total purchase amount, trade discount, cash discount, markup, sales tax, and markdown.
- Calculate surface measures and volume measures.
- Convert measures from one unit to another.

Like communication skills, math is also important on the job. Some occupations use more math than others. A carpenter, for instance, uses math more than an aerobics instructor.

Math is taught from early grade school through high school. We assume here that you have already learned basic math and measurement skills. This material does not seek to introduce new math content. Rather, it shows how basic math and measurement skills are used in the workplace.

BASIC MATH

The following examples show some common uses of arithmetic. Sometimes this is called "business math." The next part of the chapter deals with basic measurement. This is sometimes called "vocational math" or "shop math." In later chapters of the book, you will apply math skills again. You will figure interest and taxes, do comparison shopping, and other so-called "consumer math."

Total Purchase Amount

Most of your purchases involve single items. For instance, you buy a pair of running shoes for \$44.95. The total amount of your purchase is easy to figure: $1 \times \$44.95 = \$44.95$. In most states, you must add sales tax, too.

Businesses, however, often buy large numbers of the same item. A sporting goods store, for example, might buy dozens of pairs of running shoes. To find the total amount of the purchase, multiply the number of items by the price of one item (unit price).

FIGURE 16–1A **Bank tellers and company accountants use math to calculate the balance of bank accounts.**
Photo by Alan Brown/Photonics.

FIGURE 16–1B **Architects and carpenters use math to find out how much and what size lumber they need to build a house.**
Photo by Ted Cronet and Courtesy of Ford Motor Company.

PROBLEM: Figure the total amount of a purchase of 24 pairs of shoes at $32.95 each, 15 pairs of socks at $1.49 each, and 3 dozen shoelaces at $.79 each.

SOLUTION: Quantity × Unit Price = Amount

Shoes:	24 × $32.95 =	$790.80
Socks:	15 × $ 1.49 =	22.35
Laces:	36 × $ 0.79 =	28.44
Total Amount		$841.59

This skill is important for people who prepare invoices. An *invoice* is a bill for goods. Look at Figure 16–2.

Trade Discount

A *trade discount* is a deduction from the catalog (list) price of an item. Trade discounts are usually given to retailers to enable them to sell merchandise at a greater profit. In some cases, buyers get special discounts when ordering large numbers of something. The trade discount is a percentage of the list price.

PROBLEM: An office desk is listed in a catalog at $680. Business customers can buy the desk at a trade discount of 30%. How much will a business have to pay

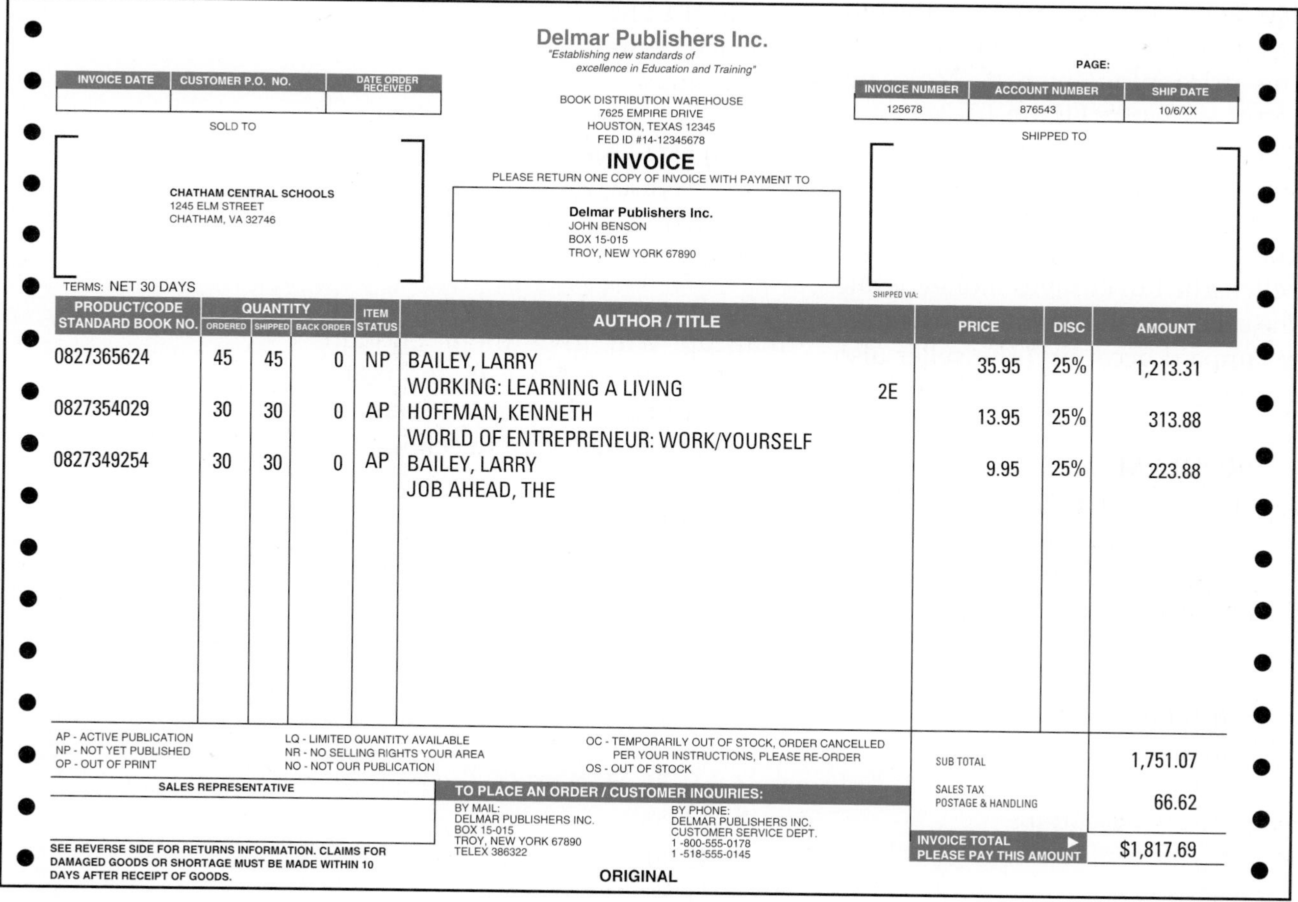

Delmar Publishers Inc.
"Establishing new standards of excellence in Education and Training"

PAGE:

INVOICE DATE | CUSTOMER P.O. NO. | DATE ORDER RECEIVED

BOOK DISTRIBUTION WAREHOUSE
7625 EMPIRE DRIVE
HOUSTON, TEXAS 12345
FED ID #14-12345678

INVOICE NUMBER: 125678 | ACCOUNT NUMBER: 876543 | SHIP DATE: 10/6/XX

SOLD TO
CHATHAM CENTRAL SCHOOLS
1245 ELM STREET
CHATHAM, VA 32746

INVOICE
PLEASE RETURN ONE COPY OF INVOICE WITH PAYMENT TO
Delmar Publishers Inc.
JOHN BENSON
BOX 15-015
TROY, NEW YORK 67890

SHIPPED TO

TERMS: NET 30 DAYS

SHIPPED VIA:

PRODUCT/CODE STANDARD BOOK NO.	QUANTITY ORDERED	QUANTITY SHIPPED	QUANTITY BACK ORDER	ITEM STATUS	AUTHOR / TITLE		PRICE	DISC	AMOUNT
0827365624	45	45	0	NP	BAILEY, LARRY WORKING: LEARNING A LIVING	2E	35.95	25%	1,213.31
0827354029	30	30	0	AP	HOFFMAN, KENNETH WORLD OF ENTREPRENEUR: WORK/YOURSELF		13.95	25%	313.88
0827349254	30	30	0	AP	BAILEY, LARRY JOB AHEAD, THE		9.95	25%	223.88

AP - ACTIVE PUBLICATION
NP - NOT YET PUBLISHED
OP - OUT OF PRINT
LQ - LIMITED QUANTITY AVAILABLE
NR - NO SELLING RIGHTS YOUR AREA
NO - NOT OUR PUBLICATION
OC - TEMPORARILY OUT OF STOCK, ORDER CANCELLED PER YOUR INSTRUCTIONS, PLEASE RE-ORDER
OS - OUT OF STOCK

SUB TOTAL: 1,751.07
SALES TAX / POSTAGE & HANDLING: 66.62
INVOICE TOTAL ▶ PLEASE PAY THIS AMOUNT: $1,817.69

SALES REPRESENTATIVE

TO PLACE AN ORDER / CUSTOMER INQUIRIES:
BY MAIL: DELMAR PUBLISHERS INC. BOX 15-015 TROY, NEW YORK 67890 TELEX 386322
BY PHONE: DELMAR PUBLISHERS INC. CUSTOMER SERVICE DEPT. 1-800-555-0178 1-518-555-0145

SEE REVERSE SIDE FOR RETURNS INFORMATION. CLAIMS FOR DAMAGED GOODS OR SHORTAGE MUST BE MADE WITHIN 10 DAYS AFTER RECEIPT OF GOODS.

ORIGINAL

FIGURE 16–2 A common use of math in business is to fill out invoices.

for the desk? (What the business pays is the net purchase price.)

SOLUTION: 30% = 0.30
$ 680.00
× 0.30
$ 204.00 Discount

$ 680.00
− 204.00
$ 476.00 Net purchase price

Cash Discount

Every sale between a business buyer and seller involves *terms.* The terms state the time limit within which the buyer must pay. A common term of sale is "net due in 30 days." This means that the buyer has 30 days in which to pay the bill. After 30 days, the buyer must pay the price plus interest. Note the terms shown in Figure 16–2.

To encourage prompt payment, the seller may offer a *cash discount* of several percent (say 3%). A cash discount benefits both the buyer and seller. The buyer saves money, while the seller has the payment instead of an unpaid account. (The seller also has business expenses to pay.)

PROBLEM: An invoice for $510 has terms of net due in 30 days with a 3% discount given for payment within 10 days. What is the amount of payment if made promptly?

SOLUTION: 3% = 0.03
$ 510.00
× 0.03
$ 15.30 Discount

$ 510.00
− 15.30
$ 494.70 Net amount of payment

Markup

A retailer buys goods from a supplier to resell. Remember the running shoes? The price the store paid is called the cost price. To make money, the retailer then added an amount (*markup*) to the cost price. (Selling price = cost price + markup.)

PROBLEM: An item costs $28.00; its selling price is $35.00. How much is the markup?

SOLUTION:
$ 35.00 Selling price
− 28.00 Cost price
$ 7.00 Markup

PROBLEM: Based on the cost price, what is the percent of markup?

SOLUTION:

$$\frac{\$\ 7.00 \text{ Markup}}{\$\ 28.00 \text{ Cost price}} = 0.25 \text{ or } 25\%$$

Businesses know how much markup will give them enough money to cover expenses and make a fair profit, so they add markup to the item before trying to sell it.

PROBLEM: A radio costs $42.00 and will be sold at a markup of 30% of the cost price. What is the selling price?

SOLUTION:
$ 42.00 Cost price
× 0.30 Markup
$ 12.60

$ 42.00 Cost price
+ 12.60 Markup
$ 54.60 Selling price

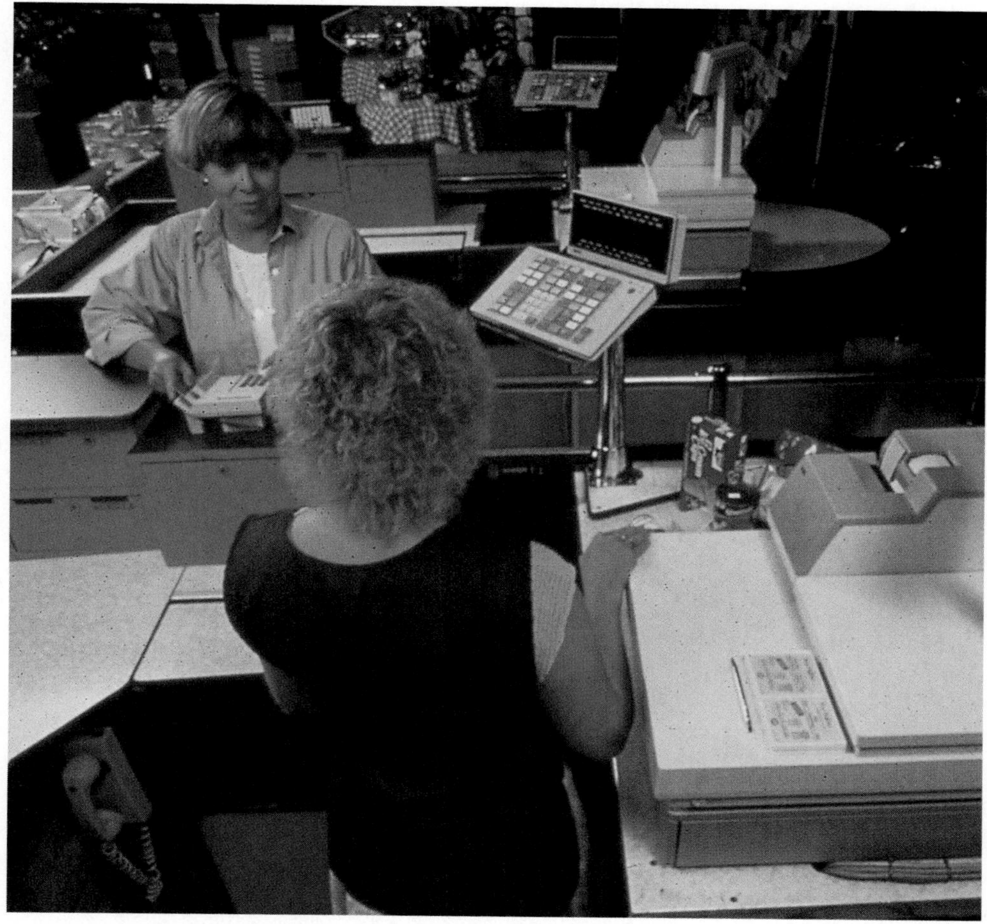

FIGURE 16–3 **Most cash registers compute sales tax automatically.**
Courtesy of NCR Corporation.

Sales Tax

Most states and cities have sales tax on goods and services. Sales taxes usually range between one and seven percent. The sales tax is added on to the purchase price of goods and services. Why is no sales tax shown on the invoice in Figure 16–2?

PROBLEM: Someone buys a sweater for $28.00 and a pair of slacks for $36.00. A 5% sales tax is added to the purchase price. What is the total amount of the purchase?

SOLUTION:

$ 28.00	
+ 36.00	
$ 64.00	Purchase price
+ 3.20	($64.00 × 0.05) Sales tax
$ 67.20	Total amount

Markdown

Most retail stores have periodic sales to move slow-selling merchandise, clear out end-of-season goods, or attract customers to the store. A reduction in the selling price of a product is called a *markdown.* The markdown is usually expressed as a percent.

? ? ? ? ? ? ? ? ? ? ? ? ? ?

WHAT WOULD YOU DO?

In observing your boss, you are surprised at the amount of math that she uses. She seems to constantly be analyzing sales data and entering numbers into a calculator. You would like to be able to move up in the company, or perhaps own a small store of your own someday. However, math has always been your weakest subject. You wonder whether you would be able to perform the math part of the business.

What would you do?

PROBLEM: A merchant is having a sale on all summer swimwear at 40% off (markdown). What is the sale price of a swimsuit that was originally priced at $45.00?

SOLUTION:

$	45.00	Original price
×	0.40	Markdown
$	18.00	
$	45.00	Original price
−	18.00	Markdown
$	27.00	Sale price

BASIC MEASUREMENT F3

Measurement is the act of determining the dimension, quantity, or degree of something. The object can be volume, area, distance, degrees, time, energy, or weight. Measurement answers the question "how much." It does so in a uniform and standardized way. This means, for example, that all inches are the same length. Many workers need to use measurement on their jobs. Such occupations include nurses, dental technicians, carpenters, drafters, machinists, and sheet metal workers. How much measurement is done on your job?

Surface Measurement

Being able to calculate the surface measures of areas and perimeters is necessary on many jobs. Construction workers, for example, must figure perimeter and area measures in order to know how much concrete, lumber, and other materials to order. Workers in the printing industry must figure perimeters and areas to cut specific sizes of paper stock.

A *perimeter* of an object is the distance around it. It is measured in any standard linear unit, including miles, feet, inches, kilometers, meters, centimeters, or millimeters. You find it by adding together the lengths of the outer edges of the figure for most shapes. For circles and some irregular figures, you will need to use simple formulas.

The rectangle is a four-sided object having a right angle (90°) at each corner. The page you are reading is a rectangle, most walls and floors are rectangles, even a square is a rectangle, Figure 16–5.

Rectangles have two pairs of sides. Each pair is equal in length. To find the perimeter, you add together the lengths of all sides. Suppose you are building a fence to enclose a dog kennel. Using measurements shown in Figure 16–5, you add the length of

FIGURE 16–4 **This carpet layer has to make accurate measurements.**
Courtesy C. H. Masland and Sons Carpet Company.

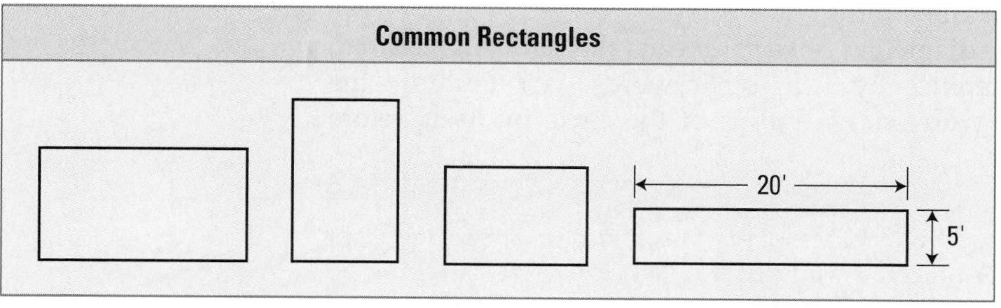

FIGURE 16–5 **The rectangle is a familiar geometric shape.**

the two 20-foot sides together with the length of the two 5-foot sides to find that the perimeter is 50. Thus, you need 50 feet of fencing to build the kennel. If all sides were of equal length, you could have found the perimeter by multiplying the length of one side by four.

The perimeter of a circle is called the *circumference.* To find the circumference, you must know the diameter or the radius of a circle. A circle with a radius of 8 inches and a diameter of 16 inches is shown in Figure 16–6. To find the circumference, you must use a formula.

The formula is:
Circumference
(C) = 3.14 × Diameter (*D*)
(*Note: The 3.14 does not change.*)

Let's say that you are going to form and install an exhaust duct in a woodworking shop. Using the dimensions shown in Figure 16–6, how wide of a piece of sheet metal will you need to roll it into a 16-inch diameter cylinder?

Step 1: Set up the formula:
$C = 3.14 \times D$
Step 2: Place values into the formula and multiply:
$C = 3.14 \times 16$ inches
$C = 50.24$ inches

You will need a piece of sheet metal 50.24 inches wide plus a little extra for the seam.

The same process in reverse will help you to determine the diameter or radius of a circle, if you know the circumference. To find the diameter, you divide the circumference by 3.14. For example, a circle with a circumference of 35 feet has a diameter of 11.15 feet ($D = 35 \div 3.14$).

An *area* is the number of square units of space on the surface of the figure enclosed by the perimeter. Area calculation uses several simple formulas, each of which is suited to a certain geometric shape. Areas are given in units of square measure such as square feet, square inches, or square meters.

For rectangles, the formula for determining area is:

Area = length × width or $A = l \times w$

For example, the area of a rectangular room that is 8-feet long and 12-feet wide is 96 square feet (8 × 12 = 96). If the room were square with each side being 12 feet, then the area would be 144 square feet (12 × 12 = 144).

To find the area of a circle, you again use a formula that contains the constant, 3.14, as well as the value of the radius. The formula is written as:

Area (A) = $3.14 \times r^2$

The r^2 means the radius is squared. In other words, you multiply the radius of the circle by itself before

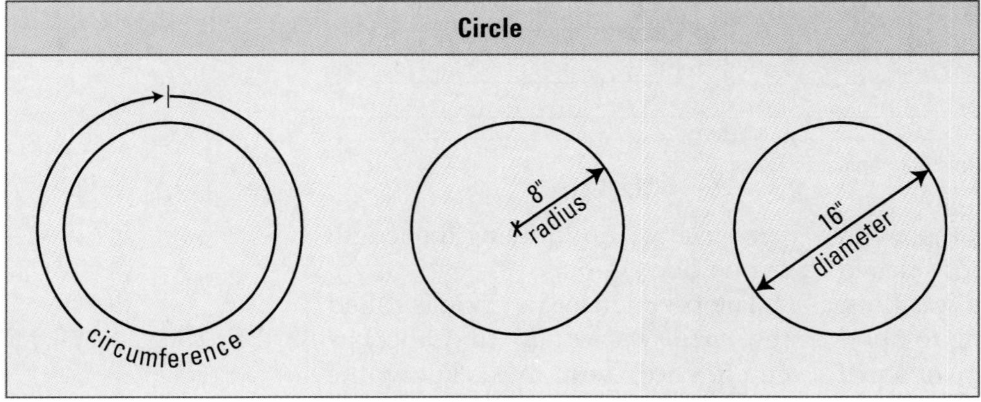

FIGURE 16–6 **The main dimensions of a circle are circumference, radius, and diameter.**

? ? ? ? ? ? ? ? ? ? ? ? ? ?

WHAT WOULD YOU DO?

You have just finished preparing the site for pouring a concrete patio. You overhear the boss saying that the job will probably require about 10 yards of concrete. That does not sound right to you. So you make a quick calculation. You come up with 12 yards. You want to tell the boss he is wrong, but you are not sure how he will react.

What would you do?

multiplying it by 3.14. The symbol for squaring is a 2, that is placed slightly above and following the number to be squared. For example, the radius of 4 squared (r^2) is 4×4 or 16.

Suppose you are going to pour a round concrete pad for a storage tank. To figure how much concrete is needed, you first must figure the area. The radius of the pad is 8 feet. You would work the problem in the following steps:

Step 1: Set up the equation.
$A = 3.14 \times r^2$
Step 2: Place values into the formula and multiply:
$A = 3.14 \times 8^2$
$A = 3.14 \times 64$
$A = 200.96$ square feet

Volume Measurement

Like perimeters and areas, volume measures are often used on the job. Volume is the amount of space an object takes up. It can be expressed in units of cubic measures such as cubic inches, cubic yards, and cubic feet. It can also be given in units such as gallons, quarts, ounces, and bushels.

To figure the volume of a figure that contains all right angles, such as a rectangle or square, the formula is:

Volume = length × width × height
or $V = l \times w \times h$

So, for example, to find the volume of a rectangular box that is 4-feet long, 2-feet wide, and 1-foot high, you multiply $4 \times 2 \times 1$, which equals 8 cubic feet.

If the dimensions are in different units, they have to be converted to the same unit of measurement before multiplying. Let's say that you are going to lay a 6-inch gravel base in a ditch before installing a sewer pipe. The ditch is 30-inches wide and 150-feet long.

Step 1: Set up the equation:
$V = l \times w \times h$
Step 2: Place values into the formula:
$V = 150$ feet × 30 inches × 6 inches
Step 3: Convert all measures to the same units. In this case use feet.
$V = 150$ feet × 2.5 feet × 0.5 foot
Step 4: Multiply:
$V = 187.5$ cubic feet

You would need 187.5 cubic feet of gravel. However, since gravel is usually sold by the cubic yard, you need to divide 187.5 by 9 (one cubic yard contains 9 cubic feet). How many yards of gravel would you need?

SYSTEMS OF MEASURE

To be effective on the job, you should be able to work with the basic units of measure in the conventional (or English) and metric systems. You should be familiar with procedures for converting measures from one unit to another

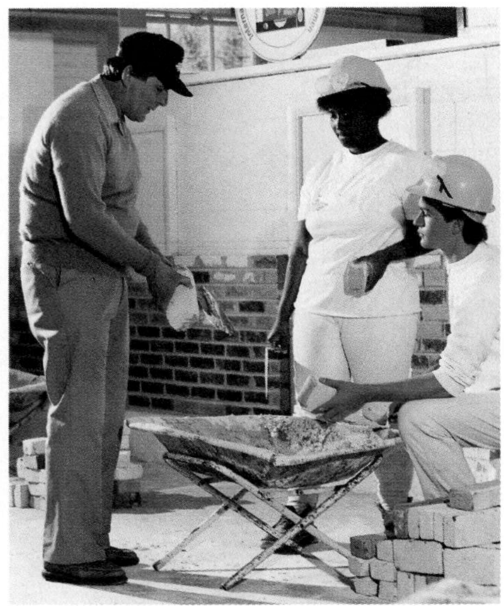

FIGURE 16–7 **Concrete, sand, gravel, and other materials used in construction are sold by the cubic yard.**
Courtesy of General Electric; photo by Mark Homan Studios.

within the same system. You also need to be able to convert measures from the conventional system to the metric system and vice versa.

You are probably most familiar with the conventional system of measure. It is the one used most often in the United States. Conventional units of measure and their relationship to each other are shown in Figure 16–8.

Within the same unit or type of conventional measure, conversion to equivalent measures usually involves division or multiplication. For example, to find the number of cubic feet required to hold 20 gallons of water, you would divide the 20 gallons by the conversion equivalent of 7.5 gallons per cubic foot:

$$20 \div 7.5 = 3.67 \text{ cubic feet.}$$

To find the number of square feet in 20 square yards, you would multiply 20 yards by the 9 square feet per yard:

$$20 \times 9 = 180 \text{ square feet.}$$

Most of the world, except for the United States, uses the metric system of measure. However, Congress passed a trade bill in 1988 that required all federal agencies to convert to the metric system by 1992.

Linear Units
1 foot = 12 inches
1 yard = 3 feet or 36 inches
1 mile = 5,280 feet or 1,760 yards

Weight Units
1 pound = 16 ounces
2,000 pounds = 1 ton
1 pint = 1 pound

Area Units
1 square foot = 144 square inches
1 square yard = 9 square feet
1 square mile = 3,097,600 square yards

Time Units
1 minute = 60 seconds
1 hour = 60 minutes
1 day = 24 hours

Volume Units
1 gallon = 231 cubic inches
1 cubic foot = 7 1/2 gallons
1 cubic foot (water) = 62 1/2 pounds
1 gallon (water) = 8 1/3 pounds
1 bushel (struck) = 2,150.5 cubic inches
1 bushel (heaped) = 2,747.7 cubic inches
1 cubic foot = 1,728 cubic inches
1 cubic yard = 27 cubic feet

FIGURE 16–8 **These are conventional units of measure.**

This means, for example, that if the Justice Department wants to buy paper, it must be measured in centimeters, not inches. If the Department of Defense wants to buy gasoline, it must do so in liters, not gallons.

This law will not force private companies to convert to the metric system. It seems likely, however, that it will encourage them to do so. Currently, some occupations and industries use the metric system a lot. The fields of medicine, engineering, and science are examples. Metric system units of measure are shown in Figure 16–9.

Conversions between and across units of measure in the metric system are in whole numbers and are divisible by 10. This is a major advantage over the conventional system of measure. For example, each centimeter is simply 10 millimeters and 20 cubic centimeters is equal to 20 milliliters. To find how many meters there are in 86.2 kilometers, you only have to multiply by 1,000:

86.2 kilometers × 1,000 = 86,200 meters.

There are times on the job when you will work with both conventional and metric units of measure. It often becomes necessary to convert measurements from one system to another. To do so, you can use the conversion chart shown in Figure 16–10.

Let's say that you want to express 30 square feet in terms of square meters. Since 1 square foot is about 0.09 square meter, you must multiply the number of square feet by 0.09:

$$30 \text{ ft}^2 \times 0.09 = 2.70 \text{ m}^2$$

The conversion chart is very useful to make quick and easy conversions from metric to conventional and from conventional to metric. However, keep in mind that the converted values will be only *approximate.* If greater accuracy is needed you should consult a table that has the conversion values listed to three decimal points.

Linear Units

1 millimeter (mm) = 0.001 meter
1 centimeter (cm) = 0.01 meter
1 decimeter = 0.1 meter
1 meter = 10 decimeters, 100 centimeters, 1,000 millimeters
1 kilometer = 1,000 meters

Weight Units

1 milligram = 0.001 gram
1 centigram = 0.01 gram
1 decigram = 0.10 gram
1 gram = 1,000 milligrams, 100 centigrams, 10 decigrams
1 kilogram = 1,000 grams

Area Units

1 square centimeter = 100 square millimeters
1 square meter = 10,000 square centimeters
1 square kilometer = 1,000,000 square meters

Volume Units

1 milliliter = 1 cubic centimeter
1 milliliter = 0.001 liter
1 centiliter = 0.01 liter
1 deciliter = 0.10 liter
1 liter = 1,000 milliliters, 100 centiliters, 10 deciliters
1 kiloliter = 1,000 liters

FIGURE 16–9 These are metric units of measure.

FROM METRIC TO CONVENTIONAL

Symbol	When You Know	Multiply by	To Find	Symbol
		LENGTH		
mm	millimeters	0.04	inches	in
cm	centimeters	0.4	inches	in
m	meters	3.3	feet	ft
m	meters	1.1	yards	yd
km	kilometers	0.6	miles	mi
		AREA		
cm^2	square centimeters	0.16	square inches	in^2
m^2	square meters	1.2	square yards	yd^2
km^2	square kilometers	0.4	square miles	mi^2
ha	hectares (10,000 m^2)	2.5	acres	
		MASS (weight)		
g	grams	0.035	ounces	oz
kg	kilograms	2.2	pounds	lb
t	tonnes (1,000 kg)	1.1	short tons	
		VOLUME		
ml	milliliters	0.03	fluid ounces	fl oz
l	liters	2.1	pints	pt
l	liters	1.06	quarts	qt
l	liters	0.26	gallons	gal
m^3	cubic meters	35	cubic feet	ft^3
m^3	cubic meters	1.3	cubic yards	yd^3
		TEMPERATURE (exact)		
°C	Celsius temperature	9/5 (then add 32)	Fahrenheit temperature	°F

FROM CONVENTIONAL TO METRIC

Symbol	When You Know	Multiply by	To Find	Symbol
in	inches	2.5	centimeters	cm
ft	feet	30	centimeters	cm
yd	yards	0.9	meters	m
mi	miles	1.6	kilometers	km
		AREA		
in^2	square inches	6.5	square centimeters	cm^2
ft^2	square feet	0.09	square meters	m^2
yd^2	square yards	0.8	square meters	m^2
mi^2	square miles	2.6	square kilometers	km^2
	acres	0.4	hectares	ha
		MASS (weight)		
oz	ounces	28	grams	g
lb	pounds	0.45	kilograms	kg
	short tons (2,000 lb)	0.9	tonnes	t
		VOLUME		
tsp	teaspoons	5	milliliters	ml
Tbsp	tablespoons	15	millititers	ml
fl oz	fluid ounces	30	milliliters	ml
c	cups	0.24	liters	l
pt	pints	0.47	liters	l
qt	quarts	0.95	liters	l
gal	gallons	3.8	liters	l
ft^3	cubic feet	0.03	cubic meters	m^3
yd^2	cubic yards	0.76	cubic meters	m^2
		TEMPERATURE (exact)		
°F	Fahrenheit temperature	5/9 (after subtracting 32)	Celsius temperature	°C

FIGURE 16–10 **These are approximate conversion charts.**

Calculator Review

The calculator is an essential tool in the workplace. Let's review its operation.

A calculator has number buttons and command buttons. The arrangement of the buttons will vary among different models.

Push [CE] if you make a mistake in your last entry.

Push [C] if you make a mistake and want to redo the problem.

Turn on the calculator. To add 34 and 57, push [3][4][+][5][7][=]. The answer appears on the screen: [91.].

Subtraction (64 – 8 =), multiplication (27 × 6 =), and division (135 ÷ 7 =) are done in a similar manner. Simply enter the first number in the calculation; press either [×], or [÷]; enter the second number; and press [=].

The calculator has no commas and no dollar signs. To add $3,618 and $4,192, push [3][6][1][8][+][4][1][9][2][=]. The screen shows: [7810.]. Write in the dollar sign and comma: $7,810.

Many calculators have these additional buttons.

[MR] button reads or displays the memory number.

[MC] button clears the memory number to zero.

[M+] button enters or adds to the memory number.

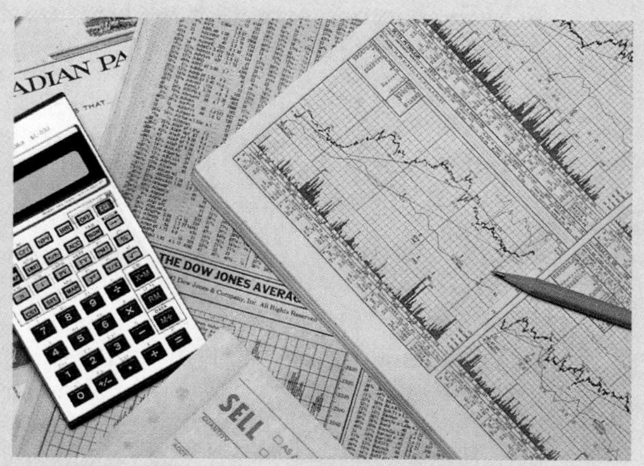

A calculator saves time and effort, but you still have to know math to use one.
© Uniphoto, Inc.

[M–] button subtracts from the memory number.

Placing a number in memory is useful for figuring sales tax, markup, and markdown. If you want to add a sales tax of 3.5%, push [3][.][5][M+]. To calculate the tax on $54.95, push [5][4][.][9][5][×][MR][%]. The answer is [1.92325], or $1.92.

If the tax increases from 3.5% to 4.0%, the actual increase is 0.5%. To increase the tax by that amount, push [.][5][M+].

To decrease the tax by 1.25%, push [1][.][2][5][M–].

Clear the memory when you have finished.

CHAPTER 16 REVIEW

CHAPTER IN BRIEF

- Basic math and measurement skills are used by many workers. One type of math skill is often called "business math." This involves being able to figure: (a) total purchase amount, (b) trade discount, (c) cash discount, (d) markup, (e) sales tax, and (f) markdown.
- Basic measurement skills are often called "shop math." This involves being able to perform surface measurement (perimeter and area) and volume measurement.
- Most countries, except for the U.S., use the metric system of measure. Even so, some occupational fields use the metric system a lot.
- You should be familiar with procedures for converting measures from one unit to another within the same system. You also need to be able to convert measures from the conventional system to the metric system and vice versa.

WORDS TO KNOW

area
cash discount
circumference
invoice
markdown
markup
measurement
perimeter
terms
trade discount

QUESTIONS TO ANSWER

1. Calculating such things as total purchase amount, trade discount, markup, and sales tax is often called "business math." Why is it called this?
2. How does a cash discount benefit a buyer? How does it benefit a seller?
3. A contractor is billed $1,850 for lumber with a cash discount of 5% offered for payment within 10 days. How much money would be saved by paying immediately?
4. What is the difference between the cost price and the selling price of a product?
5. What is the selling price of a dress that costs $60 and is marked up 40 percent? Later, the dress is put on sale at a markdown of 25%. What is the sale price of the dress?
6. Why are uniform and standardized measures necessary in business and industry?
7. How many 4 foot × 8 foot sheets of plywood are needed to cover a 16 foot × 32 foot roof?
8. How many cubic feet of storage space is contained in a warehouse that is 40 yards long and 15 yards wide and has 12-foot ceilings?

9. Name the two common systems of measure. Which system is used by most countries in the world?
10. The temperature is 78 degrees Fahrenheit. How many degrees Celsius is this?

ACTIVITIES TO DO

1. For your co-op or work experience job, list all the ways that you use math and measurement skills. Then, in class, compare your list with other students. What skills does the class find are the most common?
2. For the classroom in which you are meeting, perform the necessary measurements and calculations to answer the following questions.
   a. What is the perimeter of the classroom?
   b. How much area of floor space is contained within the classroom?
   c. How much area of wall space is taken up by window and door openings?
   d. How much volume is contained within the classroom?
   e. Identify a circular-shaped object in the classroom, such as a wastebasket. What is the circumference of it?
3. Identify as many occupations as possible that might make the types of calculations performed in Activity 2.
4. How many kilometers do you travel to work each day? What is the average distance for the entire class?
5. To find the average of a set of numbers, you can add them on a calculator and divide by the total number. For example:

   $$(140 + 145 + 146 + 149 + 144 + 146) \div 6 = 145$$

   The average is 145. Another way to find the average is to pick a "benchmark" number less than or equal to the smallest number. In the preceding example, 140 is the benchmark. Now, add the difference between each number and the benchmark. Then find the average of the difference.

   $$(0 + 5 + 6 + 9 + 4 + 6) \div 6 = 5$$

   The average difference is 5. Add this to the benchmark and you get 145. This shortcut can save you considerable time. Often, you can add the numbers in your head without using a calculator. Using benchmarks, find the averages of the following numbers:
   a. Prices of $200, $220, $210, $215, and $230.
   b. Lengths of 47 inches, 46 inches, 51 inches, 45 inches, 52 inches, 46 inches, and 49 inches.
   c. Temperatures of 80, 72, 75, 74, 73, 77, 81, and 76.

TOPICS TO DISCUSS

1. Calculators, computers, cash registers, and other machines automatically perform many math calculations on the job. This being the case, how important is it that you be able to perform math by hand?
2. Should the United States convert to the metric system? Discuss the advantages and disadvantages.

3. In "rough carpentry" work, measurements within 1/4 inch are considered "accurate." Other jobs, such as installing cabinets, require more accurate measurement. Discuss and give examples of how standards of accuracy in measurement vary among different occupations.
4. How much is the sales tax in your state? What types of goods and services does it cover?

CHAPTER 17 Safety Skills

OUTLINE

- Accidents
- Personal Safety
- Public Safety
- Chapter Review

OBJECTIVES

After reading this chapter, you should be able to:

- Describe the nature of accidents according to type and class.
- Discuss rules for personal safety in the home, at school, on the job, in recreation, and on the road.
- Explain what to do in a flood, tornado, hurricane, and earthquake.
- Name examples of government agencies and private organizations that promote public safety.
- State the three E's of safety.

Safety experts define an *accident* as an unplanned event often resulting in personal injury, property damage, or both. Accidents rank fourth behind heart disease, cancer, and stroke as a cause of death among the general public. For teenagers and young adults, however, accidents are the leading cause of death.

Even though accidents are unexpected, this does not mean that they occur by chance. Almost all accidents can be prevented by eliminating unsafe behavior and conditions and by following basic safety rules. In this chapter, you will learn more about accidents and what you can do to prevent them. Statistical data reported in this chapter is from *Accident Facts, 1993 Edition* by the National Safety Council.

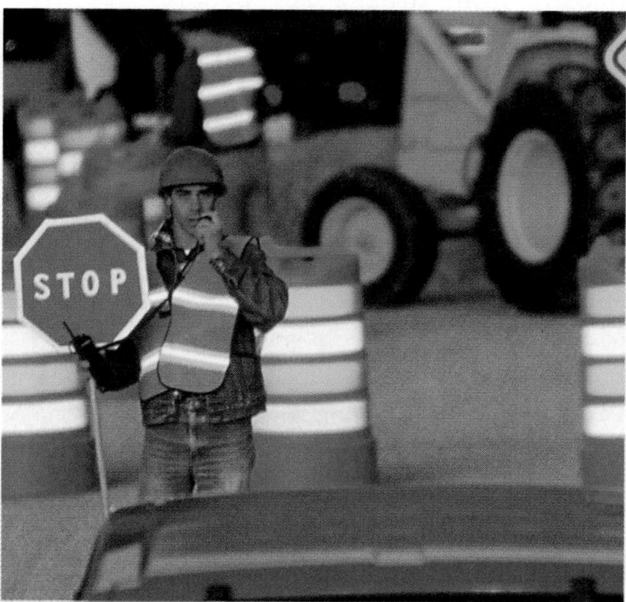

FIGURE 17–1 High-visibility colors, reflective surfaces, warning signs, and protective clothing play important roles in accident prevention.
Courtesy of 3M.

ACCIDENTS

In an average year, accidents kill nearly 83,000 Americans and injure about 17 million more. Accidents and injuries are estimated to cost the nation about $400 billion annually. There is no way to calculate the cost of human lives. Data on accidents are reported by type and class.

The *type* of accident refers to the cause of the accident. The leading causes of accidental death in the U.S. are shown in Figures 17–2 and 17–3. For people under 77, motor vehicles lead as a cause of accidental death. For young people between 15 and 24, about 80 percent of accidental deaths are caused by motor vehicles. Of these deaths, three-fourths are males.

The second-highest cause of accidental death overall is falls. But for persons age 18 to 46, it is poisoning (mostly from drugs). For people over 75, falls are the leading cause of accidental death, followed by motor vehicle accidents.

Types of Accidents	Number of Deaths
Motor vehicle	40,300
Falls	12,400
Drowning	5,200
Poisoning	4,300
Fires	4,000
Choking	2,700
Firearms	1,400
All other types	12,700
Total	83,000

FIGURE 17–2 Major causes of accidental death in the United States.
Courtesy of National Safety Council, Accidental Facts,1993 Edition.

The *class* of accident refers to where the accident occurs. More accidents take place in and on motor vehicles than any other class. Home accidents are second, followed by accidents in public places. Accidents at work trail far behind. Over the last 50 years, the death rate for all 4 classes of accidents has declined significantly.

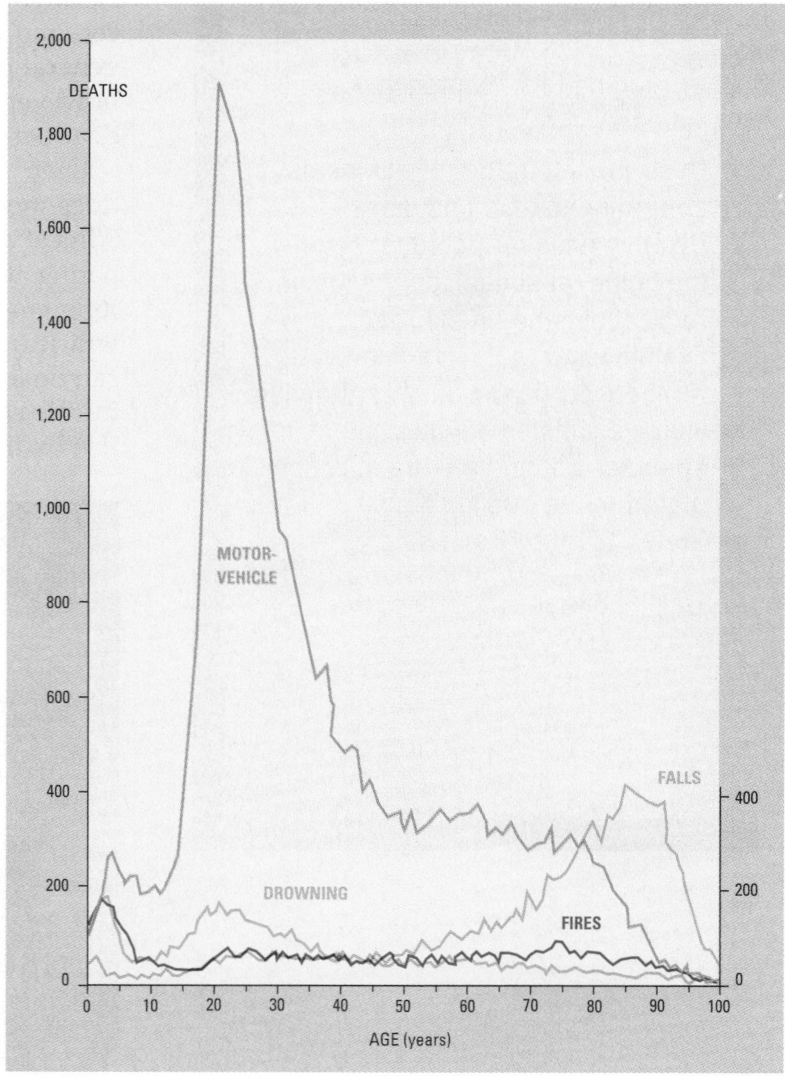

FIGURE 17–3 Leading causes of accidental death by age.
Courtesy of National Safety Council, Accidental Facts, 1993 Edition.

PERSONAL SAFETY

Safety is freedom from harm or the danger of harm. The word *safety* also refers to the precautions taken to prevent accidents. In this section, you will examine some of the things to do and avoid in order to prevent accidents at home, school, on the job, and elsewhere.

In the Home

You probably consider your home a safe place. But about one-fourth of all accidental deaths and about one-third of all disabling injuries occur in and around the home. This translates into one death every 27 minutes and one disabling injury every 5 seconds. A *disabling injury* is one causing death, permanent disability, or any degree of temporary total disability beyond the day of the accident. In addition, millions of people suffer minor (but painful) cuts, burns, and bruises.

Good housekeeping is one of the most important safety defenses. Keep everything in its proper place. Do not leave shoes, toys, books, or other objects on the floor and stairs where someone could trip over them. Put kitchen knives and utensils, tools, and household cleaners away immediately after you have used them.

In many homes, the kitchen is the busiest and most dangerous room. Climbing and reaching cause many accidents. Use a ladder or a firm chair to reach objects in high places. Store appliances and other heavy objects on low shelves. Turn pot handles toward the back of the range to avoid burns and scalds. To prevent cuts, keep kitchen knives in a rack, not loose in a drawer. Kitchens often have types of floor coverings that can become very slick when wet. Immediately wipe up water, grease, or anything else spilled on the floor.

Falls are also one of the worst dangers in the bathroom. Install nonslip strips in the tub or shower and provide handrails to prevent falls while bathing.

Water is an excellent conductor of electricity. So, dry your hands thoroughly before using a hair dryer, razor, or other electrical appliance. A plugged-in radio or other appliance could *electrocute* you if it falls into water. Unless radios, televisions, and stereos are battery operated, keep them out of the bathroom.

In the yard, lawn mowers are the cause of many injuries. Wear a shirt, pants, and heavy work shoes when operating a mower. Be alert to anything lying on the ground that might be thrown by running over it. Wear safety goggles when using string-type weed cutters.

At School

State and local laws require schools to meet certain health and safety standards. Beyond these, school officials try to make the environment as safe as possible. They conduct safety programs for students and teachers. Regular drills are conducted to prepare for fire, weather, earthquake, or other types of emergencies. Teachers provide instruction regarding proper safety practices in their particular subjects.

Accidents in school most commonly occur in gyms and on athletic fields, in vocational shops, science labs, and art rooms. It is your

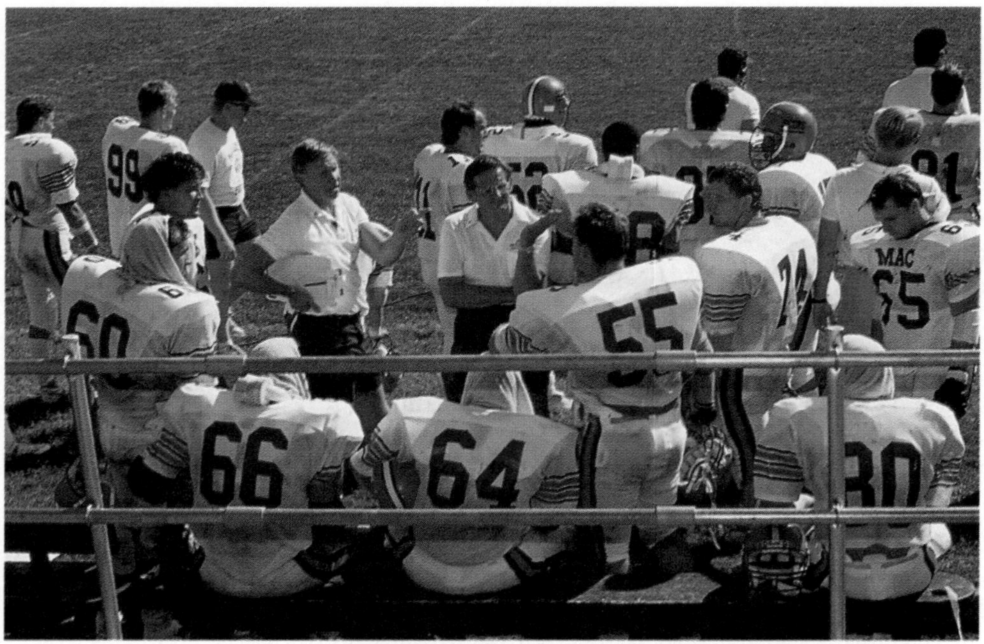

FIGURE 17–4 **Many school accidents occur in gyms and on athletic fields.**
Courtesy of Skjold Photographs.

responsibility to work with teachers and to follow their instructions in these types of classes. Accidents also occur in corridors, on stairways, and in regular classrooms. Many accidents result from students rushing to get to the next class or to go home. Stay to the right in corridors and on stairs. Do not run, crowd, or shove. In classrooms, keep your feet out of the aisles. Do not throw pens, pencils, or paper clips, which can cause serious eye injuries.

On the Job

Workplace safety has improved greatly over the years. In 1910, about 20,000 workers in the U.S. lost their lives on the job. Today, the work force is over three times as large, but the accidental death total is less than half. Still, over 8,500 workers are killed and about 3.3 million disabling injuries occur annually while at work. Your safety responsibilities as an employee are:

1. ***Learn and Obey Rules.*** Supervisors and experienced workers have learned best how to do the job. Listen, observe, and follow their instructions. Always obey rules and regulations for shop or office safety practices.
2. ***Consult Procedures.*** If you do not know how to do something, stop and consult the procedures manual or rules. Or, ask your supervisor or experienced co-workers.
3. ***Watch for Hazards.*** Many companies depend on employee assistance in identifying safety hazards and in changing safety procedures. Think about what you are doing. As you observe safety hazards or have ideas for improvements, make them known.

4. ***Report Accidents and Injuries.*** Accident reports are one of the best means of identifying safety hazards that need to be corrected. Participate in accident and injury reporting and investigation. Insurance benefits to the injured person sometimes depend on this.
5. ***Become Involved.*** Encourage other workers to act and work safely. Try to set a good example for other workers. Volunteer to participate in the shop, department, or company safety committee.
6. ***Perform as Trained.*** This is your most important responsibility regarding safety. Use the correct tools to perform your tasks. Allow enough time to finish a task safely. Avoid distractions. Follow operating procedures for using equipment and perform tasks according to training specifications. Do not operate machinery or drive under the influence of alcohol, drugs, or certain medications. Be neat and practice good housekeeping.

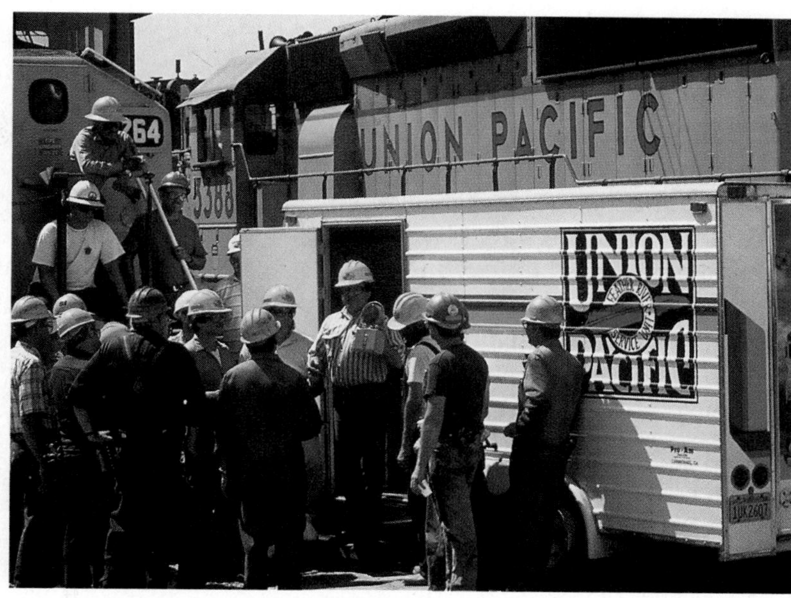

FIGURE 17–5 **Periodic review of safety procedures is standard practice at many places of work.**
Courtesy of Union Pacific Corporation.

In Recreation

Many types of outdoor recreation have some element of hazard. The major causes of accidents are inexperience, overconfidence, and fatigue. General rules for safe recreation include keeping physically fit, learning the basic skills of the particular activity, selecting a safe play area, using proper equipment and dress, avoiding overexertion, and never taking chances. Some activities present special problems.

Drownings are the fourth major cause of fatal accidents. Anyone who goes in, on, or near the water

? ? ? ? ? ? ? ? ? ? ? ? ? ?

WHAT WOULD YOU DO?

It is your turn to work the Saturday evening shift. Normally, you do not mind working until 9:00 p.m. Tonight, though, you badly want to see the game. If you hurry, you may be able to see the last half.

At quitting time, you quickly lock the door and start cleaning up. It only takes you a few minutes to wipe off the tables, clean the counter, and empty the trash. By 9:15, you are on your way.

As you arrive at the gym, the image of a coffee pot flashes through your mind. Coffee pot!!! Did you remember to turn off the coffee pot? You think so, but you are not sure.

What would you do?

should learn how to swim. Two important rules to follow are never to swim alone and always be aware of your limitations.

Boating accidents have become an increasing problem. The chief causes of boating accidents are speeding, poor judgment, and recklessness. Operator fault is a factor in half the boating casualties. Boaters should know the safety limitations of their craft and never exceed the safe speed. The U.S. Coast Guard establishes and enforces boating regulations. A boat operator should learn to follow such regulations.

Rifles, pistols, and shotguns are deadly weapons. Never point a gun at anyone. Guns should be unloaded before cleaning or storing. All firearms should be kept in a locked case or cabinet. Ammunition should be stored away from the firearms in a locked container.

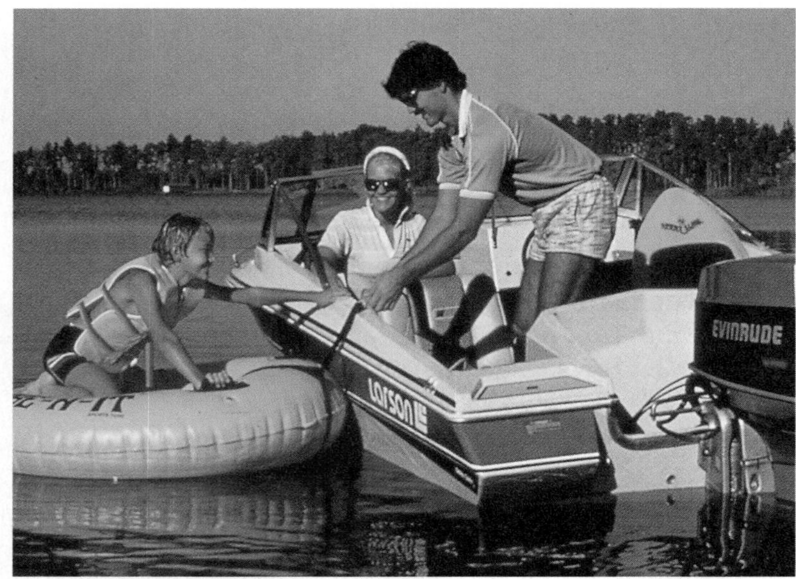

FIGURE 17–6 **When people are having fun, safety precautions are often forgotten.**
Courtesy of Outboard Marine Corporation.

On the Road

Today's automobiles and roads are built to be safer than ever before. More people are using seat belts. As a result, the death rate has dropped in relation to the number of miles driven. The current rate of less than 2 deaths per 100 million miles of travel compares with the rate of about 7 deaths in 1950. But the actual number of accidents keeps rising. This is due to the fact that there are more drivers and more autos on the road every year.

The causes of traffic accidents are difficult to determine. A number of things contribute to every accident. Improper driving of some kind is involved in about 90 percent of all accidents. This includes speeding, failure to yield the right-of-way, following too closely, and driving left

FIGURE 17–7 **Mandatory use of safety glass is only one example of how motor vehicles have been made safer.**
Courtesy of Ford Motor Company.

of the center line. Alcohol is a factor in about 50 percent of fatal accidents. Unsafe vehicles are a factor in at least ten percent of accidents.

Pamela cannot wait for classes to begin next semester. She will be enrolled in driver education. She looks forward to learning how to drive and being able to use the family car. She is wise to take driver education. It is one of the most valuable tools in traffic safety. People who have taken driver education have fewer accidents.

You can help prevent auto accidents and injury by following common-sense rules. Use seat belts every time you drive. Obey the speed limit. Adjust your speed to traffic and weather conditions. Be a courteous driver. Stay a safe distance behind other vehicles and signal when you plan to turn or change lanes. Never drive under the influence of drugs or alcohol. Keep your car in good running order.

Emergency Situations

Many accidents and deaths result from *natural disasters*. Such tragedies often strike suddenly. You can lessen the risks, however, if you know what to do during a flood, tornado, hurricane, or earthquake. Some safety rules apply to all natural disasters.

Flood conditions typically build up over hours and days. Leave a flood area as soon as a warning is announced. Do not be caught in a low-lying area. After returning from a flood, have electrical wiring and appliances checked before using them. Boil drinking water until health officials say that the water supply is safe.

Tornados occur most frequently in late spring and early summer. Be alert to threatening weather during these periods. If you hear a warning or see a tornado coming, go to a basement or inside room without windows. If you cannot move to another room, get under a heavy table or lie flat on the floor. If you are in a car, do not try to outrun the tornado. Get out of the car and lie in a ditch.

Hurricane forecasting has improved tremendously in recent years. Weather bureaus work

Location	Type	Date	Number of Deaths
Galveston, TX	tidal wave	September 1900	6,000
Johnstown, PA	flood	May 1889	2,209
Florida	hurricane	September 1928	1,833
Ohio and Indiana	flood	March 1913	732
New England	hurricane	September 1938	657
Illinois	tornado	March 1925	606
Louisiana	hurricane	September 1915	500
San Francisco, CA	earthquake	April 1906	452
St. Francis, CA	flood (dam burst)	March 1928	450
Florida	hurricane	September 1935	409

FIGURE 17–8 **The ten largest U.S. natural disasters in terms of fatalities. Why have there been fewer deaths in recent years?**

Courtesy of the National Safety Council.

closely with local radio and television stations to broadcast information about hurricanes and other weather-related problems. After learning of a hurricane warning, keep your radio or television on for further information. Follow the instructions of local officials to know what to do. After the storm, avoid loose electrical power lines and report them immediately to the power company.

Earthquakes are the most sudden of any natural disaster. In an earthquake, you must react within seconds to the danger. If you are indoors, take cover under a table or desk. If you are outside, move away from buildings or other structures where you might be struck by falling objects. If you are in a car, stop immediately in a safe area and stay in the car.

? ? ? ? ? ? ? ? ? ? ? ? ? ? ?

WHAT WOULD YOU DO?

You have had a great time at the picnic. The weather was good and the food was delicious. You enjoyed seeing your old friends. It is now time to hop in the car for the long drive home.

About half-way back to the city, the sky starts to darken. The wind begins to blow, and you see lightning in the distance. After a few more miles, the first drops of rain hit the windshield. The rain is soon coming down in torrents. It is only 4:30, but it is so dark that you have to turn on the headlights. The windshield wipers are going full speed. Even so, you can barely see the center line. You wonder what would happen if you had to stop suddenly. You would like to pull off the highway, but are not very familiar with the road.

What would you do?

PUBLIC SAFETY

Safety is everyone's business. The role of employers was explained in Chapter 8. In this chapter, you have learned about the individual's safety responsibilities. In the following section, you will learn what government agencies and private organizations do to promote working for public safety.

Public safety refers to all efforts by federal, state, and local governments to protect persons and property. These include legislation, such as traffic ordinances and building codes, and regulatory activities, such as control of air pollution. Police and fire protection services are examples of public safety. The schools and public transportation systems also play important safety roles. For instance, if you have flown in a commercial airliner, you know that the flight attendants provide safety instruction before each departure.

Government Agencies

Many agencies of the United States government are devoted to safety. Following are several examples. The Consumer Product Safety Commission protects consumers from unsafe household goods. The National Transportation Safety Board works to ensure the safety of all types of transportation. The Federal Aviation Administration creates and enforces air safety regulations. Safety in motor vehicles is the responsibility of the National Highway Traffic Safety Administration.

Earlier in Chapter 8, you learned how the Occupational Safety and Health Administration works to reduce hazardous job conditions. Most state, county, and city governments also have departments concerned with safety and health.

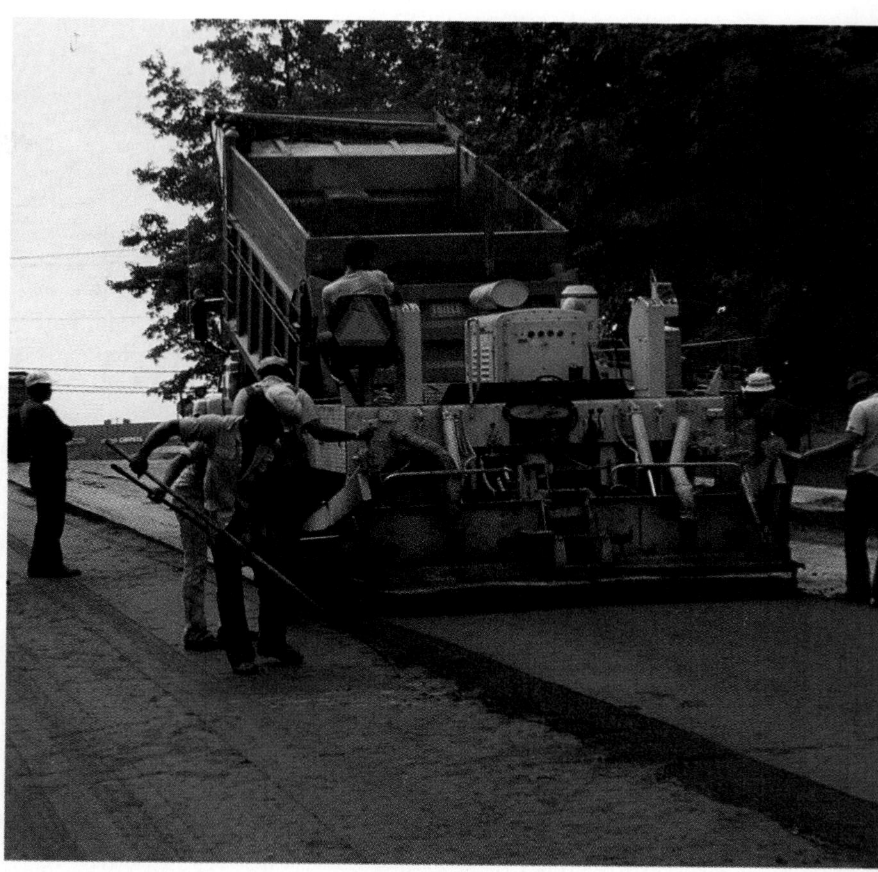

FIGURE 17–9 **Street and road maintenance is a simple example of public safety.**

Private Organizations

A number of nonprofit, private organizations engage in activities to promote personal and public safety. Following are the most common. The National Safety Council collects and distributes information on every aspect of accidental prevention. It publishes the *National Safety News* and other magazines; issues pamphlets, bulletins, and posters; and aids in developing community safety programs. The American Red Cross conducts instructions in first aid and in water safety. It also issues safety information. Underwriters Laboratories tests and certifies electrical appliances, automobile and boat safety equipment, and burglar and fire alarms.

The Three E's of Safety

The three *E*'s of safety are engineering, education, and enforcement. Proper engineering of buildings, highways, machines, and appliances eliminates many accident hazards. Through *education,* people can be made aware of accident problems and the ways to prevent them. Enforcement of safety rules prevents many accidents. The three *E*'s of safety require expenditures of time and money. But these are small compared with the savings in human suffering, compensation costs, medical expenses, and lost time.

FIGURE 17–10 **A UL seal on a product means that it has been checked for safety from fire, electric shock, and other hazards.**
Courtesy of Underwriters' Laboratories.

Focus On Health and Safety

Safety-belt Laws Start to Click

The United States is the only industrialized nation in the world that does not require its citizens to buckle up. Even though there is no federal law, most states have passed their own safety-belt laws. The first state law took effect in New York in December 1984. By late 1993, 42 states plus the District of Columbia had such legislation. All 50 states and DC have mandatory child safety seat laws.

The simple reason behind safety-belt laws is that they save lives and help prevent serious injury. According to the National Highway Traffic Safety Administration, manual lap and shoulder belts are about 45 percent effective in preventing moderate to critical injuries. The majority of the 2.2 million disabling injuries could be reduced to scratches, cuts, and bruises by buckling up. Most of the millions of "minor" traffic injuries could be avoided altogether.

Traffic deaths and injuries cost more than $150 billion a year in lost wages, medical expenses, insurance costs, and property damages. These costs could be cut sharply through safety-belt use.

When airbags are used with safety-belts fatalities are reduced by an additional 11 percent. Airbags will be required in all cars in 1997 and all light trucks in 1998.

This is what can happen when you do not buckle up when you drive.

Courtesy of National Highway Traffic Safety Administration © 1988 U.S. DOT.

CHAPTER 17 REVIEW

CHAPTER IN BRIEF

- An accident is an unplanned event. Accidents are the leading cause of death for teenagers and young adults. Almost all accidents can be prevented by eliminating unsafe behavior and conditions and by following basic safety rules.
- Accidents are reported by type and class. The leading type (cause) of accidental death is motor vehicles. More accidents take place in and on motor vehicles than any other class (location).
- Safety refers to the precautions you take to prevent accidents. Know and practice rules for personal safety in the home, at school, on the job, in recreation, and on the road.
- Natural disasters often strike suddenly. You can lessen the risks if you know what to do during a flood, tornado, hurricane, and earthquake. Some safety rules apply to all natural disasters.
- Safety is everyone's business. Individuals and employers have a major responsibility for personal safety. Many agencies of the federal government and a number of private organizations are devoted to public and personal safety.
- The three *E*'s of safety are engineering, education, and enforcement. The costs of safety are small compared with the savings in human suffering, compensation costs, medical expenses, and lost time.

WORDS TO KNOW

accident
disabling injury
electrocute
natural disaster
public safety
safety

QUESTIONS TO ANSWER

1. What is the leading cause of death among teenagers and young adults?
2. What is the leading type (cause) of accidental death in the United States? Where (class) do most accidents occur?
3. Give three examples of how good housekeeping helps prevent home accidents.
4. What is the most important thing you can do on the job regarding safety?
5. Name the major causes of outdoor recreation accidents.
6. The number of accidents and deaths on the road has increased despite safer autos and roads. Why?
7. What types of improper driving practices cause auto accidents?
8. How do natural disasters differ from other types of accidents?

9. Give two examples of government public safety efforts.
10. What are the three *E*'s of safety?

ACTIVITIES TO DO

1. The instructor will divide the class into small groups. Each group will be assigned the responsibility of preparing a bulletin board display on workplace safety. The display should be changed periodically until each group has completed its assignment.
2. Assume that you are at a party and some of the people have been drinking. The driver of your car has had too much to drink, but he insists on driving home. Do you allow him to do so? Do you ride with him? Role play this situation in which one person is the driver and the rest of the class are people at the party.
3. Have you heard of the organization called Students Against Drunk Driving (SADD)? Perhaps you have a chapter in your school or community. Invite a representative of SADD to the class to explain about the organization. Your class might take the lead in getting a chapter started in your school if you do not already have one.
4. Assume that a cook trainee badly cut her hand in the kitchen. She had to be taken to the emergency room for stitches. Try to estimate the total cost of this accident. Remember to include lost wages of the injured person and the driver, medical bills, lost productivity, and anything else you can think of.
5. Many government agencies and private organizations work in the field of personal and public safety. Select one of the following organizations. Read about it in an encyclopedia or other source, and prepare a short, written report.
   - National Transportation Safety Board
   - Federal Aviation Administration
   - National Highway Traffic Safety Administration
   - Consumer Product Safety Commission
   - Occupational Safety and Health Administration
   - United States Fire Administration
   - Nuclear Regulatory Commission
   - U.S. Coast Guard
   - Federal Railroad Administration
   - U.S. Forest Service
   - Mine Safety and Health Administration
   - National Bureau of Standards
   - National Safety Council
   - American Red Cross
   - National Fire Protection Association
   - Underwriters Laboratories
   - American Association of Automotive Medicine
   - Insurance Institute for Highway Safety
   - American Industrial Hygiene Association
   - American Society of Safety Engineers

TOPICS TO DISCUSS

1. You probably were not aware of the large number of safety agencies and organizations shown in the preceding list. Why do you think so many different groups are working to improve personal and public safety?
2. Discuss all of the things your employer does to promote safety. Name as many things as you can. All class members should contribute. Your instructor may ask you to bring in copies of safety manuals or other printed material provided by the employer.
3. Think of an accident you had at home, school, work, or in recreation. What was the cause? Discuss how the accident might have been avoided.
4. Why do you think the U.S. is the only industrialized country in the world that does not have a national safety-belt law?

CHAPTER 18 Leadership Skills

OUTLINE

- Organizational Leadership
- Vocational Student Organizations
- Parliamentary Procedure
- Chapter Review

OBJECTIVES

After reading this chapter, you should be able to:

- Define what is meant by leadership.
- Name and illustrate six types of leadership behaviors.
- Explain the purposes of a vocational student organization.
- Identify types of vocational student organizations.
- Demonstrate knowledge of parliamentary procedure.

1 When you hear the word *leadership,* what comes to mind? Many people think of a particular person, such as a high government official, a sports figure, a person of wealth, or a prominent celebrity. This view equates leadership with status, wealth, office, and celebrity. But are all such people leaders? Of course not. In this chapter, a different view of leadership is provided.

ORGANIZATIONAL LEADERSHIP

Dozens of books have been written on the subject of leadership. One book indicates that more than 350 definitions of leadership exist. We focus here on only one part of leadership—that is, leadership within an organization.

FIGURE 18–1 **Many celebrities are leaders, but not all leaders are celebrities.**
Courtesy of The National Broadcasting Company Inc.

Organizations are oriented toward achieving certain goals. An insurance company, for example, exists to sell insurance, meet the needs of its customers, and make a profit. This goal orientation is important for our definition of leadership. *Leadership* is the process of influencing people in order to accomplish the goals of the organization.

A number of writers have described the characteristics of effective leaders. John Zenger, president of a leadership training firm, identifies six types of leadership skills. They are summarized in the following paragraphs.[1] These represent actions and behaviors that most leaders seem to share. As you read them, however, keep in mind that a given leader might not be strong in all of them. Also, be aware that leaders may exhibit these characteristics in different ways.

FIGURE 18–2 Leaders are effective communicators.
© Bettman

Leaders Are Good Communicators

Leaders enjoy communicating and use every opportunity to convey their message. A leader's message often has to be repeated again and again. Leaders are effective in large meetings or in one-on-one discussions. Some rely on written or other forms of communication. For instance, they may use models or drawings to get a point across. Leaders view information as something to be shared, not to be hoarded. They use interaction with others to gather and present information.

A leader is not always the person in charge of a meeting or an organization. You can often identify the leader of a group by the way he or she communicates: Who is most persuasive? Who speaks with knowledge and authority? Who is able to express what others have been trying to say? Who do others really listen to? Who talks last on the subject?

Not all leaders are naturally gifted communicators. Lincoln and Gandhi were basically shy people. Deep beliefs about their missions drove them into the limelight. Lincoln and Gandhi gained the skill of communicating through self-discipline. They never shied away from communicating their visions and beliefs.

Leaders Develop Committed Followers

The best leaders recognize that they cannot do everything themselves. Leaders involve others.

[1]Zenger, J. H. "Leadership: Management's Better Half," *Training,* December 1985, pp. 44–53.

FIGURE 18–3 **Leaders motivate and teach others.**
Courtesy of General Electric. Photo by Brownie Harris.

They ask for advice, information, and solutions to problems. Once given, they provide positive feedback. They help make the people in the organization feel responsible for what happens.

By involving people, leaders encourage them to be self-reliant and to practice self-management. An example of this is the use of task groups, which was discussed in Chapter 9. Leaders understand the power of groups and what groups can accomplish. They meet frequently with their groups to encourage them and create a strong team spirit.

Leaders recognize that people are more productive if you help them to advance. Leaders share credit with their associates. Good work is praised and rewarded. Leaders foster and thrive on the success of others.

Leaders Inspire High Accomplishments

Leaders are not satisfied with "average" and do not tolerate poor workmanship or shoddy performance. They challenge people to stretch and reach new heights. They set high standards and expect high-quality performance. At the same time, however, leaders tolerate honest mistakes.

Edwin Land, founder of Polaroid, said: "The first thing you naturally do is teach the person to feel that the undertaking is manifestly important and nearly impossible. . . . That draws out the kind of drives that make people strong."

The leader's style *pulls* rather than *pushes* people.

Leaders Are Role Models

Many individuals earn a position of leadership because of their prior skills and successes. Leaders should represent the values of the units they lead. A captain of an athletic team is frequently the star player. A district sales manager is often a super salesperson.

Leaders know that people copy their behavior. If they work harder, the group will pick up the pace. If they slow down, the group pace slackens. Leaders send a clear signal by their own behavior. During Chrysler's financial crisis, every employee was aware that Chairperson Iacocca cut his own salary to $1 per year.

Contrast Iacocca's example with that of another executive whose company faced a similar financial crisis. He called the employees together to inform them of layoffs and budget cuts. After the presentation, he flew in a private jet to a fancy resort for a weekend of golf. Workers resented his behavior. The company's financial problems grew worse as a result of low employee morale and reduced productivity. The executive was later fired.

Leaders Search Out Key Issues and Problems

Leaders are good at uncovering and solving difficult problems. They want to know as much as possible about the matter. They ask tough questions, such as: How did this happen? How long has this been going on? What is being done to correct this? Who is responsible for it?

Leaders know how to focus attention on an issue or problem. For instance, Du Pont requires every lost-time accident to be reported to the chairperson on a daily basis. This has helped make the entire company more safety-conscious.

The president of National Semiconductor wanted to turn around the performance of a particular division. So he moved his desk next to the division's general manager. This was a clear signal that improvement was expected.

Leaders Are Involved in External Relations

Leaders do not stay chained to their desks. Leaders represent the organization and serve as links to the outside world. They get involved with outside groups. They participate in professional or trade associations. They are in frequent contact with other businesses and other leaders. They get involved in community activities and service organizations.

Summary

Only a few people will lead nations. Many more will lead companies, departments, or small groups. Some people start out with better developed abilities than others. But what have been described here as leadership characteristics can be learned by everyone. The next section describes a type of organization that can help you develop leadership skills.

VOCATIONAL STUDENT ORGANIZATIONS

Vocational student organizations (VSOs) are nonprofit, national organizations with state and local chapters. They are supported primarily by student-paid dues. Each organization is linked with an occupational area, such as business, home economics, or health occupations. These organizations function as an integral part of vocational education.

Specific goals and objectives vary from one organization to another. But all have similar overall purposes to develop leadership skills and good citizenship. The organizations provide students with opportunities to function as junior members of the trade or profession. Students apply skills learned in the classroom and interact with others in the occupational area. They develop a respect for the occupation and its *code of ethics* (rules for professional practice and behavior). Other outcomes include providing service, developing decision-making skills, and building confidence.

The national organization generally produces written guidelines for teacher/advisors, student handbooks, and promotional materials. In addition, the organization may sponsor national conferences, leadership development workshops, competitive contests, and award programs. Following is a brief profile of each VSO.

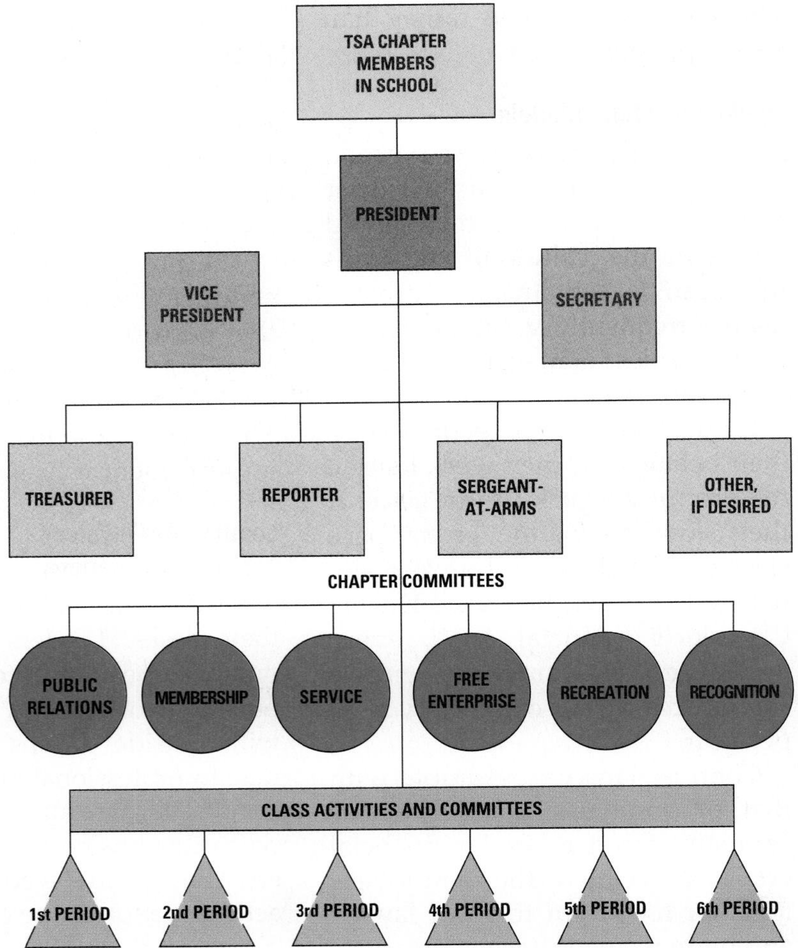

FIGURE 18–4 This chart shows how a local student organization might be structured.
Courtesy of Technology Student Association.

Business Professionals of America (BPA)

Prior to July 1988, BPA was known as the Office Education Association. The name was changed to reflect the fact that business education is incorporating new and expanding areas, such as mid-management and entrepreneurship. The BPA is for students enrolled in business and office education programs at the secondary and post-secondary levels. Its goal is to prepare students for rewarding and successful careers in business and as business leaders.

Distributive Education Clubs of America (DECA)

DECA is an organization for future leaders in marketing, merchandising, and management. One purpose of the organization is to contribute to occupational competence in distributive education. It also promotes understanding and appreciation for the responsibilities of citizenship in a free-enterprise system. Membership in the following divisions are available: high school, two-year post-secondary, college, alumni, and professional.

Future Business Leaders of America—Phi Beta Lambda, Inc. (FBLA-PBL)

FBLA-PBL seeks to bring business and education together in a positive working relationship. The purpose of FBLA is to develop vocational and career supportive competencies and to promote civic and personal responsibilities. It is for secondary students in business and office education. The purpose of FBLA-PBL is to provide opportunities for junior college and college students to develop competencies for business and office occupations or business teacher education.

National FFA Organization

First known as the Future Farmers of America (FFA), this group changed its name in November 1988. It was founded in 1928 to make instruction more interesting and more practical by combining work experience, competitive livestock judging, and agricultural leadership development activities with classroom instruction. It is part of the high school vocational agriculture/agribusiness instruction program preparing students for careers in agriculture. The National FFA Organization encourages entrepreneurship, positive work attitudes, and responsible citizenship.

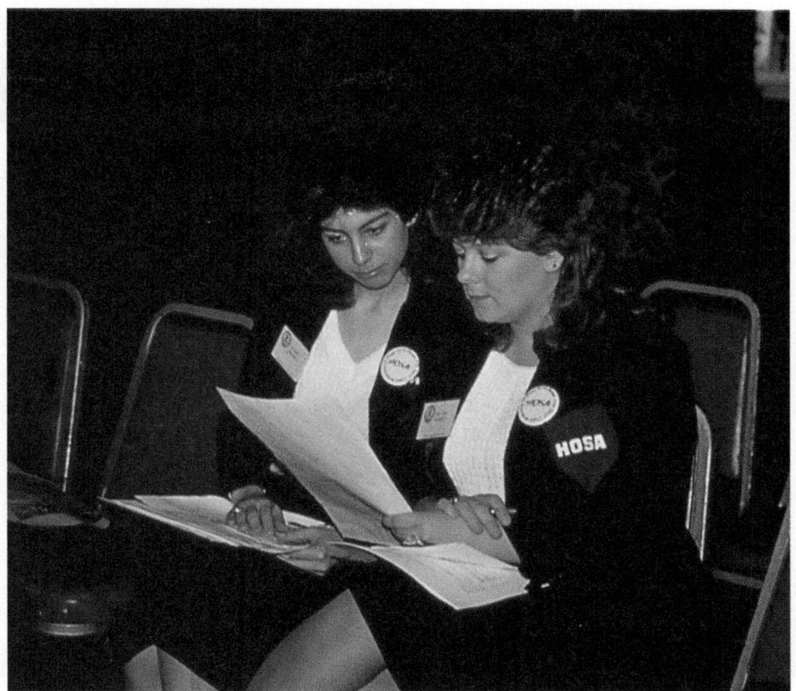

FIGURE 18–5 Vocational student organizations provide many opportunities for individuals to develop leadership skills.
Courtesy of Muhlenberg Co. AVEC KY HOSA.

Future Homemakers of America/Home Economics Related Occupations (FHA/HERO)

These two closely related organizations are for young men and women in home economics at the junior high and high school levels. Their purpose is to help youth assume active roles in society in areas of personal growth, family life, vocational preparation, and community involvement. FHA is the only in-school student organization with the family as its central focus. HERO chapters emphasize preparation for home economics occupations.

Health Occupations Students of America (HOSA)

The health care system needs workers who are technically skilled, people oriented, and capable of providing leadership as a member of a team. The focus of HOSA is to enhance the delivery of quality health care and to promote health care careers. It is for secondary, postsecondary, and adult students enrolled in health occupations.

National Young Farmer Educational Association (NYFEA)

NYFEA assists young adult farmers enrolled in agricultural education in the operation of their agribusiness. Activities focus on the utilization of resources, development of leadership and communication skills, and the improvement of rural-urban relations. A major characteristic of NYFEA is that classroom topics are identified by the members.

National Postsecondary Agricultural Student Organization (PAS)

The mission of PAS is to promote individual growth, leadership, and strong personal ethics for individuals who are pursuing agricultural careers. The organization is available to students in agriculture-related postsecondary programs.

Technology Student Association (TSA)

TSA is devoted to industrial arts/technology students at the elementary, junior high, and high school levels. Prior to June 1988, the organization was called the American Industrial Arts Student Association. Activities are designed to develop the leadership and personal abilities of students as they relate to the industrial and technical world. TSA assists students in making informed and meaningful career choices.

? ? ? ? ? ? ? ? ? ? ? ? ?

WHAT WOULD YOU DO?

Several friends approach you saying that they would like to nominate you for office in a vocational student organization. You are pleased that they respect your ability. If you were elected, it would mean extra work and responsibility. You are not sure that you have the time or could do the job.

What would you do?

Vocational Industrial Clubs of America (VICA)

VICA is for students in trade, industrial, technical, and health occupations programs in high schools and junior/community colleges. VICA offers leadership, citizenship, and character development programs to complement the student's skill training. Dignity of work, high standards in trade ethics, workmanship, scholarship, and safety are emphasized.

PARLIAMENTARY PROCEDURE

Parliamentary procedure is a way to conduct a meeting in a fair and orderly manner. It is called "parliamentary" because it comes from the rules and customs of the British Parliament. The United States Congress and other lawmaking bodies follow parliamentary procedure. The rules are used in simpler form by business and professional groups, school organizations, and social clubs. The basic principles of parliamentary procedure are majority rule, protection of the minority, and the orderly consideration of one subject at a time.

Bylaws

An organization operating according to parliamentary procedure adopts a set of bylaws. The *bylaws* define the basic characteristics of the organization and describe how it will operate. They describe qualifications for membership and procedures for selection of members. The bylaws state the duties of officers and how they will be elected. They also state how committees will be formed and what their functions will be. All members of an organization should be provided with a copy of the bylaws.

Officers and Committees

An organization usually elects a president (or chair), a vice-president, a secretary, and a treasurer. Some groups also elect a sergeant-at-arms or other officers. The president presides at meetings and supervises the work of other officers and committees. The vice-president assists the president and chairs meetings when the president is absent. The secretary notifies members of meetings, keeps the minutes, and takes care of all correspondence and committee reports. The treasurer keeps a record of income and expenses and prepares the financial reports. The sergeant-at-arms maintains order during meetings.

Most organizations elect officers once a year. This is often done at the first meeting of the new year. A member may nominate a fellow member. Usually, after two or more people have been nominated, the voting takes place by secret ballot. The person receiving the majority vote is the elected officer. A *majority* is a vote of at least one more than half of the people who vote.

Certain duties of an organization are handled by committees. Most organizations have two types of committees. One type, the standing committee, deals with regular and continuing matters, such as membership and finance. A second type, the special committee, is formed whenever it is necessary to work on a specific matter. Examples might be to plan a social event or to revise the bylaws. Special committees break up when their task is done. Committees are either appointed or elected according to the bylaws.

Holding a Meeting

Most organizations require that a quorum be present before a meeting may begin. A *quorum* is a majority of the total membership. An organizations' bylaws usually provide for an *order of business.* This is the series of steps covered in a meeting. A standard order of business is shown in Figure 18–6. An actual meeting proceeds according to a list of items to be taken care of called an *agenda.* A typical agenda for a vocational youth organization is shown in Figure 18–7.

An important part of any business meeting involves making, discussing, and disposing of motions. A *motion* is a brief statement of a proposed action. There are four types of motions:

1. *Main motions* are the tools used to introduce new business.

PARTS OF A CHAPTER MEETING

It is customary for every group to adopt a standard order of business for the meeting. When the organization's by-laws do not provide for or require a specific order, the following is in order.

1. **Call to Order**
   "Will the meeting please come to order."
2. **Roll Call**
   "Will the secretary please call the roll."
3. **Reading and Approval of Minutes**
   "Will the secretary please read the minutes of the last meeting." The minutes are read and the chairman asks:

   "Are there any corrections to the minutes?" The chair pauses to hear any corrections offered, if there are none, the chair says, "There being no corrections, the minutes will stand approved as read."

   If there are corrections, the chair recognizes the correction(s) and asks, "Are there further corrections to the minutes?" If there are none, the chair states, "There being no further corrections, the minutes will stand approved as corrected."
4. **Adoption of Agenda**
   This step is provided to insure that (1) all persons are aware of what has been proposed for discussion at the meeting; (2) that all persons are given the opportunity to have whatever matter(s) they feel is (are) important to the organization placed on the agenda for discussion; and (3) to provide a limit to and order for the matters to be discussed at the meeting.

   To achieve this, the presiding officer states, "The following items are proposed for discussion at this meeting." After reading the list of proposed agenda items, the presiding officer asks, "Are there other matters that should be discussed at this meeting?" If there are additional matters requiring discussion, the chair places them in their proper positions on the agenda.

   The chair, after insuring that all pertinent matters will come before the meeting, reads the entire agenda and states, "There being no other matters that should come before this meeting, the agenda for this meeting will stand as read."
5. **Report of Officers and Standing Committees**
   Officers, boards, or standing committees should be called upon to report in the order in which they are mentioned in the constitution or by-laws of the organization.
6. **Report of Special Committees**
7. **Unfinished Business**
   "We have now come to unfinished business. Our agenda lists the following matters as unfinished business." The chair reads from the agenda and states, "We will hear these matters in the order in which they have been mentioned."
8. **New Business**
   "We have now come to new business. Our agenda lists the following items as new business . . ."(Chair reads from the agenda). He states, "We will hear them in the order in which they were mentioned."
9. **Program**
   Programs such as exhibitions, demonstrations, etc., which are incidental to the business meeting, will be scheduled for presentation at this time.
10. **Adjournment**
    Unqualified form:

    Proposer moves for adjournment; motion is seconded; chairperson calls for a vote; action depends upon majority vote. The motion cannot be discussed.

    Qualified form:

    Proposer moves for adjournment within a definite time or adjournment to meet again at a specified time; motion is seconded; the chair calls for discussion; a vote is taken; action depends upon majority vote; can allow for legal continuation of the meeting.

FIGURE 18–6 Typical parts of a chapter meeting.
Courtesy of Technology Student Association.

PLANNING AND CONDUCTING A MEETING

Planning and conducting a meeting are two tasks that every member should be able to perform correctly and with ease. To do this, certain knowledge and skills should become part of your repertoire.

The President, with assistance from the chapter officers, should meet prior to the time of the regularly scheduled meeting to plan the business to come before the membership. Minutes from the previous meeting should be examined so that any unfinished business can be ascertained and noted for discussion at the upcoming meeting.

The agenda is a listing of those activities to be engaged in and those items of business to be brought before the membership for discussion at the next meeting. A standard order of business is used when preparing an agenda. You should be aware of and apply the order of business in the planning and conducting of all meetings. A typical chapter agenda is shown below.

SCHOOL CHAPTER AGENDA

DATE September 16, 19--

TIME 1:30 p.m.

PLACE Mills Godwin High School

I. **CALL TO ORDER**

II. **OPENING CEREMONY** (Roll call, introduction of visitors)
- Visitors: Mr. Joseph Long, Miss Laura East

III. **READING OF MINUTES**

IV. **OFFICER AND STANDING COMMITTEE REPORTS**
- Treasurer's Report
- Enterprising/Finance Committee to report on fund-raising activities

V. **SPECIAL COMMITTEE REPORTS** (none)

VI. **UNFINISHED BUSINESS**
- Halloween Dance to be held October 30 — Selection of Band

VII. **NEW BUSINESS**
- The purchase of TSA blazers for chapter offices

VIII. **ANNOUNCEMENTS**
- Members who have not turned in their money for the trip to Washington, D.C. must do so today.
- The Executive Committee will meet on September 25 in the Technology Education Lab at 12:00 noon. Bring your lunch with you. Milk will be served.

IX. **PROGRAM**
- Miss Laura East, from the State TSA office, will speak on the Virginia TSA Annual Conference to be held in May.

X. **CLOSING CEREMONY**

FIGURE 18–7 **A typical chapter agenda.**
Courtesy of Technology Student Association.

ACTION	STATEMENT
Privileged Motions	
Adjourn the meeting	"I move that we adjourn."
Recess the meeting	"I move we recess until . . ."
Secondary Motions	
Postpone consideration of a matter without voting on it	"I move we table the motion."
End debate	"I move the previous question."
Have a matter studied further	"I move we refer this matter to a committee."
Amend a motion	"I move that this motion be amended by. . ."
Main Motions	
Introduce business	"I move that. . ."
Resume consideration of a previously tabled motion	"I move we take from the table . . ."
Reconsider a matter already disposed of	"I move we reconsider our action relative to . . ."
Incidental Motions	
Raise a question about parliamentary procedure	"Point of order."
Withdraw a motion	"I ask permission to withdraw the motion."
Seek information about the matter at hand	"Point of information."

FIGURE 18–8 **Common motions listed in order of their priority.**

2. *Secondary motions* provide ways of modifying or disposing of main motions.
3. *Incidental motions* arise out of business being conducted.
4. *Privileged motions* deal with the welfare of the group, rather than any specific proposal.

The most common motions are summarized in Figure 18–8. The motions are listed in order of their *precedence* or rank of priority. When considering a main motion, secondary motion, or privileged motion, no motion listed below it may be introduced. Any motion listed above it, however, may be introduced. Incidental motions have no precedence. They must be decided or disposed of before returning to the business under consideration. Different rules apply to a motion regarding whether a second is needed, whether the motion is debatable, whether it can be amended, and so on. An organization often has a *parliamentarian* to advise the presiding officer (chair) on matters of procedure. Even though motions differ, the general procedure is the same.

To make a motion, a member obtains the floor by rising and addressing the chair. The chair recognizes the member by announcing his or her name. The motion is

? ? ? ? ? ? ? ? ? ? ? ? ? ?

WHAT WOULD YOU DO?

The vocational student organization to which you belong has had a successful year in fund raising. You are meeting today to discuss how to spend the chapter's money. A motion is on the floor to authorize spending the money for a party. The discussion suggests that there is a lot of support for the motion. You too would enjoy a party, but think that it is an inappropriate way to use the money. You are not sure if you should speak against the motion. An alternative would be to amend the motion to use only a portion of the funds for a party.

What would you do?

stated, followed by a second. The chair restates the motion for the benefit of all members. It is then open to debate (discussion). Debate continues until all members who wish to speak have had an opportunity. Members then vote on the motion. Those who approve the motion say "Aye"; those against the motion say "No." If the majority of members vote to accept the motion, it is approved.

Parliamentary procedure does not have to be mysterious and complicated. However, it is something that takes time to learn. One of the best ways to learn it is to join and participate in a vocational student organization.

Focus On The Worker

Trade and Professional Associations

Trade and professional associations are an important part of our economic, social, and working lives. A trade association seeks to advance common business interests of members.

Some trade associations cover a business function, such as manufacturing, distribution, or retailing. For instance, several retail stores may form a trade association. Others are based on the types of goods or services produced. Peanut farmers, service station operators, or restaurant owners, for example, may form an association.

The most important goal of a trade association is more income from its product or service. Activities of trade associations may include advertising, sponsoring research on new products, or promoting high standards. To get their message out, the group may publish pamphlets or sponsor tours. It may also publish a magazine for members and hold yearly conventions. For some trade associations, lobbying for favorable laws is a major activity. To pay for these activities, trade associations collect dues from members.

Public awareness advertising is a common promotional tool of trade associations.
Courtesy of the Catfish Institute.

A professional association is made up of people with a common occupational background such as teacher, pilot, secretary, and chef. Members often need to have an academic degree, license, or certificate to join an association. Professional associations inform members about new developments and issues. They publish journals and hold meetings and conventions. Some associations have student memberships. If a professional association related to your occupation is available, join it.

CHAPTER 18 REVIEW

CHAPTER IN BRIEF

- Leadership can be defined as the process of influencing people in order to accomplish the goals of the organization. John Zenger identifies six types of leadership characteristics:
  1. Leaders are good communicators.
  2. Leaders develop committed followers.
  3. Leaders inspire high accomplishments.
  4. Leaders are role models.
  5. Leaders search out key issues and problems.
  6. Leaders are involved in external relations.

  Leadership characteristics can be learned by everyone.
- Vocational student organizations (VSOs) function as an integral part of the vocational education curriculum. Each VSO is linked with an occupational area. The organizations provide students with opportunities to function as junior members of the trade or profession. Students apply skills learned in the classroom and interact with others in the occupational area.
- Parliamentary procedure is a way to conduct a meeting in a fair and orderly manner. The rules are used by business and professional groups, school organizations, and social clubs. The basic principles of parliamentary procedure are majority rule, protection of the minority, and the orderly consideration of one subject at a time.
- Bylaws define the basic characteristics of the organization and describe how it will operate. An organization usually elects a president, vice-president, secretary, and treasurer. Certain duties of an organization are handled by standing and special committees.
- An important part of any business meeting involves making, discussing, and disposing of motions. There are four types of motions: main motions, secondary motions, incidental motions, and privileged motions. Each motion must be disposed of in some way before another item of business can be taken up.

WORDS TO KNOW

agenda
bylaws
code of ethics
leadership
majority
motion
order of business
parliamentarian
parliamentary procedure
precedence
quorum
vocational student organization (VSO)

QUESTIONS TO ANSWER

1. Organizations are oriented toward achieving certain goals. Name an organization (other than the example in the book) and list two of its goals.
2. In what way is information viewed by a leader?
3. How do leaders involve other members of the organization?
4. Give an example of how a leader can serve as a role model.
5. What are the general purposes of a vocational student organization?
6. What types of activities are conducted by vocational student organizations?
7. What are the three basic principles of parliamentary procedure?
8. Identify and explain the two types of committees.
9. Name and describe the four types of motions.
10. Explain how a motion is introduced for debate.

ACTIVITIES TO DO

1. Identify a famous person who has been referred to as a leader. Rate her or him in relation to each of the six characteristics discussed in this chapter. Use a scale of "high," "average," and "low." What is the overall rating? As described in this chapter, could the person be called a leader?
2. Find out the types of vocational student organizations available in your school. For each one, list the qualifications for membership. Invite a representative from each organization to talk to the class. Select an organization of interest and join it.
3. If a vocational student organization is not available in your occupational area, write the national office to find out how to start one. Your instructor can provide the address. Initiating a VSO chapter would provide an excellent opportunity to demonstrate your leadership.
4. Practice parliamentary procedure by role playing a meeting in class. Elect a class president, vice-president, and secretary. The officers should then develop an agenda. The secretary should prepare and distribute the agenda. Conduct an actual meeting according to the agenda. Concentrate on making, discussing, and disposing of sample motions.

TOPICS TO DISCUSS

1. A characteristic of leaders is that they are able to develop committed followers. There are instances throughout history in which individuals have been able to develop committed followers for illegal or immoral purposes. Think of some historic or present examples. Should such people be called "leaders"?
2. A person may be named head of an organization or be elected to an office without being a leader. Discuss some of the things, other than leadership, that allow people to rise in an organization.
3. Strong leaders may be scattered throughout an organization. Identify and discuss as many examples as you can.

4. You have probably been involved in meetings or discussions that dragged on endlessly without anything being accomplished. Discuss how proper use of parliamentary procedure might have prevented that from happening.
5. It has been said that, "If you want to manage somebody, manage yourself." Discuss the meaning of this phrase.

CHAPTER 19 Computer and Technology Skills

OUTLINE

- Keyboarding Skills
- How Computers Work
- Computer Hardware
- Computer Software
- Computers in the Workplace
- The Future of Computers
- Chapter Review

OBJECTIVES

After reading this chapter, you should be able to:

- Explain the importance of keyboarding skills.
- Identify types of computers and computer hardware.
- Describe the two types of computer software.
- Name and describe the five types of computer application software.
- Summarize how a computer works.
- Show awareness of the role computers play in the workplace.
- Discuss the possible future impact of computers.

The previous four chapters deal with knowledges and skills that have always been important on the job. To those we must now add what is called *computer literacy*. Computer literacy is a general knowledge of what computers are, how they work, and for what they can be used. Chances are that your future work will involve some contact with computers.

KEYBOARDING SKILLS

Wayne graduated from high school without learning anything about computers. He lost out on several good jobs after interviewers learned that he could not use a computer. Wayne got the message and signed up for an adult-education course in computers. In that class, he learned enough to be able to do simple operations and to run application software.

FIGURE 19–1 **Tiny computer chips like this are helping change the way in which we work.**
Courtesy of Lockheed Corporation. Photo by W. J. Warren.

Wayne got a job in the parts department of a plumbing supply business. In this job, he uses a computer more often than a pen. He orders parts, does billings, keeps inventory, and does dozens of other tasks on the computer. He wonders what it must have been like in the parts department before the computers arrived.

A *computer* is an electronic tool. Like other tools, it helps people do various kinds of work. It can do simple arithmetic and can solve complex mathematical problems. With an optical device, it can read a printed page and write (display) text and graphics on a screen. If it has a voice synthesizer, it can even "talk." It can direct equipment to do work. Unlike people, a computer can work 24 hours a day without getting tired. It runs on little electricity and seldom breaks down. It can store vast amounts of information and can communicate with its human user. Perhaps the computer's greatest benefit is its ability to work at very high speeds.

Like Wayne, you will probably need to learn *keyboarding skills* (if you have not already). A keyboard is the part of a computer that looks like a typewriter. Most keyboard terminals are connected to a television-like screen called a monitor.

The arrangement of letters and numbers on the keyboard is the same as for a typewriter. You can use the computer keyboard to write letters and reports. Keyboarding, however, involves more than using the computer as a typewriter. The keyboard terminal directs the computer's operation.

A keyboard's operation will vary depending on the type of computer and the software used. Though keyboards differ in their operation, basic commands and procedures are similar. No matter what type of business or industry you work in, you will benefit by knowing how to use a computer keyboard.

FIGURE 19–2 Learning to keyboard and use application software is a valuable educational and occupational skill.
© Uniphoto, Inc.

HOW COMPUTERS WORK

In very simple terms, the computer works in three steps: (a) it receives instructions, (b) it does tasks according to instructions provided, and (c) it shares the results. These three steps are:

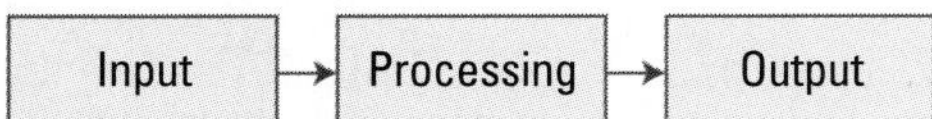

The computer solves problems much as people do. For instance, let's compare how you and the computer would add 20 + 43.

Input

You receive information by either reading or hearing the numbers.

The computer receives the information in the form of electronic signals.

Processing

You draw upon your knowledge of arithmetic in your memory. You bring together the data (20, 43) and the method (addition) and come up with the answer.

The computer draws upon a program stored in its memory. Bringing the data from input and the instructions from memory, the computer adds the numbers.

Output

You report the result (63) by writing down the answer or saying it out loud.

The computer changes the result from electronic language to human language. It presents the result in print, sound, or another form.

Now let's go beyond this simple explanation. To do this, we will need to relabel the second step and divide it into three sections. The input-processing-output sequence now appears as follows:

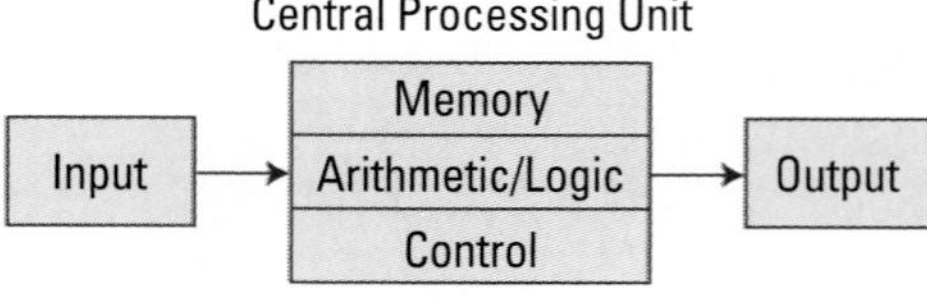

We now have the workings of a modern computer. A computer has five sections: (a) input, (b) memory, (c) arithmetic and logic, (d) control, and (e) output.

Input

The input section of a computer takes information and changes it into electronic signals the computer can use. Various devices can input data. The most common is a keyboard. As the operator types letters or numbers on the keyboard, they appear on the screen. This allows the operator to check the data.

Instead of a keyboard, a mouse may be used to control input. Other kinds of input devices include light pens, touch pads, scanners, magnetic tapes and discs, and punched cards and paper tape. A telephone and other communications equipment can be hooked up to a computer through the use of a *modem.*

Two kinds of information are fed into the computer input. One is called a *program.* A program consists of instructions on how to solve a certain problem or do a certain task. The second kind of information, data, consists of the facts and figures the program must use. From the input, the program and data go to the memory section of the computer.

Memory

The memory section is the part of the computer system that records and stores the data. These data stay in memory until other parts of the computer need it.

The memory section actually has two parts. One part is permanent memory. It is called *ROM,* which stands for *r*ead-*o*nly *m*emory. The manufacturer pre-programs the ROM. It tells the computer to do different things, depending on the uses of the computer.

The other part of the memory is working memory. It is called *RAM* (*r*andom-*a*ccess *m*emory). This part stores both current programs and data being processed. Whenever the computer is turned off, it erases all RAM data.

Arithmetic and Logic

The arithmetic and logic section is the heart of the computer. It does all the computer's math operations.

The arithmetic and logic section adds, subtracts, multiplies, divides, and compares numbers. To do complex calculations, the four operations combine into a number of steps as the program directs. This section also processes words. It does these tasks at speeds measured in millionths of a second.

The arithmetic and logic section receives its input from the memory section. After processing, the data returns to the memory section. There it will be ready for use when needed.

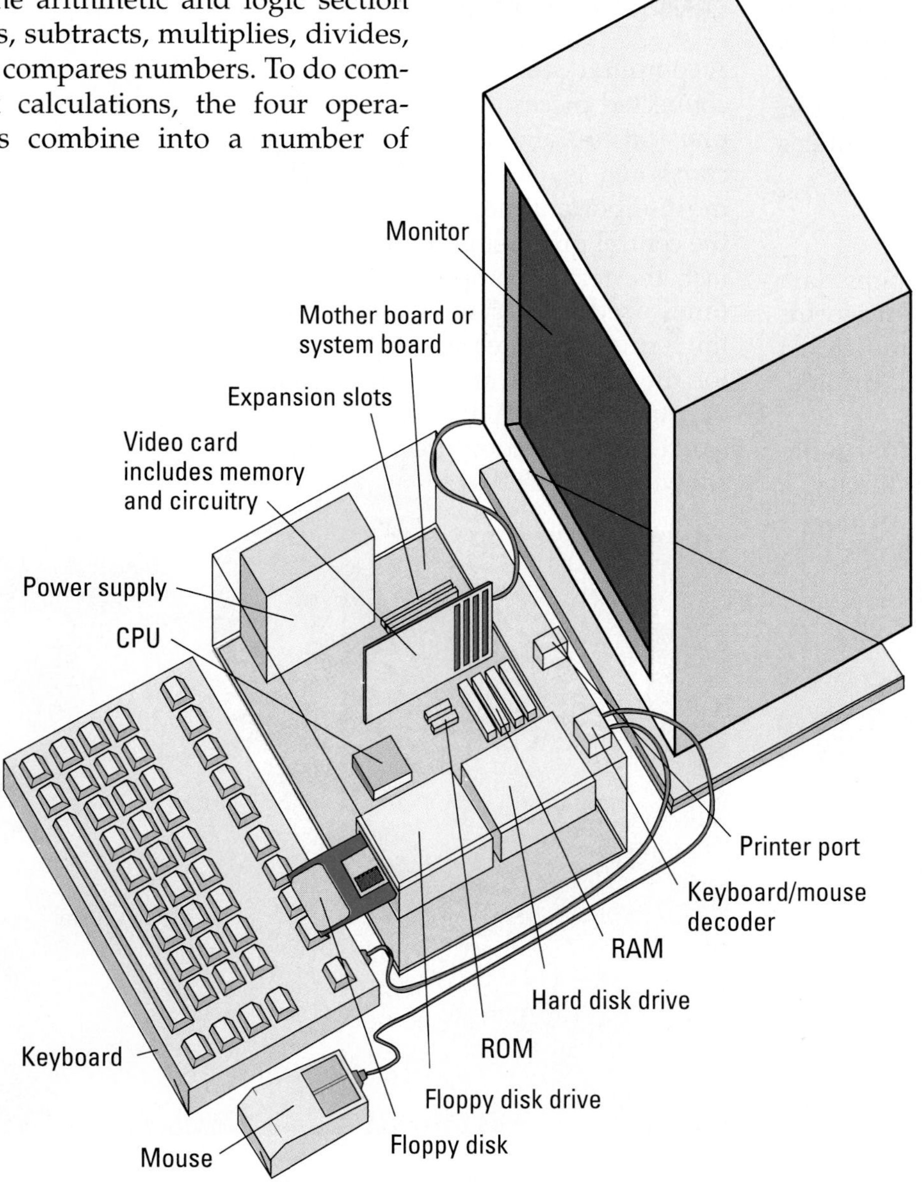

FIGURE 19–3 The main components of a standard personal computer are shown here.

Control

Part of the program of instructions a computer receives goes to the control section. The control section directs the other four sections of the computer.

Based on the program, the control section decides when to accept data and from which input device. It chooses when to send information from the input to memory and when to send it to the arithmetic and logic section. It decides when to call up a program and data from storage. And it decides when the computer's work should go to the output.

Output

The output section changes data from electronic language into forms that people can understand. Most output is either displayed, printed, or stored.

Output appears on the same monitor that displayed the input data. A printer may also reproduce the output. Sometimes magnetic tapes and discs store the data. Output devices are often the same as input devices.

Some computer systems transmit output as spoken words or music. Output can also consist of instructions that tell machines to do certain kinds of work (such as robots).

COMPUTER HARDWARE

A computer consists of several interconnected pieces of equipment. The physical equipment that makes up a computer is called *hardware.* The most important piece of hardware is the central processing unit (CPU). In fact, the term "computer" is sometimes used just for the CPU. While, the term "computer system" is used for the computer and its input and output devices. A typical home or small business computer system is shown in Figure 19–4.

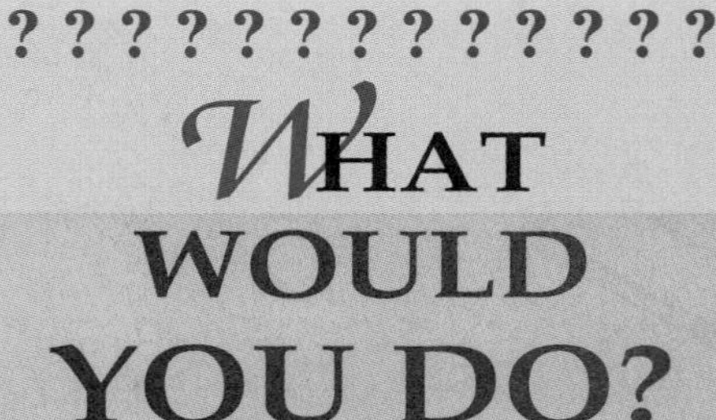

You are very interested in computers. You have subscribed to a computer magazine to learn more about them. You are saving money to buy a PC. But, the more you read, the more confusing it gets. There are so many different brand names and models from which to choose. When you do get close to making a decision, you read that a newer, more powerful, and cheaper model will be out soon. Should you buy or continue to wait?

What would you do?

FIGURE 19–4 **A typical PC system consists of a keyboard, CPU, monitor, and printer.**
Courtesy of © Tandy Corporation.

A computer system usually has several input and output devices. These devices are called *peripherals* because they are located outside of the CPU. The keyboard, mouse, monitor, printer, disc drive, and modem are all peripherals. Peripherals, of course, are part of the computer hardware.

Computers vary greatly in size, speed, storage capacity, and cost. The most familiar computer is the personal computer, or simply PC. The standard PC is a general-purpose computer designed for home and office use. A PC system can sit easily on a desktop and perform a wide variety of software applications. Smaller, portable PCs are called notebooks. An even smaller pocket-sized computer, known as a palmtop, is available.

The smallest computer is the tiny "computer on a chip," called a *microprocessor.* These are computers built for a specific purpose, such as controlling fuel usage in an automobile engine. Millions of computer chips are used every year in the manufacturing of telephones,

FIGURE 19–5 The PS–1 is a standard size PC.
Courtesy of IBM Corporation.

FIGURE 19–6 **The Thinkpad 750C is portable, about the size of a brief case, and can be used on your lap.**
Courtesy of IBM Corporation.

microwave ovens, VCRs, fax machines, and hundreds of other products.

Very powerful desktop computers, which are slightly larger than the standard PC, are called workstations. They combine the ease and use of a PC with the power and functions of larger computers. Workstations are used primarily for scientific and engineering work and office automation. Minicomputer and mainframe computers are the mid- and large-size systems used in business, industry, and government. Multiple terminals (keyboard and monitor combinations) allow hundreds, or even thousands, of people to use them at the same time. Regardless of size, all computers have similar features and components.

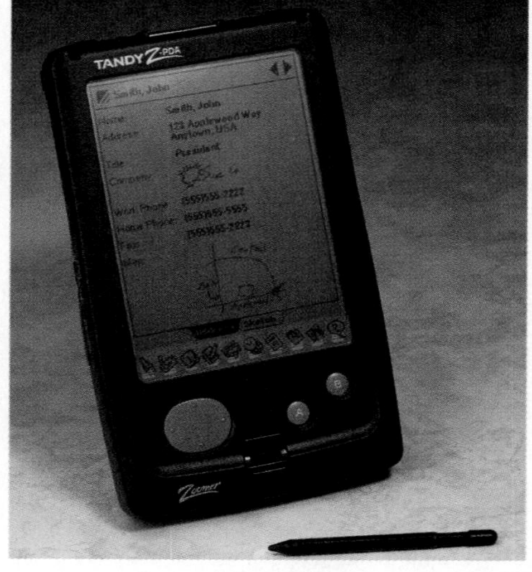

FIGURE 19–7 **The smallest of these PCs, the handheld Tandy Z, allows you to create and print sketches, handwritten or printed letters, and send and receive faxes. The Tandy Z-PDA Zoomer Personal Digital Assistant computer is about 7″ × 4″ × 1″ and fits in a pocket.**
Courtesy of Tandy Corporation.

COMPUTER SOFTWARE

Computer *software* is the programs and instructions that tell the computer what to do. There are two main types of software. One is system software, which manages what happens inside the computer. The other type is application software. These are the programs used to perform certain tasks, such as word processing.

System Software

A computer must have a program before it can do anything. Most computers are now sold with the operating system software already installed. When you first "boot up" the computer, system software is loaded into the computer's main memory. Once booted, the computer is ready to receive commands required to begin an application.

Commonly used PC operating system software includes MS-DOS, OS/2, and Macintosh. The most popular one is MS-DOS. DOS stands for Disk Operating System. The letters MS stand for Microsoft, which is the name of the company that developed it. Today, it is simply referred to as DOS, followed by numerals that indicate the latest revision (for example DOS 6.2).

The operating system is an essential link between the CPU, peripherals, application software, and user. The user controls operating software by entering commands. Each command is entered after a prompt (C>). For example, typing C> DIR and pressing Enter commands the software to display on the screen a list of files on the disk. Typing C> WP and pressing Enter loads a popular word processing program into memory. A user can also control software by selecting options from a menu.

The easiest method of controlling software is with a *graphic user interface (GUI)*. This approach was first popularized by the Apple Macintosh. The GUI uses small pictures called *icons* instead of words. For example, the outline of an eraser may represent the function of erasing the screen. To erase, a mouse is used to move the cursor to the erase icon. By clicking the mouse, a command is given to the software to erase the screen. A GUI, called Windows, has been developed by Microsoft Corporation to work with DOS, see Figure 19–8.

Application Software

The widespread use and acceptance of computers in the workplace are due to their ability to accomplish useful tasks. This is done through the use of application software. Following is a description of five basic types of software.

Document Production. The most common use of PCs is for word processing. This involves using the computer as a sophisticated typewriter. Letters and characters, called text, are *keyboarded* into the computer. The text can be edited and revised on the screen. Copies of the finished document are reproduced on a separate printer. The text can be stored electronically and recalled later for future use.

An advanced form of word processing is called desktop publishing. Text can be combined with graphics (charts, diagrams, drawings, pictures) in different page layouts and

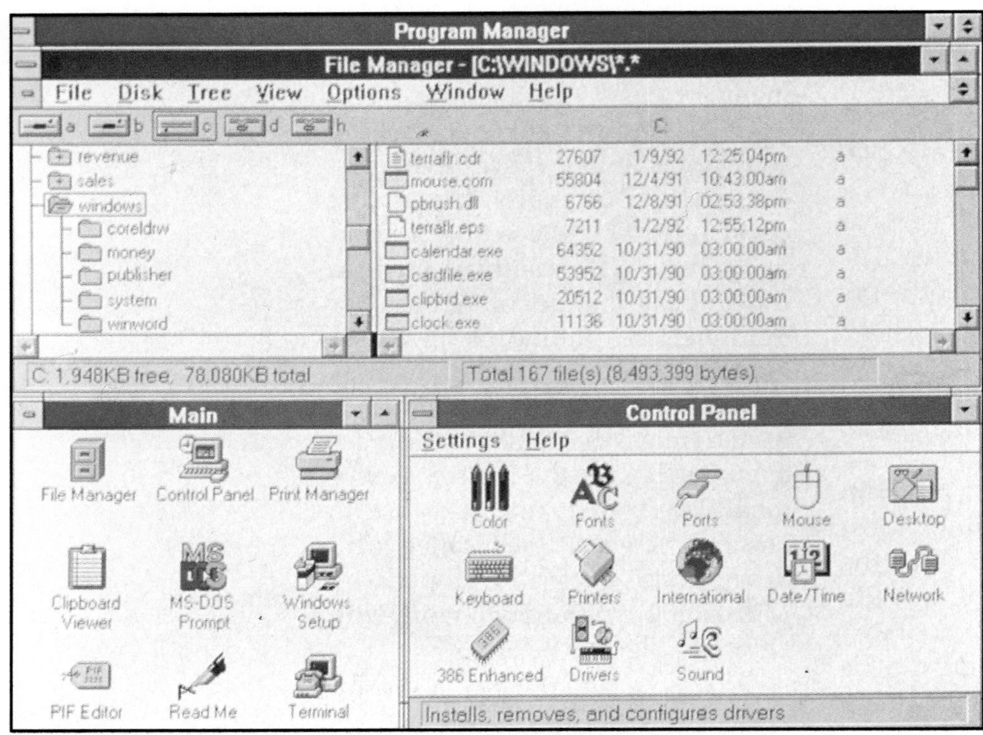

FIGURE 19–8 The windows-type interface is the easiest way to control software.
Courtesy of Microsoft Corporation.

type styles. High-quality reports, newsletters, pamphlets, and similar materials can be produced with desktop publishing software.

Spreadsheets. The financial records kept by accountants and bookkeepers are called spreadsheets. Almost any problem in which data are put into rows and columns and used in calculations can be prepared with spreadsheet software. It is used for budgeting, sales forecasting, income projection, and investment analysis. As new data are added, calculations can be performed automatically.

Data and File Management. Magazine publishers, insurance companies, airlines, manufacturers, and many other businesses maintain huge files of customer and inventory data. Your public library may have its card catalog stored in a computer. This is done with database management software. Such software is used to organize, store, and retrieve information from a database.

Graphics. This software is used to create charts and graphs. Some graphic software called "paint" and "draw" programs can be used to create complex pictures and diagrams. The output of graphics programs is often incorporated into desktop publishing or used to create slides and transparencies for presentations. A specialized type of graphics software called computer-aided drafting (CAD) is used to create three-dimensional designs and drawings.

FIGURE 19–9 A AND B **Graphics software is used to create a variety of charts, graphs, and other interesting visuals.**
Courtesy of IBM Corporation.

Communications. Transferring data from one computer to another is done with communications software. This is one of the fastest growing applications of computers. A computer that is linked together by electronic cable with another computer is called a *network.* Networks are used to enable individual computers to share printers, software, data files, and the like. Most large businesses and government institutions have their computers connected together into a local area network (LAN).

In the mid-1980s, a voluntary movement began to join LANs together to form regional, national, and international networks. Now, a world-wide "network of networks"

FIGURE 19–10 **Communications via electronic networks is becoming one of the fastest-growing computer software applications.**
Courtesy of TRW Inc.

has been created called the Internet. Collectively, these networks join universities, school systems businesses, government agencies, and numerous other groups worldwide.

Millions of people currently use the Internet. All that is required is a personal computer, a modem, and the correct software (some of which is free). There are three primary uses of the Internet:

- *E-mail,* which allows a user to send and receive electronic messages and other information. For example, you can keyboard a memo and send it to several friends thousands of miles away and they can read it on their computers seconds later.
- *Computer conferencing,* which involves simultaneous communication among individuals or groups. For example, a group of students interested in a particular subject might conduct a computer conference on that topic. Communication is accomplished by keyboarding "conversation" into the computer.
- *Information access,* which is available through a variety of electronic databases. This application is like having a library at your fingertips. You could, for example, search for information at the Library of Congress, read a news release from the White House press secretary, find out airline flight schedules, or learn about tourist attractions at a location you plan to visit.

By the year 2000, the majority of schools will be hooked to the Internet. Find out whether your school has access and get yourself plugged into the Information Superhighway.

Summary. The five types of general application software described are commonly known as stand-alone programs. This means that they work by themselves. A user, however, often needs to switch between applications (for example, to create a bar chart from the statistical data in a spreadsheet for use in a presentation).

To make it easier to switch applications, integrated software has been developed. One common integrated software package includes spreadsheet, graphics, and database management. Another package includes all five of the common stand-alone programs. Integrated software has many advantages for home, office, and small business users.

COMPUTERS IN THE WORKPLACE

Computers play a very important role in our working world. Following is only a sample of their varied uses.

Business and Industry

Offices now do routine tasks by computer. These may include checking inventories and managing payrolls. In many offices, the typewriter is disappearing in favor of the word processor. And in some offices, even the secretary is disappearing! That is, some secretaries are staying home to do their work.

Many companies are experimenting with what is called telecommuting. This refers to a workstation in an employee's home. Work assignments go to the employee via a phone modem. The employee does the work on a PC and then relays it back to the office.

American auto manufacturing was once considered to be the best in the world. By 1980, however, the auto industry had many problems, including recession, foreign competition, and high interest rates. The major U.S. auto companies were losing billions of dollars. Auto companies launched a major spending program to modernize production. Computers and robots appeared. They began to do hundreds of tasks, such as precision welding, painting, and alignment. In only a few years, production costs went down and quality improved. Some auto experts think that U.S. cars are once again among the best in the world. The computer played an important role in this recovery.

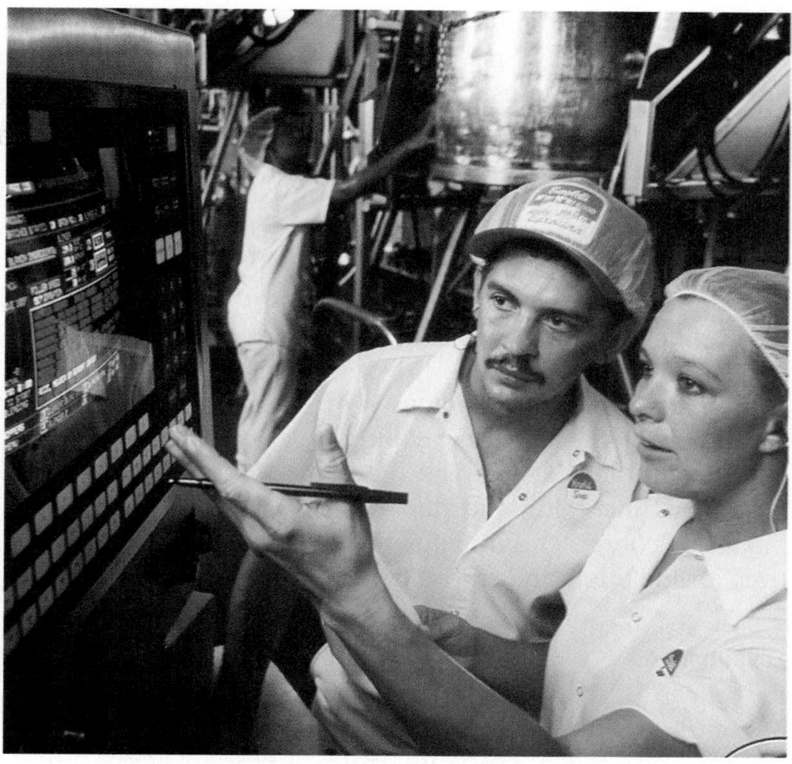

FIGURE 19–11 **Quality control during manufacturing is maintained with the aid of computers.**
Courtesy of Campbell Soup Company.

Government

The federal government was the earliest user of computers. Today, the government could not operate without computers. The Census Bureau relies on computers to update population figures. The Internal Revenue Service uses computers to check millions of tax returns per year. The FBI uses computers to compare a suspect's fingerprints with those in a computer database. Computers are a vital part of the radar defense system that guards the United States. They also launch, guide, and land spacecraft.

Communications

A writer doing a story used to rely only on printed reference materials. Now, the writer may have a computer and modem linked to an electronic database. Databases may provide general or specialized information. Some databases cover stock prices or airline schedules. Others deal with movie review. What's more, the information in an electronic database is up-to-date. With printed reference materials, the data are probably a year or more old on the day they come off the press.

Other uses of computers in communications include computer-to-computer hookups that allow mail to be sent electronically. Computers also route telephone calls automatically without the need for a human operator. The computer even tells you when you dial a wrong number.

Transportation

The transportation industry relies on computing systems for controlling and planning the use of trains, aircraft, ships, and highway traffic. Railroad companies use computers to keep track of equipment scattered over many locations. Many cities in the United States have computerized traffic lights that change according to how much traffic is flowing. One of the most important uses of computers is in air traffic control. Here, computers keep track of the location of incoming and departing planes. A computer simulator helps train airline pilots and ship captains.

Education

You can probably see many uses of computers in your school. Computers help teach students from kindergarten through graduate school. Guidance counselors also are using computers to help students plan careers.

Isaiah made an appointment at the career center for a session on "self-guided career exploration." When he arrived at the career center, a worker directed him to a computer terminal. He "booted up" a floppy disk and completed an interest inventory. When he finished, a profile of his interests was printed out. The computer also gave him a list of occupations he might wish to explore.

He then met with a counselor who helped him interpret his profile. Later, he returned to the computer for printouts on several occupations that interested him. He also got a listing of schools in his state that provided training in those occupations.

Other school personnel also use computers. Administrators plan course schedules, keep track of teachers' assignments, and store records of students' grades. Coaches use the computer to keep team and individual statistics in all sports. The school dietitian plans the lunch menu and stores recipes on the computer.

Science and Engineering

All science occupations rely on computers. Chemists and physicists use computers to control and check laboratory instruments and to analyze data. Through computers, astronomers guide telescopes and process photos of planets and other objects in space. In biology labs, computer-controlled machines scan and measure slides of genes and blood cells. Meteorologists use computers to track and study weather patterns.

Without computers, it would be impossible for engineers to solve certain problems. Architectural and civil engineers use computers to design bridges and other structures. They even use computers to make actual drawings. Before road construction starts, computers often analyze photographs. The results help people decide exactly where the roads should go.

Medicine

In medicine, computer use began with keeping records. Now, doctors use the computer as a diagnostic tool. One clinic has computers in each doctor's office. The computers are connected to a network containing some 4,000 symptoms for more than 500 diseases. When a doctor

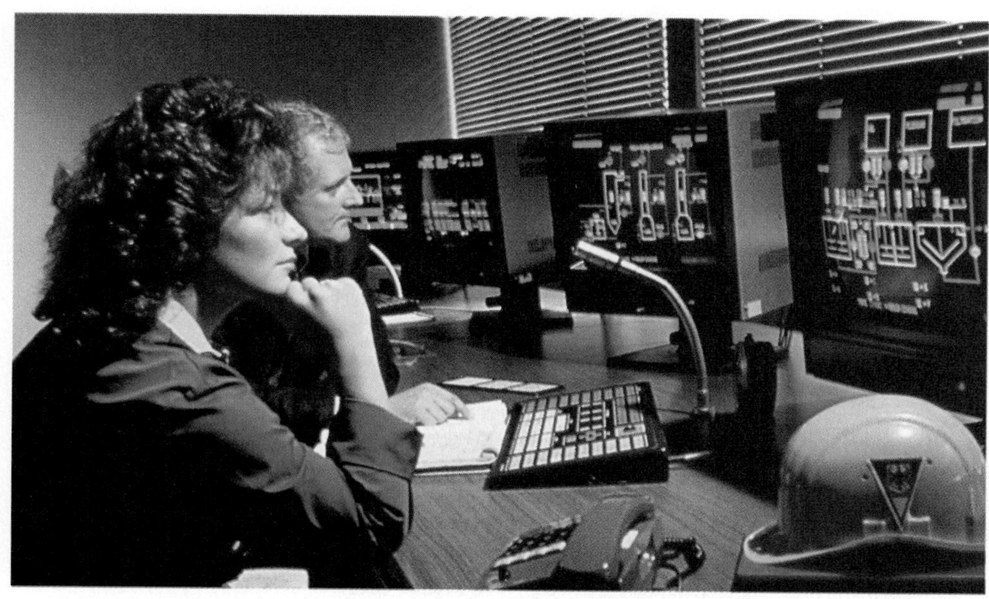

FIGURE 19–12 **The operation of electrical power generating equipment is checked automatically by computers.**
Courtesy of Westinghouse Electric Corporation.

types a list of symptoms into the computer, it prints out a list of possible diseases.

Computers are also a help in the care and treatment of patients. Computers can control heart pacemakers. Computers can also pump measured quantities of insulin into diabetics. They can test blood samples for hundreds of different allergies. In the future, computers may stimulate deadened muscles with electric impulses. This may allow many paralyzed people to walk.

Dr. Evers uses her computer for information on various drugs. By typing in the word *rhinitis* (inflammation of the nose), she can get a list of specific medications from among thousands of drugs.

THE FUTURE OF COMPUTERS

The rapid development of computer technology should continue

? ? ? ? ? ? ? ? ? ? ? ? ? ? ?

WHAT WOULD YOU DO?

You work for your grandparents in a small, family-owned business. After taking a computer course in school, you have become aware of what computers can do. You see a number of ways that a computer could be used in the business. You suggest to your grandfather that he buy a computer.

"Son, we do not have the money to buy an expensive computer," he says. "Besides, the old-fashioned way has been working just fine for years."

You are disappointed, but still believe that a computer would be a wise investment.

What would you do?

in the future. Computers will get smaller, more powerful, and less expensive. At the same time, computers will become easier to use. Programming will be simpler and it will become possible to give spoken commands to computers. All of these changes will have a great impact on the workplace. Predicting the future is risky. However, the following changes seem likely:

- The number of occupations that require computer literacy and keyboarding skills will continue to increase. Eventually, most occupations will involve computer use.
- Employment in areas involving computers and robots will increase dramatically. One source, for instance, estimates that two million robot technicians will be working by the year 2000.
- Computer technology will create many new industries and occupations. (Try to guess what some of these might be.)
- Electronics will surpass auto manufacturing and oil as the world's largest industry.
- The use of industrial robots will expand from the assembly line to all phases of manufacturing. In the totally automated factory of the future, robots will replace humans in many cases.
- The automation of offices and other service industries will increase. In the office of the future, most communication will be carried out electronically. Electronic storage and transmission of information will lead to the "paperless office."
- Major shifts in job patterns will occur. Computers and robots may eliminate as many as 25 percent of present jobs.
- Technology can also create new jobs. Many experts believe that, in the long run, technology will produce more jobs than it takes away.
- Workers losing their jobs to automation must be willing to retrain. To keep up with new technology, all workers will need continuing education and training.

You live in a very exciting time. Not since the Industrial Revolution has the workplace undergone such changes. Indeed, some people are calling the modern era of electronics the "second industrial revolution." The computer is leading this revolution. Your generation will be the first to grow up in the world of the computer.

How much knowledge and experience do you have with computers? If it is limited, think about doing something to correct it. Take a course or try to get a friend to start teaching you keyboarding skills. Not being able to use a computer could hold you back from getting or advancing in a job.

FOCUS ON

Health and Safety

Repetitive Motion Injury

We usually associate on-the-job injuries with occupations like police officer, coal miner, and farmer. One of the fastest growing types of occupational injury, however, is found among people who work with computers. It is called repetitive motion injury (RMI).

This disorder arises whenever a person must repeat movements of the hands, fingers, or arms thousands of times a day. Keyboarding is highly repetitive and users often sit with arms and shoulders in awkward or cramped positions. When the wrist is repeatedly flexed and extended, tendons in the wrist may become irritated and swell. The swelling presses on nerves that result in tingling and numbness in the fingers and hands. Pain may also occur in the arm, elbow, or shoulder.

This injury can often be avoided by setting up a computer work station for maximum comfort and efficiency, as follows:

- Adjust chair height so the thighs are horizontal and feet are flat. The back and neck should be erect. Upper arms should be perpendicular to the floor.
- Forearms and wrists should be as horizontal as possible. The idea is to prevent wrists from bending back and forward. Padded wrist rests placed in front of the keyboard are helpful.
- Adjust the computer screen height so that the top is just below eye level. This reduces tension on the back and neck.
- Frequent short breaks from keyboarding are essential. Fifteen minutes of a non-typing task for every hour of intensive typing is recommended.

Working long hours at a keyboard does not necessarily mean that one will develop RMI. This disorder, like most on-the-job injuries can be prevented.

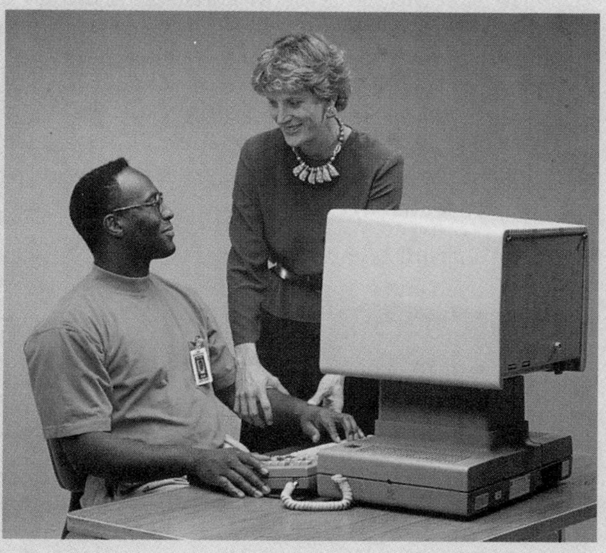

Many companies show employees who use computers frequently how to sit and move to avoid repetitive motion injuries.
Courtesy Knight-Ridder Inc.

CHAPTER 19 REVIEW

CHAPTER IN BRIEF

- Computer literacy is a general knowledge of what computers are, how they work, and for what they can be used. A computer is an electronic tool. It helps people do various kinds of work.
- A keyboard is the part of a computer that looks like a typewriter. Keyboards are similar in terms of basic commands and procedures. You will benefit by knowing how to use a computer keyboard.
- The computer works in three steps: it receives instructions, it does tasks according to instructions provided, and it shares the results. This is called the input-processing-output sequence.
- A computer has five sections as follows:
  1. *Input.* This section takes information and changes it into electronic signals the computer can use.
  2. *Memory.* This section records and stores the data. One part is permanent memory (ROM). The other part is working memory (RAM).
  3. *Arithmetic and logic.* This is the heart of the computer. It does all of the computer's math and logic functions.
  4. *Control.* This section directs the other four sections of the computer.
  5. *Output.* This section changes data from electronic language into understandable forms.
- A computer system consists of the CPU and several interconnected pieces of hardware called peripherals. Computer systems vary greatly in size, speed, storage capacity, and cost.
- There are two main types of computer software. System software manages what happens inside the computer. Application software is used to perform certain tasks, such as word processing, spreadsheets, database management, graphics, and communications.
- Computers play a very important role in the working world. They are used in all major fields of work.
- The rapid development of computer technology should continue in the future. The number of occupations that require computer literacy and keyboarding skills will increase. If your knowledge of computers is limited, think about doing something to correct it.

WORDS TO KNOW

computer
computer literacy
graphic user interface
hardware
icons
keyboarding skills
microprocessor
modem

network
peripheral
program
RAM
ROM
software

QUESTIONS TO ANSWER

1. Name two characteristics of a computer keyboard.
2. What are the three major steps in the operation of a computer?
3. List the five sections of a computer. Briefly tell what each section does.
4. Name five different types of input devices.
5. What is the difference between ROM and RAM?
6. Name two computer output devices.
7. Rewrite the following steps in the proper sequence:
   a. Processed data returned to memory
   b. Numbers typed into keyboard
   c. Processed data shown on monitor
   d. Stored data moved for processing
   e. Calculations performed
   f. Typed data stored in memory
8. What three components make up a "computer system"?
9. Name and define the two types of computer software.
10. Identify the type of application software used for each of the following tasks:
    a. Storing lists of customer addresses
    b. Writing a business report
    c. Transmitting an electronic message
    d. Creating a bar graph
    e. Preparing a budget
11. What is meant by telecommuting?
12. Computer technology both eliminates and creates jobs. Give an example of each.

ACTIVITIES TO DO

1. Identify as many ways as you can that computers are being used in your school. Do not limit your answers to just instruction.
2. Choose an occupation in which you are interested. Find out how workers in that occupation use computers. Present your findings in an oral report to the class.
3. The increasing popularity of computers has led to many new occupations and new businesses. Look in the Yellow Pages of your phone book to find out the numbers and types of different computer businesses in your area. Also, examine the classified section of your Sunday newspaper. How many job ads can you find for computer-related occupations? Discuss your findings in class.
4. Identify as many sources as possible in your school or community regarding how you might learn or improve your computer skills.

TOPICS TO DISCUSS

1. Computer critics say that computers are putting too many people out of work. They believe that someday computers will take over most of what workers now do. Do you agree? Discuss in class the human costs and benefits of computers.
2. People are often reluctant to use new technology such as computers. Why do you think this is so? How might you change the attitude of someone who feels this way?
3. In what types of occupations do computers have the greatest potential use? The least potential use? Explain your answers.

CHAPTER 20 Entrepreneurial Skills

OUTLINE

- Nature of Small Business
- Advantages and Disadvantages of Self-employment
- Ingredients for Success
- Are You the Type?
- Choosing a Business
- Chapter Review

OBJECTIVES

After reading this chapter, you should be able to:

- Name contributions that small business makes to our society.
- Discuss advantages and disadvantages of self-employment.
- Outline what it is like to own and operate a small business.
- Identify ingredients necessary for a successful business.
- Evaluate your own self-employment traits.
- Describe factors to consider in choosing a business.

As a cooperative education or work experience student, you are working in a business owned or managed by someone else. In the future, you may continue to work as an employee for another person, or you may decide to become an *entrepreneur.* An entrepreneur is someone who runs his or her own small business. The person is *self-employed.*

NATURE OF SMALL BUSINESS

Small businesses are found in agriculture, construction, sales, services, and every other type of industry. They are located throughout the country. Many are in big cities, but a large number are in small towns. Small businesses are as scattered and different as the people who own them.

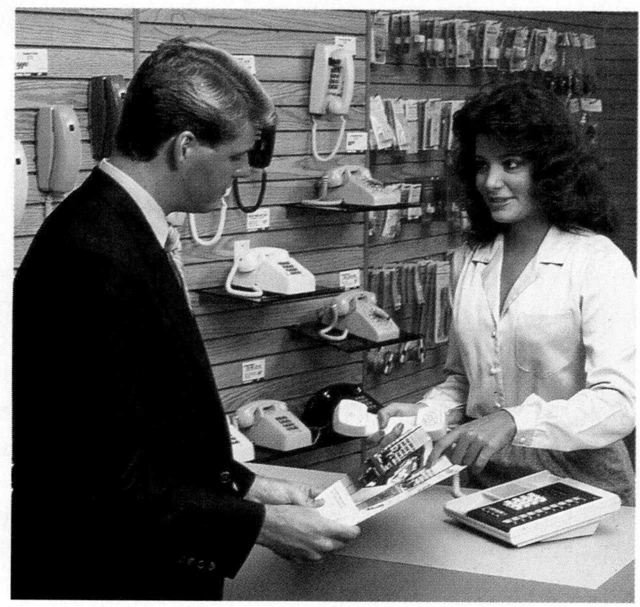

FIGURE 20–1 **This woman has reached a goal to which many people aspire. She recently opened her own telecommunications store.**
Courtesy of Tandy Corporation.

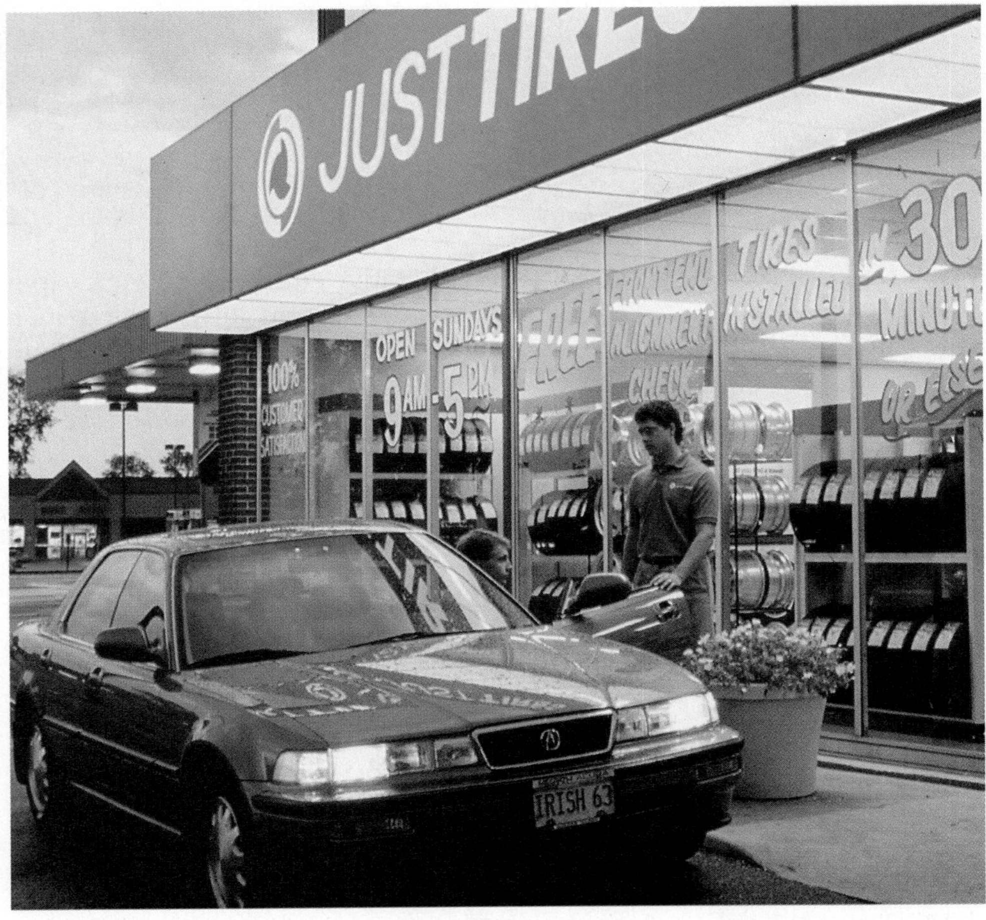

FIGURE 20–2 **Many small businesses are part of the service industry, like this auto repair and maintenance shop.**
Courtesy The Goodyear Tire and Rubber Company.

Importance of Small Business

Small business makes many important contributions to our society. One is the creation of new jobs. As new businesses begin and expand, they hire new workers. The majority of all new jobs are provided by businesses employing fewer than 20 people.

Another contribution is that small businesses often recycle old buildings. It is not unusual, for example, to find a restaurant or a dry cleaners housed in what used to be a service station. Can you think of examples in your town or neighborhood?

A third contribution is that small business provides opportunities for women and minorities to get started in business. About 39 percent of all self-employed people are females and 9 percent are minorities. The percentage for both groups is increasing steadily each year.

The most important contribution of small business comes from new inventions, products, and services. Many of the great success stories of American business have been the result of people who had a new idea or a better way of doing things.

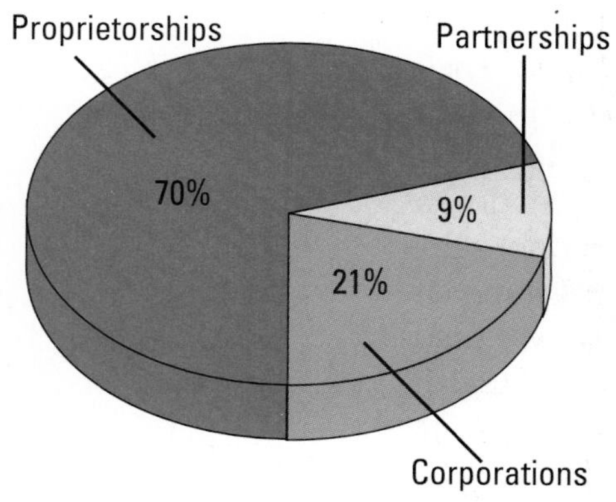

FIGURE 20–3 **Proprietorships make up about 70 percent of all small businesses.**

Form of Organization

A business can be organized in one of three ways: proprietorship, partnership, or corporation.

Proprietorship. This is the simplest and most common form. A *proprietorship* is a business owned by one person, who receives all the profits. The owner may have employees.

Partnership. A partnership is a business that has two or more co-owners. In fact, *partnerships* often come about because proprietors need additional money or want help running the business. Owners in a partnership share in both the company's management and its profits.

Corporation. A *corporation* is very different from the other two forms of business. In return for a fee paid to the state, a corporation receives a *charter,* which allows the business to carry on certain activities. The owners of a corporation are called *stockholders* and they elect a *board of directors.* The board, in turn, makes major decisions about the company and hires the company president.

? ? ? ? ? ? ? ? ? ? ? ? ? ?

WHAT WOULD YOU DO?

The company you work for is losing business to foreign competition. The owner says he cannot compete if he has to continue paying high labor costs. He is looking for a buyer. If he cannot sell the business, he is going to shut it down.

A group of employees has been meeting to help find a solution. One option being considered is for the employees to buy the company and run it themselves. This has been done successfully in a few businesses.

What would you do?

ADVANTAGES AND DISADVANTAGES OF SELF-EMPLOYMENT F12

Being self-employed is different from working for someone else. Before starting a business, you should consider the advantages and disadvantages of working for yourself. We asked some entrepreneurs about the benefits of self-employment. Here is what they told us:

"I never really liked working for other people. I like to try new things. That can be a problem when you are an employee. In my business, I can take full advantage of new ideas that appeal to me."

"Being self-employed, I can make my decisions quickly. I used to work for a large corporation in which decision-making was very slow."

"I enjoy having a flexible schedule. Last week, my wife took two vacation days. I arranged my schedule so we could go camping."

"In the shop where I worked, I did only one task. Now I can work on a project from beginning to end. I can use *all* my skills. And, I am working toward goals that are important to me."

"I am proud to be a business owner. Four years ago, we opened this small supermarket. We now have three, which will belong to our kids someday."

"When you work for yourself, no one can fire you!"

All work situations have negative points. Self-employment is no exception:

"In the beginning, the appliance-repair business brought in little money. But we still had to pay rent and other expenses."

"I am a free-lance graphic artist. My income varies a lot. It is either 'feast' or 'famine' it seems."

"We are store owners in a one-industry town. As soon as the plant started laying off, we were affected. And it wasn't our fault! If this keeps on, we may have to close. We could lose the money we have put into the business. And we could lose our house and other property, too. We are hoping for the best."

"Being self-employed is high pressure. All the decisions are my responsibility. If I make a major mistake, all of us around here could be out of work."

"I often put in 60- or 70-hour weeks."

Even when you are self-employed, you will not be your own boss entirely. No matter what business you choose, you must satisfy your customers. And your *creditors* and your competitors will influence what you do. For instance, suppose the store down the street has a two-for-one sale. You may have to do the same at your store, too. The law also touches your business. Health authorities and insurance people will expect you to meet certain standards and to follow certain regulations. You will have to abide by wage and hour laws and keep proper tax and business records as well.

No one person can represent the experiences of all entrepreneurs. The following case study will give you a good idea of the advantages and disadvantages of self-employment. The workday of Ann Kirsten (the person in the following case study) shows many of the freedoms, uncertainties, and responsibilities shared by small business owners.

Self-employment Case Study

As an entrepreneur, Ann Kirsten does many types of work tasks. In a large business, each work task would probably be done by a single person. As you read this piece, which has been reprinted and slightly adapted from the *Occupational Outlook Quarterly,* keep in mind the variety of things that Ann has to be able to do.

The Day Begins. On a typical workday, Ann Kirsten arrives at the Country Gifts 'n Crafts, her small gift and card shop, at about 10 A.M. Stepping inside, she takes a sharp owner's look around the store,

FIGURE 20–4 **Ann Kirsten, owner of Country Gifts 'n Crafts, is beginning her usual long, 10-hour day.**
Photo by David W. Tuttle.

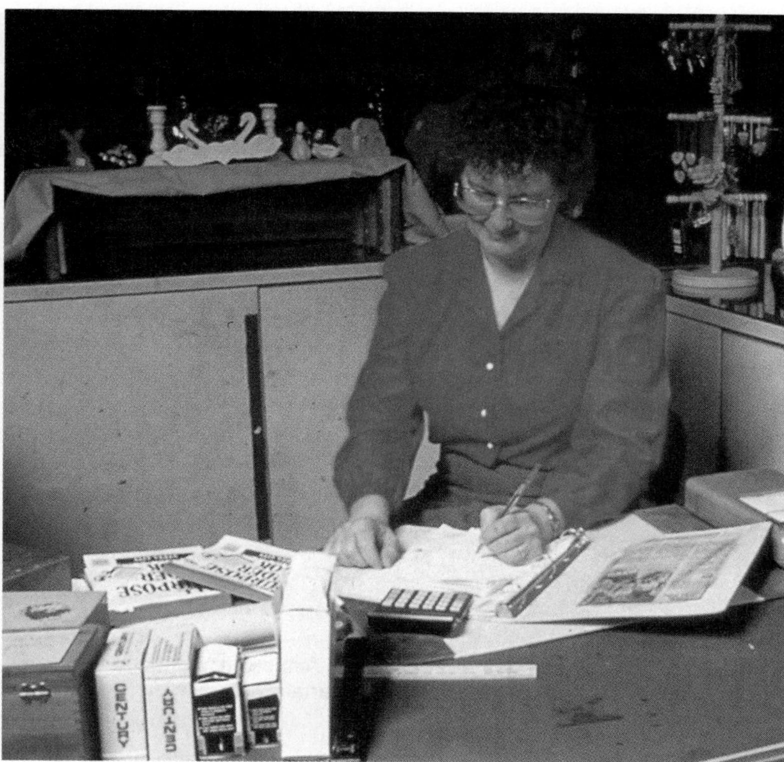

FIGURE 20–5 **Ann must keep up with correspondence and other types of paperwork because it is an important part of her business.**
Photo by David W. Tuttle.

which holds a miscellaneous assortment of wares: crystal salad bowls, candles, neckties, placemats, scented soap, and toys are among the many items in stock.

The store opens at 11 A.M. and Ann hurries to make sure everything is in order. She makes a fresh pot of coffee—a bonus for early customers—and checks to see that the store's shelves are well-stocked and tidy. Spotting a few gaps, she tells the two full-time salesclerks who have just arrived to shelve supplies of candle holders and ashtrays. She also instructs the employees to unpack a recently arrived carton of stainless steel serving bowls, tag them with the prices she has determined, and display them near the coffee mugs.

Answering the Mail. Satisfied that everything is in order, Ann takes the morning mail upstairs to a small room filled with so many cardboard boxes that it looks more like a stockroom than an executive office. Settling down at her old wooden desk, she opens the mail, taking special note of new merchandise catalogs, bills, and a customer check that has bounced. She answers some of the letters and files the rest into appropriate piles for future action.

Ann spends the rest of the morning in her office filling out several government forms required of

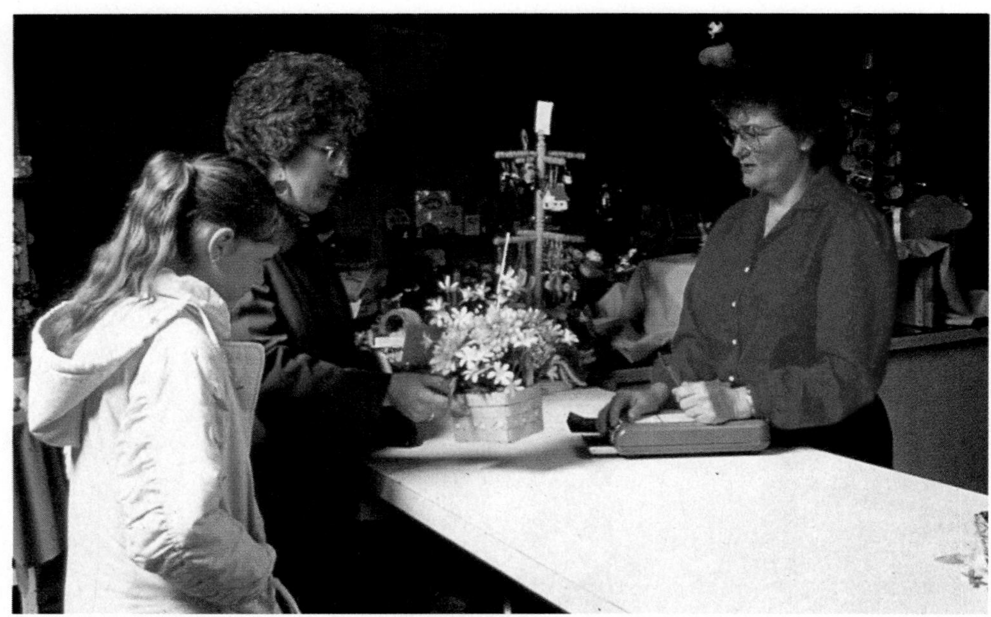

FIGURE 20–6 **Having her own business gives Ann a sense of satisfaction and independence that makes up for the long hours and economic uncertainty she has.**
Photo by David W. Tuttle.

self-employed persons. She is interrupted by a telephone call from a *supplier* who regrets that Ann's last order will be delayed for three weeks. Annoyed, but unable to do anything about the shipment date, Ann shrugs off the incident.

Unexpected Caller. A few minutes later, a sales representative unexpectedly walks in and tries to sell Ann a new line of paper placemats and napkins. Ann generally buys her merchandise from *wholesale houses* in New York City (which she visits about six times a year). But occasionally, she does buy from a visiting salesperson. Today she declines, however, believing that her current line of paper table items is adequate. Ann takes her time about making this decision, since her income hinges on her ability to make sound judgments about what her customers will buy. If she invests in an item that does not sell, she loses money.

Waiting on Customers. At 1 P.M., Ann goes back downstairs to relieve her clerks during their lunch hours. Before starting the store seven years ago, Ann enjoyed a 15-year career in public relations. She likes working with people and enjoys waiting on and talking to customers.

The clerks return and Ann grabs a quick lunch at a neighborhood delicatessen before running a business errand at the post office. She then takes time out for a haircut. Inasmuch as she is her own boss, Ann can take time off whenever she wants. Generally, however, she is reluctant to spend too much time away from the store, since there is always so much work to be done.

FIGURE 20–7 **Ann enjoys being able to leave work when she chooses for a short time to run errands or have lunch with a friend. This is one of the advantages of self-employment.**
Photo by David W. Tuttle.

Bookkeeping, Too! Back at the office, Ann goes over the books with her accountant, who keeps track of income and outgo and evaluates the store's performance. Looking at recent sales income and expenses, Ann briefly remembers the days when she received a fixed yearly income. In those days, she regularly collected a paycheck from which her employers had already withheld money for state and federal income taxes. Her share of payments for social security benefits, a health insurance plan, and other programs that assured her income during old age or periods of sickness had also been deducted. And like most employers, the organizations for which she worked had paid part of the cost of these benefits.

Looking over the books, Ann is happy to see a good rate of profit. If the store's income had not met expenses for the last several months, she would have to make up the difference out of her own savings. This rarely occurs nowadays, but, like many new businesses, the store lost money during its first several months of operation.

Ann recalls, too, how she had to borrow money to start the business and persuade a lender that she could succeed. Then there had been the years of meeting payments on the borrowed money as well as interest for its use. These payments had to be made regularly, for a merchant is helpless without a good credit rating. As she looked back, Ann was gratified to see that it had all paid off.

End of a Long Day. Ann finishes conferring with her accountant at 6 P.M. and then goes downstairs to help wait on customers until the shop closes at 7. Several boxes of merchandise have arrived during the day, and Ann stays for an hour after closing to unpack and shelve a few items. She generally puts in at least a nine-hour workday—not counting "time off" when she reads magazines to keep up with buying trends or thinks about new ideas for the store—and works six days a week.

Every once in a while, Ann remembers the days when she was salaried and worked a forty-hour, Monday-through-Friday week. She strongly believes, however, that the present freedom and challenge of being her own boss and the knowledge that her efforts are paying off in money that goes into her own pocket more than make up for the long hours and other disadvantages.

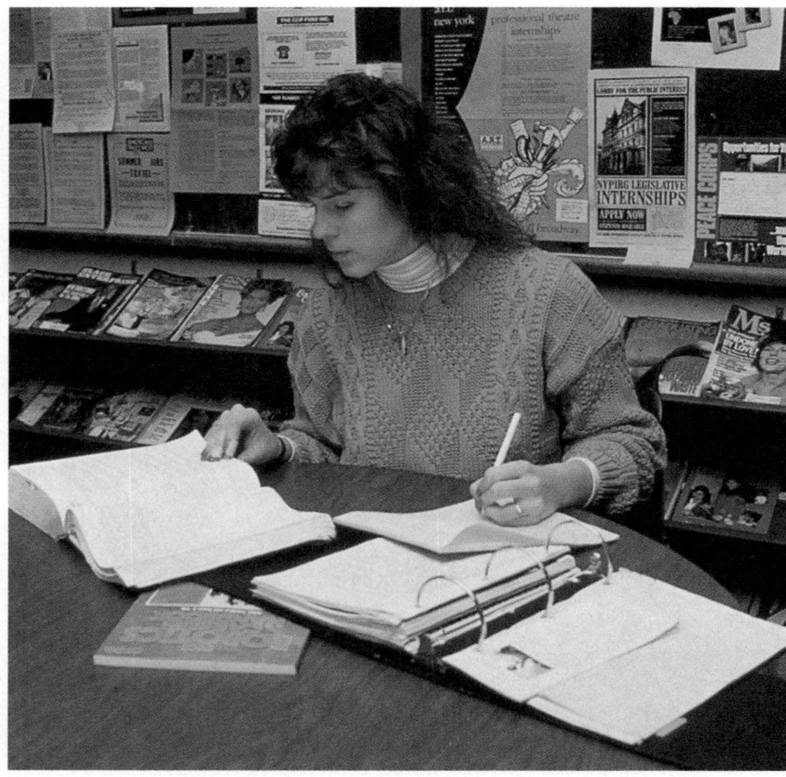

FIGURE 20–8 **The traits of a good student, such as working hard, meeting deadlines, and attending to detail, are similar to the traits needed to be a successful entrepreneur.**
Photo by David W. Tuttle.

INGREDIENTS FOR SUCCESS

A successful business requires more than just interest and a desire to make money. Studies of businesses and conversations with business owners suggest that three things are necessary for a successful business: the right personality, know-how, and money.

Personality

Not everyone has the personality needed for self-employment. Success in the business is not based on wishful thinking. If you want to be your own boss, you need to be honest about your strengths and weaknesses. The traits needed by a self-employed person are:

1. Ability to take action when needed
2. Ability to lead others
3. Being dependable and trustworthy
4. Being a good organizer
5. Ability to work hard
6. Ability to make good decisions
7. Having a positive attitude
8. Being honest and open
9. Ability to accomplish goals
10. Desire to succeed
11. Willingness to take risks

Know-how

Self-employed people need some knowledge in various areas of business. These include finance, economics, management, marketing, accounting, and commercial law. Business know-how is usually learned through coursework and on-the-job training. Before starting out on their own, most entrepreneurs work in others' businesses.

Pat King started his own restaurant last year. He had worked many years as a manager for a national chain before making his decision. Even after their business is started, many owners enroll in management training programs and take workshops and study materials provided by the Small Business Administration (SBA).

The SBA is an agency of the federal government. Its purpose is to encourage, assist, and protect the interests of small business. The SBA produces and distributes low-cost, management assistance publications and conducts management workshops and courses. The agency also makes loans to small businesses. Your public librarian can help you find the location of the nearest SBA office.

Before starting a business in a trade, technical, or professional career, it is necessary to learn the required skills. For example, Kerry and Jill got training in electronics, worked for someone else, then started their own electronics repair business.

Another way to get business know-how is to buy a *franchise.* A franchise is a contract with a large company to sell goods and services within a certain area. Some well known franchises are H. R. Block, Domino Pizza, Subway, Midas, and Nutri System. Franchise fees range from several thousand dollars to several hundred thousand dollars.

Money

The third key to successful self-employment is money. An entrepreneur must have enough capital (money) to start a business. Often this money can be borrowed from banks and other lending institutions. Business owners must pay rent, utilities, and other operating expenses. Equipment and supplies must be purchased. *Retailers* must be able to buy a large enough supply of merchandise to attract and hold customers. Any employees must be paid first. And, of course, there must be enough left over for the owner's salary.

The cost of going into business depends on the type of business, the location, size, and other factors. Often, the business that can be started with a small amount of money is also the business with the

? ? ? ? ? ? ? ? ? ? ? ? ? ? ?

WHAT WOULD YOU DO?

You are a very good auto mechanic and take pride in your work. You can diagnose difficult problems that other mechanics often cannot solve. Customers also know your work is good. Many of them specifically request that you work on their cars. This irritates some of your co-workers.

Recently, several customers have remarked that you are too good of a mechanic to work for someone else. They say you ought to consider starting your own business.

What would you do?

least potential for profit. On the other hand, businesses with good profit potential are out of the reach of most people because of the money required to begin.

Most small businesses start out slowly. It takes time for a new business to establish a reputation and build up a supply of loyal customers. The Small Business Administration says that it takes four to six months for some businesses to be self-supporting. Others take even longer. Unfortunately, some businesses never succeed and must close.

ARE YOU THE TYPE?

To succeed in business, you must honestly evaluate your strengths and weaknesses. You will be your most important employee. If you recognize that you are weak in a certain area, you may be able to find a partner or hire an employee to help you. The exercise shown in Figure 20–9 will help you to discover if you have the traits needed for self-employment.

ENTREPRENEUR RATING SCALE

1. I am a self-starter. I get things done.	YES	NOT SURE	NO
2. I like people. I can get along with just about anybody.	YES	NOT SURE	NO
3. I am a leader. I can get most people to go along when I start something.	YES	NOT SURE	NO
4. I like to take charge of things and see them through.	YES	NOT SURE	NO
5. I like to have a plan before I start. I'm usually the one to get things lined up when our group wants to do something.	YES	NOT SURE	NO
6. I like working hard for something I want.	YES	NOT SURE	NO
7. I can make up my mind in a hurry if I want to.	YES	NOT SURE	NO
8. People can trust me. I do what I say.	YES	NOT SURE	NO
9. If I make up my mind to do something, I'll see it through.	YES	NOT SURE	NO
10. I am always careful to write things down and to keep good records.	YES	NOT SURE	NO

FIGURE 20–9 **Complete this exercise to see if you have the traits to be a successful entrepreneur. (Do not write in this book.)**
Source: Starting and Managing a Small Business of Your Own, Small Business Administration.

How did you do? Count up the number of *YES* answers. If most of your answers are *YES,* you may have what it takes to run your own business. Review your answers again. Make sure you did not answer *YES* because of wishful thinking.

If you have several *NO* or *NOT SURE* answers, you should probably not risk your money and your time in starting a business. You should recognize, however, that you can take steps to improve yourself and increase your chances of success.

CHOOSING A BUSINESS

If you are serious about going into business, you will first need to identify the business in which you want to be in. You need to be clear about the kind of business even though you may not know exactly which one. For example, you may be sure you want to go into retailing, but not know what sort of store to open. Or you may decide that some other business is better than the one you originally considered. The time to change your mind is before you start a business, not after.

You might also begin by writing out a summary of your background and experience. Include what you learned on jobs, in school, and from hobbies (that relate to your business interests). Then write down what you would like to do. Try to match up what you have done with what you would like to do. If you do not like the business you choose, your lack of interest will probably lead to failure.

The more experience and training you have, the better your chances of success. So pick a field you know the most about. The best way to learn about a business is through actual experience. Seek a job working for somebody else in the business you are considering. Try to pick a well-managed, successful company. Once hired, learn as much management know-how as you possibly can.

Education will help, too. While there may be no educational requirements for starting your own business, the more schooling you have, the better equipped you should be. For example, in most businesses, you must know how to figure interest and discounts, keep simple and accurate records, and take care of correspondence. How might you learn these skills in school?

Get all the facts you can about the kind of business you want to start. Find out what the appropriate trade association is, what it publishes, and what assistance it offers. Visit similar businesses to get a first-hand idea of how they operate. Read magazines, newspapers, and newsletters on the subject. Collect as much information as possible from other sources, even the competition. Talk with the local Chamber of Commerce, local business groups, banks, and the like.

Next, try to determine whether potential customers need or want the type of business in which you are interested. Do not take anything for granted. Even if certain products and services meet certain needs, people may want something different.

The business you are thinking about should be in tune with the trends of the time. Choose a field in which growth is expected. You will need to do studying and seek advice from people who are in a position to know. Successful business owners are those who can make accurate predictions about the future.

FIGURE 20–10 **This man opened a home inspection service when he learned that this need was not being met by other businesses in the area.**
Courtesy of American Electric Power.

FOCUS ON The Workplace

THE GROWTH OF SMALL BUSINESS

The first settlers to this country arrived from Europe. They came seeking freedom to live, speak, work, and worship. Many Colonial Americans chose business as a way of life. These early business-people were some of the first to speak out against British rule. Paul Revere, for example, was a silversmith before he became a revolutionary. Almost everyone who signed the Declaration of Independence was a businessperson or professional of some kind. For these individuals, the ideal of "life, liberty, and the pursuit of happiness" included the freedom to be one's own boss.

The stock of many small businesses is traded in the same way that large corporations are bought and sold.
Courtesy of New York Stock Exchange.

For about a century after the Revolutionary War, small business people and farmers provided most of the country's goods and services. Thousands of hardworking businessmen and women realized the American dream. They helped to lay the foundation for the Industrial Revolution of the late 1800s.

Machines invented during the Industrial Revolution led to the building of great factories. Gradually, more people went to work in cotton mills, steel mills, auto assembly plants, and other manufacturing industries.

In recent years, the economy has changed from an emphasis on goods production to providing services. An important fact about this change is that service businesses are more likely to be small businesses. Small businesses are being incorporated at a rate about twice the number from a decade earlier. No one knows how many proprietorships and partnerships are being formed. The trend, however, is clearly that more and more people are going into business for themselves.

CHAPTER 20 REVIEW

CHAPTER IN BRIEF

- Small businesses are found in every type of industry. They make many important contributions to our society. Small business creates new jobs, recycles old buildings, provides opportunities for women and minorities, and creates many new products and services. A business can be organized as a proprietorship, partnership, or corporation.
- Self-employment has many advantages and many disadvantages. Entrepreneurs work for themselves, make their own decisions, have a flexible schedule, do a variety of tasks, and take pride in owning their own business. On the other hand, entrepreneurs have big responsibilities, work long hours, have fluctuating incomes, and risk the possibility of failure. The case study of Ann Kirsten illustrates many of the advantages and disadvantages.
- Being a successful businessperson requires the right personality, know-how, and money. Before considering starting a business, you should honestly evaluate your strengths and weaknesses. Not everyone is suited to owning their own business.
- If you are serious about going into business, pick a field you know the most about. The more experience and training you have, the better your chances of success. Find out all you can about the kind of business you want to start. Try to determine whether potential customers need or want the type of business in which you are interested. Choose a field in which growth is expected. Successful business owners are those who can make accurate predictions about the future.

WORDS TO KNOW

board of directors
charter
corporation
creditors
entrepreneur
franchise
partnership
proprietorship
retailers
self-employed
stockholders
supplier
wholesale houses

QUESTIONS TO ANSWER

1. Why isn't there such a thing as a typical small business?
2. Name the four important contributions that small business makes to our society.
3. Name and briefly explain the three forms of business organization.
4. Give four advantages and four disadvantages of self-employment.

5. Ann Kirsten performs many different types of work tasks, such as supervising employees and ordering new merchandise. Name five additional work tasks she performs.
6. Name the three main ingredients that are necessary for self-employment.
7. What is the SBA? What does it do?
8. Are you the type of person who might be a successful entrepreneur? Why or why not?
9. Why are the first six months often crucial in getting a new business started?
10. Why is having a trade or a technical skill a good first step in becoming an entrepreneur?

ACTIVITIES TO DO

1. You learned earlier that the most important contribution of small business is new inventions, products, and services. With your classmates, try to identify as many inventions, products, and services as you can that small businesses have introduced in the last several years.
2. Select someone who has achieved success in a business that he or she started. (A good resource is *Entrepreneurial Megabucks,* which contains a list of the 100 greatest entrepreneurs over the past 25 years.) After gathering information, write a two- to three-page biography. Turn in the paper to your teacher.
3. Contact two or three small business owners in your community and explain to them you are working on a class project. Ask them to identify their main reason for going into business. In class, pool your findings and discuss the results.
4. Check the reference section of your local public library for copies of franchise directories. (A good source is the *Franchise Opportunities Handbook* published by the U.S. Government Printing Office. It lists all the franchises available in the U.S.A. and people to contact for more information.) Select a franchise in which you are interested. Write to the franchisor and ask for their franchise package for prospective owners. Report your findings to the class.
5. Arrange with your instructor to duplicate copies of the "Entrepreneur Rating Scale" shown in Figure 20–9. Complete one yourself. Next, give one to a parent or family member and one to your supervisor at work and ask them to rate you. Compare ratings to see how well they agree. Discuss the results with your teacher.

TOPICS TO DISCUSS

1. New businesses are often started because they provide something better or different. Name and discuss products and services that you are dissatisfied with that could possibly lead to the creation of a new business.
2. Think about recent trends and how society is changing. Discuss the types of businesses that are likely to be successful five years from now. Provide reasons for your predictions.
3. During the late 1970s and early 1980s, dozens of young computer and software whizzes became millionaires while still in their teens. How were they able to accomplish so much at such a young age?

SECTION 5

MANAGING YOUR MONEY

In Chapter 21, you will learn about economics and the American free enterprise system. Economics is the study of how goods and services are produced, distributed, and used.

A consumer is someone who buys or uses goods and services. In Chapter 22, you will learn about consuming and your rights and responsibilities as a consumer.

Checking accounts are one of the most commonly used banking services. How to open and manage a checking account is explained in Chapter 23.

A person's financial well-being is related to how they spend and manage money. In Chapter 24, you will learn how to get the greatest benefit from your money by developing and using a budget. The chapter also deals with saving and investing money.

People buy insurance to protect themselves from risk due to fire, accident, illness, or other catastrophes. In Chapter 25, you will learn about health, life, home, and auto insurance.

In Chapter 26, you will learn about taxation and types of taxes. A tax is a required contribution of money that people make to the government.

Government programs that help people meet social and economic needs are called social security. The six most common types of social security programs are explained in Chapter 27.

Co-op Career SPOTLIGHT ON

Georgia (Joy) Morris, *Undercover Narcotics Agent*

"My wardrobe is kind of versatile," says Joy Morris. She is about to pack up her business suit and high heels and exchange them for jeans, leather motorcycle jacket, and boots. These are the clothes she needs for her new assignment as an undercover narcotics agent for a state task force. Joy began the career that lead to this position when she was a co-op student at Hernando High School in Hernando, Mississippi.

"I got dressed for my high school prom in the sheriff's department," said Joy Morris, head of administration and narcotics for a county sheriff's department in Mississippi. Her father was deputy sheriff and she decided to follow in his footsteps and make law enforcement her career. She was 16 when she started work at the department as a one-person dispatcher. As a dispatcher she received the emergency medical, fire, and police calls to the station. She had to stay cool and professional and contact the closest patrol car, fire department, or helicopter to go to the scene.

"I was the heartline from communications to the man in the field," she says about the operation that has grown from that one-person job to a computerized, ultra high-band radio system that requires two or three people to run it. She worked for the sheriff's department while she was a co-op student. After she graduated in 1985, Joy attended Northeast Community College, where she earned an associates degree in criminal justice.

Joy says the lessons she learned in co-op helped her launch her exciting career.

"Co-op taught me how to use the resources I had as an individual. It taught me how to be a professional, how to handle myself to talk with different types of people, how to ask the right questions, and to know what agencies or organizations can give you the information you want."

CHAPTER 21 Our Economic World

OUTLINE

- Principles of Economics
- Economic Systems
- The American Free Enterprise System
- Economic Growth
- Economic Freedom
- Chapter Review

OBJECTIVES

After reading this chapter, you should be able to:

- List the four factors of production.
- Explain the circular flow of economic activity.
- Illustrate how supply and demand influence market prices.
- Name and describe the two basic types of economic systems.
- Summarize characteristics of the American free enterprise system.
- Name the three things required for economic growth.
- Discuss types of economic freedom you enjoy.

Over 130 million people are employed in the work force. They work in hundreds of thousands of offices, stores, factories, farms, and other places. These men and women produce trillions of dollars worth of goods and services a year. This activity occurs without the government telling people where to work or what to produce.

The main reason why our system works so well is that people are free to make economic decisions and to improve their financial well-being. To continue to succeed, our economy

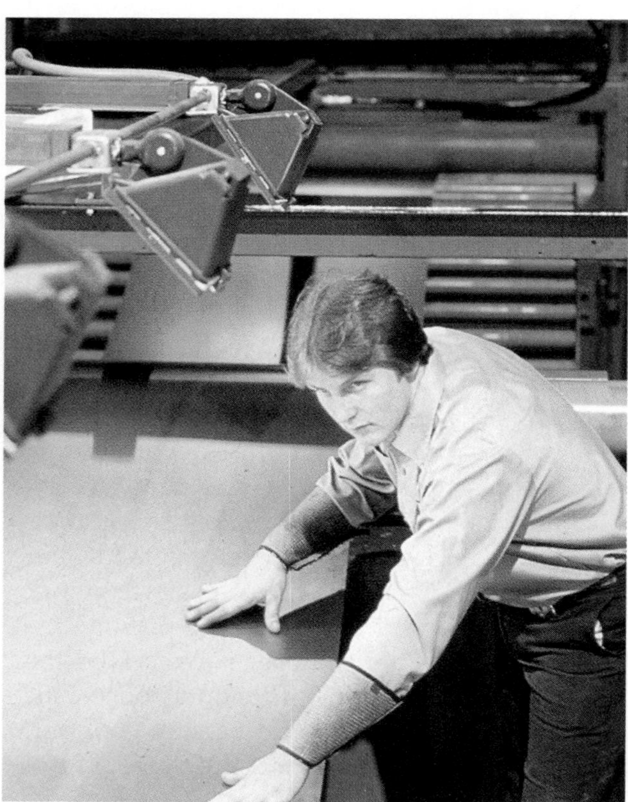

FIGURE 21–1 The economic strength of America is due largely to the efforts of individual workers.
Courtesy of USX Corporation.

needs the support of us all. We have responsibilities as both consumers and producers. In this chapter, you will learn about the American economic system and your part in it.

PRINCIPLES OF ECONOMICS

Economics is the study of how goods and services are produced, distributed, and used. Economics is also concerned with how people and governments choose what they buy from among the many things they want. You probably do not have much trouble spending your paychecks. The hard part involves making choices from among the many things you need and want. Federal, state, and local governments have the same types of choices to make.

The city of Centerville, for example, would like to build a new swimming pool at the city park. However, there is not enough money left in the budget after the city pays employees' salaries and bills. These expenses include street maintenance, garbage collection, and snow removal. A city, like an individual or family, has only so much money to spend.

Factors of Production

Meeting the needs of people and nations from what is available leads to the economic activity called *production.* Production takes place when a farmer grows corn, a nurse cares for patients, or a barber cuts hair. In one way or another, all production involves the following four resources.

Natural Resources. Materials provided by nature are important to production. Soil, water, mineral deposits, and forests are all examples of a nation's resources. Human beings do not create them.

FIGURE 21–2 **Millions of economic choices are made every day by people of all ages.**
Courtesy of Campbell Soup Company.

Labor. Labor includes all of the people employed in the work force. Both the skill of the work force and the amount of labor help to determine the amount of production.

Capital. Most people think of capital as money. To the economist, however, capital (sometimes called capital goods) is any person-made means of production. Tools, machines, and factories are examples of capital goods. Capital used skillfully can greatly increase productivity.

Management. Management refers to the people who organize and direct the other three factors. In Chapter 20, we called this entrepreneurship. Managers assume the risk of operating a business. Good organization and management apply to both single-person businesses and large corporations.

Consumption

Several kinds of economic activities help people satisfy their needs and wants. Production is one such activity. A second kind of economic activity is *consumption.* This is the process of using goods and services that have been produced. Buying a pair of shoes, drinking soda, and going to a movie are all different kinds of consumption. All of us are consumers.

There is a close relationship between consumers and producers. This is called the circular flow of economic activity. Here is how the circular flow works. Suppose that you work in the business or industry shown in Figure 21–4. The inside bottom arrow shows that you give your services to a producer who employs you. The business or industry (producer) gives you wages for your work as indicated by the outside bottom arrow. But you also receive goods and services from producers, as the inside top arrow shows. For these goods and services, you pay money to producers, as indicated by the outside top arrow.

The Market

Whenever goods and services are bought and sold, a *market* is created. A market may be a neighborhood grocery store or an international grain market. Buyers and sellers may meet in person, or they may conduct their business by telephone, mail, or satellite transmission.

FIGURE 21–3 **This farmer is involved in production as well as consumption. Can you explain how?**
Courtesy of Deere & Company.

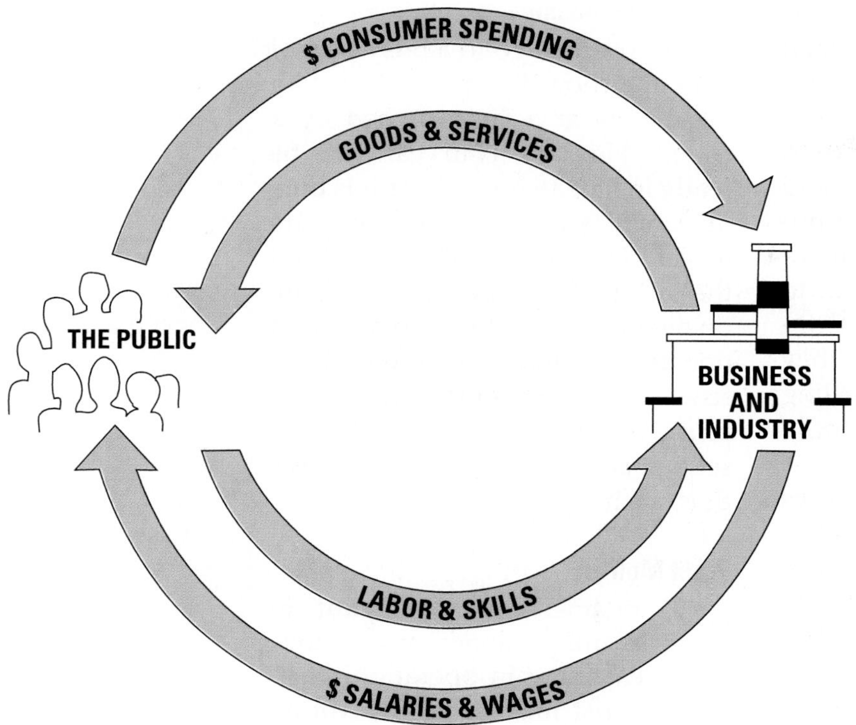

FIGURE 21–4 **A circular flow of goods, services, and money takes place between consumers and producers.**

In a free economy, market prices rise and fall according to *supply* and *demand.* When the demand is greater than the supply, the seller will often raise the price of the goods or services. This encourages the producer to provide a greater supply of goods or services. Eventually, the supply begins to catch up with the demand. If the supply becomes greater than the demand, the seller may lower the price to help get rid of the excess supply. Can you provide an example of such a product or service?

In a market, *competition* helps to keep prices down. Suppose there is only one seller for a product or service. Prices will be high. Consumers have no real choice. But if there are many sellers, each competes with the other. Shoppers benefit from the lower prices that result.

ECONOMIC SYSTEMS

Countries do not solve their basic economic problems in the same ways. There are different economic systems. One major type is the centrally planned economy. Under this system, the people have no voice in economic decision-making. A central authority (government) owns all resources and sets wages. The group in power also controls all production and distribution. For example, the central government decides how much production should be devoted to consumer goods, such as automobiles and washing machines.

A second major type of economic system is free enterprise. In such an economy, people and industries can do more or less as they please. Private individuals and industries own and control the resources and means of production and distribution. People can work for themselves or they can sell their labor to someone else for wages. Consumers can buy and sell as they choose. Such buying and selling creates markets in which supply and demand influence prices.

In actual practice, neither of these economies is ever found in pure form. Historically, the former Soviet Union leaned heavily toward a centrally planned economy. In the late 1980s, however, the former Soviet Union and other Communist nations of Eastern Europe began to relax government control of the economy. And, private ownership of farms and factories began to be allowed.

The United States leans heavily toward the free enterprise economy. The government, however, owns many resources and runs various industries. It also controls certain prices. In addition, laws prohibit companies from making unsafe products. Both the United States and the countries of the former Soviet Union, then, are "mixed economies."

THE AMERICAN FREE ENTERPRISE SYSTEM

The United States is said to have a free enterprise economy, even though it does not exist in a pure form. For the most part, the American economy runs by itself. People and industries make most of their own economic decisions. Let's look more closely at this system.

Private Ownership

Suppose you go to a busy part of your town or city. You stop for an oil change at a shop owned by a friend. He says your car will be ready in half an hour. Since it is time for lunch, you go next door to a cafe to eat. The auto service shop and the cafe are two examples of private ownership. They are owned and operated by individuals who have risked their own money to make a profit. For the most part, people can set up any legal kind of business they wish.

Profit Motive

All business owners want to make as much money as possible. To at least stay in operation, businesses must make a profit. Not all of them succeed.

Gino was surprised to learn that one of his favorite restaurants was going out of business. The restaurant had been owned by the same family for more than 30 years. The food was excellent and fairly priced. The restaurant seemed to have many loyal customers.

Since Gino had wanted to own a restaurant, he checked into buying it. In examining the financial records of the business, Gino discovered why it was being sold. Mr. Colletti, the owner, may have known how to prepare good food, but his knowledge of running a business was sadly outdated.

Gino figured that the costs of operation were about 20 percent higher than they should have been. He concluded that by using good business practices, such as wholesale buying, quantity purchasing, and control of overhead he could make a good profit. What's more,

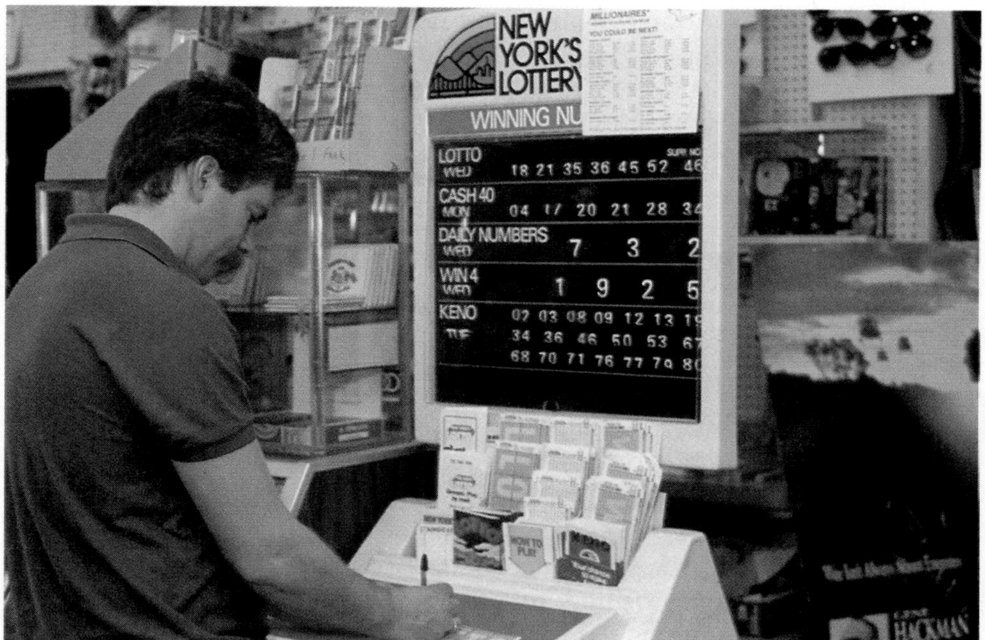

FIGURE 21–5 **State governments are also driven by the profit motive. This state-run lottery provides millions of dollars for education.**
Photo by Ruby Gold.

he could do it without sacrificing quality or service.

Competition

Jenny wanted to buy a certain brand and style of shoes. Each store that carried the shoes wanted a different price. What did Jenny do? She bought from the store where she would get the most for her money. If one company had a *monopoly* on the shoe business, Jenny would not have had a choice. A monopoly is exclusive control over the supply of a product or service. Every pair of shoes in all the stores would have been the same price.

Free enterprise needs competition. It forces producers to be efficient and encourages a wide variety of goods and services. Competition is so important to the American economy that the government has passed laws to forbid monopolies.

Freedom of Choice

You have already read that people having certain resources can start a business. They are not the only ones who have choices. Consumers and workers do too.

Consumer choices influence the types of goods and services produced. For instance, if consumers stop buying a certain product, it will probably disappear from store shelves. Buyers also help determine the prices of goods. Marketers will price as highly as they think the market will bear. If they are wrong, prices will fall. Prices also go down if heavy competition appears.

A similar situation exists with workers. They seek to be paid as much as possible. In a free enterprise economy, they are able to work for whomever they choose. And people who want to change jobs can do so.

FIGURE 21–6 **Why do you think the price of this garment keeps going down?**
Photo by Ruby Gold.

? ? ? ? ? ? ? ? ? ? ? ? ? ?

WHAT WOULD YOU DO?

A new brand of exercise shoes has just been introduced. They are "hot." Merchants can hardly keep them in stock. You go to the store to buy some. You love the shoes, but are shocked by the price. They are about $25 more than the shoes you usually buy. You would have to charge them since you do not have enough cash. Your mom suggests that you wait a few months until the price comes down. You doubt that they will be any cheaper later on.

What would you do?

Profit and competition help control this system. Some say that in free enterprise, markets are self-regulated. This means that supply and demand help set prices for goods and wages for workers.

ECONOMIC GROWTH

The United States economy has grown steadily throughout the years. In order for this growth to continue, several things must occur. First, a portion of the nation's resources must be used to produce capital goods. Second, individuals and businesses must use a portion of their income for savings and investments. Third, the nation must use a portion of its resources for education and training. These influences on economic growth will now be illustrated.

You have read about the factors of production. As you will recall, these are natural resources, labor, capital, and management. Companies use these factors to provide capital goods and consumer goods. But a country cannot grow if it uses all of its resources to produce consumer goods and services. These do not produce anything of further value. Think about it. Once you buy them, a pair of jeans loses value. Capital goods, on the other hand, create future economic worth. Suppose a trucking company puts money into new rigs and loading docks. Workers use the docks over and over to load goods onto the trucks. These, in turn, carry cargo to distant markets.

When buying new capital goods, businesses often borrow money. For example, Mrs. Luna decides to add

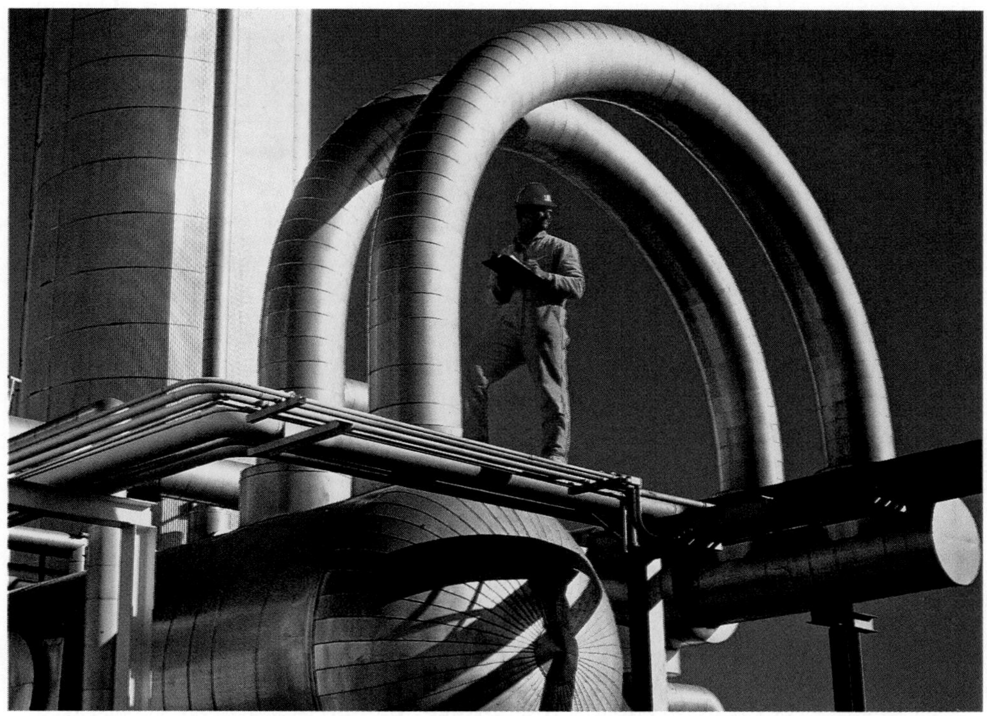

FIGURE 21–7 **Investing in new plants and equipment helps companies compete.**
Courtesy of CSX Corporation, Richmond, VA.

on to her flower shop. She does not have all the funds she needs. The bank gives her a loan. Where does First City bank get this money? It comes from deposits from people like you. When the savings rate is high, banks have more money to lend to businesses. The economy can grow.

Capital goods produce value. So do workers and managers. Offering further training to employees benefits a business. Skilled workers and managers contribute to future production and growth. Many employers pay for this education.

Patterns of Economic Growth

A free enterprise economy goes through various cycles. Tracing these shifts is like following the path of a roller coaster. A period of expanding economic growth is known as *prosperity.* During these good times, unemployment is low. Workers receive steady pay raises because companies make high profits. Since so many people are working, they buy many consumer items. This leads to increasing production. The supply of goods meets the demand, so prices stay down.

A downturn in the economy is called a *recession.* Let's see what can happen. Suppose there is a strong national feeling that the economy will turn bad. While scared consumers save more of their incomes, goods stack up on shelves. Companies make production cutbacks, which lead to worker layoffs. Young people seeking their first jobs cannot find work. People then have less money to spend, so they buy even fewer goods.

If a recession gets worse, a *depression* can result. In this situation, very large numbers of people become unemployed. Consumers purchase only what they really need. Business failures increase. Production drops further and even more workers lose their jobs.

Major fluctuations in economic growth have occurred for decades. Yet, there is much disagreement (even among economists) regarding causes and solutions. Many heated national debates result from disagreement among politicians and others over inflation, recession, and unemployment.

? ? ? ? ? ? ? ? ? ? ? ? ? ?

WHAT WOULD YOU DO?

Business has been great at the shop where you work. You received a raise and are working a good deal of overtime. You are using the extra money to buy clothes and other things you have always wanted. One day at break, you show a co-worker a picture of the new watch you put on layaway.

"It is neat," he says. "But if I were you, I would not spend all of my paycheck. Good times will not last forever."

"I thought business was good," you say.

"It is," he responds. "This is the way it always is before things slow down and we get laid off."

You have not thought about that. You wonder if you should go ahead and buy the expensive watch.

What would you do?

Inflation

A serious problem of our economic system is often *inflation.* This is when prices of goods and services rise rapidly. A *slight* upward trend in prices is very typical of free enterprise and is not very serious. Wages usually increase along with prices. When prices go up much faster than wages, though, money loses some of its value. Let's see how this can happen. Workers at The Jiffy Company do not think their wages are keeping up with the cost of living. Through their union, employees bargain for pay increases. To cover the raises, the company raises the prices of its products. Consumers buying a Jiffy food processor, for example, will now pay more for it. If there are price increases throughout the economy, Jiffy's workers will continue to seek higher wages.

What causes inflation? There is no single, easy answer. However, economists generally agree that the following factors fuel inflation:

1. Excessive consumer demand.
2. Government spending and *deficits.*
3. Increased energy costs.
4. Decreased productivity.
5. Government regulations.
6. Fear of future inflation.

Even though the causes are complex, inflation can be curbed. All segments of society, including government, business, labor, and consumers, must work together to control it.

ECONOMIC FREEDOM

You have learned that in a free enterprise system, individuals make most of the economic decisions. Another way of saying this is that people in a market economy enjoy economic freedom. Economic freedom is a collection of the following rights, which allow people to make free choices:

1. The right to choose an occupation.
2. The right to change occupations or jobs.
3. The right to engage in business and to make a profit.
4. The right to spend money as one chooses.
5. The right to offer our goods or services at prices we decide.
6. The right to reject prices on goods or services we may want to buy.
7. The right to use property and wealth to produce income.
8. The right to succeed, limited only by one's ambition and ability.

Economic freedom is not available to everyone in the world. Like other freedoms, people often take economic freedom for granted. Economic freedom can be lost or weakened if individuals, businesses, and governments fail to act as responsible consumers and producers.

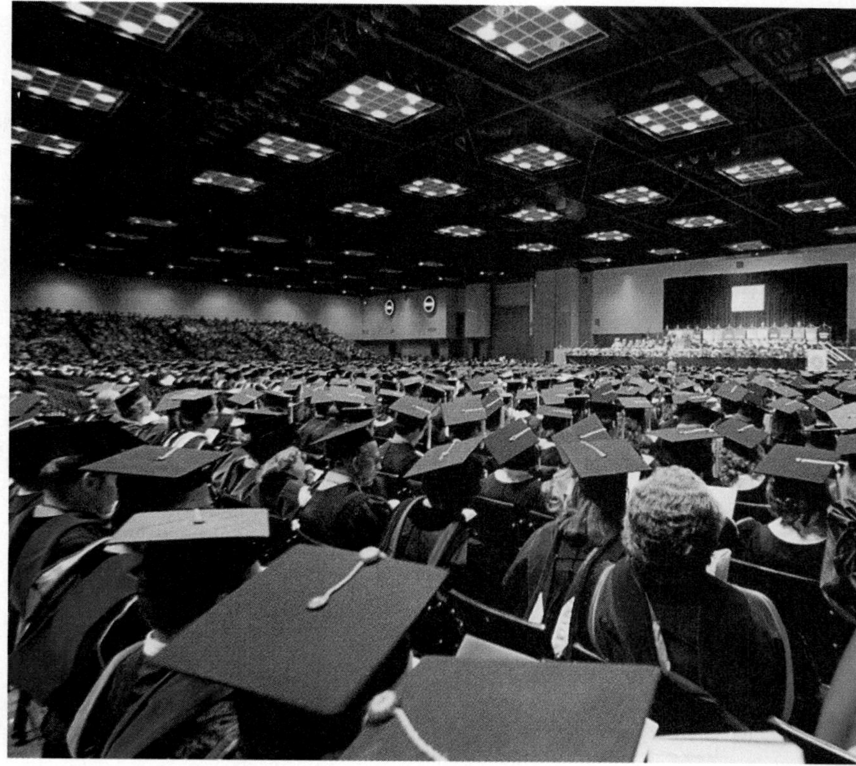

FIGURE 21–8 You will have the good fortune to make choices about your future when you graduate from high school or college that less advantaged people do not have.

FOCUS ON

Skills For Living

Counterfeit Goods Undercut the Economy

Few customers are aware that they may be buying counterfeit goods. An estimated 250 different fake products have flooded the market. These include jewelry, jeans, handbags, auto parts, toys, electronic appliances, perfumes, and even prescription medicine.

The economic toll is staggering. Counterfeit goods cut into company profits, reduce taxes paid, and cost jobs. Health and safety are also major concerns. Imagine driving around with fake brake shoes on your car! The death of a helicopter pilot was linked to the failure of a fake rotor assembly part. Many people are taking drugs and using health care products that contain ineffective or wrong ingredients.

Here is an example of how fake products are produced and distributed. A dishonest importer signs up a foreign manufacturer to make a shoddy oil filter. The manufacturer produces the filters. They are packaged into large crates generically labeled "oil filters" to pass U.S. Customs. The importer receives the filters and packs them in boxes printed with a real brand name. They are sold to a legitimate wholesaler as "overstock." The wholesaler (who is unaware they are fake) sells to reputable retail outlets. Consumers then come along and buy the phony filters at gas stations, auto dealers, chain stores, and the like.

Many expensive products, like this Rolex watch, are copied to look the same, but sell for lower prices. These copies are called "knock offs."

Courtesy of Rolex Watch U.S.A. Inc.

There are a number of things you can do to protect yourself. Be wary when looking for hard-to-get toys and other fad items. When shopping for a product having a high status trademark, read labels carefully and pay close attention to workmanship. Look for sloppy printing, misspelled words, and altered logos on packages. Do not buy a product when the packaging is missing or not up to standard. Buy only at reputable places of business. If you do happen to get taken, you will be more likely to get a refund.

CHAPTER 21 REVIEW

CHAPTER IN BRIEF

- Economics is the study of how goods and services are produced, distributed, and used. Economics mainly deals with how things that people need and want are made and brought to them. It is also concerned with how people and governments choose what they buy from among the many things they want.
- Meeting the needs of people and nations from what is available leads to the economic activity called production. All production involves four resources: natural resources, labor, capital, and management.
- Consumption is the process of using goods and services that have been produced. All of us are consumers. Consumers and producers are linked together by what is called the circular flow of economic activity.
- Whenever goods and services are bought and sold, a market is created. In a market, competition helps to keep prices down.
- There are two major types of economic systems. In a centrally planned economy, the government owns all resources and controls production and distribution. In a free enterprise economy, private individuals and companies own most of the resources and control production and distribution.
- The American free enterprise system has four main characteristics: private ownership, profit motive, competition, and freedom of choice. The system runs largely by itself without government interference.
- In order for economic growth to continue, several things must occur. First, a portion of the nation's resources must be used to produce capital goods. Second, individuals and businesses must use a portion of their income for savings and investment. Third, the nation must use a portion of its resources for education and training.
- A free enterprise economy goes through various cycles. A period of expanding economic growth is known as prosperity. A downturn in the economy is called a recession. A very serious recession can lead to a depression.
- Inflation is when prices of goods and services rise too rapidly. This problem is caused by many factors, including: excessive consumer demand, government spending, increased energy costs, decreased productivity, government regulations, and fear of future inflation.
- Economic freedom is not available to everyone in the world. It can be lost or weakened if individuals, businesses, and governments fail to act as responsible consumers and producers.

WORDS TO KNOW

competition
consumption
deficits
demand
depression
economics
inflation
market
monopoly
production
prosperity
recession
supply

QUESTIONS TO ANSWER

1. What is the most important economic issue with which individuals and governments must deal?
2. All production involves four factors. Name them and briefly describe each one.
3. What phrase is used to describe the relationship between consumers and producers?
4. Explain how market prices rise and fall as a result of supply and demand.
5. Name two differences between a centrally planned economy and a free enterprise economy.
6. List the four characteristics of free enterprise.
7. Why is it important for individuals and businesses to save and invest money?
8. Why is it important for companies to invest in training for workers and managers?
9. The economic growth of a free market economy goes through cycles like the path of a roller coaster. Give an example.
10. How do the following factors contribute to inflation: (a) government spending, and (b) decreased productivity?

ACTIVITIES TO DO

1. As a class, identify someone in your community who has lived in a country with a centrally planned economy. Invite the person to class to share personal experiences. Before the person arrives, prepare questions that you want to ask.
2. You often read or hear news reports about the gross domestic product (GDP). What is the GDP? How is it figured? How is the GDP used as a measurement of economic growth? Use encyclopedias or other resources to answer these questions.
3. Does someone you know remember The Great Depression? As a class, invite some people to speak about what it was like. Be sure to prepare questions ahead of time.

TOPICS TO DISCUSS

1. The early 1980s was a very difficult period for automakers. There were low sales and foreign competition. Large companies such as General Motors, Ford, and Chrysler lost billions of dollars. Thousands of autoworkers lost their jobs. Yet, during this period, the price of new cars continued to rise. This seems to differ from what we have learned about the law of supply and demand. Discuss this situation in class.
2. You have learned that inflation's causes are many. Discuss how the following individuals might contribute to inflation:
   - A union leader negotiating a labor contract.
   - A merchant setting prices for goods.
   - A factory worker assembling car parts.
   - A consumer shopping for a video cassette recorder.
   - An elected official preparing a new budget.
3. What are some of the things the government often does during periods of recession to help stimulate the economy and relieve unemployment?

CHAPTER 22 The Consumer in the Marketplace

OUTLINE

- You as a Consumer
- What is Consuming?
- Advertising and the Consumer
- Consumer Rights
- Consumer Responsibilities
- Consumer Complaints
- Chapter Review

OBJECTIVES

After reading this chapter, you should be able to:

- Give examples of goods and services that are consumed.
- Name and describe the three stages involved in consuming goods and services.
- Identify different advertising techniques.
- Discuss types of consumer rights.
- Describe responsibilities of consumers.
- Summarize steps to take in dealing with consumer problems.

A market is anywhere two or more parties come together to buy and sell. At one time, the market was a clearing along the river. There were few goods to buy and little choices available.

Now, the market may be a department store, service station, grocery store, movie theater, or barber shop. All markets operate basically the same. That is, sellers wish to attract buyers and then make a profit on the sale. Buyers, on the other hand, look for good quality at a low price.

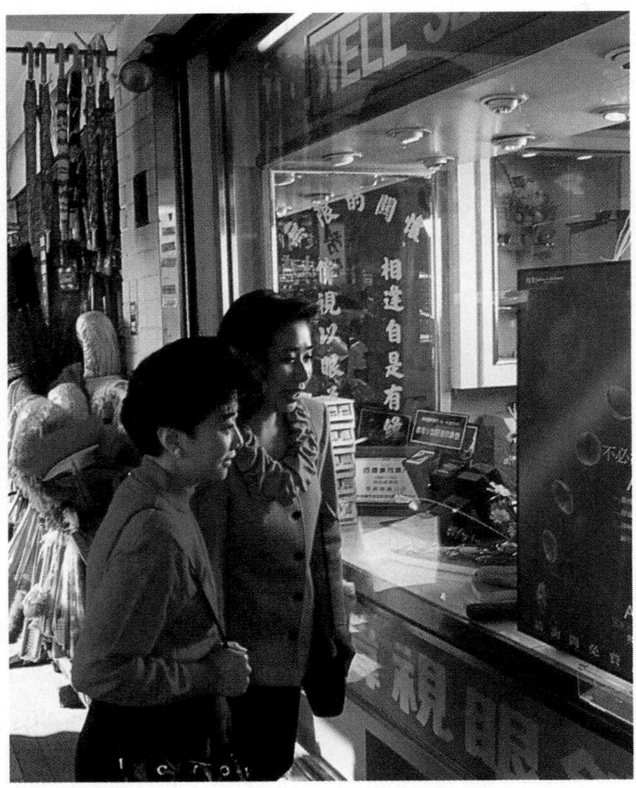

FIGURE 22–1 **Learning to make wise choices as a consumer is an important life skill.**
Courtesy of Johnson & Johnson. Photo by Ted Kawalerski.

As a buyer, you will make decisions all your life. Today, you may choose between two brands of shampoo. In a few years, you may need to make more important choices, such as which house to buy. Making a mistake then could be very costly. By learning wise consumer skills now, you might save yourself problems later.

YOU AS A CONSUMER

A *consumer* is someone who buys or uses goods and services. *Goods* are articles that are produced or manufactured. Some goods, such as food, are used up almost immediately. Other goods, such as tools, last for many years. A house is also a type of good. If properly built and maintained, a house may last for a long time.

Services differ from goods. Services involve the payment of money to people and to businesses for work performed. Having a suit dry cleaned and getting a haircut are personal services. We pay fees to doctors, dentists, and lawyers in exchange for their knowledge and skills. Buying life insurance or obtaining a credit card involves the use of business services. Many common services that we use are for maintenance and repair work, such as having an automobile tuned up or a television fixed. Entertainment and recreation are also types of services that we often purchase.

Money buys food, clothing, and other necessities of life. We also buy goods and services that we want but may not need. A pair of designer jeans and a concert ticket are examples of things that we may want. People often use the term *need* when they really mean *want*. To say that you need a new pair of designer jeans to wear to the game is probably not true. You may want the jeans, but you do not actually need them. Needs are necessities; wants are luxuries.

FIGURE 22–2 **Many of us *want* to own a camera, but a professional photographer *needs* one or more of excellent quality.**

WHAT IS CONSUMING?

Being a consumer is more than simply paying money for something. Consuming involves three stages—choosing, buying, and using.

Making Choices

Buying always involves choosing or making choices. You have to eat in order to stay alive, so that really is not a choice. However, you *do* have to make decisions about what you eat. Do you eat a balanced diet or only frozen pizzas and soft drinks? Do you prepare meals at home or eat in restaurants? Are you like Mike? He often skips meals in order to spend money on movie tickets.

Sometimes, you have to choose between two similar products or services. Suppose you are going to buy a pair of shoes. The two pairs of shoes you like vary in price and quality. How do you decide which pair to buy? Some choices involve different kinds of products or services. Let's say you would like to have a hair permanent and a sweater. But you only have enough money for one of these. Which will you decide to buy? Another type of choice is that between spending your money or saving it. This may be the most difficult choice of all. If you save some of your money, it will mean doing without some things that you would like to have now.

Buying Wisely

This stage begins once you have decided to buy. Knowledge and planning are very important to wise buying. There are several ways to learn about different products and services. You can talk with friends and family, attend special classes, and read consumer magazines. *Consumer Reports* is perhaps the best-known consumer magazine. It rates various products in terms of price, quality, and other factors. Knowing which products are rated highly can save you shopping time as well as money. There are still other things you can do to be a good shopper.

FIGURE 22–3 **Visit your local public library and find out what consumer magazines it has.**
Photo by Paul E. Meyers.

? ? ? ? ? ? ? ? ? ? ? ? ? ?

WHAT WOULD YOU DO?

You live in the city where you work and share an apartment with several friends. You all pool grocery money and take turns shopping and cooking. You are more thrifty than your roommates. You often buy store brands and generics rather than more expensive brand-name foods. As you are unloading groceries, one of your roommates comes into the kitchen.

"What is this stuff?" she bellows. "I am not eating this generic junk. We can afford to buy some decent food."

What would you do?

Bill Martin is a wise consumer. Let's see how he saves money on food and clothing. First of all, Bill never shops for food when he is hungry. He knows that when he is hungry he tends to buy food on impulse. To avoid exceeding his food budget, Bill plans what he will buy. He writes everything on a list and follows it. Bill knows the grocery stores in his town run sales on weekends, so he shops then when possible. He buys *generic products* when he can, because the quality is good and the prices are lower.

Large sizes of cereal and canned food are often good buys, and Bill is always sure to use up these products. If some of the food is wasted, a large size isn't a bargain. Last week, Bill saw some dented cans in a bin. He passed the bin without buying because the food might have been spoiled. Buying spoiled food, no matter how cheap, is no bargain.

Recently, Bill went to a department store to look for a new shirt. He found four he liked, but rejected two right away. The care label on one said "dry clean only." Over several years, dry cleaning can be expensive. The other rejected shirt was 100 percent cotton and would need to be ironed. Of the two remaining shirts, one was better made than the other.

However, before buying the better-made shirt, Bill decided to do some *comparison shopping*. He first checked prices in a mail-order catalog. They were slightly cheaper than the store's, but he would have to wait for the shirt to be delivered in the mail. He would also have to pay postage. Then Bill saw a discount store's newspaper ad for shirts. When Bill reached the store, a clerk was putting shirts on a shelf. Two of them were exactly what Bill wanted. The labels showed they were *brand-name* shirts. Best of all, the shirts were on sale for 25 percent off.

Buying wisely also involves the careful use of credit. Some businesses may sell products cheaper when you pay cash. If you charge a purchase, it is important to know how much more the product or service will cost you. Usually, if you pay within a certain amount of time, the credit is free. If you do not pay right away, though, credit may be expensive.

FIGURE 22–4 **You can get more value for your money by comparison shopping.**
Courtesy of Sears, Roebuck and Company.

Using Goods and Services Properly

Wise consuming does not end after you bring a product home. If a product is ruined because of carelessness, you have wasted money. Treat products as if you want them to last forever. Suppose you just bought a new hair dryer. Be sure to save the receipt in case you have to return the product. Then, read the instructions carefully *before* trying it out. Once you are sure the item works, check the carton for the warranty card. A *warranty* is a guarantee or promise that a product is free from defects. Fill out the card and send it in right away.

You are now ready to enjoy your new hair dryer. Always use it according to directions. Remember that if you misuse a product, *you* are responsible for any damage. The company that made the hair dryer will not honor the warranty on a misused product.

Being a wise consumer of services is also important. For example, the price of an oil change may vary by ten dollars or more depending on where you have a car serviced. Watch for advertising by automobile dealers, discount stores, service stations, and tire and appliance service centers. Such businesses frequently lower the price on oil changes simply to increase business and get you into their store. If you want to save the most money, buy the oil and filter at a discount store and change it yourself.

ADVERTISING AND THE CONSUMER

Sellers of goods and services use *advertising* to attract potential buyers. Advertising is any type of public notice or message. It is all around us. It is in newspapers and magazines. Ads also appear on television, buses, signs, and billboards. Do you receive advertising in the mail? This form is called *direct-mail advertising.*

Advertising is very important for both the seller and the consumer. From a business point of view, the purpose of advertising is to sell goods and services. For consumers, advertising provides information about goods and services for sale.

What are some ways that advertising helps you, the consumer? Well, suppose you see two newspaper ads for A-1 tents. One store's price is cheaper than the other's. Without leaving your home, you can decide where to buy the tent at the better price. This way, you do not have to go from store to store to check prices. You will save time and money.

The next day, you hear a radio spot in which the announcer talks

FIGURE 22–5 **How does an advertising sign like this benefit the community?**
Photo by Paul E. Meyers.

about a bargain tune-up at Smith's Garage. A while later, you see an ad in the window of Pope's Auto. On the same tune-up, they offer a better price than Smith's. Again, by comparing advertising, you are able to save money.

Do you complain about ads on radio and television? Without advertising, many of your favorite programs would go off the air. This is because most of the costs of producing these programs are paid for by advertising. Newspapers and magazines are also operated with money made through advertising. As you can see, without advertising our world would be quite different than it is now.

Advertising also has disadvantages. Consumers pay for it. The cost of advertising often ranges from 0 to 5 percent of the selling price of a product or service. So $.50 of a $10 price tag could be advertising costs.

Advertising can be expensive in yet other ways. It can convince us to buy things we may not actually need. Jason knows this . . . now.

Jason had been saving his hard-earned money for a used motorcycle. He already had $250. Last winter, he kept seeing ads for leather coats. Jason already had a nice coat, but many of his friends had leather ones. They were nice. On the way to the bank one day, Jason passed the clothing store and went in. He entered with $250 and left with a leather coat and a few dollars. After several weeks, he was sorry he had not saved the money. Jason had to start saving for a
11 motorcycle all over again.

Sometimes, we need a product or service. There may be so many ads for it that we have trouble deciding. Consumers might make choices based on false advertising claims. Most advertisers, though, are honest. A few make false promises or cheat the public in other ways. How to deal with such situations is discussed later in this chapter.

Advertising Techniques

To get us to remember their products or services, advertisers use means such as pictures, slogans, and jingles. In fact, we may often use a brand name to refer to a whole class of products. For example, how many times have you heard the brand name "Scotch tape" used instead of cellophane tape? Also, how about Kleenex tissues, Xerox copies, and Levis jeans? Can you think of other examples?

Once people are familiar with a product's name, they may buy it. But advertisers do not take chances. To achieve their aims, advertisers use proven methods, such as the following.

Endorsements. Famous people present the advertising message. For example, a famous athlete may tell you she uses a Whammo tennis racquet. If the racquet is good enough for her, it should suit you. Right? That is what the advertiser wants you to think.

Familiarity. You hear a jingle, musical theme, or slogan over and over. The advertiser wants you to become familiar with a product and remember it.

Association. This approach often is seen during the holiday season. Here is an example. A horse-drawn sleigh passes by a beautiful, snow-covered landscape. This pleasant scene is then associated with the product being advertised.

Goodwill. Some advertisers work hard to create a good public image. They may provide health tips or engage in other activities. A major fast-food restaurant chain, for example, paid for the swimming and diving facility used at a recent Olympic Games.

Successful Living. These approaches appeal to people's desire for success, wealth, status, or beauty. For instance, one manufacturer of men's shoes uses the advertising phrase "Shades of the Sophisticated Man." The message is that you will be more sophisticated if you wear their shoes.

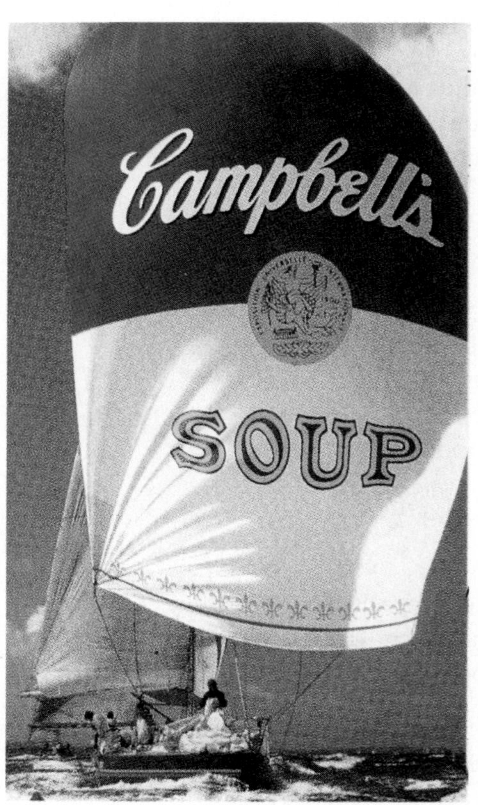

FIGURE 22–6 **Which type of advertising technique is used here?**
Courtesy of Campbell Soup Company.

Emotional Appeal. Many ads contain messages related to happiness, friendship, and other pleasant emotions. "Buy a diamond for someone you love" is a theme that frequently appears.

Economic Appeal. Messages about spending, saving, and making money are featured in many ads. An example is, "No money down, no payments until after Christmas."

Conformity. In this approach, you are encouraged to buy something because others have it. You may hear "Our product is used by millions of satisfied customers." An example of a slightly different approach is, "By using this camera, you, too, can be an expert photographer."

Scare Tactics. We all want to avoid unpleasant situations, such as danger and embarrassment. Who wouldn't want to prevent an auto accident? Sure-Grip tires will keep you from having one. This advertiser wants you to think you may have an accident if you do not use its products.

Intellectual Appeal. Many products claim to help you become more informed or better educated. Or they appeal to your intelligence. Does the following sound familiar? "Smart people have found this dishwashing soap to be the better product."

Health and Comfort. This approach is used in ads for products, such as aspirin, skin creams, and vitamins. The ads tell you how the product will make you healthier or feel better.

Sales Traps to Avoid

There is nothing wrong with advertising as long as it is honest. If you dislike an ad's message, you

FIGURE 22–7 **Advertisers use creative visuals to attract attention.**
Photo by © Rubbermaid Inc.

can choose not to buy. Problems occur when the advertising is misleading. Be alert to the following deceptive (misleading) practices.

False Pricing. When consumers see an item that has been marked down, they naturally believe it is a bargain. Sale prices are usually lower than the regular ones. However, some merchants will raise the regular price on a sales ticket *before* marking it down. Let's say that the suggested price for a watch is $60. After the seller changes the price tag to read $100, the price is then "marked down" to $60. A consumer buys it believing that $40 has been saved. The truth is that the watch was bought at the regular price.

Bait and Switch. This occurs when an ad offers a product or service that is not available. For example, a butcher shop advertises a cut of meat at a bargain price. When you get to the store, you find out that the meat has all been sold (or maybe they had none to begin with.) The ad was used as "bait" to get you to the store. The clerk then tries to show you a more expensive cut (the "switch").

Referral Sales Plans. A few sellers of services and expensive products use this technique. How does it work? Suppose someone contacts you about siding for your house. You are offered a "special introductory deal" on new siding. The seller explains

RAINCHECK

Fay's® DRUGS

THIS RAINCHECK ENTITLES THE BEARER TO REDEMPTION OF THE ITEM LISTED BELOW.

ITEM ______ (ADVERTISED ITEMS ONLY) MODEL / SIZE ______

REG. PRICE ______ SALE PRICE ______ LIMIT ______

AD DATE ______ STORE NO. ______ FAY'S AUTHORIZED SIGNATURE

EXP. DATE: Item must be claimed within 7 days from postmark date.

NAME ______

ADDRESS ______

CITY ______ STATE ______ ZIP ______

HOME PHONE ______ BUSINESS PHONE ______

CUSTOMER COPY - RETURN FOR REDEMPTION

FIGURE 22–8 **Merchants who sell out of an advertised product sometimes give "rainchecks." What does a raincheck mean?**
Courtesy of Fay's Drug Company Inc.

that you will receive a bonus of $100 for each new purchaser you refer to them. Unfortunately, you pay the full price for the siding job. You then discover that it is very difficult to find customers for the builder. (Their bad reputation is probably known.) The sellers may even have left town. Most consumers are never able to earn their bonus money.

Unclear, Untrue, and Overstated Claims. Some products are advertised as being "improved" or "lasting 50 percent longer." Look carefully at such ads. Are the advertisers keeping facts from you? Do they tell you *how* a product has been improved? If so, does what they say make sense? If a product is said to last longer, ask yourself "Longer than what?" Your question might not have an answer.

Other ads use words such as "stain resistant" or "never needs ironing." The terms used may have several meanings. For example, a coat that is "stain-resistant" cannot be expected to resist *all* stains. Ads that say a product is "guaranteed" are often unclear and untrue. If you are told a product is guaranteed, make sure the *guarantee* is in writing. Another problem phrase is "lasts a lifetime." Few products do. If a claim for a product seems too good to be true, it probably is not true.

Clever Sales Tactics. You have studied an ad and believe that it is not misleading. Wise consumerism does not stop there. Remember, salespeople use various techniques to get you to buy. For instance, some salespeople use high-pressure or fast-talking approaches. Others flatter you or are very friendly because they want to make it difficult for you to say "no." Sometimes, a salesperson who is having trouble getting you to buy will turn you over to a second salesperson. A favorite sales trick is to say that "the price is going up tomorrow." A similar line is "this is the last item available."

? ? ? ? ? ? ? ? ? ? ? ? ? ?

WHAT WOULD YOU DO?

You see an advertisement in the paper for an item you have wanted. You stick the ad in your pocket and head for the store. You find the item on the store's shelf and take it to the checkout counter. The clerk rings up the item at the regular price. You point out the item is on sale. The clerk brushes off your comment and says that the ad in the paper is in error.

What would you do?

CONSUMER RIGHTS

Consumers have not always had rights. Until this century, there were few laws to protect buyers. If consumers bought defective products, it was their problem. Since they had no legal responsibility, producers often paid little attention to safety and quality. After many consumers were harmed by unsafe products and faulty merchandise, the public began to demand tougher standards.

Laws now require manufacturers to make safety their concern. Consumers have a right to expect that what they buy is safe. Laws also now protect consumers who buy faulty merchandise. After an item is sold, the producer must stand behind it. Consumer rights regarding credit, interest rates, insurance, housing, and so on, are discussed throughout the remainder of Section 5.

Cathy bought a Brewbetter coffeemaker. After she had used it for several months, she read a *recall* notice in the newspaper. Many people had reported problems with the product. It had even caused several fires. When Cathy took the coffeemaker back to the seller, she got a new one.

Laws protect buyers in another way. When purchasing a good or service, consumers must have choices. At one time, a single company could control an industry, such as oil. This is referred to as a monopoly. (You learned about monopolies in Chapter 21.) The company could charge whatever it wanted and consumers had to pay. Laws keep these situations from happening now.

Until the 1960s, there wasn't much information available about products and services. People often bought according to what they had heard from advertisers and friends. Now the government and many private associations and businesses provide a wide variety of consumer information and services. Smart shoppers take advantage of their right to obtain consumer information.

CONSUMER RESPONSIBILITIES

Along with consumer rights come responsibilities. First of all, you owe it to yourself to learn how to choose, buy, and use goods and services. This chapter has given you some tips on wise consuming. In the remaining chapters of Section 5 of this text, you will read more about smart shopping. Your study

FIGURE 22–9 **Consumers have a right to expect safe and satisfactory performance from the products they buy.**

of consumerism will not end here, though. Such learning is a lifelong process.

Assertiveness

To protect yourself and other consumers, you have a responsibility to speak out. Be *assertive.* If you think a business has not behaved properly, speak politely but firmly to a salesperson. Whenever you are not satisfied with the salesperson's response, see the manager. Should you continue to receive poor products and services, take your business elsewhere. Buying goods and services is somewhat like casting a vote. Through the things that you buy (or do not buy), you vote for or against a business.

Honesty

You expect businesses to be fair and honest with you at all times. As a responsible consumer, you should also be fair and honest. You may not realize it, but all consumers pay a penalty for a few dishonest people. When a person steals from a department store, for example, the store may suffer a temporary loss. However, to make up for this loss (and others), the store will raise its prices.

CONSUMER COMPLAINTS

Most of the time, you will be satisfied with goods and services you purchase. Sometimes, however, you may be disappointed. Here is a list of the most common consumer problems.

- Difficulties in getting a product repaired or replaced as promised in the warranty.
- Misleading advertising, labeling, or packaging.
- Defective products; for example, a cassette tape may break the first time you use it.
- Being overcharged for a product or service.
- Poor service or work of bad quality.
- Goods that were ordered and paid for but never received.
- Errors in computerized billing.

Suppose such a situation happens to you. How will you solve it?

Before Complaining

If you have a consumer *complaint*, do not write a nasty letter or hire a lawyer. In fact, you should never write a nasty letter to a business! Review the whole situation and try to resolve it in the simplest manner possible.

Save Everything. Keep track of all paperwork related to what you buy. This includes copies of order forms, receipts, and warranties. It is difficult to settle a complaint without proof of purchase.

Think it Through. You may have a faded blouse or a broken tool, but who is at fault? The reason the blouse faded was because you washed it with hot water instead of cold. The tool broke because you used it improperly. You should not expect the seller or manufacturer to replace such a product.

Many products do not work properly because people fail to follow instructions. This is often true for electrical appliances. If a product does not do what it should, reread the instruction book. Look at the product again. Ask a friend or family member to do the same. *Then* return the item or call a repairperson.

Give the Seller a Chance. If you know there is a problem and you are not at fault, take the product back to where you bought it. Make sure you have the receipt and anything else you might need. Be prepared to explain the nature of your problem. Think over what you want the merchant to do. For example, do you want a replacement, a refund, or do you want the product repaired?

Ask to see someone who can handle your problem. Many larger

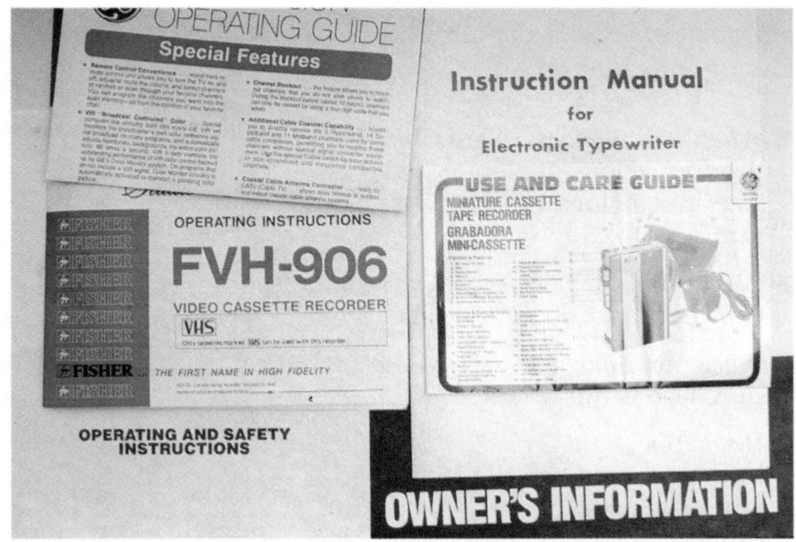

FIGURE 22–10 You can extend the life of many products by following instructions in the owner manuals.
Photo by Paul E. Meyers.

stores have a complaint (or customer service) department. If so, go there. Explain your case to the person in charge. Do not be either too timid or too aggressive. Usually, if you are fair and reasonable, the other person will be also. You may be surprised at how quickly the problem is resolved. Sellers do not want to lose customers.

436 Lincoln Road
Waterton, MI 67459

June 12, 19--

Mr. Gerald Morris
Customer Service Manager
Barkley Tackle Company
1003 Seventh Street
Henderson, WI 37849

Dear Mr. Morris:

On June 7, 19--, I purchased a 5'6" Barkley casting rod (Model No. 96) at Lunker Sporting Goods Store in Waterton, MI. The selling price was $39.95, which I paid in cash. Attached find a photocopy of the receipt.

Several days later, I used the rod for the first time. As I tried to make a routine cast, the rod snapped in half. I had only used it for about an hour.

Then I took the rod back to the store and explained what had happened. I was told by the store manager, Mr. Robert Stark, that the rod was not guaranteed. I insisted that I had used it only once, but he said there was nothing he could do.

I'm very sorry that the rod broke, but I do not believe that I was at fault. I have always used Barkley fishing products without any previous problems. This is to request that you provide me with a replacement rod or a refund. I'm sure you will agree that this problem should not have happened.

Sincerely yours,

Brad Corder

Brad Corder

attachment

FIGURE 22–11 A sample letter of complaint.

Making a Formal Complaint

If the local merchant cannot or will not help you, the next step is to complain to the manufacturer. Ask the seller how to contact the manufacturer. If you cannot get this information, check the product. It should have the manufacturer's name and address. If you cannot find the address, ask your local librarian for help.

When you do not have the name of a person at the company, address the letter to the customer service department. The Better Business Bureau says that a complaint letter should contain the following information:

- *What You Bought.* Describe the product. Does the item have a size and color? Is there a serial number?
- *Where You Bought It.* Give the complete address of the seller.
- *When You Bought It.* The date of purchase is important.
- *How You Paid For It.* Specify how you paid for the item. Did you use cash, a check, a credit card, or a money order? Attach copies of necessary papers. (Never send originals.) Paperwork may include receipts, cancelled checks, and sales contracts.
- *What the Problem Is.* Let the facts speak for themselves.
- *What You Want.* Do you want a refund? Would you like them to repair the item? Be clear.

Make a copy of the letter for yourself. You should receive a response within two or three weeks. If you do not, contact your local Better Business Bureau or consumer rights group for help.

FOCUS ON

Skills For Living

BUYING A USED CAR

For most of us, car ownership begins by buying a used car. In fact, used car sales outnumber new car sales by about two to one. Many people simply cannot afford the cost of buying a new car. Others, though, actually prefer a used car to a new one. They say that used cars are a much better value for the money.

The majority of used cars are bought from private owners, new car dealers, used car dealers, and auto rental companies. Each source has advantages and disadvantages. A good car at a fair price may be found through any of the four sources. New car dealers, however, are probably the best overall source. New car dealers sell used autos that have been traded in for new ones. They usually keep only the newer and better cars on their lots. Cars are usually reconditioned and offered with some type of warranty. The dealer wants you to be satisfied and come back later to buy a new car. However, used car prices at a new car dealership are usually higher than elsewhere. This is because of the greater cost of doing business.

Once you have located a car that interests you, make a careful inspection. You do not have to be an expert on cars to spot major problems. Look for body damage and signs of rust. Look under the car for holes in the exhaust system and for evidence of fluids leaking from the engine, radiator, transmission, or brakes. Drive the car and listen for noises, rattles, and vibrations. Note anything about which you feel suspicious or uncomfortable. Not all problems are serious. But find out what things will need to be fixed or replaced if you decide to buy.

A careful examination of a used car and a test drive should help you eliminate unacceptable ones. Before agreeing to buy, however, take several more steps:

1. Get an idea of the price for the year and model car that you are considering. Check the *Official Used Car Guide* published by the National Automobile Dealers Association (NADA). The NADA guide can be found at most credit unions, banks, and public libraries.

Check everything from price to tires when you buy a used car. Then relax and enjoy it!
Photo by Pictor/© Uniphoto, Inc.

2. Confirm the mileage. The law requires that the seller provide the buyer with a signed statement indicating the current mileage. Anyone who illegally tampers with an odometer, or who fails to provide the required disclosure statement may be sued.
3. Take it to a mechanic for an inspection. You should not rely solely on your judgment about a car. Hidden problems in the engine, transmission, or rear axle are of the most concern because these are costly to repair.
4. Contact the previous owner. Federal law requires dealers to have this information. Most reputable dealers will give you the name and phone number of this person. Call the person and explain that you are thinking about buying his or her previous car. You may be surprised at how cooperative and honest this person can be.
5. Check out the warranty. In May 1985, a new Federal Trade Commission rule took effect. The rule requires sellers of used cars (except private owners) to place a large "Buyers Guide" window sticker on each car. The guide makes clear what type of warranty is provided with the car. Many consumer experts say not to buy a used car "as is." Get a warranty, even if it is just for thirty days. A warranty provides important financial and legal protection.

Now you are ready to finalize the deal. Most buyers and salespeople expect to haggle a little over the price. However, do not expect the salesperson to lower the price much. Or do not expect the seller to do a log of free repairs as part of the deal. The margin of profit on a used car is fairly low.

Dealers try to make it easy for you to buy a car by providing financing. However, their rates will often be higher than you can find elsewhere. Do not be afraid to tell the salesperson that you will get your own financing. To hold the car, you may be required to leave a small deposit.

Once you pay for the car, it is yours. You will then need to arrange for insurance, license plates, and a new title. After that, you can sit behind the wheel, buckle up, and take your car for a cruise. Drive carefully.

CHAPTER 22 REVIEW

CHAPTER IN BRIEF

- A consumer is someone who buys or uses goods and services. Goods are articles that are produced or manufactured. Services involve the payment of money to people and businesses for work performed.
- Being a consumer is more than simply paying money For something. Consuming involves three stages: making choices, buying wisely, and using goods and services properly.
- Advertising is important for both sellers and consumers. For the seller, the purpose of advertising is to aid in selling goods and services. For the consumer, advertising provides information about goods and services for sale. Sellers use various advertising techniques to accomplish their purpose.
- There is nothing wrong with advertising, as long as it is honest. Problems occur when the advertising is misleading. Always be on the lookout for misleading advertising practices, such as: false pricing; bait and switch; referral sales plans; and unclear, untrue, and overstated claims.
- A number of steps have been taken to protect the rights of consumers. Laws have been passed regarding safety, faulty merchandise, and competition in the marketplace. Government and private agencies also provide a wide variety of consumer information and services.
- Along with consumer rights come responsibilities. You owe it to yourself to learn how to choose, buy, and use goods and services. You have a responsibility to speak out regarding poor products and services. You should also be fair and honest in your business dealings.
- Sometime, you will probably have a consumer complaint. Try to resolve the problem in the simplest manner possible. Make a formal complaint if simpler approaches do not work. Be businesslike in your efforts to resolve a consumer complaint.

WORDS TO KNOW

advertising
assertive
brand name
comparison shopping
complaint
consumer
direct-mail advertising
generic products
goods
guarantee
recall
services
warranty

QUESTIONS TO ANSWER

1. How are the goals of a buyer and seller different?
2. What is a need? A want?
3. The process of consuming has three stages. Name and briefly describe these three stages.
4. Give three reasons why Bill Martin is a wise consumer.
5. Why should you use and care for a product properly?
6. Advertising has advantages and disadvantages for consumers. Name two of each.
7. Which type of advertising technique is used in each of the following ads?
   a. A famous person speaks for the product.
   b. A company provides athletic uniforms with their name on them.
   c. A company explains how their product will make you more attractive.
   d. You are told how a certain service will save you money.
   e. An accident or other dangerous situation is shown.
8. What is meant by "bait and switch"? Give an example.
9. What are your rights and responsibilities as a consumer? Name two of each.
10. How is buying a product or service similar to casting a vote?
11. What should you do before writing a formal letter of complaint?
12. What six points should be included in a complaint letter?

ACTIVITIES TO DO

1. Prepare a list of five different grocery items. Visit a number of different stores (at least three) and record the price of each item. What were your findings? Which store is the most expensive? The least expensive? Which stores carry generic brands? Were those items priced lower than brand-name products?
2. Find examples of the advertising techniques discussed in this chapter (endorsements, familiarity, association, and so on). You will probably need to do this over several days. Pool your ads with classmates. Choose the best ads for a bulletin-board display.
3. Conduct an election for your class's or school's favorite television commercial. Nominate candidates. Prepare an election ballot and circulate it to classmates. Count the ballot and declare a winner. Send a letter to the winning company explaining what the class has done.
4. Think of a problem you have had with a product or service. Write a sample complaint letter to the manufacturer. Follow the guidelines provided in this chapter. Turn in the letter to your teacher.
5. As a class activity, develop a list of things to look for in buying a used car. Include things to examine visually and through a test drive.

TOPICS TO DISCUSS

1. Think of a major purchase you have made recently. Did you do comparison shopping before buying the item? If so, explain how you went about it. If not, explain why.
2. Until recently, doctors and lawyers have been prohibited from advertising their services. It is still a controversial issue. What is your opinion on this practice?
3. Have you ever ruined a new product by failing to read or follow instructions? If so, discuss your experiences in class.
4. You have probably heard someone say that buying a certain thing is "false economy." What does this phrase mean? Discuss examples of consumer practices that illustrate false economy.
5. Have you ever been cheated by a dishonest seller or misleading advertising? If so, discuss your experiences in class.
6. You or other members of the class have probably bought used cars. Car owners should share experiences in order to learn more about buying a used car. Discuss the following questions: Where was the car bought? Was a fair price paid for the car? Were any hidden problems discovered after the sale? Was the car covered by a warranty? You can probably think of additional questions.

CHAPTER 23 Banking and Credit

OUTLINE

- Financial Institutions and Services
- Checking Accounts
- Managing a Checking Account
- Credit and Its Use
- Chapter Review

OBJECTIVES

After reading this chapter, you should be able to:

- Name and describe the four major types of financial institutions.
- Describe how to open a checking account.
- Illustrate how to write and endorse a check.
- Illustrate how to maintain a check register and reconcile a bank statement.
- Illustrate how to make a bank deposit.
- Discuss how electronic banking may change money management.
- Name and describe the two basic types of credit.
- Calculate the cost of credit.

As you grow older, your use of money will probably change. Rather than pay cash for all of your purchases, you will find that it is often more convenient to write a check. There may be times also when you do not wish to use cash or a check. In those cases, you may want to use credit instead. The credit you use may be in the form of a loan or a charge purchase. Knowing how to use checking, credit, and other financial services is an important life skill for everyone.

FINANCIAL INSTITUTIONS AND SERVICES

A bank used to be the place to go when you wanted to save money, borrow money, or open a checking account. Today, there are four major

FIGURE 23–1 **It is not a good idea to carry large amounts of cash. Deposit your paycheck into a checking account and only keep a small amount of cash in your wallet.**
Photo by Paul E. Meyers.

types of financial institutions that provide these services and others.

Commercial Banks

Commercial banks may also be known as "bank and trust companies" or "community banks." Commercial banks are the most common type of financial institution. They are *full-service banks*, which offer a variety of services. These include checking and savings accounts, loans, safety deposit boxes, money orders, travelers checks, and so on. Borrowers and savers can find almost every convenience and service in these places.

Mutual Savings Banks

These began early in the nineteenth century in order to service ordinary people what commercial banks often overlooked. In theory, mutual savings banks are owned by their depositors. However, a board of trustees directs the bank's operations and acts in the interest of the depositors. There are only about 18 states that charter mutual savings banks. Most are in the Northeast.

Such banks generally provide the same services as commercial banks. In addition, they offer some of the services of a savings and loan association. One of the main attractions of mutual savings banks is that they often pay a slightly higher rate of interest than commercial banks.

Savings and Loan Associations

Other names for these institutions are "building and loan associations," "cooperative banks," "savings associations," and "homestead associations." They started in the early 1800s when people pooled their savings. Each, then, in turn, could borrow enough money to build a house. Savings and loan associations are now in all states. Such institutions provide more home mortgage business (home loans) than all other lenders combined.

Credit Unions

Credit unions (CUs) are nonprofit savings and loan cooperative associations. They are made up of people who have something in common. This could be a place of employment, a union membership, or the like. For example, all employees of a particular school district might form a credit union. Members govern the credit unions. They only accept savings from and make loans to those who belong. At the end of the year, a well-run credit union often has a surplus to distribute to its members.

Credit unions provide savings accounts, consumer loans, and financial counseling. A convenient feature of CUs is that members can often make deposits and loan payments through payroll deductions.

Changes in Financial Institutions

During the early 1980s, many banking laws were changed to allow financial institutions to be more competitive. Now financial institutions can pay higher rates of interest than before. Another result of the changes is that the four major types of financial institutions have begun to offer similar services.

Financial institutions now actively compete for business. This is good news for the consumer. It means, however, that consumers should shop around and compare services,

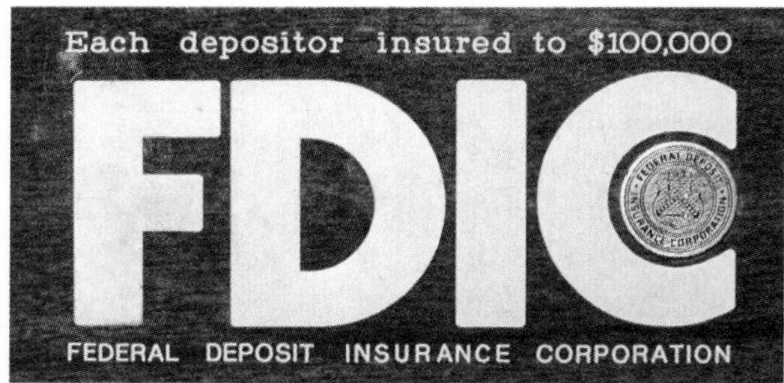

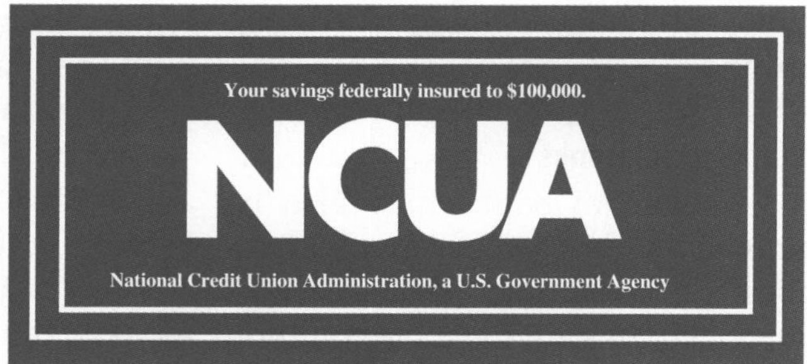

FIGURE 23–2 **Look for these seals at your bank or credit union. The Federal Deposit Insurance Company (FDIC) insures deposits in banks. The National Credit Union Administration (NCUA) insures savings deposits in credit unions.**
Photo by Paul E. Meyers; b. Courtesy of National Credit Union Administration.

charges, and rates of interest. This will ensure that they get the best deal.

The experience of Teresa Romero is a good case in point. When Teresa learned that her bank was raising the service charge on checking accounts, she began to ask about charges elsewhere. She discovered that she was eligible to join the credit union where her mother worked. After becoming a member, she received no-cost checking. In addition, she was paid monthly interest on her checking account balance.

CHECKING ACCOUNTS

Checking accounts are one of the most commonly used banking services. Checking accounts have two main advantages: safety and convenience. Checks provide a safe and convenient way to pay bills. It is unsafe to carry large amounts of cash. Also, keeping large amounts of money at home is unwise. Michael found this out.

Michael never thought he needed a checking account. He liked to go to the bank on Friday evenings and cash his paycheck. He then paid for all of his purchases in cash. The cash he did not carry with him was kept inside an empty tennis ball can that was stored on the hall closet shelf. No one would ever think of looking there for money, he thought.

Michael returned from a movie late on Friday night to discover that his apartment had been burglarized. His portable television and VCR were the only things he noticed that were missing. As he sat down on the couch to think about what to do, he remembered his money. He went to the hall closet. As he opened the closet door, an empty tennis ball can rolled off the top shelf.

He had insurance to cover the cost of replacing the television and VCR. But he was heartsick to lose the money he needed to live on the rest of the month. Needless to say, Michael opened a checking account the next time he got paid.

Checks can be used as freely as cash. Unlike cash, however, only the person to whom the check is made out can get the money. A second advantage of checks is that they make it easier to keep good financial records. A canceled check is legal proof of payment. Be sure to save your canceled checks.

Without the use of checks, our economic system could not function. Individuals and businesses write billions of checks each year. A very elaborate national system allows millions of checks to be processed daily. Let's see how the system works.

Assume that you take your car in for repairs and the bill comes to $45. Rather than pay the mechanic in cash, you write a check. That is, you write instructions to your bank, the American National Bank, to deduct $45 from your account and pay it to Joe's Garage. Joe then takes your check to his bank, Mid-America Bank, where he deposits the check. His account is credited in the amount of $45.

The Mid-America Bank does not collect payment directly from the American National Bank. It would be ridiculous for a bank to pay separately for every check written by a customer and receive separate payment for every check credited to a customer's account. Instead, a bank sends all of its checks to a centralized clearinghouse. The checks are added up at the clearinghouse each day. Each individual bank then makes or receives just one daily payment to or from its fellow banks.

After the check has been cleared, it is returned to the American National Bank where the bank subtracts $45 from your account. The check is stamped "paid" and will be returned to you along with other canceled checks.

Types of Checking Accounts

In the past, banks offered only two basic types of checking accounts: regular and special. A regular account, often called a minimum balance account, requires that the customer maintain a certain minimum balance. As long as the minimum balance is in the account, there is no extra charge. If the balance drops below the minimum amount, however, the customer will have to pay a service charge.

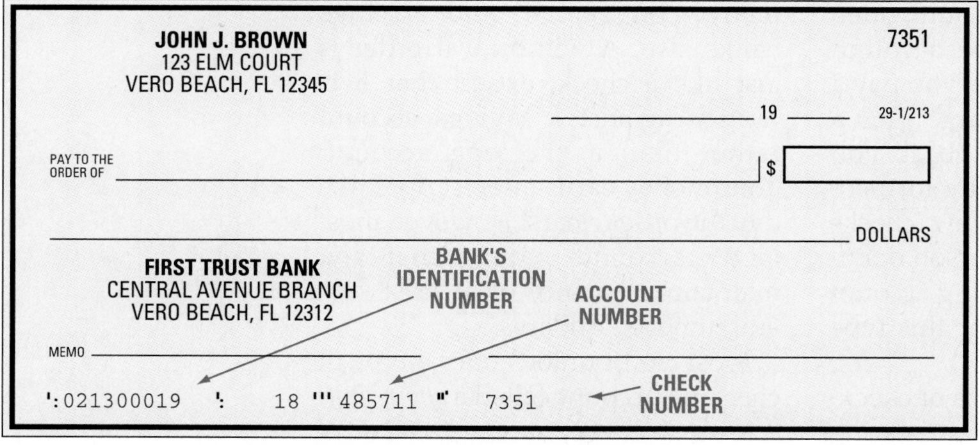

FIGURE 23–3 The coded numbers at the bottom of a check are read by a computer. This speeds up check processing considerably.

JANE A. SMITH
999 Main Street
Troy, Illinois 12000

727

March 20, 19 --

80-289
518

PAY TO THE ORDER OF *United Insurance Co.* $ *54.00*

Fifty-Four and 00/100 DOLLARS

STATE EMPLOYEES
CREDIT UNION
Troy, Illinois 12000

FOR: *Acct # 43072-18* *Jane A. Smith*

⑆021989478⑆ 756420855808⑈ 0727

JANE A. SMITH
999 Main Street
Troy, Illinois 12000

$ 727

CHECK HERE IF TAX DEDUCTIBLE ITEM ► ☐

March 20, --

BAL FOR'D	
THIS PAYMENT	*54.00*
BALANCE	
OTHER	
BAL FOR'D	

United Insurance Co.

Fifty-Four and 00/100

STATE EMPLOYEES
CREDIT UNION
Troy, Illinois 12000

Acct # 43072-18 *Jane A. Smith*

NOT NEGOTIABLE

⑆021989478⑆ 756420855808⑈ 0727

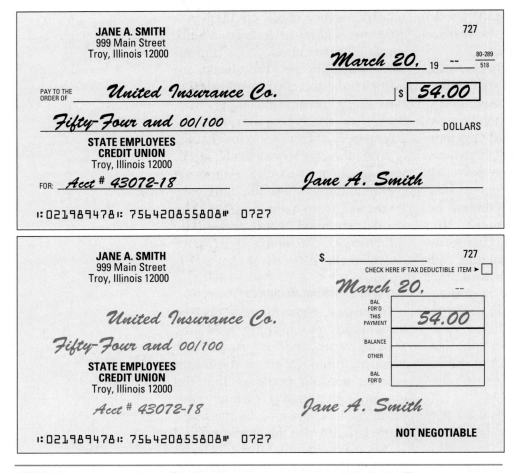

FIGURE 23–4 **Some banks and credit unions do not return canceled checks. They use a two-part form instead that provides customers with a record of the transaction.**

A second basic type of checking account is the special account, often called a cost-per-check account. With this type of account, you pay a flat monthly service charge plus a small amount for each check you write. Special accounts are for people who only write a few checks each month. A young person opening his or her first checking account should carefully consider this type of account.

One of the newest types of checking accounts is an interest-bearing account called a *negotiable order of withdrawal (NOW)* account. These started with savings and loan associations and are now offered by many commercial and savings banks also. A withdrawal order is just like a check, except that it is written against a savings account rather than a checking account. Your money earns interest up to the day the order clears. However, most NOW accounts require that you maintain a balance of at least several hundred dollars.

Most credit unions offer a type of checking account called a *share-draft account.* It is very similar to a NOW account. You write drafts (checks) against a credit union savings account. Your money earns interest until the draft clears. Many credit unions have no monthly service charges at all. However, to earn interest on the account, the credit union often requires a minimum balance of $500 to $750.

If abused, a checking account can become very expensive. For example, if you write a check for more than you have in your account (an *overdraft*), the check will be returned. Your bank will then charge you a fee for every check that "bounces." If you write a check to someone, and decide to "stop payment" on it, the bank will usually charge you for this also. As you are shopping around for a place to open a checking account, request an information sheet that describes all of the institution's services and charges.

Opening a Checking Account

Once you have decided on a bank and checking account plan, opening an account is very simple. You need only fill out a *signature card.* The signature card asks for your name, address, phone number, social security number, and similar data. At the end of the card, there is a place for your signature. The signature that you put on the card should be your legal name, not a nickname.

MANAGING A CHECKING ACCOUNT

Maintaining an accurate up-to-date checkbook requires knowledge and practice of a few important rules. Here are some important steps and guidelines to follow.

Writing a Check

A blank check requires five kinds of information. One additional kind is optional. Each of these will now be discussed. Refer to Figure 23–5 as you read about each part.

Date. Record the date on the check. This will help you keep accurate records. Never date a check ahead of time *(postdating)* because you do not

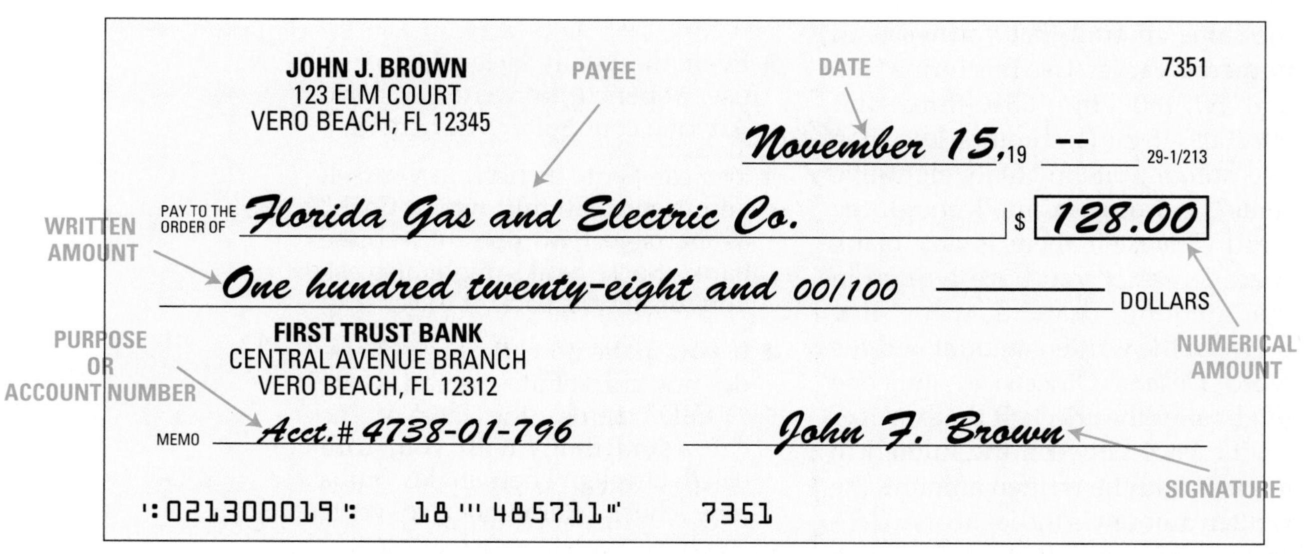

FIGURE 23–5 **A correctly written check.**

have enough money in your account. If the payee cashes the check, you might overdraw the account.

Payee. The person or institution to whom you write the check is the *payee.* It is proper to ask someone how they would like the check made out. On their bills, many businesses indicate how to write the check. If the name is a long one, it is acceptable to abbreviate. However, use common abbreviations, such as "Inc.," "Co.," and "Assoc."

Numerical Amount. You record the amount of the check in two places. At the end of the line where you fill in the name of the payee, you write the amount of the check in dollars and cents. For example, "10.50." If the check is for under a dollar, put a "0" in front of the decimal point and insert the word *cents "$0.85 cents."* To keep someone from altering the check easily, place the figures close to the dollar sign.

Written Amount. On the long line near the middle of the check, you will see the word *Dollars.* Here you write out the same amount that you wrote in numerals earlier. Use this form: "Ten and 50/100" or "Fifty-three and 00/100." If the amount is less than one dollar, write in "Only eight-five cents" and draw a line through the word *Dollars.* If there is any blank space left after you have written in the amount, draw a wavy line between the written amount and the word *Dollars.* Otherwise, someone might alter the check. If there is ever a difference between the numerical amount and the written amount, the written amount is the legal one. Generally, however, a bank will contact the writer before it will accept a check with differing amounts.

Purpose. In the lower left-hand portion of a check, there is a space that is indicated as "For" or "Memo." This space does not have to be filled out. But it is always a good idea to do so. This is where you indicate the purpose of the check. For example, "auto tune-up" or "birthday gift." In paying bills, some companies may ask you to write a policy or account number on the check. Next to "Memo" or "For," you would write "Acct. #4738-01-796" if that were your number. Routinely filling in this line can help you later as you review a budget or prepare an income tax return.

Signature. The bottom right-hand portion of the check is where you sign your name. Sign it exactly as it appears on the signature card you filled out when you opened the account. Do not use the words *Mr., Miss, Mrs.,* or *Ms.* as part of a signature.

In addition to following the procedure discussed for filling out checks, also keep in mind the following guidelines:

- Even though it is legal, do not use a pencil to write a check. Anyone could alter your check.
- You can write a check to yourself and cash it. Simply write "Cash" as the payee and present it to the bank. (Some banks might also ask you to sign the back of the check.)
- If you make an error on a check, do not correct it. Instead write "VOID" across the face of the check and file it with your canceled checks. Then make out a new check. Remember to write "VOID" in your register, too.
- Do not sign a blank check and let someone else fill in the amount.

- Do not leave your checkbook or blank checks in a place where someone can take them.
- Do not loan a blank check to someone because they have forgotten theirs. The bank's computer will read *your* electronic number and subtract the money from your account.

? ? ? ? ? ? ? ? ? ? ? ? ? ? ?

WHAT WOULD YOU DO?

You like having a checking account, but the checkbook is just something else to carry. You often put it in the glove box of your car. It is safe enough since you always keep your car locked. After a movie one evening, you return to your car to find that it has been burglarized. Your stereo is gone and so is the checkbook. You are very upset.

What would you do?

Keeping a Check Register

After you open an account, you will receive a supply of imprinted checks and a separate *check register.* The register is where you keep a record of checks written, deposits, and other transactions. One checkbook style has a check stub attached to the check itself. There is no separate check register. However, the check register style is the most popular.

A common mistake people make in maintaining a checking account is not recording checks in the register. This often happens when someone is in a hurry. Get in the habit of filling out the check register *at the time you write a check.* If you don't, you won't know the correct balance and might overdraw the account.

Overdrawing a checking account can be very embarrassing. One day Jackie Brown got a phone call from her friend Barbara who worked at The Clothes Rack. Barbara called about a check that Jackie had written to buy a new outfit. The bank had returned the check to the store because of "Insufficient Funds." Jackie felt humiliated.

In looking over her check register, Jackie found that she had not recorded a check written to the gas company. It was near the end of the month when she wrote a $53.46 check to The Clothes Rack. There was only $46.20 in her account and the check "bounced." Jackie immediately took another check to Barbara.

Figure 23–6 shows two common ways to maintain a check register. Study each part of the illustration. Both ways work well, so choose the one that you prefer. The column next to the "payment/debit" column may be used to check off items cleared when you balance a statement. Or, if you prefer, you can indicate in this column which items are tax deductible (T).

Endorsing a Check

Suppose a friend writes you a check. What do you do with it? You take it to your bank and endorse it there. An *endorsement* is your signature on the back/left side of a check. Your written name enables a bank to cash the check. There are three common types of endorsement: blank, restrictive, and full (see Figure 23–7).

ONE-LINE ENTRY

RECORD ALL CHARGES OR CREDITS THAT AFFECT YOUR ACCOUNT

NUMBER	DATE	DESRCRIPTION OF TRANSACTION	PAYMENT/DEBIT (-)		✓ T	FEE (IF ANY) (-)	DEPOSIT/CREDIT (+)		BALANCE $	
									282	34
7341	3/25	Cash	$ 150	00		$	$ 255	67	388	01
7342	3/25	Florida Telephone	25	00					363	01
7343	3/27	Metropolitan Life Ins.	8	70					354	31
7344	3/27	John Hancock Ins.	5	78					348	53
7345	3/27	Capital Cablevision	19	75					328	78
7346	3/27	State Bank	400	00			305	67	234	45
7347	4/1	Chrysler Credit Corp.	257	62			485	45	462	28
7348	4/1	Town and Country Motel	68	00					394	28
7349	4/1	Fairway Super Market	36	11					358	17
7350	4/3	Linens and Things	90	91					267	26

TWO-LINE ENTRY

RECORD ALL CHARGES OR CREDITS THAT AFFECT YOUR ACCOUNT

NUMBER	DATE	DESRCRIPTION OF TRANSACTION	PAYMENT/DEBIT (-)		✓ T	FEE (IF ANY) (-)	DEPOSIT/CREDIT (+)		BALANCE $	
									282	34
7341	3/25	Cash	$ 150	00		$	$		150	00
		Car repair							132	34
Deposit	3/25	Deposit Check					255	67	255	67
									388	01
7342	3/25	Florida Telephone	25	00					25	00
		Telephone Bill							363	01
7343	3/27	Metropolitan Life Ins.	8	70					8	70
		Insurance							354	31
7344	3/27	John Hancock Ins.	5	78					5	78
		Insurance							348	53
7345	3/27	Capital Cablevision	19	75					19	75
		Cable Bill							328	78

FIGURE 23–6 **Keeping a check register up-to-date is not difficult. You just have to be accurate and pay attention to detail.**

Endorse a check exactly as it is made out. Do this even if your name is improper or misspelled. When there is an error, you endorse the check first as is, followed by the correct way. For example, suppose a check to Sharon Robbins is made out incorrectly to "Sharon Robins." She would first endorse it as "Sharon Robins" followed by "Sharon Robbins." Or a check to Skip Turner would be endorsed "Skip Turner" followed by "James A. Turner."

A recent federal law guarantees customers of financial institutions timely access to money they deposit. The law also requires customers to use new uniform standards to endorse checks, Figure 23–8. If you fail to follow the guidelines, you will still get your money. But it could take longer.

Making a Deposit

The process of putting money into a checking account is known as "making a deposit." To do this, you fill out the preprinted *deposit ticket* that comes with your supply of checks. A deposit ticket is used to deposit any combination of currency, coins, or checks. In making a deposit, a portion of the deposit

A **blank endorsement** is simply your written signature. Once you have signed a check , it can be treated as cash. Anyone can then present it to the bank for payment. So, never endorse a check until you are ready to cash it.

Jill Yount

A **restictive endorsement** is a message and a signature that restricts the use of the check. The most common restrictive endorsement is "For deposit only." This is usually used when you wish to send a check by mail to a bank for deposit. With this message, the check can't be used for any othe purpose.

For Deposit only
Jill Yount

A **full endorsement** is used when you want to pay someone else with a check that is made out to you. This is done by writing "Pay to the order of______" and then signing your name. This endorsement transfers the right of payment from you to a new payee.

Pay to the Order
of Sharon Weber
Jill Yount

FIGURE 23–7 **Different forms of endorsements are used for different purposes.**

can be received in cash, if desired. Figure 23–9 shows a completed deposit ticket.

When you make a deposit, the bank will return to you a receipt showing the amount of the deposit. Check this to make sure it agrees with the amount you wrote in the

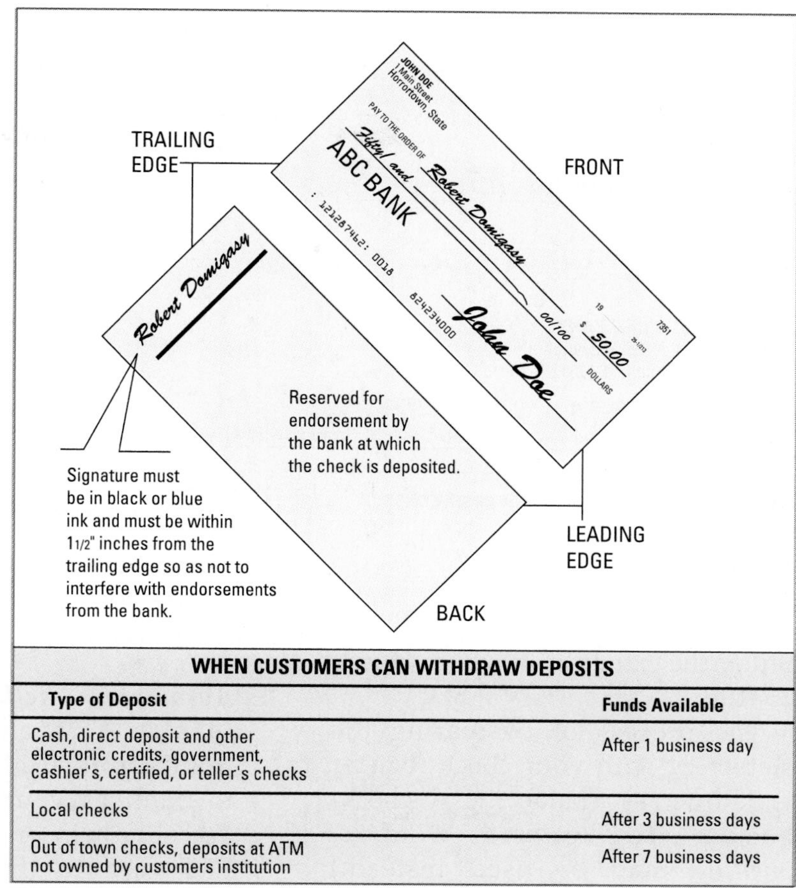

WHEN CUSTOMERS CAN WITHDRAW DEPOSITS

Type of Deposit	Funds Available
Cash, direct deposit and other electronic credits, government, cashier's, certified, or teller's checks	After 1 business day
Local checks	After 3 business days
Out of town checks, deposits at ATM not owned by customers institution	After 7 business days

FIGURE 23–8 **Follow these new check endorsing requirements.**

deposit ticket. Record the deposit right away in your check register.

Balancing a Statement

Once a month, the bank will send you a packet that includes a *statement of account* and the canceled checks that you wrote. Canceled checks are not returned if you have the type of checks shown in Figure 23–4. The statement is a summary of all your transactions for a given period. It includes the following:

- The amount of each check and the date the bank received it.
- The deposits you made.

DEPOSIT TICKET

JOHN J. BROWN
123 Elm Court
Vero Beach, FL 12345

DATE *November 15,* 19 --

CASH ➜	32 00
LIST CHECKS SINGLY	76 18
TOTAL FROM OTHER SIDE	
TOTAL ITEMS — TOTAL	108 18

29-1/213

USE OTHER SIDE FOR ADDITIONAL LISTING. ◄ ENTER TOTAL HERE

BE SURE EACH ITEM IS PROPERLY ENDORSED

FIRST TRUST BANK
Central Avenue Branch
Vero Beach, FL 12312

⑆021300019⑆ 18⑈485711⑈

DELUXE HO-14

CHECKS AND OTHER ITEMS ARE RECEIVED FOR DEPOSIT SUBJECT TO THE PROVISIONS OF THE UNIFORM COMMERCIAL CODE OR ANY APPLICABLE COLLECTION AGREEMENT.

FIGURE 23–9 A completed deposit ticket.

- Any service charges.
- Beginning and ending balances.

Study the example shown in Figure 23–10.

The process of comparing the statement with your check register is known as "balancing a checkbook." (In some cases, the word *reconciling* may be used instead.) Instructions for how to balance your account are usually printed on the back of the statement, Figure 23–11. Follow each step exactly as described. If you have a problem that you cannot figure out, do not wait until you receive the next statement. Rather, go to the bank right away and ask someone to help you.

After you have balanced your checkbook, make any necessary changes in the register. For example, you may need to record an amount for service charges or for an overdraft.

Electronic Banking

In the future, electronic banking may change the way you manage money. *Electronic banking* is a broad term used to describe various types of electronic fund transfers (EFT). There are four common types of EFT services:

1. ***Automated Teller Machines (ATM).*** ATMs are 24-hour electronic terminals that permit you to bank at your convenience. You simply insert your personal EFT card in the machine to withdraw cash, make deposits, or transfer funds between accounts.
2. ***Pay-by-Phone Systems.*** These systems permit you to telephone your bank and instruct it to pay certain bills or to transfer funds between accounts.
3. ***Direct Deposits or Withdrawals.*** Deposits, such as a paycheck, may be authorized to your account on a regular basis. You can also arrange to have regular bills, such as insurance premiums and rent payments, paid automatically.
4. ***Point-of-Sale Transfers.*** These transfers let you pay for retail purchases with your EFT or *debit card.* This is similar to a credit card except that money

FIRST TRUST BANK
Central Avenue Branch
Vero Beach, FL 12312

PAGE 1 OF 1

JOHN J. BROWN
123 Elm Court
Vero Beach, FL 12345

002 613 CY

13435711
6134357116

STATEMENT OF YOUR ACCOUNT(S) FOR PERIOD 11-15-XX THROUGH 12-13-XX

SUMMARY OF REGULAR ACCOUNT # 18 485711

BALANCE LAST STATEMENT	502.10
DEPOSITS AND OTHER ADDITIONS	1910.78
CHECKS AND OTHER SUBTRACTIONS	1306.12
BALANCE THIS STATEMENT	1106.76

TAXPAYER ID NUMBER **123 45 6789**

DATE	TYPE OF TRANSACTION	CHECKS	SUBTRACTIONS	ADDITIONS	BALANCE
11–15	BEGINNING BALANCE				502.10
11–18	DEPOSIT			405.24	907.34
11–22	CHECKS POSTED (3)	67.20			840.14
11–23	DEPOSIT			650.15	
11–23	CHECKS POSTED (1)	17.75			1472.54
11–25	CHECKS POSTED (4)	519.45			953.09
11–28	CHECKS POSTED (1)	44.00			909.09
11–29	CHECKS POSTED (3)	47.20			861.89
11–30	DEPOSIT			305.24	
11–30	CHECKS POSTED (1)	50.00			1117.13
12–05	CHECKS POSTED (3)	363.27			753.86
12–06	CHECKS POSTED (1)	149.69			604.17
12–07	DEPOSIT			305.24	909.41
12–08	CHECKS POSTED (1)	4.00			905.41
12–09	CHECKS POSTED (1)	43.56			861.85
12–12	DEPOSIT			244.91	1106.76

CHECKS POSTED (* INDICATES SEQUENCE BREAK)

CHECK	AMOUNT	DATE	CHECK	AMOUNT	DATE	CHECK	AMOUNT	DATE
7242	50.00	11–30	7249	21.20	11–29	7255	16.00	11–29
7243	44.00	11–28	7250	8.70	11–25	7256	10.00	11–29
7244	17.75	11–23	7251	47.20	11–22	7257	13.27	12–05
7245	10.00	11–22	7252	10.00	11–22	7258	43.56	12–09
7246	400.00	11–25	7253	17.66	11–25	7259	300.00	12–05
7247	50.00	12–05	7254	93.09	11–25	7260	149.69	12–06
7248	4.00	12–08						

FIGURE 23–10 **Every month your bank will send you a bank statement. This is a summary of all your transactions during that time period.**

for the purchase is immediately transferred from your bank account.

Electronic banking can be very convenient. A possible disadvantage, however, is that your EFT card and personal identification number are used for all transactions. If they should be lost or stolen, you must immediately notify your bank. With EFT, you also need to carefully examine receipts and monthly statements for errors. At the time you open an EFT account, your bank will provide you with written information on your rights and responsibilities.

"It's Easy to Balence Your Account" - Follow the instructions and use the reconcilement form below.
Reconcilement Instructions:

- Check off each paid check on your checkbook stub or register.
- Be sure that all **checks posted** and **other subtractions** shown on your checking account have been subtracted from your checkbook balance and that all **deposits** and **additions** have been added.
- List and total under "Checks Outstanding" all checks not paid by the bank during this statement period.
- Fill in the ending balance shown on this statement.
- Add the deposits made after the close of this period.
- Deduct the checks still outstanding.
- The result should be the same as the balance remaining in your checkbook.

Checks Outstanding						Reconcilement Form	
Check No. or Date	Amount	Check No. or Date	Amount	Check No. or Date	Amount		
	$	Total Forwarded	$	Total Forwarded	$	Balence as of this statement, shown on front. $	
						Add Deposits not yet shown on front	
						Total $	
						Subtract Total Checks Outstanding $	
Total or Carry Forward		Total or Carry Forward		**Total**		**This Result should agree with your check-book balance $**	

Please examine at once.
Your account will be considered correct if no report is received by our auditors in 14 days; except that matters involving your line of credit or electronic transfer(s) must be reported within 60 days (see above).

FIGURE 23–11 **You can keep your account balanced if you follow this step-by-step procedure.**

CREDIT AND ITS USE

Credit refers to the receipt of money, goods, or services in exchange for a promise to pay. People may get credit in the form of loans. This form is called loan credit. Sales credit is also available. In this type, consumers can delay their payments for goods and services.

Loan Credit

Loan credit involves money borrowed in order to buy something. Most of these loans are for major expenses. Borrowers may not have cash on hand to pay for a house, car, or college education. The buyer usually gets a loan at one place and spends the cash in another. For example, you may secure a loan from a credit union. You will then use the money to buy a car at a local dealer.

Buyers generally pay back loan credit in equal installments over a fixed time period. In the case of the auto loan, you might pay installments of $150 for 36 months.

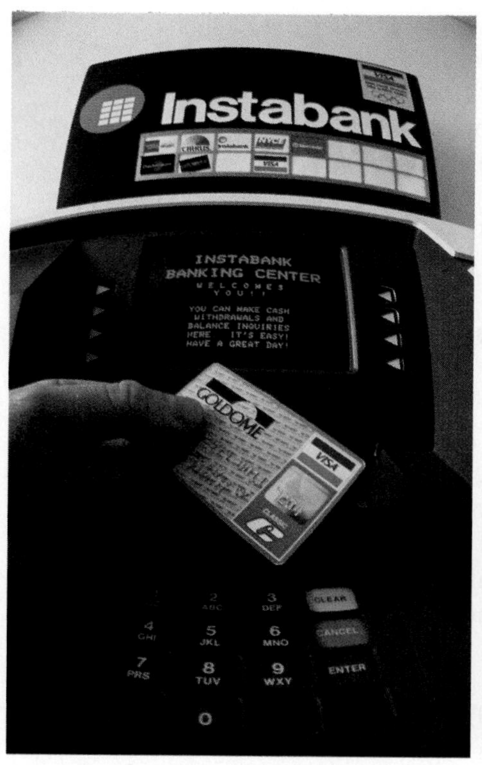

FIGURE 23–12 **Automated teller machines (ATM) are the most common type of electronic banking.**
Courtesy of Goldome.

FIGURE 23–13 **Without credit, it would be impossible for most people to buy a house, car, or major home appliance.**
Courtesy American Electric Power.

Sales Credit

When using loan credit, you borrow money. Sales credit, however, allows you to obtain goods and services immediately. You can then delay paying until later. There are three main types of sales credit: open charge accounts, revolving charge accounts, and installment accounts.

Many businesses provide open charge accounts to customers with good credit ratings. Don Marshall has a charge account at Polk's Department Store. One day, he decides to charge two sweaters there. After telling the clerk he is making a charge purchase, Don presents his charge plate. He signs a receipt and then takes home his purchase. The bill arrives a few weeks later.

The revolving charge is probably the most common form of consumer sales credit. Most of these are credit card accounts issued by chain stores, oil companies, and banks. Bank cards have names such as VISA, MasterCard, and Discover. With them, you can charge a number of goods and services. These include restaurant meals, airline tickets, and auto repairs.

Like Don, credit card customers receive a monthly statement of all transactions. Don paid his entire bill. He could also have made a minimum payment or some other amount. But had he done that, he would have paid a finance charge.

What percent of interest is paid on credit card purchases?

Installment accounts are the third major type of sales credit. People may use these to buy items that exceed the credit line of revolving charge accounts. Stores that do not honor credit cards may offer installment plans. Examples of items sometimes bought this way include furniture and home appliances.

The customer usually makes a small down payment. An installment contract that details payment terms for the balance is signed. The contract usually calls for fixed monthly payments and a finance charge. Installments are paid over several months or a few years. Finance charges are often higher than those for revolving accounts.

The Cost of Credit

The cost of credit varies from place to place. Fortunately, the law requires lenders to tell you in writing before you sign an agreement how much the charges will be. To understand the agreement, you will need to know the terms finance charge and annual percentage rate.

The *finance charge* is the total dollar amount you pay for using credit. It includes interest, service charges, insurance premiums, and other fees. For example, borrowing $100 for a year might cost you $15 in interest. If there is also a service charge of $2, the finance charge will be $17.

The *annual percentage rate* (APR) is the percentage rate cost of credit on a yearly basis. Suppose you borrow $200 for one year and pay a finance charge of $20. If you keep the entire $200 for 12 months and then pay it back in one lump sum, you are paying an APR of 10 percent. However, if you repay the $200 and finance charge in 12 equal monthly installments (a total of $220), you do not really get to use the $200 for the whole year. In fact, you get to use less and less of the $200 each month. In this case, the $20 charge for credit amounts to an APR of 18 percent.

The APR is your key to comparing credit costs regardless of the amount of credit or the repayment period. All lenders (such as banks, stores, and credit card companies) must state the cost of their credit in terms of both the finance charge and APR. The law says you must be aware of this information before signing a credit contract.

To actually compare credit costs, you must take into account the APR and length of the loan. Let's assume you are buying a car for $7,500. You pay $1,500 down and borrow $6,000. The relationship among three different credit arrangements is shown in Figure 23–14.

	APR	Length of Loan	Monthly Payment	Total Finance Charge	Total Cost
Creditor A	14%	3 years	$205.07	$1,382.52	**$7,382.52**
Creditor B	14%	4 years	**$163.96**	$1,870.08	$7,870.08
Creditor C	**15%**	4 years	$166.98	$2,015.04	$8,015.04

FIGURE 23–14 The cost of credit varies according to the APR and the length of the loan.

The lowest total loan cost is available from Creditor A. If you are looking for a lower monthly payment, you can get that by paying the loan back in four years instead of three. However, the lower monthly payment from Creditor B will add $487.56 to the total finance charge. If the four-year loan is only available from Creditor C, the 15 percent APR will add another $144.96 to the finance charge.

Other terms, such as the size of the down payment, will also make a difference in the cost of credit. Be sure to consider all aspects of a loan before making a choice.

? ? ? ? ? ? ? ? ? ? ? ? ? ?

WHAT WOULD YOU DO?

You are excited about buying your first car. You got a good deal and the finance rate is reasonable. The last step is to sign the installment sale contract. In going over the contract, you discover that the amount financed includes charges for "credit life and disability insurance" and "extended warranty." You ask the salesperson about the charges. He says they are optional, but that most people buy them. They only add a few dollars to the monthly payment. You are not sure whether you need them.

What would you do?

YOUR CREDIT HISTORY

Whenever you apply for credit, the potential merchant or lender will usually request a credit report on you. Such information is obtained from a credit bureau. A credit bureau is a private organization that provides information to businesses regarding the credit history of customers.

Your credit file contains four major types of information:

1. Personal information, such as name, address, previous addresses, marital status, and number of dependents.
2. Information about your salary, spouse's salary, and other income.
3. The status of your current accounts. What kinds of loans you now have. How well you pay your bills.
4. Any court judgments or liens against you. A lien is a charge against your property for failure to pay a debt. Accounts turned over to a collection agency are also noted.

The credit bureau only compiles information and provides it to the merchant. The merchant or lender then makes a judgment about how credit worthy you are.

Federal law gives you the right to know what information is in your file. If you are refused credit on the basis of a credit bureau report, the merchant must give you the name and address of the bureau. You are entitled to obtain a free credit report from them. If you disagree with information in the file, the credit bureau must reinvestigate. Information that cannot be backed up must be taken out.

Even if you are not turned down for credit, you may want to look at your file. A local bank or merchant can tell you the name of the credit bureau nearest you. Write or call them to ask how to obtain a credit report. You will probably be charged a fee. After you read the report, you can ask to have missing information added to the file.

People who use credit cards or who have bank loans should find out if the information in their credit bureau files is correct.

Photo by David Conklin/© Uniphoto, Inc.

CHAPTER 23 REVIEW

CHAPTER IN BRIEF

- There are four major types of financial institutions: commercial banks, mutual savings banks, savings and loan associations, and credit unions. Recent changes in laws governing financial institutions now allow all of them to offer similar kinds of services. Increased competition among financial institutions is good news for consumers.
- Checking accounts are one of the most commonly used banking services. Checking accounts have the advantages of safety and convenience. There are four types of checking accounts: regular (minimum balance), special (cost-per-check), negotiable order of withdrawal (NOW), and share-draft account.
- A blank check requires several kinds of information: date, payee, numerical amount, written amount, purpose (optional), and signature. Learn how to correctly write a check.
- The check register is where you keep a record of checks written, deposits made, and other transactions. A common mistake is not recording checks in the register. Overdrawing a checking account can be very embarrassing.
- An endorsement is a signature and a message to the bank to cash, deposit, or transfer the check to someone else. There are three kinds of endorsements: blank, restrictive, and full.
- Once a month, the bank will send you a statement of account. The process of comparing the statement with your check register is known as balancing (or reconciling) a checkbook.
- Credit refers to the receipt of money, goods, or services in exchange for a promise to pay. Credit may be in the form of loan credit or sales credit. There are three main types of sales credit: open charge accounts, revolving charge accounts, and installment accounts.
- The finance charge is the total dollar amount you pay for using credit. The annual percentage rate (APR) is the percentage cost of credit on a yearly basis. The APR is your key to comparing credit costs regardless of the amount of credit or the repayment period.

WORDS TO KNOW

annual percentage rate (APR)
automated teller machine (ATM)
check register
credit
debit card
overdraft
deposit ticket
electronic banking
endorsement
finance charge
full-service bank
negotiable order of withdrawal (NOW)
share-draft account

payee
postdating
reconciling
signature card
statement of account

QUESTIONS TO ANSWER

1. There are four major types of financial institutions. Name and briefly describe them.
2. What are the two main advantages of having a checking account?
3. Explain the basic difference between a regular checking account and a special checking account.
4. Name the five kinds of information you write on a check.
5. How should you endorse a check if your name is misspelled on the face of the check?
6. What is a mistake people often make with their check registers? How can this mistake be prevented?
7. In simple terms, what is the purpose of balancing a bank statement?
8. Name and briefly describe the four types of EFT services.
9. There are two forms of credit. Name and briefly explain each type.
10. What are the three basic types of sales credit?
11. What does the finance charge include?
12. What is the practical purpose of the APR?
13. Let's say you bought a new car for which you paid $2,000 down and made monthly payments of $178.60 for three years. What was the total cost of the car?

ACTIVITIES TO DO

1. As a class, survey the types of financial institutions in your community, suburb, or region of the city. How many institutions are there? Classify each according to the four types of institutions discussed in this chapter. Which is the most common type of financial institution in your area?
2. A group of several students should visit at least three different financial institutions. Collect information about the types of checking accounts offered. How many different types of accounts did they discover? Which type of account best meets your needs in terms of both cost and convenience? Discuss your answers in class.
3. Ask a parent or another adult to allow you to perform the following tasks for them:
   a. Write a check.
   b. Record a transaction in a check register.
   c. Make a deposit to a checking account.
4. The instructor will provide a sample statement of account and check register. Follow the procedure shown in Figure 23–11 to reconcile the bank statement.

5. Obtain an application for a credit card at a financial institution or other business. Read the application carefully and answer the following questions:
   a. Is the card free or is an annual fee required?
   b. What is the APR?
   c. How is the finance charge figured?
   d. What is the credit limit?
   e. What is the minimum monthly payment required?
6. Find out the interest rates being charged in your area for consumer loans. Compare the rates for a number of different sources, such as savings and loan associations, commercial banks, and finance companies. Which one offers the best rates?

TOPICS TO DISCUSS

1. Discuss advantages and disadvantages of electronic banking.
2. Some futurists are saying that we are headed for a "checkless" or "moneyless" society. Do you think this time will ever come?
3. Many people like to order merchandise from mail order catalogs. Which of the following methods of payment are the safest and offer the greatest consumer protection: money order, check, or credit card? Discuss reasons for your answer.
4. A young person applying for credit is often required to have a parent or other adult co-sign the application. What does this mean? Do you think the requirement is fair?

CHAPTER 24 Budgeting, Saving, and Investing Money

OUTLINE

- Income and Spending Patterns
- Developing and Using a Budget
- Saving Money
- Types of Savings Accounts
- Figuring Interest Rates
- Investing Money
- Chapter Review

OBJECTIVES

After reading this chapter, you should be able to:

- Identify your own personal income and spending patterns.
- Name and describe the four steps involved in developing and using a budget.
- Discuss the importance of setting aside a portion of income for savings.
- Name and describe the two basic types of savings accounts.
- Compute interest rate returns on savings.
- Explain the following types of investments: stocks, bonds, and money market funds.

People often refer to someone's financial status by use of terms such as *rich, middle class* and *poor.* Financial well-being, of course, is related to how much money you earn. The way in which you spend money, however, is also important.

Many people who earn average incomes live comfortably and securely. They have learned how to get the greatest benefit from their money. Wise money management depends on knowledge and skill in the areas of budgeting, saving, and perhaps investing money.

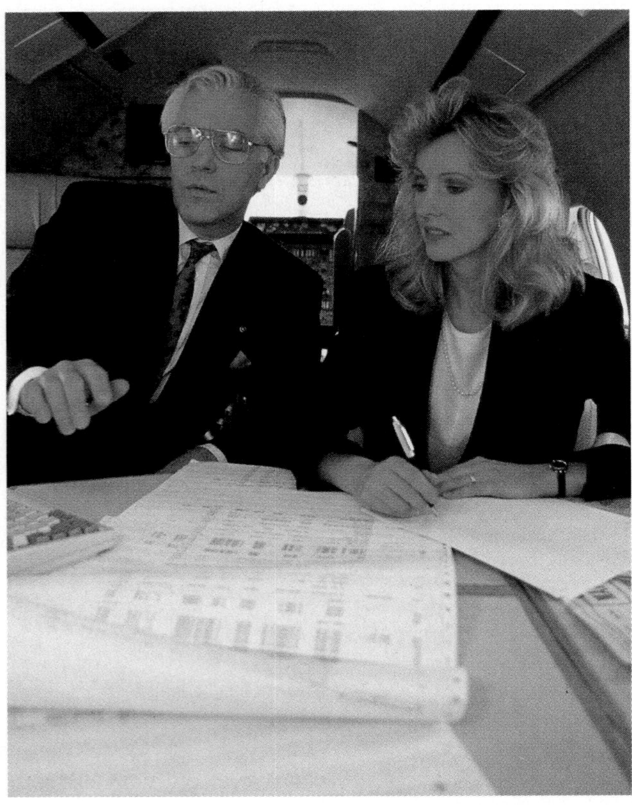

FIGURE 24–1 **Individuals and families should operate within budgets like businesses do.**
Photo by Pictor/© Uniphoto, Inc.

INCOME AND SPENDING PATTERNS

A good first step in learning how to manage money is to find out where your money is coming from (income) and where it is going (expenditures). You will do this by maintaining a record of *income* and *expenditures*. A simple form for doing this is shown in Figure 24–2. You can use a form to cover a week or any time period you choose.

RECORD OF INCOME AND EXPENDITURES

Week *Feb 4-10* 19 *--*

Cash on hand *42.45*

Date	Item	Income	Expenditure
4	Allowance & lunch money	25.00	
4	School lunch ticket		8.75
5	Gas in car		20.00
6	Babysitting	35.00	
7	Basketball game		3.50
	Soda and snack afterward		5.00
8	Movie w/friends		7.00
	Pizza afterward		5.00
9	Shopping (new music CD)		14.00
10	Personal care items		10.00

End of week cash balance *30.20* Totals *60.00* *73.25*

FIGURE 24–2 **Records like these help determine patterns of income and expenditures for individuals, families, and businesses.**

To fill out a form like this one, begin by inserting the total amount of cash on hand at the beginning of the week. (Don't include savings.) Then, start keeping detailed records of all income and expenditures. For income, include take-home pay as well as tips and any money you receive from gifts or allowances. In the column provided, list all expenditures, regardless of how small. At the end of the week, total up all income and expenditures. How much money is left at week's end? It should equal initial cash on hand plus or minus income and expenditures. Say your initial cash on hand is $75. You spend $50, and your aunt sends you $15 as a birthday gift. The end-of-week cash balance would be $40.

Once you have kept your records for a few weeks, figure your average income and expenditures. Add up all the income for the period, then divide by the number of weeks covered. Do the same for expenditures. Keeping a record of income and expenditures over a period of time can help you understand your financial condition and spending habits. The data in Figure 24–2 shows, for example, that the pattern of expenditures cannot continue much longer. You can then use this information to set up a budget for yourself.

DEVELOPING AND USING A BUDGET

A *budget* is a plan for managing income and expenditures. Such a spending plan will help you get the most benefit from your earnings. The four steps involved in developing a budget are:

1. Establishing goals.
2. Estimating income and expenditures.
3. Setting up the budget.
4. Following and revising the budget.

The process is similar for everyone—individuals and families, young people and adults.

Establishing Goals

Goals should be set before you work out the details of your budget. Identify what you need and want. As you decide on goals, discuss them with your family. If the budget is for a family, all family members should participate. Goals should be kept realistic in relation to present and expected future income.

To focus on your goals, list them according to time periods. Be as specific as possible. Bear in mind that there are short-range, medium-range, and long-range goals.

PERSONAL (OR FAMILY) GOALS

Goals for this year: ____________

____

____

Goals for the next five years: ______

____

____

Long-term goals: ____________

____

____

FIGURE 24–3 **Write out your financial goals so you will know what you are working toward.**

Naturally, goals change along with situations. For example, if you are single and live at home, your goals are probably different than they will be when you leave home. If you marry, your goals will change again, as they will if you have children. With two people working, the family goals may be different than they would be if only one were working, and so on.

Once you have decided on your goals, write them down. Save your list. You will need to refer to it as you plan the budget.

Estimating Income and Expenditures

Once you have decided on goals, estimate your income and expenditures. A budget may cover any convenient budget period. Most people like to plan a budget around how often they get paid, such as weekly, bimonthly, or monthly.

If you have kept records of income and expenditures for a four- to six-week period, you should be able to arrive at fairly close estimates. If the budget is for a family, records of income and expenditures should be kept over a three- to six-month period. Figure out your average income per budget period. Now review. Did you include all regular income, such as wages, salary, and tips? How about variable income, such as bonuses, gifts, interest, and dividends.

Individuals whose income varies present special problems. Examples of such people include seasonal workers, salespeople on commission,

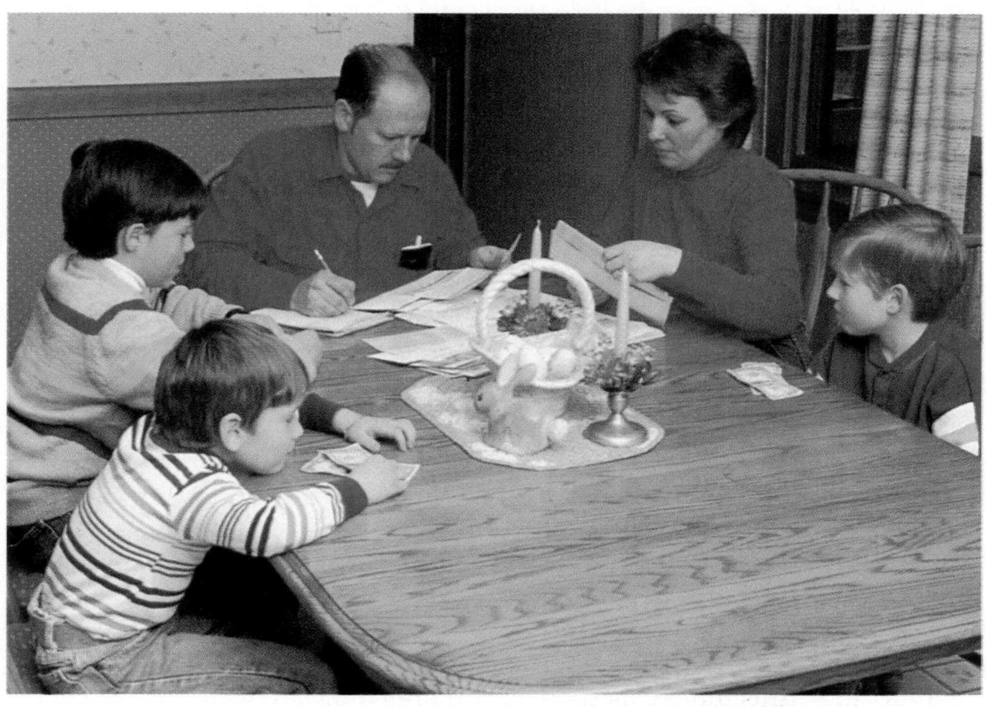

FIGURE 24–4 **Families can learn to live within their budgets more successfully when the whole family is involved in paying the bills.**
Photo by David W. Tuttle.

farmers, and other self-employed people. In these cases, it is usually better to base the budget estimates slightly below the average income. It is always easier to spend the extra money than it is to come up with a shortage.

Ann is a sales representative who earns most of her income from commissions. The more she sells, the more she earns. During the last six months, her income has been about 30 percent above normal. Business has been so good that she decided to trade her car in on a new one. She can make payments with the extra commissions she is earning.

She got a call today at the office from one of her best clients. "Hello, Ann, this is Cliff at Dramon Corporation. I'm afraid I'll have to cancel that big order you wrote up for me last week. My field representatives are telling me that business is starting to slow down. We could be moving into a recession."

What if an economic slowdown is on the way? Ann's future commissions will probably fall. Ann now wishes she had not gone in debt for the new car.

Regarding expenditures, your previous records should help you identify the major categories of items. Next, review the list to make sure you have not left out a seasonal expenditure or some other item that does not show up in your records. A checkbook register together with bills and receipts can help you remember such information.

As you review your record of expenditures, decide whether to continue your present spending pattern or to make changes. If you are satisfied with how you have saved your money, allow similar amounts in your budget estimates. Suppose your records point out poor buying habits or overspending. In that case, you must decide to make changes.

FIGURE 24–5 **Farmers often receive a big paycheck at harvest time, but there is usually a long wait between harvests.**
Courtesy of Elanco Products Company, makers of Treflan®.

Setting Up the Budget

Now that you have established your financial goals and have estimated income and expenditures, you are ready to set up your spending plan. The sample budget form shown in Figure 24–6 consists of three main parts.

The first part of the budget is for *savings*. It is important to set aside this money as soon as you are paid. If you wait until the end of the budget period, there may be nothing left for savings. You should save a regu-

HOUSEHOLD BUDGET FORM

Month *Jan.* 19 -- Estimated Income $ *1420.00*

Expenditure	Estimate	Actual	Difference (+ or -)
Savings			
Emergency reserve	35	35	0
Goals	50	30	+ 20
Regular Expenses			
Rent or mortgage payment	300	300	0
Utilities	165	196	– 31
Insurance	100	100	0
Auto payment	0	0	0
Credit or loan Payment	80	80	0
Other ( )			
Variable Expenses			
Food and beverage	350	345	+ 5
Clothing	50	77	– 27
Transportation	100	95	+ 5
Household	40	40	0
Medical care	30	23	+ 7
Entertainment	60	68	– 8
Gifts and contributions	30	25	+ 5
Taxes	30	30	0
Other ( )			
TOTALS	1420	1444	– 24

FIGURE 24-6 **Using a budget form like this can improve the quality of your life and help you meet future goals successfully.**

lar amount of income for use in an emergency. For a family, the amount should equal *at least* one month's total income. Once you have reached your figure to set aside for emergencies, start shifting money to savings goals and investments.

The next two parts of the budget include regular and variable expenditures. *Regular expenditures,* sometimes called fixed expenditures, are those essential monthly payments that are usually the same amount each month. *Variable expenditures* are day-to-day living expenses. They may change depending on the time of year, spending habits, and so on. Here is a list of common regular and variable expenditures.

Regular Expenditures

- ***Rent or Mortgage Payment.*** This fixed expenditure covers your basic housing needs. Renters pay their landlord. Buyers of a property make payments to the lender that granted the mortgage. A mortgage payment usually includes amounts for property taxes and insurance.
- ***Utilities.*** These include services such as electricity, telephone, gas, and water. *Even though these amounts vary,* you should list them as regular expenses because they are essential monthly payments. Suppose you have trouble deciding how much to budget for utilities? Check with the utility companies. Many of them have a plan whereby you can pay a fixed amount each month based on your average utility usage.
- ***Insurance.*** Include here all insurance premiums not covered by payroll withholding and mortgage payments. Life and auto insurance are two common examples.
- ***Auto Payment.*** This is an optional expenditure. However, many people make monthly installment payments on an auto loan.
- ***Credit or Loan Payments.*** These are also optional expenditures. They may include payments on charge accounts or student loans, for example.

Variable Expenditures

- ***Food and Beverage.*** This includes food and beverages purchased for home use as well as essential meals eaten away from home, such as school lunches. Optional purchases, such as a snack after the game, should be listed under "Entertainment."
- ***Clothing.*** Include here the cost of buying new clothing. Be sure to consider expenditures for repairs, alterations, dry cleaning, and laundry charges.
- ***Transportation.*** Include here the cost of using public transportation. If you own a vehicle, be sure to consider expenditures for gas, oil, repairs, tolls, and license plates.
- ***Household.*** This includes the cost of buying and maintaining furniture and home appliances. (Furniture payments could be included in "credit payments.") If you rent, the owners may or may not provide furniture. Everyone, though, must buy cleaning supplies. Homeowners may have extra expenses, such as paint, and lawn-care products.
- ***Medical Care.*** You can plan ahead for some of your medical care. For example, you know if you have to take regular medication or have periodic check-ups. Try to set aside some money for variable medical and dental expenses not covered by insurance.
- ***Entertainment.*** This includes vacations, hobbies, concert tickets, sporting events, and the like. If you have children, babysitting might be a related expense.

FIGURE 24–7 You can save money by doing your own home repairs and maintenance.
Courtesy of The Pillsbury Company.

- *Gifts and Contributions.* Besides gifts, be sure to consider contributions to charity, churches, and political parties.
- *Taxes.* Include here amounts for taxes not withheld from your paycheck or included in a mortgage payment. Keep in mind that it is often necessary to pay extra income taxes at the end of the year.

These items are the expenditures that most families have. You should feel free to *add or subtract items as necessary.* If you choose, *rearrange them in a way that works best for you.* Once you have developed a list of expenditures for your budget, enter on the budget form a dollar amount for each item. The total of all items in the "Estimate" column should equal the amount of "Estimated Income."

Following and Revising the Budget

Following a budget involves the *allocation* of income to various budgeted items, and keeping accurate records of expenditures. One way to allocate income is simply to deposit all or most of the income in a checking account. You can then write checks for items as necessary. Another common way of allocating income is to first cash the paycheck. After you have divided the cash according to budget categories, place it in separate envelopes. These should be labeled with the names of your main budget headings. You then take money out of the envelopes as needed.

A good choice is probably a combination of the two methods. Place most of your paycheck in a checking account. The remaining is kept on hand for frequent purchases. Regardless of which method you use, refer to the budget often. Otherwise, your spending plan is useless.

Keeping accurate records is an important part of maintaining a budget. Because you will probably pay them by check, major expenditures are easy to keep track of. Be sure, though, to write everything in your check register. Small cash purchases can be another matter. Because you make so many of them, it is tempting to ignore them. Failure to note these items makes your budget useless.

To account for cash purchases, use a form such as the one shown in Figure 24–2. If that form does not meet your needs, modify it or develop a new one. Another approach is to get an expandable manila file and label each pocket according to the items in the budget. Use this file to keep track of receipts. To jot down items for which you do not have a receipt, keep a notepad and pen near the file. All family members who spend money should get in the habit of saving and filing receipts.

At the end of the budget period, collect your receipts and records. Then, transfer the information to the column labeled "Actual" using the budget form in Figure 24–6. Write in the total amount spent for each *line item* in the budget. In the next column, record the difference between the "Estimate" and the "Actual" amounts. For example, if you estimated $70 for transportation, but only spent $65, write in "+$5." However, suppose you spent $85. In that case, you would put down "–$15."

After you have filled in all information, add up the totals for the "Actual" and "Difference" columns. Now you must face up to reality. How does your spending compare to your estimates? If the figures are similar, you should be proud of yourself. If not, try to find the problem. Perhaps your estimates were not accurate or realistic. Or, maybe the estimates were good, but you had trouble sticking to them. If there is a problem with the estimates, revise them. When the problem is with you, resolve to do a better job next time.

You should not expect to have a perfect budget the first time you set one up. A budget is something you must keep working and reworking. Even after you arrive at a budget that is right for you, you will need to change it from time to time.

? ? ? ? ? ? ? ? ? ? ? ? ? ? ?

WHAT WOULD YOU DO?

You have done your best to develop and follow a budget. You are careful to stick to budget estimates, but every month there is an unexpected expense. It never seems to be the same type of expenditure. One month it is a car repair, the next month a medical bill, another month an increase in insurance, and so on. You are very frustrated and about ready to "trash-can" the budget.

What would you do?

SAVING MONEY

If all of your paycheck goes for bills, you are working for someone else! Ask Ralph. On the first of the month when he gets paid, Ralph writes checks for all of his monthly payments. Checks go for rent, a car payment, utilities, and various credit card accounts. After putting aside amounts for groceries and insurance, Ralph has little left. He keeps his fingers crossed every month. Ralph knows that an illness or emergency would be a financial disaster.

One weekend at a family gathering, Ralph was talking about finances with his Uncle John. Uncle John, a banker, listened patiently until Ralph had finished. Then he said, "Ralph, you must learn to *pay yourself first.*" What Uncle John meant was that Ralph should reward himself for working. He should take a portion "off the top" of his paycheck and put it into savings.

The word *savings* refers to cash that has been set aside in a bank account. There are two reasons to do this. First of all, you will have some funds to meet a financial emergency. Suppose Ralph follows his uncle's advice and opens a savings account. Then should his old car need urgent repairs, Ralph won't wonder how he will pay for them. Secondly, a savings account allows you to achieve financial goals. Ralph, for example, may want to save toward a compact disc player.

Where to Save

In Chapter 23, you read about the four types of financial institutions offering checking accounts. Those institutions—commercial banks, mutual savings banks, savings and loan associations, and credit unions—accept savings deposits as well. Bear in mind that it is not necessary to have both checking and savings accounts at the same place. Do some comparison shopping. Teresa Romero did.

FIGURE 24–8 This car may need new brakes and shocks soon. The owner can be prepared to pay for them if he begins saving money now.
Photo by David W. Tuttle.

You may also remember from Chapter 23 how Teresa Romero saved money on her checking account by moving it to a credit union. So, when it came time to open a savings account, she reviewed the material she had already collected about financial services.

After comparing various plans and interest rates, Teresa decided to open a savings account at a mutual savings bank. It is close to her home and does not close until 8:00 P.M. on Friday evenings. Her money, on which she receives a good interest rate, is insured. She can withdraw funds at any time. Teresa is satisfied to know that she is using her money wisely.

Because of certain changes in federal and state regulations, institutions

? ? ? ? ? ? ? ? ? ? ? ? ? ?

WHAT WOULD YOU DO?

You see an ad in the newspaper regarding the grand opening of a new mutual savings bank. The bank is offering a clock radio to new customers who deposit a certain amount. You already have a passbook account and a CD at another bank. But you are considering switching banks to get a free gift.

What would you do?

now offer about the same types of services. Shop carefully for the right ones for you. You have many choices. For example, even within one institution, you may discover a variety of savings plans. In the end, your efforts will gain you more interest for your savings dollars.

TYPES OF SAVINGS ACCOUNTS

Financial institutions may advertise many different savings account plans. These plans are generally of two basic types: regular savings accounts and time deposits.

Regular Savings Accounts

Regular savings accounts, also called "passbook accounts," are very convenient and flexible. You can make deposits and withdrawals at any time. These accounts get their name from the passbook used for recording deposits, withdrawals, and interest payments. Most regular accounts, however, are being converted to computerized statements. A statement may be provided at the time a transaction is made. A summary statement may also be mailed monthly or quarterly to the customer.

It is easy to open a regular savings account. You simply sign a signature card and make a deposit. An individual account number will be assigned, and the institution will give you a passbook or an identification card for your account.

SAVINGS WITHDRAWAL DATE ____________

PAY TO ____________________________ Or Bearer

____________________________ Dollars

I HEREBY CERTIFY ALL PERSONS NAMED IN THIS ACCOUNT ARE STILL LIVING

ACCOUNT NUMBER ☐ CASH ☐ CHECK AMOUNT WITHDRAWN $

TELLER'S STAMP CHECK NUMBER ____________

SIGNATURE

SUPERVISOR ____________ SIGNATURE

C - 153 500M 2/89-T PASS BOOK MUST ACCOMPANY THIS ORDER

SAVINGS WITHDRAWAL FORM

SAVINGS DEPOSIT DATE ____________

ACCOUNT NUMBER

	DOLLARS	CENTS
CASH		
CHECKS LIST SEPARATELY BE SURE EACH ITEM IS ENDORSED		
TOTAL DEPOSIT		

NAME ____________

ADDRESS ____________

TELLER'S STAMP

SUPERVISOR ____________

All unpaid items will be charged back to the depositor.

C - 153 500M 2/89-T

SAVINGS DEPOSIT FORM

FIGURE 24–9 **There are separate forms for making deposits and for making withdrawals from a bank account.**

Regular savings accounts offer safety, convenience, and *liquidity.* In return for these benefits, depositors receive slightly less interest than they would on other accounts. The lower return is due to the fact that passbook accounts are expensive for institutions to service.

Time Deposits

If you can deposit a lump-sum amount for a longer period of time, you may be interested in time deposits. These special accounts may be called *certificates of deposit* (CD) or they may have names such as "Golden Passbook Accounts" or "Bonus Savings Accounts."

Most time deposits work in the same way. A depositor puts in money for a fixed period of time. This may be six months, one year, or longer. The saver agrees not to withdraw money from the account during that period. In return for agreeing not to withdraw the money for a fixed period of time, the institution pays a higher rate of interest. Also, the longer the saver agrees to keep the money in the account, the higher the rate of interest will be, Figure 24–10. What if the depositor *needs* to withdraw the funds? It can be done, but the interest rate will be greatly reduced.

Time deposit accounts often require a minimum deposit. The advantages of time deposits are that they are safe and provide a guaranteed rate of return for a fixed time period. On the negative side, they do not permit deposits and withdrawals and are not as liquid as regular savings accounts.

First Trust Bank
Central Avenue Branch
Vero Beach, FL 12312

SUBJECT TO CHANGE

DEPOSIT RATES EFFECTIVE May 3, 19--
THRU May 9, 19 --

Type	Minimum	Current Rates
Time Deposits 32–91 days	$500	6.30
Time Deposits 92 days–1 year	$500	6.55
Time Deposits 13–18 months	$500	6.65
Time Deposits 19–30 months	$500	7.25
Time Deposits 31–48 months	$500	7.45
Time Deposits over 48 months	$500	7.75

FIGURE 24–10 **This is an example of how time deposit interest rates vary for different time periods.**

FIGURING INTEREST RATES

Savings account interest rates fluctuate from time to time. In the early 1980s, for example, interest rates were over 10 percent. By the early 1990s, they had dropped below 3 percent. Rates vary according to the type of savings plan selected. Determining the best interest rates for different savings plans requires effort on your part. To start, look at this newspaper ad:

> Save more at University Bank: 5¼% interest compounded daily, paid quarterly on passbook savings. Yield 5.390.

From the ad, you learn the amounts of the annual interest rate (5¼%) and annual percentage yield (5.390). University Bank also tells you how often interest is compounded (daily) and when interest is paid (quarterly). Let's now discuss these four points in detail.

Annual Interest Rate

The law requires banks and other financial institutions to clearly state in their ads the true annual interest rate paid on savings. In the preceding ad, the figure "5¼%" is the annual interest rate. This means that on each $100 of savings, the institution pays you $5.25 in interest. Interest rates are figured by multiplying rate x time (in years) x principal (0.0525 x 1 x $100 = $5.25).

Frequency of Interest Compounding

It is easy to understand the annual interest rate. You want the most interest for your money. But the highest advertised annual rate may not be the best deal. More important than the interest rate is how often the interest is compounded. When an institution adds interest, an account's balance rises. There is then more money to earn interest later. This process is called *compounding*. A 6-percent interest rate that is compounded annually is one in which the interest is added every 12 months. So, if $100 is in your account, $106 will be the balance after one year. At the end of the second year, you will have $112.36. The institution figured that interest rate on $106. How much, then, would you earn the third year?

If the interest rate of 6 percent on $100 is compounded semiannually, you will have $103 at the end of six months. After a year, you will have $106.09, and at the end of two years, $112.55. The more often the interest compounds, the more money you make. Figure 24–11 shows how the value of a $1,000 deposit varies according to the rate of compounding.

Frequency of compounding	After 1 year	After 5 years	After 10 years	After 20 years
Daily	1,054.67	1,304.90	1,702.76	2,899.41
Quarterly	1,053.54	1,297.96	1,684.70	2,838.20
Semiannually	1,053.19	1,295.78	1,679.05	2,819.21
Annually	1,052.50	1,291.55	1,668.10	2,782.54

FIGURE 24–11 **More frequent interest compounding results in higher returns. The figures are based on a $1,000 deposit at 5¼ percent.**

Interest Pay Periods

How often does the financial institution credit interest to your account? The ad for University Bank says that they compound interest daily and pay it four times a year (quarterly). Should you close the account in mid-quarter, you would lose all the interest for that three-month period. You may want to look instead for an account that pays interest from day-of-deposit to day-of-withdrawal.

Annual Percentage Yield

When comparing one savings account with another, it is useful to know the annual percentage yield (APY). That figure will tell you the actual yearly interest rate per $100 left on deposit. The number takes into account both the rates for annual interest and compounding. In general, the higher the APY, the better the deal you receive (see Figure 24–12).

Other Information

The four factors discussed here are not the only ones that influence

5¼%, compounded	APY
Daily	5.47%
Quarterly	5.35%
Semiannually	5.32%
Annually	5.25%

FIGURE 24–12 **The APY is the best indicator of how much interest you will earn.**

Weekly deposit	After 1 year	After 3 years	After 5 years	After 10 years	After 20 years
$ 5	$ 267.16	$ 845.95	$1,489.54	$ 3,431.69	$ 9,265.67
10	534.32	1,691.89	2,979.08	6,863.37	18,531.35
15	801.48	2,537.84	4,468.62	10,295.06	27,797.02
20	1,068.63	3,383.79	5,958.17	13,726.74	37,062.70
25	1,335.79	4,229.74	7,447.71	17,158.43	46,328.37

FIGURE 24–13 **Over the years, a small amount of savings can add up to a large amount. (Figures based on 5¼ percent interest, compounded daily.)**

savings interest. One bank ad, for instance, contained this statement: "Deposits made by the tenth of the month earn interest from the first. Interest is figured on the low balance per month and there must be a balance at interest-paying days in order to earn interest."

This example illustrates only one of the many different methods that savings institutions use to compute interest. However, if you know the basic principles of figuring interest rates, you should be able to understand and compare the methods used by different institutions.

If you shop around, remember that savings institutions may differ a great deal as to how they figure interest. Try to narrow down your choices to a few institutions offering the highest APY. Speak with bank personnel about requirements. Your best choice will probably be the institution having the highest APY and the fewest restrictions and penalties.

Following this advice will bring you financial rewards. Why settle for just any institution? It is *your* money. Study Figures 24–13 and 24–14 to see how different amounts of savings can grow according to different interest rates and time periods.

Interest rate	After 1 year	After 3 years	After 5 years	After 10 years	After 20 years
4½%	$ 615.13	$ 1,932.88	$ 3,376.53	$ 7,618.34	$ 19,641.57
5	616.84	1,948.41	3,422.06	7,831.35	20,832.93
5¼	617.70	1,956.25	3,445.16	7,940.88	21,463.05
5½	618.55	1,964.11	3,468.42	8,052.13	22,115.27
6	620.28	1,979.99	3,515.63	8,281.10	23,496.83
6½	622.01	1,996,02	3,563.61	8,518.04	24,982.45
7	623.74	2,012.22	3,612.46	8,763.73	26,583.82
7½	625.48	2,028.60	3,662.20	9,018.48	28,310.47
8	627.23	2,045.16	3,712.83	9,282.67	30,173.06

(Based on a $50 a month deposit, compounded daily.)

FIGURE 24–14 **This table shows the importance of shopping for the highest interest rates. (Figures based on a $50 a month deposit, compounded daily.)**

INVESTING MONEY

Investing is the process of using money not required for personal and family needs to increase overall financial worth. Investing is different from savings in that investing is a long-term financial strategy. Money for investing comes from funds left *after* meeting basic expenditures and short- and medium-range savings goals.

The investor wants to make as much money as possible. In order to make a lot of money, though, there is usually a risk of losing money. For example, buying stock in a new, unproved company is very risky. High-risk investments, however, can sometimes produce big payoffs. Let's take another example. Buying bonds of a large, financially stable corporation involves a relatively low risk. However, lower risk investments generally produce smaller profits.

When investing, you must learn to balance risks. Probably the best way to balance risks is to *diversify* investments. This means to spread out money over several different types of investment options. Let's now examine three popular types of investments: stocks, bonds, and money market funds.

Stocks

One of the most popular forms of investment is the purchase of shares of *stock.* When you buy stock in a company, you are buying part of the ownership of that company. Shares of stock vary in price from a few dollars a share to a few hundred dollars. Stock is most often sold in 100-share lots.

Stocks are usually bought from individuals called *brokers* who specialize in selling stocks and other investments. Stock prices vary from day to day. The purchase price for a stock is the current selling price plus a small fee, called a *commission,* charged by the broker.

You can make money on stocks through *dividends,* through *capital gain,* or both. Dividends are the profits that a company divides among the stockholders. Let's say you bought stock in a company for $24 a share. If the company paid a $.50 per share dividend each quarter, you would make $2 a year on each share of stock that you owned. The return on your investment would be 8.3 percent.

Capital gain refers to an increase in the selling price of the stock. For example, if the stock you bought at $24 increased in price to $30 a share, the capital gain would be $6 per share. In this case, your return on investment would be 25 percent. The $2 share dividend plus the $6 capital gain results in a total return of 33 percent. Be aware, however, that the dividend can be reduced and that the stock price can go down.

Instead of buying individual stocks, you can purchase shares of stock in a *mutual fund.* A mutual fund is an investment company that pools the money of thousands of investors and buys a collection of stocks called a *portfolio.* The advantage of a mutual fund is that prices do not vary as much as those for an individual stock. Like individual stocks, profits on mutual funds can be derived from dividends, capital gains, or both. Mutual funds are generally recommended over individual stocks for the beginner and for the small investor.

Bonds

You have learned that stock represents shares of actual ownership in a company. *Bonds* represent a loan to a company or government agency. Let's say a large corporation needs 10 million dollars to expand its plant. One way to raise the

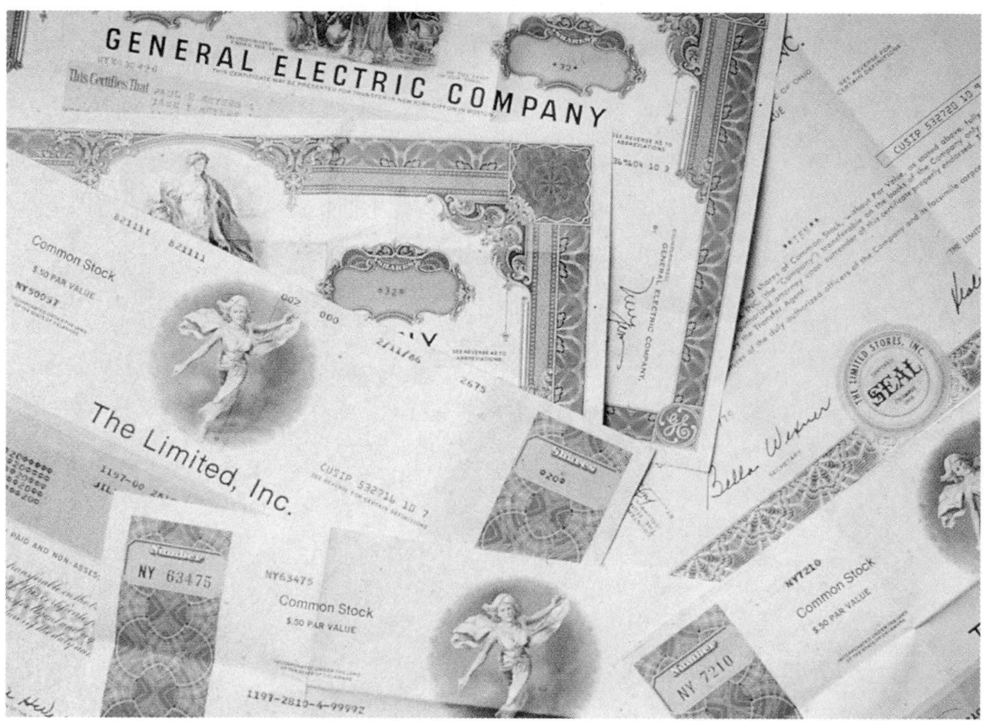

FIGURE 24–15 **A stock certificate is evidence of ownership in a particular company.**
Photo by Paul E. Meyers.

money is to sell shares of stock in the company. Another way is to issue bonds. A bond is a pledge to repay the borrowed sum plus a certain amount of interest.

To be more specific, Lunar Manufacturing Company issues $1,000 bonds, paying 8.5 percent interest with a maturity date of 2010. If you purchase one of these bonds, Lunar Manufacturing Company will pay you $85 interest per year until 2010, at which time they will return your $1,000 dollars.

Bonds issued by private companies like Lunar Manufacturing Company are called corporate bonds. Government agencies also issue bonds to raise money for roads, schools, sewer systems, and so on. Those issued by state, city, county, and other units of local government are called municipal bonds. When the federal government issues bonds, they are known as government bonds. The idea behind all bonds is the same. They are a piece of paper that represents a promise to repay a specific borrowed amount in the future along with a fixed interest rate.

Bonds can be purchased through the same brokers that sell stocks. Like stocks, bonds are available individually or through mutual funds that specialize in bonds.

Money Market Funds

This is a type of mutual fund run by an investment company or a financial institution. Money is pooled from many investors and

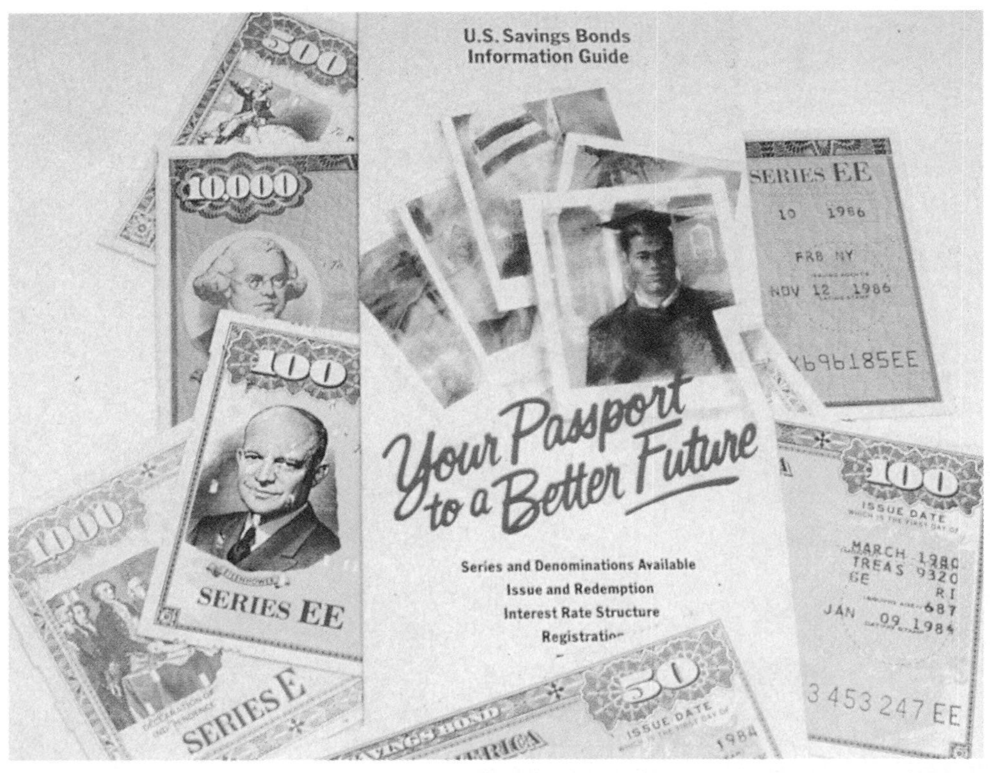

FIGURE 24–16 The federal government is the largest borrower in the country. It borrows money by selling savings bonds and other securities.
Photo by Paul E. Meyers.

used to purchase short-term corporate notes, U.S. treasury notes, and certificates of deposit. The objective is usually to earn the highest possible safe interest rate. *Money market funds* provide a way for the small investor to take advantage of the higher interest rates that were once available only to the large investor. Most funds require a minimum deposit (often as little as a few hundred dollars).

Money market shares can be purchased directly from an investment firm, through a financial institution, or from a broker. The interest rates on these funds go up and down according to the general economy. Money market funds are not insured or guaranteed, but they are regarded as very safe. Shares in these funds can be sold (redeemed) at any time.

Investing is part of an overall process of budgeting and saving money. Decide on your personal or family goals and stick to them. Do not get greedy. Stay away from hot tips that promise instant wealth. To avoid losing money, be wary and investigate any investment very carefully before turning over any money.

Credit Billing Blues

It is difficult enough to manage a budget without being billed for things you do not owe. Problems can be taken care of, however, if you know how to use the Fair Credit Billing Act. To be protected under the law, here is what you need to do:

1. Write the bank or merchant who issued the credit. A telephone call *does not* trigger the legal safeguards provided under the act. Your notice must be received within 60 days after the bill containing the error was mailed. Include in the letter your name and account number; the date; type and dollar amount of the incorrect charge; and why you think there was a mistake.
2. Send the letter to the correct place. Do not put your letter in the same envelope as your payment. Your bill will usually explain where you should address inquiries. You may wish to send a certified letter to make sure the creditor receives it.

If you follow this procedure, the creditor is required to acknowledge your letter in writing within 30 days after it is received. The alleged error must be investigated. Within 90 days, the mistake must be corrected, or you must be given an explanation and proof of why the bill is accurate.

If you continue to have problems, you should contact your local or state consumer protection agency. Under the law, the creditor cannot close your account just because you disputed a bill.

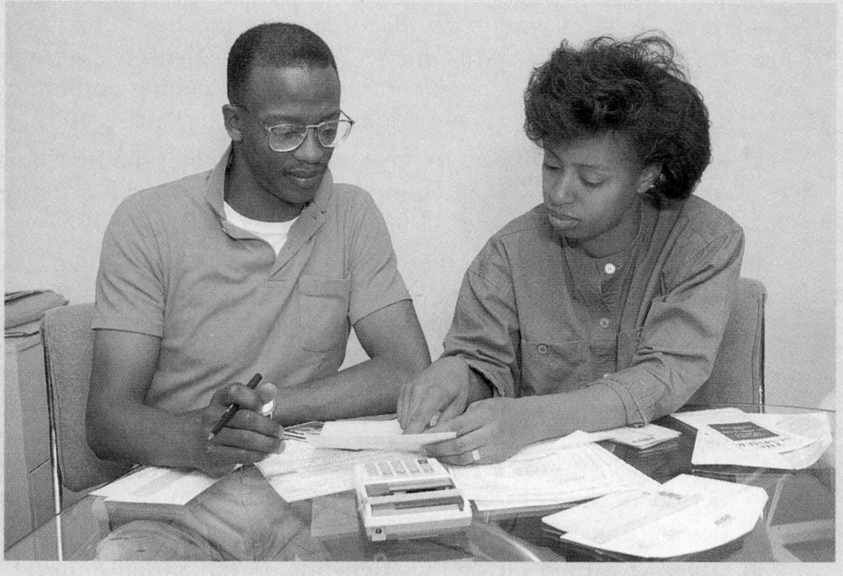

Do not despair—billing errors do happen occasionally. Correct any errors by checking your records carefully, then write your creditor and tell them about the mistake. They will usually clear up the matter quickly.
Photo by © Robert Brenner/Photo Edit.

CHAPTER 24 REVIEW

CHAPTER IN BRIEF

- A good first step in learning how to manage money is to identify sources of income and spending. You will do this by maintaining a record of income and expenditures. This will help you understand your financial condition and spending habits. Such information is then used to set up a budget.
- A budget is a plan for managing income and expenditures. Such a spending plan will help you get the most benefit from your earnings. The four steps involved in developing a budget are: establishing goals, estimating income and expenditures, setting up the budget, and following and revising the budget.
- Goals should be set before you work out the details of your budget. List goals according to different time periods. Goals should be realistic and achievable. Write them down and use them to plan the budget.
- Once you have decided on goals, estimate your income and expenditures. Base estimates on actual records. Budget periods are usually planned around how often one gets paid (weekly, bimonthly, monthly, or the like).
- A budget consists of three main parts: savings, regular (fixed) expenses, and variable expenses. Items can be added or subtracted from these three parts or rearranged in a way that works best for you.
- Following a budget involves allocation of income to various budgeted items. A good way to do this is to place most of your paycheck in a checking account. Write checks for larger expenses. Keep the remaining cash on hand for frequent purchases. Keeping accurate records is an important part of maintaining a budget.
- You should not expect to have a perfect budget the first time you set one up. A budget is something you must keep working and reworking until it "fits."
- Savings refers to cash that has been set aside in a bank account. Savings are important for two reasons. First, to have funds for a financial emergency. Second, to meet personal and family financial goals.
- There are two basic types of savings accounts. With a regular savings account (passbook account), you can make deposits and withdrawals at any time. They offer safety, convenience, and liquidity. A time deposit account is where you deposit a certain lump sum for a fixed period of time. They are safe and offer a higher rate of return than passbook accounts.
- Interest earned on savings depends on the annual interest rate, frequency of compounding, and when the interest is paid. In comparing savings options, it is useful to know the annual percentage yield (APY). Generally, the higher the APY, the better the deal.

- Investing is the process of using money not required for personal and family needs to increase overall financial worth. Investing involves the risk of losing money. A good way to balance risks is to diversify investments.
- There are three popular types of investments. Investing in stocks involves buying shares of actual ownership in a company. Money on stocks can be made through dividends, capital gains, or both. Another way to invest is to purchase paper certificates called bonds, which provide a fixed interest rate. Bonds represent a loan to a private company or government agency. Money market funds are a type of mutual fund that invests in corporate and government notes and certificates of deposit. Money market rates vary monthly according to overall interest rate trends.

WORDS TO KNOW

allocation
bonds
brokers
budget
capital gain
certificates of deposit
commission
compounding
diversify
dividends
expenditures
income
investing
line item
liquidity
money market funds
mutual fund
portfolio
regular (fixed) expenditures
savings
stock
variable expenditures

QUESTIONS TO ANSWER

1. Two factors influence a person's or family's financial well-being. Name them.
2. What is the purpose of keeping a record of income and expenditures?
3. What four steps are involved in developing a budget?
4. How does goal-setting differ for a single person and a married person?
5. Why is the first part of a budget devoted to savings?
6. Explain how to allocate income to budgeted items.
7. In following a budget, you might discover that your actual expenditures are quite different from your estimated expenditures. What two things might cause this problem?
8. Explain what is meant by the phrase "pay yourself first."
9. There are two reasons to set aside savings. Name them.
10. What are the two basic types of savings accounts? Briefly describe each.
11. On what two things is the annual percentage yield (APY) based?
12. How is investing different from saving money?
13. What is the basic difference between a stock and a bond?
14. Name the type of bond issued by a private company. By a local government.
15. What is the main advantage offered by a money market fund?

ACTIVITIES TO DO

1. Write down income and expenditures on a form similar to Figure 24–2. Keep records for a week. Then, study them. List at least three things you noticed about your spending. Discuss your findings in class.
2. Think about your financial goals. Write down your financial goal(s) for the next year. Then note your financial goals for the next five years. Discuss your goals in class. How do they compare to your classmates' goals? Also discuss how your goals might be different if you and your classmates were all five years older.
3. Consider the case of a family consisting of a husband, wife, and one young child. Assume the family's net monthly income is $1,800.00. As a group, in-class activity, prepare an estimated budget for this family. Use or adapt the budget form shown in Figure 24–6.
4. After completing Activity 3, invite a qualified person to class to review the budget. Ask him or her to examine and discuss your class's budget for the family.
5. In groups of two or three, visit several different financial institutions in your area and collect information on their regular (passbook) savings account. (Or individuals or teams could be assigned to visit specific institutions.) Compare the alternatives with respect to: (a) interest rate paid, (b) how the interest is computed, (c) when the interest is paid, (d) annual percentage yield, (e) minimum size of deposit, (f) service charges, and (g) rules and restrictions. You may wish to prepare some type of a chart to help you compare alternatives. Discuss your findings in class.
6. Let's assume that you deposited $500 in a savings account paying 6 percent annual interest. You do not disturb the money for a year. Interest is compounded quarterly. At the end of the year, how much money is in the account? What is the annual percentage yield?
7. Let's assume you bought 100 shares of stock at $25 a share. The stock pays a $.40 dividend each year. How much total dividend do you receive in two years?
8. Locate the listings for the New York Stock Exchange in the financial section of a newspaper. Select a stock of interest in the listing and answer the following questions: (a) Does the stock pay a dividend? If so, how much? If so, what is the yield? (b) How many shares were sold the previous day? (c) What were the previous day's high, low, and closing prices? (d) What was the net change? (e) For what does the "P/E ratio" stand?

TOPICS TO DISCUSS

1. Philanthropy is the act of giving away money. How do you feel about giving money to charity?
2. A big problem for the federal government is staying within a budget. The government routinely spends more than it takes in (called deficit spending). Why do you think this is the case?
3. It is not unusual to read about the financial difficulties of high-paid professional athletes, entertainers, and other famous people. What are some of the "problems" created by fame and instant wealth?
4. What is the advantage of using payroll deductions to save and invest money? Are payroll savings and investment options available where you work?
5. Have you ever saved money over a long period of time and then used it to buy something? Describe how it made you feel to accomplish a savings goal.
6. There is an old saying that "you shouldn't invest more in stocks than you can afford to lose." How true do you think this statement is?

CHAPTER 25 Insuring Against Loss

OUTLINE

- Nature of Insurance
- Health Insurance
- Life Insurance
- Home Insurance
- Auto Insurance
- Chapter Review

OBJECTIVES

After reading this chapter, you should be able to:

- Explain the basic idea of insurance.
- Name and describe the five types of health insurance.
- Summarize the advantages and disadvantages of term and cash-value life insurance.
- Outline different characteristics of home insurance.
- Name and describe the six types of auto insurance coverage.
- Identify factors that influence the cost of auto insurance.

Major purchases, such as a home or car, can be very costly. Once you have bought such items, you do not want to lose them. Things do happen, though. Suppose you purchase a new car. A week later, you park in the lot of the local library. When you leave the library, the car is gone. The next day, the police call to say your car has been found. Your joy disappears upon learning that the car was wrecked badly.

Deciding if you need insurance, evaluating different policies, and comparing costs and coverage can be difficult. This chapter will help answer your questions. The material will deal with the nature of insurance, and then discuss the specifics of the four most important kinds of insurance: health, life, home, and auto.

NATURE OF INSURANCE

Throughout history, people have used insurance to protect themselves from *risk* due to fire, acci-

FIGURE 25–1 **Auto insurance will help this person pay for the repairs on his car.**
Photo by David W. Tuttle.

dent, or other *catastrophes*. Few people can bear such catastrophes without serious hardship. Society, as well, may suffer from an unexpected loss. For instance, if someone dies, the community may need to support a dependent family. When a building burns and a business is forced into bankruptcy, creditors lose money and employees lose their jobs.

The basic idea of insurance is that a large group of individuals pay a yearly premium that goes into a common fund. When disaster strikes one member of the group, the pooled funds pay for the loss. Insurance shifts probable loss from the individual to the group.

In simple terms, when you buy insurance, you are substituting a known expenditure (insurance premium) for protection against risk of a large uncertain loss. The kinds of risks against which people seek protection may be grouped in this way:

- *Personal Risks.* These are catastrophes affecting individuals. Examples include accident, illness, disability, and unemployment.
- *Property Risks.* There is always the possibility that property will be damaged or destroyed. Losses include automobile accidents, natural disasters, fire, and vandalism.
- *Liability Risks.* Certain events may affect the person or property of others. Injury may result from an automobile accident that you caused. Or, a visitor to your home might be hurt.

In addition to providing protection against financial loss, insurance gives people greater peace of mind. Knowing that you have minimized your risks can contribute to your emotional security.

FIGURE 25–2 The first mutual fire insurance company was founded in 1725 with the help of Benjamin Franklin.
Courtesy of The Franklin Institute.

HEALTH INSURANCE

The purpose of health insurance is to pay expenses resulting from illness or accident. This is probably the most necessary form of insurance because the expenses resulting from illness or accident can be enormous. The costs, for example, of minor surgery and several days in a hospital are likely to be several thousand dollars. Major surgery and an extended hospital stay can amount to tens of thousands of dollars.

Jim was painting the house. He fell about twenty feet from a ladder. Jim was badly injured. Over the next five years, he was in the hospital twenty-two times for surgery and other medical care. His total medical expenses were nearly a million dollars. This is a rare case, but it does show why insurance is so important.

Most people obtain health insurance through some type of group plan. This may be through an employer, union, or professional association. The group policy may only cover the individual enrolled, or it may include dependents as well. Persons not eligible for group coverage may buy individual plans. However, group plans usually provide more coverage and are less expensive than individual plans.

In the traditional approach to health insurance, an insurance company pays a doctor or hospital for service performed in treating an illness or accident. Routine office visits are not covered. During the last decade or so, the *health maintenance organization (HMO)* has been growing. It is an alternative to traditional health insurance. Members in an HMO (or the employer) pay a regular fee as they would for an insurance policy. The difference, however, is that HMO members are entitled to unlimited professional services and treatment. This includes regular office visits and checkups as well as treatment for illness and accidents.

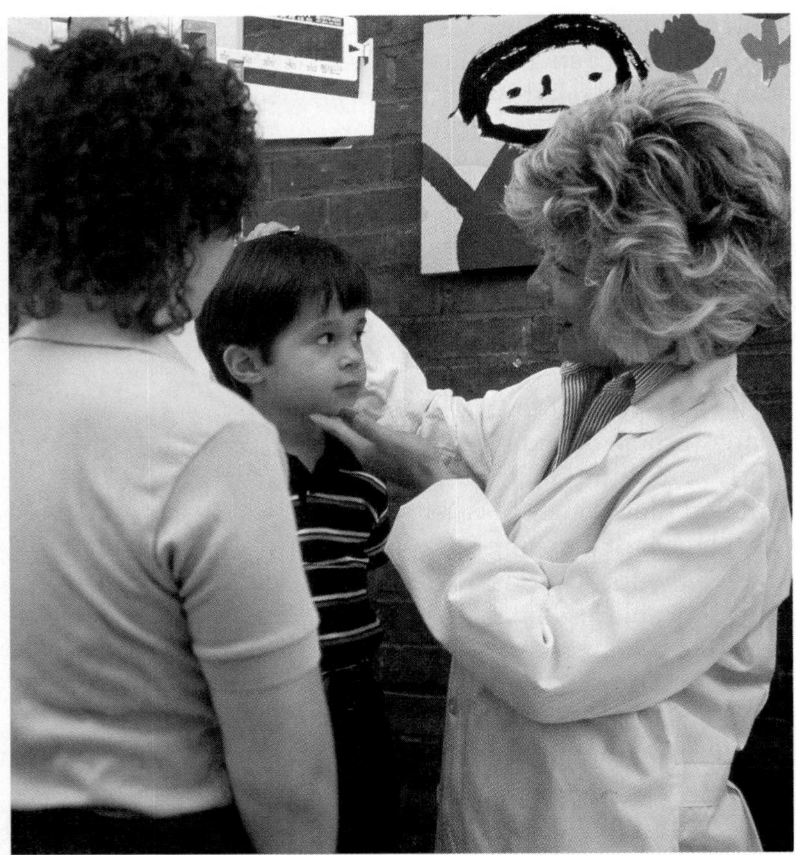

FIGURE 25–3 **HMOs encourage preventative health care to avoid serious illness and the high insurance costs needed to treat them.**
Courtesy of Empire Blue Cross and Blue Shield.

Even though regular insurance plans protect against huge medical expenses, most of them are not free. A typical health insurance plan, for example, might require you to pay the first $100 for a hospital stay (called a *deductible*) and 20 percent of the remaining amount. Many policies contain a *stop-loss provision,* which prevents your out-of-pocket expenses from rising above a certain amount.

Health insurance packages usually cover hospital, surgical, medical, and major medical expenses. If you want disability insurance, though, you will have to buy a special policy. For full-time employees, employers often pay all or part of the cost of health insurance.

? ? ? ? ? ? ? ? ? ? ? ? ? ?

WHAT WOULD YOU DO?

You are employed as a library assistant at one of the state universities. You have received information about the new health insurance plan that covers all state employees. Beginning June 1, you will have the choice of continuing with the regular health insurance or switching to a new HMO option. The premium, which is paid by the state, is the same for both plans. You are not sure which plan to select.

What would you do?

Hospital Expense

This coverage provides for hospital charges such as room and meals, operating room use, laboratory fees, and drugs. The policy may specify a certain maximum-per-day room charge or may limit the number of days in the hospital the policy will cover. This type of health insurance is the most common.

Surgical Expense

Coverage here involves a wide variety of medical procedures and operations, ranging from sewing up a cut to replacing a heart valve. Depending on the procedure, it may be performed on an inpatient or outpatient basis. A policy may contain a list of covered surgical procedures and the amount that will be paid for each one.

Medical Expense

Medical expense, also known as physician's expense, is usually combined with hospital and surgical-expense insurance. The three together form what is known as *basic* coverage. Medical expense coverage pays for the doctor's medical visits while the patient is in a hospital. Some policies provide benefits for home and office visits as well.

Major Medical Expense

This type of insurance protects against huge expenses resulting from a serious illness or accident. Covered expenses generally include the same types of charges as those for basic coverage. Major medical contains a *co-insurance* feature that requires a policyholder to share in the expenses beyond the deductible amount. One of the most common plans is an "80-20" policy in which the insurance company pays 80 percent and the policyholder takes care of the other 20 percent.

In one group plan, for example, the insurance company pays 80 percent of the first $15,000 of covered expenses and 100 percent thereafter up to a maximum of $250,000.

Disability Coverage

Paying benefits to someone unable to work because of illness or injury is the purpose of disability insurance. The coverage is sometimes called loss-of-income insurance. A typical policy may pay between 50 and 75 percent of the

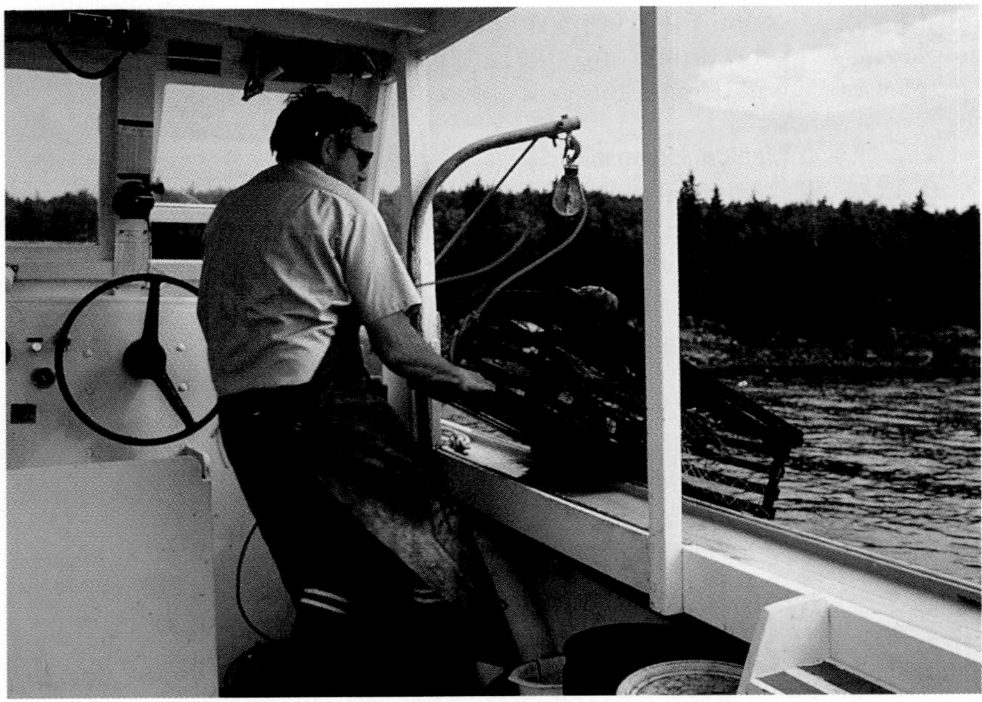

FIGURE 25–4 **Self-employed people need disability coverage to protect their businesses in case they become too sick or injured to work.**
Photo by Paul E. Meyers.

worker's normal earnings for a specified period. This insurance may not be as important for people already covered by such benefits as paid sick leave, workers' compensation, and social security.

Helen was in a hurry to get to work and failed to notice that a light rain had fallen and then frozen during the night. As she stepped from the covered porch onto the sidewalk, she slipped and fell. She cried out in pain. A neighbor who was leaving for work at the same time saw her fall. He helped her into the house and called an ambulance.

Helen's injury was diagnosed as a broken hip. Surgery on the hip was required, followed by a long period of rest and physical therapy. It was six months before Helen was able to return to work. Fortunately, she had a disability insurance policy that provided her with income while she could not work. Without the disability policy, she would have had to dip into her retirement savings.

LIFE INSURANCE

Life insurance involves a contract written between an insurance company and a policyholder. The document specifies an amount of money (*face value*) to be paid in the event of the policyholder's death. Also stated in the contract is the price of the policy (*premium*) and the name of the person (*beneficiary*) to whom the death benefits are to be paid. The main purpose of life insurance is to provide financial security for dependents after the insured's death.

Individuals differ in terms of their need for life insurance. A young, single person without dependents, for example, has little need for life insurance. All that may be required is a small policy to pay funeral expenses and to cover outstanding debts.

People with children have the greatest need for life insurance. If the wage earner (or wage earners) should die, the family would need an income to pay day-to-day living expenses. Insurance would help a family member or friend raise surviving children and perhaps provide them with higher education.

Traditionally, the primary wage earner has been the man of the house. Today, however, women often earn as much or more than their husbands. Many women are head of the household. They have great insurance needs. Even a person not working outside the home should be insured in order to cover added expenses in the event of death.

As with health insurance, both group and individual life insurance policies are available. Most life insurance, though, is in the form of individual policies. Two basic types of life insurance are available: term and cash value.

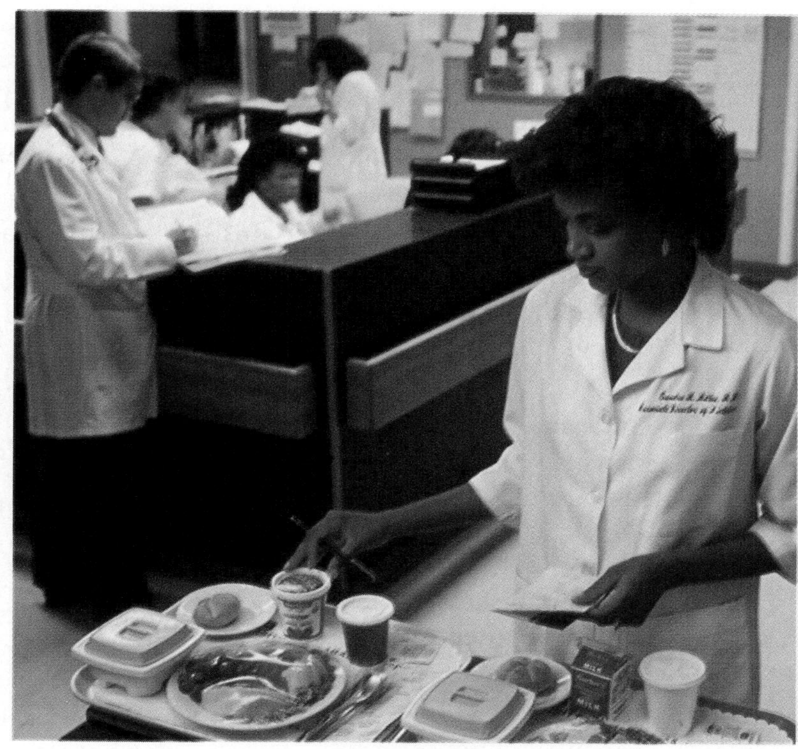

FIGURE 25–5 Health insurance is usually part of the compensation paid to full-time staff employees.
Courtesy of Marriott Corporation.

Term Insurance

Term insurance is often called pure insurance because it provides protection only. The policy has no cash value or loan value. People buy term insurance for a specified period of time. Under term insurance, you pay as long as you need the coverage. Then you drop the policy or it terminates automatically. For example, you might purchase a twenty-five-year policy to provide protection while you are making big house payments and your children are growing up.

As you grow older, the likelihood of your dying increases. This is why term insurance premiums go up as you age. Premiums are low at first and then increase steadily throughout the course of your life. By the time you reach age sixty, you may be paying fifteen times what the same amount of protection cost you at age eighteen.

In the example just described, the face value of the policy remains steady and the premium increases yearly. Such insurance is called *level term*. Another type, called *decreasing term* insurance, works differently. In that kind of policy, the premium remains steady, but the face value decreases yearly. In year one, for example, you might have a face value of $50,000. In year two, it drops to $48,000; year three to $46,000; and so on.

Cash-value Insurance

Under cash-value insurance, protection is teamed with the gradual buildup of a savings account. Cash-value insurance is also called permanent insurance because when the policy is paid up after a certain number of years, the policyholder owns the insurance. For example, if you purchase a plan called life paid-up at sixty-five, you pay premiums until you are sixty-five. At that point, you have a permanent policy that will pay the face value upon your death. Other names for cash-value insurance are whole, ordinary, and straight life insurance.

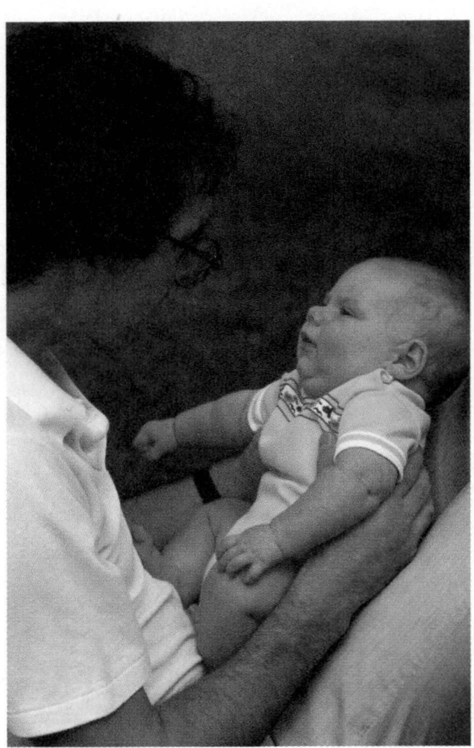

FIGURE 25–6 **Some life changes require changes in life insurance. For instance, when a baby is born into a family, the parents may want to increase their life insurance.**
Photo by Edith Raviola.

The premium and the face value for cash-value insurance remain the same each year. You pay the same premiums for as long as you live. Or, you can purchase plans that are paid up in twenty or thirty years. A portion of the premium is set aside and accumulates in a type of savings account. The interest rate, however, is usually less than other forms of savings. If the policy is dropped, the cash value is returned to the policyholder.

Which Type to Buy?

There are advantages and disadvantages to both term and cash-value insurance. The primary advantage of term insurance is that it is less expensive than cash-value insurance. But with cash-value insurance, you have protection combined with savings.

Most experts on the subject (who do not work for insurance companies) seem to agree that term insurance is the better value. They point out that the main purpose of life insurance is protection. About the only way young people can realistically afford the amount of insurance necessary to protect their families is to purchase term insurance. You may want to buy term insurance and save the difference between that and cash-value insurance. Later, you may want to consider cash-value insurance as part of an overall life insurance program. But do not get saddled with a big policy and a big premium at a time when you can least afford it.

How Much Insurance Will You Need?

The amount of life insurance coverage depends on your personal situation and what you want to protect. The needs of a young, single person are very different from those of someone with a family, or a middle-aged couple who have their home paid for and their children raised. Some insurance agents provide the general guideline that you need insurance equal to about four to eight times your annual income.

HOME INSURANCE

For most people, a home is the largest expenditure in their budget. In addition to the home itself, household furnishings and personal belongings represent a sizable investment. For this reason, it is very important to protect a home and the contents against damage or loss. The basis for all home insurance policies is coverage against the various damages or *perils* shown in Figure 25–7.

Another important feature of home insurance policies is the provision for living expenses. For example, the Alfano's home was damaged by a storm and they could not live in it. The insurance company paid for the family's lodgings, meals, and related expenses elsewhere until the house was livable again.

Liability coverage is also a part of home insurance policies. The most important type of *liability* coverage is personal liability, which protects you against a claim or lawsuit resulting from an accident or injury occurring on your property. The same coverage will also protect you if someone in your family causes an injury away from home.

1. Fire or lightning.
2. Windstorm or hail.
3. Explosion.
4. Riot or civil commotion.
5. Aircraft.
6. Vehicles.
7. Smoke.
8. Vandalism or malicious mischief.
9. Theft.
10. Damage by glass or safety glazing material which is part of a building.
11. Volcanic eruption.
12. Falling objects.
13. Weight of ice, snow or sleet.
14. Accidental discharge or overflow of water or steam from within a plumbing, heating, air conditioning, or automatic fire protective sprinkler system or from within a household appliance.
15. Sudden and accidental tearing apart, cracking, burning, or bulging of a steam or hot water heating system, an air conditioning or automatic fire protective sprinkler system, or an appliance for heating water.
16. Freezing of a plumbing, heating, air conditioning, or automatic fire protective sprinkler system, or of a household appliance.
17. Sudden and accidental damage from artificially generated electrical current (does not include loss to a tube, transistor, or similar electronic component).

FIGURE 25–7 **These are the dangerous situations (perils) against which property is insured. The first 11 represent basic homeowners' insurance.**
Courtesy of Insurance Information Institute.

To meet the varying needs of customers, insurance companies have developed various kinds of homeowners insurance. Whether you live in a house, apartment, mobile home, or condominium, there is a policy designed for you. Ann and Mark learned this fact the hard way.

Ann and Mark were newlyweds who had just moved into their first apartment. They were awakened one night by the sound of a fire alarm. They got up quickly, threw on coats, grabbed the puppy, and fled the apartment. As they raced down the back exit, they heard the siren of the fire truck coming. The fire was on the floor above theirs.

The fire company put out the blaze in a few minutes. It was not a serious fire, but there was a lot of smoke and water damage. All of Ann's and Mark's clothes and upholstered furniture was ruined.

The next day, the couple went to the apartment manager's office to find out about getting their clothes and furniture replaced. The manager told them that his insurance only covered damage to the building. Apartment tenants have to carry insurance on their personal property. Ann and Mark were upset. They had assumed that the building owner carried insurance that also covered their property. They should have had a renter's policy. The fire proved to be a costly lesson for Ann and Mark regarding the need to understand home insurance.

? ? ? ? ? ? ? ? ? ? ? ? ? ?

WHAT WOULD YOU DO?

You have just moved into an apartment with a couple of friends. As you unpack, one of your roommates asks if you have purchased renter's insurance. You laugh and say that you do not have enough possessions to worry about insurance.

"You would be surprised," says your roommate. "It would cost quite a bit of money to replace everything in this room."

"I will think about it," you say. "But I really cannot afford insurance for a couple of months."

What would you do?

AUTO INSURANCE

The topic of auto insurance is very important to young people. Unfortunately, they are the ones who most need it. Drivers under age 25 are involved in about 30 percent of all auto accidents.

Everyone who drives a motor vehicle is responsible for operating it safely and paying for any damage the vehicle might cause. All states now have what are called financial-responsibility laws that require drivers to pay for damages they cause to people or property. Rather than risk having to come up with thousands of dollars as a result of an accident, most people buy insurance to show proof of financial responsibility. About half of the states have laws specifically requiring registered automobile owners to have liability insurance of some kind.

Types of Auto Insurance Coverage

An auto policy may provide six basic types of coverage:

Bodily Injury Liability. This coverage applies if you kill or injure someone in an accident in which you are at fault. The person may be a pedestrian, a rider in your car, or someone in another car. The policy covers bodily injury expenses and claims, including your legal expenses if you are sued.

Property Damage Liability. What if you damage another person's car or property? This type of insurance won't repair your car, but it will cover the other person's car or property. Property damage liability also provides legal expenses should you be taken to court.

Protection Against Uninsured Motorists. This coverage applies to bodily injuries that you may suffer as a result of a hit-and-run accident. The policy also covers you in the event of an accident in which the other driver does not have insurance.

Keith was sitting in his car at a stoplight waiting for the light to change. Suddenly, a car from behind smashed into him. The other driver was adjusting the radio and not paying attention to the intersection ahead. Keith's car was badly damaged.

The police came and filled out an accident report. They gave Andy, the other driver, a traffic citation for reckless driving. Keith and Andy exchanged information regarding addresses, phone numbers, and so on. Andy said that he could not remember the name of his insurance company, but that he would call Keith later with the information. The call never came.

In the meantime, Keith contacted his insurance company. They told him to go ahead and have his car fixed and they would collect from Andy's insurance company. As it turned out, Andy did not have auto insurance. However, since Keith was covered by uninsured motorists' protection, his insurance company assumed the cost of having the car repaired.

As for Andy, he was found to be in violation of the state Motorists' Responsibility Law. His driver's license and automobile registration were taken away. In order to get them back, Andy will have to pay Keith's insurance company the $1,200 it cost to repair Keith's car.

Medical Payments. Under this coverage, your insurance company agrees to pay medical expenses resulting from accidental injury. Medical insurance includes you and family members whether in your car or someone else's. It also applies if you are struck by a car. Payment is made regardless of who is at fault.

Auto Collision. Your car is covered by this type of insurance. The insurance company will pay to have your car repaired or replaced regardless of who is at fault. Keep in mind, though, that collision insurance does not cover repairs greater than the actual cash value of the car. Collision is the most expensive form of coverage. Most collision insurance is sold with a deductible (usually $200 or $250).

Auto Comprehensive. This coverage protects your car against loss from theft, vandalism, fire, windstorms, and other perils listed in the policy. If your car is damaged in an accident, collision, not comprehensive, will cover it.

The Cost of Auto Insurance

Basic rates for automobile insurance vary from area to area. Each state is divided into rating territories that indicate the losses paid in various parts of the state. The price of insurance is then set based on the loss experience of the rating territory. This means that rates in an area having heavy losses will be higher than in places where losses are not so great.

Many factors influence the price of insurance. These include the year, make, and model of the car. The sex, age, marital status, and driving record of the operator are also factors. In addition, driving a car a long distance every day will raise premiums. If you have more than one vehicle insured, you might receive a discount.

Even though you cannot do much about influencing basic insurance rates, you do have some control over the final cost. How many types of coverage do you wish to have? The first four mentioned previously are too important not to have. However, whether you purchase collision or comprehensive depends on how much your auto is worth. It would be foolish to have collision on an old car worth only a few hundred dollars.

You can also reduce the cost of car insurance by choosing higher deductibles. For example, raising the deductible on collision or comprehensive coverage from $100 to $250 can save you about 20 percent.

Motorcycle insurance is similar in coverage to that for cars. By knowing the basics of auto insurance, you should have no trouble understanding policies covering motorcycles.

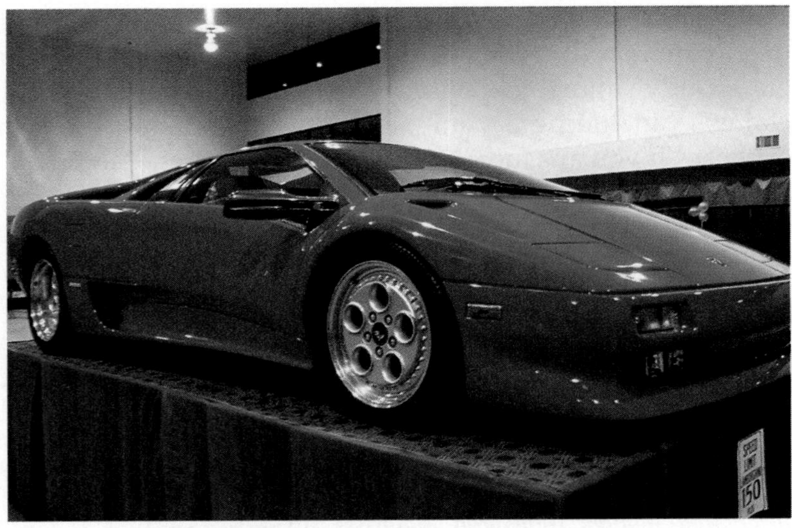

FIGURE 25–8 **Auto insurance rates are higher for sports cars and certain other types of vehicles.**
Photo by Jeff Greenberg.

No-fault Insurance

A problem for insurance companies is determining who is at fault in an accident. This process often requires the service of lawyers and may lead to long delays and expensive legal fees. Courts award generous compensation to some victims. Others receive little or nothing.

In order to reduce time, costs, and provide fair settlements to victims, about half of the states have developed no-fault insurance. Under the no-fault system, each person's losses and expenses are paid for by his or her insurance company regardless of who caused the accident. Lawsuits are permitted only under certain conditions.

No one enjoys paying insurance premiums, especially for something that you do not see or may never use. Do not, however, be tempted to take a chance and go without insurance. You only have to have one big loss to realize why it is so important to have insurance protection.

Health and Safety

WALK-IN MEDICAL CLINICS

What would you do if you severely cut yourself while slicing vegetables or if you woke up on a Sunday morning with a bad earache and high fever? You would probably head for the emergency room of the nearest hospital. Some people now have another option. It is called the walk-in medical clinic.

These new health clinics are one of the hottest trends in medical care. Thousands of them have sprung up across the country in the last several years. Regional and nationwide chains are being created just like fast-food restaurants. They are legitimate medical facilities staffed by licensed doctors and other professional personnel. They provide competition and are changing the way we make decisions about medical treatment.

The clinics take patients without appointments. They are open 12-to-16 (some 24) hours a day, seven days a week. They can treat most typical illnesses or accidents. But they do not do major surgery or handle serious emergencies like auto accidents. Fees for a normal visit are the same or slightly less than those for a regular doctor. For emergency treatment, however, the clinics can be substantially less. Treatment of a cut requiring stitches, for example, can be a third to a half of what is charged by a hospital emergency room. Health insurance usually covers such emergency treatment.

Cost and convenience, however, are not the whole story. In our mobile society, many people do not have a regular physician. When they need a doctor, walk-in clinics can provide that service.

Walk-in medical clinics help hold down costs of many medical services.
Courtesy of Healthshield—The Community Health Plan.

CHAPTER 25 REVIEW

CHAPTER IN BRIEF

- Insurance shifts probable loss from the individual to the group. The basic idea of insurance is that a large group of individuals pay a yearly premium that goes into a common fund. When disaster strikes one member of the group, the pooled funds pay for the loss. People buy insurance to protect themselves against three types of risks: personal, property, and liability.
- The purpose of health insurance is to pay expenses resulting from illness or accident. The expenses resulting from illness or accident can be enormous. There are four major types of health insurance: hospital, surgical, medical, and major medical. These are usually sold together in various combinations of health insurance packages. A fifth type of health insurance, disability, is usually sold separately. It provides income to people who are out of work because of illness or injury.
- The main purpose of life insurance is to provide financial security for dependents after the insured's death. The two basic types of life insurance are term and cash value. Term insurance provides protection at a low cost. It has no cash or loan value. Cash-value insurance provides protection along with the gradual buildup of a savings account. The amount of life insurance coverage you need depends on your personal situation and what you want to protect.
- For most people, a home and its contents is their most valuable investment. For this reason, it is very important to protect a home and contents against damage or loss. An important feature of home insurance is the provision for living expenses. This pays for food and lodging while your home is being rebuilt or repaired. Liability coverage is also important. It protects you against a claim or lawsuit for an accident or injury occurring on your property. There are various kinds of homeowners' insurance, depending on the type of coverage desired and whether you live in a home, apartment, condominium, or other dwelling.
- All states have financial responsibility laws requiring drivers to pay for damages caused to people or property. Most people buy insurance for this purpose. An auto policy may provide six types of coverage: bodily injury liability, property damage liability, protection against uninsured motorists, medical payments, auto collision, and auto comprehensive.
- The cost of auto insurance varies from one geographic area to another. Rates are also influenced by a number of factors, including the year, make, and model of the car; the driving record of the operator; the distance driven daily; the type of coverage and deductibles desired; and so on. About half of the states have no-fault auto insurance. This pays for losses and expenses regardless of who caused the accident.

WORDS TO KNOW

beneficiary
catastrophe
co-insurance
deductible
face value
health maintenance organization (HMO)
liability
perils
premium
risk
stop-loss provision

QUESTIONS TO ANSWER

1. Explain how insurance shifts probable loss from the individual to the group.
2. Insurance protects against three kinds of risks. Name them.
3. What is meant by basic health insurance coverage? What is major medical coverage?
4. Which individuals are most in need of disability coverage?
5. Describe an advantage and a disadvantage of both term and cash-value insurance.
6. Which type of term insurance has the same face value throughout the life of the policy?
7. What four things are usually covered by homeowners insurance?
8. Which type of auto insurance coverage applies to the following situations?
   a. You run into someone's parked auto.
   b. Your car is damaged when you back into a utility pole.
   c. A tree falls on your car during a windstorm.
9. Name four factors that influence the cost of auto insurance.
10. Explain the idea underlying no-fault auto insurance.

ACTIVITIES TO DO

1. Mrs. Owen has just recovered from a serious illness. Her hospital stay resulted in a bill of $12,340. She has health insurance that contains the following provisions:
   a. A $100 deductible for each hospital visit.
   b. Co-insurance in which the plan pays 80 percent of the next $5,000, and 100 percent of the costs thereafter.

   How much of the bill does Mrs. Owen have to pay?
2. As a class, obtain a policy or descriptive information about disability insurance. What types of illnesses and injury does the insurance cover? How much will the policy provide? What is the cost of the policy?
3. As a class, obtain cost estimates for a twenty-year-old individual on three different $50,000 face-value policies of the following types:
   a. Five-year renewable level-term plan.
   b. Thirty-year decreasing term plan.
   c. Thirty-year cash-value plan.

What is the annual cost for each plan at age 20, 30, 40, and 50? What is the average yearly cost for insurance over the thirty-year period? Is this a fair way to compare the cost of life insurance? What other factors (if any) need to be taken into consideration?

4. Obtain a policy or descriptive information about renter's insurance. What does the policy cover? How much is the annual premium? Does a young person moving into an apartment for the first time need such insurance? Why or why not?
5. Arrange to have an insurance agent or broker visit the class to discuss auto insurance. Ask him or her to discuss how rates are established and how final premiums are computed. Ask for recommendations about liability, medical payments, and uninsured motorists' coverage. Ask the agent to discuss the pros and cons of having comprehensive and collision coverage. If you wish, also find out how to decide between different levels of deductibles.
6. Learn your state's requirements for auto insurance coverage. Also, is no-fault insurance available in your state?

TOPICS TO DISCUSS

1. Hospitals have traditionally been operated as nonprofit community agencies. More and more hospitals and clinics are now being operated as private businesses. Why have these changes come about? What is your opinion of health providers becoming business persons?
2. People differ in terms of their need for life insurance. Identify and discuss family situations in which there is a great need for life insurance.
3. Home insurance perils are related to where you live. Identify and discuss different perils that are more common in one part of the country than another.
4. In what ways can you help to control the amount you pay for auto insurance?

CHAPTER 26 Taxes and Taxation

OUTLINE

- Taxation
- Types of Taxes
- The Federal Income Tax
- Filing an Income Tax Return
- Chapter Review

OBJECTIVES

After reading this chapter, you should be able to:

- Explain the purpose of taxes.
- Identify and explain the major types of taxes.
- Illustrate the difference between a graduated tax and a flat tax.
- Summarize the general process by which the amount of income tax is determined.
- Complete a Form 1040EZ.

John Nye had just completed two weeks on his new job. He could hardly wait to get his first real paycheck. His supervisor handed him the check as he was leaving on Friday afternoon. He took the paycheck and put it into his jacket pocket, not wanting to appear too excited.

After he got on the bus headed for home, John unfolded the paycheck and looked at it. He was disappointed. He had known that deductions would be taken from his paycheck. But he had not realized the amount would be so large.

When he got home, John asked his mother why he had to pay taxes. "After all," he said, "I don't make very much money." John's mother explained how every citizen is expected to pay part of the cost of government. Mrs. Nye also explained the types of taxes, and John's future need to file an income tax return. This chapter will help you to understand more about the purpose and types of taxes.

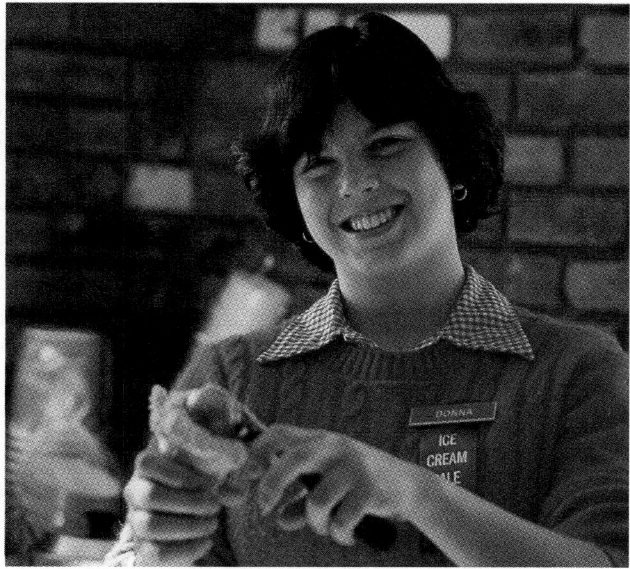

FIGURE 26–1 **Every worker who earns income above certain minimum levels must pay federal income tax.**
Photo by Ruby Gold.

? ? ? ? ? ? ? ? ? ? ? ? ? ?

WHAT WOULD YOU DO?

You are working about fifteen hours a week as part of a work experience program. In looking over your pay statement, you discover that money has been withheld for federal and state income taxes. You try to recall back to the time you filled out Form W-4, Employee's Withholding Allowance Certificate. You think that you claimed exemption from withholding because you did not expect to owe any taxes this year. Perhaps you made a mistake on Form W-4.

What would you do?

TAXATION

Local, state, and federal are the three levels of U.S. government. These units of government provide a wide variety of services. Supporting schools, building and maintaining roads, and providing for the nation's defense are examples. The process by which the expenses of government are paid is called *taxation.*

Purpose of Taxes

A *tax* is a compulsory (required) contribution of money people make to the government. Calling a tax compulsory helps to distinguish it from other types of payments. For example, when you buy a postage stamp you are paying for a government service. The difference between that purchase and taxation is that you are not required to buy a stamp. The main purpose of taxation is to raise *revenue* to pay the cost of government. Most taxes are revenue taxes.

Direct and Indirect Taxes

For centuries, governments have used direct and indirect ways of raising money. A direct tax is paid directly to the government. Examples include paycheck deductions and property taxes.

If you buy gasoline, you pay an indirect tax. The oil company pays tax on the gasoline it produces. These increased costs are then passed on to you at the pumps. Passing on taxes to the consumer is known as "shifting the tax burden."

Sometimes, a direct tax can become an indirect tax. Karen's landlord told her that the rent was going up $20 a month. When she asked why, Karen learned that property taxes on the building had risen about $600 last year. What the owner did was to pass the property taxes (a direct tax) on to Karen and other renters in the form of an indirect tax.

The consumer is often aware of indirect taxes. When you buy gasoline, for example, the price you pay for excise tax is clearly shown on the pump. Or, when you buy automobile tires, the bill will list the amount of federal excise tax. How much tax is included in the cost of gasoline where you live?

Some kinds of indirect taxes are "hidden." For instance, the price you pay for a stereo receiver includes taxes paid on the labor and raw materials used to produce the product. Taxes were collected on the factory and equipment used in manufacturing. Shipping costs to get the product to market include taxes paid by the transportation company. In fact, hidden taxes may make up as much as 20 percent of the cost of goods you buy.

TYPES OF TAXES

Individuals and businesses pay a variety of direct and indirect taxes for the purpose of raising revenue. The major types of taxes are: income; payroll; sales and excise; and estate, inheritance, and gift.

Income Taxes

You pay taxes on the money you earn and businesses are taxed on their profits. Governments collect the majority of taxes in this manner. The federal government, most state governments, and a few local governments collect income taxes. You pay income taxes not only on salary, wages, and tips, but on savings and investment income as well.

FIGURE 26–2 Food does not have a sales tax in most states.
Courtesy of Esselte Business Systems Inc.

Payroll

Income taxes pay for the overall costs of government. Payroll taxes, however, only go to support social security insurance programs. If you work for an employer covered by social security, both you and the employer make a contribution. These funds will help to provide you with a retirement income and other benefits. Some workers, such as teachers and government employees, pay into a state retirement program rather than into social security. You will learn more about social security in the next chapter.

Sales and Excise Taxes

Most state governments and some local ones have a *sales* tax. When you buy something, a few cents per dollar is added to the amount of the sale. Taxes on large items can be very high. For instance, on a car purchase, the sales tax can amount to several hundred dollars.

Excise taxes are a type of sales tax placed on specific items. These taxes are most commonly found on such items as gasoline, tires, and amusements. Why do you suppose the government taxes these things?

Estate, Inheritance, and Gift Taxes

When a person dies, the government may collect two types of taxes. An *estate tax* is assessed on the value of the dead person's wealth and property *before* it passes on to the heirs of the estate. In addition, an *inheritance tax* may be taken out of each person's share of the will. The federal government collects only an estate tax. Some state governments levy both inheritance and estate taxes.

You may wonder why people do not just turn over large sums while living so heirs can avoid these taxes. Gifts up to a certain amount are tax free. Beyond the figure, however, the person receiving the money must pay a *gift tax*.

THE FEDERAL INCOME TAX

In 1913, Congress passed the 16th Amendment to the Constitution, which gave the government the right to tax incomes. A few months later, an income tax on individuals and corporations was imposed. Since 1913, income tax laws have changed many times, and income tax rates have increased greatly.

In 1911, Wisconsin became the first state to tax income. The success of this tax led many states to pass similar laws. By the mid-1970s, almost all states had passed some form of income tax. After World War II, many cities also adopted income taxes. Added revenues were needed to catch up with needs neglected during the war.

Who Must Pay?

Unless excused by law, individuals, corporations, trusts, and estates must pay income tax. For example, the government does not tax certain individuals and families who have

FIGURE 26–3 **The first income tax was imposed in 1862 to help pay the costs of the Civil War.**
Photo from the Library of Congress.

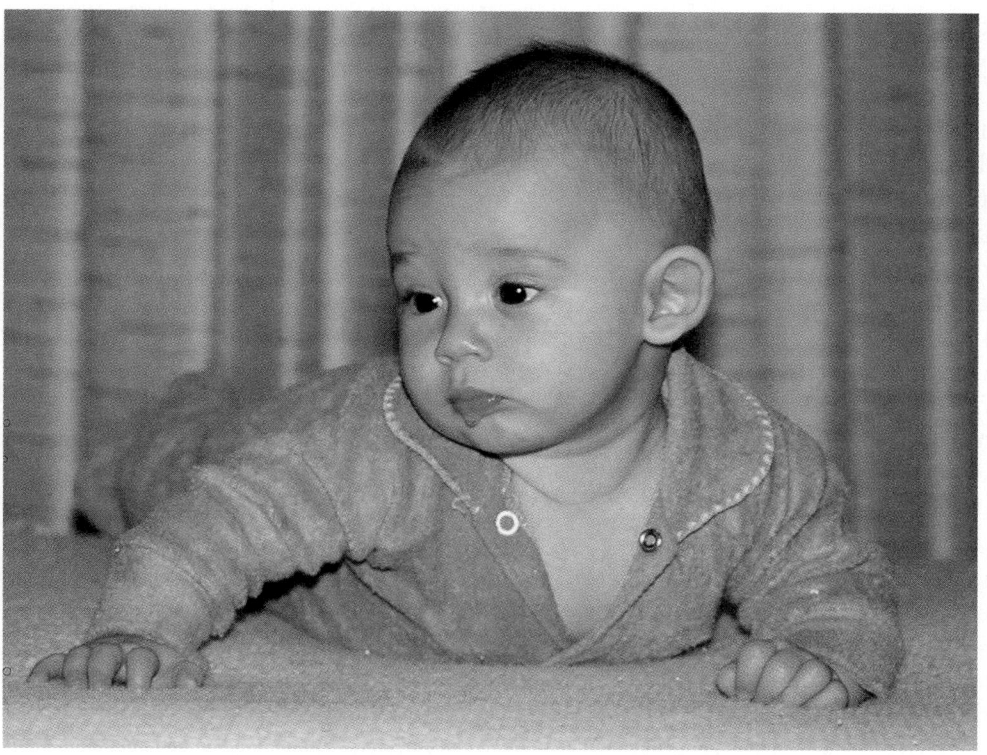

FIGURE 26–4 **This baby has to pay federal income tax. Her grandfather left her a large inheritance and the interest it earns is taxable.**
Photo by Paul E. Meyers.

low incomes. Nonprofit organizations such as churches, charities, and hospitals are also tax exempt.

Aliens, who are citizens of other countries who live and work in the United States, must pay income taxes. All corporations pay income taxes. Small businesses do not pay corporate taxes (unless they have been incorporated). Instead, owners of such businesses pay individual income taxes on their shares of the business income.

The Graduated Income Tax

Most Americans recognize that paying taxes is a necessary part of being a good citizen. The income tax is seen by most of us as being the fairest type of tax. People who earn more money should be able to pay more taxes. A system in which taxes are tied to one's income is called a graduated tax. See Figure 26–5.

Each taxpayer is allowed a certain level of tax-free income. The amount of tax-free income is determined by marital status and number of dependents. Based on recent tax rates, a single person without additional dependents paid no tax on the first $6,250 of earned income ($3,800 standard deduction plus $2,450 personal exemption). Marie and Frank are a married couple with two children. The family paid no taxes on the first $16,150 of earned income ($6,350 standard deduction plus four personal exemptions). The standard deduction for most students who can be claimed as a dependent on another person's return is limited to not more than $3,800 earned income.

The income tax rate, then, requires nothing from people with very low incomes. Large families pay less in taxes than small families. Married people pay less than single people.

Most state and local income taxes are also graduated. Some state and local governments, however, use a flat tax. This means that a flat percentage (usually one to six percent) is assessed on income regardless of its amount. If the flat rate were five percent, a $20,000 income would be assessed $1,000. Someone earning $30,000 would have to pay $1,500 in taxes.

Over the years, many kinds of exemptions and deductions have been written into the tax laws. Some of them are called *loopholes* because they permit certain individuals to reduce or avoid income taxes. Loopholes are criticized by some people because they are regarded as unfair. A so-called loophole, however, is a legal tax provision of which any eligible person can take advantage. For example, one loophole involves interest paid on a home mortgage. People buying homes can deduct the interest paid from their taxes. People paying rent have no such deductions.

How the Tax Is Determined

Your total income for a given year consists of money you earned from your job plus income from savings, investments, and other sources. But you do not have to pay taxes on your total income, Figure 26–6.

Schedule X—Use if your filing status is **Single**

If the amount on Form 1040, line 37, is: *Over—*	*But not over—*	Enter on Form 1040, line 38	*of the amount over—*
$0	$22,750	-------- **15%**	**$0**
22,750	55,100	**$3,412.50 + 28%**	**22,750**
55,100	115,000	**12,470.50 + 31%**	**55,100**
115,000	250,000	**31,039.50 + 36%**	**115,000**
250,000	---------	**79,639.50 + 39.6%**	**250,000**

Schedule Y-1—Use if your filing status is **Married filing jointly** or **Qualifying widow(er)**

If the amount on Form 1040, line 37, is: *Over—*	*But not over—*	Enter on Form 1040, line 38	*of the amount over—*
$0	$38,000	-------- **15%**	**$0**
38,000	91,850	**$5,700.00 + 28%**	**38,000**
91,850	140,000	**20,778.00 + 31%**	**91,850**
140,000	250,000	**35,704.50 + 36%**	**140,000**
250,000	---------	**75,304.50 + 39.6%**	**250,000**

Schedule Z—Use if your filing status is **Head of household**

If the amount on Form 1040, line 37, is: *Over—*	*But not over—*	Enter on Form 1040, line 38	*of the amount over—*
$0	$30,500	-------- **15%**	**$0**
30,500	78,700	**$4,575.00 + 28%**	**30,500**
78,700	127,500	**18,071.00 + 31%**	**78,700**
127,500	250,000	**33,199.00 + 36%**	**127,500**
250,000	---------	**77,299.00 + 39.6%**	**250,000**

FIGURE 26–5 The rate at which you pay tax is based on the amount of taxable income you earn and your filing status.
Source: Internal Revenue Service.

To determine income subject to tax, first subtract certain nontaxable items called adjustments. *Adjustments to income* may include alimony paid and contributions to an Individual Retirement Account. After you subtract adjustments, you are left with an *adjusted gross income.*

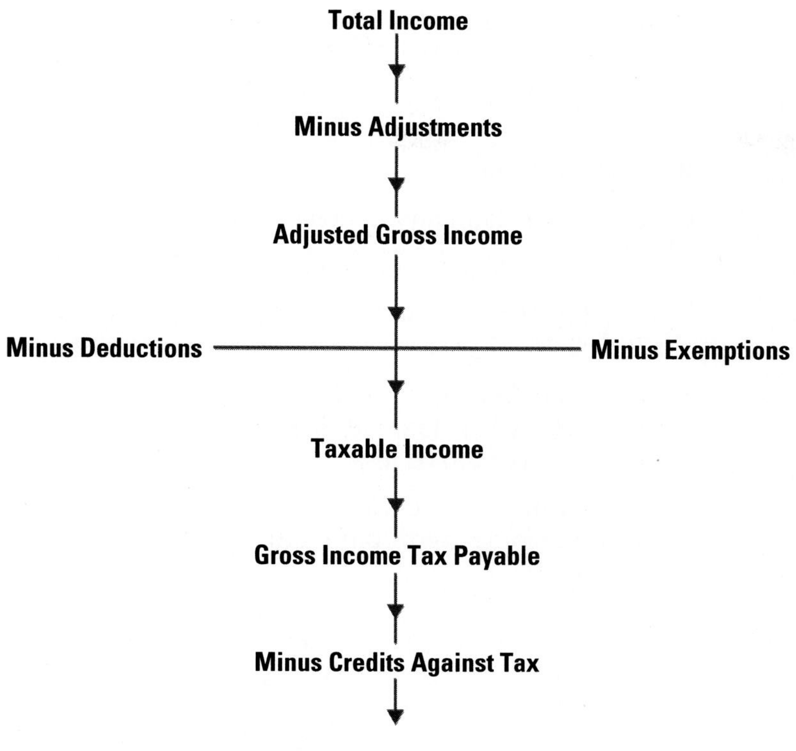

FIGURE 26–6 **This is the general process used to determine the amount of federal income tax owed. The actual process varies among individuals.**

Next, you are allowed to subtract various *deductions*. For example, mortgage interest, property taxes, contributions to charity or churches, and other expenses can be deducted. Next, you may subtract a set amount for each dependent. These are your *exemptions*. A married couple with one child, for example, would have three exemptions. Subtraction of amounts for deductions and exemptions leaves you with your *taxable income*.

Determine the amount of tax owed by using the appropriate tax table, Figure 26–7. For example, suppose you are married and filing a joint return. If you made $23,430 in taxable income, the tax is $3,514. A single person earning the same amount would owe $3,602.

Your figure from the tax table may be reduced if you are eligible for any *tax credits*. These include child care and certain other expenses. The amount left after subtracting credits will be the amount of federal income tax you owe.

A final step in determining your tax is to compare the amount owed with the tax you have already paid. Because your employer withheld taxes from each paycheck, most or all of your tax obligation should be satisfied. If too much tax has been withheld, you can claim a refund. However, if too little has been withheld, you will have to pay an additional amount.

You must sign and mail your return and any attachments by

If line 37 (taxable income) is—		And you are—			
At least	But less than	Single	Married filing jointly *	Married filing sepa-rately	Head of a house-hold
		Your Tax is—			
23,000					
23,000	**23,050**	3,490	3,454	3,977	3,454
23,050	**23,100**	3,504	3,461	3,991	3,461
23,100	**23,150**	3,518	3,469	4,005	3,469
23,150	**23,200**	3,532	3,476	4,019	3,476
23,200	**23,250**	3,546	3,484	4,033	3,484
23,250	**23,300**	3,560	3,491	4,047	3,491
23,300	**23,350**	3,574	3,499	4,061	3,499
23,350	**23,400**	3,588	3,506	4,075	3,506
23,400	**23,450**	3,602	3,514	4,089	3,514
23,450	**23,500**	3,616	3,521	4,103	3,521
23,500	**23,550**	3,630	3,529	4,117	3,529
23,550	**23,600**	3,644	3,536	4,131	3,536
23,600	**23,650**	3,658	3,544	4,145	3,544
23,650	**23,700**	3,672	3,551	4,159	3,551
23,700	**23,750**	3,686	3,559	4,173	3,559
23,750	**23,800**	3,700	3,566	4,187	3,566
23,800	**23,850**	3,714	3,574	4,201	3,574
23,850	**23,900**	3,728	3,581	4,215	3,581
23,900	**23,950**	3,742	3,589	4,229	3,589
23,950	**24,000**	3,756	3,596	4,243	3,596

FIGURE 26–7 **Sample tax table.**
Source: Internal Revenue Service.

April 15. In signing your name, you signify that everything contained on the form is accurate and truthful. If you mail the form late, you will have to pay a late penalty. People who do not file their forms at all are practicing *tax evasion.* If they are found guilty of this charge, they will have to pay a heavy fine and perhaps serve a prison sentence.

FILING AN INCOME TAX RETURN

The term *filing* is used to refer to the process of completing and submitting an income tax return. Filing a tax return can be simple or complex, depending on your filing status, source(s) of income, number of deductions, and so on. The easiest form to file is Form 1040EZ. You can use this form if:

- Your filing status is single.
- You do not claim any dependents.
- You are not 65 or over, or blind.
- Your taxable income is less than $50,000.
- You had *only* wages, salaries, and tips, and your taxable interest income was $400 or less.
- You did not receive any advance earned income credit payments.
- You were not a nonresident alien at any time during the previous year.
- Your total wages were not over $55,500 if you had more than one employer.

In a recent calendar year, John Nye worked afternoons during school and all day on Saturdays at Barden Ruddens ice cream parlor. During the summer months, he worked a full forty-hour week.

John's W-2 Form appears in Figure 26–8. Form W-2 Wage and Tax Statement is an IRS form that your employer prepares and sends to you by January 31 of the following year. The form summarizes the total earnings and tax withholding.

When John got his W-2, he went to the IRS office and picked up a copy of Form 1040EZ. A copy of John's completed return is shown in Figure 26–9.

As you can see, it was not difficult for John Nye to file an income tax return. Not all returns, however, are as simple as this. Because John's older sister had dividend income from stock, she had to use Form

a Control number	OMB No. 1545-0008	
b Employer's identification number 37-5732196	1 Wages, tips, other compensation 4,560.00	2 Federal income tax withheld 197.83
c Employer's name, address, and ZIP code Barden Ruddens Inc. 1640 W. Main Street Carbondale, IL 72901	3 Social security wages 4,560.00	4 Social security tax withheld 282.72
	5 Medicare wages and tips 4,560.00	6 Medicare tax withheld 66.12
	7 Social security tips .00	8 Allocated tips
d Employee's social security number 315-20-4024	9 Advance EIC payment	10 Dependent care benefits
e Employee's name, address, and ZIP code John R. Nye 1612 Fredrick St. Carbondale, IL 72901	11 Nonqualified plans	12 Benefits included in box 1
	13	14 Other
	15 Statutory employee ☐ Deceased ☐ Pension plan ☐ Legal rep. ☐ 942 emp. ☐ Subtotal ☐ Deferred compensation ☐	

16 State	Employer's state I.D. No.	17 State wages, tips, etc.	18 State income tax	19 Locality name	20 Local wages, tips, etc.	21 Local income tax
IL	0348-4321	4,560.00	137.14		4,560.00	.00

Form **W-2** Wage and Tax Statement **19--**

Copy 1 for State, City, or Local Tax Department

Department of the Treasury–Internal Revenue Service

FIGURE 26–8 A W-2 Form, Wage and Tax Statement will be sent to you by your employer in late January following each year that you worked.

1040A. John's parents used a third type of common form, Form 1040, because they itemize deductions and also receive income from a property they rent.

As a result of completing his own Form 1040EZ, John discovered that he enjoyed this type of work. When he asked his sister and parents if he might help them with their forms, they quickly accepted his offer. By helping to fill out their forms, John learned a great deal more about income tax returns. Why don't you offer to help a family member or friend with income tax preparation? You will probably learn a lot, too!

? ? ? ? ? ? ? ? ? ? ? ? ? ? ?

WHAT WOULD YOU DO?

You are in the process of filling out your income tax return. The next line on the form deals with "charitable contributions." You go over your canceled checks and discover several that qualify as deductions. You can remember several other cash contributions, but you do not have the receipts. Also, you had some out-of-pocket expenses for church activities. These are allowable deductions. But you do not have records for those either. You are not sure how much you should claim for charitable contributions.

What would you do?

Form 1040EZ

Department of the Treasury–Internal Revenue Service

Income Tax Return for Single and Joint Filers With No Dependents (0) **19 - -**

OMB No. 1545-0675

Use the IRS label (See page 12.) Otherwise, please print.

LABEL HERE

Print your name (first, initial, last): John R. Nye

If a joint return, print spouse's name (first, initial, last):

Home address (number and street). If you have a P.O. box, see page 12. Apt. no.: 1612 W. Main St.

City, town, or post office, state, and ZIP code. If you have a foreign address, see page 12.: Carbondale, IL 72901

Your social security number: 315 20 4024

Spouse's social security number:

See instructions on back and in Form 1040EZ booklet.

Presidential Election Campaign (See page 12.)

Note: *Checking "Yes" will not change your tax or reduce your refund.*

	Yes	No
Do you want $3 to go to this fund? ▶	X	
If a joint return, does your spouse want $3 to go to this fund? ▶		

		Dollars	Cents
Income Attach **Copy B of Form(s) W-2 here.** Enclose, but do not attach, any payment with your return.	1 Total wages, salaries, and tips. This should be shown in box 1 of your W-2 form(s). Attach your W-2 form(s). 1	4,560	
	2 Taxable interest income of $400 or less. If the total is over $400, you cannot use Form 1040EZ. 2	42	
	3 Add lines 1 and 2. This is your **adjusted gross income.** If less than $9,000, see page 15 to find out if you can claim the earned income credit on line 7. 3	4,602	
Note: *You **must** check Yes or No.*	4 Can your parents (or someone else) claim you on their return? [X] **Yes.** Do worksheet on back; enter amount from line G here. [ ] **No.** If **single**, enter 6,250.00. If **married**, enter 11,250.00. For an explanation of these amounts see back of form. 4	3,800	
	5 Subtract line 4 from line 3. If line 4 is larger than line 3, enter 0. This is your **taxable income.** ▶ 5	802	
Payments and tax	6 Enter your Federal income tax withheld from box 2 of your W-2 form(s). 6	198	
	7 **Earned income credit** (see page 15). Enter type and amount of nontaxable earned income below. Type / $ 7	No	
	8 Add lines 6 and 7 (don't include nontaxable earned income). These are your **total payments**. 8	198	
	9 **Tax**. Use the amount on **line 5** to find your tax in the tax table on pages 28–32 of the booklet. Then, enter the tax from the table on this line. 9	122	
Refund or amount you owe	10 If line 8 is larger than line 9, subtract line 9 from line 8. This is your **refund**. 10	76	
	11 If line 9 is larger than line 8, subtract line 8 from line 9. This is the **amount you owe**. See page 20 for details on how to pay and what to write on your payment. 11		

Sign your return Keep a copy of this form for your records.

I have read this return. Under penalties of perjury, I declare that to the best of my knowledge and belief, the return is true, correct, and accurately lists all amounts and sources of income I received during the tax year.

Your signature		Spouse's signature if joint return	
John R. Nye			
Date	Your occupation	Date	Spouse's occupation
2-20-19--	*fast-food worker*		

For IRS Use Only—Please do not write in boxes below.

For Privacy Act and Paperwork Reduction Act Notice, see page 4. Cat. No. 11329W **Form 1040EZ (19 - -)**

FIGURE 26–9 **Most young workers can use Form 1040EZ.**

FOCUS ON

Skills For Living

Electronic Tax Preparation and Filing

Almost anyone who files a tax return can now file a 1040PC return. The 1040PC is prepared on a personal computer using tax preparation software. Software packages can be purchased from any retail store or mail-order company that sells computer software.

Most software uses a question-and-answer format. You simply enter the data requested. The software will perform the necessary calculations and print the return in a form acceptable to the Internal Revenue Service (IRS). You can then mail the completed form to the IRS or file it electronically by computer.

Electronic tax filing was begun in 1986 on an experimental basis. The first year, 25,000 returns were filed. Today, millions of returns are transmitted this way. The process is designed to cut down on paperwork. Traditionally, IRS employees opened the envelopes, organized and read the information, and keyed the data into a computer. By filing direct, these steps are eliminated.

The next step, after eliminating paper forms, may be "returnless" systems. In the future, IRS computers may keep wage, interest income, social security, and other taxpayer data on file. Then each year, the IRS would send either a bill or a refund without a return ever being filed.

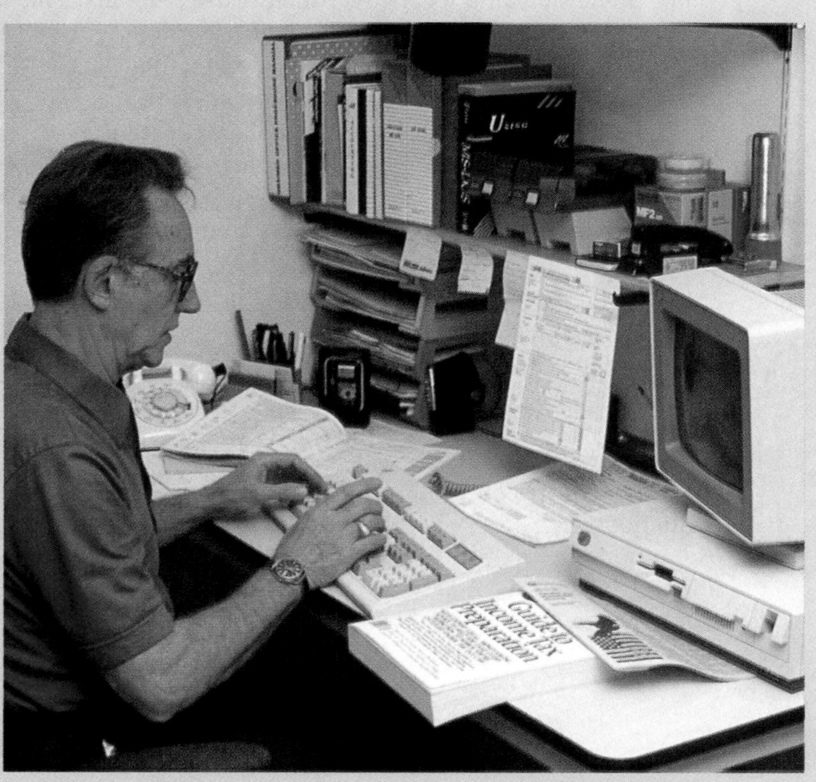

Electronic tax preparation and filing are other uses for computers in our society.
Photo by Paul E. Meyers.

CHAPTER 26 REVIEW

CHAPTER IN BRIEF

- The process by which the expenses of government are paid is called taxation. A tax is a compulsory contribution of money people make to the government. Most taxes are revenue taxes.
- A direct tax is paid directly to the government. Examples include payroll deductions and property taxes. An indirect tax is one that is included in the cost of goods and services you buy. Excise taxes are one of the most common types of indirect taxes.
- Individuals and businesses pay a variety of direct and indirect taxes. The major types of taxes are: income; payroll; sales and excise; and estate, inheritance, and gift.
- Most individuals and corporations pay income taxes. Income from a small unincorporated business is taxed as individual income rather than as corporate income.
- The graduated income tax is one in which the amount of tax paid is tied to income. The more you earn, the more you pay. The federal government, and most state and local governments, levy a graduated income tax. Some state and local governments use a flat tax. This means that a flat percentage is assessed on income regardless of its amount.
- To determine income subject to tax, first subtract certain nontaxable items called exclusions and adjustments. This leaves you with an adjusted gross income. Next, you are allowed to subtract various deductions and exemptions. This leaves you with your taxable income. You figure your tax based on this amount. This amount can sometimes be further reduced by subtracting tax credits. The resultant figure is the amount of federal income tax you owe.
- The easiest tax form to file is 1040EZ. Most teenage workers are eligible to use this form.

WORDS TO KNOW

adjusted gross income
adjustments to income
deductions
exemptions
filing
loopholes
revenue
tax
taxable income
taxation
tax credits
tax evasion

QUESTIONS TO ANSWER

1. Why do all of us need to pay taxes?
2. What is a revenue tax?
3. Is an excise tax on tires a direct or an indirect tax?
4. Name and briefly describe the seven major types of taxes.
5. Do aliens working in the U.S. have to pay income taxes? Why?
6. What is a flat tax? How is a graduated tax different?
7. How are owners of small businesses taxed?
8. Based on Figure 26–7, how much tax does a married couple filing jointly owe on an income of $23,945? How much does a single person owe on the same amount?
9. If you are married, can you use Form 1040EZ to file your federal income tax?
10. What happens if you have earned income and fail to file an income tax?

ACTIVITIES TO DO

1. As a class, obtain a copy of the most recent federal budget. What is the total amount of the budget? What is the primary budget expenditure? What specific items are included in this category? How much is the budget deficit? Discuss your answers in class.
2. Get a copy of and instructions for Form 1040EZ. Fill out the form using the following figures: wages of $12,648, tips of $943, and $183 in interest income. Federal income tax in the amount of $1,766 was withheld. What is the amount of tax? Your instructor may assign additional problems including use of 1040PC.
3. If your state has an income tax, obtain a copy of the income tax form and instructions. Using the amounts shown in Figure 26-18, see if you can complete the form by yourself. When finished, ask your instructor to check the figures.
4. Let's assume you make $305 a week in salary for 52 weeks. You pay $2,070 a year in federal income tax, and $482 in state income tax. You also pay $218 in sales tax, $73 in property tax, and $990 in FICA tax. A variety of other taxes add an additional $132. What is the total amount in taxes paid during the year? How many weeks must you work just to pay taxes?
5. Obtain a copy of Publication 910, "Guide to Free Tax Services" at your nearest IRS Forms Distribution Center. Using the publication, find out what the IRS offers regarding:
   a. Toll-free telephone assistance.
   b. Recorded tax information (Tele-Tax).
   c. Tax publications and forms.
   d. Taxpayer Educational Programs.

   Your instructor may arrange to have you view a film or video cassette.

TOPICS TO DISCUSS

1. Why do you think so many people dislike paying income taxes? How do you feel?
2. Which do you think is more fair, the graduated tax or the flat tax?
3. In what ways might the federal income tax system be improved? Give specific illustrations.
4. Have you ever heard of the "underground economy"? To what does it refer? Give examples.

CHAPTER 27 Social Security

OUTLINE

- Social Security
- Major Social Insurance Programs
- Eligibility and Financing
- Individual Retirement Accounts
- Chapter Review

OBJECTIVES

After reading this chapter, you should be able to:

- Identify the two forms of social security.
- Name and describe the six major federal and state social insurance programs.
- Explain how state workers' compensation is financed.
- Describe who is eligible for federal social security payments and how the program is financed.
- Explain the purpose of an Individual Retirement Account (IRA).
- Name two tax benefits of an IRA.

You know that your employer withholds money from your paycheck for federal, and perhaps state and local, income taxes. A sum is probably also withheld for *social security* taxes.

You may have little interest in social security now. After all, it will be a long time before you retire. However, you need to be aware that social security is more than just a retirement program. Social security is actually a broad state and federal effort consisting of various types of social insurance. These programs will be explained later in this chapter.

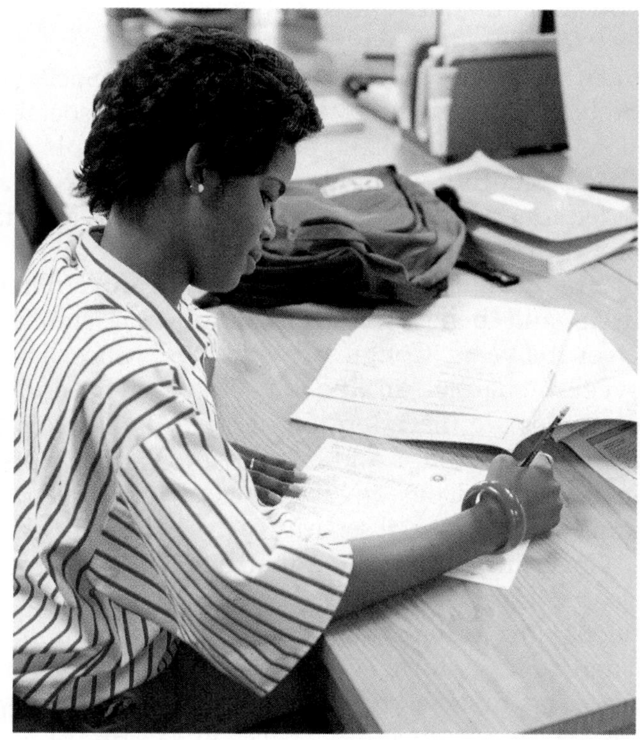

FIGURE 27–1 **When this student's father died suddenly she could afford to stay in school because she received social security benefits.**

SOCIAL SECURITY

At one time, most Americans lived in rural areas and were farmers. Rural families lived off the land. They built their own homes; raised their own food; and traded or sold surplus food, crops, and livestock. Families and neighbors helped each other during difficult times.

Gradually, the country began to change from an agricultural economy to an industrial one. Increasing numbers of people moved to cities and took jobs in factories. Instead of living off the land, families began to depend on wages paid by an employer. If the income stopped for some reason, such as a worker's illness or old age, the whole family suffered.

The Great Depression of 1929–1933 showed on a large scale how painful unemployment could be. To help deal with unemployment and the many other social problems brought on by the Depression, Congress, in 1935, passed the Social Security Act. This law provided for a system of old-age (retirement) pensions, unemployment insurance, aid for dependent children, and benefits for the blind. Over the years, Congress has made several changes in the act. Two examples are the extension of *benefits* to more groups and an increase in tax rates. Does anyone in your family receive social security?

Government programs that help people meet social and economic needs are called social security. There are two forms of social security. The first is known as public assistance (or welfare). This program aids the needy regardless of their work record. General taxes finance public assistance.

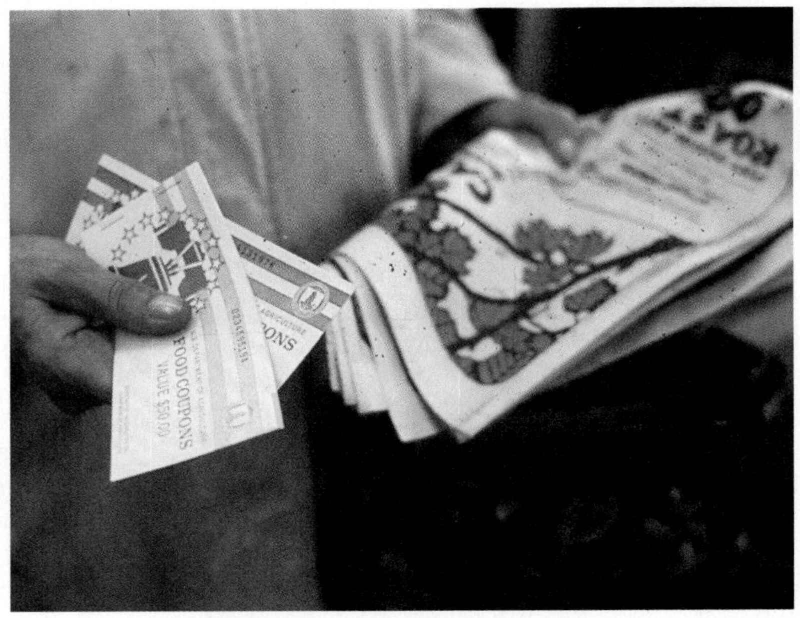

FIGURE 27–2 **The food stamp program is one type of public assistance. It helps people who have low incomes or temporary unemployment to buy food.**
Courtesy of United States Department of Agriculture.

Social insurance, the second form of social security, pays benefits to people who have earned them by working and paying social security payroll taxes. In some cases, a worker's family can receive benefits. In many ways, social insurance is similar to other types of insurance. During your working years, you and your employer pay taxes that go into special funds. The risks and costs are thus spread among many people. When your earnings stop because of retirement or certain other situations, you receive benefits. If you die, payments are made to your survivors.

MAJOR SOCIAL INSURANCE PROGRAMS

National and state systems of social security have changed greatly from the way they were in 1935. The six major social insurance programs in the United States are shown in Figure 27–3. The general nature of each of these programs is described in this chapter. As some of the rules are quite technical, no effort is made to explain all details regarding eligibility and payments. More specific information can be obtained from your local Social Security Administration (SSA) office. More than 1,300 such offices are located across the country.

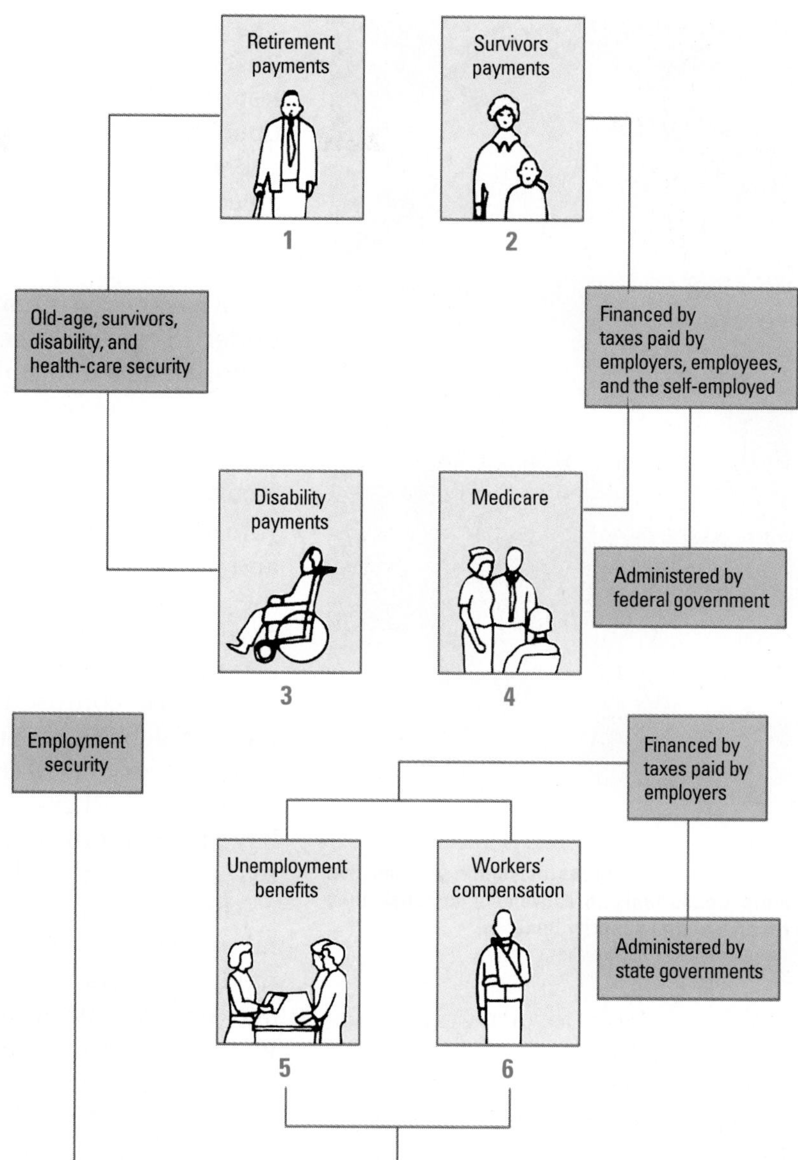

FIGURE 27–3 **These are the six major types of social insurance programs in the United States. Most people call the first four "social security."**

Retirement Payments

This is the best known social security program. It provides a monthly *pension* to retired workers who reach age 65. Individuals may choose to retire at age 62. If so, they will collect on 80 percent of the rate established for a person retiring at age 65. The amount of monthly benefits received is based on your average annual earnings.

Benefits under the program are also payable to the spouse of the retired worker. A spouse's benefit equals about 50 percent of the worker's benefit. Under certain conditions, unmarried children of the retired worker may also be eligible for benefits.

Retirement-age rules will change in the future as a result of revisions made in 1983 to the Social Security Act. Between the years 2003 and 2027, the retirement age will gradually increase from 65 to 67. This means that if you are a high school student now, you will not be eligible to receive full retirement benefits until you reach age 67. Early retirement benefits (age 62) will be reduced to 75 percent by 2009 and to 70 percent by 2027.

Survivors Payments

If you are insured and you die (either before or after retirement), your dependents may be eligible for survivors payments. These benefits are of two types. First, a *lump-sum payment* is made to your spouse or child. Second, your dependents

FIGURE 27–4 **Millions of senior citizens live more comfortably in retirement because they receive social security benefits.**
Courtesy of Sears, Roebuck and Company.

may be eligible for a monthly survivors benefit.

Monthly payments may be made to a surviving spouse age 60 or older. Under certain conditions, surviving unmarried children and dependent parents may also receive payments. The amount of monthly payments is based on the benefits the worker was getting at the time of death. Suppose the person had not yet retired. The survivor would then be entitled to the benefits the deceased worker would have received.

Disability Payments

If you are unable to work because of a severe physical or mental disability, you may be eligible for benefits. The disability must have lasted at least twelve months or be expected to last that long. Payments can start upon the sixth full month of disability.

Benefits are also paid to a disabled worker's spouse. A dependent spouse may collect full benefits at age 65 or reduced benefits at age 62. Unmarried children under 18 can also receive benefits. If a worker has a disabled child, special benefits may apply.

Medicare

In 1965, Congress added hospital and medical insurance benefits to the social security program. This coverage, known since as Medicare, is for people age 65 or older. (This is sometimes confused with Medicaid, which is a health service program for welfare recipients.) Disabled workers under 65 who have received disability benefits for two years are also eligible.

Medicare consists of both hospital insurance and supplementary medical insurance. Hospital coverage (Part A) pays for nursing care as well as hospital expenses. The insured person must pay an initial amount (a deductible) for each hospital stay. Medicare then pays the rest of the hospital expenses for up to 60 days. Once a stay lasts over 60 days, additional limitations apply.

The hospital insurance part of medicare is automatically provided to eligible workers (and spouses). However, the medical coverage (Part B) is an *optional* health insurance plan. It pays the cost of doctor's fees and other medical services not included in hospital insurance. If you want medical coverage, you must pay a monthly premium for the service. Under this plan, you must pay a deductible each year. The program then pays 80 percent of the remaining expenses.

Unemployment Benefits

Unemployment insurance, which was included as part of the original 1935 Social Security Act, is not a federal program. The purpose of the law was to motivate states to pass their own laws. Each state finances and administers its own unemployment insurance program.

Unemployment insurance provides weekly cash payments to workers who have lost their jobs. Paul Miller, for instance, was laid off from his job at the Black Gold Coal Mine. He had to go to the local state employment service office to register for unemployment benefits. Paul has started receiving weekly checks amounting to half of his normal full-time pay at the time. He is eligible to receive payments for up to 26 weeks. However, during the time he is receiving unemployment benefits, Paul is required to accept any suitable job that the employment service has available.

The amount of the weekly payment and the number of weeks of eligibility varies from state to state. Otherwise, state programs of unemployment insurance operate in the same general manner.

Workers' Compensation

Every state in the United States has a workers' compensation law, which helps people who are injured or who develop a disease as a result of their job. The program pays the cost of medical care and helps replace lost income. Workers' compensation also pays death benefits and pensions to dependents of workers killed on the job.

Benefits vary among states. How much workers receive depends on the type and duration of the disability and on the worker's weekly earnings. States have minimum and maximum benefit limits and benefit periods. But injured workers typically receive less than half of what they would have earned. In return for compensation, workers give up their right to sue an employer for damages arising from their disability.

In most states, employers are required to participate in a workers' compensation program. However, many states do not cover farmworkers, household workers, and employees of small firms. And some states refuse to extend protection to workers in dangerous jobs.

? ? ? ? ? ? ? ? ? ? ? ? ? ?

WHAT WOULD YOU DO?

You injured your leg badly in a warehouse accident. The leg was put into a cast. You have been confined to bed for several weeks. It will probably be months before you can go back to work. You are glad you have workers' compensation benefits.

Your co-workers stop by to see you every few days. During one visit, you remark that you cannot wait to get the cast off and go back to work. Your buddy laughs and says that if he were you, he would lie about the leg hurting and stay home as long as possible. He says that a lot of people do it.

What would you do?

ELIGIBILITY AND FINANCING

In the previous section, you learned about four federally administered social security programs and two state administered ones (review Figure 27–3). This section explains how the federal program is financed, as well as how you become eligible for federal social security benefits. Eligibility and financing for state programs vary widely among states.

Who Is Eligible

To be eligible for social security benefits, you must earn a certain amount of *work credit* in jobs covered by social security. Work credit is measured in *quarters of coverage.* A three-month period equals one quarter of coverage. Currently, you receive a quarter of coverage for each $620 of covered annual earnings. The amount of earnings needed for a quarter of coverage increases periodically. You are limited to four quarters of coverage per year no matter how much money you make.

There are two different eligibility statuses—fully insured and currently insured. A *fully insured* worker has earned forty quarters of coverage. Fully insured workers are eligible to receive complete retirement, survivors, disability, and health benefits. A *currently insured* worker has earned at least six quarters of credit during the 39 months before death or disability. Such a worker is only eligible for limited survivors benefits.

Financing the Program

You and your employer share equally the cost of financing federal social security. This tax is called the *Federal Insurance Contributions Act (FICA)* tax. Your employer deducts your share of FICA tax from your paycheck. Your employer then adds an equal contribution and sends the Treasury Department the total amount monthly or quarterly. The department then distributes the money among the various funds that will pay benefits.

Up to a certain limit, taxes are figured on your gross annual wages. The salary limit is called the *wage base.* In 1937, when the first FICA taxes were collected, both the worker and employer paid 1 percent tax on the first $3,000 (wage base) of earnings. Currently the tax rate is 7.65 percent on the first $60,600 of earnings. Earnings in excess of the wage base are not subject to FICA tax. However, you must continue to pay 1.45 percent for Medicare on all earned income.

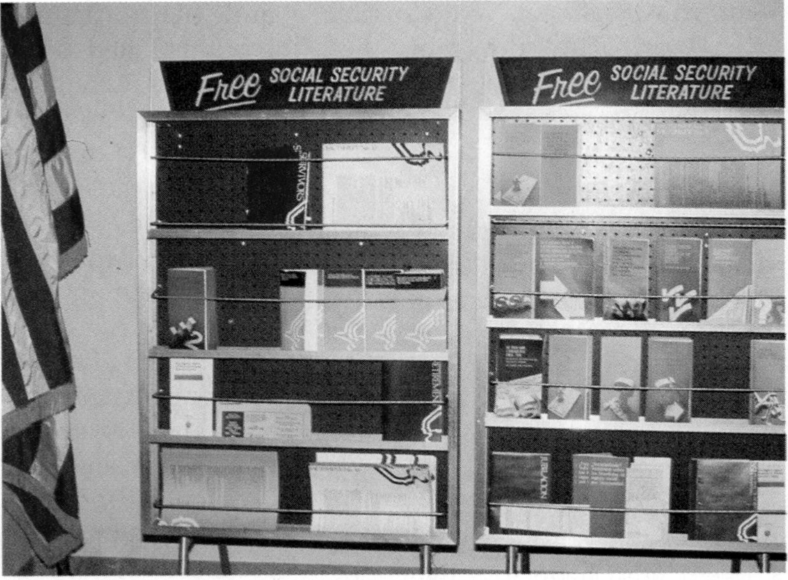

FIGURE 27–5 **There is a great deal of information available at Social Security offices.**
Photo by Paul E. Meyers.

FIGURE 27–6 **Plan your retirement while you are young so you can enjoy your old age.**
Courtesy of Eastman Kodak Company

INDIVIDUAL RETIREMENT ACCOUNTS

The social security retirement program is designed to provide a minimum standard of living for retired workers. Social security was never designed to meet *all* of a retired person's financial needs. To live reasonably well in retirement, it will be necessary for you to supplement social security retirement income with other sources. These might include savings, investments, or private pension coverage.

About 95 percent of all employed workers are covered by social security. Approximately half of these are also covered by a private pension plan. To encourage more people to establish private pension programs, Congress passed legislation in 1981 making almost every working person eligible for an *Individual Retirement Account (IRA).*

Anyone who earns income from working and is under age 70½ can open an IRA. You are eligible to put up to $2,000 a year into an IRA. When your spouse also works, you can each invest up to $2,000 per year. If your spouse does not work outside the home, you can still both open an account. However, in this case, you are limited to a combined total of $2,250. This amount can be split in any combination, but no more than $2,000 can be put in either account each year.

Tax Benefits

An IRA has *two* big tax benefits. First, people can deduct IRA contributions from their income tax. This depends, however, on whether you have a retirement plan at work and on how much you earn. A person who is not covered by a retirement plan at work is able to put up to $2,000 a year into an IRA and deduct the full amount. People who have retirement plans at work are able to get the full deduction only if their incomes are below a certain level, see Figure 27–7.

Let's say that a married couple had taxable income of $35,000. By placing $2,000 into an IRA, they would only pay taxes on $33,000. This would result in a tax savings of $300. It costs this couple, in effect, $1,700 to make a $2,000 investment. For people earning higher incomes, the savings are even greater.

The second tax benefit of an IRA is that interest and other earnings on

Yearly Income	If You or Your Spouse are Covered by a Retirement Plan	If You or Your Spouse are not Covered by a Retirement Plan
Married $40,000 & under Single $25,000 & under	Full Deduction	Full Deduction
Married $40,000–$50,000 Single $25,000–$35,000	Partial Deduction	Full Deduction
Married $50,000 & above Single $35,000 & above	No Deduction	Full Deduction

FIGURE 27–7 This chart will help you determine whether or not you can deduct your IRA contribution based on your annual adjusted gross income.

the IRA investment are not taxed until they are withdrawn. This allows an investment to compound at a much greater rate than if taxes were deducted. Examples of how an IRA investment can multiply are shown in Figure 27–8. You can see that it is possible for a young person like you to accumulate several hundred thousand dollars before retirement. The amounts shown would increase dramatically if you put in a full $2,000, and you earned a higher yield. Remember that inflation will probably increase over the years, too.

21 Even if you cannot put $2,000 into an IRA, try to put in what you can afford. The key to getting the most from an IRA is to start early, put in as much as you can, and make a contribution each and every year.

Age Open IRA	Age 65	Age 70
18	$288,680	$395,675
19	270,870	371,634
20	254,097	348,994
25	183,793	254,097
30	131,710	183,793
35	93,125	131,710
40	64,540	93,125

FIGURE 27–8 This table shows what an IRA could earn based on a $1,000 annual contribution at 6 percent compounded daily.

Opening an IRA

Companies that offer IRAs include banks, savings and loan associations, insurance companies, stockbrokers, credit unions, and mutual funds. To open an account, you only have to complete a simple application form and make an ini-

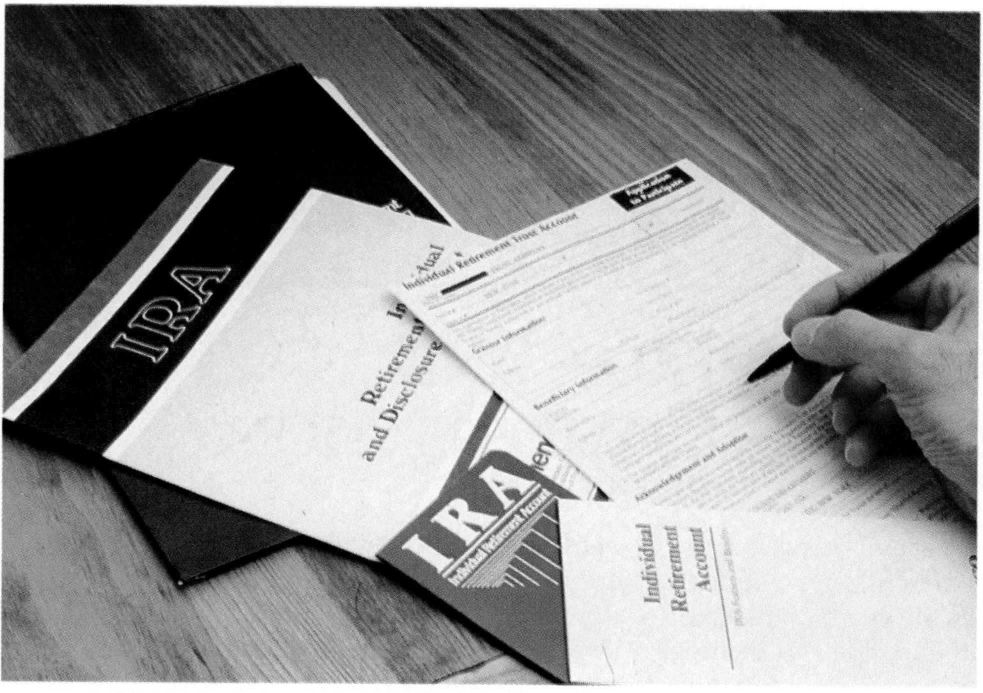

FIGURE 27–9 **Completing a simple form is all that is required to open an IRA account.**
Photo by Paul E. Meyers.

tial deposit. In most cases, you can make contributions to the account any time during the year and in any amount.

The type of investment you select is very flexible. You can use your contributions to purchase certificates of deposit, U.S. treasury securities, bonds, stocks, mutual funds, and many other types of investments. You may even purchase several different types of investments and build up a diversified account. Also, you are allowed to switch from one investment to the other as you wish.

? ? ? ? ? ? ? ? ? ? ? ? ? ? ?

WHAT WOULD YOU DO?

You work for a large company that employs hundreds of workers. Every several months, the personnel department conducts "brown-bag" lunches for interested employees on such topics as investing, tax planning, and the like. An announcement is included in your pay envelope indicating that a program on IRAs will be offered next week. You are supposed to mark and return the form if you are interested. You do not think you will go. You still have about forty years before retirement.

What would you do?

FOCUS ON

Health and Safety

JOB STRESS AND WORKERS' COMPENSATION

In the early 1900s, several states passed laws to provide benefits for workers injured on the job. Over the years, the idea of workers' compensation expanded to include all states, most occupations, and most job-related accidents and illnesses.

In 1955, workers' compensation took a new turn. Two men had been working on a scaffold when a rope broke. One fell to his death. The other was caught by the rope and dangled in the air until he was rescued. His most serious injury was a rope burn. But the guy was a psychological wreck. He was afraid to get on the scaffold ever again. So he filed a claim for workers' compensation. After a lengthy legal battle, Texas courts upheld an award for the man.

Since then, state courts have allowed compensation for three new categories of workers: (1) those who suffer a physical injury that leaves a psychological after-effect; (2) those who suffer mental trauma that leads to a physical ailment; and (3) those who suffer mental strain that leads to more serious mental problems. The last type is the most controversial. Here is an example.

The department in which an employee worked was eliminated. The employee transferred to another job. She developed chest pains and suffered an emotional breakdown. She quit working and filed a workers' compensation claim against the company. She argued that the job transfer caused her breakdown. Ultimately, the state supreme court awarded her payment of medical bills and two-thirds of her salary.

Job-stress cases such as this have mushroomed. Seven states, currently recognize everyday mental stress as grounds for workers' compensation benefits. But courts in nine states have rejected all such claims. This is likely to remain a hot issue for a long time to come.

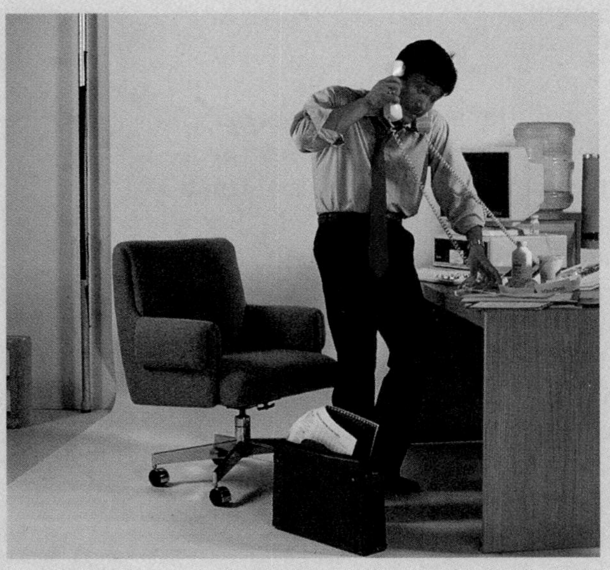

Experts on worker stress believe the computer age is causing workers mental strain.

Courtesy of Knight-Ridder Incorporated.

CHAPTER 27 REVIEW

CHAPTER IN BRIEF

- Government programs that help people meet social and economic needs are called social security. One form of social security is known as public assistance (or welfare). General taxes finance public assistance. The second form of social security is social insurance. It is financed by taxes on earnings paid by workers and employers.
- The four social insurance programs (most people call them social security) administered by the federal government are: retirement payments, survivors payments, disability payments, and Medicare. The two types of state-administered social insurance programs are unemployment benefits and workers' compensation.
- To be eligible for federal social security benefits, you must earn a certain amount of work credit in jobs covered by social security. Work credit is measured in quarters of coverage. A fully insured worker has earned forty quarters of coverage. He or she is eligible to receive complete benefits.
- The four federal social security programs are financed by payroll taxes on earnings. Currently, the tax rate is 7.65 percent on a wage base of $60,600. Your employer contributes an amount equal to what you pay. State-administered employment security programs are financed through taxes paid by employers only.
- Anyone who earns income from working and is under age 70½ can open an Individual Retirement Account (IRA). You are eligible to put up to $2,000 a year into an IRA. An IRA can provide two big tax benefits. First, IRA contributions can be deducted from income taxes. (Restrictions apply to people earning more than a certain amount.) Second, interest and other earnings in an IRA are not taxed until they are withdrawn. An IRA started at an early age can compound to a large amount of money prior to retirement.

WORDS TO KNOW

benefits
Federal Insurance Contributions Act (FICA)
Individual Retirement Account (IRA)
lump-sum payment
pension
quarters of coverage
social security
wage base
work credit

QUESTIONS TO ANSWER

1. There are two forms of social security. Name them.
2. List and briefly describe the six major types of social insurance programs.

3. How long must you be disabled in order to receive social security disability payments?
4. Name the two types of Medicare insurance. Which type is not automatically provided to eligible workers?
5. How many quarters of coverage are required to be a fully insured worker? A currently insured worker?
6. How is federal social security financed? How is state employment security financed?
7. What percentage of a worker's income is currently withheld for FICA tax? What is the wage base?
8. How much can a single worker contribute annually to an IRA? A married couple in which both work? A married couple in which only one works?
9. What are the two tax benefits of having an IRA?
10. IRA contributions are tax deferred, not tax free. Explain what this means.

ACTIVITIES TO DO

1. Have you ever worked at a job in which FICA tax was withheld from your paycheck? If so, prepare a list of all such jobs and the length of time you were employed in each. Then, figure out how much work credit (quarters of coverage) you have accumulated to date. Compare your results with those of your classmates.
2. Go to your local social security office and pick up several "Request for Statement of Earnings" forms. Complete and mail one of the forms. If you have not worked at a job covered by social security, fill out copies of the form for one of your family members.
3. Last year, Shirley Jefferson earned $26,700. The FICA tax rate was 7.65 percent. How much money was withheld for social security from Ms. Jefferson's income? What was the total amount paid by Ms. Jefferson and her employer last year?
4. Assume that three single workers had taxable incomes of $17,000; $21,000; and $25,000, respectively. Each is planning to make a $2,000 contribution to an IRA. Using a current federal tax table, figure out how much tax each person will save. Now, figure out how much each $2,000 contribution "actually" costs each person.
5. Invite a banker or stockbroker to class to discuss IRAs. Ask him or her to explain the various kinds of investments that can be purchased with an IRA contribution.

TOPICS TO DISCUSS

1. Assuming they have no house or rent payment to make, about how much monthly income do you think a retired couple would need to live comfortably?
2. Why is inflation such a major concern for most retired people?
3. Some people would like to make federal social security optional. In other words, people could take the 7 percent or so withheld for FICA and invest it in their own retirement programs. Discuss the positive and negative aspects of such a change.

SECTION 6

INDEPENDENT LIVING

The nature of law and the two main types of law, civil and public, are dealt with in Chapter 28. The general process by which laws are enforced and how court works are summarized. Guidelines for choosing and working with a lawyer are also provided.

In Chapter 29, different housing alternatives are examined. You will learn how to locate and evaluate an apartment. Understanding a lease and landlord-tenant relationships are also covered.

Healthful living is related to your productivity and success in work and life. There are three aspects of healthful living: nutrition and diet, controlling stress, and physical fitness. These are explained in Chapter 30.

The responsibilities of citizenship and the importance of voting are discussed in Chapter 31. Registering to vote and casting a ballot are summarized. Distinguishing among rumor, opinion, prejudice, allegation, bias, propaganda, and fact when choosing a candidate or a position on an issue is discussed.

Will your education end upon graduation from high school? Additional education and training will be one of the best investments you can make in your future. Chapter 32 explains the six most common types of education and training: on-the-job training, apprenticeship, vocational and technical schools, community and junior colleges, colleges and universities, and military training. Sources of educational information and financial aid are included.

Co-op Career SPOTLIGHT ON

James McAndrews, *Automobile Dealership Co-Owner*

"My goal was always to own whatever business I was in. When I was in high school I wanted to own a McDonald's restaurant," says 29-year-old Jim McAndrews. Jim is now co-owner of a large automobile dealership in Arlington, Texas, only 11 years after graduating from Sam Houston High School.

Jim plans to own this dealership eventually, become a millionaire, retire at 50, and play with his grandchildren. Jim says his family and the lessons he learned in co-op have given him the confidence to set high goals. His career shows that he is reaching these goals because he knows what he wants, works very hard to achieve it, and never gives up.

He began working toward his goals at age 15. It was then that he began dating his wife, Kelly, and got a part-time job at a local McDonald's as a cook. During high school, while he was a co-op student, he worked up to manager of the store by the time he was a senior. In his junior and senior years, he also owned a landscaping and sprinkling business. His clients were the 28 McDonald's stores in the Arlington area.

Jim married Kelly when they graduated from high school, but he had a hard time getting the right job. He wanted to make a career at McDonald's and eventually own his own store, but he quit because a McDonald's policy would not allow him to be promoted until he was 25 years old. After he quit and tried to get a job as an automobile salesperson, he was told again that he was too young. "I tried ten different dealerships, but no one would hire me because of my age and the fact that I looked 14," he said. He finally got his chance at the company he co-owns. He worked 70-hour weeks, selling cars for 2 years until he became sales manager at age 21 and moved up to general sales manager at age 24. Two years later, he became general manager and replaced the man who hired him.

Jim works so hard to succeed because he wants to have the family and financial security he did not have as a child. (He was raised by grandparents with little money.) He says his wife "standing beside him" and his co-op experience have helped him reach his goals.

"I feel the vocational work program instilled the work ethic in me. In my case I didn't have parents who showed concern, but the teachers showed a lot of interest in me and made me feel that I could accomplish something." He says the opportunity to speak in front of people in co-op activities also gave him confidence. Now he feels he can do anything.

"If co-op did anything, it instilled in me the belief that I can achieve anything in life that I want to. If I wanted to be president of the United States, I could be."

CHAPTER 28 The Legal System

OUTLINE

- The Nature of Law
- The Court System
- Legal Services
- Chapter Review

OBJECTIVES

After reading this chapter, you should be able to:

- Explain the difference between civil and public law.
- Describe the general process by which laws are enforced.
- Summarize how a court works.
- Identify situations that may require legal advice.
- Explain how to go about choosing a lawyer.
- Name the three types of legal fees.

Hopefully, you will never become involved with the legal system because of law-breaking. Even if you never break the law, though, you might sometime be accused of a crime that you did not commit. Or you may become an innocent victim of crime.

Not all law deals with crime. For example, Terry and Susan adopted a baby. To finalize the adoption, they had to hire a lawyer and appear before a judge in a law court.

Law, then, is concerned with many everyday matters, too. Understanding laws and the court system is an important part of informed citizenship. It is also necessary to know how to find legal help. It is good to learn this *before* needing such services.

FIGURE 28–1 **No person is above the law. In 1974, President Richard Nixon resigned from office rather than face an impeachment trial.**
Photo from National Portrait Gallery.

THE NATURE OF LAW

Law is the body of enforced rules by which people live together. If all people did as they pleased, society could not function. For example, what would happen if everyone drove an auto as fast as they wanted or an employer decided to ignore the safety rules? The law defines and makes clear the relationships among individuals and between individuals and society. Law tries to give as much freedom to each person as possible, while protecting the freedom of others. Current laws are developed from the long-established customs (unwritten rules) of a people. This is called common law.

FIGURE 28–2 **A dispute between a worker and an employer may involve civil or public law depending on the issue.**
Photo by Carol Lee/©Uniphoto, Inc.

Branches of the Law

The two main types of law are civil and public.

Civil Law. Sometimes called private law, civil law determines a person's legal rights and obligations in activities that involve other people. Examples include credit purchases, renting an apartment, and signing a job contract. Judges and lawyers spend most of their time on civil matters. Most civil law cases are settled out of court. Even so, more than a million lawsuits are tried yearly in U.S. courts.

Public Law. The purpose of public law is to define citizens' rights and responsibilities under local, state, federal, and international laws. Criminal law is the most familiar kind of public law. Public law also deals with different divisions of government and their powers. An example of public law is the requirement that all cars have seat belts. Workers' wages and hours and public safety also come under public law.

Law Enforcement

Most of us obey laws. But what about people who do not? The police may arrest anyone they see violating the law. They may also arrest someone they reasonably believe has committed a crime. In some cases, a court order called a *warrant* is required before a police officer can make an arrest.

After the suspect has been arrested, a charge is entered in the arrest book. The criminal evidence is then turned over to a government attorney or prosecutor. An *arraignment* (hearing) is then held before a judge. During the arraignment, charges are brought against the arrested person. This is called an *indictment.* The person being held can answer the charges. If the individual pleads guilty, the judge gives a sentence or sets a future date for sentencing.

If the accused pleads not guilty, a trial to determine guilt must be held. Rather than remain in jail until the trial, an individual is usually released on *bail.* This is a certain sum of money paid to the court to guarantee that the person will show up for trial. For certain serious crimes, someone may be held without bail. A person without bail money must remain in jail until the trial. If he or she cannot afford an attorney, the judge provides one.

The purpose of a trial is to decide the case. Attorneys for both sides present their evidence. A decision of guilty or not guilty is then made. If the defendant is found guilty, the judge imposes a sentence.

Criminal laws generally specify the minimum and maximum prison terms for which a criminal can be sentenced. Not everyone goes to jail, however. In certain cases, the judge may decide to release a person on *probation* instead. In such instances, the person must report regularly to a parole officer. For some crimes, the judge may impose a fine as part of the sentencing.

What to Do If Arrested

Any law enforcement person, such as a police officer, sheriff, state trooper, or game warden can make an arrest. What if a law enforcement officer wants to arrest or search you? Do not resist. Your guilt or innocence can be determined later. If the arrest is legal and you resist,

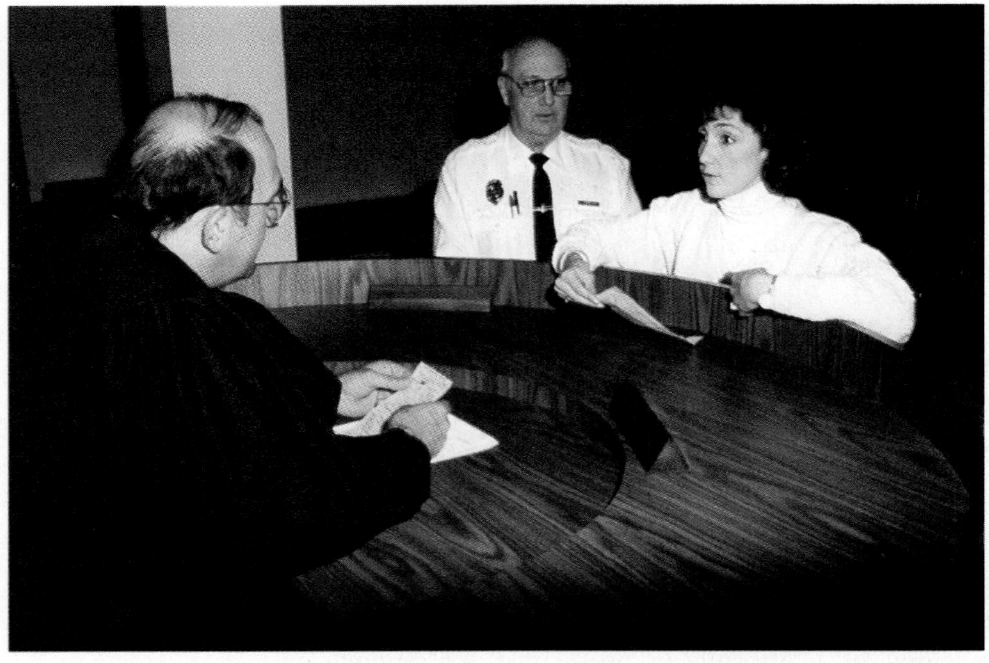

FIGURE 28–3 **People accused of a crime are guaranteed the right to present their case before a court of law. This person is disputing a speeding ticket.**
Courtesy of Police Department, Town of Colonie, NY.

you may be guilty of the crime of resisting arrest. If the arrest is illegal, you can bring an action for false arrest against the arresting officer.

Even if you are not arrested, an officer may stop you if he or she has reason to believe that you have committed or are about to commit a crime. The officer may ask your name and address and an explanation for your actions. You may be searched for weapons if the officer suspects you might attack.

WHAT WOULD YOU DO?

You go to answer the door. You open it and are surprised to find a police officer. It seems that a car like yours was seen last night leaving the scene of a gas station holdup. The officer wants you to come to the station to answer some questions.

What would you do?

THE COURT SYSTEM

A court is the branch of government having the power to settle disputes.

Courts are an essential part of government. Without courts to interpret them, laws would be meaningless. Although they differ in some ways, all courts decide civil disputes between individuals or other parties, determine the guilt or innocence of accused persons, and impose punishment on the guilty.

Types of Courts

The two types of U.S. court systems are state and federal.

State Courts. Each state has its own court system. The lowest or first courts are the magistrates' courts in cities and the justices of the peace in villages and rural communities. There may also be various special and municipal courts.

Above the magistrates' courts are general trial courts. These courts, also known as county or circuit courts, deal with civil and public matters.

Many states have appellate courts, which are between the general trial courts and the state supreme court. Appellate courts hear appeals from the trial courts. The highest appellate court in a state is usually called a supreme court. Several judges (usually five to seven) sit on a state supreme court.

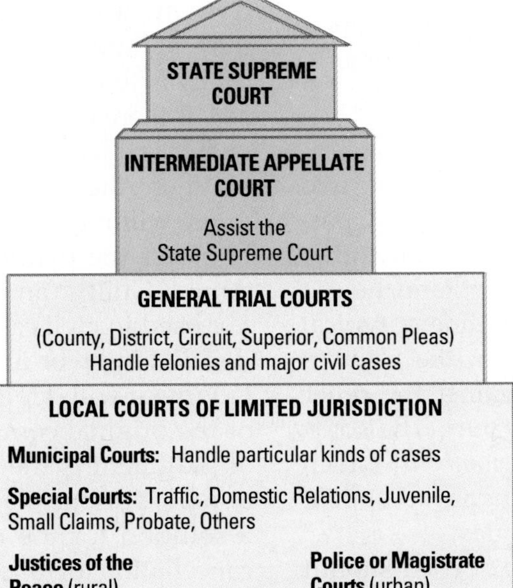

FIGURE 28–4 Although court systems vary from state to state, this pattern is typical.

Federal Courts. The United States Constitution provides for a federal court system. Federal courts handle cases involving the Constitution, violations of federal laws, and cases in which the U.S. government is a party.

The lowest courts of the federal system are the U.S. district courts. The trial of both civil and public cases begins in the district courts. The manner of arrest, indictment, trial, and appeal is very similar to that of state courts.

Above the trial level are the circuit courts of appeal. These courts operate about the same way as state appellate courts. A court of appeal is made up of three judges.

The highest federal court is the Supreme Court of the United States. This court is made up of nine justices (judges). It is presided over by one of them who is called the Chief Justice of the United States. Most cases the Supreme Court hears are appeals from the circuit courts and appeals from state supreme courts if they present federal questions.

FIGURE 28–5 **Serving on a jury is an important civic duty.**
Photo by © Billy E. Barnes/PhotoEdit.

How a Court Works

Disputes may arise between two or more persons over money, personal injury, property, or many other issues. To better understand how a court works, let's outline a typical civil case. One person (the *plaintiff*) files a complaint against the other (the *defendant*) in a court. The court clerk then issues a *summons,* which commands the defendant to appear in court on a certain day.

The defendant must then submit a written report that tells his or her side of the story. By comparing the two sides, the court can see where the difference of opinion lies. If grounds for a suit are present, the judge sets a trial date.

When the trial is held, attorneys for the plaintiff and defendant produce evidence to try to show the truth in the case. Part of the evidence may be supplied by other persons called witnesses. The judge, or the jury if there is one, decides questions of fact and reaches a verdict.

When the case is decided, the judge will make a *judgment* in favor of either the plaintiff or the defendant. ("Guilty" and "not guilty" are not used in civil cases.) If the case is decided in favor of the plaintiff, the judgment will depend on the nature of the original complaint. One type of judgment is the award of a sum of money to the plaintiff. Another is a solution for the dispute, such as cancellation of a contract. A third type of judgment is for the court to *decree* (order) the defendant to stop doing whatever he or she was doing that harmed the plaintiff.

? ? ? ? ? ? ? ? ? ? ? ? ? ? ?

WHAT WOULD YOU DO?

In sorting through the day's mail, you find a postcard addressed to you. It says that you have been chosen for jury duty. You are instructed to appear at the courthouse next Wednesday at 9:00 A.M. for possible jury selection. "I cannot go," you think to yourself. "I have to work."

What would you do?

LEGAL SERVICES

During your lifetime, you will probably face many legal problems. You may be able to resolve some of them yourself. If you cannot, you will need an attorney.

Deciding If You Need a Lawyer

Whether or not you need a lawyer depends on your situation. Following are some types of situations that may require legal advice:

1. Being charged with a crime.
2. Buying a house.
3. Starting a business.
4. Suffering accident or injury.
5. Buying a faulty consumer product or service.
6. Being discriminated against in employment.
7. Preparing a will.
8. Declaring bankruptcy.
9. Getting a divorce.

A lawyer is not absolutely necessary in all these cases. The more you learn about the law and legal services, the better able you will be to decide whether you need a lawyer.

Choosing a Lawyer

Lawyers, like doctors, are in either a general or specialized practice. Most lawyers are general practitioners who handle a variety of legal work. For most situations, a general attorney will be adequate. General lawyers who cannot handle a particular problem will usually refer clients to a specialist.

Choosing a lawyer is similar to selecting a doctor, banker, or other professional. Ask enough people and the same name may come up repeatedly. This is a good sign that you are on the right track.

In 1937, the American Bar Association established the Lawyer Referral Service (LRS). Its purpose is to

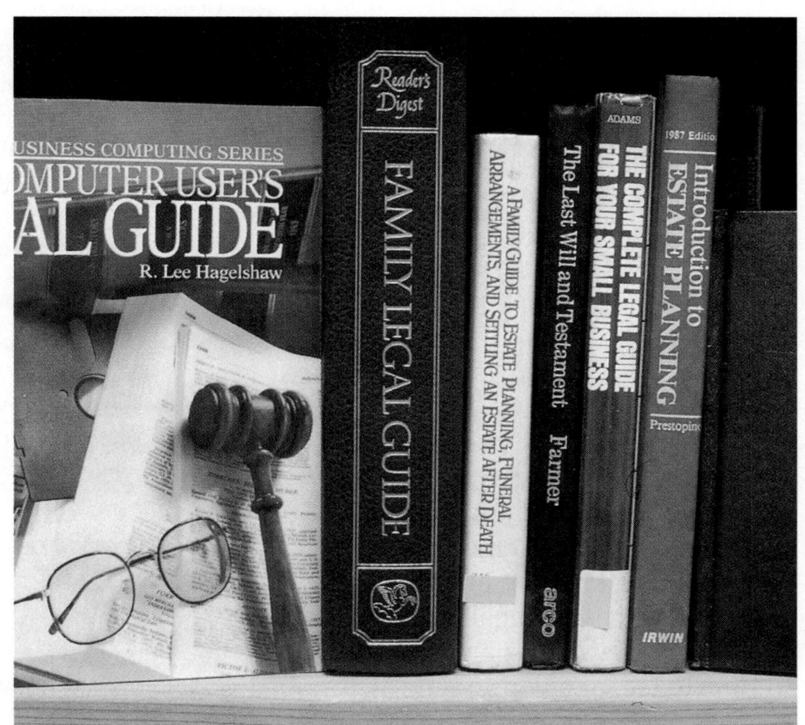

FIGURE 28–6 **People can solve their own legal problems with the help of how-to books, but sometimes the problems are too serious and a lawyer should be consulted.**
Photo by Paul E. Meyers.

help people obtain legal assistance at moderate costs.

In over 250 U.S. cities, the LRS is administered through the local bar association. You can contact the LRS by looking in your phone book's Yellow Pages under "Lawyer (or Attorney) Referral Service."

Another way to choose a lawyer is through advertising. In recent years, lawyers have been able to advertise their services, although few do so. If you read or hear an ad that you like, give the attorney a try. Many attorneys provide a free initial consultation. Before deciding on an attorney, it may be wise to meet with several different ones.

If you cannot afford a lawyer, you have several options. In a criminal case, the court will provide a lawyer for you. For civil cases, there are more than 800 free legal services and defender programs in the United States. You can find such agencies by looking up "Legal Aid" or "Legal Assistance" in the phone book. Another source is the *Directory of Legal Aid and Defender Services,* which is available in many libraries.

Legal Fees

The fees lawyers charge vary depending on the type of situation you have. Do not be afraid to ask about fees at your first meeting. You are entitled to know in advance the approximate cost of legal services.

Lawyers may charge a flat fee, an hourly fee, or a contingency fee. A *flat fee* often covers routine services that take about the same amount of time in all instances. Examples might be a real estate closing or an uncontested divorce. An *hourly fee* is a specific amount paid for each hour the lawyer spends on your case. Rates per hour may range from $50 to several hundred dollars.

The *contingency fee* is used for certain kinds of cases, such as personal injury or medical malpractice. It is called a contingency fee because you do not pay unless the case is won. If the attorney does win, you must pay a certain percentage of the amount awarded. A one-third contingency fee is common. For example, if you receive $15,000 in a legal judgment, the attorney will receive $5,000.

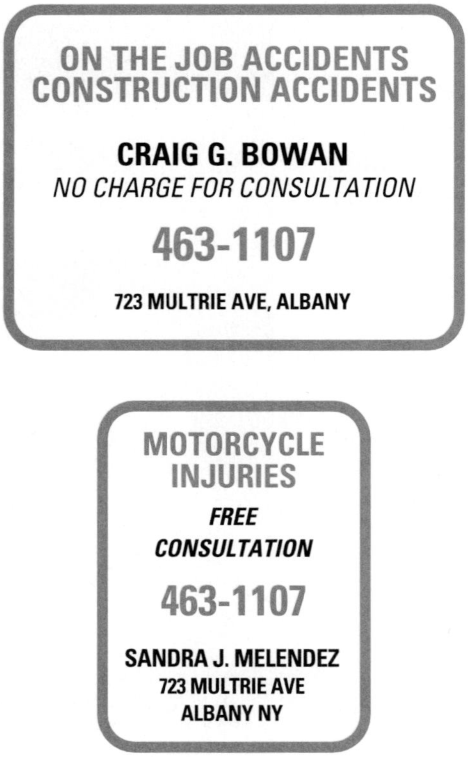

ON THE JOB ACCIDENTS
CONSTRUCTION ACCIDENTS

CRAIG G. BOWAN
NO CHARGE FOR CONSULTATION

463-1107

723 MULTRIE AVE, ALBANY

MOTORCYCLE
INJURIES

FREE
CONSULTATION

463-1107

SANDRA J. MELENDEZ
723 MULTRIE AVE
ALBANY NY

FIGURE 28–7 **More and more lawyers are advertising their services.**

Small Claims Courts

There may be times when you do not need a lawyer. Small claims courts, sometimes called people's courts, have been around since 1913. They allow you to sue someone without using an attorney. For example, let's say that you worked two days for Ms. Adams, a local businessperson, and she refuses to pay you. To get your money, you could file a claim in small claims court.

The amount of money that can be recovered in small claims court varies among states. Usually though, the amount is limited to several thousand dollars. You cannot sue for lost time or hurt pride and you cannot collect damages beyond your loss.

A small claims court is usually part of the general trial court in a county or city. To learn more about the court in your area, call the office of the county or city government.

FOCUS ON

Skills For Living

COMMON LAW

The system of law used in the United States is called *common law,* except in Louisiana where the Code Napoleon is followed. Common law originated in England as a way of settling disputes. The law at first was based on customs. But in the twelfth century, the king's courts began to take over settling disputes from the local customary courts.

The decisions of the king's justices were supposed to be based on customs. On occasion, there were no customs. The courts then had to reach a decision based upon logic and reason. As a result, a body of common law grew up from the judges' decisions.

The early colonists who settled America brought with them the practices of common law. After the American Revolution, the tradition of English common law continued. Over the years, American judges gradually changed the common law to make it more suitable for our society.

As new conditions arose, common law often did not apply. A new source for law emerged. This type of law is called statute law, or legislation. Statute law is that type of law made by Congress and state legislatures. In present society, legislation and judge-made law are equally important.

The U.S. legal system, except in the state of Louisiana, is patterned on English law, which evolved from the Middles Ages. This picture shows an English courtroom scene in the nineteenth century.
Photo from Stock Montage.

CHAPTER 28 REVIEW

CHAPTER IN BRIEF

- Law is the body of enforced rules by which people live together. The law defines and makes clear the relationships among individuals and between individuals and society. The two main types of law are civil law and public law.
- The police may arrest anyone they see violating the law or they reasonably believe has committed a crime. A charge is then entered into the arrest book. An arraignment is held and the arrested person is indicted. If the accused pleads not guilty, a trial is held. Evidence is presented at the trial and a decision is made regarding guilt. If the defendant is found guilty, the judge imposes a sentence.
- If a law enforcement officer wants to arrest or search you, do not resist. Your guilt or innocence can be determined later.
- A court is the branch of government having the power to settle disputes. All courts basically do the same three things: decide civil disputes between individuals or other parties, determine the guilt or innocence of accused persons, and impose punishment on the guilty. The two types of court systems are state and federal.
- In a typical civil case, the plaintiff files a complaint against the defendant in a court. A summons is issued for the defendant to appear in court. The defendant must then submit a written report of his or her story. If grounds for a suit are present, the judge sets a trial date. Attorneys for both sides present evidence at the trial. The judge (or jury) reaches a verdict. When the case is decided, the judge will make a judgment in favor of the plaintiff or the defendant.
- Someday, you will probably face a situation in which you will need an attorney. Choosing a lawyer is similar to selecting a doctor, banker, or other professional. The Lawyer Referral Service is available in over 250 cities to help people obtain legal assistance at moderate cost.
- The fees lawyers charge vary depending on the type of situation. They may charge a flat fee, an hourly fee, or a contingency fee. Do not be afraid to ask about fees at your first meeting.
- There may be times when you do not need a lawyer. Small claims courts are available to allow an individual to sue someone without using an attorney. A small claims court is usually part of the general trial court in a county or city.

WORDS TO KNOW

arraignment
bail
common law
decree
defendant
indictment

judgment
law
plaintiff
probation
summons
warrant

QUESTIONS TO ANSWER

1. Why do we have laws?
2. Name the two main branches of law. Give an example of each.
3. What happens if a person is arrested and cannot afford to hire an attorney?
4. If you are stopped by a police officer and arrested for a crime that you did not commit, how should you act?
5. What are the three basic things that courts do?
6. What is the name of the highest federal court in the United States? Who presides over this court?
7. In a court case, who does the prosecuting attorney represent? Who does the defense attorney represent?
8. Explain the purpose of the Lawyer Referral Service.
9. Name three methods of paying for legal services.
10. What is the purpose of a small claims court?

ACTIVITIES TO DO

1. The United States Supreme Court has a very important role in our society. With the help of your teacher, identify a recent Supreme Court decision. Investigate this decision and then give a short oral report to the class.
2. As a class, invite a department store manager to talk about the problem of shoplifting and how a shoplifter is dealt with.
3. Invite a member of SADD (Students Against Drunk Driving) to class. Talk with him or her about the legal issues surrounding drunken driving.
4. Find out the location of your nearest small claims court. Contact the clerk's office and obtain a copy of any written guidelines and forms regarding how to file a complaint. Discuss in class the types of situations that might be taken to small claims court.

TOPICS TO DISCUSS

1. How might you be influenced in the future by having a criminal record?
2. What is meant by the term *white collar crime?* Do you think white collar criminals should be treated differently than other criminals?
3. In what types of legal situations would you probably need a specialized lawyer (as opposed to a general lawyer)?
4. A great deal has been said and written about the United States being a "litigious-intensive society." This means that we have a tendency as a people to file too many lawsuits. Do you think this is true?

CHAPTER 29 Where to Live

OUTLINE

- Choosing a Type of Housing
- Rent or Buy?
- Apartment Hunting
- The Rental Agreement
- Landlord-Tenant Relationships
- Chapter Review

OBJECTIVES

After reading this chapter, you should be able to:

- Identify types of housing alternatives.
- Discuss advantages and disadvantages of renting and buying.
- Name and describe factors to consider in apartment hunting.
- Summarize items included in an apartment lease.
- Explain rights and responsibilities of a tenant.

Jack's life is changing very rapidly. In a few weeks, he will graduate from high school. He has accepted a job as a mechanic at Porter Tire and Auto. Although he does not mind living at home, he would like a place of his own.

At some point in your life, you will probably leave your parents' home. When that time comes, deciding where to live will become important to you. The choice is a difficult one that involves both personal and financial considerations. Young people who have never before lived away from home may not know what is involved in renting or buying their own place. They may also underestimate the total cost of a house or an apartment.

CHOOSING A TYPE OF HOUSING

If you decide to get a place of your own, housing will probably be the largest single expense in your budget. In many areas, rents and home prices are high and costs continue to increase. But cost is not the only problem. Many desirable communities have housing shortages.

Since housing is such a major expense, plan carefully. Begin by analyzing your needs and wants. Based on what you learn, you can then decide whether buying or renting is best for you.

Housing Needs and Wants

The "perfect" place to live may not be available or affordable. So it may be necessary to make some compromises that suit you and your budget. Nonetheless, it will be important to consider needs and wants in a place to live. Identify your needs and wants *before* you start looking.

FIGURE 29–1 Places to live differ a great deal in size, style, features, and price.
Left, courtesy of Jay Whitney.

It is a good idea to make a list of the features you think are essential or important in a place to live. That way you will not be attracted by some eye-catching feature that you do not really need or want. Know the difference between *essential* and *important.*

Rosanna is looking for an apartment. She does not want a long commute to work. For Rosanna, being near her office is essential. She also thinks having a garage is important. But if she found a place near the office that did not have a garage, Rosanna would probably rent it anyway.

Individuals and families differ greatly in how they feel about housing. For some people, a house or apartment is simply a place to stay. For others, their lifestyles, hobbies, and goals revolve around their home.

Housing Alternatives

Different types of housing are available. One alternative is the single-family detached house. This kind of house usually offers more space, a larger yard, and more privacy than other types of housing. Also, many people consider a house the most convenient and desirable place to raise children. A detached house is often the most expensive type of housing.

Attached houses, also called *townhouses,* are common in some communities. This kind of housing often includes a small yard. The houses may also share common properties such as a pool, tennis courts, and other extras.

Housing is also available in apartments. These may range in size from one room to many rooms. An apartment usually does not include a yard. A townhouse or

FIGURE 29–2 **Some apartments have recreation facilities, such as swimming pools, to attract renters.**

apartment may also be called a *cooperative* (a share of an apartment building complex) or *condominium* (ownership of a specific unit).

Still another housing alternative is a mobile home. Mobile homes may have several rooms. They are usually located on small lots in mobile home parks in or near a city or a town.

RENT OR BUY?

To get the type of housing that you or your family needs and wants, should you rent or buy? Now that you have analyzed your needs and wants and considered the types of housing available, give some serious thought to this question.

Buying and renting have advantages and disadvantages. In deciding which is best for you, you will want to consider various factors. These include the number and ages of the people in your family, your financial situation, your lifestyle, and the housing alternatives available in your community. Remember that buying generally means making a down payment and then paying a mortgage every month for fifteen to thirty years.

Renting

Some advantages of renting are:

- Rent is usually a fixed amount for the term of the lease. Renters face no unexpected costs.
- Renting only obligates you for the length of the lease. If you want to move, you can make other arrangements when the lease expires.

- Renters have limited responsibility. You are not responsible for taxes and repairs.
- Overall expenditures for renters are usually lower than those for buyers.
- If a job opportunity in another city comes along, it is easier to move if you are renting.
- When you are new to an area, renting gives you an opportunity to learn about the community. After you have been there for a while, you may decide to move somewhere else.
- When future housing needs are uncertain, you can postpone a decision by renting.

Renting may involve different costs and responsibilities depending on what you rent. If you rent a detached house, you will probably have to pay not only the rent, but also all the normal expenses for running a home. You will probably also be responsible for all maintenance tasks and repairs. Likewise, if you rent a townhouse, you will probably have some maintenance and repair responsibilities.

If you rent an apartment, you will generally not be responsible for maintenance or repairs. These will be provided by the landlord. Also, if you do not want to buy furniture, you can find apartments where the major pieces are provided. For all these reasons, renting an apartment is probably the most common choice of young people who are living away from home for the first time.

Buying

Some of the advantages of buying a home are:

- Spending money to buy a home is a fairly safe form of investment. Unlike most investments, a home can be used.
- During inflationary times, property values rise. If you have a mortgage loan, you will be paying it off with cheaper dollars.
- Owning your home saves money on income taxes through deductions for mortgage interest and real estate taxes.
- The *equity,* or money invested in a home, can be used as security for a loan.
- Home ownership can improve your credit rating.
- When you own your own home, you can decorate the way you wish. You may also make structural or landscaping alterations. These alterations sometimes increase the value of the property.

Buying involves different costs and levels of responsibility depending on what you buy. When you buy a house, you pay not only the mortgage, but also all expenses for home operation, upkeep, and repairs. Maintenance and repair work are also your responsibility.

When you buy a cooperative or a condominium, you are sharing with others the responsibilities, obligations, and maintenance costs. Very often, cooperative and condominium owners form a homeowners association or a maintenance association. Monthly fees are paid to the association. The money is then used to provide for maintenance and improvements to common properties such as grounds, tennis courts, and other areas. A maintenance fee may add considerably to the cost of owning a cooperative or condominium.

Mobile homes are much less expensive to buy than houses. Mobile homes allow more people to enjoy the benefits of home ownership. However, mobile homes do not increase in value as much over time as houses and apartments generally do. Mobile homes may also be unsafe in storms and high winds.

? ? ? ? ? ? ? ? ? ? ? ? ? ?

WHAT WOULD YOU DO?

You want to get an apartment closer to work, but have not located anything you can afford. You get a call one evening from a person who works at an office near yours. She heard from a mutual acquaintance that you were looking for an apartment. The caller's roommate has left and she is looking for someone to move in and share expenses. You write down the information and indicate that you will think it over. You are uneasy about the idea of sharing an apartment with someone you do not know.

What would you do?

APARTMENT HUNTING

Let's assume you have decided to rent an apartment. Available rental housing is often listed with a real estate agency or an apartment-finding business that charges fees for their services. More often, people find an apartment by checking the newspaper classified ads, by following through on tips from friends or co-workers, or by just walking or driving through a particular neighborhood. College students can often find an apartment through the school's housing office.

Things to Consider

Suppose you and a friend are looking for separate places at the same time. What you consider important in a rental may not be important to your friend. But both of you will need to be concerned about certain things.

Location. The neighborhood in which an apartment is located is important. However, the location is usually not as critical to a renter as it is to a home buyer. Renters have no financial investment in the property. So their interest is limited more to convenience factors. Depending on the person, finding an apartment that is near work or school, has

FIGURE 29–3 A college dorm room is often a person's first experience living away from home.
Courtesy of SIUC Photocommunications.

nearby shopping, and is accessible to public transportation may be important.

Safety. Because of the nature of apartment living, you should pay careful attention to several things. The first one is safety. Well-lighted and uncluttered entrances, hallways, and stairways contribute to security. A locked outside entrance is another good feature. Apartment doors should be securely constructed and contain deadbolt or other types of strong locks. Basement or first-floor apartments should have special window grills or locking features in addition to the regular window latches.

Another aspect of safety is fire protection. Each apartment should have one or more fire alarms in good working order. The kitchen area ought to have a fire extinguisher available. (*Buy one yourself if it doesn't.*) Check to see if the apartment has an external fire-escape exit. If not, is there an evacuation plan to follow in case of fire?

Privacy and Noise. Find out what type of people currently live in the building. If possible, meet and talk with some of the tenants. Remember that you may be sharing a relatively small area with dozens or even hundreds of other people.

Since apartment residents live closely together, noise can be a real problem. Noise can come either from outside streets and parking lots, or from within other apartments. Buildings should be soundproofed to dampen the sounds of talking, plumbing, and music between apartments and between hallways and apartments. Noises from apartments above are usually more noticeable than sounds from apartments below.

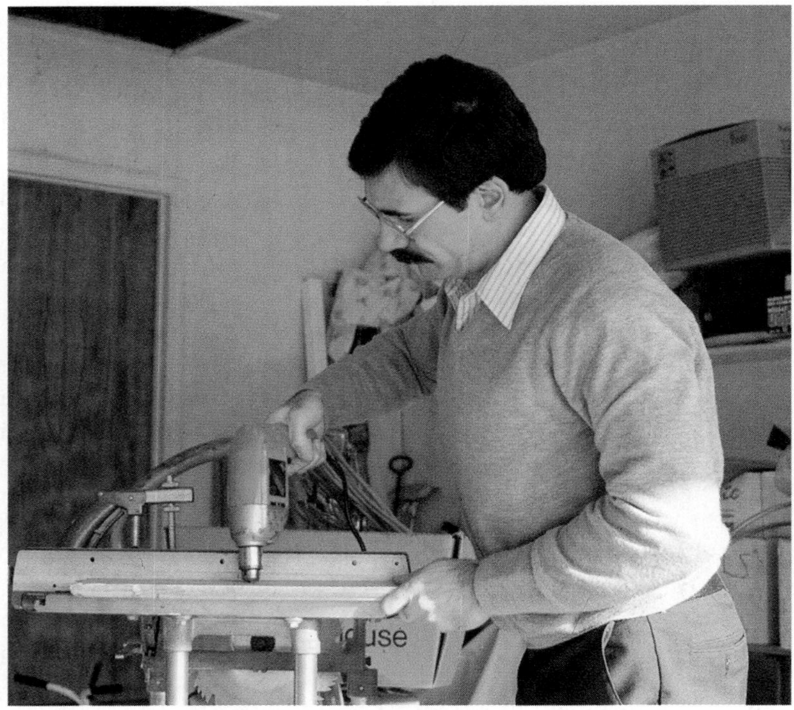

FIGURE 29–4 **If you live in an apartment, be considerate of the rights and comfort of people living in other apartments. One way is not to make loud noises very early in the morning or late at night.**
Photo by Paul E. Meyers.

Scott and Sandy Foster, for instance, have an upstairs neighbor who works from 3:30 to midnight. He usually wakes them up about 12:20 A.M. when he gets home and opens the apartment door. A few minutes later, he is heard taking a shower. Off and on throughout the night, Scott and Sandy are awakened by sounds of footsteps, closing doors, music, and so on. Their neighbor is not unusually loud or inconsiderate. He just happens to live a different lifestyle than they do. This is not an unusual situation for apartment dwellers.

Ventilation. Can air enter easily? Most apartments that have air conditioning are well ventilated. In places without this feature, cooking odors and stagnant air may be problems. Does the stove have an exhaust fan for ventilating the kitchen? Is the number of windows adequate, and do they all open easily? Besides permitting good air circulation, windows provide natural light that adds to a place's cheerfulness.

Other Considerations. Check appliances such as refrigerators, stoves, and dishwashers. Do they work well? Be sure you know who pays for utilities. Is the electricity your responsibility? How about heat? Can you give other examples? Ask for an estimate of typical costs for utilities and other services for which you will be responsible.

You probably have friends or relatives who live in apartments. If so, ask them to describe how they found their living quarters. Also, find out if they have any advice to share about what to look for.

FIGURE 29–5 **Do not rent an apartment unless you inspect it first.**

How to Approach a Landlord

Looking for a place to live is a great deal like getting a job. As with a potential employer, it is important to make a good impression on the *landlord* or apartment manager. Apply for an apartment in person and be courteous and friendly.

Most landlords will ask you to fill out an application. The landlord is interested in checking your past rental record and credit references. Fill out the application form completely and honestly without blank spaces.

Some landlords will charge an application fee. Before you pay such a fee, ask if you will get it back. Also find out if you must rent the unit if your application is accepted. Be sure you know when you will be notified of the landlord's decision.

THE RENTAL AGREEMENT

Most apartments are rented according to an agreement called a *lease.* This is a written legal contract between you and the landlord. For agreeing to pay rent and following the leases's rules, you are allowed to rent the apartment. The lease is often a preprinted form that contains most or all of the following parts and rules:

- The names of the landlord and *tenant* (renter).
- The address of the property.
- The beginning and ending dates of occupancy.
- The amount of rent and when and where it is to be paid for the term of the lease.
- The amount of the security deposit. If the renter obeys the lease, the money is to be refunded after the lease ends.
- Limits on the number of renters. Any rules against pets should be made clear also.
- Responsibilities for normal maintenance and repairs. The renter must repair any damage caused by carelessness.
- Responsibilities for electricity, trash pickup, and the like.
- (For furnished places) An attachment that shows an inventory of the items and their condition.
- Sublease permission. Suppose a renter needs to move before the lease is up. Can he or she rent it out (*sublet*)?
- When the landlord can enter the apartment. The lease should explain such conditions.
- The procedures to be followed when the tenant wishes to end the lease. An automatic renewal clause may also be a part of the lease.

Any special arrangements between you and the landlord should be written into the lease.

? ? ? ? ? ? ? ? ? ? ? ? ? ? ?

WHAT WOULD YOU DO?

You come home from work to discover the landlord leaving your apartment. He seems surprised and says that he was checking on the furnace. Several times over the next month, you notice little things that suggest someone has been in the apartment. You are aware that the landlord has the right to enter your apartment for emergencies, maintenance, and the like. But you are upset by the thought that he may be in the apartment for other reasons.

What would you do?

Read the lease very carefully before signing it. When you put your name on a lease, you say that you understand and accept all conditions contained in it. Make sure you are provided with a signed copy of the agreement.

LANDLORD-TENANT RELATIONSHIPS

The relationship between you and a landlord is a legal one. Both of you have certain rights and responsibilities.

Rights and Responsibilities of Landlords

The landlord has the right to set reasonable rules and regulations for the management of the rental units. Unless you have agreed to repair or maintain the property, the landlord must keep the place in reasonable repair. This means the landlord must keep the premises in a clean, safe condition.

Rights and Responsibilities of Tenants

Your rights as a tenant are essentially the reverse of the landlord's responsibilities. You pay rent for housing and you expect to receive a safe and livable apartment. If something goes wrong, it should be repaired in a reasonable amount of time. You are entitled to peace, quiet, and privacy. You should not be cheated, or overcharged.

On the other hand, you have the responsibility to follow the rules in the lease. These basically deal with paying the rent on time, keeping your area clean and safe, and not abusing the landlord's property or the rights of other tenants.

Beyond your responsibilities as a tenant, try to maintain a proper business relationship with the landlord. Report all problems as they occur. The landlord will appreciate knowing this information as soon as possible. In addition, have in writing all communication with the landlord and make copies of everything. The landlord is used to dealing with people on a businesslike basis, and will appreciate this behavior.

A landlord-tenant relationship is like any other personal or business association. For the relationship to work, both parties must fulfill their obligations. Do your part by understanding your obligations and then carrying them out.

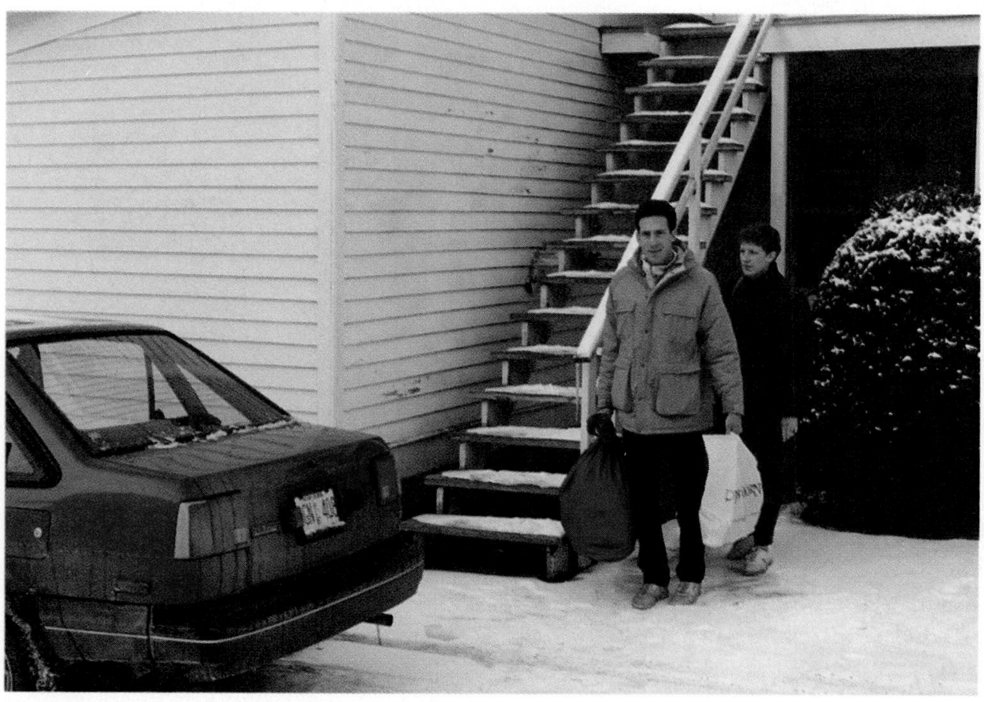

FIGURE 29–6 If you leave your apartment for a few days, it is a good idea to tell the landlord and leave a number where you can be reached in case of emergency.
Photo by Paul E. Meyers.

FOCUS ON

Skills For Living

Dealing with a Roommate

Most people have a roommate at one or more times in their lives.

Living with a roommate is a business relationship because money is exchanged. But it is also an emotional relationship.

Before choosing or becoming a roommate, you should have a serious discussion with the other person. Items you will need to agree on in advance include: housework and laundry; food and beverage supplies; overnight guests; the security deposit and how it will be refunded; pets (and who takes care of them); smoking; boy or girl friends; and stereos and musical instruments. Particularly important are the terms for moving out. It is a good idea to have an agreement to give each other a thirty- or sixty-day notice. Without any prearranged agreements, a nonleaseholding roommate does not have much in the way of rights.

Here is how one group of four roommates have been able to get along. Each person signs a separate form outlining all the financial responsibilities involved and what will be shared. Each person contributes a fixed amount each week for household staples such as milk, toothpaste, garbage bags, and newspaper. Each person takes turns going out to buy what is needed. Apart from this, they buy their own food and do their own dishes. They occasionally cook a meal together for a holiday dinner or other special event.

Utility bills are divided equally. Each roommate has a separate phone and no one answers anyone else's phone. Every two weeks, the group meets to discuss any problems.

Sharing living space can be difficult. But many roommate crises can be easily prevented or resolved. Set ground rules from the start. Discuss your feelings and expectations with your roommate. And always be willing to negotiate and compromise.

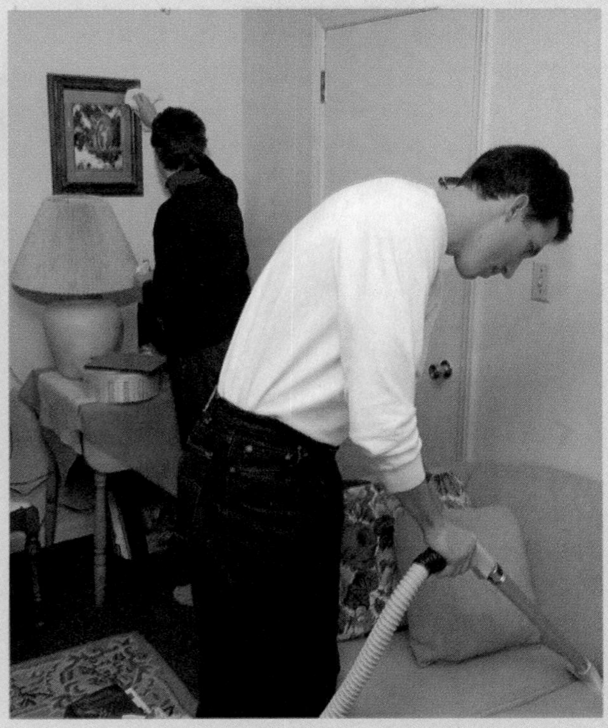

When you live with a roommate, be prepared to share chores in addition to other living experiences.
Photo by Paul E. Meyers.

CHAPTER 29 REVIEW

CHAPTER IN BRIEF

- At some point in your life, you will probably move from your parents' home. When that time comes, deciding where to live will become important to you. The choice is a difficult one that involves both personal and financial considerations.
- Since housing is such a major expense, plan carefully. Begin by analyzing your needs and wants. It will probably be necessary to make compromises that suit you and your budget. Your housing alternatives may include a detached house, townhouse, apartment, or mobile home.
- Buying and renting have advantages and disadvantages. Become familiar with these. Renting an apartment is probably the most common choice of young people who are living away from home for the first time.
- When hunting for an apartment, you need to be concerned with certain things such as type and location of neighborhood, personal safety and fire protection, privacy and noise, ventilation, furnishings available, and so on. Looking for a place to live is a great deal like getting a job. It is important to make a good impression on the landlord or apartment manager.
- Most apartments are rented according to an agreement called a lease. It is a written legal contract between you and the landlord. Know what to expect in a lease. Read it carefully before signing.
- You and the landlord have certain legal rights and responsibilities. Your rights as a tenant are to receive a safe and livable apartment. You are entitled to peace, quiet, privacy, and fair treatment. You also have the responsibility to follow the rules in the lease. Deal with the landlord in a businesslike manner.

WORDS TO KNOW

condominium
cooperative
equity
landlord
lease
sublet
tenant
townhouse

QUESTIONS TO ANSWER

1. What is the first step in deciding where to live? Why is this important?
2. What are the four major types of housing alternatives?
3. There are reasons for renting and buying housing. Name three of each.
4. In what three ways do most people locate an apartment?

5. What two types of fire protection devices should you look for in an apartment?
6. Explain how renting an apartment is similar to getting a job.
7. What is the purpose of a security deposit? Do you think it is fair to require one?
8. If a furnished apartment is rented, what should be attached to the lease?
9. What is the landlord's basic responsibility? The tenant's basic responsibility?
10. In what way is the landlord-tenant relationship like any other association?

ACTIVITIES TO DO

1. Assume you are going to move to a nearby town in a few months to begin a new job. A friend who works for the same company is also moving. The two of you decide to share a place to live. Prepare a list of what you need and want in housing. Turn the list in to your instructor. Then discuss this subject in class.
2. As a class, invite a landlord or apartment manager to visit and discuss landlord-tenant relationships. Prepare well. You may want to begin by asking the person what he or she looks for in a person who comes to rent an apartment.
3. Check local classified ads to find out the cost of renting in your area.
4. Find out if your state or city has a tenancy law, tenant ordinance, or housing code (not building code). What is the warranty of habitability? Can a tenant be evicted from an apartment? How may a tenant resolve complaints with a landlord?

TOPICS TO DISCUSS

1. Sharing an apartment with others is a good way to economize on housing. However, living with roommates can be difficult at times. What do you think might be the most common problems with roommates? How can they be avoided?
2. Does your community have a neighborhood watch, neighborhood patrol, or other type of citizen-oriented crime prevention program? Discuss how such programs operate.
3. The price and availability of housing is often an important factor in the decision to accept a first job or to relocate in another job. Discuss and provide illustrations of this.

CHAPTER 30 Healthful Living

OUTLINE

- Nutrition and Diet
- Stress and Its Control
- Physical Fitness
- Chapter Review

OBJECTIVES

After reading this chapter, you should be able to:

- Describe how the Food Guide Pyramid is used in choosing a healthful diet.
- Identify your own recommended weight and daily calorie needs.
- Name and illustrate the three major ways to reduce or eliminate stress.
- Discuss benefits of physical exercise.
- Name and describe the three types of exercises that should be included in a workout.

Sherri had not been feeling well for a long time. Her appetite was poor and she always seemed tired. She was spending a great deal of time in her room and had little interest in going out with her friends. She had frequent headaches. Sherri's parents became very concerned and took her to the doctor for a checkup.

After a complete exam and several tests, Dr. Williams sat down with Sherri to explain the results. "Well, Sherri," said the Doctor, "I don't find any major problems. But I don't think you're in very good health."

The doctor's statement confused Sherri. Dr. Williams then explained to Sherri that being

FIGURE 30–1 **Healthy people of any age are ones who have good eating habits, exercise regularly, and engage in activities with other people that are fun and relaxing.**
Photo by © Carl Yarbrough/Uniphoto.

healthy means more than just being free from illness or disease. Good health involves a person's overall physical and mental well-being.

Dr. Williams told Sherri that achieving and maintaining good health depends on nutrition and diet, stress control, and exercise. In this chapter, you will read about what Sherri learned from her doctor. Good health is related to your success and productivity at school and on the job.

NUTRITION AND DIET

Nutrition is the process by which plants and animals take in and use food. What we eat provides certain chemical substances needed for good health. These substances, called *nutrients,* serve as fuel to provide energy, help regulate body processes, and furnish basic materials for building, repairing, or maintaining body tissues.

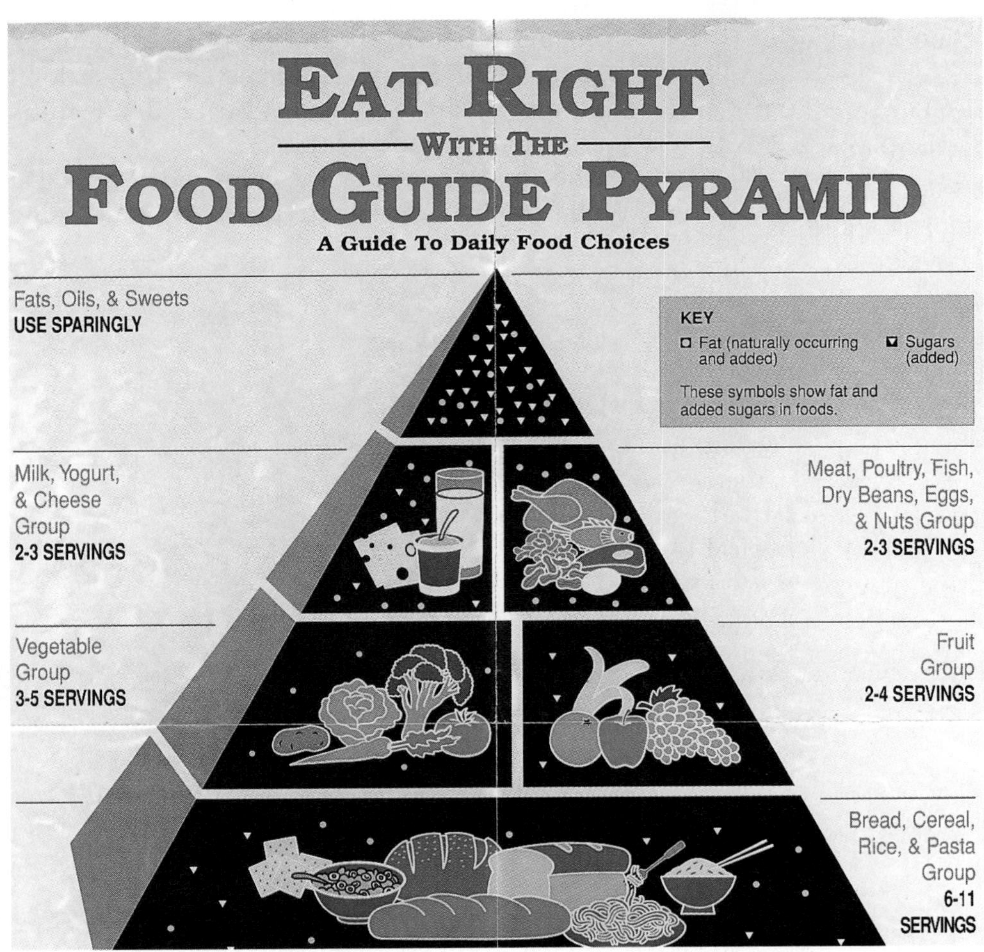

FIGURE 30–2 How closely does the food you eat daily follow this food guide?
Source: United States Department of Agriculture.

Daily Food Guide

Nutrients are supplied by foods that people eat. Foods vary in the kinds and amount of nutrients they contain. Nutrition scientists have developed the easy-to-use daily food guide shown in Figure 30–2. The Food Guide Pyramid emphasizes foods from the five major food groups shown in the three lower sections. Each of these food groups provide some, but not all, of the nutrients you need. Foods in one group cannot replace those in another. No one food group is more important than another. You need them all for good health.

At the base of the Pyramid are foods from grain. You need the most servings of these foods each day. The second level includes foods that come from plants. Most people need to eat more of these foods for the vitamins, minerals, and fiber they supply. On the third level are two groups of foods that come mostly from animals. These foods are important for protein, calcium, iron, and zinc.

The small tip of the Pyramid shows fats, oils, and sweets. These are foods such as salad dressings and oils, cream, butter, margarine, sugars, soft drinks, candies, and sweet desserts. These foods provide calories and little else nutritionally. Most people should use them sparingly.

Energy Requirements

Calories are units of food energy needed for continuous body functions such as breathing and heart rate. To carry out work and leisure activities, we all need calories. How many calories you need depends on your age, sex, size, and how active you are. The National Academy of Sciences has suggested the following approximate calorie levels: *1,600* calories for many *sedentary* women and some older adults; *2,200* calories for most children, teenage girls, active women, and many sedentary men, and *2,800* calories for teenage boys, many active men, and some very active women.

Now, let's look at the Food Guide Pyramid again. Note that a range of servings is shown for each food group. The number of servings that are right for you depends on your calorie level (low, medium, high). For example, an older adult needs 3 servings from the vegetable group; a teenage girl 4 servings; and a teenage boy 5 servings.

When the foods you eat provide more energy than you need to meet the demands of the body, your body stores the extra energy as fat. If you regularly eat too much food, you gain weight. On the other hand, if your energy level requires more calories than you take in, the body uses stored fat. You then lose weight.

Ideal weight varies among individuals. You can get an idea of your desirable weight from the table shown in Figure 30–3. For example, if you are a six-foot tall male, your ideal weight should be between 145 and 182 pounds. The range takes into account that there are small, average, and large body frames.

The number of calories used by the body each day to maintain weight is called the daily calorie need. Part of this is for continuous body functioning called *basal metabolism.* The remainder is used by the body as it carries out various work and leisure activities.

DESIRABLE BODY WEIGHT RANGES		
Height without shoes	Weight without clothes	
	Men (pounds)	Women (pounds)
4'10"		92-121
4'11"		95-124
5'0"		98-127
5'1"	105-134	101-130
5'2"	108-137	104-134
5'3"	111-141	107-138
5'4"	114-145	110-142
5'5"	117-149	114-146
5'6"	121-154	118-150
5'7"	125-159	122-154
5'8"	129-163	126-159
5'9"	133-167	130-164
5'10"	137-172	134-169
5'11"	141-177	
6'0"	145-182	
6'1"	149-187	
6'2"	153-192	
6'3"	157-197	
Note: For women 18-25 years, subtract one pound for each year under 25.		

FIGURE 30–3 Recommended weights for young adults.
Source: USDA.

FIGURE 30–4 Food can be tasty and still be nutritious and low in calories.
Photo by Alan Brown/Photonics.

Controlling Weight

For good health, it is wise to maintain your recommended weight. Do this by controlling the amount of food intake (calories) or level of activity, or both. To maintain the same body weight, the amount of calories eaten must balance the amount of calories used. To lose weight, you need to take in (or use up through exercise) fewer calories than your body needs. To gain weight, extra calories must be consumed. For each pound you want to gain or lose, you must take in about 3,500 calories more or less than the body uses.

If you are interested in gaining or losing weight, the first step is to learn about the number of calories that various foods contain. Charts showing the calorie values of common foods appear in most cookbooks. If you cannot find a calorie chart on your own, your public librarian can help you.

If you are trying to gain or lose weight, remember that you still need proper nutrients. Even though the number of calories may vary, you need the appropriate number of servings from each level of the Food Guide Pyramid. It is a good idea never to go below 1,200 calories a day. By taking in less than that, you probably will not get the vitamins and minerals you need.

STRESS AND ITS CONTROL

Stress, an unavoidable part of life, is a response the body makes to any demand made upon it. Causes of stress, called *stressors,* may be physical, biological, or emotional; they may be good or bad; and they may range from mild to severe. Following are the most common causes of stress:

- Daily activities, events, frustrations, and challenges cause stress. Examples might include missing a bus to school, giving a speech, taking a test, overcooking dinner, or going out on a blind date.

??????????????

WHAT WOULD YOU DO?

It seems like you are always on a diet. You do not eat much, but still cannot lose weight. For instance, all that you have had today is a couple of donuts for breakfast and an order of french fries and a soft drink for lunch. You guess that you will just have to get used to dieting continually.

What would you do?

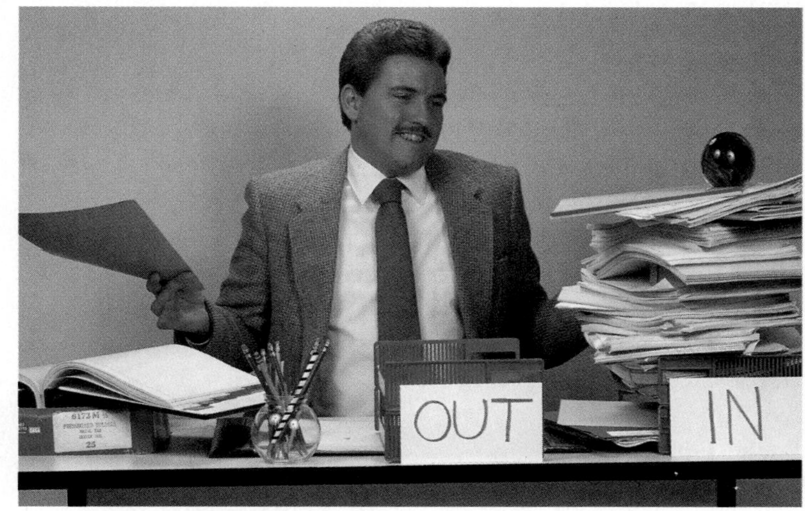

FIGURE 30–5 **Stress is a normal part of life. Healthy people recognize this fact and learn to handle it so stress does not harm them.**

- Illness adds to stress because it forces the body to use its defenses. Stress also results when the body must heal an injury or adjust to conditions such as extreme heat, noise, air pollution, or the like.
- A life change is often stressful. Examples might include moving into a new house, getting married, or changing schools. Such changes require many adaptations to new surroundings and situations.
- Life crises produce the greatest stress. These events might include the death of a parent, the loss of a job, or a divorce. The more serious the crisis, the greater the stress.

An event that causes great stress for one person may only be a minor problem for another. Your existing physical or mental condition influences your ability to handle a new stress. Your response may also depend on whether you feel in control of the situation. A difficulty may cause little stress if you can predict it, overcome it, or at least understand it.

Most people are able to cope with life's everyday stresses. However, when stressors build up faster than you can solve them, your capacity may be overloaded. Continual stress exhausts the body's resources that maintain energy and resist disease. The result may be anxiety, depression, or serious illness.

Coping with Stress

A well-balanced life can help you prevent and reduce stress. Managing stress may include alternating mental activity with physical activity, sharing emotional feelings with others, reading inspirational books, and having interests outside of school or work. In addition, developing positive emotions such as hope, confidence, faith, and love can enable you to develop a lifestyle that will help you resist daily life stresses. Worrying less and having a sense of humor also helps a great deal. The three major ways to reduce or eliminate stress are: plan how to deal with stress, learn to relax, and change your life.

Plan How to Deal with Stress. Some crises and other types of stressors cannot be predicted. For instance, a loved one may die suddenly. Other stressors, though, such as taking a test, leaving home to go to school, or giving a speech are known in

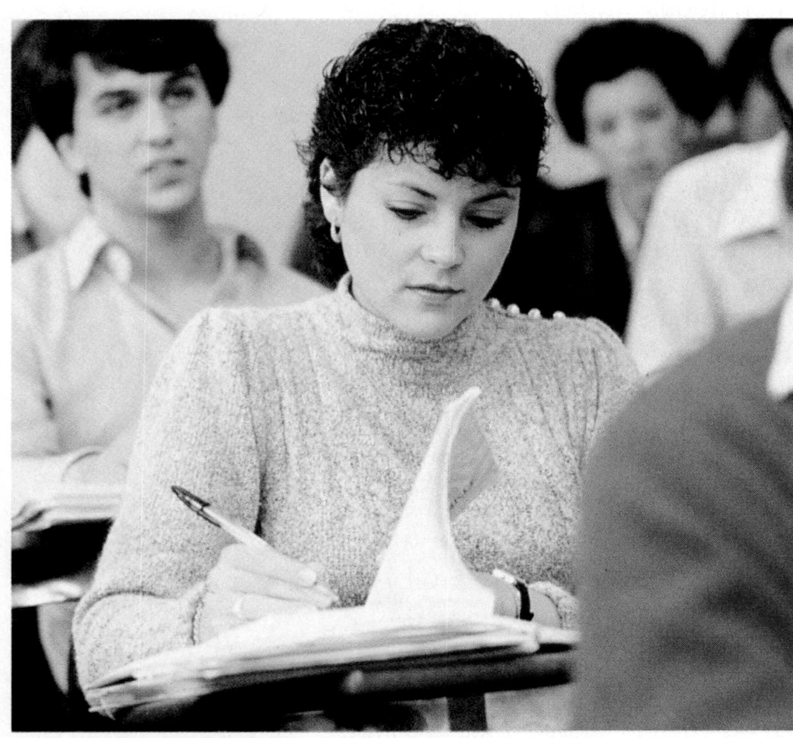

FIGURE 30–6 **Have you ever felt wiped out after taking a test? This feeling is the result of stress.**
Courtesy of Johnson & Wales College.

advance. For those kinds of stressors, you do not have to wait for them to happen. Plan and prepare for them. For example, reduce stress associated with test-taking by thoroughly studying the test material until you are confident that you know it well.

If possible, do not schedule several stressful activities during the same time period. When you know a stressful activity or event is coming up, learn to pace yourself. During stressful times, eat well, get plenty of rest, and exercise at an enjoyable pace.

Learn How to Relax. Because stress is unavoidable, it is very useful to learn a method that reduces or eliminates stress.

One doctor suggests this very simple relaxation method. Sit or lie in a comfortable position in a quiet place where you will not be disturbed. Close your eyes, and silently repeat the word *one* over and over for ten to twenty minutes. This activity seems to produce bodily changes that are the reverse of the ones stress causes. Muscle tension is reduced and a variety of other changes occur in the heart, blood, and respiratory systems. In order to learn and use a meditation technique, it should be practiced once or twice a day.

If meditation does not appeal to you, learn some other method that will help you relax and have a calming effect. The activity may be jogging, listening to music, walking in the park, riding a horse, or sitting in a suana. Use whatever works for you. Bear in mind that the bodily changes associated with stress can be reversed if you take steps to do so.

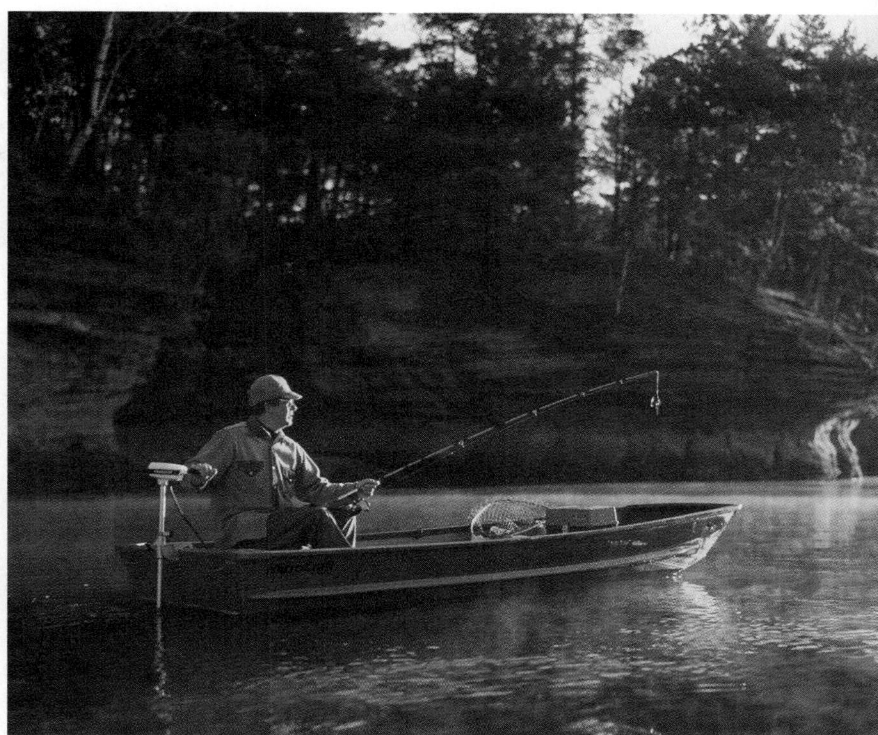

FIGURE 30–7 Fishing relaxes this man. What activity relaxes you most?
Courtesy of Outboard Marine Corporation.

Change Your Life. The methods previously mentioned are some important ways of managing stress. However, if the same stressor is always present, stress-release techniques may not be very beneficial. You may have a situation in your life that simply makes you miserable. This may be a class at school, a job, a roommate, or some other situation or relationship. If these situations cannot be relieved through other means, your last resort may be to drop the class, quit the job, or find a new roommate.

Of course, turning away from all stressful situations would be bad. But some situations and relationships are so stress-producing, that it is often better to change them than to continue.

? ? ? ? ? ? ? ? ? ? ? ? ? ? ?

WHAT WOULD YOU DO?

You have been studying all weekend for a test on Monday. You feel tense and your neck and shoulders ache from leaning over a desk. One of your friends calls asking you to go to the recreation center for a workout. You would like to go, but do not feel that you can take time away from studying.

What would you do?

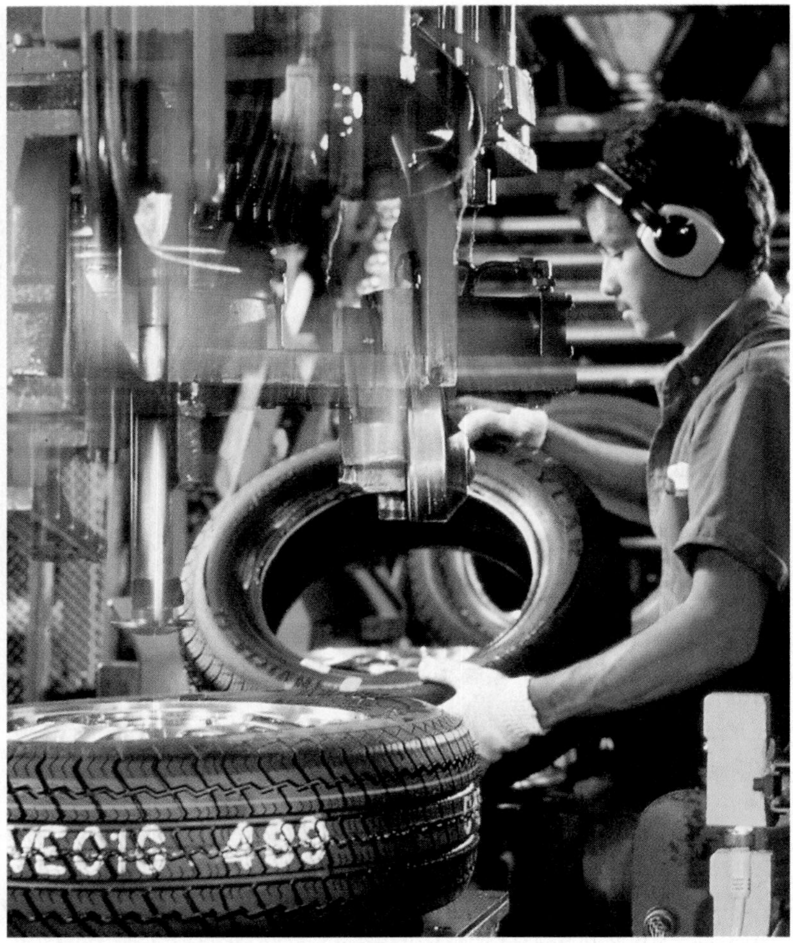

FIGURE 30–8 **Some workers have jobs that give them a lot of exercise.**
Courtesy Goodyear Tire & Rubber Company.

PHYSICAL FITNESS

No matter how good your diet or how well you control stress, you cannot be healthy without physical fitness. People have different ideas about what fitness means. For some, it is not being ill, while for others, it is having a trim body.

Physical fitness refers to how well your heart and other organs function. Your physical fitness is determined by such factors as age, heredity, and behavior. Although you cannot control your age or heredity, your behavior can help you become physically fit. People vary greatly in their capacity for physical fitness, but almost anyone can improve by exercising regularly.

All of us need physical exercise. The years between adolescence and middle age are generally the peak period for physical fitness. However, people of all ages can stay fit if they maintain good health habits and get regular exercise. According to the American Medical Association, exercise:

1. Improves strength, endurance, and coordination, thus increasing the ease with which daily tasks are accomplished.
2. Aids weight control, thus helping to ward off heart disease, arthritis, diabetes, and other ailments often associated with being overweight.
3. Helps ensure the proper growth and development of young bones and muscles.

4. Improves the ability to avoid and recover from illnesses and accidents.
5. Strengthens muscles that support the body, improving posture and appearance.
6. Increases poise by developing grace and ease of movement.
7. Reduces stress, thus acting as a natural tranquilizer.

Types of Exercise

Your level of physical fitness depends largely on how often and how hard you exercise. Experts say that you should exercise at least three times weekly for at least thirty minutes at a stretch. Improvement in fitness may occur faster with even more frequent workouts.

The President's Council on Physical Fitness and Sports recommends a thirty-minute workout of continuous exercise. To be beneficial, the exercise does not have to be difficult or strenuous. But, as your condition improves, you should increase the number of times you do each activity. Every workout should include exercises for flexibility, endurance, and strength.

Flexibility Exercises. These stretch the connective tissues and move the joints through a wide range of motions. Such exercises include touching the toes, swinging the arms in circles, rotating the upper body from the waist, and jogging slowly. These should be performed before and after each workout.

Endurance Exercises. Running, cycling, skipping rope, swimming, and brisk walking speed up action of the heart and lungs. These are called *aerobic exercises.* Such exercises strengthen the heart, blood vessels, and lungs.

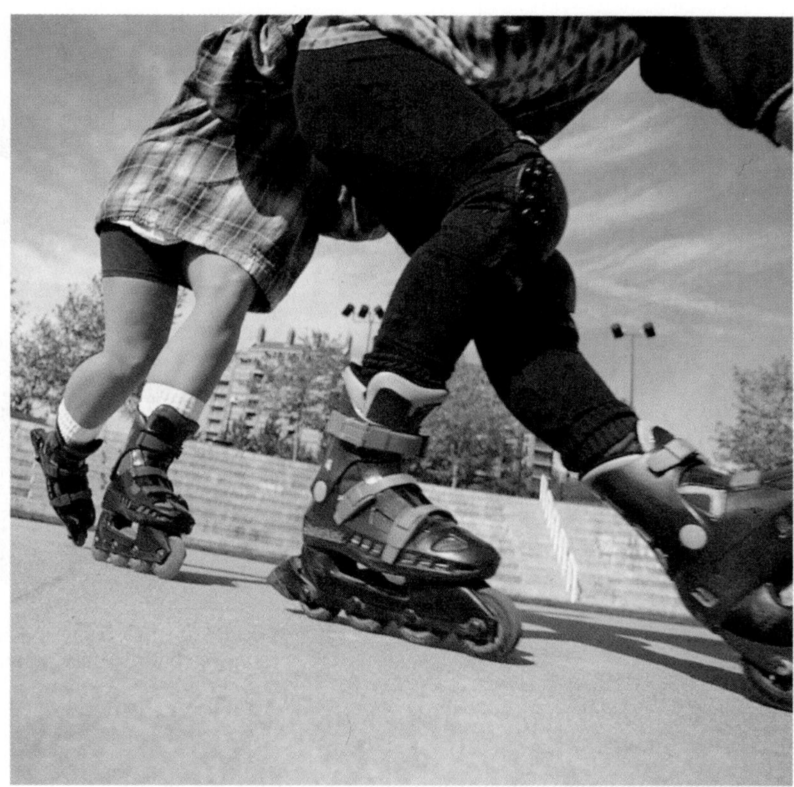

FIGURE 30–9 **Rollerblading is wonderful exercise and can be done with family or friends.**
Photo by Mimi Ostendorf/Photonics.

Strength Exercises. Pullups, pushups, situps, lifting weights, and other exercises increase the strength and endurance of the body's major muscle groups. For example, lifting weights increases the strength of arms, shoulders, and back muscles.

Guidelines for Physical Fitness

Exercise is basic to healthful living. Beginning or maintaining an exercise program should be done with the following guidelines in mind:

1. Do not keep finding excuses not to exercise.

2. Do not think of fitness as a crash program. To avoid injury and fatigue, start slowly and build yourself up.
3. Enjoy yourself. Exercise can be fun.
4. Do not set unrealistic expectations. Remember, you are not training for the Olympics.
5. To avoid boredom, vary your exercise routine.
6. Once you get in shape, keep up your exercise program. If you get lazy and quit, your fitness level can deteriorate rather rapidly. The longer you allow yourself to be inactive, the harder it is to get back in shape.
7. Harmful health habits such as drugs, smoking, alcohol, and lack of sleep can undo the results of regular exercise.

As a young person, you have most of your life ahead of you. The quality of that life will depend a great deal on your physical and mental health. Begin now to follow the guidelines in this chapter regarding nutrition and diet, reducing stress, and physical fitness. This will better allow you to live and enjoy your life to its fullest.

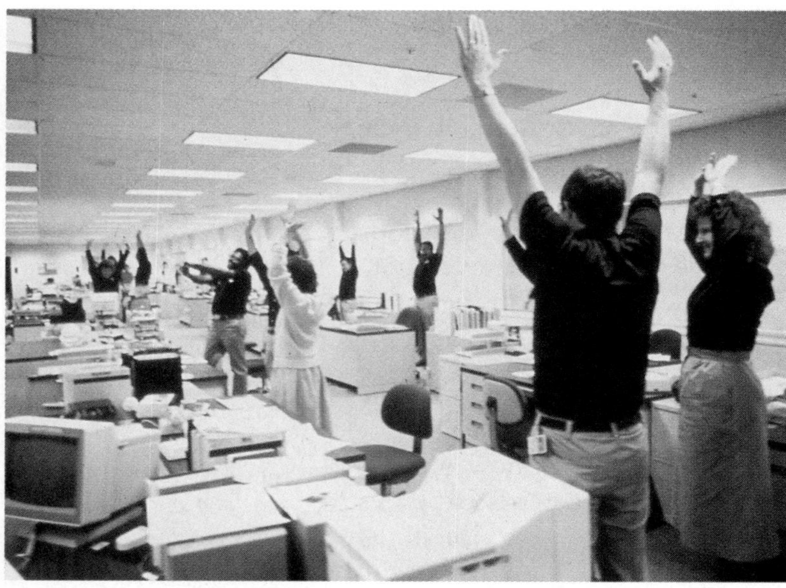

FIGURE 30–10 **Some companies begin the workday with a few minutes of stretching exercises.**
Courtesy of Toyota Motor Manufacturing, U.S.A., Inc.

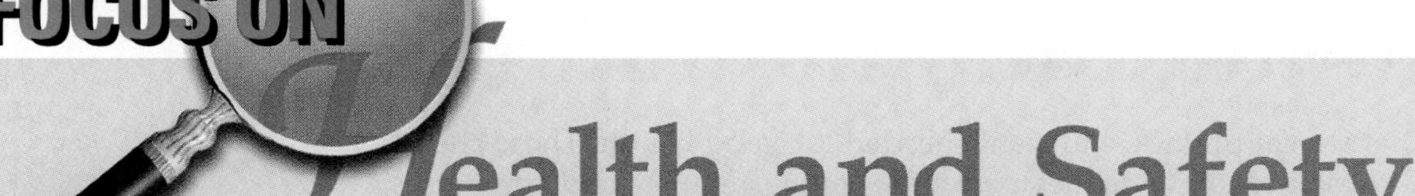

Corporate Fitness Programs

Faced with spiraling medical costs and insurance premiums more companies are promoting preventive health care. This may include health screening for employees, educational seminars and workshops, and opportunities for physical activity.

Here is how the program operates at one large corporation. The program, called "Live for Life," offers classes on stress management and how to quit smoking. It teaches employees the importance of blood pressure testing, weight control, and exercise. The company has a fitness center on site.

In the center, an aerobics instructor leads exercise classes before and after work and at lunch time. Free laundry service is provided. The company distributes a monthly newsletter on fitness and sponsors regular seminars on good nutrition and other topics.

The program is voluntary, but incentives to participate are provided. For every twenty minutes of exercise, employees get $1 of "play money." They can use it to purchase jogging suits, ankle weights, and other health-related items. About 60 percent of the company's 30,000 employees participate.

Research has shown that fitness programs such as this pay off. There are fewer illnesses and accidents, reduced absenteeism, and a more vigorous, creative, positive work force. In one company, it was found that the average yearly medical cost for exercisers was less than 50 percent of that for nonexercisers. Some companies even share the reduced medical costs with employees.

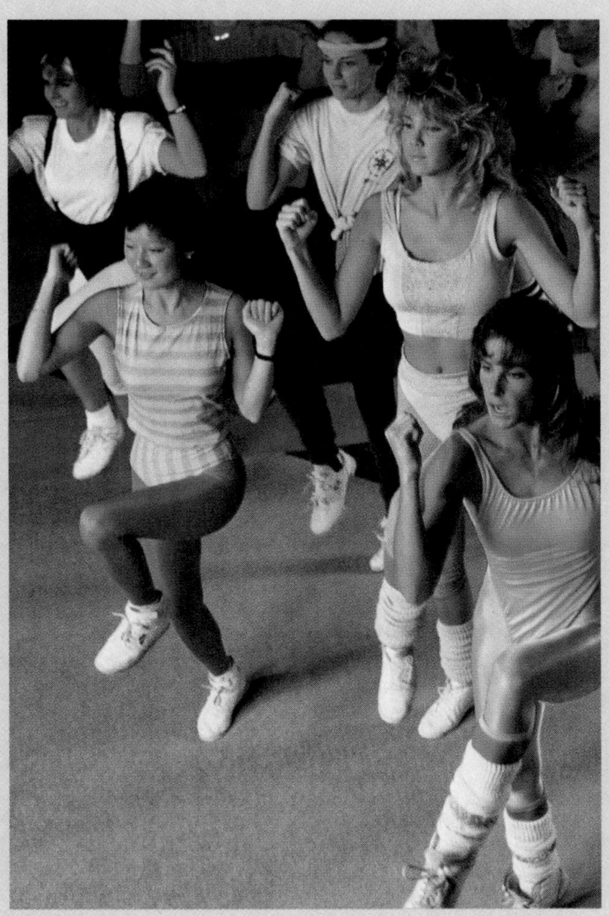

Fitness programs benefit both businesses and employees.
Courtesy Health & Tennis Corporation of America.

CHAPTER 30 REVIEW

CHAPTER IN BRIEF

- What we eat provides nutrients needed for good health. These chemical substances serve as fuel to provide energy, regulate body processes, and furnish basic structural material for building, repairing, and maintaining body tissues. To make sure you get the required nutrients, you need to eat a variety of foods each day.
- Calories are units of food energy needed for basal metabolism and for energy. The number of calories used by the body each day to maintain weight is called the daily calorie need.
- For good health, it is wise to maintain your recommended weight. Do this by controlling your calories or your level of activity, or both.
- Stress is a response the body makes to any demand made upon it. The most common causes of stress are daily activities, frustrations and challenges, illness or injury, life changes, and life crises. Continual stress exhausts the body's resources that maintain energy and resist disease. The result may be anxiety, depression, or serious illness.
- A well-balanced life can help you avoid or reduce stress. Three major ways to reduce or eliminate stress are: plan how to deal with stress, learn how to relax, and change your life.
- No matter how good your diet or how well you control stress, you cannot be healthy without physical fitness. This refers to how well your heart and other organs function. Physical fitness is determined by your age, heredity, and behavior.
- Your level of physical fitness depends largely on how often and how hard you exercise. You should exercise at least three times weekly for at least thirty minutes at a stretch. Every workout should include exercises for flexibility, endurance, and strength.
- Harmful health habits such as drugs, alcohol, smoking, and lack of sleep, can undo the results of regular exercise. You have most of your life ahead of you. The quality of that life will depend a great deal on your physical and mental health.

WORDS TO KNOW

aerobic exercises
basal metabolism
calories
nutrients
nutrition
physical fitness
sedentary
stress
stressors

QUESTIONS TO ANSWER

1. Name the three functions that nutrients perform.
2. In order to eat a balanced diet, you should select foods daily from the Food Guide Pyramid. Name the five major food groups.
3. Based on the table shown in Figure 30–3, what is your ideal weight? About how many calories should you eat each day?
4. Why is it important not to go below 1,200 calories a day?
5. Stress sometimes comes from a positive event. Give an example.
6. Do people respond the same to stress? Answer and explain your answer.
7. Name three possible ways to cope with stress.
8. Name four benefits of exercise.
9. Briefly explain the three basic types of exercise.
10. Harmful health habits can undo the results of exercise. Name four unhealthly habits.

ACTIVITIES TO DO

1. For one full day, keep track of everything you eat and the approximate amount of each. After you have done this, compare what you have eaten with the Food Guide Pyramid shown in Figure 30–2. How well does your diet compare with the recommendations? What foods, if any, are missing from your diet?
2. Using the Food Guide Pyramid and a calorie chart as references, plan a sample menu for one day. Be sure to include snacks, too. The total calories of all menu items should be enough to maintain your weight. Turn the menu in to your teacher.
3. Learning a relaxation method can be very helpful. For several days, practice the method described under "Learn How to Relax" on page 439. In class, discuss whether you notice any difference in how you feel as a result of the meditation.
4. As a class, survey various businesses and industries in your area (or search for information at a library) to find out what things employers do to encourage workers to be more physically fit. How do employers benefit from having exercise breaks, exercise rooms, and related activities and facilities?
5. In May 1994, new federal rules took effect that require food companies to put nutrition labels on their packaged food products. The rules require labels listing calories, total fat, saturated fat, cholesterol, carbohydrates, and sodium. All are listed as percentages in a recommended daily diet.

   Bring a label from one of your favorite foods to class. Compare the nutritional value of the food product you selected with the recommended daily intake shown at the bottom of the label. Discuss how such nutritional information can help you make better food choices.

TOPICS TO DISCUSS

1. It has been said that Americans are the most "overfed and undernourished" people in the world. Why might this be true?
2. Eating disorders such as anorexia and bulimia have become serious health problems. What are some of the possible causes of these?
3. In what ways may short-term stress be beneficial?
4. How does physical fitness differ from body building?
5. A good diet, control of stress, and physical exercise are all interrelated. Discuss how one may benefit others.

CHAPTER 31 Responsible Citizenship

OUTLINE

- Responsibilities of Citizenship
- Voting and Self-government
- Thinking Clearly
- Chapter Review

OBJECTIVES

After reading this chapter, you should be able to:

- Explain the four responsibilities of citizenship.
- Summarize the process of registering to vote and casting a ballot.
- Discuss the importance of voting in local, state, and national elections.
- Identify and describe those things that get in the way of clear thinking.

One of your most important roles in life is that of a citizen. *Citizenship* is a part of daily living. It involves participation in home, school, community, and work life. In this chapter, you will learn more about citizenship and how to be a more effective citizen.

RESPONSIBILITIES OF CITIZENSHIP

The responsibilities of citizenship involve *personal, economic, political,* and *national-defense* activities. On the personal level, good citizens are considerate of the needs of others. They help develop and preserve basic institutions such as home, family, and community. They adhere to the customs and laws of society. Good citizens stand up for what they believe is right and take action against what they know is wrong.

FIGURE 31–1 **Economic citizenship includes being a productive worker.**
Courtesy Goodyear Tire & Rubber Company.

Economically, being a good citizen means producing efficiently and consuming wisely. It also means helping to protect the rights of others to work. Good citizens use their talents and abilities to further the economic welfare of the society.

In the political area, every citizen of age should be a registered voter and participate in all elections. A good citizen keeps up with politics and informs politicians of his or her opinions. People can serve the government directly in such ways as performing jury duty when asked. They also can contribute to the national defense.

Some full-time workers belong to the military reserve. Dan Hartley, for instance, is a member of the Air National Guard. His regular job is working as a cabinetmaker at Blue Ridge Woodworks. Dan also attends monthly reserve meetings and spends two weeks at reserve summer camp. In a national emergency, Dan could be called into active duty.

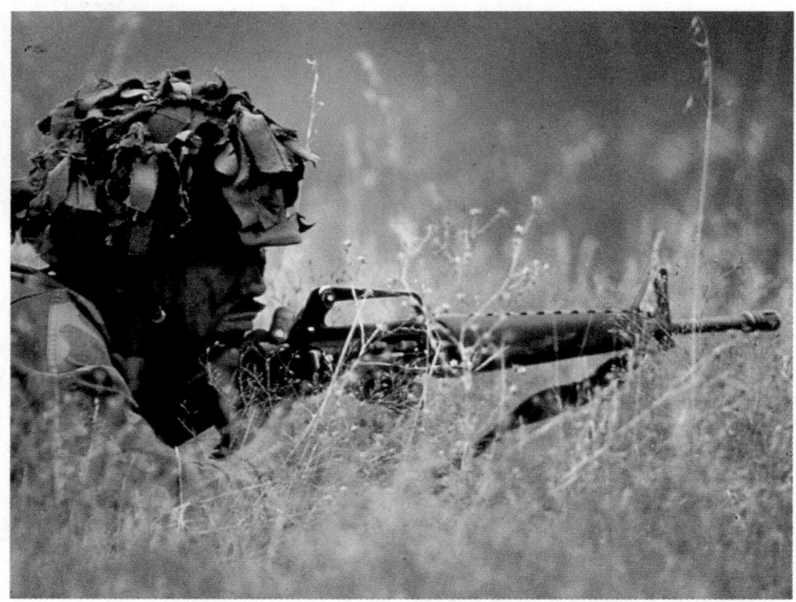

FIGURE 31–2 **Men and women serving in the U.S. Armed Forces have kept this country free.** *Courtesy of the U.S. Department of Defense.*

VOTING AND SELF-GOVERNMENT

Voting is both a privilege and a right. You have the responsibility to vote in local, state, and national elections. If everyone refused to vote, self-government would come to a standstill. "What difference will my vote make?" you ask. Election outcomes often hinge on a few votes. Yours might make the difference!

Voting Qualifications and Procedures

In all states, voters must be U.S. citizens of at least eighteen years of age and meet state residency requirements. For state and local elections, residency requirements vary among states. For national elections, it is thirty days.

Once you are eighteen and meet residency requirements, you should register to vote. In the registration process, a person's name is added to the list of eligible voters. In many areas, voters may register in person or by mail. To be eligible to vote in an election, it is usually necessary to register at least thirty days beforehand. In most states, registration is permanent unless the voter moves to another town or fails to vote for several years. If you ever move to a different place in the same town, notify the appropriate county office. They will need to update their records.

Casting a Ballot

In the United States, each county or ward of a state is divided into voting districts called *precincts.* A person must vote at the polling place for the precinct in which he or she lives. The polling place may be a public building such as a school, in a place of business, or even a private home. At the polling place, election officials check eligibility for voting, distribute ballots, and count the votes after the polls close.

? ? ? ? ? ? ? ? ? ? ? ? ? ?

WHAT WOULD YOU DO?

The school board has voted to make drastic cuts in the district's vocational education program. The board says that it is too expensive to operate. Many students are very upset. A group of them is meeting after school to discuss what they might do. You have been asked to come to the meeting. You are concerned about the cuts, but are not sure you want to get involved.

What would you do?

Basic to our system of voting is the right to cast a secret ballot. At every polling place, some type of private booth is provided. Only one voter at a time is permitted to be in the voting booth. The voting itself is made as easy as possible. Voters either mark a printed ballot or use some type of voting machine.

When voting for various offices, people may vote a "straight ticket" or "split" their ballots. Voting a straight ticket is when someone simply votes for all candidates of a particular party. Splitting a ticket is voting for some candidates of one party and some of another. For example, someone might vote for a Democratic candidate for president and a Republican candidate for governor. And if they desire, people may also write in the name of someone whose name is not on the ballot. Any issues and questions on the ballot require only a "yes" or "no" vote.

The Election of Candidates

In most elections, the candidate with the most votes is the winner. This is probably what happens in your school elections. Suppose that in a class election Leroy Johnson receives 98 votes, Tiffany Anderson 95 votes, and Eric Washington 80 votes. Leroy Johnson would be the winner.

FIGURE 31–3 **Voters approved a bond referendum to build this new sewer system.**
Courtesy of American Electric Power.

In some elections, though, a candidate must have a majority of the votes cast. If that were the case in the class election, Leroy Johnson would not be the winner. He failed to receive at least half of the 273 votes. When a candidate like Johnson does not receive a majority, a "run-off" election is usually held between the top two candidates. Johnson runs against Anderson. The one with the most votes is the winner.

Voting Behavior

Our ancestors struggled to earn the right to vote. Unfortunately, too many people now take this privilege for granted. Middle-aged and older citizens are much more likely to vote than are young adults. Less than half of the people under twenty-five vote. In the last three presidential elections, an average of about 35 percent of the eighteen-to-twenty age group voted. In "off-year" Congressional elections, only about 20 percent of eighteen-to-twenty year olds vote.

Too many people are like Roger's friend, Ted. On election day, Roger awoke before the alarm sounded. He got up and dressed quickly. This was the first election in which he was old enough to vote. After breakfast, he headed off to the polling place. On the way, Roger saw Ted jogging on the sidewalk.

"Hey Ted," said Roger, "Do you want to go with me to vote?"

"Are you nuts, man?," exclaimed Ted. "It doesn't do any good to vote. Those politicians don't care about anyone except themselves."

Roger was very disappointed in Ted's reaction. He went on to the polling place. There was a short line in front of the building, but no one seemed to mind. They quietly chatted among themselves until their turns came. Roger signed the register and got in line.

Several minutes later, a booth became available. Roger entered and marked his ballot. After he finished, Roger gave the ballot to a clerk and watched her put it into a box. He left the polling place with a feeling of satisfaction. He was glad he had voted, but could not help but think about Ted. "I wonder what I could do to change Ted's mind," he thought. Do you have any suggestions about what Roger might do?

Because of the publicity of a national campaign, more people vote in a presidential election than in any other. On the average, fewer voters participate in elections for state and local officials. This is interesting because our lives are influenced directly by the actions of our state and local officials. What reasons might people give for not voting in these elections?

FIGURE 31–4 Your political participation can make this country better.
Courtesy of Knight-Ridder, Inc.

THINKING CLEARLY

It is not always easy to choose between two political candidates or to decide which position on an issue is the correct one for you. Many issues such as nuclear power, federal spending, and the role of labor unions are not clearcut. To clarify your thinking about a candidate or an issue, gather all the *facts* you can. Remember that facts can be proven. It is fact, for example, that the earth is round and not flat. Following are a number of things that are frequently confused with facts.

Rumor

A *rumor* is a popular report or story that has not been proven. Most rumors are spread by word of mouth. People often treat rumors as if they are fact.

Opinion

An *opinion* is one person's views about something. We reveal our opinions when we show preference for a certain candidate or take a particular side in an issue. Although opinions may be based on fact, they are not fact in themselves.

Prejudice

A *prejudice* is an opinion that is based on insufficient information (a prejudgment). People might express prejudice toward a person's sex, race, religion, or some other factor. Prejudice frequently causes great harm to innocent people and is the opposite of clear thinking.

? ? ? ? ? ? ? ? ? ? ? ? ? ? ?

WHAT WOULD YOU DO?

An election will be held in a couple of weeks for class officers. Small groups of students have organized to push for certain candidates. Campaign workers are putting up posters and passing out literature. The campaign is starting to get dirty. A representative of one group has come to you asking that you not vote for Christine because "we do not want a girl for president."

What would you do?

Allegation

An *allegation* is an unproven statement about someone or something. For example, you might state that Elliot Chemical Company dumps hazardous waste into the river. An allegation is a very serious charge. Because you can be sued, you should never make an allegation unless you have the supporting facts.

Bias

When you have a tendency to lean toward something because of familiarity or preference, you have a *bias.* You might then make overexaggerated claims. For example, even though running is good exercise, joggers often exaggerate its benefits. Biases are not necessarily harmful. We all have them. But, when making choices and decisions, carefully keep in mind who is saying what.

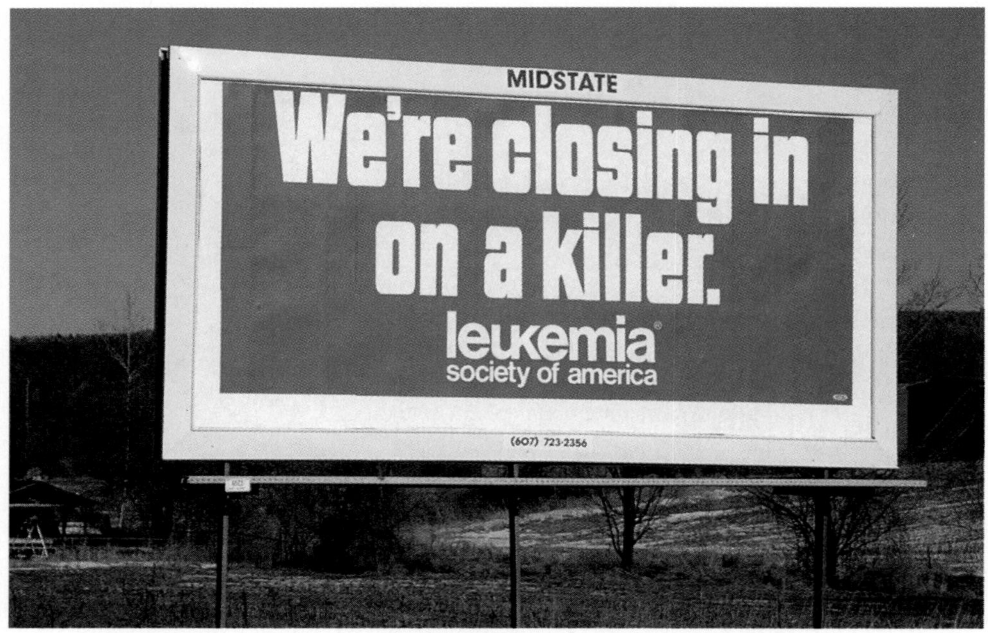

FIGURE 31–5 **Is this message considered propaganda? Why?**
Photo by David W. Tuttle.

Propaganda

Propaganda involves any organized effort or movement to spread certain information. The information may be true or false. Like biases, propaganda is not always negative. For example, the American Heart Association uses propaganda to convince people of the hazards of smoking.

FOCUS ON

Skills For Living

CITIZEN LAWMAKERS

Most laws are passed by national, state, and local legislative bodies. However, through a method called an *initiative,* citizens can introduce a law. The initiative is used primarily at the state and local levels. Twenty states in the U.S. provide for the initiative in their constitutions.

In states or cities that use the initiative, anyone can draw up a proposed law. The next step is to collect a specific number of signatures on a petition favoring it. Once the initiative petition has qualified, it is voted on.

An initiative may be direct or indirect. In the first case, the proposed law is placed on a ballot and goes directly to the voters. In an indirect initiative, the proposed law goes first to the legislature. Should the legislative body approve the initiative, it goes into law. In some states, the question is ended if the legislature votes the bill down. In other states, a rejected bill is submitted to the people. If they vote for it, the bill becomes law. The governor cannot veto a bill passed in this way.

In recent years, the following initiatives have appeared on ballots in various states:

- Create overnight shelters for the homeless.
- Remove sales tax from food products.
- Roll back tax hikes.
- Establish a state lottery.
- Regulate pornography on cable TV.
- Limit medical malpractice damages.

The initiative works in much the same way in a city as it does in a state. Whether at the state or local level, an initiative is a device that enables people to take direct political action if their elected representatives ignore their wishes.

A number of important state laws have been enacted through the process of an initiative.
Photo by David W. Tuttle.

CHAPTER 31 REVIEW

CHAPTER IN BRIEF

- Citizenship is part of daily living. The responsibilities of citizenship involve personal, economic, political, and national-defense activities.
- You have the responsibility to vote in local, state, and national elections. In all states, voters must be U.S. citizens at least eighteen years of age and meet state residency requirements. To be eligible to vote, you must register beforehand.
- A person must vote at the polling place for the precinct in which he or she lives. At every polling place, some type of private booth is provided. People may vote a straight ticket or split their ballots.
- Too many people take the privilege of voting for granted. Less than half of the people under twenty-five vote. On the average, fewer voters participate in state and local elections than in presidential elections.
- It is not easy to choose between two political candidates or to decide which position on an issue is the correct one. Many issues are not clearcut. To clarify your thinking, gather all the facts you can.
- Facts can be proven. A number of things are confused with facts. These include rumor, opinion, prejudice, allegation, bias, and propaganda.

WORDS TO KNOW

allegation
bias
citizenship
opinion
precincts
prejudice
propaganda
rumor

QUESTIONS TO ANSWER

1. Name the four types of citizenship responsibilities.
2. Give three examples of how citizens might exercise economic responsibilities.
3. What would happen if all but a very few people failed to vote?
4. In order to vote in an election, what must you do beforehand?
5. What is it called when a person votes for candidates of different political parties.
6. Why do you think more people tend to vote in a national than in a local election?
7. A prejudice can be thought of as a prejudgment. Give an example.
8. Why should you be careful in making an allegation?

ACTIVITIES TO DO

1. Identify someone (perhaps a friend or relative) in your community who is a *naturalized* citizen. Invite the person to class to talk about why he or she chose to become a U.S. citizen. Make a list of questions to ask.
2. Find out the residency requirements for voting in your community or city. Also, find out how you go about registering to vote where you live.
3. Newspaper and magazine editorials are a special type of opinion. Bring copies of editorials of interest to class. Discuss them. Are there any about which the class disagrees? If so, compose your own class opinion and send it to the proper source.
4. Bring to class a brochure or other statement that can be considered propaganda. Identify the main idea that the propaganda is attempting to communicate. Then, discuss the following questions: (a) Who wants you to believe this? (b) Why does the person or group want you to believe it? (c) Are there arguments on the other side?

TOPICS TO DISCUSS

1. If you were an employer, how might you feel if several of your employees were called away for emergency military reserve duty?
2. Citizens may be of three types. One type is like a *stone* that stays where it is, neither hearing nor responding. A second type is like a *sponge* that absorbs and retains, but does not respond. The third type is like a *generator* that converts energy into power. Generators are the people who get things done.

   What percentages of students in your school, do you think, fall into each of these three groups? In which group do you belong? Discuss your answers in class.
3. Why do you think so few young adults vote? What can be done to increase the number of young voters?
4. On federal income tax forms, there is a place to mark if you want $3 of your tax to go to the Presidential Election Fund. How is this money used? Do you support this approach?

CHAPTER 32 Education for Lifelong Learning

OUTLINE

- Education and Training
- Types of Education and Training
- Educational Information
- Chapter Review

OBJECTIVES

After reading this chapter, you should be able to:

- Discuss why additional education or training beyond high school may be needed.
- Illustrate how the amount of required preparation varies among occupations.
- Name and describe the six common types of education and training.
- Explain how education or training requirements may vary for a given occupation.
- Know sources of information regarding education and training and financial aid.

One day Lionel and several of his friends were discussing what they were going to do after high school. "I can't wait to get my diploma," said Lionel. "I'm sick of school."

"I'm going to get a job in a factory," remarked Marty. "That way, I don't have to go on to school."

"Yea," said Henry, "who wants to get more education? I have a cousin who graduated from college and she can't get a job."

"I think you people are wrong," said Samantha. *"Most jobs require some type of education or training*. And there is a lot of competition for jobs, even among people who have degrees or training."

The conversation among these students shows some truths and some misunderstandings about the relationship between education and employment. It is true that not all jobs require additional schooling. But such jobs tend to be low-paying and have little security.

It is also true that getting a college degree will not automatically guarantee you a job. Some types of degrees do not lead directly to employment. For instance, to get a job in psychology, most students will need at least one graduate degree. And, with some programs, there are more graduates with degrees than there are available jobs. So people take jobs requiring less education. These are often jobs that high school graduates usually fill. So competition for those jobs increases.

On the other hand, it is a mistake to think that you will not need more education or training after high school. Most entry-level (beginning) jobs in factories, businesses, mines, and other workplaces require on-the-job training. If you want to advance in a company, you will probably have to continue education throughout your lifetime. Your attitude toward future schooling is one of the things your employer will probably consider in judging you for a promotion or raise.

Linda and Vicki were in the same high school graduation class. After graduating, they were both hired as assemblers at General Electronics. Their work involved putting together electrical components for radio receivers.

General Electronics has an agreement with Northwest Community College to offer courses at the plant. Classes start at 4:00 P.M. after employees get off work. The company pays for tuition. Linda enrolled in the program because she wanted a more challenging, better-paying job. Vicki ignored the program, saying that the courses were a waste of time.

New jobs at General Electronics frequently open up at all levels from assemblers to supervisors. Employees with two years of experience may apply for higher level jobs. As soon as they were eligible, both Linda and Vicki applied for the first available job in the records department. Linda got the job. The personnel manager was impressed by the fact that she had the initiative to continue her education. Vicki has since been passed over for several other jobs. Could it be due to her feelings about further training?

Career ladders exist in most industries. A *career ladder* is a number of related occupations organized into ranks like steps on a ladder. Two examples of career ladders in the

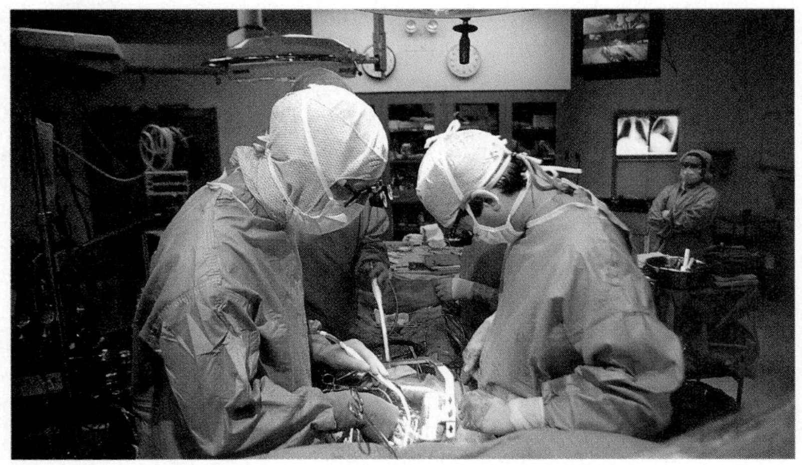

FIGURE 32–1 **Most desirable jobs require some type of education or training.**
Photo a, by Joseph Schuyler; b, © Dennis MacDonald/PhotoEdit; and c, © Mark Richards/PhotoEdit.

food service industry are shown in Figure 32–2. It is possible for one to start at the bottom of a career ladder and "climb" to the top. To do so, however, on-the-job experience and additional training are required.

Even though you are looking forward now to completing high school, do not turn your back on education at a later time. Some type of education or training program will probably be suited to your interests and abilities. Think it over carefully. Education and training will be one of the best investments you can make in your future.

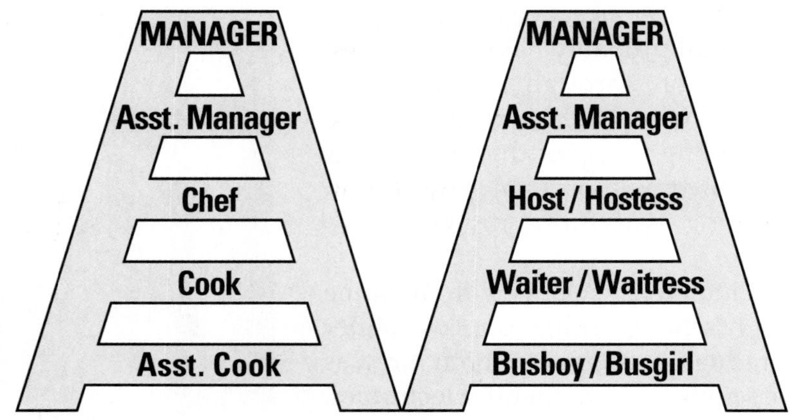

FIGURE 32–2 **These career ladders show how workers can progress in the food service industry. They master one job and then move up to the next.**
Courtesy of Educational Foundation of the National Restaurant Association.

EDUCATION AND TRAINING

Do you have any idea of how you might go about becoming a hotel manager? A toolmaker? A computer programmer? A pilot? The first thing you would have to do for each of these occupations is learn a set of skills. To work as a hotel manager, you would have to learn about accounting, hiring, employee relations, and food service management. Toolmakers need to know machining operations, math, and blueprint reading and be able to use machine tools and special measuring instruments. To work as a computer programmer, you would have to learn how to translate ideas into computer language the computer could understand and write instructions it could follow. To become a pilot, of course, you would have to learn how to fly a plane.

Like a hobby or a sport, every occupation involves knowledge and skills that must be learned. But the amount of preparation needed varies among occupations. Deciding how much time and effort you are willing

FIGURE 32–3 **Do you know what type of training it takes to become a television producer?**
Courtesy of SIUC Photocommunications.

to put into education or training is important to career planning. It does not make sense to aim for a career as a veterinarian, for instance, unless you do well in school, are interested in science, and are willing to put in at least six years of hard work and study after high school.

The best way to begin a career is to complete high school. High school courses teach basic skills that will help you be a better worker, consumer, and citizen. A high school diploma is necessary if you want to go to college, too. And you will usually need one to get into trade schools, technical institutes, apprenticeship programs, or the military. Moreover, most employers prefer to hire people who are at least high school graduates.

The choices that are open to you after high school are shown in Figure 32–4. As you can see, many options are available to get necessary education and training. The path you choose depends on the kind of occupation you have in mind—and the time and effort you are willing to put into your training.

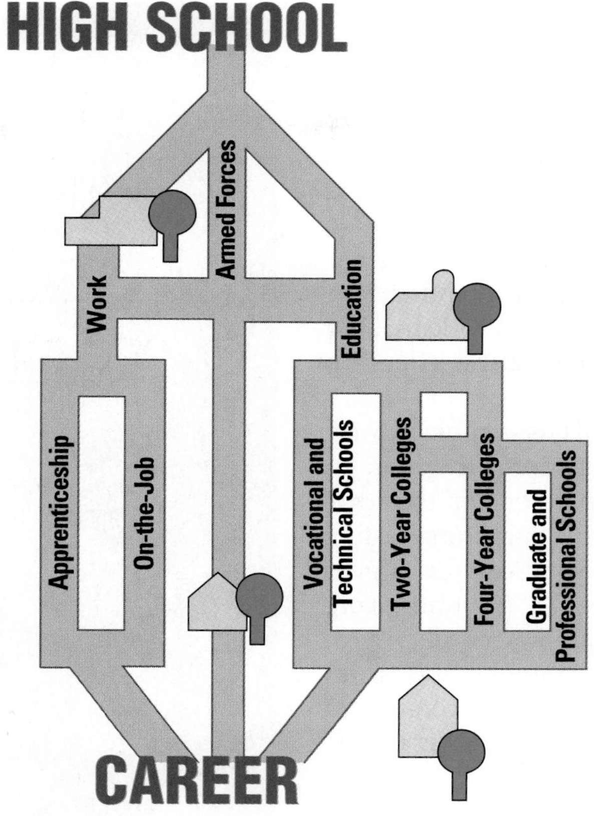

FIGURE 32–4 **Several different paths may lead to your career goal.**

TYPES OF EDUCATION AND TRAINING

From hearing people talk, you may sometimes get the feeling that almost everyone gets a college education. That is not so. About 60 percent of all high school graduates *do* continue their schooling, though not necessarily in college.

On-the-Job Training

Almost all occupations involve some sort of learning by doing, also known as on-the-job training (OJT). A skilled worker teaches you as you

? ? ? ? ? ? ? ? ? ? ? ? ? ?

WHAT WOULD YOU DO?

After several years in your present job, you have reached a dead-end. You cannot advance without additional training. But you never were a very good student. You are a poor reader, have difficulty memorizing, and nearly panic whenever you have to take a test. You do not want to admit it, but you are scared by the thought of taking a course.

What would you do?

watch. You then do the task under that worker's supervision. An advantage of OJT is that you are paid while you learn. Some jobs are almost always learned through OJT. Examples include postal clerk, machine-tool setter, shoe repairer, and furniture upholsterer. Generally, OJT is given for jobs that take more than a few days to learn, but less than formal apprenticeship would require.

Very often, OJT is combined with short-term classroom training. A power truck operator, for example, may take a safe driving course lasting several days. In some cases, OJT goes on for a few years. Air traffic controllers, for example, need two or three years of training and work experience before they are considered fully qualified to handle their jobs.

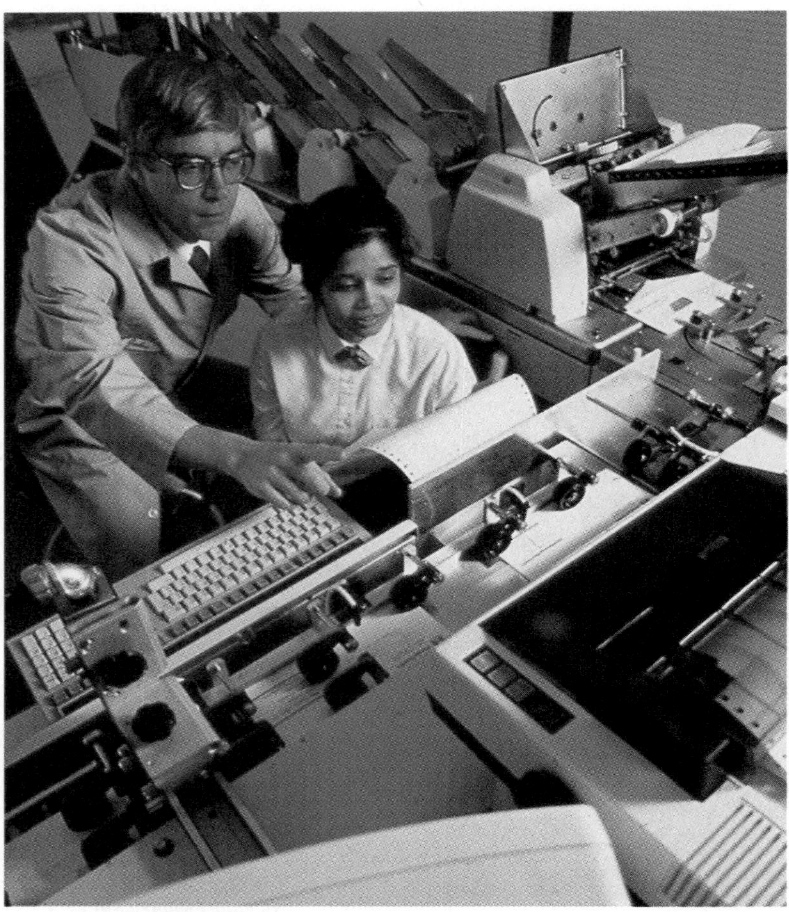

FIGURE 32–5 **On-the-job training is a continuing process for most jobs in today's economy.** *Photo by © Gary Gladstone.*

Apprenticeship

Apprenticeship is a formal on-the-job program during which a worker (called an *apprentice*) learns a trade. Extensive OJT and related instruction are involved. Apprenticeships usually last about four years, but may range from one to six years. During this time, apprentices work under *journey workers.* Under the journey worker's guidance, the apprentice gradually learns the trade and performs the work under less and less supervision. Apprentices are full-time employees. An apprentice's pay generally starts out at about half that of an experienced worker and gradually increases throughout the apprenticeship. Many programs are co-sponsored by trade unions that offer apprentices union membership.

The main drawback to apprenticeship is the stiff competition to get into a program. Generally, program sponsors seek people who seem to have the greatest chances of completing the program. To get your name placed on the *apprenticeship register* (waiting list) you usually have to take an aptitude test, have an interview, and meet the necessary physical requirements. Once on the register, the wait can last months or even years. In the construction trades alone, an estimated eight applicants are qualified for every opening.

Electrician
Carpenter
Plumber
Pipe fitter (any industry)
Sheet metal worker
Electrician, maintenance
Machinist
Tool-and-die maker
Roofer
Firefighter
Bricklayer (construction)
Cook (hotel and restaurant)
Structural steel worker
Painter
Operating engineer
Correction officer
Maintenance mechanic (any industry)
Electronics mechanic
Automobile mechanic
Millwright
Construction-equipment mechanic
Police officer I
Airframe and power plant mechanic
Diesel mechanic
Electrician, airplane
Insulation worker
Welder, combination
Line maintainer
Refrigeration mechanic (any industry)
Cement mason
Boilermaker I
Environmental-control-system installer-servicer
Fire medic
Line erector
Cook (any industry)
Tool maker
Radio station operator
Car repairer (railroad)
Stationary engineer
Telegraphic-typewriter operator

FIGURE 32–6 **More than 80 percent of all apprentices work in these occupations.**
Source: Occupational Outlook Quarterly.

Vocational and Technical Schools

Many types of schools offer vocational training to teach skills used on the job. Vocational programs are offered by high schools, vocational high schools, and area vocational centers. Common areas of study include business and office, consumer and homemaking, trade and industrial, health occupations, and agriculture.

Other sources of training include trade schools, technical institutes, business schools, and correspondence or home-study schools. Privately run schools such as these are often called *proprietary schools.* In classes lasting from several weeks to several years, these schools will teach you cosmetology, barbering, flying, office procedures, computer operations, fashion design, locksmithing, and many other skills. The cost of training at a proprietary school is often more expensive than at a public institution such as a community college.

In a vocational or technical school, you will practice in the classroom those skills you will need on the job. In business school, you might do word processing, file, use a dictaphone, or keep books. In programs for health occupations, you might operate medical equipment. People learning to be mechanics and repairers would take classes in blueprint reading and shop math.

When you complete your program, you will receive a certificate. You will then be ready to begin work, though your employer may also want to give you some on-the-job training.

Community and Junior Colleges

These two-year colleges provide two types of education. One is the college transfer program, a two-year general education program for students who plan to transfer later to a four-year college. General education courses include English, history, science, art, and music. The other type of program is the occupational or career program, which offers specialized skill training leading directly to employment. Though a typical occupational program lasts two years, some such as licensed practical nurse, can be learned within one year.

A community or junior college offers training in many occupational areas. Examples include computer service technician, dental hygienist, forestry technician, emergency medical technician, recreation leader, auto mechanic, and welder.

Community and junior colleges offer two main advantages. First, they have close ties with local business and industry and try to tailor their training programs to the needs of the local area. This makes it easier for students to find jobs after training. Another advantage is that these colleges are usually less expensive to attend. Since they are supported by local property taxes, many colleges charge low tuition.

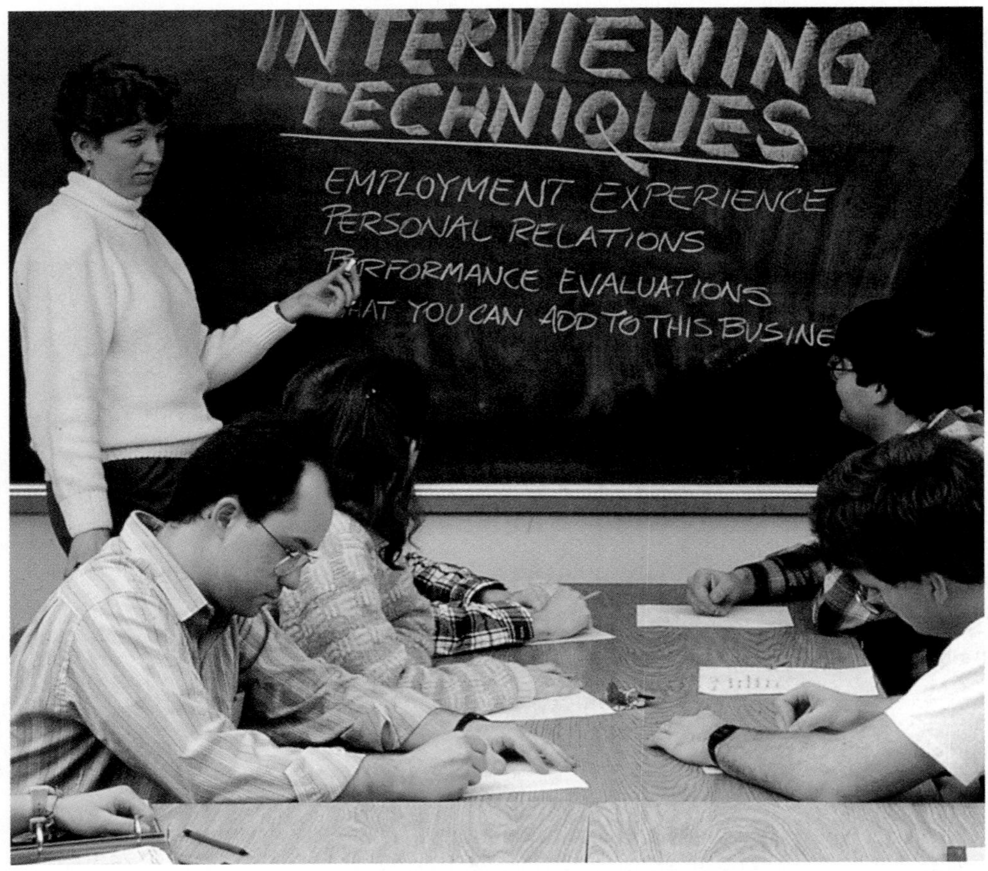

FIGURE 32–7 Working adults who attend school part-time often go to community and junior colleges.
Photo by David W. Tuttle.

Colleges and Universities

Colleges and universities are four-year institutions that vary widely in their concern for training students in specific occupations. Some are primarily liberal arts schools that offer a broad, general education. Others are very specialized and are oriented toward engineering and technology. Still others, such as large state universities, offer a combination of general and specialized education.

A typical state college or university offers 100 or more areas of study called *majors*. Common majors include Business and Administration, Journalism, Education, Engineering, Political Science, Chemistry, Economics, Plant and Soil Science, Art, Theater, and Psychology.

By and large, college does not prepare you for one particular occupation. Instead, most undergraduate programs give you a foundation upon which many careers can be built. In four years of college, you can expect to gain a basic education in your chosen field of study. In addition, you will be expected to broaden your knowledge of literature, mathematics, science, history, the fine arts, and many other areas. An advantage of college, however, is that you usually have a lot of freedom in choosing courses that interest you.

Kurt is attending a state university. His major is Administration of Justice. Within his major, he takes courses in law enforcement, correctional management, juvenile justice, and delinquency prevention. Administration of Justice graduates get jobs as police officers, corrections counselors, parole officers, and so on. Kurt plans to get additional training and hopes to become an FBI agent.

Military Training

Another way to get education and training is to join a branch of the military service—Army, Navy, Air Force, Marines, or Coast Guard. The military prepares people for a variety of occupations in which civilians also work. These include cook, nurse, computer operator, mechanic, firefighter, and hundreds of others. While in the service, you can learn occupational skills and gain work experience. Then, when you get out, you can use your skills to get a civilian job. Or you may decide to make a career of military service.

EDUCATIONAL INFORMATION

To make a good educational decision, you will need information on

? ? ? ? ? ? ? ? ? ? ? ? ? ? ?

WHAT WOULD YOU DO?

You notice an advertisement in the paper for Whitney Business College. The ad states, "Flexible hours, credit for life experiences, tuition financing arranged, guaranteed job upon graduation." The school is not too far from your home.

"This could be just what I am looking for," you say to yourself. "I think I will give them a call."

What would you do?

various schools—their courses of study, admissions requirements, costs, and so on.

Sources of Information

In Chapter 14, you learned how to use the *Occupational Outlook Handbook (OOH)* in an occupational search. For each occupation described in the *OOH,* a section titled "Sources of Additional Information" appears at the end. For each occupation in which you are interested, write to the sources listed. The information you receive will frequently list places where education and training are available.

Both private and government publishers put out guides to education and training programs. Your school guidance office or career center should have a collection of such guides. So, too, should your local public library. Many of these guides are updated annually, so be sure to use the most recent edition.

To learn more about apprenticeship, your local Job Service is probably the best source of information. In some cities, Apprenticeship Information Centers (AICs) furnish information, counseling, and aptitude testing. They also direct people needing more specific help to union

FIGURE 32–8 **The number of women enrolled in U.S. colleges and universities is greater than the number of men who attend.**
Photo by Pictor/© Uniphoto, Inc.

hiring halls, Joint Apprenticeship Committees, and employer sponsors. Ask a Job Service counselor if there is an AIC in your community.

For information about education and training in the Armed Forces, contact the local recruiting office of the branch in which you are interested. Each branch of the service has information available describing its specific program.

Financial Aid

18 The cost of education or training is an important consideration in making educational decisions. You will have to think about how much training you or your family can afford as well as how much you would like to get. The cost of schooling needed to become a doctor is much greater than the cost of training to become a lab technician.

In some cases, the training requirements for a specific occupation will vary greatly. For example, to become a registered nurse, you could attend one of three different types of programs:

- A two-year associate degree program at a junior or community college.
- A three-year diploma program operated in connection with a hospital.
- A four-year degree program at a college or university.

The costs per year of training will also be quite different.

Do not be discouraged if you want to pursue education beyond high school, but you or your family cannot afford the cost. Begin by talking to your school guidance counselor. *Financial aid* may be available. *Scholarships,* loans, *grants,* and the like are available from schools, educational foundations, business firms, religious groups, community organizations, and the government. A good section on "Sources of Financial Aid Information" is contained in the *OOH.* Make sure you use the most recent edition.

Take advantage of educational opportunities. Education is never wasted. Whether you take formal coursework, learn on the job, or study on your own, you benefit as a worker and human being by continuing to learn and grow.

FOCUS ON The Worker

TRAINING AND MORE TRAINING

In the last decade or so, the automobile industry has undergone dramatic change. Competition has forced companies to modernize plants and alter manufacturing methods to improve quality and productivity. A different type of worker is being recruited and trained. Following is the description of a typical process.

Job applicants must take general aptitude tests, drug tests, and written exams. Counseling and in-depth interviews are conducted to determine each person's company loyalty, team spirit, and versatility. Assembly-line simulations are also performed. The application and screening process takes about a day and a half per person. Employees are hired ten to twelve weeks before they are placed on the assembly line.

New hires receive three weeks of "soft training" in which they learn the basics of teamwork and company philosophy. Then they are assigned to an area such as the body shop where they get seven weeks of classroom and hands-on training. During this time, they are screened according to job capabilities. Individuals are assigned to a job for which they are best suited.

Next, they are assigned to a unit leader (similar to a foreman). The unit leader further screens the workers and decides at which point on the assembly line they will work best. Then three or four more weeks of off-line training is given.

Recruiting and training a single employee can cost more than $10,000. Companies invest such sums because they believe that the key to success is picking the best employees and training them well. Similar recruitment and training efforts are becoming standard throughout the automobile manufacturing industry. The emphasis on quality employees and training is shared by hundreds of other businesses and industries.

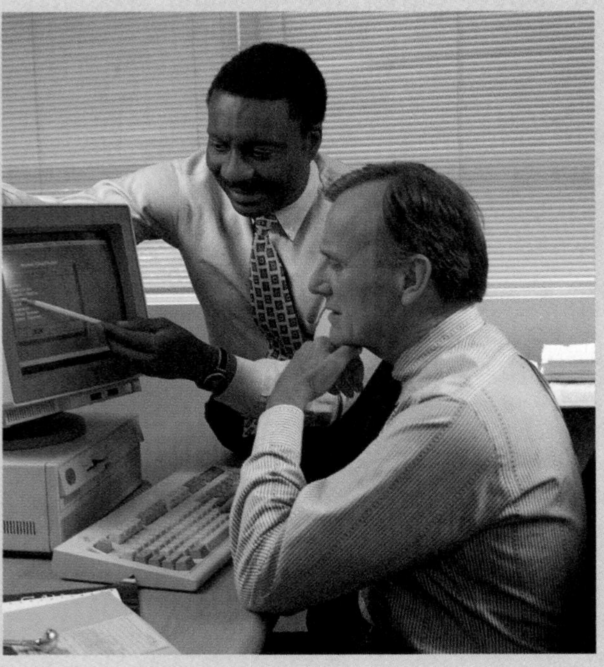

New technology and work organization have created different approaches to recruiting and training workers.
Photo by Alan Brown/Photonics.

CHAPTER 32 REVIEW

CHAPTER IN BRIEF

- Not all jobs require additional schooling. Such jobs, however, tend to be low paying and have little job security. Getting a college degree will not automatically guarantee you a job. On the other hand, it is a mistake to think that you will not need more education or training after high school. Additional education and training will be one of the best investments you can make in your future.
- Every occupation involves knowledge and skills that must be learned. But the amount of preparation needed varies among occupations. Deciding how much time and effort you are willing to put into education or training is important to career planning.
- The most common education and training options are: (a) *On-the-job training*—short-term training provided while you work. (b) *Apprenticeship*—formal on-the-job training from one to six years. (c) *Vocational and technical schools*—skill training for a specific occupation conducted in classrooms, labs, shops, and workplaces. (d) *Community and junior colleges*—two-year programs for college transfer or skill training in a specific occupation. (e) *Colleges and universities*—four-year schools offering a variety of programs ranging from general to specialized education in hundreds of majors. (f) *Military training*—training and employment in hundreds of different occupations while serving in the Armed Forces.
- To make a good educational decision, you will need information on various schools (courses of study, admissions requirements, costs, and so on). Both commercial and government publishers put out a variety of educational information and guides.
- The cost of education or training is an important consideration in making educational decisions. There are many sources of financial aid to help pay for education or training. A good section on "Sources of Financial Aid Information" is contained in the *Occupational Outlook Handbook.*
- Education is never wasted. You will benefit as a worker and human being by continuing to learn and grow.

WORDS TO KNOW

apprentice
apprenticeship
apprenticeship register
career ladder
financial aid
grants
journey workers
majors
proprietary schools
scholarships

QUESTIONS TO ANSWER

1. Give three reasons why you should consider taking additional education or training beyond high school.
2. What is the best way to begin a career?
3. Identify the six most common types of education and training.
4. What is the difference between OJT and apprenticeship?
5. Which is more expensive to attend, a public vocational/technical school or a proprietary school? Why?
6. Community and junior colleges provide two main types of programs. Name them.
7. Name three types of information that you will need to make a good educational decision.
8. Name two sources of information about apprenticeships.
9. Provide an example to illustrate how education or training requirements may vary for a given occupation.
10. What publication contains information about types of financial aid?

ACTIVITIES TO DO

1. Select an entry-level occupation of interest. Develop a career ladder for the occupation similar to those in Figure 32–2. You will probably need to ask people in related occupations for assistance.
2. Go to your school or public library. What sources of education and training information do you find there? Are there information sources about financial aid? Your instructor may assign you a specific task. List the information your teacher requests and duplicate a copy for each class member.
3. Contact your local Job Service to find out what types of information it has about apprenticeship. Also, check with them to find out the location of the nearest Apprenticeship Information Center.
4. Identify a school or college in which you may be interested. Use one of the resources listed in this chapter and find out the following information: (a) What are the entrance requirements? (b) How long does it take to complete the program you are interested in? (c) How much does it cost to attend? (d) Is any financial aid available? (e) Does the institution provide job-placement services? Summarize your findings on paper and submit your report to your instructor.
5. Invite to class a recruiter from the military services and have him or her discuss types of training programs and educational benefits provided by the military.

TOPICS TO DISCUSS

1. Most of you are probably employed as part of a work experience education program. Discuss how learning on the job is different from learning at school.
2. Has working made you more aware of the need for education or training? If so, how?

3. Many companies encourage their employees to pursue additional education (beyond that received on the job). How does this benefit the employer?
4. More and more adults are returning to college and other types of education. What is behind this trend?
5. If you are working now, find out what type of education or training you would need to move ahead in your job. Discuss this in class.

APPENDIX

LEARNING A LIVING: A BLUEPRINT FOR HIGH PERFORMANCE

In Chapter One of this book, you were introduced to "The Changing Workplace." You learned that a new economy is evolving in the United States based on knowledge and information. Then in Chapter Six, you read about the "High Performance Work Organization." This refers to a new way of combining people and technology to achieve greater productivity. Changes in our overall economic system and in the workplace have resulted in the need to rethink how students are prepared for work.

In 1990, the U.S. Secretary of Labor appointed a group called the Secretary's Commission on Achieving Necessary Skills (SCANS). Its task was to determine the skills that young people need to succeed in the world of work.

The Commission spent months talking to business owners, to public employers, to people who supervise employees, to union officials, and to workers. Across the country and in every kind of job, the Commission heard the same message. That is, good jobs depend on people who can put knowledge to work. New workers must be creative and responsible problem-solvers. They must have the skills and attitudes on which employers can build.

Based on their investigation, the Commission made three major recommendations:

- All American high school students must develop a new set of competencies and foundation skills if they are to enjoy a productive and satisfying life.
- The qualities of high performance used by today's most successful companies must become the standard for the majority of companies, large and small, local and global.
- The nation's schools must be transformed into high-performance organizations in their own right.

The Commission produced four reports explaining the historical background of our skills problem, defining workplace know-how, and outlining a system for an improved education system and a more productive national economy. It is important for teachers and students to be familiar with this material. The remainder of this section summarizes key parts of the SCANS reports.

THE WORLD HAS CHANGED

For most of this century, America took its goods to the world without worrying about competition from abroad. The quality of our goods and services was second to none. American production techniques and know-how were the envy of the world. American markets, isolated by two great oceans, belonged to American producers. Those days are behind us.

Today, telecommunications and modern air transportation have created a truly global village. More than 70 percent of American manufactured products have foreign competitors. The globalization of finance, capital, technology, and labor means that a product can be designed in one company, engineered in another, produced in yet a third, and distributed around the world. If the next generation of Americans is to enjoy increasing economic prosperity, the United States must respond to the challenge of global economic competition.

WORK IS CHANGING

The future depends on high performance work organizations and a highly competent workforce. The high performance workplace is one that empowers workers to participate and utilize their skills and knowledge. The differences between traditional workplaces and high performance workplaces are summarized in Figure A–1.

CHARACTERISTICS OF TODAY'S AND TOMORROW'S WORKPLACE	
TRADITIONAL MODEL	**HIGH PERFORMANCE MODEL**
STRATEGY	
• mass production • long production runs • centralized control	• flexible production • customized production • decentralized control
PRODUCTION	
• fixed automation • end-of-line quality control • fragmentation of tasks • authority vested in supervisor	• flexible automation • on-line quality control • work teams, multi-skilled workers • authority delegated to worker
HIRING AND HUMAN RESOURCES	
• labor-management confrontation • minimal qualifications accepted • workers as a cost	• labor-management cooperation • screening for basic skills abilities • workforce as an investment
JOB LADDERS	
• internal labor market • advancement by seniority	• limited internal labor market • advancement by certified skills
TRAINING	
• minimal for production workers • specialized for craft workers	• training sessions for everyone • broader skills sought

FIGURE A–1

In most workplaces of today, work is routinized, repetitive, and organized along hierarchical lines. It emphasizes mass production by workers who are not asked to think much about what they are doing. Defects are weeded out through inspection of the final product.

High performance workplaces, by contrast, are models for the future. In this environment, work is problem-oriented, flexible, and organized into teams. Most important, the high performance organization recognizes that producing a defective product costs more than producing a high-quality one. The solution is to design quality into the product development process itself. This is done by enabling workers to make decisions and correct defects on-the-spot.

High performance organizations are committed to excellence, to product quality, and to customer service. These are the kinds of organizations required to lead the way in international competition and to provide high-wage jobs for tomorrow's workers.

WHAT IS WORK LIKE TODAY?

In this section, several case studies are provided to illustrate what workers are expected to do when they enter high performance work environments. The case studies are drawn from five different sectors of the economy.

Manufacturing

Kareem is an electronic specialist employed in a newly designed automobile assembly plant (AAP) in the Midwest. He had previously spent two years in the Army as an electronic specialist.

The plant is a modern production facility employing nearly three thousand hourly workers. About two years ago, assembly line automation was completed with the installation of a new robotics painting system. Kareem and other production line workers were involved in the selection of this equipment.

The vendor provided initial training on setting up and programming the painting system. However, no provision was made to train people to properly maintain and troubleshoot the system. After the vendor left, Kareem found himself frequently on-call to troubleshoot problems. The other electricians, who had been hired from an older AAP plant on the basis of seniority, had a difficult time making the transition to electronics concepts.

Kareem worked with the training director at AAP and the vendor to develop an on-the-job training plan. It included a broad array of maintenance skills needed on the line. One of the goals was to reduce the costs associated with repeated calls for assistance from the vendor.

The training, which was taught by Kareem, included instruction in basic electronic concepts. It also included work in pneumatics and hydraulics. The use of computer consoles with on-the-floor simulations of equipment operation was emphasized.

One result of this training is a more confident team of electricians who can provide immediate assistance to the line. Another is a significant reduction in system downtime, which can cost automakers more than $1 million daily.

Health Services

Luretta is the registrar in the emergency room of City Hospital. This is a large public facility on the west coast. It serves a diverse, urban population. Residents of nearby low-income neighborhoods use the facility for routine health care. Accident victims from the area are frequently brought to the hospital. And, victims of gang violence end up there as well. This combination threatens to overwhelm the emergency room, particularly on weekends.

On Friday evening, the emergency room staff is just recovering from a very difficult afternoon. Seven children, injured in a school bus accident, were brought in between 3:30 and 4:00 p.m. As Luretta takes a breather, an ambulance crew brings in a local college student suffering from a drug overdose. Luretta processes his papers from information provided by the ambulance crew. She then turns him over to a licensed practical nurse (LPN). As the LPN leaves, a gunshot victim staggers in on the arm of a friend. Luretta obtains information from the friend about the victim. She has an orderly wheel the victim back to an examining room. At that very moment, a distraught mother arrives with her teenage daughter who is clearly in severe respiratory distress.

Confident that the first two patients are in good hands, Luretta turns her attention to the mother and daughter. The girl is choking. The mother, unable to speak English, becomes hysterical. Frank, a registered nurse (RN) who hears the commotion, arrives and takes the girl to an examining room. As the RN leaves he instructs Luretta to get an attending physician and an interpreter.

Luretta locates Dr. Paula Jones in the next room and asks her to come to the examining room. Next, she calls the community affairs office and gets an interpreter on the phone with the mother and herself. The interpreter informs Luretta that the girl is asthmatic and that she has been treated at the hospital before. Luretta smiles at the mother to reassure her that everything is under control. She goes to her computer terminal and locates the daughter's records. Luretta hands a copy of the records to Dr. Jones who completes an examination and prescribes medication to relieve the girl's distress.

Retail Trade

Mickey is a salesperson at a computer store on Main Street in a small northeastern city. The store carries a basic line of computers and printers. About fifeteen different pieces of hardware are maintained in inventory varying in size, price, and capabilities. The store also carries a wide range of software, from word processing to database management. Peripherals, diskettes, paper, reference books, and miscellaneous supplies are also stocked.

This week the company has a sale on laptop computers. Each salesperson who sells ten or more laptops will receive a big bonus. Mickey uses his own computer to search a customer database to identify potential clients, and begins to place calls.

At this point, a customer walks into the store. The customer owns a small real estate company. She explains that her sales agents travel so much that it is difficult for them to keep up-to-date with new listings and bank mortgage rates. As a result they are probably losing sales. Mickey tells her that, "You've come to the right place. Laptop computers can help solve this problem. And, we have a terrific sale on them right now."

"This model has a built-in modem. If you equip your sales agents' cars with phones, they could download information they need just by dialing your office from their cars. You also need a desktop computer at your office to answer the phone. And your sales agents could connect with it directly. We also have a software package which can connect you to an on-line information network. In this way you can get up-to-the minute real estate listings and mortgage rates."

The customer is interested, but worried about the costs. Mickey nods, "Even with the sale we are offering, half a dozen computers is a substantial investment. But let me ask you this. You tell me that you may be losing several sales a week because your agents can't stay on top of listings and mortgage rates. If this system helps you recoup just one of these sales a week, isn't it true that it will pay for itself in a couple of months?"

"That may be about right," responds the customer. "Let's sit down and figure out exactly how much this is going to cost me."

Food Services

Greg, Anthony, and Kathleen are on the verge of opening their own restaurant (The Three Chefs). They have each worked hard to reach this point, spending years learning the restaurant business. They have pooled their savings and borrowed from family and friends to raise needed start-up funds. Greg took out a second mortgage on his home to satisfy the bank's requirement for a security guarantee.

Greg serves as manager and "front-of-the-house" supervisor during the day. Kathleen is the lunchtime chef and evening manager. Anthony trains the staff, does the bookkeeping, and prepares the evening meals. Renovation has been completed on the restaurant. Most of the new kitchen equipment has been installed. Food servers have completed their training and have worked two practice shifts to iron out problems.

Kathleen and Anthony analyzed the "back-of-the-house" work flow during the practice shifts. They then developed a plan for improving the kitchen's output. They can improve efficiency in the kitchen by starting food preparation an hour earlier and moving a work station to the front of the house. After additional consideration, however, they realized that the changes will probably cost them between $7,000 and $10,000. This is money which they did not have. If their projections are correct, they might be able to afford it after they have made about $25,000 in sales. That is, in three to four months, if all goes well. They decide to make minor adjustments to the system and postpone expensive changes until they see how first month's sales and expenses turn out.

"Here's another way we can control costs," says Kathleen. "I've come across a new management information system that can generate inventory reports, sales reports, and pricing charts. We can integrate the inventory reports and pricing data to project costs and make menu changes. I've also been looking at several different accounting software packages. I think the software our accountant recommended is the most suitable for our needs. There is a large pool of programmers who know that software. This will make it easier for us to obtain a consultant on short notice to tailor the software to our operation."

Office Services

Verbatim Transcription Service (VTS) provides written records of meetings, legal proceedings, and conferences. The firm employs twenty-four people, including six transcribers. But, today only four of them are available. The transcriber's job is to decipher tapes received from stenographers and recorders and create a written record. Accuracy and timeliness are critical elements of the transcriber's work, and essential to the firm's success.

Gabriela is a top-notch transcriber at VTS. This has been a particularly busy week. Today she has six tapes in various stages of conversion. Three of the clients have asked for their documentation by the following morning. One law firm has a court case approaching. The minutes of a controversial school board budget hearing are to be delivered to the local newspaper tomorrow for publication. Also, the president of a local university (one of VTS's largest clients) wants immediate service on the tapes of a book he is dictating.

Gabriela doesn't think she can finish all the tapes on time. She goes to Nan, her supervisor, to discuss the problem. She and Nan decide to call in a freelance transcriber they have called on in the past. Gabriela then calls the school board president and the local newspaper. She arranges to have the minutes reviewed that evening by school board staff. This will allow her to make corrections and deliver them to the newspaper prior to their publication deadline. She then contacts the university president and negotiates an alternative allowing her to have his transcript ready two days later.

After finishing her scheduled daily work, Gabriela looks over the first draft of a new transcriber hired to work with a local teaching hospital. She wants to determine if his knowledge of medical terms is adequate. Otherwise, he will have to attend a refresher course on medical terminology. Gabriela is happy to inform Nan that they have hired a qualified person.

COMMON WORKPLACE SKILLS

What these case studies have revealed are the problems, demands, rewards, and satisfactions of high performance work environments. They capture what many individuals actually do in today's workplace. They confirm that when employers say they want people comfortable with technology and capable of solving problems, they are realistic. They confirm, also, that reading, writing, and basic arithmetic are not enough. These skills must be integrated with other kinds of competency to make them fully operational.

The elements common in each of the case studies are performance in five groups of skills, or competencies. These five competencies rest on a three-part foundation of skills and personal qualities. Collectively, the competencies and foundation skills constitute the workplace know-how needed for effective job performance.

The designation of workplace know-how is an outgrowth of research conducted by the SCANS Commission. A listing of so-called SCANS competencies is shown in Figure A–2.

The competencies are the basis of the modern workplace dedicated to excellence. The members of SCANS believe that these competencies are applicable from the shop floor to the executive suite. They are generic across industries and at many steps on a career ladder. (See Figure A–3.) In the broadest sense, the competencies represent the attributes employers seek in today's and tomorrow's employee.

Now, let us return to the five case studies described earlier. We will review how essential these five competencies are for effective performance across the job spectrum. The three foundation skills will be addressed later.

Resources

Whether it was Kareem in the automobile factory, Kathleen and her partners in the restaurant, or Gabriela at VTS, all demonstrate their

WORKPLACE KNOW-HOW

The know-how identified by SCANS is made up of five workplace competencies and a three-part foundation of skills and personal qualities that are needed for solid job performance. These are:

WORKPLACE COMPETENCIES—Effective workers can productively use:

- **Resources**—They know how to allocate time, money, materials, space, and staff.
- **Interpersonal skills**—They can work on teams, teach others, serve customers, lead, negotiate, and work well with people from culturally diverse backgrounds.
- **Information**—They can acquire and evaluate data, organize and maintain files, interpret and communicate, and use computers to process information.
- **Systems**—They understand social, organizational, and technological systems; they can monitor and correct performance; and they can design or improve systems.
- **Technology**—They can select equipment and tools, apply technology to specific tasks, and maintain and troubleshoot equipment.

FOUNDATION SKILLS—Competent workers in the high-performance workplace need:

- **Basic skills**—reading, writing, arithmetic and mathematics, speaking, and listening.
- **Thinking skills**—the ability to learn, to reason, to think creatively, to make decisions, and to solve probelms.
- **Personal qualities**—individual responsibility, self-esteem and self-management, sociability, and integrity.

FIGURE A–2

COMPETENCE NEEDED ACROSS THE BOARD

Who needs the SCANS competencies? Everyone from the entry-level clerk to managers, executives, or partners in professional corporations. Take the high-pressure world of a major law firm as an example of how competence is required across the board:

Receptionists are expected to demonstrate personable "front-desk" skills (meeting clients and identifying their needs) and to manage complex telecommunications systems without difficulty.

Secretaries are routinely called on to work with associates and partners with different, often difficult, working styles and to manipulate computer-based data, graphics, and information systems on different kinds of equipment.

Legal Administrators help select and oversee the installation of state-of-the-art telecommunications and information systems to meet lawyers' needs and they also ensure that all support personnel are trained in these systems.

Associates (junior attorneys) having spent three years learning the rudiments of the legal system and its precedents stretching back to common law, are now expected to put that knowledge to work on specialized problems situated in complex modern systems, e.g., corporations, hospitals, contracts, or civil rights law, and to search for precedents supporting the client's legal position.

The Managing Partner is responsible for ensuring that the cogs and gears of the entire firm operate as a harmonious system–that the support system meets the demands the firm places on it; that the accounting and finance systems follow and recover costs; that the background of the lawyers meshes with the legal specialty of the firm; and that potentially profitable new areas of client interest can be accommodated.

FIGURE A–3

ability to manage resources. Kareem understood that time is a resource and that downtime costs money. The three chefs had put their life savings on the line. Their analyses of costs, procedures, and the best use of their own time were designed to protect their investment. Gabriela made exceptional use of the human resources and time available to her in meeting a time crunch, one having serious implications for VTS's reputation.

Interpersonal

Interpersonal competence is the lubricant of the workplace, minimizing friction and the daily wear and tear of work. It also undergirds restructured work organizations in factories and provides the "service" in service firms. It is required if teams are to solve problems that they jointly face. All of the workers in our case studies functioned effectively in quite complicated interpersonal environments. A false step in most of these situations invites resistance from colleagues or clients and could, in some situations, threaten lives.

Kareem showed sensitivity toward the older electricians who were having difficulties troubleshooting the new electronic painting equipment. Gabriela's skills helped her negotiate a potentially troubling work conflict. Mickey took his customer's concern about costs seriously, but, he turned the issue to his advantage. Luretta, in perhaps the most pressure driven of these situations, went out of her way to reassure the distraught mother. At the same time, she was able to seek help from a doctor and an interpreter.

Information

Luretta, facing a potentially life-threatening situation, could do nothing to help until she obtained the information needed by the doctors. She calmly called in an interpreter who provided her with knowledge of the patient's history and the location of her medical records. She then manipulated a computerized information system to locate the records. Gabriela's job at VTS is essentially transforming information from one form (audio tapes or stenographic notes) to another (written record).

The heart of Mickey's job is not so much selling as showing his customers how the equipment he has to offer can solve their information problems. If he can do that, the technology often sells itself. Mickey asked for information from the customer about her needs. Using that knowledge, he was able to describe how a laptop computer and software could make information an asset instead of a problem.

Systems

All workers need to understand their own work in relation to that of others. They must think of specific tasks as part of a larger whole. Greg, Kathleen, and Anthony understood that the "front-of-the-house" could not begin to function without an effective operation in the "back-of-the-house." Moreover, they were able to view portions, menus, and inventory control as integral parts of the restaurant's overall cost structure.

On one level, Kareem's troubleshooting of the computerized painting equipment is simply part of his job. Kareem's special contribution was to understand that his job affected the entire operation and profitability of the plant. He then drew on the training department, his co-workers with outdated skills, and the strengths of the vendor.

Luretta's job as registrar placed her in a pivotal position for the systems revolving around her—ambulance crews, nursing staff, doctors, community affairs specialist, the police, and others. Luretta not only obtained information from the interpreter, but she understood how important it was to obtain the patient's records and pass them along to Dr. Jones.

Technology

Today, technology has permeated every aspect of life from home to workplace. Mickey obviously spends much of his time helping fit technologies to his client's needs, but he also used the technology himself to stay in contact with his customers. Karem worked with the engineering department to select and install the new robot painting system. His knowledge of this new technology propelled him from troubleshooter to a leadership position as trainer. At the heart of the inventory and cost control efforts of the three chefs is a technology-based information system.

Conclusion

The expert worker of tomorrow will not simply "pick-up" these competencies. Their acquisition must begin in the schools and be refined through on-the-job experience and further training. Teaching and learning the competencies must become the tasks of all teachers and students.

FOUNDATION SKILLS

The competent performance by workers described in the case studies would have been impossible without the three foundation skills. (Review Figure A–2.) The basic skills are the minimum requirement for anyone who wants to get even a low-skill job. They will not guarantee a job or access to a college education. But, their absence will ensure that the door of opportunity remains closed.

The thinking skills, by contrast, permit workers to analyze, synthesize, and evaluate complex situations. They are the raw materials from which the five competencies are built.

The personal qualities are attributes that employers would like to be able to take for granted, but cannot. They are so important that their absence can quickly disqualify any job seeker at any level of accomplishment. Schools normally do not "teach" these qualities in the classroom itself, but weave them into the life and structure of the school environment.

Effective performance in today's workplace requires high levels of performance in all three foundation skills. People who cannot read, write, and communicate cannot be trusted in a transcription service. The rude salesperson who alienates customers will not make sales. The cashier with a hand in the till cheats the business. The electrician who cannot solve technical problems threatens the production line. And restaurant owners who cannot creatively approach problems will probably not be in business for long.

The foundation of basic skills, thinking skills, and personal qualities is the point from which competence is built. It supports the possibilities and potentials that schools need to bring out. By learning the workplace competencies as the foundation skills are learned, students of today will be ready to enter and thrive in the workplace of tomorrow.

MEASURING SCANS COMPETENCIES

New approaches to teaching and learning will be required to achieve the SCANS workplace competencies. Also required will be new ways to measure and certify the SCANS skills. Standard classroom tests will continue to be used. In addition, the use of a cumulative resume is suggested. (See Figure A–4.) Following is an explanation of how it might be used.

A cumulative resume will be created for all students in the middle school years. The resume will contain information about courses taken, projects completed, and proficiency level attained in each competency. When a student reaches the performance standard for certification in a SCANS competency, the certification will be recorded on the resume. When the student has accomplished enough to meet an overall standard, the resume will show that he or she has been awarded a certificate of initial mastery (CIM).

Most students will probably earn their certificate of initial mastery by age 16. But, no age limit is imposed. Students will be able to work toward certification at their own pace. And, several opportunities to achieve the CIM will be provided.

The cumulative resume, then, is a new type of report card. A sample resume is shown in Figure D. Such a resume has a number of advantages. For the student, the resume becomes a permanent record of actual attainment. Students could use their resumes in seeking employment or further education. This information would be very useful to employers in making hiring decisions and to colleges in evaluating applications. Because of this, students would have a strong motivation to learn the SCANS foundation skills and workplace competencies. And, employers would have a strong incentive to require them. It would be up to employers, colleges, the military, and others to decide how much weight to give each element in the resume.

HYPOTHETICAL RÉSUMÉ

Jane Smith	Date of Report: 5/1/--
19 Main Street	Soc. Sec.: 599-46-1234
Anytown	Date of Birth: 3/7/--
Home Phone: (817) 555-0133	Age: 19

SCANS Workplace Competency	Date	Proficiency Level
Resources	10/--	1
Interpersonal Skills	12/--	2
Information	11/--	3
Technology	1/--	2
Systems	4/--	3

Core Academic and Elective Courses	Date	Proficiency Level
English	11/--	3
Mathematics	12/--	3
Science	2/--	3
History	4/--	2
Geography	8/--	1
Fine Arts	11/--	4
Vocational/Industrial Education	4/--	2

SCANS Personal Qualities	Average Rating	No. of Ratings
Responsibility	Excellent	10
Self-Esteem	Excellent	10
Sociability	Excellent	8
Self-Management	Excellent	7
Integrity/Honesty	Good	6

Portfolios and Other Materials Available	Reference
1. Report on Grounds Keeping (Chemistry)	Mr. Kent
2. Video on Architectural Styles (Social Studies)	Ms. Jones
3. Newspaper Article Written	Ms. French

Extracurricular Activities	Role	Date	Reference
Newspaper	Reporter	9/-- –1/--	Frank Jones (Adviser)
Basketball Varsity	Center	9/-- –6/--	Dean Smith (Coach)

Awards and Honors	Date	Source	Reference
Teen Volunteer of the Year	6/--	Rotary Club	John Grove
Class Secretary	9/-- –1/--	Lincoln High School	Emma Rice

	Earned	Required
Points Toward Certificate of Initial Mastery	300	500

(Supplied by Student)

Work Experience	Date	Place	Reference
Volunteer Work	6/-- –6/--	St. Joseph Homeless Shelter	Father John O'Connell (508) 555-0033
Summer Camp Counselor	6/-- –8/--	Camp Kiowa	Susan Miller (508) 555-0151
Office (Word Processor)	1/-- –5/--	PDQ Secretarial Help	Myrna Copper (508) 555-0102

FIGURE A–4

SUMMARY

The recommendations of the Secretary's Commission on Achieving Necessary Skills provides a blueprint for reinventing American elementary and secondary education. They call this blueprint the "Learning a Living" system. Long-term efforts will be required to prepare students for high-skill, high-wage employment. Such efforts are now underway in Florida, Indiana, New York, Oregon, and many other states to restructure education around the SCANS skills. We hope that this introduction to SCANS has been informative in explaining this important new development.

REFERENCES

The previous discussion was based on the following four reports of The Secretary's Commission on Achieving Necessary Skills:

- *What Work Requires of Schools.* June 1991.
- *Skills and Tasks for Jobs.* 1992.
- *Learning a Living: A Blueprint for High Performance.* April 1992.
- *Teaching the SCANS Competencies.* 1993.

All are available from the U.S. Government Printing Office.

GLOSSARY

accident - an unplanned event often resulting in personal injury, property damage, or both. (17)

adjusted gross income - the amount on an income tax form that results after you subtract exclusions and adjustments from total income. (26)

adjustments to income - items that can be subtracted from income when filing an income tax return. (26)

advertising - a public notice or message intended to aid in the sale of a product or service. (22)

aerobic exercise - exercise that conditions the heart and lungs by increasing the body's ability to take in oxygen. (30)

affirmative action - a series of government policies and programs designed to correct past discrimination. (8)

agenda - the list of items to be followed in an actual business meeting. (18)

allegation - an unproven statement about someone or something. (31)

allocation - the process of distributing income to the various items in a budget. (24)

allowances - the number of tax exemptions to which one is entitled. (6)

alternatives - the choices or options available in making a decision. (12)

annual percentage rate (APR) - the percentage cost of credit on a yearly basis. (23)

anxiety - a feeling of concern, worry, or unease, such as concern about a forthcoming job interview. (6)

appraise - to evaluate someone or something, such as a potential employer. (5)

apprentice - a trainee engaged in learning an occupation under the guidance and direction of a skilled worker. *See* apprenticeship. (32)

apprenticeship - a formal program of on-the-job training and related instruction by which a young worker learns an occupation under the direction of a journey worker. (32)

apprenticeship register - a waiting list for individuals who have met the preliminary requirements for entrance into an apprenticeship program. (32)

aptitudes - developed abilities; those things that one is good at doing. (13)

area - the number of square units of space on the surface of a figure enclosed by the perimeter. (16)

arraignment - a hearing before a judge during which formal charges are brought against an arrested person. (28)

assertive - firmly and positively stating one's position or point of view. (22)

authority - the power or rank to give orders or make assignments to others. (6)

automated teller machine (ATM) - one type of electronic banking in which a plastic card is used in an electronic terminal to withdraw cash, make deposits, or transfer funds to another account. (23)

automatic raise - a regular pay raise received by all employees. (10)

bail - a sum of money paid to the court guaranteeing that an accused person will show up for trial. (23)

basal metabolism - the sum of all chemical changes taking place in the cells of the body. (30)

beneficiary - the person to whom the death benefits from a life insurance policy are to be paid. (25)

benefits - financial help in time of sickness, old age, disability, or the like. (27)

bias - a tendency to favor something because of preference or familiarity. (31)

board of directors - individuals elected by the shareholders to assume responsibility for the management of their company. (20)

body language - nonspoken communication through physical movements, expressions, and gestures. (5)

bonds - interest-bearing certificates issued by a government or corporation. (24)

brand name - nationally known brand; a product made or sold by a well-known company. (22)

brokers - individuals who specialize in selling stock and other financial investments. (24)

budget - a plan for managing income and expenditures. (24)

bylaws - printed information that defines the basic characteristics of an organization and describes how it will operate. (18)

calories - units of energy produced by food when it is used by the body. (30)

capital gain - an increase in the selling price of a stock. (24)

career guidance - assisting students in career planning and decision-making. (1)

career ladder - a group of related occupations that have different skill requirements that can be arranged in a ladder-type fashion from low to high. (32)

cash discount - a discount of several percent offered to the buyer to encourage early payment on an account. (16)

catastrophe - a sudden disaster or misfortune. (25)

certificate of deposit (CD) - a type of time deposit in which an amount of savings is placed into an account for a fixed period of time at a specified interest rate. (24)

charter - a legal document giving a corporation permission to conduct certain business activities. (20)

check register - a ruled form used to record all of the transactions that occur in a checking account. (23)

circumference - the perimeter of a circle. (16)

citizenship - membership in a state or country; carrying out the duties and responsibilities of a citizen. (31)

civil service test - a pre-employment test that is administered to a job applicant seeking a government job. (4)

clients - the business customers of a professional worker. (9)

co-insurance - a provision of health insurance in which the insured person is required to share in the expenses (typically 20 percent) beyond the deductible amount. (25)

code of ethics - rules for professional practice and behavior. (18)

commission - a fee paid to a broker upon purchase of a stock. (24)

common law - the system of law used in the United States; judge-made law. (28)

communication - sending information, ideas, or feelings from one person to another. (15)

comparison shopping - the process of finding out the cost of a product or service at several different places before making a decision to buy. (22)

compatible - something that is pleasant or agreeable, such as a relationship with a job interviewer. (5)

compensation - the total amount of income and benefits received from a job. (10)

competition - the efforts of sellers to win potential customers. (21)

complaint - an expression of dissatisfaction with a product or service. (22)

compounding - compound interest; a process in which interest is periodically added to the account balance, causing savings to steadily grow. (24)

computer - an electronic tool that can store and process data, and can direct the work of other tools. (19)

computer literacy - a general knowledge of what computers are, how they work, and for what they can be used. (19)

conditions of employment - the specific details of a job offer, such as working hours, salary or wages, and fringe benefits. (5)

condominium - ownership of a specific unit in a townhouse or apartment. (29)

confirm - to verify or make firm, such as calling to confirm (check on) an appointment. (5)

consumer - someone who buys or uses goods and services. (22)

consumption - the process of using goods and services that have been produced. (21)

cooperation - getting along with and working well with others. (7)

cooperative - a share of an apartment building complex. (29)

corporation - a form of business organization in which shareholders own the business and elect a board of directors to manage the company. (20)

cover letter - a letter of application accompanied by a job resume that is sent to a potential employer. (4)

credit - the receipt of money, goods, or services in exchange for a promise to pay at a later date. (23)

creditors - persons or companies to whom money is due. (20)

debit card - a plastic card, similar to a credit card, used in electronic banking to immediately transfer funds for a purchase from a bank account. (23)

decision-making - the process of choosing between two or more alternatives or options. (12)

decision-making styles - the typical manner in which a person makes a decision. (12)

decree - an order by the court to the defendant to stop doing whatever is harming the plaintiff. (28)

deductible - a provision of insurance in which the insured person is required to pay a certain initial amount before the insurance company pays the balance. (25)

deductions - certain amounts that are withheld from the paycheck of an employee. (26)

deductions - items on an income tax form that can be subtracted from the adjusted gross income. (10)

defendant - a person required to answer charges in a lawsuit. (28)

deficits - when the government spends more than it takes in. (21)

delegate - to assign a task or responsibility to others. (6)

demand - the willingness of consumers to spend money for goods and services (when demand increases, the price generally goes up). (21)

deposit ticket - a preprinted form used to make a deposit in a checking account. (23)

depression - a severe recession marked by stagnant business activity, scarcity of goods and money, and high unemployment. (21)

direct-mail advertising - advertising that is sent to potential customers through the mail. (22)

disabling injury - an injury causing death, permanent disability, or any degree of temporary total disability beyond the day of the accident. (17)

discrimination - favoring one person as compared to another. (8)

diversify - to spread out money over several different types of investment options. (24)

dividends - company profits that are divided among the stockholders. (24)

due process - the legal right to state one's case or point of view before a decision is made. (6)

economics - the study of how goods and services are produced, distributed, and used. (21)

EEOC - the government agency that administers the Civil Rights Act of 1964. (8)

electrocute - to cause death by electric shock. (17)

electronic banking - a broad term used to describe various types of electronic fund transfers. (23)

employability skills - the general work habits and attitudes required in all jobs. (1)

employment practices - the manners and methods by which employers deal with child labor, wages and hours, and equal pay. (8)

endorsement - a signature on the back of a check used to cash or transfer ownership of the check. (23)

enthusiasm - eagerness; a strong interest in something. (7)

entrepreneur - one who runs her or his own business; a self-employed person. (20)

entry-level job - a beginning job that does not require any previous job knowledge or experience. (3)

enunciation - speaking and pronouncing words clearly. (15)

environment - the sum total of one's surroundings. (12)

equal employment opportunity - the idea that a person cannot be discriminated against in hiring or employment because of age, race, color, religion, sex, national origin, or handicapping conditions. (8)

equity - the value of a home above the amount owed on a mortgage. (29)

exclusions - items for which income taxes do not have to be paid. (26)

exempt - to be free of something, such as not having to pay taxes. (6)

exemptions - a set amount based on the number of dependents that is subtracted from adjusted gross income when filing an income tax form. (26)

expenditures - money that is spent. (24)

experiences - the sum total of events that compose an individual's life. (12)

face value - regarding life insurance, the amount of money that is paid in the event of the insured's death. (25)

fee - a sum of money charged by a private employment agency for helping someone find a job. (3)

FICA - the federal law requiring employers to deduct an amount from workers' paychecks for Social Security. (27)

filing - the process of completing and submitting an income tax form. (26)

finance charge - the total dollar amount paid for the use of credit. (23)

financial aid - a broad term that includes all forms of financial assistance (scholarships, loans, grants, and so on) to individuals pursuing postsecondary education. (32)

follow-up letter - a thank-you letter sent to an interviewer following a job interview. (5)

franchise - a contract with a parent company to use its name and sell goods or services within a certain area. (20)

full-service bank - one that offers customers a full range of financial conveniences and services. (23)

generic products - goods that state only the common name of the product on the label. (22)

goods - articles that are produced or manufactured. (22)

goods-producing industries - those companies and businesses, such as manufacturing, construction, mining, and agriculture, that produce some type of a product. (14)

goodwill - acts of kindness, consideration, or assistance. (9)

grammar - a set of rules about correct speaking and writing. (15)

grants - grants-in-aid; funds provided to qualified persons to assist them in attending college or other postsecondary education. (32)

graphic user interface - a type of software that uses icons (small pictures) and a mouse to control the operation of application software. (19)

grooming - maintaining a neat, attractive appearance. (11)

gross pay - the amount of salary or wages earned for a certain period before deductions are withheld. (10)

guarantee - a pledge that something is exactly as stated or advertised. *See* warranty. (22)

hardware - the physical parts of a computer that you can see and touch. (19)

health maintenance organization (HMO) - a type of insurance in which unlimited group health care is provided for a fixed monthly or yearly fee. (25)

honesty - a refusal to lie, steal, or mislead in any way. (7)

human relations - interactions among people. (9)

hypothetical - something imagined or pretended, such as a potential job. (5)

icons - graphic symbols representing various computer functions that are used within a graphic user interface to control software. (19)

incentive - something to work toward; a potential reward. (10)

income - money coming in. (24)

indictment - the formal statement charging a person with an offense. (28)

industries - places of employment, such as factories, hospitals, restaurants, banks, and so on. (14)

inflation - a sharp increase in the costs of goods and services. (21)

interest - feeling of excitement and involvement. (7)

interests - things that one likes to do; preferences for certain kinds of work activities. (13)

interpersonal attraction - a tendency to be drawn to another person because of similar characteristics and preferences. (9)

intuition - a feeling or hunch. (12)

investing - using money not required for personal and family needs to increase overall financial worth. (24)

invoice - a bill for goods; an itemized statement of merchandise sent to a purchaser. (16)

IRA - voluntary private pension plans that allow employed individuals to save up to $2,000 annually toward retirement and receive certain tax benefits. (27)

job - a paid position at a specific place or setting. (1)

job application form - a form used by employers to collect personal, educational, and occupational information from a job applicant. (3)

job interview - a face-to-face meeting between a job seeker and a potential employer. (5)

job-lead card - a card on which to record information and notes about a job lead. (3)

Job Service - local branches of the state employment service that help unemployed people find jobs. (3)

journey workers - skilled, experienced workers; the status achieved by apprentices upon completion of an apprenticeship program. (32)

judgment - the judge's decision in a civil suit in favor of either the plaintiff or the defendant. (28)

judgment - thinking about a problem and making the right decision. (7)

keyboarding skills - the ability to operate a computer by use of the typewriter-like keyboard terminal. (19)

landlord - the owner or manager of a rental apartment. (29)

law - the body of enforced rules by which people live together. (28)

leadership - the process of influencing people in order to accomplish the goals of the organization. (18)

lease - a rental agreement between a tenant and a landlord. (29)

letter of resignation - a letter by an employee notifying an employer of the intent to quit a job. (10)

liability - that for which one is responsible, such as an accident occurring in your home. (25)

life roles - the various parts of one's life, such as citizen, parent, spouse, worker, and so on. (13)

lifestyle - the way in which a person lives. (13)

line item - a single entry in a budget; a budgeted item. (24)

liquidity - easily converted into cash. (24)

loopholes - a legal tax provision that allows some people to reduce or avoid income taxes. (26)

loyalty - faithfulness; believing in and being devoted to something. (7)

lump-sum payment - a one-time payment of money to the surviving spouse or child of a deceased person covered by Social Security. (27)

major - the primary area of study chosen by a student for a college or other degree. (32)

majority - a vote of at least one more than half of the people who vote. (18)

markdown - a reduction in the selling price of a product. (16)

market - marketplace; the place where buyers and sellers meet to conduct business. (21)

markup - an amount added by a retailer to the cost price of goods that allows it to cover expenses and make a fair profit. (16)

measurement - the act of determining the dimension, quantity, or degree of something. (16)

merit raise - a pay raise that is based on job performance. (10)

microprocessor - a CPU contained on a single chip. (19)

minimum wage - by law, the lowest hourly wage that can be paid to an employee. (8)

minors - people who have not reached the full legal age. (3)

modem - an electronic device that allows computers to be linked through standard telephone lines. (19)

money market fund - a type of mutual fund in which the pooled funds are used to buy interest-bearing notes and certificates of deposit. (24)

monopoly - exclusive control of the supply of any goods or services in a given market. (21)

morale - a current mood and spirit, such as the attitude and emotion of employees. (6)

motion - a statement of proposed action by a participant in a business meeting. (18)

mutual fund - an investment company that pools the money of many investors and buys a collection of stocks or bonds. (24)

natural disaster - an uncontrollable event in nature that destroys life or property. (17)

negotiable order of withdrawal (NOW) - a type of interest-bearing checking account in which a withdrawal order (check) is written against a savings account rather than a checking account. (23)

net pay - the amount on a paycheck; the take-home pay of an employee after deductions are subtracted from gross pay. (10)

network - a group of computers that can communicate electronically. (19)

nutrients - chemical substances contained in food that are needed for good health. (30)

nutrition - the process by which plants and animals take in and use food. (30)

obsolete - outdated; no longer in use. (2)

occupation - name given to a group of similar tasks that a person performs for pay. (1)

occupational description - information about a specific occupation that explains what the work is like. (14)

Occupational Outlook Handbook (OOH) - a printed resource produced by the government that provides occupational information. (14)

occupational search - collecting information about an occupation of interest using some type of printed resource or data base. (14)

occupational skills - learned abilities to perform tasks or duties of a specific occupation. (1)

opinion - one person's views about something. (31)

order of business - a standard series of steps followed in a business meeting. (18)

OSHA - the government agency that sets and enforces standards for safe and healthful working conditions. (8)

overdraft - a check written for an amount greater than is available in the account. (23)

overtime - time worked beyond the standard forty-hour workweek. (8)

overtime pay - the wage received for working overtime, usually 1½ times the normal hourly wage. (10)

parliamentarian - the individual in an organization who advises the chair on matters regarding correct parliamentary procedure. (18)

parliamentary procedure - the formal rules used to conduct a meeting in a fair and orderly manner. (18)

partnership - a form of business organization in which two or more persons co-own the business. (20)

patients - persons under treatment or care by a medical practitioner. (9)

patronize - to trade with or give one's business to a certain individual or company. (9)

patrons - customers of certain service-producing businesses or institutions. (9)

payee - the person or agency to whom a check is written. (23)

pension - a regular payment of money to a retired person. (27)

performance evaluation - the process of judging how well an employee is doing on the job. (7)

perils - the possible damages from which one seeks protection through the purchase of home insurance. (25)

perimeter - the distance around the outside of an object. (16)

peripheral - a piece of computer equipment that can be attached to the main computer unit. (19)

personal data sheet - a summary of personal, educational, and occupational information used to help fill out a job application form and to prepare a job resume. (4)

personal hygiene - keeping one's body clean and healthy. (11)

physical fitness - how well your heart and other organs function. (30)

plaintiff - the complaining party in a lawsuit. (28)

policy manual - a booklet given to new employees that contains an explanation of company policies and rules. (6)

portfolio - a collection of stocks or bonds. (24)

postdating - placing a date on a check that is ahead of the current date. (23)

posture - the position of a person's body while standing, walking, or sitting. (11)

pre-employment test - a paper-and-pencil test or performance exercise administered by an employer as part of the job application process. (4)

precedence - the order of priority among the four types of motions used in a business meeting. (18)

precincts - a division of a city, ward, or county for election purposes. (31)

prejudice - a prejudgment; an opinion that is based on insufficient information. (31)

premium - the cost of an insurance policy. (25)

pride - feeling satisfied with what one has accomplished. (7)

probation - a trial period during which one's performance is being observed and evaluated. (6)

probation - releasing a convicted person on a suspended sentence under supervision and upon specified conditions. (28)

problem - a question in need of a solution or answer. (12)

production - the making of goods available for human needs and wants. (21)

productivity - the output of a worker; how much a worker produces on the job. (7)

program - coded instructions that cause a computer to perform a certain task. *See* software. (19)

promotion - advancement to a higher level job or position. (2)

promotion - an advancement to a higher-level job within a company. (10)

pronunciation - the way in which words are spoken. (15)

propaganda - any organized effort or movement to spread certain information. (31)

proprietary schools - a privately operated postsecondary vocational, technical, or business school. (32)

proprietorship - a form of business organization in which one person owns the business. (20)

prosperity - a period of expanding economic growth. (21)

public safety - all efforts by federal, state, and local governments to protect persons and property. (17)

punctuality - being on time. (7)

qualify - meeting the preliminary requirements for another job or position. (2)

quarters of coverage - a three-month period during which a certain amount of income is earned; used to determine eligibility for Social Security. *See* work credit. (27)

quorum - a majority of the total membership of an organization. (18)

RAM - an acronym for random-access memory; the working memory in a computer. (19)

reality factors - those persons, events, or situations that are real and present, such as the high cost of going to an Ivy League college. (12)

recall - to call back; a request to return something. (22)

recession - a period of declining economic growth. (21)

reconciling - the process of comparing a bank statement with one's personal check register to verify accuracy. (23)

references - names of individuals listed on a job application form or resume that are qualified to provide information about the applicant. (4)

referrals - directing a student to a potential employer for a job interview. (3)

regular (fixed) expenditures - in budgeting, those essential payments that are about the same amount each month. (24)

reimburse - to pay back money already spent. (6)

responsibility - the duty to follow an order or carry out a work assignment. (6)

resume - a one-page description of a job seeker's history and qualifications for employment. (4)

retailers - businesses that sell directly to the consumer. (20)

revenue - money that is raised through taxes to pay the cost of government. (26)

risk - the chance of an accident or loss. (25)

ROM - an acronym for read-only memory; the permanent memory in a computer. (19)

rumor - a popular report or story that has not been proven. (31)

safety - freedom from harm or the danger of harm. (17)

savings - cash set aside in a bank account to be used for financial emergencies and goals. (24)

scholarships - financial aid awarded to a student on the basis of outstanding academic achievement. (32)

sedentary - inactive. (30)

self - what you are; your personal characteristics or traits. (13)

self-direction - setting goals and working toward them. (2)

self-employed - an individual who owns and operates a business; an entrepreneur. (20)

self-information - knowledge about your self, particularly in relation to career decision-making. (13)

seniority - the length of time someone has worked for a company. (9)

service-producing industries - those companies and businesses that produce (provide) some type of personal or business service, such as transportation, finance, insurance, trade, and so on. (14)

services - work performed by individuals and businesses for the benefit of another. (22)

share-draft account - a type of checking account in which a draft (check) is written against a credit union savings account. (23)

signature card - a form that is completed to open a checking account. (23)

social security - government programs that help people meet social and economic needs; commonly used to refer to the federal system of retirement pensions, survivors payments, and hospital insurance for the elderly. (27)

software - the electronic instructions and programs that direct a computer to perform certain applications. (19)

stable job - a job considered to be permanent; may last several years. (2)

standard English - the usual form of language used by the majority of Americans. (15)

Standard Industrial Classification (SIC) - a system of grouping industries according to the type of product or service produced. (14)

Standard Occupational Classification (SOC) - a system of grouping occupations based on the type of work performed. (14)

standard workweek - by law, the completion of forty hours of work during a seven-day period. (8)

statement of account - a summary of all transactions completed in a checking account for a given time period. (23)

statement of earnings - a pay statement; the attachment to a paycheck that shows gross pay, deductions, and net pay. (10)

stockholders - individuals who purchase stock or shares of ownership in a company. (20)

stocks - shares of ownership in a company. (24)

stop-loss provision - a condition of health insurance that limits the amount of the bill for which the insured person is responsible. (25)

stress - a response the body makes to any demand made upon it. (30)

stressors - physical, biological, or emotional causes of stress. (30)

sublet - a lease by a tenant to another person. (29)

summons - an order commanding the defendant in a lawsuit to appear in court on a certain day. (28)

sunscreen - a special lotion used to protect the skin from the sun's ultraviolet rays. (11)

supervisor - a boss; one who gives directions and orders and oversees the work of others. (6)

supplier - a person or agency that distributes goods to retailers. (20)

supply - the amount of goods available for sale (when the supply is plentiful, the price generally decreases). (21)

task group - a work group formed to accomplish a particular objective. (9)

tax - a required contribution of money made to the government. (26)

tax credits - certain expenses that can be deducted from the amount of income tax owed. (26)

tax evasion - the illegal practice of avoiding payment of some or all of one's income tax obligation. (26)

taxable income - the amount on an income tax form left after all exclusions, adjustments, exemptions, and deductions have been subtracted; the amount of income on which tax is paid. (26)

taxation - the process by which the expenses of government are paid. (26)

technology - application of scientific knowledge to practical uses. (2)

tenant - renter; the person who rents an apartment. (29)

terms - terms of sale; the time limit within which the buyer must pay for merchandise received from the seller. (16)

territorial rights - unwritten rules concerning respect for the property and territory of others. (9)

townhouse - an individually owned house that is attached to another house on one or both sides. (29)

trade discount - a deduction from the catalog (list) price of an item. (16)

training agreement - a signed agreement outlining the relationships and responsibilities of the parties involved in a work experience education program. (1)

training plan - a listing of knowledges, attitudes, and skills to be developed by the student participating in a work experience education program. (1)

training station - a work experience student's place of employment. (1)

variable expenditures - in budgeting, day-to-day living expenses. (24)

vocabulary - the total of words known by an individual. (15)

vocational student organization (VSO) - nonprofit, national organization with state and local chapters that exists to develop leadership skills and good citizenship among members; each organization is composed of vocational students interested in a specific occupational area. (18)

wage base - the amount of gross salary or wages subject to Social Security tax. (27)

wardrobe - wearing apparel; one's clothing. (11)

warranty - a guarantee; a promise that the product is free from defects. (22)

warrant - a court order authorizing a police officer to make a search, seizure, or arrest. (28)

wholesale houses - businesses that sell to retailers rather than to consumers. *See* supplier. (20)

work - activity directed toward a purpose or goal that produces something of value to oneself and/or to society. (1)

work credit - a guideline used to determine eligibility for Social Security benefits; measured in quarters of coverage. (27)

work experience education - education programs designed to provide opportunities for students to explore or participate in work as an extension of the regular school environment. (1)

work history - all of the jobs that one holds during the course of a working lifetime. (2)

work permit - a form issued by school officials that gives a student permission to work during school hours as part of a work experience education program. (3)

work values - attitudes and beliefs about the importance of various work activities. (13)

world of work - an informal phrase used to describe the network of industries and occupations that exists within the American economic system. (14)

INDEX

D

E

F

J

K

L

M

N

O

P

Q

R

S

T

U

V

W